By the same author (with Herbert S. Parmet)

AARON BURR: PORTRAIT OF AN AMBITIOUS MAN

NEVER AGAIN: A PRESIDENT RUNS FOR A THIRD TERM

John Quincy Adams

John Quincy Adams

A PERSONAL HISTORY
OF AN INDEPENDENT
MAN

☆

Marie B. Hecht

The Macmillan Company · New York, New York
Collier-Macmillan Limited · London

The Macmillan Company
866 Third Avenue, New York, N.Y. 10022
Collier-Macmillan Canada Ltd., Toronto, Ontario

Library of Congress Catalog Card Number: 72-77279

FIRST PRINTING

Printed in the United States of America

To Ann

AND

David Bloomfield

With Love

Acknowledgments

The bulk of the material in this book comes from Columbia University's microfilmed copies of the Adams Papers. Thanks are due to Gail Casper, head of the Microfilm Room at the Butler library for her valuable assistance during the many months I spent in daily attendance in her domain. Permission to quote from the microfilm version of the Adams Papers was graciously granted by the Massachusetts Historical Society.

To the staff of the New-York Historical Society for their kind help in the library, the newspaper archives, and the map and print room I would like to express my appreciation. The Great Neck, Long Island library was ever pleasant and cooperative and delightfully close to home.

Herbert S. Parmet read the manuscript in its entirety and provided continual encouragement and valued criticism during the four years of production. The care and devotion of my typist, Margaret H. Crum, made the final struggle for completion both possible and relatively painless. I am indebted to Winifred N. Lynn for her willing ear. The editorial guidance of Ray A. Roberts of The Macmillan Company deserves my gratitude. And to Andrew Hecht, my appreciation for the cheerfulness with which he tolerates a writing mother.

Great Neck,
April 20, 1972

Contents

Plates

FACING PAGE 336

John Quincy Adams

Landscape for an Adams

"In the old world we have no traces . . ."
CHARLES FRANCIS ADAMS

JOHN QUINCY ADAMS's earliest memory was of a family trip, taken on the eve of the first anniversary of the Boston Massacre, to see a commemorative illustrated transparency. The small child, not quite four years old, was awed by the spectacle and also, quite probably, by being out on Boston's King Street after dark.[1]

Nevertheless, this recollection was appropriate for a child of the Revolution. Though John Quincy was too young to participate in the violent and controversial events of the times, he perceived them through the words and the actions of his parents. He was born as civil protest was sweeping through his colony of Massachusetts, and his childhood was spent in the midst of armed rebellion. His father, John Adams, was a Revolutionary. His mother, Abigail, was an ardent supporter of the patriot cause.

The founding of the Adams dynasty in America was unassuming. A number of settlers from the town of Braintree, Essex County, England, embarked from Ipswich with their pastor, the Reverend Mr. Flooden, arriving in Boston two years after Governor John Winthrop had established the Massachusetts Bay Colony. There was no room in Boston for them so they settled "probably without much examination of title," along the Bay winding around the harbor of Boston southward upon a hillock on the margin of the sea, an area which had been named Mount Wollaston by the leader of an earlier abortive settlement.

In 1634, the Massachusetts General Court voted that the town of Boston should be enlarged to include Mount Wollaston and parcelled out the lands to certain individuals on the condition of settlement. At the same time, the General Court ordered that the settlers from Braintree be removed. Fortunately this order was never carried out. Somehow the Braintree squatters came to terms with Boston and for some years appeased the larger city with the performance of militia duties and church attendance on Sundays. However, the ten miles distance from Boston made the weekly obligation inconvenient and so, in 1639, the Braintree residents formed their own church and appointed a pastor and a teacher. A year later they were rewarded with the approval of the General Court and incorporated as a separate town.

"Of this swarm from Braintree, Henry Adams was one of the working bees," John Quincy wrote of the immigrant founder of the family. Henry set up a brewery on the borders of Mount Wollaston which persisted through two generations of his descendants.

Henry was already on in years when he emigrated from England with his wife, eight sons, and an unmarried daughter. His oldest son, Henry, became Braintree's first clerk. Consequently, the first eight or nine years of the town's records were in his handwriting, thus initiating the traditional Adams role of scribe.

After the death of the Patriarch in 1656, only two sons remained in Braintree. Joseph, the youngest, who married Abigail Baxter of Roxbury, became active in local politics. He served from time to time as selectman, constable, and surveyor of highways, as did, in his turn, his eldest son Joseph.

John Adams, the second son of Joseph II and Hannah Bass, a granddaughter of John and Priscilla Alden, born in 1693, was characterized by his patrician descendant Charles Francis Adams as "a typical New England yeoman." But his own son, with much more perception, insisted that he was an unusual man, whose character and accomplishment belied his lack of education and learning. Called the "Deacon" because of his long years of service in that office at the North Precinct Church, John Adams was a staple in Braintree politics. A farmer and a shoemaker by trade, by avocation he was a tithingman, constable, militia officer, and nine times selectman. "Almost all the business of the town [was] managed by him for 20 years together," his son John asserted. The Deacon married Susanna, the daughter of Peter Boylston and Ann White of Muddy River (Brookline) and the granddaughter of Thomas Boylston, a well-known surgeon and apothecary who had emigrated from London.

No one was more aware of his family's simple origins than John Quincy Adams. "The best history of them I know is Gray's *Elegy in a Country Churchyard*," he wrote. "They were distinguished only as men of Industry, Sobriety and Integrity, living upon very small landed Estates with numerous families of children and, at the close of long lives of humble labour, returning their bodies to the soil which had nourished them and their weak and quiet spirits to the God who gave them. If their veins had swollen with all the blood of the Howards, could as much have been said for them?"[2]

Deacon John and Susanna's first child, John, who would lift the Adams family from obscurity, was born October 30, 1735. "My father had destined his first born, long before his birth to a public education and I was taught to read very early," John Adams wrote. As a youngster his "enthusiasm for Sports and Inattention to books" alarmed his father. But Deacon John closed his ears to his son's plea that he be permitted to become a farmer like his forbears instead of a college man. The child was promptly enrolled in Mr. Marsh's school, which was located just two doors from the Adams house—close enough for parental scrutiny.

In due time, Adams was admitted to Harvard College, a member of the class of 1755. Students were then seated at the college according to their rank by birth. Charles Cushing was placed first and John Adams fourteenth of a class of twenty-four young men, a position to which he was entitled only because his mother was a Boylston. Academically, however, John was among the first three scholars. He said that he "perceived a growing Curiosity, a Love of Books and a fondness for Study, which dissipated all my Inclination for Sports, and even for the Society of the Ladies."[3]

It had been determined that Adams would enter the Ministry. However, exposure to a controversy between Lemuel Bryant, the Minister of the Braintree Church, and some of his parishioners soured the youth. Bryant, who was accused, with some truth, of

unorthodox principles and light morals, was the subject of many
acrimonious debates conducted at Deacon John's house. Young
John, listening to the furor, developed grave doubts as to his calling.
The dogmatism and bigotry that he heard made him realize that if
he became "a Priest I must take my side, and pronounce as positively as any of them, or never get a Parish, or getting it must soon
leave it."[4]

John wanted to be a lawyer. He had discovered a facility for
public speaking at Harvard and was encouraged by his friends to
pursue his inclination for the law. The Deacon was willing to listen
to John as long as he wanted to pursue some profession, but other
members of the family were "full of the most illiberal prejudices
against the Law."[5] A serious obstacle, however, was the cost of legal
training. Deacon John had three other sons to educate, so the final
decision would have to wait.

In the meantime, John took a job as Latin Master at the Worcester Grammar School. He lodged with Dr. Nahum Willards, a
skillful physician whose library of medical books tempted him with
thoughts of becoming a physician. But his real love was for the law.
When he attended the Courts and heard some of the outstanding
lawyers plead, he felt an irresistible desire to become one of them.

Finally, John Adams worked up the courage to approach James
Putnam, a prominent lawyer, and asked him to take him on as a
student. They arranged that Adams would lodge at the Putnam's, at
the town's expense, while he continued to teach at the Worcester
school. John would pay Putnam "an hundred dollars, when I should
find it convenient." And so for two years, he read law at night and
taught school during the day.

At the termination of his apprenticeship, several Worcester lawyers invited John to practice in town but he refused. Ill health,
which camouflaged homesickness for "the Breezes from the Sea and
the pure Zephirs from the rocky mountains of my Native Town,"
enticed Adams back to Braintree. There had never been a lawyer in
the country part of Suffolk County so he decided to practice there
and bypass Boston, which was already inundated with members of
the profession.[6]

Events in the outside world made 1759 a critical year in John
Adams's life. Montreal surrendered to the British, an event, John
observed, "joyful to Us and so important to England if she had seen

her true interest." But, instead, she was inspired with "a jealousy which ultimately lost her thirteen colonies . . ."[7] George III's decision to have the coercive Trade and Navigation Laws reactivated against the colonists presaged the future. This imprudence brought England and her colonies in America "to a collision." Forced to take a position, Adams decided for his colony of Massachusetts. Its cause seemed just, and if he had to die for it he would do so "with a good Conscience and a decent grace, if that Tryal should become indispensable."[8]

Deacon John died in 1761 leaving his oldest son a house and barn, forty acres of land, and about one-third of his father's personal estate, a shade less than his brothers because he had been provided with an education. Nevertheless, the young lawyer continued to live with his mother and brothers until his marriage three years later to Abigail Smith. The young lady was the second daughter of Reverend William Smith of Weymouth and Elizabeth Quincy, whose parents were Colonel John Quincy and Elizabeth Norton Quincy of Mount Wollaston.

A strain of aristocracy was now introduced into the Adams line. Both the Quincys and the Nortons could trace their ancestry to gentlemen who had come from Normandy with William the Conqueror. A forbear, Saer de Quincy, was one of the Barons of Runnymede whose names and seals were inscribed on the Magna Carta.

John and Abigail lived in the small clapboard house inherited from the Deacon with the front parlor set up as a law office. John's law practice and civic duties kept him very busy and quite often absent from home. He attended the courts at Plymouth, Taunton, Middlesex, and, occasionally, Barnstable and Worcester. The Plymouth Company engaged him to handle all its cases, which called him annually to the Falmouth Superior Court.

Once more, the events of the outside world encroached on private endeavor. Thirty-year-old John Adams called 1765 "the most remarkable year of my life." When Great Britain imposed a stamp tax on the American colonies there was a loud outcry from New Hampshire to Georgia. John Adams authored the Braintree Instructions, which denounced the direct tax and denied Parliament's right to tax the colonies. The document was unanimously adopted by the selectmen and the townspeople and was sent to Ebenezer Thayer, Braintree's representative at the General Court. Though the message was a sharp one, Adams, when an old man, declared that its fault was that it conceded too much.

In July, Abigail and John's first child, a daughter also named Abigail, was born, but this did not stop Adams from political opposition. His authorship of the anti–Stamp Act "Instructions" was an open secret. However, since the Massachusetts courts were closed rather than use stamps, Adams prepared to use his idleness to advantage. He said that he would read books, reduce his accounts, diminish expenses, and spend the winter in study. "So sudden an Interruption in my Career is very unfortunate for me. . . . I have groped in dark Obscurity till of late, and had just become known, and gained a small degree of Reputation, when this execrable Project was set on foot for my Ruin as well as that of America. . . ."9

Actually, these regrettable events increased Adams's prestige. Along with James Otis and Jeremiah Gridley, he was appointed by the town of Boston to persuade the Governor to open the courts. Each representative presented a part of the colonists' case. John based his argument on the invalidity of the Stamp Act because the colonists had not consented to it and on the inability of the government to carry it out. The second point proved to be precisely correct. The Stamp Act Congress, which assembled at New York and was attended by representatives from most of the colonial assemblies, had succeeded in effecting not only the closing of the courts but also the imposition of economic sanctions on British goods. Before the end of the year, business resumed without the use of stamps and repeal of the Act was under consideration in England because of pressure from British merchants who feared an American boycott.

News of the repeal of the Stamp Act reached Boston on May 19 but John Adams was deprived of the day's joy. He wrote a week later: "A darker day than last Monday, when the Province was in Rapture for the Repeal of the Stamp Act, I do not remember to have passed." Abigail and the baby both had whooping cough and John was obliged to attend the Plymouth Court on the next day and so could not go to Boston. The real rub, however, was a painful injury to Adams's pride. Obliterated by the Diarist, but still decipherable, was a bitter complaint against Braintree's neglect of him "while almost all the zealous opposers of the Stamp Act [were caressed] by their Towns and chosen Representatives."10

This pique was unfair, because the town had recognized Adams several months before by electing him selectman in the place of

Ebenezer Miller, an Anglican close to the government. John Adams's work was now extended to include responsibility for the schools, the poor, and taxes, but he consoled himself with the observation that "It will increase my Connection with the People."[11]

The year 1767 was politically quieter than its predecessor. John Adams's recent flurry of fame in Boston as well as in his native town increased his law practice considerably. With the additional money he earned, he was able to buy books—a lifetime hunger—and invest in land. But the year's most significant event was the birth of John and Abigail's first son on July 11.

The fine, healthy baby was named John Quincy after his great-grandfather, who died on his christening day. Abigail's mother requested this tribute, which was gratefully granted by the parents, who both admired the distinguished old gentleman. Colonel John Quincy had been the town's leading citizen when John Adams was a boy. He had been speaker of the Massachusetts Assembly, Colonel of the Militia, and a member of the Governor's Council. John Adams respected him particularly because he prided himself upon being neither enslaved nor dependent on any man, an attitude that had already served as an inspiration for the new baby's father.

Urged by his friends in Boston, John moved Abigail, Nabby, his small daughter, and Johnny into the White House on Brattle Square in Boston. He had just turned down the office of selectman from Braintree, because of his absence from town, and the post of Advocate General in the Court of Admiralty, for reasons of principle. Advocate General was a plum that had always served as a first step on the ladder of royal favor and promotion. Since this was a path that Adams had renounced, all of Attorney General Sewall's pressure to reconsider could not move him. Boston loyalists later denied John's story and asserted that he began his opposition to the British government because he was not given that office. This version was included in Thomas Hutchinson's *History of Massachusetts Bay*, a brilliant work, but its Tory author did not understand a wayward son's motivation.

The landing of a British army which filled Boston with troops afflicted the Adams family very directly. Early every morning the noise of the redcoats' fife and drum corps awakened them because the troops' exercise grounds were across the street from their house. John wrote that their indignation was soothed only by "the sweet songs, violins and flutes of the serenading Sons of Liberty, under my windows in the Evening." Though he believed that the appearance of the troops in Boston was strong proof of Britain's determination to subjugate the colonies, he was not ready yet to speak out at town meetings. He did, however, continue to draw up resolutions for protesting representatives.

On March 5, John Adams was spending the evening on the south side of Boston with two of his friends. About nine o'clock they were alarmed by the ringing of bells, a signal that usually meant a fire. They rushed into the street to offer their assistance but soon learned that the excitement was caused by the British soldiers who had fired on the populace, killing some and wounding others. The episode had occurred near the Town House, but when Adams and his friends arrived there, there was nothing to see but some soldiers drawn up to protect field pieces placed before the south door. John was concerned for Abigail, who was alone with the children, and so walked down Boylston Alley into Brattle Square where he saw soldiers stationed in front of the church with fixed bayonets. Edging by them, John made his way to Cold Lane. Abigail had already recovered from her first fright and was satisfied that nothing further would occur that night.

By the next morning, the incident had been dubbed "the Boston Massacre" by a thoroughly aroused citizenry. John Adams was approached to defend the British Captain Preston, who had been refused by both Josiah Quincy and Mr. Auchmuty unless he would agree to take the case. After some misgivings, Adams accepted, saying that "the very last thing that an accused Person should want in a free Country" was the right to counsel. Furthermore, John suspected that this "was the explosion which had been intentionally wrought by designing Men, who knew what they were aiming at better than the Instrument employed."[12] There was, of course, some popular clamor and suspicion against Adams for taking the case.

However, animosity against him was short lived. In June, Adams was elected to the General Court as the delegate from Boston to replace James Bowdoin. At about the same time, the family moved back to Braintree. The death of a daughter, Susanna, and the birth of a second son, Charles, in May had sapped Abigail's strength. John, too, wanted to breathe some country air. He had been speaking in public for several hours every day, which had brought on chest pains and a lung complaint so severe that he believed his life was threatened. The hills of home, his ever lively interest in agriculture, and brisk rides on horseback restored his health and energy.

After nineteen months of commuting between the family homestead in Braintree and his Boston office, John decided to try living in Boston again. He bought a house in Queen Street opposite the Court House and, in November of 1772, moved his family into it. John Hall, who had married John's widowed mother, took charge of the Braintree farm. As a formula for survival, Adams vowed to be disengaged from public affairs and concentrate on minding his office, his clerks, and his children.

The children now numbered four—Nabby, Johnny, Charles, and the latest addition, Thomas Boylston. In spite of the constant moving, Johnny had learned how to read and write. His earliest letter, written to his cousin Elizabeth Cranch, said that he had "made But veray little proviciancy in reading. . . ." He suggested that the reason for it was "to much of my time in play (th)ere is a great Deal of room for me to grow better. . . ." It was a shrewd analysis for a youngster of six years.[13]

John Adams wrote on December 17, 1773, "Last night three cargoes of Bohea Tea were emptied into the Sea. . . . This Destruction of the Tea is so bold, so daring, so firm, intrepid and inflexible, and it must have so important Consequences, and so lasting, that I can't but consider it as an Epocha in History." Obviously he thoroughly approved of the dramatic demonstration against the British Tea Act which had bestowed parliamentary favoritism on the British East India Tea Company. The action of the band of men disguised unconvincingly as Indians, who boarded the tea ships in Boston Harbor, broke open the tea chests, and dumped them into the sea, was called high treason by Governor Hutchinson. Adams, however, thought that to have allowed the tea to land would have been to give up the principle of rejecting taxation by parliamentary authority and to have lost the ten-year struggle, thereby subjecting the colonists "forever to Egyptian taskmasters."[14]

The Boston Tea Party had considerable impact and decided repercussions for Boston, for Massachusetts, and for all the American colonies. But, in the meantime, personal matters concerned John Adams. In February of the new year he bought the house in which he had been born from his brother. He said that he wanted it very much, particularly "that beautiful Brook" which ran through the farm and had always delighted him. Abigail's health was poor again, and the decision was made to move back to Braintree, at least for the season so that the sea air might once more revive her.

Abigail had full responsibility for the children while John was at his Boston office or away on his legal journeys. Separation was to be so continually a way of life for John and Abigail that letters had to become a substitute for paternal care. In their frequent communications, John urged his wife to join him in the "effort to mould the minds and manners of our Children. . . . Let us teach them not only to do virtuously but to excell. To excell they must be steady, active, and industrious."[15]

Johnny had started his education. He was not sent to the town school but was tutored by his father's law clerks, John Thaxter and Nathan Rice. He and Mr. Thaxter got along very well, and Abigail was satisfied with the arrangement. She checked on the boy's progress in reading by having him read to her each day several pages from Rollin's *Ancient History*, a popular work translated from the French. Abigail, who found the book fascinating, hoped that Johnny would develop an interest in classical heroes from their reading. John was properly impressed with the precocity of his seven-year-old but cautioned him to stay out of the company of rude children. "I hope to hear a good account of his Accidence and Nomenclature when I return,"[16] he wrote to his wife. The absent father also advised that it was time to teach the children, "whose education is never out of my mind," the French language.

Adams, who was in Philadelphia attending the Continental Congress as a Massachusetts delegate, had to remain there until October. Upon his departure he prophesied, with unusual lack of foresight, that it was very unlikely that he would return to "this part of the world again, but I shall ever retain a most gratefull pleasing Sense of the many Civilities I have received in it."[17] Before he left, Johnny's first letter to him arrived. It was well phrased and becomingly modest. The child said that he had "been trying ever since you went away to learn to write you a Letter. I shall make poor work of it, but Sir Mamma says you will accept my endeavours, and that my duty to you may be expressed in poor writing as well as good."[18]

The year 1775 was the year of decision both for the British and for the increasingly belligerent colonists. Britain decided on their suppression by armed might and the Americans decided on armed resistance. The British were conveniently blind to the difficulties involved in subduing a people from whom they were separated by a wide ocean. They also underestimated the spur that a mutual enemy gave to unifying thirteen jealous sister colonies. John Adams said after the Peace of Paris that "the revolution was complete, in the minds of the people, and the Union of the Colonies, before the war commenced in the skirmishes of Concord and Lexington on April 19, 1775."[19]

By this time Boston and its environs were on the front lines. John Quincy Adams described the terrors a small child experienced: "My mother with her infant children dwelt, liable every hour of the day and of the night to be butchered in cold blood, or taken and carried into Boston as hostages by any foraging or marauding detachment of men. . . ." Some of it was fun, however. One day a company of militia came down from Bridgwater and camped overnight at the Adams house. John, who was at home, took the boy to visit the soldiers and, to the child's delight, had him go through the manual of arms at the command of the company sergeant.

Abigail was terrified a good part of the time because of the proximity of the Braintree house to the seacoast. There were constant alarms that the British men-of-war stationed in the Bay would send out landing parties to harass the countryside. In case of such real danger, Adams advised, "Fly to the Woods with our children."

The spring and summer of 1775 the experience of war reached Johnny. From the summit of Penn's Hill, he and his mother saw the fires of Charlestown and heard the roar of the British cannon during the Battle of Bunker Hill. The boy was particularly aware of his mother's disquiet. Fear for her children's safety, constant anxiety over her absent husband's revolutionary activities, and pity for the "poor distressed inhabitants" of Boston combined to intensify her anguish. The war sickened her but also moved her to almost hysterical outbursts of patriotism which she poured out to her oldest son.

The Battle of Bunker Hill became even more distressingly real to the Adams family when news reached Braintree that Dr. Joseph Warren, a close friend and the family physician, had fallen in the battle. Johnny remembered him for having saved his finger from amputation after a very bad fracture. During the Bunker Hill battle, Abigail moved the children inland to Elihu Adams's farm because the seacoast was considered too dangerous.

In May, John Adams's young law clerks left, Mr. Rice to join the army as the captain of a company and John Thaxter to return to his home in Hingham. This threw Johnny more exclusively into his mother's company. She taught the boy to recite one of her favorite poems, "How Sleep the Brave," by William Collins, which was written to commemorate the warriors who had fallen in the war to subdue the Jacobite rebellion of 1745. Johnny was instructed to recite the two verses daily before rising from bed each morning directly after he said the Lord's Prayer. Seventy-one years later, John Quincy Adams bragged to a friend that he was able to repeat the verses with only one small mistake.

"Portia," Abigail's chosen pen name for her letters to her husband, and Johnny lived for the letters from Philadelphia. John wrote with surprising regularity and much concern for his absent family. He tried to provide some long-distance direction, particularly about the children's education. Abigail's comment, "We have no school. I know not what to do with John," disturbed him. He advised that all the children be taught geography, the art of copying, and the skill necessary to draw plans of cities and countries, especially America. Being a good Puritan father, he was concerned most of all about their honor, truth, and morals, which he prayed would be kept pure.[20] Johnny wished that Papa would come home to him, although, he said wistfully, probably his father had so much to do that he would forget him.

Inevitably, disease came in the wake of war. A virulent epidemic of dysentery struck Braintree in the late summer. An early victim was John's brother Elihu, who had been commanding a company of militia. Abigail contracted the disease in September and Tommy soon followed. Both of them recovered in time and, fortunately, the other children escaped. As the disease spread through Braintree, it made more havoc than the war. Abigail wrote to John that "some poor parents were mourning the loss of 3, 4 and 5 children and some families are wholly stripped of every Member."[21] Her own family was not spared. On October 1, she wrote to her husband, "Have pitty upon me, have pitty upon me O! Thou my beloved for the hand of God presseth me soar." After sixteen days of agonizing suffering, Abigail's mother died, leaving Reverend Smith, "like a firm Believer and a Good Christian," trying to set "before his children the best of examples of patience and submission."[22]

John Quincy had been staying with his grandparents Smith at Weymouth when Elizabeth Quincy Smith died. Her funeral was his first experience with the death of someone he loved. He said of her that she was kind and affectionate and that his respect and admiration for women was based on his early memories of his maternal grandmother.[23]

Even with Abigail's multiplying difficulties, John doubted that he could be spared from Philadelphia. Affairs were in a critical state, he reported, "and important steps are now taking place every day. . . ." Nabby stayed with Aunt Betsy after Grandmamma's death but Johnny returned home. He suffered from sore eyes, which did not prevent him from writing to his father several times, but he only sent one of the letters because he felt that the others were not good enough. His father commented that the one he received was written "like an Hero glowing with Ardor for his country and burning with Indignation against her enemies."[24] Abigail's fiery patriotism and his father's absence completed the child's indoctrination.

In early December, John delighted the family with an unexpected visit. Congress released him because he was worn out, and also because he had to make a decision whether to assume his duties as Chief Justice of Massachusetts, a position to which he had been appointed, or stay on as a congressional delegate. Four days before Christmas John arrived in Braintree for a reunion that was to be very brief.

Abigail, once more the head of the family early in the new year, was made very unhappy by a silly story that spread through the colonial newspapers. It reported that John Adams and John Hancock had deserted the colonial cause and sailed for England aboard a British man-of-war. Abigail wrote to John about it in a light vein but added that the ridiculous report made some of their friends uneasy and "the Gaping vulgar swallowed the story."[25]

After the British evacuation of Boston, Johnny was able to inform his father that the British left their house very little damaged as a result of the siege and occupation. John replied with a moralizing lecture on the need to remember "the Losses, Dangers, and Inconveniences that have been born by your Parents, and the Inhabitants of Boston in general for the Sake of preserving Freedom for you, and yours—and I hope you will all follow the virtuous Example if, in any future Time your Countrys Liberties should be in Danger, and suffer every human Evil, rather than Give them up."[26]

Johnny successfully weathered mumps and a severe case of pleurisy that winter without any ill effects but Abigail was concerned about the outbreak of smallpox in Boston. She determined to have her family inoculated, an ordeal that John had undergone before his marriage. The two of them had discussed inoculation before the war but the cost and other factors prevented them from doing it earlier.

Dr. Zabdiel Boylston, John Adams's great-uncle, had first introduced the process of smallpox inoculation into the British Empire. Matter was taken from the pustules of a person with the disease and inserted into a healthy person, the assumption being that the disease would be contracted in a mild form by the healthy individual and, after recovery, he would have permanent immunity.

Arrangements were made with Dr. Thomas Bulfinch, a Harvard graduate who had studied medicine at the University of Edinburgh, to inoculate the Adams family in July 1776. Abigail, the children, Abigail's sister Betsy, Cotton Tufts, John Thaxter, a maid, and Abigail's old nurse made up the hospital. The group drove down from Braintree accompanied by a cow that was to provide them with milk. Hay and wood had already been stored in the barn for them. In addition, each patient was required to bring two pairs of sheets and a counterpane. The cost per person was eighteen shillings a week plus one guinea for the inoculation. Abigail figured that the family would have to stay at the hospital for about three weeks.

John received a running account of his family's progress from Abigail's lively pen. After the five of them were inoculated on July 13, each one responded differently. The little ones "puke every morning but after are comfortable." Nabby and Johnny had an inflammation of the eyes that prevented them from writing to their anxious father to reassure him. By the last of the month eruptions began to appear on Nabby and Johnny, but they were not severe enough to cause great discomfort.[27]

Several rules were to be carefully carried out at Dr. Bulfinch's. Air, all that could be obtained for the patient, was considered essential. Consequently the patient must walk or be led or ride. Windows were flung open all night while everyone lay on the carpet, straw beds, a mattress, or anything hard. Diet was controlled to exclude salt, spirits, and fats, but fruit and unseasoned vegetables were allowed.

As the process went on, Johnny turned out to be the most fortunate of all the patients. He had enough pustules to give him future immunity but not enough to make him very sick. Adams wrote to Abigail, "Tell John he is a very lucky young Gentleman, to have it so much better than his Mamma, his sister, and his brothers."[28]

Nabby had "enough of the small Pox for all the family beside," her mother observed. She was so covered with spots, so sore and swelled up, that "She can neither walk sit stand or lay with any comfort." Abigail described the eruptions as "above a thousand pussels as large as a great Green Pea."[29] Though the young girl felt terrible, Dr. Bulfinch was satisfied that she would make a good recovery.

Charley was the problem. He had three inoculations before anything happened, and then the doctor believed that he had taken "the distemper in the natural way," a hazard that always existed. By August 20, the other children were out of the hospital, but Abigail had to stay with Charles, who was delirious for forty-eight hours. He recovered slowly, but by September Abigail and the other children were all together in Braintree. The smallpox adventure had proved to be much longer and more expensive than had been estimated.

While the Adams family were at Dr. Bulfinch's, the Declaration of Independence was presented "to a candid world." John Adams, a member of the committee that prepared the draft, informed Abigail on July 3 that "the greatest Question was decided, which ever was debated in America and a greater perhaps never was or will be decided among Men." Without one dissenting Colony, a resolution was passed "That these United States, are, and of right ought to be free and independent States. . . ." He told her that in a few days she would see a Declaration setting forth the causes for this "mighty Revolution" and its justification "in the sight of God and Man." In his joy, however, he had some apprehension that he shared with his wife. He feared the "unbounded power" that the people would have because "the People are extremely addicted to Corruption and Venality, as well as the Great."[30]

On Thursday, July 18, Abigail went "with the multitude" to King Street to hear the Declaration of Independence proclaimed. From the balcony of the State House, Colonel Thomas Crafts read the document to the assembled crowd which listened in awed silence. As soon as the reading was over, there was a cry from the balcony, "God save our American states," and a response of three cheers from the people below. Bells rang, cannon were discharged, and from the harbor came the sound of firing from the privateers. "Every face appeared joyfull," Abigail reported. After dinner the King's arms were taken down from the State House and everywhere else they had been displayed and were burned in King Street. "Thus ends royall Authority in this State, and all the people shall say

Amen," wrote Mrs. John Adams.[31] Very likely Johnny, who had recovered so well from the pox, was present at the occasions that Abigail described. His mother recorded that he attended a reading of the Declaration after church service in August, a procedure that had been ordered by the Council. After the reading, the pastor, Dr. Chauncy, lifted his eyes and hands to heaven and ⸻ "God bless the United States of America."

Back at Braintree again, Johnny, who had been the mail carrier from the post office to the Boston house, resumed the chore. Although he was only nine years old, he proudly rode from Braintree to Boston and back carrying the mail. His father thought that it was excellent training for him and only regretted that his lads were not old enough for military service, training that was "a great advantage to any Character."[32] Yet, when writing to his sons about their futures, Adams did not recommend the military life. He advised Johnny to develop a taste for literature and a taste for business. Since he would not have property enough to pursue learning alone, he had better apply himself to business in order to earn a living, "but you will find learning of the utmost importance to you in Business, as well as the most ingenious and elegant entertainment of your Life."[33] Tommy, he advised, must be a politician like the great-grandfather after whom he was named, and Charles should just grow up to be good and useful.

Johnny was now able to compose letters to his father without any assistance. They were charmingly misspelled and engagingly free of punctuation, a style that he seemed to have acquired from Abigail. The child wrote about the books that he was reading and then, as he had been taught, drew the proper moral from them. Of a biography of Bamfylde Moore Carew, known as the king of the beggars, Johnny said: "He got a great deal of money yet I do not think he got his living either credibly or honestly for surely it is better to work than to beg and better to beg than to lie. . . ." John responded with the comment that "You, my son, whom Heaven has blessed with excellent Parts, will never abuse them to bad purpose. . . ."[34]

Young Johnny felt his responsibility as the oldest son in a virtually fatherless family in the midst of war very deeply. Much as he wanted to be loved and approved of by his Puritan parents, and he wanted it fiercely, being dutiful was hard work. He confessed that "I Love to receive letters very well much better than I love to write them, I make but a poor figure at Composition my head is much too fickle, my thoughts are running after birds eggs play and trifles, till I get vexd with my Self, Mamma has a troublesome task to keep me Steady, and I am ashamed of myself." Hopefully the father smiled a little at that confession and regretted the child's need to take his place.

To pl... ...ha, Johnny kept at his reading, setting himself a daily ... ...o many pages of Tobias Smollett's *Complete History of England*. John Thaxter was away at Court and could not work with the boy at all. Reaching out for his absent father, Johnny asked for "Some instructions with regard to my time. . . ." His P.S. revealed the Adams heritage. "Sir," he added, "if you will be So good as to favour me with a Blank book I will transcribe the most remarkable occurences I mett with in my reading which will serve to fix them upon my mind."[35] Johnny's resolutions netted favorable results. He said that he felt more satisfied when he had applied himself to "some useful employment" and "found much entertainment in the perus... of history."[36]

In June 1777 Abigail, who was pregnant, worried about rumors that General Howe would attack Boston. She wanted John's advice because "We have not a man either upon the Castle or at Nantasket. I believe our Enemies know it." Her condition was making her doubly anxious: "I used to have courage [but] now can but poorly walk about the House. . . ."[37]

In general, John Adams thought that the situation was improving for the rebels. "We have now got together a fine Army, and more are coming in every day," he reported, but a few months later the Congress had to flee from Philadelphia before an advancing British army.[38] From their new quarters at York, Adams wrote that, in his opinion, Philadelphia would be no loss at all.

Wherever he had to go, John sent home advice about the children. He wanted Johnny, or Mr. John as he often called him, to read newspapers so that he may be aware of the progress of the war. When he read history, Abigail was told, the boy should have treachery, perfidy, cruelty, and hypocrisy pointed out to him for his contempt and detestation.[39] She must not conceal reality from the youngster; rather the Revolution through which he was living was to be a source of instruction about human nature as well as an instrument of patriotic indoctrination. Johnny had already inherited his parents' passion for books and reading. He loved fairy tales, the *Arabian Nights,* and fiction of every kind, the more inventive the better. As an adult he recalled, "I dreamed of enchantments as if there was a world in which they existed." Abigail's volumes of Shakespeare were available to him, and he read *The Tempest, As You Like It, The Merry Wives of Windsor, Much Ado About Nothing*, and *King Lear*. As a child, he commented, he missed completely the intricacies of Falstaffian humor and the buffoonery of the clowns, but the incantations of Prospero, the love story of Ferdinand and Miranda, the ethereal, sprightly liveliness of Ariel, and the beastly grossness of Caliban "tossed me into Elysium."

John Milton was responsible for the acquisition of a habit that it took John Quincy Adams thirty years to break. Since Johnny knew that both of his parents were very fond of *Paradise Lost*, he thought that he, too, should read the epic poem. He tried twice to get through the book but only succeeded in reading half of it. Finally, ashamed to ask his parents what made the poem such a favorite, and moved to tears of frustration, he decided to make the work more interesting by trying tobacco along with Milton. After a couple of bouts of nausea the tobacco habit was acquired, but not a love for *Paradise Lost*. Johnny was thirty before he finished the poem with any pleasure.

Abigail wrote to her husband on July 9 that for the past week she had experienced strange complaints and just that day had had a shaking fit that made her fear that the baby she was carrying was dead. Two days later, on Johnny's tenth birthday, she delivered a stillborn daughter. She was keenly disappointed, as was Nabby who hoped for a sister. Though Abigail recovered her health quickly, this tragedy made Adams even more guilty about his constant absence from the family. Abigail, however, took the view that the separation was her sacrifice to her country. But she did regret that it happened to the children "at the time of life when the joint instructions and admonitions of parents sink deeper than in maturer years."[40]

An even more painful separation was in store. On November 28, 1777, Congress, now under the presidency of Henry Laurens, elected John Adams to replace Silas Deane as a commissioner at the court of France with Benjamin Franklin and Arthur Lee. Abigail learned the news before her husband arrived in Braintree and "made use of his absence to prepare my mind for what I apprehend must take place least I should unnecessarily embarras him."[41]

As his wife expected, John Adams doubted neither the dangers such a mission presented nor his commitment to undergo them. He did not fear the severity of the winter passage but was uncomfortably aware that the British must know of his appointment through their spies and might try to capture him from the *Boston*, the ship on which he was scheduled to sail. "The consequence of capture would be lodging at New Gate," he said, and then a treason trial in England. "I had no doubt that they would go to the extent of their power and practice upon me all the Cruelties of their punishment of treason." These premonitions, the responsibilities of a family man with four children, and his feelings of inadequacy for the office were put aside. The most important fact, he told himself, was "that the confidence of my Country was committed to me."[42]

Abigail proposed accompanying the new commissioner with the two older children, but John protested that it was entirely too dangerous in wartime. "My desire was you know to have run all hazards and accompany him, but I could not prevail upon him to consent," Abigail wrote to John Thaxter. And, she added, "in case of a capture my sufferings would enhance his Misery, and perhaps I would be subjected to worse treatment on account of my connection with him."[43]

Although his mother and siblings were sentenced to stay at home, Johnny, "by earnest entreaty," was able to persuade his father to take him along. Instead of getting ready to enter Samuel Moody's Governor Dummer Academy in Byfield, a preparatory school for Harvard College, as had been arranged, Abigail had to ready the lad for the trip to France.

As his mother phrased it, John Quincy Adams, ten and one-half years old, was to enter "the world in which he is to live."[44]

CHAPTER 2

The Education of a Diplomat

*"Poor Johnny is gone you tell me. I think he is now laying the foundation
of a great man."*

JOHN THAXTER TO ABIGAIL ADAMS

"MR. ADAMS. You are going to embark under very threatening
signs. The Heavens frown, the clouds roll, the hollow
Winds howl, the Waves of the Sea roar upon the Beach," prophesied
the local Cassandra. She spoke to John Adams who, with Johnny and
Captain Samuel Tucker, commander of the *Boston*, had just left
Norton Quincy's dinner table. Despite the ill omens, Adams said
that he was not enough of a Roman to believe in them. The party
just continued to walk quietly to the Moon Head, where the *Boston*'s barge waited to carry them aboard.[1]

It was mid-February 1778 and the sea was rough, but hay was
stashed in the bottom of the boat and coats were wrapped around
the passengers to keep them warm. Waiting on board the *Boston*
were the two young men who were to be Adams's charges on the
voyage. William Vernon, Jr., a recent graduate of Princeton whose
father was a member of the Navy Board, was being sent to France to
learn about commerce. Jesse Deane, the son of Silas Deane was
about a year older than Johnny.

The predictions of the seeress started to come true at once.
Storms, snow, and the ship's needs delayed sailing for a few days. By

this time Johnny was used to his lodging on shipboard—"a Cott with a double mattress, a good Bolster, my own Sheets and Blankets enough"—but not to the constant rolling and rocking of the ship. The first day out, everyone was seasick.

When Captain Tucker sighted a large ship, probably British, he told Adams that he would avoid it because his mission was to carry the new commissioner to France not to capture prizes. Adams, however, urged him to fight. He wrote in his *Diary*: "It would have been more eligible for me to be killed on board the *Boston* or sunk to the bottom in her, than to be taken Prisoner."[2]

Before the ship could go into action, a wind sprang up that quickly developed into a hurricane. Adams was persuaded to go below but sleep was impossible. He and Johnny spent the night holding themselves in bed with their hands while bracing their feet against the timbers and planking. Suddenly they heard a terrible report which they took for the British ship's guns until an officer descended to tell them that the ship had been struck by lightning and four men had been killed.

By the next day the enemy was lost, but for three days and nights the *Boston* tossed in "one of the most furious storms that ever Ship survived." No one could stand, nothing stayed put, no person and no place was dry. The sails had to be hauled down but, before the process could be completed, the foresail was ripped from top to bottom by a gust of wind. The noise, the language and behavior of the crew, the crackling from all the parts of the ship, the mountains of water breaking over the gunwales added to the nightmare quality of the storm. Adams recorded with some satisfaction that he had remained calm and collected but regretted having carried his small son into these dangers. The lad, however, surprised his father with the quality of his behavior. Though completely aware of the danger, he strove to be patient and courageous and attentive to his father.

Before the hurricane, Johnny started to learn French from Dr. Nicholas Noel, a French army surgeon, who was charmed by the youngster. Adams, now that the sea was calm and the ship repaired, tried unsuccessfully to resume his reading and his study in the little world that they were living—now so damp that he was thoroughly bored with it. But, unlike his father, Johnny became even more involved in life on shipboard. He resumed his French lessons, showing marked improvement, and the Captain taught him all the sails and the Mariner's compass.

Excitement on board the *Boston* was a steady diet that the young Adams found very satisfying. On March 10, the British ship *Martha*, commanded by Captain McIntosh, sailing from London to New York with a cargo valued at eighty thousand guineas, was captured by the *Boston*. But the next vessel that the *Boston* chased, a French brig, caused a tragedy. Attempting to fire a gun as a signal to the ship, the cannon burst shattered Lieutenant Barrons's right leg. Adams and Captain Tucker held the unfortunate man in their arms while the ship's doctor amputated the leg but, ten days later, Barrons died. Johnny was present with the rest of the ship's company when the coffin with the offending gun lashed to it was lowered over the ship's side into the ocean. It was "one of the most painfully impressive events" that he ever witnessed, John Quincy wrote a lifetime later.[3]

Gales and heavy seas persisted until March 20, at which time the weather cleared and the prospect of reaching Bordeaux without further incident looked encouraging. Johnny's first glimpse of Europe was the coast of Spain, a dramatic backdrop of snow-tipped mountains with a foreground of green extending into the sea.

On March 29, a pilot came aboard to guide the ship up the Garonne River to the city of Bordeaux. The angry ocean and miles of blue were replaced with vistas of beautiful gardens and chateaux that bordered the river. The two "simple inhabitants of the American wilderness" found the moving panorama of churches, convents and villages built of stone "very magnificent."[4] The Captain of the *Julie*, a French vessel going to Santo Domingo, invited the Adamses aboard for their first taste of French cooking which they both enjoyed, particularly after weeks of sea rations.

A few days in Bordeaux introduced the Adams party to the opera, the theater and the French ladies of fashion. Adams enjoyed the first two but was rather shocked by the ladies. After being questioned by one lady in a manner that embarrassed him hugely, he concluded that such women could never support a Republican government and care must be taken not to import them into America. He was overwhelmed also by the profuse, almost suffocating compliments that were showered upon him and his country. At a dinner in his honor, the garden was illuminated with the inscription, "God save the Congress, Liberty, and Adams."[5]

Much more disconcerting was Adams's discovery that animosity was rancorous among the three American Ministers: Benjamin

Franklin, Silas Deane, and Arthur Lee. Further, he learned that the Americans and French connected with American affairs had divided up into factions that were bitterly opposed to one another. Adams decided that he would try to be cautious and impartial.

Johnny found the journey to Paris both instructive and fatiguing. They traveled at the rate of a hundred miles a day so that the trip took four days. France's landscape was very different from Massachusetts, because every field was cultivated and trees were scarce. Beautiful as was the ride along the Loire and the thirty-mile paved road into Paris, the scenic splendor was spoiled for the Americans by the constant swarm of beggars that accosted them along the way.

Since accommodations in Paris were hard to find, the Adams party stayed only one night and then drove out to Passy to call on Ben Franklin. He and Adams had served in Congress together and had, at the time, seemed to agree on most issues so Adams expected their meeting to be very amiable. The Doctor was housed at the Hotel Valentinois which had been offered to him, rent-free, by its owner, Jacques de Chaumont, a wealthy gentleman who was heavily invested in support of the American colonies.

Passy appealed to the Adamses at once. An almost rural and fashionable suburb just a mile from the French capital, bordering the Bois de Boulogne and overlooking the Seine, its elegant houses, terraces, and gardens were irresistible. Adams accepted Franklin's offer to live at his hotel. Though he had some private misgivings about the arrangements, he rationalized that he would "put my Country to no further expense on my Account."[6]

Johnny had about a week to get used to his new surroundings before he and Silas Deane were sent to the Passy Academy. Franklin, whose grandson, Benny Bache, was a student at M. Le Coeur's, recommended the school enthusiastically. Johnny thought that he would like it there because rewards were offered to the best scholars, a system that he called "very encouraging," and Adams was impressed with the curriculum which included, in addition to the usual classical subjects, fencing, dancing, and music.

The Academy, which was situated "sur la montagne de Crève Coeur," had a strict schedule. The students were routed from their beds at six o'clock in the morning and kept at their studies until eight-thirty at night except for meals and very short recreation periods. Weekends became a necessary as well as a welcome respite. Adams looked forward to the reunions with his son but was "somewhat mortified" to find that "this child . . . learned more french in a day than I could learn in a Week with all my books."[7]

Abigail's letters to Johnny were both yearning and harsh. She assured her oldest son that he was "constantly . . . upon my heart and mind" but then promptly reminded him of the advantages that he was enjoying and his obligation to make use of his talents. Her advice was often extravagantly worded. In one excess, she said, "dear as you are to me, I would much rather you should have found your grave in the ocean you have crossed, or that any untimely death crop you in your infant years, than see you an immoral, profligate, or graceless child."[8]

To his mother, Johnny confided his resolution to start "a journal, or a diary of the Events that happen to me, and of the objects that I see, and of characters that I converse with from day to day."[9] He admitted that the observations and letters of an eleven-year-old might seem like "childish nonsense" to him in a few years but he thought a journal would help him to recollect people and events that he might otherwise forget. Not content with a black book in which to keep his records, Johnny wished for a pencil book to take with him wherever he went "to make notes on the spot to be transferred afterwards in my Diary." The boy courted his mother with the sentiment that this resolve would not only improve him but would also "enable me to be more entertaining to you."[10]

John Adams, who was terribly proud of Johnny, allowed himself unaccustomed superlatives about the boy's "assiduity to his books and his discreet behaviour."[11] But, basically, the new commissioner was very dissatisfied with the role he had to play in France. He felt decidedly *de trop* because neither he nor Lee "are looked upon of much consequence." The eyes of all Europe were fixed on Franklin, whose long and great reputation made him the most important American in Europe.[12] By December 1778, Adams was writing to Abigail that for at least two months he had longed for his recall.

Feeling sorry for oneself was a characteristic that became a kind of Adams mannerism. Among the slights that pricked the sensitive Adams skin was the French misconception that John Adams and not Tom Paine was the author of *Common Sense*. More often than was comfortable Adams would be questioned by admiring Frenchmen who would ask if he were "le fameux Adams," the author of the pamphlet that all France was praising. John wrote sadly, "I was a man of whom nobody had ever heard before, a perfect Cypher, a

Man who did not understand a word of French—awkward in his figure—awkward in his Dress—No Abilities—a perfect Bigot—and Fanatic."[13]

Therefore, it was with relief that Adams received the despatches from Congress, delivered by Lafayette's aide-de-camp in September. The American Commission was dissolved and Dr. Franklin was elected the sole plenipotentiary. The release came just in time because Johnny's education was becoming exorbitant. "Although his company is almost all the pleasure I have in life, yet I should not have brought him had I known the expense," John wrote to Abigail.[14]

In less than a month the Adamses left Passy to travel for five days by way of Versailles through "the most barren and least cultivated part of France" to Nantes. They visited Joshua Johnson, the brother of the Governor of Maryland, here. Until the American Revolution, Johnson had been the factor of an Annapolis shipping firm stationed in London, but when the war started he travelled to France, expecting to return to America as soon as he could find a ship. However, since he had several small children, he decided to settle in Nantes rather than undertake a dangerous ocean voyage. Now a successful merchant, he undertook commissions for Congress and the state of Maryland. It was here that Johnny met his future wife, who was four years old, but, of course, he was then quite unconscious of Louisa Catherine Johnson's existence. A twelve-year-old would not deign to look at a small girl.

The *Alliance*, commanded by Captain Pierre Landais, was supposed to be waiting for Adams at Nantes but a covey of forty unruly British prisoners had delayed the ship at Brest. Reluctantly, Adams had to go there to arrange a prisoner exchange so that it was the end of April before Johnny and the baggage were put aboard.

While waiting for the *Alliance* to sail, Johnny read *Don Quixote* and translated Cicero's first oration against Catiline, with the help of his father who wondered whether these "classical amusements" suited him. The confinement to the cabin bored him and made Johnny restless. Adams indulged in some fearful self-condemnation, lamenting: "There is a feebleness and a Languor in my nature. My mind and Body both partake of this weakness. By my Physical Constitution, I am but an ordinary Man. The Times alone have destined me to Fame—and even these have not been able to give me much."[15]

Adams's discontent intensified when news reached them that the

Alliance was ordered to l'Orient and the sailing would be delayed until the Chevalier de la Luzerne, the new French Ambassador to the United States, arrived, at which time they would be transferred to a French ship. Johnny profited by the delay. While the ship lay at anchor, the sailors taught him how to swim, a sport he pursued enthusiastically all of his life.

Finally, on June 12, the Chevalier and Francois Barbé-Marbois, his secretary, arrived. Five days later, the ship sailed in a convoy that included Captain John Paul Jones's *Bonhomme Richard* and several other French and American ships. On board the *Sensible*, to which they had been moved, Adams had an 8×6 cabin but Johnny and M. Marbois hung their hammocks in the large room that served as a recreation hall during the day.

The agreement on board was that English would be spoken so that the French party would have the opportunity to learn the language but, despite the good intentions, nine-tenths of the conversation was in French. Johnny contributed by teaching English to the Chevalier and M. Marbois. One morning Adams entered his stateroom to find the elegant French Ambassador seated on a cushion, M. Marbois stretched out on one cot, and his son on the other. The Chevalier was reading aloud from Blackstone's *Discourses* while Johnny was correcting the pronunciation of every word, syllable, and letter. The two Frenchmen maintained that "Mr. John" taught much better than his father for "he shews us no Mercy and makes Us no Compliments."[16]

The voyage back to the United States was as agreeable as the eastward trip had been hazardous. Good weather, French esprit, and a rousing Fourth of July celebration to honor the Americans made the trip memorable. On July 31, the Adamses left the *Sensible* at Nantasket Roads and were rowed onto the beach at Mount Wollaston. The family reunion was tender and happy but, fortunately for Abigail, she did not know for how short a time she would have her returned travellers.

Once again Congress recognized John Adams's ability by electing him Minister Plenipotentiary to negotiate peace and commerce treaties with Great Britain, which meant a return to Paris where the talks would take place. Adams, for whom duty was an unalterable way of life, informed Samuel Huntington, president of the Continental Congress, that he would accept the mission.

Once again Mr. and Mrs. Adams debated the problem of which

members of the family would accompany the Minister. It was decided that Charles, now nine years old, would replace his brother as his father's companion. John Quincy must begin a more conventional education to prepare himself for Harvard College, a decision that the boy endorsed, fearing that another European trip would lose him a college education.

But Abigail questioned the wisdom of their choice. With "the resolution and the Roman Matron's affection," she urged Johnny to leave her. One evening, after the family had been to church, she took the boy into her room, alone. Persuasively and firmly, she reasoned Johnny into the belief that it would be more advantageous to his education to accompany his father and his brother. Johnny, to his father's relief, yielded. He asked to be taken to France again. Johnny's old friends had not forgotten him—M. Marbois wrote to Adams that he had heard about the French mission and desired that "you would carry with you again . . . the Young Gentleman, Your Son."[17]

On November 13, Abigail endured another leavetaking. Once again the travellers boarded the *Sensible*, this time riding in Boston harbor. Along with the Adamses went John Thaxter to act as John's private secretary. The French vessel was crowded with 350 sailors, some of them American recruits, and many passengers. Among them was Francis Dana, a Harvard lawyer and former delegate to the Continental Congress who was accompanying Adams as the Secretary of the Commission and the Chargé D'Affaires.

The weather allowed for an easy passage across the ocean and the British warships left them alone, but the ship itself was not properly seaworthy. It developed a leak of such proportions that crew and passengers had to take turns at the pumps to keep the vessel from foundering. Finally, the Captain had to put in at Spain because he could not continue the voyage safely. Johnny took advantage of the peace of the trip to make a first attempt at keeping a journal; bravely titled, *A Journal by JQA from America to Spain, Vol. 1 begun Friday, Nov. 12 1779.* Unfortunately, the project was soon abandoned. "I hadn't the perserverance," John Quincy admitted later.

When the ship docked at Spain, Adams had to decide whether his party should wait for the ship to be repaired or proceed overland to Paris, a trip of twelve to thirteen hundred miles. There was no regular post or mail service so that a carriage and horses would have to be purchased and, he was advised, the trip over the Pyrennees was rugged. The harassed man worried about his responsibility for the children but consoled himself that he had resisted taking Abigail and the little ones.

The problem was solved for Adams when, after an examination of the injured vessel at Ferrol on December 9, it became evident that the *Sensible* would not sail again without extensive repairs. Since it was imperative that Adams reach Paris as soon as possible to carry out his mission, the party would have to proceed by land.

In typical Adams style, the enforced delay in Spain was turned to good use. A Spanish grammar and a Latin grammar in Spanish were purchased and "By the help of these Books, the children as well as the Gentlemen of our little Company were soon employed in learning the language." Though the task seemed easy at first, Adams wrote, because of his knowledge of Latin, "a Language is very difficult to acquire especially by Persons in middle life."[18] The children, however, had no such difficulty.

Johnny and Charly were enchanted with their mode of transportation to Corunna. Mounted on mules with two muleteers in attendance, one in front to serve as a guide and the other behind to pick up stragglers, the American travellers rode over the deplorable roads and high mountains of northwestern Spain through a countryside of well-cultivated and rich soil dotted with some orange and lemon trees and many nut trees. At Corunna, the Governor of the Province of Gallice called on the American Minister and insisted on meeting his sons. Polite, continual entertainment was supplied to the Americans by the French and Spanish officers. But throughout the trip the travellers suffered terribly from the "innumerable Swarms of Enemies of all repose" that infested not only the beds but the entire apartments in which they lodged. Adams wondered sometimes if they would live to see France.[19]

The day after Christmas the Americans left Corunna. At an exorbitant price, three miserable carriages and a bevy of sorry-looking mules were hired. Johnny, his father, and his brother rode in one; Dana and Thaxter in the second; Jeremiah Allen with Samuel Cooper Johannot, the eleven-year-old son of a Boston merchant who was being sent to Europe to be educated, in the third. The servants rode the mules most of the way but sometimes the passengers took turns or walked alongside the caravan. On this lap of the trip, the party carried their own beds, blankets, sheets, pillows, and provisions of tea, chocolate, sugar, milk, butter, cheese, salt, pepper, liquor, and everything that was needed. The taverns along the way provided only fire and water.

Though the scenery was wildly beautiful and the officials along the way exceedingly courteous, the trip was difficult and depressing. As Americans, the Adamses deplored the signs of poverty and misery among the people. As prudent, careful New Englanders, they were critical of the half-cultivation of the fertile countryside and the absence of "Symptoms of Commerce, or even internal Trafick, manufactures or industry." As descendants of Puritans, the Americans noted the contrast between evidences of want among the populace and the "rosy faced Priest in his proud Canonicals rambling among the rubbish of the Village."

On January 2, 1780, the travellers arrived at Astorga, where the country grew much smoother and the beds cleaner, "No fleas for the first time in Spain." Madrid was now only forty miles out of the way, a temptation to John who longed to see the city himself and to show it to the children; but lengthening the trip at the most severe season of the year and placing himself in an awkward political position because Spain had not yet recognized the United States made him abandon the idea. Instead, the party dutifully turned eastward towards Leon and Burgos and then north to Bilbao.

Though the sights along the way were diverting, the winter season was taking its toll of the travellers. Constant cold, wet and fatigue, bad nourishment and other accompanying ills gave them all such terrible colds that they travelled to the accompaniment of sneezing and coughing. The children annoyed everyone, the servants were useless, and even Thaxter elicited from John the comment that he "was as shiftless as a child. He understands neither French nor Spanish," and, strange criticism from an Adams, "all he does is write his Journal."

The fog, rain, and snow encountered during the day was no more uncomfortable than the nights in Spanish taverns, without chimneys or windows except portholes, which gave no warmth in the rooms because the only heat provided was a pan of coals. Smoke and dirt, however, was plentiful.

Not far from Bilbao, the scenery became sensational. The party travelled through a pass between two mountains with lofty, craggy precipices that marked the boundary between Castile and Biscay. The road was an artistic and engineering feat with a descent that was a real curiosity. It spiralled round and round and round the mountains, having been blown out of the rocks, until it came to a steep pitch, which was made passable for a carriage only by serpentining the road. Johnny was thrilled by it.

At Bilbao, on January 15, M. Gardoque and Son, a mercantile firm with American interests, took care of endless personal commissions, but even their kindness could not make the stay really pleasant. The violent coughs and colds hung on and some of the children were so ill that it looked as if they might be detained for a long time. But five days' needed rest made possible the three-day muleback trip to Bayonne where the Spanish men and mules were paid off. Adams was sorry to sell his mule, and the children considered the replacement, a genteel post chaise, a poor substitute.

Nevertheless, France looked good after the rigors of Spain. "Everything here was clean, sweet and comfortable," a relieved John Adams wrote. Couriers on the road directed the Adams party to the principal inns of Bordeaux. After some sightseeing in the city, they left for Paris on February 2, and a week later reached the French capital. The journey by land had taken twice as long as the passage across the Atlantic Ocean.

In a few days the Adamses were lodged in a separate house attached to the Hotel de Valois in the Rue de Richelieu, which also served as an office for the duration of John Adams's stay in the city. The Adams boys and Samuel Johannot were enrolled in a pension academy at Passy run by M. Pechigny. Johnny and Charly both liked the school, stayed in good health, and visited their father frequently.

Abigail had qualms of guilt about forcing Johnny to go to France. She wrote to him that she would not have insisted had she believed him capable of judging what was best for him. Taking refuge in moralizing, she urged the youngster to exploit his "superior advantages" under the "instructive eye of a tender parent."[20]

At his first opportunity, Johnny wrote a hair-raising account of his journey across Spain for the edification of the Braintree relatives, particularly his mother. She was his match, however, with an answer that pointed out that his preservation "was not to rove from clime to clime, to gratify your idle curiosity." On the contrary, he must strive to know himself: "You are feelingly alive, your passions are strong and impetuous: and though I have sometimes seen them hurry you to excesses, yet . . . I have observed a frankness and generosity accompany your efforts to govern and subdue them."[21]

The Adams mission made no progress partly because the commissioner, by his own judgment, succeeded only in annoying the French Minister, Count de Vergennes. Therefore, Adams decided to go to Amsterdam as a private citizen to try to persuade the Hollanders to make a loan to the United States. He was unaware that the month before Congress had acted to commission him as its temporary agent to Holland until Henry Laurens could replace him officially.

Once again the three Adamses set out, but this time they travelled through fine country, heavy with vines and comfortably stocked with cattle and sheep, a striking contrast to Spain's wild terrain. At the Hague, Adams contacted Charles William Frederic Dumas, a writer who served as an agent and correspondent to Franklin. Later on, Dumas continued his usefulness to the United States as adviser, a liaison with Dutch officials, and a translator—a trusted friend of John Adams and, later, of John Quincy.

While Adams worked at raising money for the United States, the boys were placed in a well-known latin school that dated back to 1342, located on the Singel, a canal in the heart of Amsterdam on the moat by the Mint, a building now occupied by the Amsterdam police. Johnny, usually so agreeable and adaptable, hated the school. He started out badly because he was put in a lower form due to his inability to speak Dutch.

While at school, Johnny read the *Tatler*, the *Spectator*, and the *Guardian*, and made extracts of his reading in his journal. But mainly he looked forward to Wednesdays and Saturdays when he and Charly visited their father. The clash between Rector H. Verheyck and Johnny Adams came to a head when the headmaster reported that the boy was impertinent and disobedient. Adams, after a correspondence with the rector, instructed him to send his son home.

In the meantime, Adams made arrangements with Benjamin Waterhouse, a medical student who was studying in Leyden, to acquire "a little of the Dutch phlegm." John Thaxter would be lodged with the two boys at Waterhouse's place on the Langeburg, not far from Kloksteeg, the site of the church where in 1620 John Robinson preached to the English Separatists before they sailed to Plymouth Rock. Thaxter was to arrange for the boys to study Latin and Greek under good masters and to attend the university, at that time considered the most distinguished in Europe. John wrote to Abigail that this was a much more satisfactory arrangement for their sons because the air was purer and the company and conversation much better than in Amsterdam.[22]

Johnny was much more relaxed at Leyden. He wrote for "a pair of scates" and leather breeches and boots for riding, so he was having some fun as well as "writing in Homer, the Greek grammar, and the Greek Teſtament every day."[23] Thaxter was able to report that the boys were making good progress in the classical tongues and behaving themselves.

In January 1781, John visited the children and observed their progress at first hand. Johnny's progress was so impressive that Adams decided to try to get him admitted to the university. The Rector Magnificus of Leyden University reviewed the child's qualifications and admitted him, pending his declaration that he would do nothing against the laws of the university, the city, or Holland. Despite a heavy load of classical studies, Johnny kept up a lively intellectual correspondence with his father on such diverse subjects as Pope's poems, French drama, and Dutch history and jurisprudence. He even reminded Adams that before he left he had promised him lessons in algebra.

Abigail, who had not heard from her sons since their arrival in Holland, was very conscientious about writing to them frequently. She praised Johnny's account of Charly's progress, written from Paris, and reported the home news. Tommy suffered from very bad rheumatism "taken by going too early into the water" but was now recovered and planned to write. Nabby, whose nose was a little out of joint because, although the oldest, she had never had the opportunity to travel, told her brother that he should be grateful "for the presence of your Poppa. . . . It has hitherto fallen to my lot to pass my time in a very contracted sphere. I have scarcely visited as many towns as you have kingdoms. . . ."[24]

Charly was very ill in the spring of 1781. His anxious father brought him to Amsterdam to recover but when it became obvious that a good part of the boy's problem was homesickness, the best plan was to send him back to Braintree as soon as a suitable guardian could be found to take him. Johnny, however, was offered a unique opportunity.

Francis Dana was commissioned to travel to Russia to attempt to secure sympathy for the American cause and perhaps recognition of the United States from Empress Catherine II. He needed a secretary who understood French, the language of the Russian court, so that he could act as an interpreter. Fourteen-year-old Johnny Adams had the requirements and, with his father's consent, accepted the post.

For almost two months, the two Americans travelled night and day across Eastern Europe, a distance of 2,400 English miles. Johnny's observations were piercingly honest, touched with the candor of youth and seen through the eyes of a new American. He noted the contrast between his own country's freedom and the worst of the oppression that dominated the Old World. The teachings of John and Abigail Adams were constantly reflected in his keen comments.

The first place of consequence in which the travellers spent time was Berlin, the capital of the kingdom of Prussia. Johnny observed that it was a pretty town in the process of being improved by the King's housing program. Wherever there was a row of low, small houses, the owners were sent away, their dwelling torn down and a large elegant dwelling built in the same place and then returned to the owner. But this exercise in urban renewal did not make the King popular with his subjects, the boy wrote, because he treated them like slaves. "If a farmer has two or more sons, the oldest inherits all the land and the others become soldiers at about 2 pence a day," Johnny reported. Throughout his trip, the debasement of farmers by their masters outraged young Adams, a descendant of farmers. He observed that in Courland, "which belongs to Poland but Russia has more influence there," the farmers were "bought and sold like so many beasts and were sometimes exchanged for dogs or hogs." He was further horrified to find out that if a master killed one of these unfortunates he paid only a trifling fine. Theoretically, the slaves could buy their own freedom but seldom were allowed to earn sufficient money to do it. Physically the trip was uneventful except for the breakdown outside of Berlin of their carriage, which had to be replaced with a new one.[25] On August 21, the travellers reached St. Petersburg. The Russian capital, still uncompleted, was situated on the Gulf of Cronstadt in the midst of nine branches of rivers, which gave it distinction even though seven of them were no more than creeks made into canals about as wide as the Singel in Amsterdam. The streets were large and the houses well built, mostly constructed of brick plastered over in imitation of stone. Although Johnny predicted it would probably take another century before the city was completed, he thought it more handsome than Berlin. At the time, only 400,000 people lived in St. Petersburg, but the new summer palace was one of the most beautiful structures in Europe and the villas around town were of "surprising magnificence . . . some with waterworks surpassing those at Versailles," Johnny wrote to his mother, who had never been far from Braintree.[26]

Schooling for Johnny proved to be a major problem in St. Petersburg. There was no school or academy and a scarcity of private teachers. Mr. Dana, when he discovered the exorbitant fees that the tutors commanded, hesitated to spend so much of John Adams's money without specific orders. Johnny's solution was to go on with his studies independently, but he had left his Latin-English dictionary behind in Amsterdam and was unable to buy another. He wrote to his father to send the missing book on the first vessel that could get into the winter-locked ports in the spring.

Adams, appalled at the cost of masters—ninety pounds a year for an hour and a half a day of instruction—considered the possibility that Johnny should return to Leyden in the spring. In the meantime, he urged the boy not to be troublesome to Mr. Dana and to continue as well as he could with his studies. Actually he regretted Johnny's absence very much because Charly had returned to America under the care of Dr. Waterhouse.

The reason for the lack of schools in the Russian capital became apparent to Johnny. He wrote: "There is nobody here but Slaves and Princes. The slaves can't have their Children instructed and the nobility that chuse to have theirs send them into foreign countries."[27] Left on his own, the boy read voraciously, studied some, and took advantage of Dana's subscription to an English library. But he was rather lonesome because he had no companions of his own age. As the winter progressed, Adams began to regret that he had allowed his son to go to Russia. Though Johnny's skill at language was formidable, his father mused that "it is a mortification to one to find that you write better in a foreign language than in your Mother tongue." His letters "showed a Judgement beyond your Age," but the style was unformed either in French or English. Another worry that he expressed was: "Alas! I regret that the Friendships of your Childhood can not be made among your own Countrymen."[28]

Nabby, writing from Braintree, expressed the same sentiments. She told her brother that Charly was back after a long and perilous journey that extended from early August 1781 to late January 1782 and was re-established as a favorite in the family circle. "You, my Brother, are far, very far removed from your friends and connections, it is a painful reflection to those who have parted with a Son and Brother."[29]

Dana's Russian mission was getting nowhere because the Empress was afraid to risk a quarrel with England. News from Amsterdam was much more positive. Adams wrote that "the Independence of your country" was acknowledged by Holland and he wanted Johnny back with him because even Mr. Thaxter was leaving for America. The problem was how to get Johnny from Russia to Holland since Dana planned to spend another winter in Russia.

On October 30 Johnny left St. Petersburg in the company of Count Greco, an Italian friend. They travelled by way of Helsinki to Stockholm, where they arrived on November 25 after encountering terrible weather and frozen water passages which forced them to stay in the Swedish capital for six weeks. Johnny liked the Swedish people's friendliness to strangers and their manners, which reminded him of his own country. The last of December he left Stockholm alone but had to stop at Norrkoping, about 120 miles away, for another fortnight. Another three-week delay at Gottenburg kept him from his rendezvous with Count Greco in Copenhagen. When the two friends finally met, they booked passage on a vessel for Kiel, Germany, and then, after waiting three weeks for a good wind, the harbor froze. Johnny thought the Danes less "openhearted" than the Swedes but nevertheless enjoyed his stay. Finally he and the Count proceeded by land to Hamburg on March 11 and then to Bremen where, Johnny wrote, "I drank . . . some Rhenish wine about 160 years old." About a month later he reached Amsterdam and then the Hague where he waited for his father, living with the family of M. Dumas until his father arrived at the end of July.[30]

During Johnny's travels, Adams was out of touch with him for months at a time and "suffered extreme Anxiety on his Account." For the first few months of 1783, the officers of the French and Dutch diplomatic and consular services were constantly scouring the Baltic and North Sea ports for the fifteen-year-old lad. "My Younker ought to think himself highly honoured by the Notice that has been taken of him by so many respectable Personages," his father said.[31]

During this period Adams had been involved in the peace talks with Great Britain which started in Paris in April between Franklin and Richard Oswald, the representative of the Rockingham Ministry. Henry Laurens, now released from his internment in Britain after being captured in 1780, was sent to the Hague to see Adams.

He arrived at the conclusion of Adams's successful effort to gain Dutch recognition. Adams then succeeded in floating a two-million-dollar loan from the Netherlands bankers in June and, in October, negotiating a treaty of commerce with the Dutch government. Arriving in Paris on October 26, John Adams joined Franklin and John Jay, who had come north from Madrid in June. Rockingham's death and the Earl of Shelburne's elevation to the post of Prime Minister had not changed Oswald's position. However, the American commissioners failed to consult with France on the peace offers, as they had agreed, because the British terms were so good. Count Vergennes was justifiably outraged but agreed to accept Franklin's tactful explanations. The next job for the commissioners, squeezing out favorable commercial concessions from the former mother country, was not so easy. Negotiations dragged on through the spring. Adams concluded, quite correctly, that no concessions would be made, a position that became obvious on July 2 when a British Order in Council excluded American ships from their West Indian ports. Consequently, he went back to the Hague to consolidate America's position with Holland and to bring Johnny back to Paris.

In September, John Thaxter returned to America carrying the Treaty of Peace with him. Adams, who had been very overworked, fell ill with a violent fever. His physician, Sir James Jay, advised him to go to Bath in England and to drink and bathe in the waters there. He and Johnny set out for London at once. While in the English capital, the Adamses visited John Jay and Joshua Johnson, now returned from Nantes and lodged at Cooper's Row, Great Tower Hill, which became John's official mailing address.

Through the influence of Benjamin West, now a fashionable court painter, the two Adamses were taken on a tour of Buckingham Palace, whose library they particularly admired. Sightseeing became a compulsion. From the Houses of Parliament to the Wedgwood factory, to Westminster Abbey, to St. Paul's and Windsor Castle, they were tireless in their pursuit of their English heritage. Inevitably, the frenetic activity harmed John Adams's health so that they finally decided to try the healing virtues of Bath. However, before the efficacy of the cure could be tested, bad news came from America and Amsterdam. The Holland loan had been exhausted and Adams must return to the Netherlands to float a new one. He was not optimistic about his chances.

While in England, Abigail heard from Johnny after a two-year silence. She was relieved that he was well and safely returned to his father but advised him to return home and attend "our university" in the course of the year. However, she added, he should get a good look at England first.

Adams doubted whether he could stand the rigors of a sea voyage in the midst of winter but, having no choice, he and Johnny went to Harwich, where they stayed in a seedy, uncomfortable inn devoid of books or company until a violent storm abated enough to allow them to sail. The voyage was a disaster. Finally, the exhausted Captain was forced to land his passengers on a desolate shore on the island of Gooreethe, the province of Zeeland, five miles from the nearest town with no available transportation.

The measure of young John Quincy Adams showed in his good-humored and attentive care of his ailing father. The roles were reversed while Johnny walked slowly by his father's side, encouraging him step by step until they reached the village of Goree. Their difficulties were not yet over because they had to cross several islands before reaching the mainland. However, a wagon with a horse and driver was available to carry them over frozen roads to the inn at Overflacken, which, thankfully, was comfortable. They had still to endure the ordeal of a trip by ice-boat.

The ice-boat was a large ferryboat with runners fastened onto it. It was rowed in the water until it came to ice. Then the skipper and his eight or ten men leaped onto the ice and hauled the boat on its runners after them. The passengers were required to get out and walk beside them on the ice. On the spots where the ice was thin and brittle, the boat would slide into the water, at which point the sailors would leap into it and break away the ice floes until the boat came to a place where the ice was thick enough for the passengers to get in. This miserable process was repeated again and again until the exhausted travellers were wet and "chilled to the heart." The passage took all day.

In a series of carriages, some primitive, all uncomfortable, Johnny and his father were carried to the Hotel des Etats Unis in The Hague on January 12. Almost immediately, they had to press on to Amsterdam where the depressing voyage was crowned with unexpected success. Adams was able to negotiate a loan for 2,000,000 guilders, although on terms he considered exorbitant.[32]

On May 15, Johnny was sent to England to await the arrival of his mother and sister, who were to join them there. This time he had an easy trip from The Hague to London, where he waited a month, using the time to observe England's lawmakers in action. He recorded that, in his opinion, Mr. Pitt was the best speaker in the House; Fox had striking ideas but stammered; and Lord North was "very cool."[33] When the family failed to appear in a month, Johnny returned to the Netherlands.

The reason for Adams's consent to Abigail's proposal to join him in Europe, for which she had been urging him for two years, was a domestic crisis. Nabby was being courted by Royall Tyler, a Harvard man who had become a lawyer and settled in Braintree. Though there was no outright objection to the suitor, Abigail and Adams both preferred to see if the attraction could survive a separation.

Abigail delayed her departure until she was absolutely sure that a vacillating Congress would appoint her husband one of the negotiators of the European commercial treaties. Therefore, it was June 20 before the ladies embarked on the *Active*, which carried them across the Atlantic in a month. When Adams had news that his wife and daughter were in England, he wrote that he felt "twenty years younger than I was Yesterday." Unfortunately, he could not leave at the time to meet her but he would send "you a Son who is the greatest Traveller, of his age, and without partiality, I think, as promising and manly a youth as in the whole world."[34]

On July 30, Abigail sat in her room at the Adelphi Hotel writing when a servant came in, breathless, crying, "Young Mr. Adams is come!"

"Where? Where is he?" she and Nabby both demanded.

"In the other house, Madam," the servant replied. "He stopped to get his hair dressed."

When Johnny entered the room, Abigail drew back unbelieving, until he said: "O, my mammy and my dear sister!"

Abigail recognized her son only by his eyes.[35]

On August 7, John Adams joined the family group and the next day he took them all to Paris. He had rented the Hotel de Roualt at Auteuil, a very large house by American standards and decidedly chilly. It had thirty rooms that were furnished only with the bare necessities; furniture was minimal as were the carpets, the curtains, and the table utensils. Abigail realized at once that housekeeping would be a nightmare because the red-tiled floors could not be kept clean and the area to be taken care of was enormous. The great bare house's sole attraction was its five acres of gardens and its location on the Bois de Boulogne.

Johnny once again had a mother to wake him up in the morning and to provide a hearty New England breakfast. He studied his Latin by himself and mathematics with his father's assistance. They translated Euclid into Latin and then did trigonometry, geometry, and conic sections. More important perhaps was the close relationship that developed between Johnny and Nabby, who travelled around Paris together, visiting the shops and theaters, sharing their ideas and their impressions.

Nabby was very appealing, perhaps because she was in love and separated from Tyler. The French thought that although she was not beautiful she had an air about her which they characterized as "triste." Johnny, too, was recovering from a mild but hopeless romance. While in Holland he and Mlle. Dumas had enjoyed long talks together while Johnny read poetry to her. Their similar experiences made the brother and the sister sympathetic to each other.

The Auteuil summer was idyllic. When he was not with his parents or his sister, Johnny was often in the company of Jefferson, the American Minister to France, or the Marquis de Lafayette. They both found the younger Adams a delightful, intelligent young man. During the summer Johnny went with his family to Versailles to be presented to the newborn prince who was given the title of Duke of Normandy and sometime later attended a Te Deum sung at Notre Dame in honor of the baby.

At the end of the summer John Adams's appointment to the Court of St. James precipitated Johnny's decision on whether to stay in Europe as his father's secretary or return to America to round out his haphazard education with some years at Harvard. The idea of settling down to the role of schoolboy after seven years of travel all over Europe and acceptance in the adult world was not appealing. How could he endure being "subjected to all the rules which I have been so long free and then to plunge into the dry and tedious study of the Law for three years?" Johnny asked.[36] His answer was the practical decision to return to Braintree and seek entrance into Harvard.

In May, while his family prepared to move to England, Johnny took passage on the French packet, *Courier de l'Amerique.* John Adams, bulwarked by Abigail and Nabby, sent his son off with a load of letters and ambitious plans for him. The hardest parting for Johnny was from his sister who had become his confidante. They promised to write to each other daily and Johnny agreed to meet Royall Tyler and try to become friendly with him. Vale Europe! Ave America!

CHAPTER 3

The Education of an American

"Fifteen months of Harvard maybe saved me from early ruin."
JOHN QUINCY ADAMS

T HE PASSAGE FROM FRANCE to New York was tedious. For fifty-six days the ship floated in a calm that allowed it to move no more than eight to ten leagues each day. The captain utilized Johnny's bilingual skill by requesting him to stay on deck all night to translate the pilot's orders. "Form to yourself an idea how I was puzzled to translate English sea terms that I did not understand to French sea terms which I knew no better," he wrote to Nabby.[1]

New York City struck Johnny, who had turned eighteen while at sea, as a very political place. Everywhere that he went he heard talk about the new country's predicament. The British, instead of giving up the ports, as they had agreed to do in the peace treaty, were bringing in reinforcements of troops and precluding the Americans from the fur trade. Everyone wanted to tell the American Minister to England's son that they were waiting impatiently to hear from his father what to do.[2]

Rufus King and James Monroe were very attentive to John Quincy and Richard Henry Lee, now the president of the Continental Congress, insisted on housing him. But the warm summer days were not wasted entirely on elderly political gentlemen.

Johnny joined the young set for their rounds of parties and excursions. An overnight trip was made to the home of Colonel William Smith's family where young Adams met Smith's five sisters. He commented that only Sally was really handsome. Later she and his brother Charles were married.

By mid-August there was no valid reason to tarry longer in New York, so Johnny prepared to travel to Braintree. He chose the land route, in order to see his native countryside for the first time. With Le Ray de Chaumont, a young Frenchman, as his travelling companion, he set out for Boston via Stamford, New Haven, Hartford, and Springfield.

Hartford proved to be the highlight of the trip. It was pleasantly nostalgic to renew his acquaintance with his boyhood travelling companion, Jesse Deane, who lived there. But it was through Colonel Jeremiah Wadsworth, at whose elegant home he dined, that John Quincy was introduced to some literary works that made him talk of an American literary renaissance. Wadsworth gave him a present of "M'Fingall," written by John Trumbull, a cousin of the painter. This popular poem, modelled on Butler's *Hudibras*, burlesqued the battles between the Whigs and the Tories during the American Revolution. Johnny thought it was an immensely important work which, along with Timothy Dwight's epic, *The Conquest of Canaan*, gave adequate proof that a genuine American literature existed. The Connecticut Wits, as they were called, had no more enthusiastic supporter than the youthful returned expatriate who felt a strong need for a true native poetry.

Johnny's return to the Boston area made an understandable stir among the Adams's friends and relatives, who engaged in the customary game of deciding which parent the young man most closely resembled. The consensus was that Johnny's short, stocky build and general stance favored his father but that, feature for feature, he was like Abigail Smith.

The adulation of relatives, who marvelled at the young man's adventures and wanted to hear his descriptions of castles and cities and foreign courts, was flattering but was not furthering the purpose of Johnny's return, which was to be admitted to Harvard with advanced standing. John Adams had said rather proudly that Johnny "was eminently a self made man in the broadest sense." In the groves of academe, however, the young man's unorthodox training and irregular education proved to be unappreciated.

After interviewing young Adams, President Joseph Willard concluded that the prospective student had better make up his deficiencies, particularly in the classics, before the college could admit him to the junior class. John Quincy withdrew unhappily from the encounter, particularly chagrined because his younger brother Charles, who had prepared in the usual way, was well established at the college.

President Willard had indicated that if Johnny met the requirements he would be admitted in the spring. Therefore, the former world traveller and companion to foreign ministers had to go to the small town of Haverhill, Massachusetts, to be tutored by his uncle, Reverend John Shaw. He boarded at the Shaws where he became a member of an already crowded household. Besides the Shaws and their children, Tommy Adams and two young ladies lived there. This was an additional hardship for John Quincy, who was used to commodious, often luxurious quarters and to quiet and privacy. In order to solve part of his problem, Adams placed himself on a different schedule from the rest of the family, rising later and retiring later than the others.

Ten hours a day was allotted to John Quincy's individualized cram course. The strain of the intensive study made him anxious and irritable. Accustomed to admiration and encouragement, he reacted negatively to his uncle's bluntness. Uncle Shaw thought his clever young nephew rather presumptuous and somewhat arrogant, a trait that even his admiring parents had detected. Consequently, Johnny grew thin and suffered constantly from sore eyes, an affliction that became chronic. New friends and the company of young people relieved some of his tension, but Johnny enjoyed most his visits with John Thaxter, now a practicing lawyer in Haverhill. With him he could relive his more exotic past.

The tutoring months were enlivened by an abortive little romance that involved Johnny and Nancy Hazen, one of the Shaw's female boarders. The seventeen-year-old girl, an orphaned niece of the Revolutionary War General Moses Hazen was, Johnny said, not quite a beauty but had a fine shape and magic in her eyes. Her main attraction was a sophistication that the local girls lacked. That he was "never in greater danger" from his emotions, John Quincy admitted to his diary, confessing that he had escaped "Passion" up to this time only because of good fortune and now he was to be "put to a trial."[3] He was relieved when Nancy went away, for upon her return the stricken lover was able to convince himself that she was a coquette.

Very likely had everyone stayed out of it the anemic little romance would have faded away quietly. But Johnny's Puritan relatives found it necessary to inform Abigail, who then confronted her son. John Quincy answered his mother on December 28 that though Nancy had many amiable qualities, she need not fear for her son. However, the alarm went out when Aunt Eliza found a poem that Johnny had addressed to "Delia" and immediately concluded that its subject was her boarder.

Shortly afterward Nancy left the Shaws, either voluntarily or as a result of the episode. The romance, such as it was, cooled—or, rather more accurately, froze. Johnny admitted to "being more attached to her, than I would wish to be" but claimed that his feeling was of short duration and that her character "acquires a person's affection, much easier than she preserves it."[4] At a later meeting, he professed to be relieved by her coldness.

The uncomfortable distraction was resolved by a message from Harvard. Since certain lectures were to be given earlier than expected, it said, Mr. Adams had better seek admission at once. Johnny mounted his horse on March 14 and rode the thirty miles to Cambridge.

The next morning at nine o'clock, President Willard, four tutors, three professors, and the librarian examined John Quincy on Latin, Greek, Watts's *Logic* and Locke's *Essay on Human Understanding*. His performance, on his own admission, was mediocre. But the president, after reading his translation of some Latin lines, said to him, "You are admitted."

John Quincy shared an upstairs room in Hollis Hall with Henry Ware, an older student who was already a Bachelor of Arts. He followed the college curriculum which was rigidly classical with much time spent on exercises in declamation because most of the students were planning for a career in the ministry, law, or teaching.

John Quincy had mixed feelings about his college years. Though he was now with his peers instead of being a child among men, and in his native setting instead of in foreign capitals, he felt alienated. These suitable young men were strangers to him, not his childhood friends. His father's college, though close to home, was not really familiar. Except for his intellectual activities, Adams was always a spectator, never a participant in the Cambridge scene.

Consistently critical of the faculty and of the administration, John Quincy said that the tutors were too close in age to the students and too ignorant to merit respect. He hated Mr. Hale, the metaphysics teacher, and thought the mathematics tutor "very prejudiced and very vindictive." The Greek tutor often betrayed ignorance so that, of them all, only Mr. James, the Latin professor, had merit. He knew his subject and was a gentleman. In general, he said, the faculty treated the students like "brute beasts," which attitude, John Quincy conceded, might teach him some needed humility.[5] Harvard's president fared no better than his staff from Adams's vitriolic pen. Although a sociable man, Johnny said he was "stiff and formal" and, as a preacher, "not an elegant compositionist nor a graceful orator"; sometimes he would try so hard that he would make faces "which do not render his harsh countenance more agreeable."[6]

Student scrapes and student rebellions were often recorded in the *Diary* entries for these years. Although usually sympathetic and sometimes apologetic for his fellow students, Adams never participated in their scrapes. The tutors were the butt of student anger when inebriated students set off the "high goes." Students broke faculty windows and then booed, groaned, clapped, and hissed when tutors rose to leave the dining hall. On one occasion, Borland, a classmate of Johnny's, collared a tutor, threw a handful of gravel in his face, and cursed him. Adams thought Borland's punishment, which was to read a confession and be degraded to the bottom of the class, much too severe. Others, he commented, had been just as drunk and "behaved quite as ill."[7]

Adams's broadminded attitude towards student self-expression was amusingly presented in a long satirical poem about some members of the junior class who expressed their opposition to the distribution of parts for an exhibition by staging a drunken mini-riot. The poem, called "Lines Upon the Late Proceedings of the College Government" by a student, was written and circulated during Johnny's senior year. It began:

> I found the Juniors in a high rant
> They called the President a tyrant.

The tutors took turns making accusations against the students to the president, who answered:

The Crime is great, I own
Send for the Juniors one by one!
By this almighty wig I swear
Which with some majesty I wear,
And in its orbit vast contains
My dignity, my power, and brains,
That Weir and Prescott both shall see
That college boys must not be free!

One of the tutors declared that he soon "would teach them to be still":

Their wicked rioting to quell,
I'd rusticate, degrade, expel;
And rather than give up my plan
I'd clear the college to a man.

President Willard, however, was more lenient. He warned the culprits "to beware":

Of drinking more than you can bear.
Wine an incentive is to riot,
Destruction of the public quiet.
Full well your tutors know this truth
For sad experience taught their youth,
Take then this friendly exhortation!
The next offence is rustication.[8]

Whether John Quincy's sympathetic and yet passive role in these situations was due to inhibition, lack of spontaneity, or age and experience, he never seemed able to get down to the level of the others, a difficulty that followed him through life.

Adams worked hard to perfect his public-speaking technique so that he could participate in the public exhibitions. Harsh criticism of his early efforts by both his peers and his teachers spurred him to persevere until he became one of the recognized experts. After presenting his arguments on the question "Whether the immortality of the human soul is probable from natural reason," he delivered an address before the A.B. literary society which he had just been invited to join. The thesis of his maiden address was that the relationship between happiness and education was negligible. Knowledge of Newton, he declaimed, was not guaranteed to make man happier, nor was the political system nor civilization itself. From his own experience, Adams observed that he had seen more evidence of "cheerfulness and contentment" in a despotic monarchy than any-where else. Education's function was utilitarian, he said. Its purpose was to raise the individual from his natural state to a sense of duty that would turn his attention from considerations of personal hap-piness to those of patriotism and wisdom.

By August 1786, the senior class had to choose its valedictory orator and the collectors of the theses. John Quincy was chosen the collector of mathematics theses, an appointment that, he wrote to his father who had held that same post, "will confine my studies for the ensuing year much more to the mathematics than I should have done if I had been left to my own disposal."[9]

News came from London that Nabby was married to Colonel William Smith on June 11. Royall Tyler, that gifted but eccentric man who would become a famous American dramatist, had missed out on becoming a member of the Adams family. John and Abigail Adams were pleased with their daughter's choice. Their son-in-law was handsome, dashing, well educated, well mannered, and well connected—a perfect mate, they thought. The young couple set up housekeeping in an apartment in Wimpole Street not far from the American ministry.

In September, on a visit to Holland, Mr. and Mrs. John Adams were entertained by the faithful Dumas. Both Monsieur and Ma-dame Dumas sent affectionate greetings to Johnny but there was no word from their lovely daughter with whom the young man had sung duets, played the flute, and fancied himself in love. The Marquis de Vere, who was now the French Minister to Holland and had been in St. Petersburg with John Quincy, also enquired for him. He remarked to Abigail that were she dressed in Johnny's clothes, he should have taken her for him.

Because of heavy snows and a shortage of wood, President Willard gave the students an eight-week vacation beginning in mid-Decem-ber. John Quincy stayed in Cambridge at the home of Professor Wigglesworth, where he studied, read Montesquieu and spent an agreeable portion of his time with Miss Wigglesworth and her friends.

At dinner with the young ladies, Johnny commented, "The con-versation turned on divers topics, and among the rest upon love, which is almost always the case when there are ladies present." It was rumored that young Adams was interested in Peggy Wiggles-worth's cousin Catherine Jones but his *Diary* mentioned many girls.

Of a Miss Ellery from Newport with whom he "had a deal of chat,"
he wrote, she had "a larger share of sense than commonly falls to an
individual of her sex."[10]

While John Quincy was at Harvard, Western Massachusetts was
in turmoil. Farmers, many of them veterans of the Revolutionary
War, were so debt-ridden that their farms were being foreclosed. In
several places anger and outrage over the situation had driven them
to mob action. On September 26, Daniel Shays, formerly a Captain
in the Revolutionary War, now a dissident farmer, gathered a small
army of about 500 equally desperate men and attacked the militia
who were protecting the Supreme Court sitting at Springfield. They
succeeded in forcing the Court to adjourn.

The July before this, John Quincy had participated in his first
debate for the Phi Beta Kappa Society on the subject: "Whether
civil discord is advantageous to Society." He had been assigned the
affirmative, which he had argued with little enthusiasm, stating that
civil discord could be useful because too much calm might be the
forerunner of a storm. When he first heard of the Shays' uprising, he
commented that in a Republican government such disturbances
could be productive but, if allowed to get out of hand, they could
lead to the horrors of civil war.

The first college exhibition of the school term took place on September 26, the same day as Shays' rebellion. Its subject was, appropriately, the relationship between equality and liberty. Young
Adams asserted that democracy was the greatest tyranny and that the
current rebellion proved that too much equality meant less liberty.
In November, he spoke at the A.B. society on the same subject, this
time asserting that the causes for the uprising were the familiar
classical Roman ones: the decay of public virtue and the decadence
that always set in after the heroic days of a Revolution.

By December 20, John Quincy's attitude toward the disturbance
became clear to him. Harvard was involved because, for a time, it
was used as an emergency military headquarters. Since rumors persisted that the insurgents were on their way to Cambridge, some of
the college students had formed companies and started to drill but
Johnny was not among them. He wrote to his mother that he had a
"great aversion'" even to thinking about public affairs and "near as
we are to Boston, I should know nothing concerning them if riots,
insurrections and anarchy were not at this time the only topics of
conversation." He thought that the "present insurrections" were

not immediately dangerous for the government had "sufficient vigor and energy to suppress them at once." However, "I suspect that the present form of government will not continue long . . . the men of property and consideration think the constitution gives too much liberty to the unprincipled citizen," he added.[11]

In the Spring Exhibition, which was to be a conference, in English, on the comparative utility of law, physics, and divinity, John Quincy was assigned the defense of the law, Nathaniel Freeman and Moses Little the other parts. Not only did Adams dislike the part to which he was assigned but he also dreaded comparison with his chief rival, Freeman. Both of these reasons reinforced his conviction that he lacked talent in rhetorical composition. All in all he wished the conference to the devil and wrote his lines with the greatest difficulty.

The composition that John Quincy turned out had in it echoes of Shays' rebellion, which had been quelled in February. It also expressed something of its author's doubts about the value of his future profession. He declaimed:

At a time when the profession of the Law, labours under the heavy weight of popular indignation; when it is upbraided as the original cause of all the evils with which the Commonwealth is distressed; when the legislature have been publicly exhorted by a popular writer to abolish it entirely, and when the mere title of lawyer is sufficient to deprive a man of the public confidence, it should seem this profession would afford a poor subject for a panegyric; but its real utility is not to be determined by the short-lived frenzy of an inconsiderate multitude. . . .

Despite his frequent antagonism to the legal profession John Quincy never seemed to have considered seriously the pursuit of any other profession. His parents, of course, assumed that he would follow his father's career. As early as Johnny's junior year at Harvard, John Adams had written to Dr. Cotton Tufts, his agent: "What are we to do then about John? What lawyer shall we desire to take him, in town or country? And what sum must be given him? And what will his board and clothing cost? And when shall we get the money to pay all these expenses?" In his transport of fatherly concern, Adams suggested, half seriously, that he ought to return home to take all his sons into his own office. Dr. Tufts made arrangements for young Adams to enter the office of Theophilus Parsons, a distinguished Newburyport lawyer. John Quincy and his mentor met for the first time at a dinner given by Judge Francis Dana, who still took an interest in his young former secretary. The plan was that John Quincy would go to Newburyport after his college graduation.

"O Lord! O Lord! I hope it will rain hard that all their white wigs may be wet that would not let us have a private commencement," John Quincy lamented. He disliked his commencement topic, which he thought was too controversial and, once again, he feared unfavorable comparison with his constant rival, Freeman. As it turned out, his fears were not unwarranted.

Johnny's prayers unanswered, graduation day was sunny though unseasonably cool. Aunt Cranch had prepared the traditional feast for her two graduates, her son Billy and Johnny Adams. Everything had been cooked at Braintree, to avoid the exorbitant prices of the Cambridge merchants, and then transported by wagon. She worked a week to prepare the two shoulders of beef a la mode, four boiled hams, and six tongues. The day before graduation she baked dozens of biscuits and a tremendous plum cake that took twenty-four pounds of flour. Cider and wine in quantity went along with the feast, which would be served on the college grounds on tables and benches specially constructed by Braintree carpenters so that they could be dismantled, carried to the college, and then set up for the celebration.

Harvard Commencement Day resembled a town outing. Alumni, friends and relatives of the students, officials of the college, and the graduates were only a small part of the crowd. The Governor and other state and local officials, the sheriff of Suffolk County, and a military company were augmented by the general populace who came to see the festivities and added to the holiday atmosphere. They milled around while the college band, which included Charles and John Quincy as flutists, played loudly.

Second in rank among the fifty-one Baccalaureate candidates of the class of 1787, John Quincy was in eighth place on the program when he got up to speak in the meeting house where the graduation orations were delivered. His relations noted that he was becomingly nervous and, with remarkable facial contortions, acquitted himself well. One of two English orations given, his subject was: "Upon the importance and necessity of public faith to the well being of the community."

After the presentations, the college gave a dinner which, it was observed, was not as luxurious as in "some former years of public tranquillity" but did, at least, "give the satisfaction of literary entertainment." After the repast, the guests regrouped at the meeting house for the distribution of the degrees. An honorary Doctor of Laws was given, in absentia, to Thomas Jefferson.

It was a relief to John Quincy when the ordeal was over, but unpleasantness was yet to come. The Boston *Centinel* of July 21 ran an extensive, highly critical account of the ceremony. It referred to the plenitude of "scholastic jargon" and "fulsome syllogism," and then complimented President Willard for the "brevity of his address." Each of the candidate's efforts was examined but special comment was reserved for Billy Cranch and John Quincy Adams. Cranch's topic was: "Upon the impossibility of civil liberty's long subsisting in a community without three orders in the government, vested with such powers as to be mutual checks upon and balances to each other." The reporter observed that the author obviously relied on John Adams's newly published, *Defence of the Constitution.* "If he appeared to some persons to have adopted many sentiments of the author, without sufficient examination, they may impute it to circumstances both rational and natural," he wrote. "Mr. Adams is undoubtedly a great man. He is likewise the orator's uncle!"

The pro-Shaysite *Centinel* was even more pointed in its handling of John Quincy. After calling his performance manly and sensible, the reporter added, "The public expectations from this gentleman, being the son of an Ambassador, the favourite of the Officers of the College, and having enjoyed the highest advantages of European instruction were greatly inflated. . . . He is warmly attached to the republican system of his father and discanted upon the subject of public justice with great energy." In the next statement, the reporter struck. "Mr. Adams's indisputable superior in style, elegance and oratory, is the graceful *Mr. Freeman.* It was thought almost impossible for him to exceed his accomplished rival who spoke before him, but to *Freeman* everything was easy."[12]

The *Centinel* hurt poor Johnny's most sensitive spots. It was also most unfair. He was not a favorite of the college, he insisted, and resented particularly the references to his European education, which obliquely branded him as an alien. His nagging fear of public comparison with Freeman had been all too completely realized.

Some pleasant results also developed from the commencement oration. John Adams wrote from London that he had read the speech and judged it spirited and manly. And, Reverend Jeremy Belknap, who had been present at the graduation, requested a copy for publication in the *Columbian* magazine, a Philadelphia literary venture. The oration appeared in the September 1787 issue, but there had been some difficulty about it which exposed the depth of John Quincy's sensitivity. In his correspondence with Belknap, young Adams agreed to the publication of his work but wanted it to appear without his name. Belknap answered diplomatically. "A young Gentleman of acknowledged Genius," he said, should not want to deprive his countrymen of the satisfaction of seeing "ye features of the Parent in the son, and may I not add your country will have a pledge of a succession of abilities in the same Family still to add to her Cause and espouse her interest."[13]

The *Centinel* struck again in mid-September with an anonymous lampoon in the form of an open letter called "To the *Overseers* of An University" by "The Students." The piece asserted that "partiality in the extreme" was the ruling criterion for distinction at the university. It was unclear whether the authors meant the attack to be directed against Adams but, nevertheless, Johnny was reminded once again of the difficulty of being the son of a public man.

The contents of John Quincy's address had become secondary to its author's family connections. However, the address did have some merit. It contained one memorable phrase, its characterization of the era as "this critical period." It stated also, with much oratorical flourish, that republican opinions were superior to monarchical and advocated that public promises should be kept, citing Roman examples of the "punctilious observance of all the contracts in which she was engaged."[14] John Quincy had proved himself to be his father's son.

Once again John Quincy Adams had to start a new life pattern. On a very warm afternoon in mid-August, he rode to Newburyport to call on Mr. Parsons. The town not only failed to fill him with "favorable expectations" but, on the contrary, aroused extreme anxiety. "About three weeks hence," he wrote, "I am to become an inhabitant of the place. Without friends or connections I am to stand on my own ground." He was expected to spend three years there preparing for entrance to the bar, which, he observed, might or might not turn out to be agreeable. However, he predicted, "The presages within my breast are not such as I should wish realized."[15]

Despite his uncertainty, John Quincy assured his mother that he

did not regret the Harvard years, though they cost the price of a
deflated ego. "It had reduced my opinion of myself and of my future
prospects to a nearer level with truth so that making allowances for
the general exaggerations of youth I do not overrate myself more
than people in general are apt to do," he wrote.[16] His greatest
regret was that he had not entered the college a year and a half
sooner and become a more solid member of his class.

Until he was due in Newburyport, John Quincy stayed in Boston
visiting friends and reading voraciously. He liked *Tom Jones*, "one
of the best novels in the language," because it was realistic and,
though it did not give a favorable opinion of human nature, also did
not give a false one. Best of all, he enjoyed Jefferson's *Notes on
Virginia* for "its learning without ostentation, and a spirit of philosophy equally instructive and entertaining."[17]

At three in the morning, on September 7, young Adams left for
Newburyport. He arrived in the early afternoon and took possession
of his room at Mrs. Leather's, located on State Street just a block
from Parsons' law office. He then proceeded to the office, determined to give the law profession an honest trial. Quiet and tedious
were the words John Quincy most frequently used to describe his
Newburyport experience. He obediently followed Parsons's reading
list, starting with Robertson's *History of Charles V*, which gave an
account of feudal institutions, although he had read it before. Actually, he found Rousseau's *Confessions* much more interesting—"the
most extraordinary book I ever read in my life,"[18] he said.

Parsons expected his students to work eight hours a day in his
office and four more at home. Johnny thought that three years of
such a diet should give him some stock of law but he hoped that his
health would hold up. Frequent dizzy spells and a tendency to acid
stomach threatened to interfere with his studies. Friends wrote to
Abigail that the young man pursued his task with too much ardor
and was endangering his health.

The world of John Quincy was not limited to hard work. He
acquired a set of friends with whom he pursued the youthful plea-
sures of wine, women, and song. One Saturday night, he reported,
he and a group of young men went out to a tavern, where they got
to singing and passing the bottle around with great enthusiasm.
Johnny's resultant hangover kept him from attending church on
Sunday and for three nights afterwards he was unable to write at
all.

As for the young ladies, he recorded that it was easy to be sociable with Mercy Brooks from Medford. Hannah Emery had "a beautiful countenance, an elegant person, and (I am told, an amiable mind.)"[19] One evening, tired of studying, Johnny went to a dance hall, where he danced until three A.M. with a collection of ladies that were strangers to him but almost all beautiful.

As a matter of fact, said John Quincy, dissipation was so fashionable that he decided to take advantage of Mr. Parsons's three weeks' absence and take a vacation. He rode to Thaxter's where there was a party going on with singing and drinking. After a couple of hours, almost all of the others were under the table but he took pride in the fact that he had been moderate enough to recover after a good dose of fresh air. Arrived at Quincy, Johnny spent most of his time in his father's library reading his journals from 1769–1776, which he found entertaining.

During the summer of 1787, delegates from all the states had been meeting in Philadelphia behind locked doors to write a new constitution for the United States. After the convention approved its final draft and adjourned on September 17, the document was carried back to the states for ratification. In order to be adopted, it needed the approval of nine states. Mr. Parsons favored the new constitution but his new apprentice did not. It was calculated to increase the power and wealth of those who had it already, "a grand point gained in favour of the aristocratic party," John Quincy said. Although willing to take his chance with the new government, he found it hard to give up the old and to "confess that a free government is inconsistent with human nature."[20] However, most of the people the young man talked with favored the constitution and, on November 20, at the town meeting it was unanimously approved.

John Quincy's firm anti-federalist position was supported or, perhaps, inspired by his fellow boarder, Dr. Daniel Kilham, a Harvard graduate, an apothecary, a bachelor about sixteen years older than Johnny and a delegate from Newburyport to the Massachusetts legislature. Of Kilham's unpopular stand, John Quincy said: "I think he is perfectly right in preferring his independency to his popularity." Later, after Kilham's speech in General Court against the constitution, Adams added that "he is very much to be applauded for that independence of spirit which disdains to sacrifice a sentiment to the breath of popularity." A much older John Quincy Adams had second thoughts about his own anti-federalist position.

Though he did not doubt his youthful sincerity and earnestness, he said that his opinions were "monumental errors" and his series of letters, written to Judge Cranch to explain his opposition, "a lesson in humility."[21] However, he would never retract one word about Kilham's right to his position nor did he ever give up the belief that independence of spirit was preferable to popularity.

Nowhere in J.Q.A.'s voluminous papers did he express enthusiasm for the profession of the law. After two months' study he complained that twenty years of study would not give him the knowledge that he needed. The "more I do, the more I find to do," he complained. Intensifying his feeling was a rising public animosity against the legal profession, which followed the mushrooming in their numbers. Inevitably, available business would have to be divided, "but I am determined not to despond," Adams wrote.[22]

He grew ill instead. His eyes began to fail and he had continual colds and general malaise. More serious was an intense depression of the spirits. Insomnia plagued him and when he did sleep his disturbing, extravagant dreams drove him to Dr. Swett, who, he said, had a mean attitude towards human nature, possibly because doctors "see humanity in a state of humiliation and it is no wonder if they have no idea of its glory."[23]

The future was Johnny's monster. He admitted that his prospects seemed darker to him daily and if he could look into the future he would shrink from the opportunity. He did not seek fortune or honors and, he philosophized, "the bubble reputation" was deceitful. These statements were as deep as he allowed his self-analysis to go. Unmentioned, perhaps unrealized, were fears that he would not be able to meet his parents' soaring hopes for him and that his father's career, far from having yet reached its peak, would be hard to equal.

Dr. Kilham at least kept the young man from being as solitary as a hermit. The society in town was agreeable but he didn't go to meet it. Even the future of the country looked gloomy. "We're probably on the eve of revolution," he prophesied, and on the last day of the year he reflected only on the shortness of human life.

Melancholy dominated all of John Quincy's days. Writing in his journal, he said, was just for the pleasure of complaining and the rest of the time he was wasting talking to Parsons or reading for pleasure. He lamented his lack of industry. "Though no stranger to the midnight lamp but do not make good and rapid progress," he complained.[24] The winter cold only made life more unbearable because Mr. Parsons objected to a fire in the office when he was not there and sometimes Johnny was forced to drop his pen because of the stiffness of his fingers.

The big news that winter, the ratification of the federal constitution by the Massachusetts convention, reached Newburyport on February 7. There was almost universal rejoicing but John Quincy could not share in it, having accepted the anti-federalist position. He was soon converted, however, for he asserted, "In our government, opposition to the acts of a majority of the people is rebellion to all intents and purposes."[25] Despite the noble sentiment, the new convert stayed home reading and writing while the rest of the town turned out to welcome home the delegates from the convention.

When Johnny's fellow law clerks left the office to be sworn in as lawyers, he became aware that his turn would soon come. He cautioned himself to let time take its course but was unable to take his own advice. Finally, tired of waiting to hear from his parents, who were expected home in the spring, he decided to return to Braintree where his father's new house was being prepared for the family's return.

The house had been built by Major Leonard Vassall, a West Indian planter, in the early eighteenth century. During the Revolution, Vassall's widow returned to England with her fellow Tories and the house was sequestrated. Adams bought it from Leonard Vassall Borland for six hundred pounds. It was a handsome house with a parlor panelled in West Indian mahogany and well proportioned to receive Abigail's new furniture, purchased in France and England. A new ell was being built to further gratify the returning Adamses. John Quincy was dissatisfied with the job that the contractors were doing and, perhaps, resented the abandonment of his childhood home. He said that he would never make the pretentious new house his permanent residence but would "pass much of my time here."[26]

The Braintree vacation revived John Quincy for a short time but soon his health broke again. Together with his physical complaints were the nagging problems of his prospects. He rehearsed them—two more years of boring study, no chance of supporting himself through this period, no fortune to expect, and, finally, entrance into an already crowded profession.

After more false reports, on May 18, 1788, a letter from Tom Adams confirmed the information that John and Abigail Adams were in Boston. Two days later John Quincy was in Boston seeking his parents. He found out that his father had gone to Braintree but his mother was at the Governor's house. Johnny rode there at once and "enjoy'd all the satisfaction that can arise from meeting so near and dear a friend after a long absence." Together mother and son set out for Braintree for the reunion with John Adams. Discussing politics with his father, Johnny asked why John Hancock had been elected Governor when at the last election it was declared that the constitution would be destroyed if he were elected. Now the same men who had opposed him had done everything to get him in office. "And the other side are equally capricious," he observed. The quixotic nature of party politics was never fully accepted by John Quincy Adams, though he spent a long lifetime in the midst of it.

There was no opportunity for Johnny to study while he helped his parents get settled in the new house. The packages, when unwrapped, revealed a great deal of damage but the precious books were unharmed. It was a major task to unpack and arrange the many volumes that Adams had purchased abroad and Johnny could not resist perusing each volume, just for a moment, before he placed it on the shelf. One of the great ties between John Adams and his oldest son was their mutual love of reading. The list of books with which John Quincy seasoned his daily records was overwhelming and each one was suitably commented upon and then catalogued in his mind.

On July 11, the occasion of his twenty-first birthday, with some humor, Johnny wrote:

This day completes my twenty-first year. It emancipates me from the yoke of parental authority, which I never felt, and places me upon my own feet, which have not strength enough to support me. I continue therefore still in a state of dependence. One third of the period of my professional studies has also now elapsed; and two years more will settle me, should life and health continue; in a situation where all my expectations are to center.[27]

In September, before Governor Hancock, the college officials and some officers of a French squadron harbored in Boston, John Quincy delivered the Phi Beta Kappa oration. It was a tame effort compared to some of his college presentations, possibly because the subject, "Ambition for a Young Man," was too personally threatening a topic to be treated in any other way. The orator recommended a life

of service and extolled the virtues of the lawyer who defended innocence and truth and rejected intrigue and cunning. But, allowing
his own preferences to show, he awarded the accolade for the most
virtuous ambitions to the vocations of literature and science. At
dinner, the French consul complimented young Adams profusely.

Shortly after this vapid performance, Johnny succumbed completely to ill health. All of his former symptoms reappeared in aggravated form and were little helped by Dr. Swett's opiates. In
desperation, Johnny rode to Haverhill to visit Aunt Eliza Shaw to
"recruit my health." She tried affectionate care and her own medicinal tea but he did not improve. Abigail received a letter from her
sister that asked if they had done something to him at Braintree
the past summer, such as telling him a "woeful story."[28] His battle
for health lost, study became impossible, so John Quincy decided to
return to Braintree until he recovered.

A regular regimen of exercise, medicine, and sports was set up
under the care of his parents. Johnny rode for hours at a time,
tramped through the fields and marshes with his gun, but failed to
conquer either his insomnia or his depression. In November Abigail
went to New York to be with Nabby who was expecting another
baby, but John Quincy stayed home with his father. Finally, in
December, he returned to Newburyport. He felt just as ill as before
but his conscience would not allow him to stay away any longer. In a
few weeks, however, he had to return to Braintree where he resumed the cure—riding, skating, hunting partridges and quails, and
some limited social activities. He stayed there until March.

John Adams, now the first Vice President of the United States,
elected by 34 of the 69 votes—which gave him more votes than
anyone else but not a majority—travelled to New York to take office
in the temporary capital. Johnny returned to Newburyport for the
rest of his stint. By a curious swing of the pendulum, the serious law
scholar turned into a social butterfly. Heeding the advice of his
friends and relatives to take the business of living more lightly, he
proceeded to act on it with accustomed thoroughness.

John Quincy's poetic muse was constantly at his side during the
winter of his recovery. He had made a hobby of composing pleasant
and unpleasant verses about young ladies of his acquaintance. The
spring before, he had been the author of a nasty set about Miss
Rebecca Cazenau, a friend of Alice Tucker. It was included later in
a garland of verses that he published under the title, "A Vision."

> Belinda next advanc'd with rapid stride
> A compound strange of Vanity and Pride
> Around her face no wanton cupids play,
> Her tawny skin, defies the God of Day
> Loud was her laugh, undaunted was her look,
> And folly seemed to dictate what she spoke.
> In vain the Poet's and Musician's art
> Combine to move the Passions of the heart,
> Belinda's voice like grating hinges groans
> And in harsh thunder roars a lover's moans.[29]

Versifying was part of a miniscule literary revival that filled the columns of bi-weeklies and magazines published in Boston and environs. There was much interest in rebuses that carried the names of local ladies and in the many stanzas of romantic verse that half concealed their identities. It was an amusing game to try to identify the originals of the Delias, Dianas, and Daphnes praised or reviled in the stanzas. Johnny was an avid participant, providing pages of copy.

John Quincy's long poem, "A Vision," was probably completed by late spring 1790. Its theme was a young poet's search for female loveliness, during which he encountered a number of ladies who failed the test until one—Clara, his ideal—succeeded. He wrote:

> Come, and before the lovely Clara's shrine
> The mingled tribute of your praises join:
>
> The partial gods presiding at her birth,
> Gave Clara beauty and yet gave her worth;
> Kind nature formed of purest white her skin,
> An emblem of her innocence within;
> And called on cheerful Health her aid to lend,
> The roses' colors in her cheeks to blend,
> While Venus added, to complete the fair,
> The eyes blue languish and the golden hair;
> But far superior charms exalt her mind,
> Adorned by nature, and by art refined,
> Hers are the lasting beauties of the heart,
> The charms which virtue only can impart.
> On thee thy ardent lover's fate depends,
> From thee the evil or the boon descends;
> Thy choice alone can make my anxious breast
> Supremely wretched or supremely blest.[30]

There is doubt about the identity of "Clara." Was she a particular girl or an ideal? The two most probable candidates for "Clara" were Catherine Jones and Mary Frazier. "Katy" had been the subject of a rebus as early as 1787 but so had several other young ladies. However, James Bridges, John Quincy's closest friend, wrote to him in February of 1789 in a manner that suggested that Catherine Jones was extremely partial to Adams. Miss Jones, whom Bridges met by chance one day, "spouted away upon her favourite topic with so much tenderness and warmth of friendship," he wrote, and Johnny, of course, was "the favourite topic."[31] But sixteen-year-old, blonde, beautiful, blue-eyed Mary Frazier was the girl with whom local legend most persistently, then and later, linked young Adams, who was a frequent visitor at her home. A definitive identification is difficult because an exact date cannot be assigned to the poem.

Even as late as 1844, John Quincy was enigmatic. At that time, a friend sent him a copy of "A Vision," republished in a newspaper in January of that year. JQA answered: "Portraits were from life, shaded by Fancy, to bring in the beloved image. . . . The lines were the effusion of a genuine but not a fortunate passion . . . forty years have passed away since the unrivalled beauty of Clara was consigned to the soil. . . ." The dating and the other clues point unmistakably to Mary Frazier, who died in 1804.[32]

Much improved by June, now in the last stage of his apprenticeship, Johnny tried to see "the practical part of the profession." In September he visited his parents in New York, where he enjoyed nightly visits to the theater. On a visit to the House of Representatives, he noted, acidly: "The eloquence had all been exhausted, but the spirit of contention still remained.

Newburyport was honored in November by a visit from President George Washington. John Quincy drafted the address presented to him and rode in the welcoming procession. At dinner, young Adams was exceedingly flattered that he was remembered from the New York visit. When the President left, Johnny rode with him in the procession that escorted him to the New Hampshire border.

That winter a bout of flu caused some return of the "ancient quarrel between the powers of drowsiness and me" and a "few nervous twitches."[33] But these inconveniences did not preclude visits to Miss Frazier and other social activities. A great deal of worrying about the future continued to take place. The relative merits of Newburyport, Braintree, and Boston as an appropriate place to practice law were carefully weighed. John Quincy wrote to his father that Newburyport already had Parsons and Bradbury; Braintree would have William Cranch and so did not need Adams; Boston would have to be the place. That he did not want to be a burden to his parents any longer was reaffirmed, but he would like to have his father's law library moved from Braintree.[34]

In July John Quincy received his Master of Arts from Harvard after participating in a disputation on the unalienability of citizenship delivered at the Harvard commencement. Almost at the same time, he became twenty-three years old and was admitted to practice at the bar in Essex County.

CHAPTER 4

The Reluctant Lawyer

"There is not in the profession [law] many gentlemen inhabiting this town whose characters are remarkably formidable from their respectability."

JOHN QUINCY ADAMS

BOSTON, IN 1790, was the metropolis of New England, a 780-acre peninsula inhabited by 18,000 people and surrounded by a large harbor. The city's population was homogeneous, made up mostly of Congregationalists of English stock. It looked much the same as it had at the time of the American Revolution—narrow and crooked streets paved with beach stones, white wooden houses with tiny gardens, and, everywhere, the smell of the sea. Faneuil Hall was its most distinguished landmark, along with the Long Wharf and Beacon Hill. Among the New England city's chief products were rum, beer, spermaceti, tallow candles, and glass. Often characterized as a conservative, self-satisfied town, Timothy Dwight disagreed. He said that on the contrary, it had a lively imagination and an adventurous spirit.[1]

John Quincy Adams, his formal education completed, paid Theophilus Parsons the promised $100 and, on August 9, 1790, set out for Boston. He took possession of his law office on Court Street, but considered himself a stranger in town because he had been educated elsewhere. Though he had family and friends in town, he expected nothing from them. His major concern was to make his own way because his parents had two younger sons to educate.

Adams experienced the normal frustration of an eager young professional. He waited for clients, at first hopefully and, finally, with what grace he could manage to muster. When they failed to make an appearance, Johnny filled some of his time reading Cicero, Tacitus, Burke, Clarendon, and Hume. But "I had troubles of the heart, deep and disturbing," he recalled over twenty-five years later.[2]

The reference was to the destruction of his romance with Mary Frazier, effectively accomplished by his parents, particularly his mother. Abigail had learned nothing from her meddling with her daughter's attachment to Royall Tyler, although Colonel Smith had proved to be a poor provider. Nabby had just given birth to her third son while her husband moved from scheme to scheme, unable to get settled. Nonetheless Abigail did not hesitate to advise John Quincy not to form a connection until he was able to support a family. She even hinted, in classic maternal style, that he might consider the wisdom of marrying a wealthy girl. The candidate she had in mind was Nancy Quincy, who had in fact just married. Johnny commented that his cousin Nancy was too fat and a prude as well.

There was an absence of youthful rebelliousness in the makeup of the young lawyer. He wrote to his father resignedly, "Happiness in life I am fully persuaded must be derived principally from domestic attachments: but a foundation must be laid before the superstructure can be erected. I hope I am in no danger from this quarter."[3] Abigail, rather cruelly, pretended that she had just heard about Johnny's love affair from his brother Tom. She advised him flatly to refrain from getting entangled, though she said, wickedly, perhaps his attachment might mend his careless dress. The name Mary Frazier was never mentioned in the mother-son correspondence, and by the end of November Johnny's affair had been successfully squelched.

Abigail used several unoriginal but effective techniques to discourage serious developments. Her own ill health was the background to all her remarks, which were, of course, very reasonable. Since Johnny could not afford to be formally engaged, she said, would it not be cruel to the girl and only a source of misery to him to continue his attentions? Though Abigail reproached herself for failing to be more explicit earlier, she had won the battle. John Quincy answered her that now he lived forty miles from Mary, so distance alone made it impossible for him to indulge his weakness. "If you knew the object, I am sure you would excuse," he wrote plaintively. And from a perspective of thirty-eight years, he later said that his "troubles of the heart . . . gradually wore away."

Nabby, who had reason to know, had warned her brother the previous spring that prudence crushed early romance. However, realistically, Johnny accepted the fact that he could not marry at once and, more important, he hated to hurt his parents. Their approval was a lifelong need that he seldom jeopardized.

Mary's role in this sad, abortive romance was strangely passive. There is a record of her having visited Johnny in Medford in October but, when he failed to declare himself, she withdrew. It is likely that her parents advised the pretty young girl not to waste her time on a reluctant suitor. Local legend persisted in the story that Mary Frazier vowed not to marry before John Quincy Adams. She remained single until several years after him, at which time she married Daniel Sargent, Jr., one of John Quincy's friends. Abigail may eventually have regretted her part in the story because Mary Frazier was, at least, a Massachusetts belle.

In late summer all of Boston was excited by the arrival of an American ship, *Columbia*, commanded by Captain Robert Gray, which had just completed a trip around the world. John Quincy wrote to Abigail that the most curious sight he had ever seen was "Owyhee," a native of the Sandwich Islands whom one of the travellers brought back as a servant. The native spoke English, which was remarkable, but even more striking was his "feather cloak of golden suns set in flaming scarlet that came halfway down his brown legs; created with a gorgeous feather helmet shaped like a Greek warrior's. . . ."[4]

In October John Quincy tried his first case. Unfortunately, it was given to him with only three hours' notice and consequently he was dissatisfied with his performance. Harrison Gray Otis was his opposing attorney. "My talent at extemporary speechifying" was always negligible, he complained and admitted to tremendous agitation during the trial. The family all had comments to make. Charles said it was not astonishing to have been "somewhat confused upon your first exertion," and suggested that the audience might have found it "rather pleasing." Honest John Adams wrote that Dr. Thomas Welsh, with whom Johnny was living, had reported, "your diffidence was remarked and your tremor observed, when you opened at the Bar."[5]

The winter was a rather miserable one. Johnny's health was poor again, unresponsive to the ministrations of Aunt Eliza and Aunt Mary Cranch. Abigail diagnosed his illness as impatience and fretting over his lack of a legal practice. When she saw him in Philadelphia, however, she was shocked by his pallor and his listlessness. Though still certain that his vitality would return if he had some clients and some money. No one mentioned Mary Frazier. Actually, the Philadelphia visit was a dismal failure. Tom, recovering from a painful attack of his chronic rheumatism, was still confined to the house. Charles, usually the life of the family, was strangely subdued, and Nabby was out of town.

By March the young lawyer was back in Boston, still awaiting clients. He tried to distract himself with card parties, assemblies, and all the other activities offered to a young gentleman with an excess of leisure, but he was not amused. He read romantic poetry, copying it into the blank pages of his *Diary*, which contained only occasional entries—such as an account of the eclipse of the sun which he viewed from Beacon Hill and which, he said, hurt his eyes because he did not have a glass to protect them. The *Diary* had little else except for lists of books read, mostly on poetry and history.

Though Johnny admitted the tedium and monotony of his life, he seemed only to half-regret his coldhearted decision to give up Mary. "Should my Heart ever yield itself to the voice of Love, I hope my judgment will approve, though it must never pretend to direct the passion," he promised on April 9. His papers reveal no indication that he considered renewing his suit or even his friendship with Miss Frazier, but later references indicate that he never entirely forgot her.[6]

John Quincy achieved a little more peace of mind at this time. Abigail convinced her husband that he should send his son a regular stipend of twenty-five pounds per quarter. In return, John Quincy was delegated to handle his father's Boston estate. Financial security made a foray into the field of literature possible.

For some time John Quincy had been collecting books and newspaper articles in preparation for a work on the national government. He had read Edmund Burke's pamphlet on the French Revolution, which interested him, but Thomas Paine's answer to it, *The Rights of Man*, drove him to compose a response. He wrote the eleven essays that were published as a series of letters by the *Columbian Centinel*, from June 8 to July 27, while living at Braintree with his parents.

John Quincy's use of a nom de plume, Publicola, caused a great deal of confusion in the public mind. John Fenno's *Gazette of the United States* had just printed John Adams's *Discourses on Davila,* a series of heavy-handed attacks on the French Revolution, which were severely condemned by the pro-French republicans who immediately dubbed the Vice President a monarchist and a supporter of the aristocracy. Just at this moment, Thomas Jefferson's laudatory preface to *The Rights of Man* was printed. Though Jefferson had not expected his remarks to come out in print, they accurately reflected his point of view. John Adams said that certain passages were deliberate attempts to injure him in the public eye. One of them was Jefferson's remark that "despite the 'political heresies' that had sprung up among us of late," he did not doubt that American citizens "would rally again around the standard of Common Sense."[7] Although offended, Adams decided not to respond to the Secretary of State because he felt that it would have a negative effect on national unity. John Quincy Adams felt no such restriction on his pen.

Johnny's prose differed greatly from his father's. James Madison, a notable stylist, remarked that Publicola's work displayed more method and "less clumsiness and heaviness of style" than the writings of the Vice President.[8] A serious student of literature and well aware that to tangle successfully with Tom Paine, publicist par excellence, would require more than mere scholarship, John Quincy prepared his work carefully. He attempted to inject wit, grace, and some dry humor into his prose, for he wanted to accuse his opponent of flippancy about serious matters.

Publicola stated his intention was not to defend the principles of Edmund Burke but to present the truth. "I shall without hesitation refuse my assent to every principle inconsistent with that, whether it proceeds from Mr. Burke, Mr. Paine, or even from the illustrious National Assembly of France."[9] Much of the work, however, was a lively defense of the Anglo-Saxon political system, quite in the spirit of John Adams.

Paine's assertion that there was no English constitution was called an absurdity. If a constitution was simply a written piece of paper, John Quincy wrote, then all constitutions except for the American would fail to qualify. A constitution may be defined as "the system of fundamental laws by which the people have consented to be governed, which is always supposed to be impressed upon the mind of every individual, and of which the written or printed copies are nothing but evidence. Paine's exhortation to the English people to destroy their present government was one of his 'flippant witticisms,'" John Quincy accused. "Mr. Paine seems to think it is as easy for a nation to change its government, as for a man to change his coat."[10]

Seemingly for satirical purposes, Paine claimed that the Norman conquest was the central event in British history. William the Conqueror's shortcomings, starting with his bastardy, provided good copy for Paine's jibes. John Quincy answered him. "The English government did not originate in the Norman conquest," he said. For his source, he quoted William Blackstone—"as good an authority as Mr. Paine's," he suggested. The jurist had made the point that the victory at Hastings was over Harold and did not alter the nature of the government."[11]

Publicola found the contemporary French government full of flaws and "inherently dangerous." The American government, he asserted, had the advantages of both the French and English and avoided their evils by establishing federalism, which divided power between the two levels of government. One of France's greatest flaws was her intricately indirect method of electing members to her legislature. The National Assembly, Adams said, had refined their representation "through so many strainers" in order to avoid the tumult and bloodshed of English elections that instead they had created an expensive system that "must open a thousand avenues to every sort of intrigue and venality," resulting inevitably in a body that would be "an aristocracy without responsibility." America had managed so far to enjoy its natural rights along with peace and tranquillity.[12]

Paine's assertion that the French constitution was more liberal than either the British or American on the subject of game laws allowed Adams a humorous rebuttal. To Paine's assertion that in France "the universal freedom of the chase" was placed beyond the control of their legislature, Adams answered that the preservation of game was an object of public concern and the legislature of every country ought to have the power of making game laws for the benefit of the public. An enthusiastic hunter in the marshes of his native Braintree, John Quincy had once remarked that though game laws were reputed to curtail the hunter's liberties, "where there are none, there never is any game."[13]

In the area of foreign affairs, Adams again found Paine's reasoning to be faulty. The French method of allowing their National Assembly complete power of negotiation on war and peace would just "open a thousand enemies for base intrigue, for furious faction, for foreign bribery, and domestic treason," John Quincy said. "Let us not substitute our liberties for the unsubstantial fabric of visionary politicians," he added.

Paper Number XL, published on July 21, said clearly that the Vice President had neither written nor corrected any of the papers. Publicola challenged all of Tom Paine's supporters to point to any passage in the published papers that recommended "either a monarchy or an aristocracy to the citizens of these States." But John Quincy's final words that "the candour of the public will not take misrepresentation for reason, nor invective for argument" did not silence the excitement that the articles caused.

Despite all assertions to the contrary, it was generally assumed that Publicola was John Adams. Jefferson wrote to Madison that "nobody doubts here who is the author of Publicola, any more than of Davila."[14] Madison answered that John Beckley, the clerk of the House of Representatives, told him that Publicola was probably the manufacture of John Quincy Adams "out of materials" furnished by his father.[15] Tom Paine had no doubt about the identity of his antagonist. "I had John Adams in my mind when I wrote the pamphlet and it has hit as I expected," he said.[16]

The furor resulted in the publication of the letters on both sides of the Atlantic. In France, Paine saw to it that Publicola was published and refuted. In London, the papers were attributed to John Adams, which made them very acceptable. Jefferson was quite accurate when he said that it was Publicola who gained attention for Paine's *Rights of Man.*

Many writers hastened to answer Publicola in the American press. The *Independent Chronicle* alone carried responses from "Agricola," "A Republican," "The Ploughman," and "The Watchman." The answers, however, were not serious discussions but merely commented on the now familiar charge against the Adamses of supporting monarchy and aristocracy. Satirical references to John Adams as the "Duke of Braintree" and deliberate distortion of his writings had been standard republican tactics for some time. Jefferson indignantly denied that he had a hand in any of this kind of activity. "I never did in my life, either by myself or any other have a sentence of mine inserted in a newspaper without putting my name to it; and I believe I never shall," he asserted.[17]

Both John and John Quincy Adams suffered from the Publicola experience. They defended themselves promptly and capably but the Vice President particularly regretted the coolness that developed between him and Jefferson. In a letter to John Adams, Jefferson blamed Publicola for the ill-feeling, which upset John Quincy even more, and perhaps accounted for his sore eyes, which he complained made him "almost blind." But, at the same time, John Quincy enjoyed some very positive results from his first venture into public controversy. He had tilted with one of the most successful practitioners in the art of political polemics and had been taken seriously. More important, George Washington was said to know the true identity of Publicola and to have noted it.

Young Adams, like many new lawyers, involved himself in local politics. The northern part of Braintree was being incorporated into the town of Quincy and John Quincy served on a committee to expedite the process. He was also appointed a member of a committee of twenty-one to report to the town on police reform. However, experience on the grass-roots level of politics caused him to question the much admired democracy of the New England town meeting. He said to his brother Tom that the 700 men present at the meeting looked as if they had been collected from all the jails on the continent and promptly outvoted everyone of wealth and ability. This was "a confirmation of my abhorrence and contempt of simple democracy as a Government," he concluded. John Quincy said nothing publicly at the meeting, although he realized that it could have been the start of a political career. He gave a variety of reasons for his silence, but it was chiefly "a want of confidence in myself," he admitted, and looked forward to the time when he would not be "oppressed by my diffidence."[18] Part of his reluctance to engage in political activity was his belief that he should not become known politically until he had established a professional reputation. He wanted to remain obscure rather than "appear as a politician without any character as a lawyer."[19]

There had been a flurry of legal business during the winter but it was soon taken care of and did not develop into a steady stream of clients. Abigail's encouragement barely kept John Quincy from complete despair. He read history and poetry and wrote some poetry, participated without much spirit in the antics of the Crackbrain Club, and even became interested for a short time in a girl named Sally Gray. But he absented himself from Harvard for the Phi Beta Kappa exhibition, probably because he was dissatisfied

with his undistinguished career, and once again he endured insomnia. His few *Diary* entries were cryptic and melancholy.

Once again the pen became the means of dissipating John Quincy's restlessness. This time his cause was the theater and its actors.
One of the few foreign tastes that the Adamses acquired in Europe
was a love of the theater. JQA had been acquainted with Shakespeare's plays from childhood because of Abigail's enthusiasm for
the Bard. She quoted him often in her correspondence and used the
nom de plume of Portia for her wartime letters to her husband. In
their diaries, John and John Quincy Adams often recorded their
attendance at plays, commenting on the actors and actresses who
played in them.

But devotion to the stage was only one of the reasons for John
Quincy's defense of the players which he published in December
1792. Another was the opponent whom he challenged, Attorney
General James Sullivan, lately an enemy of the Adams clan. Among
other reasons, Sullivan had lost favor because he had backed John
Hancock for the Vice Presidency in 1788. John Adams warned his
son not to cross the traitorous Sullivan lest he try to harm his
embryo law practice.

The present controversy arose over Sullivan's article, written
under the name "A Friend to Peace," which appeared in Boston's
Independent Chronicle on December 13, 1792. The previous January, despite the failure of a Boston petition for the repeal of the
Massachusetts State prohibition against the theater, construction of
an "exhibition room" was started. The theater, because that was
what it really was, a remodelled livery stable, seated about 500 and
opened, finally, in August. At first, John Quincy reported, it presented only very inferior vaudevillelike productions, but by October
a poor production of *The Miser* was offered, followed by a "fair"
Hamlet and a "miserable" *Marriage à la Mode*.

The authorities tried to find an informer or a Grand Jury willing
to supply an indictment but, failing to do either, arrested an actor
during a performance. Though the audience rioted in sympathy
with the players, "Board Alley" thought it best to shut up the theater. On the following day, Sullivan wrote an explanation and a
defense of the administration's policy. As soon as Adams read the
article, he prepared to answer it.

Using the pseudonym "Menander," who was a witty, sophisti-
cated Athenian playwright of the fourth century whose plays were

not discovered until the twentieth century, Adams set out to refute Sullivan. He used one of his favorite arguments from the Publicola papers: "In a free government the minority never can be under an obligation to sacrifice *their rights* to the will of the majority, however expressed." Even more boldly, he asserted that "no obedience is due to an unconstitutional act of the legislature."[20]

With a youthful lack of judgment, in Menander 2, John Quincy attacked Governor Hancock for prodding the legislature into action against the theater and for encouraging a number of people to "unlawfully collect" in front of the theater for the purpose of "pulling down the building where performances had been exhibited."[21] Menander's last appearance, four days later, was considerably subdued. He had to withdraw his accusation against the Governor because it was false, just as John Adams had surmised when he read his son's installment in New York.

In the balance, the exchange was unsuccessful for Adams, providing another frustration for the dismal year of 1792. "I am the more desirous to keep myself altogether unconnected with political topics, because my sentiments in general I find are as unpopular as my conduct relative . . . to the theatrical questions. I have no predilection for unpopularity as such," John Quincy wrote to his father early in 1793. Though his words were sincere at the time, they proved inaccurate. By the end of April, Johnny was in print again.

The *Columbian Centinel* carried another series of articles by the prolific John Quincy Adams. This time the subject was more congenial to the author. It concerned American neutrality in the war between France and England. Writing under the name Marcellus, a Roman general, the first article was published two days after Washington's "Declaration of Neutrality" was made. Marcellus attacked privateering, which he said was "a depredation upon the commerce of one of the parties under the authority of another," a violation of the laws of nature and much the same as piracy. He condemned it even among nations formally at war, proudly pointing to the treaty between the United States and the King of Prussia which renounced privateering between warring nations, "the first instance in which two great nations have adopted this system of benevolence and humanity."[22]

In the two Marcellus essays subsequent to Washington's proclamation, citizens were cautioned to suppress their private reactions to the foreign war and to understand their position "as the citizens of a nation at a vast distance from the continent of Europe; of a nation whose happiness consists in a real independence, disconnected from all European interests and European politics. It is our duty to remain the peaceable and silent, though sorrowful spectators of the sanguinary scene." Adams never moved far away from this early statement of foreign policy. He told his countrymen that the United States had a seacoast of 1,200 miles open to invasion "and where is the power to protect it?" Since the country was destitute of all the apparatus of war and burdened with public debt, "to advise us to engage voluntarily in the war, is to aim a dagger at the heart of the country."[23]

In answer to the sensitive question of American obligation "to take the part of the present government in France," particularly if the British attacked the West Indies, Adams said that it was a difficult problem because the Law of Nations generally accepted the continuity of treaties through revolutionary change. He therefore advanced the principle "that no stipulation contained in a treaty can ever oblige one nation to adopt or support the folly of another." Applying this to French administration of its West Indian colonies, he pointed out that the islands had been kept in a constant state of rebellion and civil war and that it had been reported that a formal deputation from the colonies had solicited British protection. "There would be something singularly absurd and iniquitous," he wrote, "to see the United States support the French in a plan of oppressive administration over their colonies, as a reward for rescuing them from the oppression of Great Britain."[24] Therefore, he concluded, the French obligation was "dissolved or at least suspended. . . . We cannot take part with the French Republic without uniting all the rest of Europe against us," which would be "dooming ourselves to inevitable ruin and destruction."[25] A law that superseded all others, therefore, was that of Hobbesian self-preservation which would command the United States to stay at peace.

Marcellus was accused by those who disagreed with him of blatant pro-British propaganda, or of being the advocate of a double morality. The opposition pointed out that avoiding the obligation to France could be turned around. Suppose France had used Marcellus's logic and had refused to help the American colonies revolt against the British?

Possibly had more clients made their way to John Quincy Adams's law office on Court Street, he would not have had the time to fill the pages of the *Boston Centinel* with yet another anonymous series of controversial articles. These, however, would have significant results.

Adams's final set of polemics was written at a time when the country was divided over the activities of an aggressive French revolutionary, Edmond Genêt, Minister of the United States from the new government of France. Assuming that the United States was the ally of France under the Treaty of Alliance of 1778, Genêt further assumed that he could make the country a jumping-off place for the French conquest of the Spanish Floridas and her former colonies, Louisiana and Canada. He also expected that the United States would allow the French to equip privateers for use against the British.

The consistent rebuffs that Genêt suffered from the American government contrasted strangely with his brilliant reception on a kind of triumphal progress from Charleston, South Carolina, to the capital. In Philadelphia Genêt was given a magnificent dinner attended by all the city's prominent citizens. "La Marseillaise" was sung with enthusiasm. Genêt was certain that he was in a strong position when he observed what seemed to be encouragement from Secretary of State Jefferson.

But President Washington was displeased with the public clamor for the French Minister and the approval of his cause that it affirmed. The knowledge that the puny American Navy could not realistically counteract the privateers already commissioned by Genêt was a frustrating and irritating predicament for Washington.

In August 1793, the irrepressible Frenchman outdid his own excesses. He threatened to go to the American people, over their Chief Executive's head if necessary, and demand that Congress be called into special session to discuss the matter of France. This audacity turned Jefferson against Genêt but not against his cause. However, Hamilton advised that the Frenchman's recall be demanded at once. In Boston, John Quincy Adams was denouncing the French upstart with vehemence in a series of papers, written under the name of Columbus, that were to turn the American people away from their enchantment with Genêt.

According to rumor, John Quincy had known Edmond Genêt when he was at school in France, a fact that the American had either forgotten or chose not to acknowledge. However, an entry in John Adams's *Diary* for March 3, 1779, said that he and Edmond Genêt and Johnny "went to see the Menagerie."[26] There is no further evidence of subsequent meetings between the boys, nor would it have been surprising, because Edmond was a precocious lad four years older than young Adams. Nevertheless, John Quincy stated in his Columbus paper: "I have no personal acquaintance with the man (Genêt) nor feel any personal resentment or animosity against him. My sentiment for his country, like those of every true American, are those of partial attachment; but as in my opinion his actions bespeak him the most implacable and dangerous enemy to the peace and happiness of my country, I hold it to be a moral and religious duty to support the opinion with the reasons upon which it is grounded."[27] Genêt's audacity in challenging the authority of the President was, he said, "an insolent outrage" against the people's "common friend and Benefactor" by a "petulant stripling" who presumed to "place himself in opposition to the father of *their country*." The people realized that the President had been delegated by them to negotiate with foreign ministers, said Adams, and therefore no longer reserved to themselves the right to judge so that "the intention of the Minister, was no less hostile to the Constitution than insulting to the government of the Union."[28]

The growth of democratic-republican societies modelled on the Parisian Jacobin societies struck John Quincy as a symptom of "an imported distemper," part of a movement by Genêt to arm one part of America against the other and to divide the parts in order to rule the whole. Athens, he reminded his readers, was an example of the dangers that encompass the liberties of a republican state when foreign influence intrudes on its administration. In the last quarter of a century the same cause had been fatal to the liberties of Sweden, Geneva, Holland, and Prussia—"the association of internal faction with external power."[29] The American people must examine these examples and "remember that the eye of the basilisk is less to be dreaded, than the designs of such a man."[30] To solve the problem, John Quincy agreed with Hamilton—the President must dismiss "such a criminal agent."

Washington did, indeed, demand the recall of Genêt but the charismatic Frenchman did not return home. A new regime had gained power in France and, fearing for his head, Genêt elected to settle on Long Island. He eventually married Cornelia Tappen Clinton, the daughter of Governor George Clinton, became an American citizen, and lived out his life in the United States.

Columbus's articles were very popular with the federalists. They were copied widely and elicited many answers. Most significant, however, was that the President and the Cabinet and Congress, also "formed the same judgment of Columbus," John Adams recorded happily. "Partisans will rail but sound reason will enlighten and prevail," he added.

It would have been much better if John Quincy, now writing as Barneveld, had ignored Columbus's critic, Americanus, who was JQA's old antagonist James Sullivan. Sullivan maintained that the American government had changed since 1776 and now the people were supreme so that even the Chief Executive must bow to their sovereignty. And then, once again sounding the anti-Adams battle cry, he accused them of not really accepting the American Revolution and of preferring the rule of an aristocracy.

Unable to control his anger, John Quincy abused Americanus bitterly, charging him in savage tones with falsehood, absurdity, and inconsistency. Sullivan, older and better controlled, answered effectively with some humor.

The public had mixed reactions to the exchange. The partisan *Columbian Centinel* carried a sonnet addressed to Columbus but the *Chronicle* reported that "the *petulance* and *affected* wit of Columbus and Barneveld" was a "sort of *literary plagiarism* from Junius." The same paper commented on the *"aspirations of family pride"* and *"the Juvenile author"* and "the high station of his sire." JQA denied that the gibes perturbed him but admitted to being hurt by the coolness with which some of his friends received his work.[31]

Though John and Abigail were pleased with their son's pamphleteering, they were critical of his excesses. Abigail wrote to John Quincy that Sullivan's age merited some respect and both parents advised their son to remember that he was a gentleman even if his opponent had forgotten it.[32]

John Quincy's personal life continued to be unhappy. He was gaining weight, partly, he admitted, from overindulgence in wine and partly, very likely, from overeating due to frustration. His *Diary* entries referred to excessive imbibing and the uncomfortable effects he endured the next day. There were some cryptic references to late evenings and casual encounters on the Commons. Regarding these, Adams promised his *Diary* that he would reform and apply himself to serious work. An indulgence for which Adams offered no excuse, however, was the theater, which could now be enjoyed legally. He was a sponsor who faithfully attended performances three or four times a week.

John Quincy's law practice improved. "It gives me bread," he wrote to his father and told him that he would no longer require his allowance. John Adams urged his son to become active in town meetings and to join a political club. "But I am afraid of all these things," John Quincy answered. He wanted to make "some provision for fortune" before seeking public office.[33] Nonetheless, when President Washington failed to appoint him federal Attorney General for New England as had been predicted, JQA was very disappointed. He was not opposed to that kind of public recognition, only to elective office gained through political channels.

The President had noticed young Adams. John Adams wrote that "Washington was indeed under obligation to him [JQA] for turning the tide of sentiment against Genêt and he was sensible of it and grateful for it." Secretary of State Edmund Randolph hinted to the Vice President that there was a possibility of a foreign mission for his son. In fact, he had been asked to find out about John Quincy's life and character from the members of Congress. After his inquiries, Randolph informed Adams that he was prepared to make a favorable report to the President.[34]

The Senate unanimously confirmed George Washington's appointment of John Quincy Adams as Minister Resident to The Hague to succeed William Short who was to go to Spain to deal with the Mississippi question. The appointment was considered an excellent choice because young Adams had lived in Holland as a boy, studied there, and knew the language. He was acquainted with Europe and familiar with its courts. He was a lawyer and, more unique, a scholar who appreciated history, philosophy, and literature, and had made international law his avocation. In his writings, despite some youthful excesses, JQA had demonstrated a concern and a grasp of basic foreign policy that had integrity and a flair for originality. There were phrases and basic principles in the Columbus papers that appeared later in Washington's farewell address of 1796, suggesting that the President had either kept them for reference or retained them in his memory.[35]

Shortly before the Senate confirmation, Adams wrote to Abigail that "the President has it in contemplation to send your son to Holland" so that she might "recollect" herself and "prepare for the event." He admonished her to keep the news a secret but "our son must hold himself in readiness to come to Philadelphia." With characteristic caution, Adams added, "Perhaps the Senate may negative him."[36]

Abigail who stayed in Quincy because of her health, suppressing her anxieties, congratulated John Quincy on his good fortune. Martha Washington's letter of congratulations helped the ailing mother to accept the separation. While praising John Quincy's abilities and reflecting on his future prospects, the First Lady understood the sadness with which Abigail must contemplate another departure.

The news reached John Quincy first in a letter from his father. His appointment, John Adams pontificated, was "Proof that Sound Principles in Morals and Government are cherished by the Executive of the United States, and that Study, Science and Literature are recommendations which will not be overlooked."[37] "This intelligence was very unexpected and indeed surprising," John Quincy said when he heard of his mission. He had mixed feelings about the event. Understandably, he commented, "I wish I could have been consulted before it was irrevocably made. I rather wish it had not been made at all."[38] But there was never any serious possibility that he would have turned down the opportunity.

John Quincy had, in reality, ample reason to welcome a change of scene. The American years had been difficult after a rather idyllic youth. Most significant, however, was that the diplomatic appointment was the first indication that John Quincy Adams would fulfill his parents' expectations. They had prepared him carefully for a brilliant public career. Just that spring, John Adams had written to his wife—"my good and worthy son. . . . All my hopes are in him, both for my family and country."[39]

CHAPTER 5

Mission to Holland

*"Go on, dear son, and by a diligent exertion of your genius and abilities,
continue to deserve well of your father, but especially of your government."*
JOHN ADAMS

ON HIS TWENTY-EIGHTH birthday, John Quincy, in Philadelphia
at Secretary of State Edmund Randolph's request, received
his commission to the Dutch post. The suddenness with which the
news of his appointment had arrived forced him to liquidate his law
practice and prepare for his departure in less than two weeks.

Always a careful scholar, Johnny took advantage of his time by
going through the six large folio volumes that contained his father's
despatches sent from Europe to the Congress. Though they did not
relate directly to his own diplomatic assignment, John Quincy said
that "they have proved such a fund of information and of entertainment to me as I have seldom met with in my life."[1]

The new Minister, permitted a secretary at an annual allowance
of $1,380, offered the post to his brother Tom, who hesitated about
making such a major decision without consulting his father. However, since time did not allow for this nicety, Tom agreed to go. He
was the only member of his family who had never been abroad and
he welcomed the opportunity of acquiring some experience in diplomacy.

John Quincy's departure was delayed until Alexander Hamilton, whose instructions were essential to the mission, returned to the capital. It was more than a little disturbing to Adams when he discovered that his dealings with Holland were to be mostly financial. Such a limited assignment made it impossible for him to calculate the length of his residence in Europe and though he wanted to serve his country, he did not want to "feed upon her for nothing."[2]

At the end of a hot July, Johnny fretted that he was "lolling away" his time and "sweating away" his person with nothing to do. The longer he waited, the larger his abandoned law practice grew in size and attraction. He speculated that he could not return to it without a tremendous loss because a three-year interruption would put him behind in his studies and place his peers far ahead of him. Even more upsetting to his imagination were the well-remembered agonies of expatriation. An American in Europe, Adams mused, because of his distance from his country and peer communication, could not fail to lose "to some measure his national character. The habits, the manners, and the affectations insensibly undergo an alteration." Inevitably, by the common changes to which society is prone, he would lose contact with many of the friends that he left behind and have no others to take their places. He, more seriously, tended to follow "the course of the stream into which he has been banished" and gradually, "takes an European disposition, becomes a stranger to his own country, and, when at length he returns, finds himself an alien in the midst of his own fellow citizens."[3]

When Hamilton returned to Philadelphia at the end of August, he confirmed the fact that the mission was basically economic. Adams was instructed to discuss the admission of United States consuls to the Dutch Islands in the vicinity of the United States, to forward the $800,000 loan to ransom Americans held in Algiers, and to keep a daily memorandum and a letter of progress. Randolph had important despatches to be delivered to John Jay and Thomas Pinckney in London and so directed that the first leg of the trip must be to England.

Hamilton's delay had been caused by his participation in quelling the Whiskey Rebellion which had flared up over opposition to the collection of the excise tax on liquor. Angry farmers in Western Pennsylvania had burned down a collector's house and then clashed with a company of soldiers. Johnny wrote a full account of the episode to his mother, replete with the current gossip which asserted that there was friction in the President's Cabinet over the hostilities.

After composing the letter, he realized, with mock dismay, that henceforth his correspondence could not be quite so free. "It will take some time to case myself in diplomatic buckram completely," he observed to Abigail.[4]

Fortunately, the Adams brothers were able to return to Quincy to make their farewells to the family because their ship sailed from Boston. These scenes of parting were painful re-enactments of earlier ones for Johnny but a fresh experience for Tom. Nathan Frazier, Jr., Mary's cousin, and Daniel Sargent, Jr., her future husband, accompanied the travellers as far as the lighthouse. That chance had chosen these two for the parting was suitably symbolic but Johnny, in his *Diary*, made no special point of it, merely remarking on the pain of separation from friends and country.

The voyage was unnecessarily unpleasant due to the shortcomings of the ship, The *Alfred*, and its Captain, Stephen Macey. John Quincy observed that were it not for the fact that the equinoctial gales were light and of short duration, the 28-day trip in the "flimsy, crazy," leaky vessel which was so inexpertly managed might have been a disaster. Just the week before, hundreds of vessels had gone down in the Channel due to terrible storms. "I think hereafter I'll avoid embarking in an eggshell to cross the Atlantic," he commented.[5]

The returning traveller, viewing England after an eleven-year absence, found it beautiful beyond description, and with an air of vast wealth. Johnny's chief complaint, a familiar one to Americans in Europe, was the constant need to hand out gratuities. If he were an absolute monarch, he mused, servants would be properly paid by their masters. "I would never allow of this privileged beggary, which will neither fix its demands, nor acquiesce in what it received."[6]

Just before the post chaise that carried the Adams party from Deal crossed London Bridge, Johnny heard a rattle and then a noise as if a trunk had fallen. He stopped the carriage and leaped out to find that all his trunks were missing, including the one containing the public despatches. Tom, seeing his brother's look of distress, joined the search until one trunk was located under the carriage and the other a few rods behind.

In the interval during which the baggage was missing, John Quincy speculated with horror on the field day for malice and slander the loss of the papers would have caused. Included in the official diplomatic bag were original documents about the depredations to American commerce that were essential to Jay in his treaty negotiations and a confidential account of the insurrection in Western Pennsylvania, meant only for the eyes of Thomas Pinckney, the American Minister to England.

After calming down some, the brothers agreed that the carriage straps must have been cut while they stopped to pay the toll at the turnpike. It was most likely that a child had crept under the vehicle because there was no room for adults. Hopefully the motive was simple theft, though John Quincy could not rid himself of the idea that it was something more sinister. Hence, unable to rest comfortably at the Virginia Coffee House where they were lodged, Johnny took the papers and drove with them to Jay's apartment at the Royal Hotel in Pall Mall. Though Jay was ill and confined to his room with a rheumatic complaint, he admitted the young man at once. After a desultory chat with the ailing negotiator, John Quincy, much relieved that his papers were safely in hands other than his own, returned to his hotel.

The Adamses stayed in London for ten days, moving to Osborne's Hotel, "our old station," as Johnny wrote nostalgically to his father. But there was little time for anything but official business. Jay and Pinckney invited Johnny, who was immensely flattered by their attentions, to go over the plan of the treaty with them article by article. John Quincy, well aware that the terms of the treaty would not please many people in America, although he felt that they were honest and necessary and maintained the national honor, observed that "The national interest will suffer infinitely less than it would by the most successful war we could wage."[7] Closer analysis of the treaty did not change his conclusions. British depredations on American commerce, the chief grievance to be negotiated and the principal object of Jay's mission, were provided for as amply as could be expected. The delivery of the western forts by the British was postponed more distantly than desirable, he admitted, but the compensation offered was a sufficient equivalent. Similarly, he regarded the partial opening up of the West Indies as indemnity for deprivation of the fur trade and for the Negroes carried away contrary to the peace treaty. The fledgling diplomat concluded his critique of the Jay treaty with the observation that neither Jay nor Pinckney was satisfied with the document but believed it to be preferable to war. Realistically, Adams asserted, no commerce treaty with Great Britain would be of much use until the Navigation Acts ceased to be the cornerstone of their foreign policy.[8]

Though he knew it to be impossible, John Quincy wished that the American people would find the treaty terms acceptable. Since the people and government of England had no genuine feelings of friendship for America no better arrangement could be achieved. It was just as well that there was no great love lost, he asserted, for otherwise the influence of the former mother country might be too great. "A free commercial intercourse and peace is all that can be beneficial to us," he said.[9]

John Quincy's frequent letters to his father were crammed with reports, comments, and vignettes of events that he witnessed or heard about from his many contacts in Europe. Full despatches were dutifully directed to his superiors as well, but, he confessed, he was able to write more freely to his father, and valued his father's advice and reactions above anyone else's.

A "servant of my country" for the first time, Johnny appreciated the acceptance and hospitality that Jay and even Pinckney, whose wife had just died, offered to him and to his brother. Public business required too much attention for Abigail's request for miniatures of her two sons to be fulfilled, but there had been time for frequent visits to the theater. John Quincy admired Mrs. Siddons' performances at the Drury Lane and reported Miss Wallis to be a captivating Juliet.

The current European situation was complicated and menacing. On July 28, Robespierre had been executed and then succeeded by "a party called Moderates in power in Paris." Although at this time there was less use of the guillotine, large numbers were released from prison, and some mercy was extended to emigrés, John Quincy was more skeptical than hopeful about the new leadership. By the summer of 1794, the French army had crossed the Pyrenees into Catalonia, occupied the Italian Riviera, invaded the Rhineland and Belgium, and penetrated into Holland as far as the area south of the Rhine delta.

Adams predicted France's memorable final victory because of her superior numbers, unexhaustible resources, and high morale. The British forces shared the defeat of their allies, except for their naval victories. However, the French had 10,000 British seamen as prisoners whom they refused to exchange, causing a prodigious shortage of men for the English Navy. There seemed to be no remedy for

England's want of seamen and the resultant suffering to her commerce.

The effect on Holland of the struggle between France and England was immense. William V, the Dutch Stadtholder, a weak and ineffectual ruler at best, was unable to rouse his people to resistance. "I call upon you. . . . Here are the arms and powder. . . . Take them! . . . Soldiers, citizens and peasants, let us all unanimously assemble!" he ordered. But the Prince of Orange's appeal fell on deaf ears. His practical subjects were too civilized to hear their monarch's plea. How different was the response to the rallying cry of France's leaders—"The French people risen against tyrants!"—which brought soldiers in large numbers to support their leaders.[10]

Before he left Quincy, Vice President Adams had advised Johnny on what to do if he arrived in Holland and found no States General and no Stadtholder. Now the possibility of such a situation was a real one. The French were in full possession of Flanders and Brabant and, unless the Dutch agreed to a general inundation, it looked as if the invasion of Amsterdam was inevitable. The situation was complicated by a petition, signed by 9,000 Hollanders, that forbade the entrance of allied troops into the city, a measure directed against the British. Though there was a statute against petitions in time of danger to the state, the document had been delivered. It was generally believed, however, that William V would admit the English Duke of York with his troops into Amsterdam and lay the country under water. "The fate of the Netherlands is suspended," Johnny wrote to his father, thus describing the position he was in as well.

Holland's precarious situation made it imperative that the American Minister proceed there without delay. He reassured his mother that she need not worry about danger from the French army. "We are neutrals, and peaceable men," he wrote, "friends of both parties, and shall take no share in their contests on either side."[11] John Jay advised Johnny on the proper public conduct during the Dutch crisis. He must avoid taking sides and do no business with a new government unless instructed by the State Department. If it became necessary to retire, he should go to Hamburg, a neutral city, rather than to either of the two belligerent nations, England and France. If conquest extinguished the government of the Netherlands, he should go home.

On October 29, John Quincy and Tom travelled from London to Harwich through "the enchantingly beautiful" autumnal countryside that almost realized the "fictions of fairyland." They endured a chilly, rainy passage to Holland and made their way to The Hague where, on November 4, they put up at the Heeren Legement. Immediately they discovered that the Stadtholder was absent, probably with the army.

Outwardly, the country seemed peaceful and unruffled, completely unlike an invaded nation. However, there had been some reprisals against the backers of the petition and other dissidents, some of whom had fled the country or were in prison. From three to five thousand troops had been posted to Amsterdam to check the people but, surprisingly, they had met no resistance. The French armies, stopped by the rainy, cold weather, were expected to go into winter quarters, which would make Amsterdam safe for the season. John Quincy believed that the Dutch Patriotic Party would rather submit to the French than make peace because, it had been observed, the French army respected property in the nations which they had conquered and left the populace alone except for the circulation of assignats (paper money), used in payment for their purchases.

Since "a total revolution of the government and even of the Constitution here seems to be inevitable," John Quincy asked Randolph what the President wanted him to do. If his commission were terminated, should he return home or await further orders? He had not been able to take up the object of his mission, the $800,000 loan arranged by Hamilton, but, he reported, American credit was higher in Holland than in any other country.[12]

When Adams presented his credentials to the Dutch court, he was told that commissions were received only in Dutch, French, and Latin, and that he would have to translate his into one of the accepted languages. The young diplomat's first impulse was to take offense at the slight but, upon further reflection, he decided to translate the papers himself into French. The documents were accepted then as agreeable to the High Mightinesses.

Dutch apathy in the midst of incipient revolution continued to amaze Adams. There was "no symptom from any part of the people of feeling or interest in the fate of their country," he told his father. "It is a new thing under the sun to see a people anxious to be conquered and praying for the success of their enemies."[13] Johnny, still in dread of committing some impropriety to paper, sent formal reports to Randolph and much livelier, fuller ones to John Adams. Somewhat guilty about it, he told his father that if any facts in his letters were important to the President or the Secretary of State, he hoped that they would be relayed.[14]

The painless settlement of the credentials problem was succeeded by a much more difficult one. General John Eustace, an aide to General Charles Lee during the Revolutionary War, who had, subsequently, served with France, was arrested in Holland. The American Minister was asked to intercede with the Dutch authorities but, before any action was necessary, Eustace was released for lack of evidence. John Quincy said that he would have interceded but later found out that Eustace had been employed by the Dutch Patriots to act as a liaison with Paris.[15]

Difficulties with loans and trade were hard to handle in the midst of Holland's civil difficulties, the presence of British allies who sometimes behaved like an army of occupation, and the threat of a French invasion. Adams could not even judge whether the 1782 Treaty of Commerce with the Netherlands was working because the books he needed for consultation had not arrived from England. Lacking them, he could not assess the complaint that American shipping was suffering heavier impositions on spices than had been negotiated because it was still being treated like a British colony.

News zeroed in from informants in Holland and from American Ministers and consuls all over Europe to John Quincy Adams's listening post at The Hague. He became the scribe who circulated the information among them and also channeled it home. However, due to wartime conditions, letters could not be sent directly from American to Holland but had to be directed to England first. Abigail was instructed to write to her sons via Thomas Pinckney or Joshua Johnson, who would then forward them.

A typical case that the American Minister had to deal with under the United States-Dutch commercial treaty concerned the *Wilmington Packet*. This American vessel, on a voyage between Bordeaux and St. Thomas, was captured by a Dutch privateer and carried to St. Martin's. There it was condemned by the Admiralty for carrying enemy property, a clear violation of the treaty. Though Holland and France were at war, the United States, as a neutral, had the right to trade with France. Adams contested the American ship's right under the "free ships, free goods" clause of the treaty, a favorite Adams principal. The case dragged on all through John Quincy's tenure as Minister and was not successfully decided until his successor's term of office.[16]

From his observation post at The Hague and, sometimes, Amsterdam, Adams watched the French Revolution come to Holland. His ears were open to the sounds that all the factions were making and his pen was always ready to record his impressions, formally for Randolph, informally for John Adams. In either case, they reached President Washington. Very much like the war correspondents of later times, Adams reported the moving scene back to the United States but his audience was limited to the Administration, some family and some friends. His *Diary*, a fair indication of his state of mind, reflected no anxiety for himself or Tom from the events that he was observing. He reacted to the French occupation with as much complacency as did the Dutch.

Even the weather aided the advance of the French troops. Severe cold made travel over the inundated land easy. However, in spite of Johnny's excellent connections with people in all camps, news at that time was hard to come by. He wrote to Sylvanus Bourne, the American consul in Amsterdam, that there was nothing at The Hague but "the millions of tongues of rumour." They must communicate frequently to pool their knowledge.[17] Nothing was certain except Holland's abandonment of the British alliance, now distasteful because of the military ineptitude of the Duke of York and the disgracefully undisciplined behavior of his troops. The domestic situation was complicated by a rift between the Patriot Party that favored full submission to France and the moderates.

When Adams arrived in Amsterdam on January 18, 1795, he found it in a state of transition because news had reached the city that Utrecht had already been taken. The tricolored cockade was being openly displayed, the "Marseillaise" could be heard all night, crowds milled around but there was no mischief. By the following day, the tricolor was waving over the State House and a Batavian revolutionary committee had sent a delegation to the Regency to inform them that their services were no longer needed. In an orderly manner, political prisoners were released and a tree of liberty was erected in front of the State House. John Quincy marvelled that the Revolution had taken place with no more than twenty-five or thirty French hussars in the city. Rumor had it that the Stadtholder and his family were already on their way to England.

The Revolution's progress continued to be rapid. General Pichegru, the French commander of the armies of the north, arrived in Amsterdam with two to three thousand men on the twentieth. It was just a matter of days, the American Minister reported, before the French forces would have control of Holland. Still, all remained tranquil in the city even though troops were quartered on the citizens. However, credit had to be given to the admirable discipline of the French army, which created no disorder, did not pillage, and refrained from any personal insults to the occupied province.

John Quincy immediately gave notice to the proper authorities that the neutral privileges of American property must be respected. He was, just as quickly, reassured by the French that they did not come as enemies of the Dutch. But the American received their courtesies with caution, assuring Randolph that he would keep careful count of the roster of American vessels and the value of the property that United States citizens had left behind.

The French representative behaved with disarming cordiality to the American Minister. He asked about General Washington's age and expressed the hope that he would enjoy his glory for a long time. He recounted with great emotion the story of James Monroe's ovation from the French National Convention and was pleased to hear that John Quincy had lived in France and had been a student there.

At the end of January, Adams returned to The Hague. M. Dumas, though ill, was in marvelous spirits now that the Revolution that he had hoped for was a reality. The French authorities continued more than cooperative—"generous," John Quincy said. But the diplomatic corps was almost depleted. The Ministers of Great Britain, Spain, Prussia, and Sardinia had left at the approach of the French armies.

Peter Paulus, president of the Assembly of the Provisional Representatives of the people of Holland, summoned Adams with the hope that he would negotiate a treaty of commerce with the new government. Paulus, who claimed to have been a good friend of John Adams and to remember Johnny from his earlier trip to Holland, declared: "Our sister Republics" must be friendly, "as the number of such sisters is very small, they had a particular value to friendship."[18] John Quincy answered, tactfully, that he had not received his orders from America but certainly hoped for friendship and harmony. His recommendation to Randolph was that such a treaty would be profitable if the right of neutrality was observed.

The orders from America directed that Adams was to follow the government of the people. If Holland remained independent, he was to accept any new constitution that the people devised but if the

Netherlands became a dependent of France his mission was terminated. Prudence was to be his guide. However, a doubtful situation would be best handled by retiring to the provinces until the State Department could arrange communications. If personal danger was feared, Randolph ordered, use "your own judgment and discretion. But without the most unequivocal necessity, it is thought best that you should not quit the country until you shall be so instructed."[19]

In the midst of this crisis, or perhaps because of it, John Quincy started to keep his *Diary* regularly. From his March 1, 1795, entry, it grew into nineteen quarto volumes of about five hundred pages a volume. In a small, neat, legible script, fifty years of an active life would be conscientiously chronicled except for an occasional break caused by tremendously pressing business.

Though the new government was basically friendly to the United States, inevitably circumstances caused breaches of full neutral rights. Adams had to intercede in order to establish his countrymen's right to take their money out of the Netherlands and to stop obstructions to the free flow of American vessels. On a personal level, when John Quincy objected to the indignity of having French soldiers quartered in his domicile, they were withdrawn.

The Hague was tranquil but its people were beginning to suffer from the inconveniences of conquest. More than a hundred thousand troops were now quartered on them. Food and clothing was requisitioned, and, most irksome, paper money was used as legal tender. The Dutch balked some when an April order required that all gold and silver plate be melted to make coins for the public use.

The establishment of the Batavian government stimulated party rivalry. A prime irritant was the preponderance of popular societies or revolutionary clubs that had grown up all over the country and had prepared the way for the French takeover. Very much akin to the French Jacobin clubs, they grew "as a monstrous wen upon the body of liberty," Johnny wrote to his mother. People on all levels of society belonged to them, sometimes only to ensure protection against insult from the French. The societies were a pernicious force because, although the government tried to be conciliatory and humane to the members of the former administration, the clubs urged retaliatory measures against them. The American Minister had been asked to join one of these clubs more than once. Though he begged off on the grounds of being a stranger and of the impropriety of taking part in the politics of his host country, some ardent club members resented his position. John Quincy commented that as a result he had lost friends because he neither joined clubs nor marched in processions.[20]

In a very short time, the new Dutch government, dependent on French protection, became "universally odious" to the people. Adams was certain that sooner or later the Stadtholder would be restored with, inevitably, subservience to either France or England. At the moment everything was stagnant in Holland. The British commanded the Channel and the North Sea, which meant that commerce in Holland was at a halt. "We are quiet and in danger of nothing but hunger," Johnny reported to Abigail. Scarcity of provisions was beginning to be severely felt in almost every part of Europe.[21]

The best that the Dutch Patriots could say about their treaty with France was that any government was better than that of William V. The disappointing terms required that the Batavian government declare war on England, maintain French occupying troops at their own expense, accept French paper money as legal tender, cede Flushing at the mouth of the Scheldt to France, and pay a huge indemnity. This was severe treatment for an ally, Johnny commented sarcastically. He had predicted correctly that the terms would be sensationally advantageous to France.

The hope for peace in Europe was dwindling rapidly and there were fresh rumors of a new alliance between Great Britain and Russia. Though there was a possibility that the scarcity of provisions felt on the continent might speed pacification or that internal changes in France might stop the war, John Quincy believed that it was more likely that Austria, Russia, and Britain would unite against the rest of Europe.[22]

The French were constantly quizzing the American Minister about the Jay treaty. Citizen Emanuel-Joseph Sieyes, a medium-sized man with a pale face, strong features, and a bald head, who later became a prominent Bonapartist, asked bluntly for an explanation of the object of the treaty. Adams answered that it was to terminate the difference between Great Britain and the United States over forts, navigation, and commerce. It was secret, he explained, because it was being debated in Congress. Sieyes remained unconvinced that the document did not contain some secret anti-French stipulations. Consequently, John Quincy warned his father that the French influence in the United States would try to prevent ratification of Jay's treaty and to foster war between America and England. If the treaty was rejected, he added, the French will be even more active among us.[23]

America seemed to be an intriguing subject to the French. John Quincy was most interested in a discussion about music with a Monsieur Richard. At dinner one evening, the French gentleman asked if there was much taste for music in America. No, Adams confessed, although the American genius was very much addicted to painting and had produced in that art some of the greatest masters of the age. "Some particular construction of our fibres," he explained, "deprived Americans of an attachment to music." In illustration of his theory, Johnny noted that in seven years of battling for their liberty the Americans composed not one single song or tune which, like "The Marseillaise," "was resounded by every voice." He confessed to Richard that he played the flute very badly.[24]

The Frenchman then asked if the United States owned any originals of the great masters. When John Quincy had to answer very few, M. Richard declared, "We will send you some. You must form a National Gallery," and then wanted to know how such a gift would be received. "With gratitude," answered Adams, fervently.[25]

A whimsical conversation with Madame Palm Daelders, an enthusiastic supporter of the French Revolution and of women's rights, annoyed young Adams. She visited him and then promptly sent him her complete political writings, which he found full of the usual commonplaces on the subject. "Political subserviency and domestic influence must be the lot of woman, and those who have departed most from their natural sphere, are not those who have shown the sex in their most admirable light," Abigail's oldest son wrote in his *Diary*.[26] She, no doubt, would have been as angry at these remarks, had she seen them, as she had been when Tom, in his first jury address, made remarks derogatory to the female character.

The Batavian Republic could not get together to form a convention because of the different interests of the country's factions. Also, interestingly, John Quincy said, the mass of the people were still attached to the House of Orange, proving their loyalty by deserting in large numbers from the armed services. Perhaps, too, they were becoming disillusioned with the barbarous nature of the Revolution that pervaded Europe. "The French Revolution of the last six years has contributed more to the restoration of Vandalic ignorance than whole centuries can retrieve. . . . The mymidons of Robespierre were as ready to burn libraries as the followers of Omar," John Quincy mourned. He sent his father publications received from Paris, commenting, "The man that can read them and retain an ardour for revolutions must indeed possess more philosophy than humanity."[27] The child of the American Revolution found the European version too strong for his stomach.

The Administration appreciated the well-organized, pithy reports from the European war theater that arrived at regular intervals fresh from the Minister of Holland's facile pen. The President said that the "American Minister at The Hague had been very regular and intelligent in his correspondence," an accolade from the usually reticent George Washington. The Secretary of State declared that the communications were "well digested, well arranged and well connected." But to the Vice President, the despatches were the fulfillment of his dearest hopes. Honest John Adams, when truly pleased, could be fulsome in his praise. "I have no language to express to you the pleasure I have received from the satisfaction you have given to the President and the Secretary of State,"[28] he purred. He told Johnny, with unrestrained pride, that his correspondence was as much esteemed as that of the former American Minister and more admired, for a "brilliancy of style and a freedom, independence and boldness of sentiment as well as a sagacity equal to any . . ."[29] This was strong praise for a young man and sufficient encouragement for him to continue to gather information, sift it, and analyze it.

One of the themes that ran through all of John Quincy's reports was his conviction that France had a fixed intention to draw the United States into war with Britain. However, he perceived Britain as an even more dangerous enemy who sought proof of American folly and extravagance, because the form of government of the United States was so indigestible to her. Despite the years of war, Britain remained a formidable enemy with unexhausted resources and a great power of recuperation. Her finances, John Quincy judged, were in much sounder condition than those of either France or Holland. France, on the other hand, though consistently victorious in battle, was internally unsettled. Her new constitution, sure to be accepted, would probably meet the same fate as the previous two and trigger another precipitous change in government.

The difficulty that Jay's treaty was encountering at home fulfilled

John Quincy's expectations but filled him with regret. He saw the issue as a pragmatic one. "Of all the guides that a nation can follow," he wrote to Daniel Sargent, "passion is the most treacherous and prudence the most faithful."[30] The people of the United States, in his opinion, had the choice between peace and prosperity or war with Great Britain, which would result in the total destruction of American commerce. It was common sense to accept the fact that the United States could never have a treaty with England that would please them. "The interests of the two nations must inevitably militate against each other." He regretted the personal enmity displayed against Jay, particularly because it came close to home. Part of it, he suspected, was a desire on the part of the anti-Adams faction to stir up rivalry for the Presidency between Jay and John Adams. "Whoever may be the successor of the present first magistrate will hold a situation so uncomfortable and so dangerous that there is nothing in its possession to make it desirable," Johnny observed to his brother Charles.[31]

In mid-October, John Quincy was surprised by a letter from Randolph, dated August 14, ordering him to repair without delay to London where documents and directions would be waiting. The purpose of his trip was relative to Jay's treaty. With that meager information he had to be contented until he arrived there. However, Randolph warned, he must be particularly careful to observe the protocol usual to temporary absences, "so as to obviate any impressions, if such should arise, which may be made by your going to London."[32]

This letter to John Quincy Adams was one of Randolph's last duties as Secretary of State. In August, President Washington, who was not yet committed to support or reject Jay's treaty, was summoned to Philadelphia from Mount Vernon by most distressing information. Evidence was presented to him that Randolph had been intriguing with the French Minister, Fauchet. In 1794, while Fauchet had been travelling home, a British ship sank his vessel. He escaped to France, but some of his papers were captured and retained by the British until the most favorable use could be made of them. That moment was deemed to be July 1795, at which time William Hammond, the British Minister, handed them over to the American government. Their contents seemed to reveal that Randolph had exposed state secrets to Fauchet and had suggested that the French bribe several important Pennsylvania republicans in order to re-establish peace in Western Pennsylvania, a proposal that Fauchet declined to act on. Later Randolph explained much of this, giving the contents of the papers an entirely different interpretation. However, after the President read the Fauchet papers, he was convinced that, whatever the extent of the entanglement, Randolph was now useless to the Administration. At a Cabinet meeting, Washington required Randolph to read Fauchet's address aloud. All the members watched the Secretary's face for some sign of guilt. Upon questioning him further, his answers did not satisfy the members of the Administration and Randolph, painfully aware of this, resigned. After his retirement to Virginia, he wrote *A Vindication of Mr. Randolph's Resignation.*[33] The Randolph episode resulted in Washington's decision to favor the treaty, although he claimed that he was not influenced by the charges against his Secretary of State.

Timothy Pickering, "at this time executing the office of Secretary of State," wrote to John Quincy explaining what had happened to Randolph, citing a number of reasons why he believed that his predecessor had sided with the opposition to Jay's treaty. Randolph's object, Pickering said firmly, "was to defeat the treaty altogether." When Adams received the letter in London, in November, he was completely shocked, writing to Pickering that he could not have believed the news had it come from anyone else.[34]

"This business is unpleasant and unpromising, but I have no election," Johnny recorded about his new assignment. He was irritated that he was being taken away from his business at The Hague at a time when he was attempting to institute some reforms. Earlier he had suggested to the State Department that passports were essential for American travellers. Sometimes, he said, real citizens of the United States had no proof of citizenship while a great number of impostors claimed to be Americans. The United States flag suffered a similar abuse; a neutral flag being useful to some vessels, it was simply appropriated by ships unentitled to use it whenever expedient. Another area of abuse was the treatment of consuls who lacked necessary power to do a satisfactory job and were very poorly compensated. However, since there was no choice, Adams had to make preparations to go to England. He left the Ministry in the hands of his brother, which consoled him somewhat. The departure was made less awkward by Mr. Paulus's willingness to accept the voyage to England as a necessity in no way unfriendly to Holland. To avoid any misunderstanding, John Quincy also paid a formal call on Joseph Michel Noël, the French Minister Plenipotentiary. He also accepted the mission, but in an attempt to turn a diplomatic compliment Johnny feared that he had mangled the effort badly. He told Noël that he had a very good opinion of Citizen Adet, the new French Minister to the United States, "but that I should have been much gratified had he himself been employed on that mission." In his *Diary*, the American recorded that he was sincere about the compliment but it was "too barebosomed."[35]

On October 21, Johnny left The Hague to take ship for Helvoet-sluys. He had a maddening time trying to make the passage to England. The wind refused to blow, some of the passengers found that they lacked the necessary credentials for sailing and had to return to the capital to get them, the pilot disappeared, and, to crown the fiasco, the weather grew stormy. On board ship, waiting, Adams read and wrote letters but couldn't concentrate, though he wrote to Tom that "the only remedy against moral as well as physical evil must very often be patience."[36] When, at the end of October, it seemed obvious that the captain of his ship had no intentions of sailing for England, he looked around for another vessel. It was not until the ninth of November that further delays, most of them due to stormy weather, allowed Adams to board the *Aurora* under Captain Furnald. A fresh wind carried the tardy Minister to Margate, where there was evidence of an even worse storm than off Holland. By dint of travelling night and day, he reached London by the 11th.

CHAPTER 6

A Romantic Interlude

"I have been accustomed all my life to plain dealing . . . and am not sufficiently versed in the art of political scoundrelry to be prepared for negotiating with an European Minister of State."

JOHN QUINCY ADAMS

"A faithful and anxious lover rather than a romantic lover."

JOHN QUINCY ADAMS

JOHN QUINCY ADAMS arrived in London too late to execute his mission. Just as he feared when he first learned of the assignment, it proved to be a setback rather than an advance in his diplomatic career. "The service upon which I am now ordered has nothing to please in prospect," he complained to his father. Jay's treaty had resulted in "a furious persecution" for its author so that any association with it had to be "nothing attractive to ambition or flattering to hope." That any failure on the part of the Minister to Holland "would extend to my nearest friends, and lavished more on them than me," also disturbed him, and, perhaps most pertinent, he doubted his own competence for such a delicate trust.[1]

A return to America in three years' time, the master plan that John Adams had designed for his son, suited the young man, who doubted that he would be promoted to a higher diplomatic office. Elevation would have to be either to the English or French Ministry. "I consider the English as an Object of aversion and the French of indifference" was Johnny's summary. But he liked The Hague, which, he said, was adequate to his talents. Indeed it was preferable to the prospect of waiting in a law office for business which never came and, when it did, "was scarcely sufficient to give bread." He decided to go back to Boston only if no other honest resource was left.[2] The matter in hand, consequently had to meet with some success or his Holland Ministry might also be in jeopardy.

After checking into Osborne's Hotel in the Strand, John Quincy breakfasted and then proceeded to Cumberland Place to see William Allen Deas, Pinckney's private secretary, who was not at home. The next day, when he caught up with Deas, he discovered that the first part of his assignment, the exchange of ratifications of Jay's treaty, had been executed. The Secretary of State had ordered that if the Minister to Holland did not arrive in London before October 20th, Mr. Deas was to perform the duty. However, since instructions for the rest of the mission had not yet arrived, John Quincy was left with nothing to do but await them.

The theater was a pleasant way to fill in time. "Shakespeare's attractions are irresistible," Johnny wrote about Mrs. Jordan's performance as Viola in *Twelfth Night*. He did not like the current version of *King Lear*, which substituted a happy ending for the Bard's tragic one. On a visit to a Mr. Ireland, he was shown several Shakespeare manuscripts reputed to be originals, and memorabilia such as a love letter to Anne Hathaway with a lock of her hair, three or four sheets of *Hamlet*, and the manuscript of an unknown tragedy called *Vortigern and Rowena*. John Quincy commented that "this will cause controversy," which indeed it did.[3]

John Quincy's London mission started with a comedy of errors about his title and accreditation to the British court. Unfortunately, Adams emerged from it looking somewhat ridiculous. As soon as Gouverneur Morris met Johnny in London, he asked him whether he was accredited at court or only a commissioner with full powers. "Neither," Johnny answered, which puzzled the ex-American Minister to France. John Quincy resented Morris's unrestricted advice on the theory and practice of negotiation. President Washington received a letter from Morris commenting on young Adams's surprising behavior. "I offered him any assistance which I could give, but to my surprise, he told me that he was here merely as a private individual," Morris wrote. "A day or two afterwards Lord Grenville gave me very different information," he added.[4]

The first British diplomat with whom Adams was confronted was George Hammond, Under Secretary of State in Lord Grenville's office. The two had met first when Johnny was in Paris with his father in 1783. Since then Hammond had been the first British Minister to the United States and had married a Philadelphia girl. Hammond's style was intimate and confiding. Unofficially, of course, he was exceedingly critical of Mr. Deas, whose letters, he declared, were violent and irritating. When he expressed the flattering wish that Adams were the American Minister, and thus succeed his father in the English post, Johnny snapped, "In my country there is nothing hereditary in public offices." He told his *Diary*, "If I stay here any time, he will learn to be not quite so fond nor yet so impertinent."[5]

Hammond thrived on confidences. He enlightened John Quincy with the news that there was not the smallest doubt that Edmund Randolph had been bribed by the French. He himself had intercepted Fauchet's despatches and had seen the evidence. At every opportunity the Englishman sniped at the anti-federalists. Pinckney's treaty with Spain made him particularly unhappy because, John Quincy analyzed, now there was the prospect of "one enemy the less for America and one more for Britain."[6] There was such an atmosphere of intrigue about Hammond that John Quincy suspected him of having examined his letters.

Communication with Lord Grenville was on a much more dignified level. The serious differences between Britain and the United States provided an ample challenge to the young diplomat's abilities. Easily achieving an amicable settlement on terms of payment for the commissioners empowered to carry out the terms of Jay's treaty, the American was encouraged to introduce the subject of his countrymen's claims in the prize courts. John Quincy told Lord Grenville that the President of the United States had been apprised that during the last summer numerous American ships laden with provisions had been captured by order of the King. "I was directed to inquire into the existence of such an order," John Quincy told Lord Grenville, who promised to send him a copy of the order. Grenville explained that he had not wished to communicate with Mr. Deas on the subject because he did not like his manner. He also hinted that there were cases in which articles that had not generally been considered contraband might become so. Using Vattel as his authority, he claimed the right to detain vessels upon suspicion of their holding property belonging to the enemy. John Quincy remonstrated, "Provisions are more valuable, proportionally speaking to us than to any other commercial nation; a restraint therefore has . . . the appearance of being specially pointed against us."[7] Grenville answered that he could prove that nations operating on the Baltic suffered more from the law than did the United States.

As to the long-overdue evacuation of the western posts by the British army, Grenville said that he believed orders to that effect were on their way. However, he added, "It can not be surprising! . . . upon seeing in what manner the treaty has been received in America, and the opposition which it has met . . . we should think it necessary to be upon our guard." The American responded that in his country it was customary for opposition to be open and active.

"With respect to the impressing of seamen," that perennially sensitive subject, Grenville pointed to a notice issued the day before that directions had been given not to press any more men who were regularly protected. The sparring matches with Lord Grenville made John Quincy hope that Pinckney would return soon to relieve him of this thankless task.

For several reasons, Adams's proper official designation in this English mission was deliberately misrepresented by the host country. First, Lord Grenville sent him a card informing him that the audience he had "solicited" with the King was granted. It was addressed to Adams as the Minister Plenipotentiary of the United States. "I am not honored with that character," and "the credential letter, which I have the honor to bear from the President of the United States to his Majesty, styles me Minister Resident of the United States of America at The Hague," Johnny answered. If this precluded him from the audience he would stay away.[8]

British officialdom then inserted a paragraph in one of the ministerial newspapers reporting that Mr. Adams, "the new envoy from the United States," had delivered his credentials. Mr. Hammond clarified the error somewhat by explaining that without such a designation John Quincy could have only an informal audience with the King who "will not admit a foreigner in the character of a Minister to another government than his own."[9] To Johnny's precise reasoning, this meant it was Hammond's intention "to construe" him into being a Minister to Great Britain, which was a deliberate snare and might be of some use to them but what he did not know.

Finally, on December 17, Johnny allowed himself to be presented at court but in the character of the Minister Resident at The Hague. Royalty offered its usual banal conversational gambits. The

Queen asked how long he had been in Holland and whether he was any relation to the Mr. Adams who had been there several years ago. The King asked if the winters in the United States were not more severe than in England.

Disbelief in British good intentions towards the United States influenced John Quincy's dealings with Lord Grenville and his subsequent official reports back home. The dispute over potash was an example. Lord Grenville said that the substance would, in the future, be considered as contraband. Since it was used in the manufacture of gunpowder, it had "lost its character of innocence." After Adams pointed out that the treaty had been signed long after the new use of potash by France was notorious and that it had not been restricted in the treaty, Grenville backed down and accepted the point as it related to the United States.[10]

Shortly after this exchange, Pickering received a letter from John Quincy reporting that a British expedition of 25,000 troops had sailed for Santo Domingo. He advised that their success would be harmful to the United States because possession of the French islands in the West Indies would serve to strengthen British supremacy on the seas and revive their policy of exclusion of the United States from that area.

Further experience with the British State Department intensified Johnny's feelings that he was out of his depth. Although Lord Grenville was plausible but insincere, Adams believed Hammond was merely cunning. Pinckney's swift return therefore was the only hope for relief from the awkwardness of his position. He celebrated the end of 1795 by attending a performance of Shakespeare's *Comedy of Errors*, which, he said, played better than it read, and in this presentation had some of the scenes of indecency left out. At the year's close, John Quincy wrote, piously, that he was "desirous to repair by the future the deficiencies of the past."[11]

On January 13, at the King's levee, John Quincy heard with great relief that Thomas Pinckney was back in London. Shortly afterward, the newspapers reported that Adams took leave of the King. However, Johnny recorded, George III did not speak to him at all. "I suppose it is a hint to me," the young man commented. But before returning to Holland, he had to await orders. In the interim, Hammond renewed his campaign of unsubtle flattery, telling Johnny that his government would much prefer treating with him than with Pinckney, whom they viewed as unfriendly to England.

Hammond might have felt differently had he seen John Quincy's letters to his father. England, said Johnny, affected a great regard for the United States only because there was too much else on their minds "to quarrel with us." We have "no more rancorous enemies than the executive machine of this country. They dread our tranquillity."[12] Nevertheless, though we cannot have cordiality, peace may continue. Consequently, he dreaded the mischief that the English publication of Randolph's *Vindication* would cause on that part of the nation that was well disposed to America.

Gouverneur Morris, still in London, heard with alarm John Quincy's outpouring of anger and frustration against the British government. The pro-British American called his youthful countryman, "mad" and a "war monger," although he did recognize that the young man's verbal excesses were momentary and were controlled when he acted professionally. However, Morris did worry that Adams might be overheard and his sentiments repeated by the wrong people. John Quincy, commenting on the same conversation, observed that Morris was "decidedly the more English the more I see of him."[13]

That his son was not a favorite with the people of England did not dismay John Adams, who shared Johnny's belief that there would never be cordial kindness and friendship with Great Britain. "Don't suffer their little Contemptable Passions and Sordid Insolence to hurt your feelings," Adams advised.[14] Privately, Adams told his wife that he was not sorry that their son went to England because he had opportunities of improvement and gaining information there.

On April 26, John Quincy received permission from the Secretary of State to return to The Hague but he did not leave Great Britain until a month later. The reason for his delay was a romance with Louisa Catherine Johnson, the second daughter of Joshua Johnson, the American consul in London.

When the Adams brothers had passed through London on their way to The Hague, business had prevented John Quincy from going with Tom and John Jay to dine with the Johnsons and their seven daughters. On that evening, Mary Johnson, the oldest sister, for some reason called Tom "Abel," which left the title of "Cain" for his absent older brother. "Cain" was unable to see the Johnsons on that visit, so it was not until his return to London that he accompanied Colonel John Trumbull, a close friend of the Johnson family, to their house.

Johnny made an unusually agreeable first impression that night. He was in high spirits and particularly witty. However, after he left, the Johnson sisters had a private laugh over his clothes, which they thought were completely Dutch and very unfashionable. Colonel Trumbull, taking the prerogative of a family friend, suggested that Mr. Adams was a fine fellow who would make a good husband. The girls, however, continued to mock his appearance, contrasting him unfavorably with his elegant brother-in-law, Colonel Smith, whom they had known and admired.

Young Adams's frequent visits to the Johnson household that autumn and winter were thought to have been inspired by Nancy Johnson, which made Louisa feel relaxed and natural in his presence. Mrs. Johnson liked John Quincy, but the consul, having a southerner's mistrust of a Yankee, reserved judgment.

"I never observed anything in Mr. Adams . . . towards me that indicated the smallest preference," Louisa wrote. On the contrary, he often expressed dislike for some of the songs that she sang. It was then in all innocence that, having heard that he was a poet, she asked him to write a poem for her which became a subject of constant banter between them. Louisa not only believed that her sister was Johnny's favorite but, more pertinent, she thought herself less attractive and less appealing than her sisters, a self-image that had been encouraged by the family's behavior to her. Her parents and sisters, she said, constantly admonished her for awkwardness and bashfulness and ridiculed her love of reading and music.

Johnny started to visit the Johnson home regularly in November. At the end of February he gave his mother some intimation of what was going on in a letter telling her that he was sending the cloaks that she had requested. They were chosen, he added, by Mrs. Johnson and her second daughter, "a very amiable young lady bearing the name of Louisa Catherine. . . ."[15]

One evening, at the Johnson supper table, Johnny handed a paper to Louisa saying that it was a song he had written. She opened it and started to read it aloud when Miss Henning, the children's governess who had been reading it over her shoulder, snatched it out of her hand and whispered to her to stop reading. Poor Louisa "blushed like a fool" and ever after remained convinced that the foolish governess read into the verses a meaning that had never been intended. Nevertheless, for many days afterward the family was in confusion. Miss Henning argued her point of view so effectively "that my vanity was enlisted and without a particle of affection at the time I suffer'd myself to be waxed into an affection that lasted probably much longer than would have done love at first sight."

At a ball that the Johnsons gave, John Quincy permitted his attention to Louisa to be publicly noted. Her jealous sisters, consequently, made Louisa suffer so much that she commented that her "first lessons in the belle passion were pretty thickly strewed with thorns." Nancy was particularly vindictive. The other sisters shunned her but Nancy subjected her to unforgiving silence and only the governess's entreaties kept Louisa from confiding the whole sorry situation to John Quincy.

Nancy had always been acknowledged the prettiest and most talented of the older trio: Nancy, Louisa, and Caroline Johnson. Louisa was, even as a young girl, considered proud and haughty. At school, she herself reported, she was respected but not loved. Her timidity kept her from shining at the musicals and ballets that the girls presented.

At fourteen, Louisa recalled, she spent her New Year's money on Milton's *Paradise Lost and Paradise Regained,* "a curious selection for so young a child," but she loved its subject. Perhaps, she speculated, it taught her "to scrutinize too closely into motives and to look too closely at the truth."

Louisa and Nancy were presented to society together, which was not to the younger sister's advantage. Not only less mature than her sister, Louisa was afflicted with chronic timidity and shyness, a constant victim of her own reserved and cold disposition.

The Johnsons circulated mostly among the Americans in London and had little to do with the English. Although Mrs. Johnson, formerly Catherine Nuth, was English-born, because of a family rift she rarely saw her people. The Johnsons were, actually, rather aggressively pro-American. Louisa declared that George Washington was her idol. And the Johnson menage became a kind of headquarters for visiting Americans, not the least of its attractions being a houseful of pretty and eligible young ladies.

In a roundabout way, Johnny prepared his mother for the future. "I begin to think very seriously of the duty incumbent upon all good citizens to have a family. If you think this the language of a convert, perhaps you will enquire how he became so? I am not yet prepared to answer that," he wrote.[16] It was uncharacteristic of the young man to be so cold with his parents but in the area of personal emotions he had been shown cause to doubt them.

Just prior to John Quincy's return to Holland, a foolish misunderstanding almost parted him from Louisa. The night before a party Louisa jokingly advised Johnny to dress handsomely for the occasion. He became very angry because he thought that she was laughing at him. Coldly, he bade her goodnight and mentioned that if the family planned to go to Ranelagh the following evening he would be at the Adelphi, but other engagements would keep him from seeing her sooner. When they called for him, he was handsomely dressed in blue. At the party, while strolling around the room arm in arm, Louisa complimented him on his dress. He answered sharply that his wife must never take the liberty of interfering in such particulars. Offended at his making such a serious grievance out of a casual comment, Louisa told him that she resigned all pretenses to his hand and left him free for a lady who was more discreet. She then dropped his arm and stayed with her mother for the rest of the evening. On the way home, Johnny apologized, but Louisa said, "If lovers' quarrels are a renewal of love, they also leave a sting behind which apparently heal'd reopens on every trivial occasion. . . ."[17]

John Quincy returned to Holland on May 5, "unaccompanied," he wrote his mother, "but only because of the voice of prudence. My choice is irrevocably made." Louisa had been told that the engagement was for an indefinite period because Johnny could not name a date but that she should correspond with him and, in the interim, improve her mind. He laid down a course of study for her to follow until they met again, "which might be in one year or in seven."[18]

Louisa was desolate. She had begged John Quincy to marry her before he left so that she might be spared the insinuating jests to which engaged ladies were subjected. The disturbances in Holland were, she thought, the reason for the postponement of the marriage, and as soon as the country settled down she expected that her fiancé would send for her. She was mistaken, as she soon found out.

On his return to The Hague, the American Minister found the people in the midst of "Saturnalian electioneering holidays." Having dissolved the Staats General, supreme authority was now in the hands of a national assembly. The president of the assembly, Vos Van Steenwyck, was also ex officio president of the diplomatic committee. John Quincy called on him.

A new assessment of the European scene convinced Adams of the pattern of French strategy. The land war concluded, the Italian states, Spain, Denmark, Sweden, and even Hamburg and Bremen would be stimulated by France to shut the Baltic and Mediterranean Seas against British commerce. The United States, he was sure, would be offered inducements to do the same. There was no doubt, the American Minister wrote, that French influence accounted for a good part of the negative reaction to Jay's treaty by many Americans. That the French wanted to involve the United States in war and "to new model our executive" was also certain.

At this time, John Quincy first enunciated his basic conviction about American policy—the continuance and preservation of the union. In a letter to his brother Charles, he asserted his belief that a war with Great Britain would result in a dissolution of the Union and so must be avoided. "We shall proceed with gigantic strides to honor and consideration, and national greatness, if the union is preserved," he predicted. But, "once broken, we shall soon divide into a parcel of petty tribes at perpetual war with one another, swayed by rival European powers."[19]

The United States must remain in a position of inferiority to Britain as long as it had no naval power and the American people refused to carry out the expense of a Navy. France's efforts to stimulate a war between the United States and England must be frustrated. She would try to use the unusual weight of her influence, which she carried from Americans arriving from Europe or writing to their friends. France appealed to Americans, John Quincy wrote, because "the French manners are captivating, the English are repulsive." And, practically speaking, many Americans have debts owed them from speculation on confiscated estates or assignats. In England, however, Americans were debtors to the British government so that a war, they conjectured, would sponge their debts or relieve them for a long time. The question now was whether Britain would honor her commitment by delivering the forts, particularly Niagara. France was certain that her enemy would not but this was one of her party maneuvers.[20]

On June 11, John Quincy was surprised to receive a commission to Portugal as Minister Plenipotentiary. It was a rise in rank and particularly gratifying to him because it had been unanimously approved by the Senate. However, he was advised by Pickering to remain in Holland until his replacement, who had not yet been chosen, arrived. In the meantime the Secretary of State wrote, "consider the new appointment what it is in reality, a decided proof of the President's high opinion of your talent, integrity and worth."

John Quincy was faced now with making a major decision about his personal life. He missed Louisa, wrote to her that his thoughts kept returning to their visits, and promised that he would try to shorten his stay in Holland. Although he had not received a letter from her, his mind was made up and not to be changed by his family's reactions to his choice of a wife. The last of June, Abigail received a letter from her oldest son explaining that he had left "a highly valued friend" behind in England because he did not have sufficient salary to support a family. Nevertheless, their separation should terminate in about a year. At the end of that time, he would return to the practise of the law, although he would prefer other possibilities of equal advantage. Under consideration also was settlement in one of the southern states, for its financial advantage. But, said Johnny, this would "remove me from my native spot and more especially from you."[21]

In London, Louisa had been going through a private agony. She was terrified at having to answer the letters of her intellectual fiancé. Her limited education had not offered her instruction in the art of letter writing so that she allowed the officious, overromantic governess to be her Cyrano. Miss Henning was convinced that she gave the letters "tone." Louisa, however, counted the hours until the letters from Holland arrived and, when they did, suffered such uneasiness about having to answer them that her health deteriorated and her appearance was spoiled.

John Quincy weathered the separation in his usual well-organized manner. He had adopted his father's dictum of early rising, thus giving himself from six A.M. to plan his day. The daily regimen included a morning hour devoted to reading words of instruction, intervals of walking and work, until he retired at 11 P.M. For a start, he read Pope's translation of the *Odyssey*. On his thirtieth birthday, Johnny judged the past year as culpable, only because so much of it had been spent in relaxation and "the weakness of the heart." But he added that none of the years for a long time "have been so innocent. Yet none of them have been more exposed to temptation."[22]

Announcing her aversion to letter writing, Louisa answered Johnny. She offered her congratulations on his father's nomination for the Presidency. Defensively, she said, "You know, *my friend*, I am not ambitious of anything but your affection and in that my wishes are unbounded."[23] Twenty-year-old Louisa was inclined to be guileless, almost simple. At the end of July, when she had not heard from her friend in five weeks, she wrote anxiously that "you have frequently endeavoured to teach me fortitude. I knew not then how much I should need it."[24]

It had been said by those who knew John Quincy Adams best that he loved his mother more than any other person in his life. This may have been true but, at this time, he needed to feel that he was the master of his own destiny rather than the malleable son who allowed his future to be determined for him. Nothing in the letters, diaries, or memoirs of either John Quincy or Louisa suggested a grand passion. There was affection and love, perhaps, but it appeared to be reasonable and restrained on Johnny's part and somewhat mannered and partially hysterical on Louisa's. Nevertheless, young Adams was adamant about his choice, or, at least, about being the one who made the choice.

In answer to Abigail's reminder of the prior claims of "Maria," obviously Mary Frazier, John Quincy reasserted that the attachment he had made was "irrevocably fixed." He and Mary, said Johnny, had parted forever, not because of necessity or an angry moment, but "it was a mutual dissolution of affection, the attractive principle was itself destroyed. The flame was not covered with ashes, it was extinguished with cold water. . . . I have satisfied the only claim to which Maria was entitled. It was that I would never marry a woman . . . unworthy of a place which she had held." John Adams's wish that his son would make an attachment in America could not be fulfilled.[25]

John Quincy, seemingly secure in his decision, waited quietly for his replacement, spending his time reading and studying. Translations from the Dutch, Italian, and Latin occupied him daily. He particularly enjoyed Ovid's *Metamorphoses* because it was the source for many of Shakespeare's ideas and allusions.

Since there was not much diplomatic business to attend to Johnny developed some of his ideas on the improvement of the American foreign service. He urged the State Department to train a consular service of responsible, impartial men. In a maritime war such as was then occurring, he argued, the peace of the United States could depend upon the behavior of the consuls. If their conduct had been distinguished for "integrity, veracity and impartiality or even neutrality toward belligerent powers our commerce would have been less harassed," he said.[26]

In a few months, or as soon as orders came to proceed to Portugal,

John Quincy planned to make a detour to London. Little as he liked the British capital, "I shall anxiously wish to see it once more for the sake of taking you as the companion for the remainder of the Journey or Voyage and of my life," he wrote.[27]

With great relief, Johnny heard from his mother that his Portuguese appointment had been completely unknown to his father and was the last nomination that President Washington made before Congress's rising. He was surely not surprised to read in the same letter about Abigail's anxieties regarding his engagement. Abigail asked her son if the young lady's parents were willing to let her go into the world at so early an age. And, reminiscent of her letters during the Frazier entanglement, she speculated on the inadequacy of a Minister's allowances. Her real misgiving, however, emerged in the question she asked about Louisa's ability to adapt to American ways after having been exposed to the dissipation of a foreign court.[28]

John Quincy answered: "If upon the whole I have done wrong I shall be the principal sufferer . . . and if I had waited until all the requisites . . . I should have been certainly doomed to perpetual celibacy." Somewhat painfully, Johnny swallowed his father's news that Harrison Gray Otis and other young Boston lawyers would enjoy a faster spreading fame than his own. "Foreign service is ostracism," John Quincy observed. It had also placed him in a falsely elevated position. "I must always be ready to return to private life and no fortune," he warned Louisa.[29]

The JQA-LCJ letters during the fall were hesitant and apologetic on her part, reassuring and gracefully affectionate on his. Louisa wrote of her fear that she would be awkward when thrust upon the world, and asked that her friend tell her when he would come so that her parents might prepare for the separation from her. "Between us two, my lovely friend, let there be peace," Johnny rhapsodized. Above all there must be no suspicion nor distrust between them. However, about practical arrangements he remained vague, though hopeful and uncertain about either the time of his departure from Holland or even the feasibility of a London detour. His lyrical outbursts came easily. "If the most ardent wishes of my heart could give me a conveyance, the wings of the wind would loiter in comparison with its rapidity."[30]

In Quincy, John Adams was tending his fields with an absorption meant to distract him from electioneering strife. John Quincy approved of his father's indifference toward "possible future competition" and his determination to be passive. They both agreed that Paine's pamphlet war against President Washington, French in origin, would brush off on John Adams.

"Electioneering goes as you would anticipate," John wrote at the end of October. He accepted the fact that his son would take with him to Portugal "an help meet, and may God grant you and her a double Portion of his choicest Blessings." However, the Vice President disapproved of Johnny's plan to quit the foreign service or settle in a southern state. Whoever is President, he asserted, will not promote others over you. "Even if your Father should be the person he will not so far affect a Disinterest as to injure you."[31] In a later letter, Adams observed, "If you become a Southern man who shall I give my hill to? I have given it the name 'Peacefield.' Shall Charles or Thomas have Peacefield?"[32]

Abigail relented also, possibly in recognition of her son's stubborn determination. She advised him to marry before going to Portugal so that "Tom could return to us. You whose chief delight is in Domestick Life, must feel yourself in a desert without a companion. . . . Give my Love to her and tell her I consider her already as my Daughter. . . ."[33]

A serious complication in the young couple's plans arose over Joshua Johnson's decision to return to America in early spring. Since as the months went by it seemed likely that it would be late spring or early summer before Johnny could leave Holland, he wrote regretfully to Mr. Johnson that the marriage might have to be postponed until his own return to America.

The period of waiting which her fiancé seemed to be able to fill comfortably with study and business was destroying sensitive Louisa. Her sisters continued to harass her and John Quincy admonished her about her lack of self-control. When he did not find a letter from her enclosed with her father's, he wrote that he hoped that this was not due "to any remains of the temper which I was sorry to observe in your last letter." He then informed her gently that news from America made a long wait probable. But he tried to reassure her that he suffered, too. Society, he said, no longer attracted him—neither balls, nor public assemblies, nor parties—because she was not there. He preferred to be alone with his books and "the remembrance of you. . . . Please write," he concluded.[34]

Once his mother chose to take a reasonable attitude towards his marriage, Johnny was pleased to confide in her. "My friend," he said, was accomplished in mind and person. Yes, it was possible that she would have some difficulty adjusting to her native country. But neither she nor he would succumb to the allure of foreign courts. John Quincy reassured Abigail that he had been explicit with Louisa about his future prospects, "which I have not presented as flattering." Louisa, Johnny wrote, was possessed of a delicate sense of propriety and a mildness of disposition. With all his fiancée's virtues, however, Johnny declared that he could never be happy living a distance from his parents.[35]

John Quincy continued to endure the prudent postponement of his wedding with the fortitude he often recommended to Louisa. If they started life in America, he suggested, they would be saved from starting out on a scale from which they must inevitably descend. "As long as we cannot command events," he wrote smugly, "we must necessarily learn to acquiesce in them. . . ." Louisa failed to carry her disappointments so gracefully. A particular humiliation overtook her when she acted too hurriedly on a comment in one of Johnny's letters that she be prepared for a sudden departure. Taking the suggestion literally, Louisa and her mother purchased all the wedding finery "to the most minute article." When this proved to be a false alarm, Mrs. Johnson had all the things locked up and all the preparations concealed "as if," Louisa recalled with bitterness, "I had committed some crime in having made them."[36]

The unhappy girl tried a strategem to promote her marriage. She wrote to Johnny that she would endeavor to prevail on her father to embark for America from Holland as she happened to know that he had a vessel there. Louisa pleaded for strict silence governing this plan because she had not yet consulted her parents.[37] Her fiancé's reaction humiliated her. He rejected a brief meeting in Holland as a satisfaction of such brevity that the voyage would be a great inconvenience to the rest of the Johnson family. Her fiancé reminded Louisa that she had discouraged him from passing through London en route to Lisbon if she could not then accompany him there. "The completion of our union here would be impossible," he said definitively. Present conditions in Holland were precarious politically and he could not take her from a happy family life into uncertainty. The fateful letter concluded with, "Still believe me your ever faithful and constant friend."[38]

For Louisa, this letter meant increased misery. She wrote pathetically that she was much altered physically and quite ill from the separation. "I think that when we meet you will cease to love me as I really am not the Louisa you were acquainted with. I am so miserably dull, stupid, and wan that I have gained the appellation of the Nun. . . ."[39] John Quincy had proved his self-characterization: "A faithful and anxious lover" rather than "a romantic lover."[40]

In the meantime, the American Minister to Holland mulled over foreign policy, a subject he believed to be very closely linked to John Adams's election to the Presidency. Citizen Adet, the French Minister, had scandalously exceeded his diplomatic position by conferring with republican party leaders to convince them to accept his strategy for defeating Jay's treaty. He was active also in planning the French invasion of Louisiana, which would be achieved by using the United States for an army staging base and in some other ubiquitous projects to effect the secession of the sections of the United States west of the Appalachian Mountains. Monsieur Adet had been recalled in mid-August, Johnny wrote to his father, and would be succeeded by Michel-Ange Bernard Mangourit, former consul at Charleston. James Monroe, Adet's opposite in Paris, was in difficulties also. Washington's attempt to balance the foreign office by putting a federalist in London and a republican in Paris had proved an unsuccessful experiment.

One of Monroe's chief problems was his friend, Tom Paine. The pamphleteer was living in the American Minister's house until his presence became too much of an embarrassment. John Quincy believed that Paine's influence on the Directorate made Monroe's position as the American Minister less useful.[41]

The French Grand Design—Louisiana by cession from Spain and England by conquest—might not be carried out as intended because matters on the continent were very pressing for the Directory. Johnny was not too worried, however, because he had a great faith in the American electorate and a firm belief that its nature was incomprehensible to the French. Even if that nation succeeded in promoting Jefferson to the Presidency he would follow the same foreign policy as his predecessor.[42]

The Washington Administration deplored Monroe's unneutral conduct in relation to Jay's treaty. Convinced that close ties with France was the only answer to British affronts, Pickering could not persuade him to modify either his view or his actions. When the news of Monroe's recall reached John Quincy, he received it with mixed feelings because there was no doubt that Monroe had the confidence of the Directory, great public influence with them, and was greatly beloved in France. General Pinckney, his successor, John Quincy predicted accurately, would not be received.[43]

Though George Washington was considered almost godlike by young Adams, he did not share the European view that the prosperity and union of the United States depended on the personal character of its first President and that when he retired the union would divide into the North and the South. This analysis, he asserted, was wishful thinking because the prosperity of the American people was a "reproach to the rulers of Europe whether monarchical or republican."[44]

In letters to his father, Johnny refrained from any but the most delicate references to his presidential hopes. But, privately, he cared. In his summary of the year 1795, recorded in his *Diary*, he admitted anxiety about the two objects nearest to his heart: his country and his father. It was painful, he said, to appear cheerful to the world. But what of Louisa?

John Quincy's continued complacency about his thwarted marriage was a vivid contrast to his fiancée's excessive suffering. At twenty, Louisa admitted that she was as unworldly as a girl of fifteen, particularly about the reactions of people. Before her engagement to Johnny she had never been left alone with a man. During the summer of 1796, Joshua Johnson rented a small house at Clapham Common and installed Louisa in it with only a young servant, Celia, as a companion. This curious arrangement was expected to give the young girl the opportunity to follow Johnny's course of study away from the distractions of the busy Johnson household. Perhaps it was also meant to spare her the continued hostility of her sisters. Louisa, who hoped that knowledge would lessen the distance between her and her future husband, worked hard, but the isolated summer was still a painful one.[45]

Her return to the family home had not lessened Louisa's unhappiness. In January of 1797, she wrote to John Quincy that she had been very ill but was now recovered enough to attend a dance. There was a coldness in tone that pervaded the letter which, at the same time, tried to be light and gay. Both qualities may have been lost on the recipient. Johnny sounded even colder in his letter to Louisa's father responding to the suggestion that the Johnsons visit The Hague before proceeding to America. The American Minister stated firmly that he could not marry at this time. "My own situation is at present so unsettled and precarious," he explained, "that the assumption of a family and its necessary appendages would be an act of folly."[46] To Louisa he was equally firm. In the eyes of the world, for her to come to Holland would give "an appearance consistent neither with your dignity nor my delicacy," he explained. A softener was added as an afterthought: "Assure me of the continuance of your affection."[47]

Letters flew back and forth between Louisa and Johnny, often crossing each other. Realistically, Louisa declared, "Our doom it appears is fixed," but she was, nevertheless, angry at Johnny's rejection of the Holland detour. She claimed that there was no change in her affection but was not too convincing about it, because her letters were stiff and formal. Of his father's election to the Presidency by five votes, she said, "It was a mark of distinction which is highly flattering though . . . dearly purchased at the present crisis of affairs."[48]

John and Abigail seemed to have accepted their son's match with good grace. Louisa's brother Tom, returned from a trip to Boston, reported that everyone there supposed that the young people were already married. He told Louisa that Mr. and Mrs. Adams approved of her marriage to their son.

Foolishly, Louisa had dared to tread on dangerous ground with an Adams. "You will be angry but I do not progress on the harp," she wrote to Johnny by way of introduction. Then she added unwisely, "my harp has not like your *Books*, usurped the primary place in my heart."[49] The rejection of the Holland visit gnawed at her. She returned to the subject constantly in her letters until it became a certainty to her that it represented a rejection of her person. "When you were here you said you could see no fault in your Louisa but how you have changed . . . erase from your memory that unfortunate letter which has been productive of our mutual anxiety."[50]

John Quincy placed his public responsibilities above his private wishes. Though he sent Louisa's mother and sisters gifts and, for Louisa, a beautiful pair of bracelets, he offered no hope for an early meeting. His country, he said, was "the first and most imperious of all obligations." Remaining in Europe was an obligation, though his own personal advantage would be better served by an immediate return to America, because it was not at a distance from the United States "that an ambitious American is to rise." He hoped that Louisa was spending her time cultivating her virtues, improving her under-standing, and correcting her defects.[51]

Louisa's outbursts angered young Adams, who was quite capable of answering them with severity. "My *dignity*, my *station*, or my *family* have no sort of concern with any subject of debate between you and me." In answer to her earlier letter, he denied that he ever believed her without fault but may have said so "in the blindness of an irrational Love." He conceded that she had "a Virtuous Heart, an intelligent Mind, an accomplished person and a gentle disposition." But, he admonished, "never again try my temper by a formal and professed assertion of your Spirit."[52]

Johnny was aware that there was a change in his feelings towards his future wife. Absence, he confessed, had restored "sober reason and reflection." London had been a time of delight but also a time of overindulgence. "The duties of life my friend are vigorous," he warned, and hoped that she would not like him less for being now "a much more estimable and respectable man."[53]

A week later, upon rereading his letters to Louisa, "and now being totally calm," he said that he had sometimes replied to her with acrimony and perhaps what he had thought was firmness was, in truth, "only temper"—a generous confession from rigid Johnny Adams. What really hurt him, however, was her attack on his love for books. "I hesitate to say anything about my books which seem to be obnoxious to you."[54] Louisa was even more contrite. She was sorry that she had sent the nasty letters and entreated his pardon. Obviously the separation was damaging the relationship between the pair.

His romantic entanglement was only one phase of John Quincy's concern. He fretted about the ill will of the French to America and particularly the personal animosity of highly placed Frenchmen such as Sieyes to John Adams. This alarm at France's activities was shared by many Americans in Europe, Johnny wrote to his father. James Monroe, who visited Holland in February, where he was en-tertained splendidly, saw Johnny almost every day of his visit. Mon-roe, John Quincy reported, said nothing about his recall, although it seemed to be continuously on his mind.[55]

In a letter to George Washington praising him for his "Farewell Address," John Quincy prayed that his countrymen would found their future foreign policy on his words. He gave no indication, however, that he recognized any similarities between the address and his own "Columbus" letters.[56] But the retiring American President had not forgotten his young admirer. He wrote to John Adams that he had a "strong hope" that merited promotion would not be withheld from John Quincy Adams "because he is your son. . . . Mr. Adams is the most valuable public character we have abroad . . . his country would sustain a loss if these were to be checked by over delicacy on your part."[57]

The packet containing Johnny's recall from Holland and commission as Minister Plenipotentiary to Portugal arrived on March 9. With it came the request that Tom come home as soon as William Vans Murray, Johnny's successor, arrived in the Netherlands. "I hope to have one of my sons near me," the President wrote fretfully to Abigail. He complained that none of his family had been with him at the Inauguration, "which was one of the most affecting and overpowering scenes I ever acted in. I was very unwell, had no sleep the night before, and really did not know but I should have fainted in the presence of all the world."[58]

Meantime, the relations between France and America worsened because, John Quincy analyzed, the Directory hoped to insult and injure the United States and to provoke her into war. To effect this plan, France decided to condemn all American vessels and merchandise bound to or from any British ports. The drive started with the use of a new form of ship's paper called an arrêté, without which no American ship would be exempt from capture and condemnation. According to John Quincy, all European nations regarded the United States with "a little envy and a little fear," in the same manner as an old nobleman looked on a parvenu.[59]

The Directory's plan to entice the United States into war was linked with the belief that the southern states could be influenced to form an independent republic which would then ally itself with France. Johnny was convinced that Tom Paine was returning to the United States with yet another scheme for separating the western states from the union.[60] The Dutch listening post also received the news that Portugal might be raided by a foreign army. Louisa was informed promptly that such an emergency would make a residence in Lisbon unpleasant for a lady. John Quincy never spared her any bad news about Europe which made her advise him not "to contemplate so constantly the dark side of things."[61]

Happily, when John Quincy's Portuguese orders arrived, his doubts about marriage vanished. He determined to reach London somehow and put an end "at length to a separation so painful to us both." The problem was that the voyage could not be taken in an English vessel which would be subject to capture by the French. He must find an American ship on its way to Lisbon that planned to stop for a few days in England. Failing to find such a transport, Johnny wrote to Louisa in despair, they must reconcile themselves to waiting until they might be reunited in America. Even in the midst of this major disappointment, John Quincy could not refrain from mentioning Louisa's preoccupation with his devotion to books. He said: "Instead of weakening, the ardent love of literature tends to confirm, to increase, to exalt every virtuous and laudable affection. I shall love you the more. . . ."[62]

At this time, General Pinckney, completely bewildered by his rejection at the hands of France, visited John Quincy at The Hague. France had transferred her anger to him from his brother Thomas Pinckney, who had refused to communicate Jay's treaty to them when he passed through Paris to his Spanish mission, Johnny explained. France had wanted the credit for getting the United States free navigation of the Mississippi River, hence Thomas Pinckney would not be forgiven for securing it, "not as a charitable donation from France, but as a fair bargain in our own right."[63] That the French would receive John Adams's Presidency with great unfriendliness was no surprise since their support of Jefferson had been quite open. "You have everything to expect from France but justice and good will," Johnny commented to his father. He also observed that Napoleon Bonaparte, then relatively unknown, was "the comet of the day . . . certainly no ordinary man."

On May 20, President Adams sent a message to the Senate nominating John Quincy Adams Minister Plenipotentiary to the King of Prussia. After some delay, the Senate approved the nomination. It was not the candidate that caused the delay but the mission, which concerned the renewal of a treaty with Prussia which was about to expire, as was a treaty negotiated with Sweden by Ben Franklin. John Quincy was transferred from Lisbon to negotiate directly renewal of the Prussian treaty, indirectly to handle the Swedish treaty. His grade would be the same as that of the Portuguese post, but his duties in Prussia would be both more arduous and more important. News of the change in plans, however, did not reach Johnny for several months.

"Our difficulties are ended," Louisa wrote to her fiancé at the end

of May. Suffused with happiness, she added, "the more I know you
the more I admire, esteem and love you, and the greater is my
inclination to do everything in my power to promote your happiness and welfare." Joshua Johnson had offered to solve the Minister's
transportation problem by fitting out one of his ships, the *Maryland,* sending it to carry him from Holland to England, and thence
to Portugal.[64]

Louisa's entire outlook changed. She hardly minded when Johnny
wrote to her, testily, that her continual use of the appellation,
"my Adams," was not to his taste because it "looks too much like
that of novels. . . . I have endeavoured to habituate myself to it
. . . but it looks to me more and more uncouth and awkward."[65] Her
enthusiasm frightened him. "But you have too much gilding upon
your prospects," Johnny warned. "You have promised yourself too
much, and I regret already your disappointment."[66] And by early
June he was putting a damper on the scheme. There was still some
uncertainty about his going to England and, he told Mr. Johnson, it
was neither his intention nor his hope that a ship would be sent to
Lisbon just for Louisa and him. If Mr. Johnson had an opportunity
to employ the vessel in another way, "I hope you will not on that
account omit any offer."[67]

Tom, just returned from a trip to Paris, decided to accompany
his brother to London. About the same time, in early June, William
Vans Murray, the new American Minister to the Netherlands, arrived at The Hague. John Quincy was pleased to be able to brief his
successor but, just before he left the country, he had one of his crises
over conduct. The usual practice of the Dutch government was to
present a departing foreign minister with a gold chain and medal.
Aware of this custom, Johnny informd Mr. Van Leyden that under
the United States constitution, such a gift could not be accepted.
Van Leyden said that his country had the same regulation but perhaps Congress, if appealed to, would allow him to accept the gift.
John Quincy wrote to the Secretary of State, but in his letter to
Pickering he said: "the mere solicitation of liberty to receive a
present from a foreign power seems an approximation of what the
Constitution has by a rule forbidden, and I shall not certainly set
the example."[68]

Finally, John Quincy arranged his own passage to England, leaving The Hague on June 28. He was delayed at Maasluys for a period
of ten days, but when he finally landed at Gravesend, on the morn-

ing of July 12, though regulations were tight, some were waived for him because of his "public character." He was able to set out for London, by coach, that same afternoon and about five in the evening he reached Osborne's Hotel.

Due to some trifling accident, the reunion between John Quincy and Louisa did not take place until the next day. Only Louisa's account has been recorded. "I met him with feelings of mortified affection more bitter than I could express . . . and with dread of parting from my parents," Louisa wrote much later.[69] Apparently, the long separation had spoiled the spontaneity of their love. Joshua Johnson felt the tension also. On July 19 he wrote to Johnny that there seemed to be "a matter of delicacy on your part" that "retards your union with my child." He urged him to accept Mrs. Johnson's invitation to lodge with them and to use the house for a headquarters from which he could conduct his business.[70] By this time a letter from John Adams had arrived telling his son that he should not go to Lisbon but to wait for his commission to Berlin.

Finally, John Quincy asked Louisa to name a date for their wedding. He seemed surprised when she set it promptly for the 26th of July, just a few days later. Mrs. Johnson openly announced her disapproval of such an early date because she had not been consulted. Louisa felt ashamed.

At nine in the morning, accompanied by his brother Tom, John Quincy went to the Johnson home on Tower Hill where the wedding party gathered. They proceeded to All Hallows Church, Barking, where at eleven o'clock, Reverend John Hewlett married John Quincy Adams and Louisa Catherine Johnson. Also present at the simple ceremony were James Brooks, Joseph Hall, and the Johnson family. Immediately after the marriage, the couple went to see Tilney House, one of the splendid country seats of England.

Although sobriety rather than passion seemed to characterize the couple's entry into marriage, two happy weeks followed. Then Louisa suffered "a blow that prostrated my pride, my pretensions, I will say my happiness forever."[71]

The intensity of emotion with which Louisa recorded her "tragedy" stretches credence but, because the family correspondence has constant reference to the episode, its impact on her must be accepted at her own evaluation.

The details of the disaster were buried in hysterical outpourings. What mattered was that Joshua Johnson was swindled by his partner, a friend of twenty-four years' standing. When a remittance he expected failed to arrive, as did a large East India ship he had financed, Mr. Johnson had to stop payment on a 500-pound check. As a result, the Johnsons had to leave the country quickly and in disgrace. Louisa realized that the sequence of events would suggest that she and her family had deceived John Quincy into marriage, concealing the precarious state of their affairs until after the wedding. The young bride concluded that she had lost her husband's esteem forever because, for a man in public life, family disgrace was awkward and compromising. "From then on all confidence was destroyed in me and mine," Louisa said.

Added to Louisa's misery was the pathetic parting with her family, especially with her adored father, who now looked like a broken man. The new bride described herself as "the worst wretch that the sun ever smiled upon." When John Quincy placed the management of the family concerns in the hands of a Mr. Whiteson, she called the act "short and rigid justice." Every rap on the door was a possible creditor who hoped that Mr. Johnson had left money with his children to settle his debts. Worst of all, an insulting letter came to Johnny calling upon him to save his father-in-law's honor.

The distraught, guilt-ridden young woman had only Mrs. Court, an old family friend, to turn to and Tom Adams, who was kind and affectionate. He assured her that he believed her innocent, as did Rufus King and his wife when they returned to London. Louisa's health failed, along with the wilting of her spirits.

John Quincy's dignified reticence kept him from referring to his reaction to his father-in-law's plight. But it would be hard to imagine a reversal of fortune more difficult for young Adams to accept. Whether this event colored his relationship to his wife cannot be assessed and there was no previous period of time during which they were married with which to compare his behavior. Louisa admitted, however, that he was often affectionate and kind but also that at times he displayed a coldness. How much of the latter was either her vivid imagination or his reserved nature defies analysis.

Meanwhile, John Quincy's powers of observation and recording pen continued to work for his country. Bonaparte's coup d'etat was duly noted, as had been the continuing animosity of France to the United States and, particularly, to her second President.

At the end of September, the Berlin commission in their hands, the young Adamses prepared to leave London. Even the leavetaking was marred by an unpleasant domestic scene. Celia, who considered herself Louisa's personal servant, was angry that she had to be left behind. And as the young people's coach pulled away, she showered her former mistress with every kind of angry imprecation. The abuse did not cease until the post chaise carried Mr. and Mrs. John Quincy Adams out of range of her voice.

CHAPTER 7

At the Prussian Court

"The year has not in any respect been a profitable one to me. The only acquisition of any value that it has afforded is that of reading German very indifferently."

JOHN QUINCY ADAMS

JOHN QUINCY, WHO tended to take a pessimistic view of change of any kind, was not pleased that he was going to Berlin instead of Lisbon. Abigail wrote that it gave her "real pain" to read that he felt so "personally inconvenienced." She agreed with him that had Washington been President he would not have been sent there. But, she revealed, "I can tell you where you would have been employed— as one of the envoys to France. This was the desire and opinion of all the Ministers and nothing but your near connection with the Chief Magistrate prevented. . . . He had a delicacy upon the subject, and declined it."[1]

Since he had no choice, John Quincy left Gravesend with his wife, his brother, and Epps, Louisa's maid. They arrived in Hamburg eight days later, Louisa in a deplorable state after the buffeting of the stormy voyage. Once there, the Swedish Minister confounded John Quincy with the news that the King of Prussia was mortally ill and if not already dead was expected to live only a few days longer.

Travelling in a coach to Berlin through pines and sands on very poor roads was an ordeal for Louisa. She was so sensitized by her experiences that when the liveried footman was ordered to take a seat in her carriage, she felt that it was an insult proffered because of the downfall of her family. Abigail was right about her fears that Louisa's values were European rather than American.

John Quincy suffered a kind of culture shock himself when he arrived at the Berlin gate. A dapper Lieutenant did not know "Who the United States were" until he was enlightened by a private. The Adams party took rooms at the Soleil d'Or, otherwise known as the Hotel de Russie.[2]

"So I am to be here six or eight months without admission," the American Minister despaired after delivering his credentials to Karl Wilhelm, Count Finck von Finckenstein, the principal Prussian Minister of State. The Count could not accept them because of the King's illness and the new King would require new credentials. It was an inauspicious beginning that could be improved only if the dying King, who favored the treaty, had a remission long enough to grant an audience. However, since his illness was dropsy and he had lost the use of his limbs, the King would not be able to sign a paper.

Happily, John Quincy's fears did not materialize. On December 5, the new King, Frederick William III, accepted the argument proferred by Count Finckenstein that the United States was a great distance from his Prussia, and received the American with his old credentials. The Count hovered over him, his old head "full of forms and procedures and titles, and all the trash of diplomatic ceremony."[3]

King Frederick William, an unpretentious man with a severe face, dressed simply in a plain uniform and boots, was gracious and cordial to Adams. He asked how long his father had been President and whether Washington had now entirely abandoned all connection with the Administration. As to the treaty, he was happy to maintain and renew the connection with the United States. The similarity of the two countries' commercial interests should produce mutual benefit, the King said, speaking quickly but with a pleasing smile. He promised to attend to the subject in due time.

More visits with royalty followed Johnny's presentation. America was a subject of curiosity to the court, particularly to Prince Ferdinand and Princess Radziwill, his daughter. They all expressed a great respect for George Washington and seemed to follow America's progress in the newspapers. Prince Ferdinand, Frederick II's brother, asked about the epidemic raging in Philadelphia, and

Prince Henry, declaring that America was rising while Europe was declining, asked if the American union was strong enough to stay together.

However, domestic problems multiplied for the Adams family. Louisa's illness became chronic. Alone in a strange country with only two young men and a seventeen-year-old maid to look after her, she grew desperately lonely and homesick. Fortunately, Dr. Brown, an English physician who treated the court, was sympathetic and able to help her. The Browns and their children, particularly their beautiful daughter Isabelle, became close friends with the Adamses. Tea at the Browns was a familiar reminder of home to English-born Louisa. Tom's health also failed at this time. He had an alarming sore throat that triggered his rheumatism.

Family illness made it necessary for John Quincy to be launched on his social career alone. Louisa resented his "sea of dissipation" and complained that their quarters, located at the Brandenburg gate added to her misery. The guard room was located under her window so that few hours passed that she did not hear the screams and blows bestowed upon the soldiers. Her weak nerves were not helped by the scenes of suffering. But it was some months before a suitable apartment within their means could be located. While her husband made his social rounds, Tom's kindness kept Louisa from a complete breakdown.

The social whirl was a necessary part of a Minister's job. As the first American Minister to the court, John Quincy had to establish his position. That he was so well received was most heartening. His keen political radar soon searched out the coolness between the Prussian court and those of Vienna and London. For France, he observed, there was friendship without cordiality, but the Prussian relationship with Russia had improved since the death of the late Empress. The new King was not without experience, particularly of a military nature, which was inevitable in a country that was little more than "a nation of soldiery." He was extremely active, sober, and domestic—"a grave man, almost harsh without any weakness, indolence, or tendency to dissipation."[4]

The diplomatic family also received John Quincy Adams cordially. Popular Antoine-Bernard Caillord, the French Ambassador, who remembered the American from the time he had been secretary of the French legation, conversed freely with him. Several other Ministers, including Baron Schultz von Aschenade of Sweden, knew John Adams.

But the formal court life was not really agreeable to young Adams, who disliked its pretension and, particularly, the dress. He suggested to his father that the problem of dress could be solved if the United States, like France, would adopt a particular uniform for its diplomatic agents. It would save expense while allowing the individual to conform more to republican simplicity without offending the host country. The uniform could differ only in color from daily dress. Decidedly, asserted John Quincy, the substitution of good, plain broadcloth for the silks, velvets, lace, and embroidery now expected would be agreeable to every American "who now undergoes these metamorphoses, and an appropriate dress would have the advantage of designating a character which should not be confounded with every tribe of courtly butterflies in Europe."[5]

In America, the most controversial and explosive issue was the adventures of the three American plenipotentiaries to France who had been sent to negotiate peace with Talleyrand and the Directory. The XYZ affair, as it came to be known, succeeded in enhancing John Adams's reputation and bestowing upon him, for a time, an unfamiliar popularity. John Quincy followed the progress of the envoys carefully so that he might report home, often in cipher, any information he could pick up at the Prussian court. But Berlin was not as accessible or as satisfactory a listening post as The Hague.

Basically, Talleyrand had no compunction about developing his position as Minister of Foreign Affairs into a profitable business. Austria, Prussia, Portugal, the Elector of Bavaria, the Grand Duke of Tuscany, the Batavian Republic, and the Grand Vizier had all paid tribute for secret articles in treaties or other services that they required. Elbridge Gerry, one of the commissioners, said aptly, "A small cargo of Mexican Dollars would be more efficient in the Negotiation at present than two cargoes of Ambassadors."[6] Neither he nor his colleagues, John Marshall of Virginia and Charles Cotesworth Pinckney of South Carolina, were naïve. They were just too shrewd to agree to pay up before they got what they had come for. Having been humiliated by being left to sit unnoticed in the anterooms and corridors of the Director's offices, after the French agents, designated as XYZ, approached them for $250,000 bribe money as a prologue to negotiations, they asked for their passports. The other quid pro quo, an apology from President Adams for his anti-French remarks in his May 15, 1797, message to Congress, was just as unacceptable.

As John Quincy followed the progress of the affair, he was relieved that he had not been sent to France. The malignity in that country against his father would have made his position there intolerable. He wrote to Elbridge Gerry his regrets that he and his colleagues were experiencing such humiliation and had so little hopes of a successful termination to the mission.

Talleyrand was deliberately delaying the culmination of the negotiations, hoping to repudiate Jay's treaty and its authors and supporters, the federalists. With the intention of dividing the commission, he withheld Gerry's passport, thus preventing his leaving with the others and enabling him to continue his conversations with Gerry started secretly before the mission officially ended. The other commissioners had not been completely deceived. Pinckney wrote to Rufus King in December, 1797, that some civilities had been shown to Gerry and none to the others.

John Quincy was sorry to hear that Gerry had not returned with his colleagues, agreeing with William Vans Murray that it promised only mischief. Any arrangement that such a man could obtain from France would only be degrading, said Adams. France wanted us in this "mongrel condition between peace and war. They plunder us as enemies but they don't want war with us because they are occupied in Europe." Citing historical precedent, he stated that temporizing would work no better than when it was tried by Venice, Genoa, and the Swiss Republic.[7]

In April, 1798, the public became aware of the XYZ Affair through the publication of the despatches. America went wild with indignation and patriotism. Pinckney's statement, "It is no, no, not a sixpence," was magnified by a newspaperman into the rallying cry, "Millions for defense but not one cent for tribute." John Adams basked in unexpected and unaccustomed adulation to the tune of "The President's March" which became one of the popular songs of the day.

Probably unaware of his father's new-found popularity, John Quincy rather regretted the publication. He feared that the revelation of the secrets of the negotiations, without proof, would just bring French denial of the charges and retribution to the Americans in France. Talleyrand was furious, though he denied everything, stressing the fact that the proposal for the bribe came from an unofficial source. His defense was lame, young Adams observed, but it served for logic and would have its effect on "our Frenchified patriots."[8]

The home life of the newly married Adamses became more comfortable after they took a handsome apartment on the Bearen Strasse. The library, the finest room of the house and, of course, Johnny's favorite, had a carpet, well-made bookcases, a mahogany desk, a second-hand sofa, and a few chairs. The other rooms were more makeshift. There was no carpet in the bedroom and the bedstead had only white cotton curtains of the coarsest quality ornamented by a border of calico which Louisa had sewn herself to match the curtains she had made. A pinewood toilet table with a muslin cover and a simple toilet glass completed the room, which had no fire in winter. The apartment had, in addition, two drawing rooms, one of which had been made into a pretty dining room. For getting about, John Quincy had purchased a second-hand chariot and a pair of horses.[9] The household consisted of Whitcomb, Epps, a footman, a housemaid, and a woman cook.

At the start of the New Year, somewhat restored in health, Louisa was presented to the young Queen, Luise Auguste Wilhelmina Amalie, Princess of Mecklenberg-Strelitz, whom she thought "full of grace, affability, sweetness and the most irresistable beauty."[10] Almost paranoid, ill and frightened, Louisa had convinced herself that her husband, ashamed of her, didn't want her seen at court. There had been gossip about the American Minister's wife's absence, which reported that she was very ugly and had a horseface. When Louisa was presented at last and was seen to be young and attractive, she enjoyed much more success than she would have without the unpleasant rumors.

Court life appealed to Mrs. John Quincy Adams. She was undemocratically aware that she was the wife of a foreign minister and the daugher-in-law of the President of the United States, always addressed as "Your Excellency" and sometimes called "Princess Royal." However, and Louisa always blamed her attitude on her English upbringing, she declared that "an American Minister was *to me* a very small personage."[11] His salary was too low to make him equal to others, she complained, although in Prussia he earned about $9,000 a year, about double his salary as Minister Resident to Holland.

John Quincy's new credentials arrived in May but progress on the treaty was still delayed. The King's absence was caused by a twelve-day annual review of the troops which was held on an open plain about two miles from Berlin. The Americans who were invited to attend were duly impressed with the formidable appearance made by the 15,000 troops that paraded.

Sweden also had delayed answering the proposal to renew her treaty with the United States. John Quincy informed Pickering that although he had presented his proposal to Mr. Engestrom upon his first arrival in Berlin, he now suspected that there was some motive for their procrastination. Most probably the culprit was France, whose treatment of Sweden was as highhanded as if the government were her own. Sweden, on her part, needed to conciliate France. To test his theory, the American Minister wrote a warning letter to Sweden, threatening that if there were any further delays and the United States got involved in war, she would be amply justified in "considering enemy's property on board Swedish vessels as prize. . . ."[12]

John Quincy was perfectly willing to act as the clearing house for European information and then to relay it back to the United States, but he insisted on secrecy at that end. A man in office, he explained, would not say anything confidential to an American Minister if his words were then, six months later, "open to the knowledge of all Europe." The danger was not detection—a cipher was used to deal with that—but publicity.[13]

On July 5, the King received the American Minister and the French Minister, Citizen Sieyes, at Charlottenburg. The next day the ceremony of the oath of allegiance by the people took place at the royal palace. In the morning, the King, his generals, and his Ministers went in procession to the Dom Church and returned at noon to the White Hall in the palace where the King ascended a throne. In a box, at the right of the throne, all the foreign ministers and their secretaries were seated. The Adams brothers were present, but all eyes were watching Sieyes and his secretary. Before the throne, the assembled burgers from different parts of the country and deputies from several states took the oath with a surprising lack of fervor. After many addresses, the procession left the hall for the large square in front of the palace, which was filled with seventy to eighty thousand of the King's subjects. Johnny observed that the weak cheer offered by the sober, orderly, and apathetic throng would have been surpassed by five hundred Americans. Tom agreed that it was an insipid spectacle, at least by his country's standards.[14]

The purpose of the mission to Prussia could now be accomplished. In his instructions, John Quincy had been advised to abandon his favorite maritime principle, that free ships guarantee free goods, or that enemy properties carried in the ships of free nations were safe from capture. Young Adams objected to modification of the principle, particularly in this case because Prussia had established the principle before the world. Count Finckenstein took Adams's carefully prepared draft to the King for study.

No event escaped Johnny's observation and comment. He was fully aware of Dr. George Logan's arrival in Hamburg with letters from Jefferson and other prominent republicans and of the fact that Lafayette's influence with the French agent there had provided him with a passport to Paris. Logan, a Philadelphia Quaker and Jacobin, was on a "curious mission." John Quincy guessed right when he wrote to Murray that Logan was probably going to France to persuade the French Directory against war. Murray was able to supply more accurate information. Logan, an anti-Adams man, was on a republican-party mission to persuade Talleyrand that war between the United States and France would destroy the party and that, since the federalists would probably not continue in power, it would be the best arrangement for Franco-American peace.

In 1799, Logan returned to the United States, saying that the Directory was willing to stop hostilities. Federalists, angered by Logan's mission, passed the Logan Act, which imposed fine and imprisonment on any private citizen found guilty of holding correspondence with foreign governments or their agents, in relation to the United States.[15] When Logan arrived in Paris he dined with the President of the Directory, who took full credit for France's raising of the embargo on almost all the American vessels in the ports of France. It was reported, however, that Talleyrand had not encouraged Logan and preferred to work with official representatives of the American government. The lifting of the embargo, Johnny observed to Abigail, was a sensible new attitude for France, who now had to face an alliance against her, composed of Austria, Russia, Turkey and Naples. But he did not guess the real reason for France's move, which was Louisiana.[16]

It became obvious that the Swedish treaty would not materialize because of Sweden's fear of giving offense to France. President Adams considered the possibility that both Prussia and Sweden might refuse to make treaties unalarming. American commerce, he said, was more important to them than theirs to the United States. Only in the case of a war with France would it be important that the

United States not be bound to permit Prussian, Swedish, or Danish ships to supply France with anything, even American produce.[17]

Thomas Boylston Adams left his brother's service at the beginning of October, embarking from Hamburg with letters from John Quincy to the State Department and the President. Admittedly his confidante, the loss of Tom was hard for the American Minister, who now had Thomas Welsh, the son of the doctor, to take his brother's place as secretary to the legation. But to Louisa, her brother-in-law's departure was a tragedy. He "soothed me in my afflictions, corrected gently my utter want of self-confidence, flattered me judiciously, and by his unerring judgment often prevented me from committing mistakes natural to my inexperience," Louisa wrote. Most important, she felt that he respected as well as loved her and did her justice when she needed a powerful friend.[18] She missed him "beyond expression." He had often been her companion when her husband was on official business and when he accompanied Mr. and Mrs. John Quincy Adams on their excursions he added some spontaneous gaiety often missing in their behavior.

Rufus King's request that the American Minister arrange for the purchase of 10,000 muskets from Prussia could not be met. Count Haugwitz explained that the King would require the entire annual production of the one small-arms manufacturer in Prussia for his own troops this year. The King was sorry, he said, that he would be unable to display his friendship for America but John Quincy believed that the excess supply had already been promised to Switzerland.

The continual round of balls, parties, and gatherings that composed the life of the Prussian court grew monotonous to both Mr. and Mrs. Adams. Louisa complained that her husband often left her to fend for herself because he was at the card table or she would stay for supper and he would go home. There was hardly an evening from one month to the other without some engagement in company, Adams complained. Though unavoidable, he thought that it was an unprofitable life and, in his summing up of the year 1798, wrote that his sole accomplishment was learning to read German, "very indifferently."

The foreign policy of all the European nations, whether friend or foe of France, was so closely linked to that country's activities that John Quincy in his letters and despatches, was almost obsessed with hatred for her. France was also his father's greatest enemy. With some justice, both Adamses attributed a good part of the President's internal difficulties to the influence of the "French party." John Quincy was just as glad that, in Berlin, he saw less of his countrymen who made their way to Europe than he had at The Hague listening post because the travellers were mostly pro-French. "They are almost without exception men whom, cold and phlegmatic as I am, I could not see without feeling the blood of indignation boil within me," he wrote.[19] He was particularly annoyed with Lafayette, although he had done what was possible to achieve his release from Olmutz, because of his "ungovernable ambition in disguise," his propensity for "intrigue not calculated to inspire confidence, his rights of man fanaticism and his loose political morality."[20] The republican party, he believed, was ready to fall into line with France to achieve dominance. Symptoms of republican desperation for power were the Virginia and Kentucky resolutions, "the tocsin of insurrection" together with Logan's mission. Nevertheless, he favored the appointment of a new Commission to be sent to France, for he detected that Talleyrand's anxiety for negotiations was sincere and he preferred to carry out the diplomacy in Paris rather than in Philadelphia.

The Senate, which according to John Quincy reflected the growing strength of the French party, refused the President's appointment of William Vans Murray to the French post and then a new Commission to confer with France. Internal politics were not clear to the American Minister operating out of Berlin so he underestimated the power of the Hamiltonian faction, which also opposed reopening negotiations. Hamilton's fervor for military honor, eventually to be a factor in leading to his fatal duel, made him oppose Adams's will for peace, a goal which would cost the second President his re-election.

Although her health was poor and she had suffered the discomfort and anguish of several miscarriages, Louisa participated actively in court socials. The lovely young Queen was kind to her—too kind, John Quincy thought. On one occasion, seeing the pale face of the American Minister's wife, the Queen offered her a box of rouge. Johnny, disgusted down to the Puritan marrow of his bones, forbade her to use the paint and insisted that she refuse the offer. A number of months later, when his wife applied the rouge surreptitiously, her husband gently but firmly washed it off her face.

In March, while standing at a window in the library, Louisa saw a child run over by a cart. She fainted and fell, causing the loss of the child that she was carrying. Her husband was kind and affectionate but could not conceal his disappointment. Her miscarriages numbered at least three by this time.

Progress on the Prussian-American treaty was slow but consistent. The King had received the full report from Count Haugwitz by May and it was now a matter of working out some of the nagging details. President Adams instructed his son that he was willing to accept the old articles of contraband set out in the former treaty. On John Quincy's thirty-second birthday, July 11, the treaty was signed.

Other than the Adams principle of free ships, free goods which had been sacrificed, most of the articles were identical with those of the earlier treaty. A novel provision of the Treaty of 1785 providing compensation for intercepted contraband was continued in 1799 and renewed throughout the nineteenth century.

Changes included some additions in the list of contraband, such as ships' timbers and naval stores, modification of the salvage rules for recaptures, and a clause that conformed to Jay's treaty negotiated with England.[21] The satisfactory conclusion of the treaty was a result of patience and good fortune. The Prussian Ministers had been opposed to the changes at first but the long period of waiting until new credentials arrived from the United States enabled John Quincy to establish personal relations with them, which helped to convince them to accept the modifications.

The Swedish treaty did not meet with the same good fortune. Working at long distance from the Swedish court, Johnny first made overtures to Mr. Aschenade, the Swedish Minister at Berlin who died shortly thereafter. His successor, Baron D'Engestrom, accepted renewal of the subject but did not pursue it with any interest. The treaty expired, another victim of French power exerted not too subtly on her satellites. Sweden also had a number of gripes against the United States: her failure to respond to an invitation to join the Armed Neutrality of 1794 and her refusal to participate in the Swedish King's plan of a joint effort on the part of the United States, Sweden, and Denmark to protect ships against the Barbary pirates. John Quincy favored the King's plan but it was never acted on in America.

His mission accomplished, John Quincy Adams decided to accept Dr. Brown's advice and take Louisa, who was suffering from a recurrence of her earlier illness, on a tour of Dresden and Toplitz. She had to be lifted into the carriage to begin the journey but by the time they teached Dresden was recovered enough to participate in the sightseeing and visits. At Toplitz, where they had a spacious apartment, the Adamses met all kinds of royalty: Prussian, Russian, and Austrian, which seemed to entertain Louisa. John Quincy had a terrible fever in August but as soon as he recovered they resumed their visits to the art galleries, museums, palaces and churches.

The two-month vacation improved Louisa's health but in December she suffered another misfortune. While assisting the doctor in taking care of a friend who had broken her leg, Louisa fainted and continued to have fainting spells all night. Once again she lost her baby and "had the misery to behold the anguish of my husband's blighted hopes."[22]

News of General Washington's death on December 15 reached Berlin by way of London in February. Johnny was deeply affected. No other public figure escaped the sharp end of his pen at one time or another. For the first President, he had only praise. "He is gone to a better world," he wrote to Murray. "But where all are glorious he will shine with more than a common luster." To his friend Pitcairn, he added, "His character will remain to all ages a model of human virtue, untarnished with a single vice. The loss of such a man is a misfortune to mankind. To our country it is a heavy calamity." He was gratified that First Consul Bonaparte had paid tribute to Washington by ordering black crepe to be hung from the flags and colors of the French armies for ten days and the bust of Washington placed in the Tuileries. In Berlin, the French Minister and his whole legation paid a condolence call on the American Minister.[23]

The remainder of John Quincy's residence in Berlin was more literary than diplomatic. For a good part of the winter of 1800 he worked on a translation of Wieland's *Oberon,* a popular German poem. Started as an amusement, it absorbed him so completely that he hated to stop even for an hour, although he was dissatisfied with the finished product. He was, of course, keeping his experienced eye on the adventures of Napoleon, whom he regarded as the major force in European politics. "The stagnation of political events during the winter months was mostly due to Napoleon," John Quincy reported to the State Department. Though the man was unprincipled and overambitious, the American Minister recognized that he had been generous in his treatment of neutral states and had rescinded the right to plunder. For the United States, it was significant that Napoleon's newly set-up Council of Prizes had decided its first case in favor of Americans. This promised well for the fate of the new American Commission in Paris for talks with Napoleon. Of the victory of Marengo, Johnny could only admit to Tom that, "The Corsican ruffian is beyond all doubt a hero in the common acceptance of the word."[24]

In the summer of 1800, once again with Louisa's health as the goal, John Quincy arranged a tour of Silesia, a rarely travelled region that was, until after World War I, a province of Prussia. The area, located in the southeastern part of the kingdom, was noted for its wild mountainous beauty and for its manufactures of glass and linen.

In a series of letters to Thomas Boylston Adams, afterwards published in forty-four weekly installments in *The Portfolio*, a Philadelphia literary periodical, Johnny recorded his impressions in a mannered but nevertheless graceful descriptive style. The *Letters from Silesia* enjoyed some popularity and was published in London in 1804 in a pirated edition. The same year, a German translation appeared with notes by a local historian, Friedrich Albert Zimmerman, published at Breslau, the leading city of the region. A French translation published in Paris enjoyed popularity there three years later.

On August 2, the Adamses travelled to the snow pits of the Reisenbirge, one of the scenic attractions. John Quincy's account of it was a good example of his prose style. After a jolting ride uphill for two hours, the party proceeded on foot up a steep hill that was "about equal to the steepest part of Beacon Hill in Boston," he wrote. The hour-long ascent was broken by a stop at a Silesian bunde (hut) for rest and refreshment. After another hour of "toiling and panting," they reached the Reisenbirge, the summit of the whole range. There they found a boundary stone that marked the limits between Bohemia and Silesia, two rival provinces whose border ran along the summit. Another half hour's ascent up a shallow hill brought them to a precipice nearly 1,500 feet deep, which "opened its ghostly jaws before us; a sort of isthmus or tongue of land, however, allowed us to proceed about an hundred rods further, until we could fix ourselves against the side of a rock, and look over into the immense depth. We had then the precipice on both sides of us, and it passes by the respective names of the Great and the

Small Snow-pit. They are so called because generally the snow at the bottom remains unmelted the whole year around; although there was no snow at all at the moment." The elevation was 4,000 feet. At the bottom of the "dreadful precipice" lofty pines slanted downwards "while beyond the foot of the mountains, our eyes ranged to almost an unmeasurable distance over hills and dales, cornfields and pastures, cities and villages, until they were lost in the gray vapours that bordered the far extended horizon." Louisa returned to the bunde from this spot but John Quincy travelled another hour and a half to visit the source of the Elbe, which required a mile descent on the Bohemian side.[25]

The next day Johnny was disappointed to find that he was not the first American to visit Silesia. At Hempel's bunde, which was the start of the climb up the Reisenkoppe, or Grant's Head, he saw the name of a Philadelphian who had been there a year before inscribed in the guest book.

Sunrise from the summit of the Reisenkoppe, a Silesian tourist attraction par excellence, aroused John Quincy at 2 A.M. to start the climb accompanied by a guide. Louisa had too severe a headache to go with them. They reached the summit, which had a chapel dedicated to St. Lawrence built by the hereditary counts who owned the entire range, in time to see the sun come up. From the top, Johnny wrote, "The Spectator has but to turn on his heel and all Silesia, all Saxony and all Bohemia, pass in an instant before his view; it is therefore truly sublime, but as it has the defect usually attendant upon sublimity of being indistinct, and in some sort chaotic, the lover of beautiful objects must content himself with a smaller elevation."[26]

About halfway down, the mountaineers met Louisa, her headache gone, and so Johnny turned back and reascended the second time. On his return, he wrote a poem describing the "sentiments of devotion I have always found the first to take possession of the mind on ascending lofty mountains."[27]

One of the chief objects of the tour, a typically New England one, was to obtain information respecting the manufactures of the country. Bohemian glass, John Quincy observed, should be an advantageous product for trade with the United States. So, dutifully, the Adams party travelled in a peasant's cart, open and without springs or proper seats, with only a couple of boards fixed across the cart and covered with straw, to the glass houses of Hirschberg.

Another local product, linen, offered the possibility for export. At the time, great quantities went to England from whence they were resold to America. Adams thought that they might be sold directly to America, furnishing linen and broadcloth at a more advantageous price than England or Ireland.

The Silesian cities were built with a square in the middle, in the center of which was the town house. Around the square, all the houses, one of them always an inn, had piazzas like the ones in Covent Garden, London. The square was the center of all business and markets were held there. As in Holland, the houses were built with the gable end to the street but in Silesia they were plastered white and the façades were marred by wooden spouts. Landeshut, one of the oldest towns, second in wealth and industry of all the mountain cities, had a very violent history. It had been sacked three times; in the fourteenth century, during the Thirty Years War, and during the Seven Years War.

Although the Silesian peasants were excessively dirty (housed under the same roof as their animals) and often dishonest (gouging travellers for milk, brown bread, and butter) they had a freedom of spirit about them that was missing in the other parts of Prussia. They alone had the privilege of not having soldiers quartered on them, which gave them "more of a republican than of a monarchical cast," John Quincy observed.[28]

This general equality among the people also gave them a social turn. In every mountain town, there was an assembly where citizens in comfortable circumstances, with their families, met once a week or oftener for conversation and social amusements.

After Louisa's achievement, ascending Grant's Head, she left the mountain climbing to her husband. He went alone to climb some of the other famous peaks in the area of Glatz.

In mid-September, his Silesian vacation ended, John Quincy observed that it was one of the pleasantest tours he had ever made. Not the least of its assets had been that, for two months, he enjoyed "the great and unwonted pleasure of hearing and knowing scarcely anything that is going forward in the political world."[29] It had been a quiet summer for warring Europe but "The trade of human butchery, I am told, is now about to commence again," Johnny wrote. However, "the balance is now so preponderant on the side of France, that it is not in the power of Fortune to turn it against her."[30]

Before returning to Berlin, the Adamses visited Dresden and

Leipzig, where they purchased prints of Corregio's *Night* and Andrea del Sarto's *The Sacrifice*. John Quincy hoped that one day these would "give some idea to our friends in America of what these high-famed paintings are." One of his duties, he believed, was to carry European culture home. He only regretted that scanty money made large purchases impossible. Both Adamses returned to Berlin in very poor health. Louisa was so ill that she caused serious alarm. Once in the city, however, Johnny recovered quickly and even Louisa responded to the attention of her friends.

John Quincy's communications were now directed to John Marshall, the new Secretary of State. It was with great reluctance that he accepted the accusation against Pickering that he had deliberately withheld papers of importance from the President, though he was well aware that Pickering was unalterably opposed to the last mission to France and could not reconcile himself to it. The theory that Pickering might have been influenced by the pro-English Essex Junto, being an Essex man, did not seem plausible to John Quincy who believed that the Junto's influence was mainly in Massachusetts. He also believed that the Junto were bad party men and generally unpopular with the bulk of federalists.

The unlikelihood of John Adams's reelection to a second term was apparent even to his son in Berlin. John Quincy wrote to his father that since a change would take place "which will leave you at your own disposal, and furnish one more example to the world, how the most important services to the public and a long laborious life, anxiously and *successfully* devoted to their welfare, are rewarded in popular governments," he must not allow this to prey on his mind and to make him ill.[31] He must keep busy in the pursuit of farming and literature. "Your triumph," his son told him, "was to have succeeded in settling the French quarrel without the smallest sacrifice of national honor and dignity. Had you not negotiated peace, the United States would be little better than a colony of Great Britain."[32] To his brother Tom he added, "If a President of the United States to secure his reelection must sacrifice his country's interests to his party's passions and prejudices, Heaven be thanked that the present Chief Magistrate disdained to set the example."[33] However, Johnny worried about his father's financial situation because "he has been so far from growing rich in the service of the public." He directed Tom to put any of his own property completely at his father's disposal, but if his father did not need it, Tom was not to mention the offer.

John Quincy did not know that his own funds were completely depleted. Charles Adams, the most affable and charming of the three brothers, and, apparently the weakest, had suffered business reverses and then consoled himself with liquor and gambling. The remonstrances of his parents made him feel contrite but failed to change his behavior. Abigail despaired, "His father has renounced him—but I will not."[34] When she was in New York in November, she visited him, now living apart from his wife and daughters in dilapidated lodgings. She and her daughter Abigail Smith removed him, at the point of death, to the Smith home where he could be taken care of. His mother had to return to Washington where the presidential family was now housed in the unfinished "palace" built for the Chief Executive.[35]

The course of Charles's disease, a dropsy in the chest, was very rapid because his constitution was destroyed. He suffered patiently and talked of making reparations for Johnny's money, which he had lost partly through Dr. Welsh's bankruptcy but mostly because he had given Colonel Smith money to save him from immediate imprisonment for debt. This was the money that John Quincy had entrusted to him, eked out from his meager salary, so that he would have some capital with which to get started upon his return to the United States. On December 1, Charles died. "Let silence reign forever over his tomb," Tom wrote to John Quincy.[36] Johnny had already heard the news from William Vans Murray, who had read it in the newspaper.

Abigail wrote pathetically about her lost son. "It becomes me in silence to mourn; mourn over him living, I have for a long time." She asked her oldest son to think of him with compassion and of his penniless widow and children. The Adamses would return to Quincy. "We have been a scattered family," she wrote. "If some of my children could now be collected round the parent Hive . . . it would add much to the happiness of our declining years."[37]

Once he failed to be re-elected, John Adams thought that it was his duty to recall his son home. He confided to John Marshall that, in justice, John Quincy should be sent to France or England. But Rufus King filled the post at the Court of St. James perfectly well and Paris was, no doubt, "destined to some other character."[38] The letter of recall was dated February 3, 1801, but did not reach its destination until April 26.

Although his father was out of the race, John Quincy could not fail to be intrigued by the Jefferson-Burr tie. He said that the worst that would happen if Burr won would be that the man not one citizen wanted to be President would have succeeded, which would point up a flaw in the election system requiring change. He predicted that Jefferson, whom he preferred, would win—"I know him, know he has long esteemed me beyond my deserts, and I have reason to believe contributed much by his testimony, if not by his recommendation to the first President to introduce me into the public service. The other I never saw."[39]

Literary composition occupied John Quincy's winter. He was pleased with the idea of becoming an irregular contributor to *The Portfolio*, whose editor had handled the Silesian Letters so satisfactorily. John Quincy offered to send poetical offerings but only under the condition that the pieces were signed with one of the letters forming the name of Columbus. The public, he said, was not ready to accept a poet as a public servant due to "some prejudice, some Cherokee contempt of literature, some envious malignity towards mental accomplishments. . . ."[40]

On April 12, George Washington Adams, the first son of John Quincy and Louisa Catherine, was born. Louisa, who had been ill all winter, had an almost fatal delivery. A drunken midwife handled her so roughly that, for a short time, she lost the use of her left leg and for five weeks was in critical condition. Lord and Lady Carysfort were the baby's sponsors, which led to a story that spread all over Europe and eventually reached the United States. The gossip was probably started by the French Ambassador in Berlin who said that the King and Queen of England were the sponsors of the Adams baby and the Carysforts were their proxies. More important, Louisa continued to be so ill that Dr. Brown thought that she had tuberculosis.

Unaware of his father's decision to recall him, John Quincy speculated on whether the new President would remove him from office. He decided that if this happened, he would submit and not insult Mr. Jefferson "by blubbering to the House of Representatives an insolent complaint against him for recalling me."[41] There is no evidence about John Quincy's reaction to his father's letter of recall. He simply acted on it by travelling to Potsdam, where the King and Queen were in residence, to present it. Their majesties were very gracious, told him of their pleasure at his handling of the mission, and discussed Silesia with him.

The departure of the Adams family was delayed because Louisa could not either walk or stand. John Quincy, while he was waiting for her recovery, sent home a small library of German books. He wrote to his father that he did not know where he would house them "but I might not perplex myself about lodging them while I know not where to lodge myself and my family." He knew, however, that this was one "perplex" that John Adams would understand very well.[42]

In mid-June, the three Adamses left Berlin. Louisa, who was still very weak, had to be lifted, fainting into the carriage. Dr. Brown, who had misgivings about her ability to survive the trip home, advised her to nurse George for six months longer in the hope that her constitution would change.

The voyage from Hamburg to the United States took fifty-eight days. Fortunately, it was reasonably calm because the baby had dysentery so badly that his anxious parents were afraid that they would lose him. By the second half of the trip, however, he recovered and the sailors enjoyed holding and playing with him. On that trip, Louisa heard for the first time about Mary Frazier. The other girl's beauty, great attainments, and the elegance of her letters, Louisa wrote, made her feel "little" but not jealous. She had confidence in her husband's affection but thought herself a poor, faded creature whose only consolation was that she had a son.[43]

The transition to the American scene would be a major adjustment for Mr. and Mrs. John Quincy Adams. Louisa had never seen America nor did she know her husband's parents. John Quincy would have to start a new career. His law practice had been dissolved while his competitors had a seven-year advantage. He returned to his country with added years, experience, and confidence, but with the added burdens of a wife and a child.

CHAPTER 8

An Introduction to Politics

"I must square every vote I give to some principle, and not say aye or no as the mere echo to my file leader."

JOHN QUINCY ADAMS

J OHN ADAMS WAS SO HAPPY that his son was "on American ground" that he could not wait to tell him of the many projects for his future that he and Abigail had discussed. However, he warned, whatever John Quincy did must be "very modest, very humble, very unassuming." In the meantime, he hastened to offer the family residence as "your home for yourself, your Lady and Son."[1]

Tom Adams, who met the travellers when they landed in Philadelphia on Stepternber 4, 1801, tried to conceal his shock when he saw Louisa's emaciated figure. The heat of the American city and Dr. Benjamin Rush's kind attentions helped her leg but she was anxious to go on to Washington to visit her family. So, with Epps and baby George, John Quincy put her on a stage to Baltimore.

Louisa hated to present herself to her father in her miserable state but she felt that she had no choice because she believed that she had not long to live. Mr. Johnson found his daughter so changed in appearance that although he had been waiting on the steps of his house to greet her, when she alighted from the carriage he did not recognize her. He, too, was very much changed. In spite of John Adams's generosity in appointing him Director of Stamps, his spirit seemed broken. He was quiet and seemed interested only in the pranks of his grandchildren.

With equal anxiety and love, John Quincy travelled north to Quincy and there "had the inexpressible delight of finding once more my parents. . . . This pleasure would have been unalloyed but for the feeble and infirm state of my mother's health."[2] The former Minister's future was discussed exhaustively with some indication that parental pressure swayed his decision. "I have determined for the sake of peace, and for want of better employment to resume my residence and my profession in Boston," he told Tom. He was convinced, however, that he would want to have nothing to do with politics because there was no party for an honest man "and I feel myself rather more strongly attached to my principles" than to ambition or to power.[3]

His career settled, Johnny went househunting. He decided on 39 Hanover Square—"not as much as I would wish," he told Louisa. It would not be ready for their occupancy for a few months, but they could stay with John and Abigail until it was. Louisa must persuade her sister to accompany her back to Massachusetts, her husband suggested.[4]

On October 21, John Quincy joined Louisa in Washington. The young Adamses were entertained in the new capital by many of its leading lights, including the President and Secretary of State James Madison. They made a pilgrimage to Mount Vernon to pay their respects to President Washington's widow, who wanted to be remembered to John and Abigail. The visit had to be terminated, however, for fear that winter weather would close down the roads to the north. Just before the young couple left, in November, Joshua Johnson became seriously ill. Johnny was thoughtful and sympathetic, sitting up nights with his ailing father-in-law, but he finally had to insist that they leave. Caroline, of course, could not accompany them as planned and stayed to nurse her father. Louisa was certain that she would never see her father alive again.

A screaming child, rough roads, and a depressed wife made the trip to Philadelphia a nightmare. His brother found Tom in good health "and fattening on celibacy. I wish his estate were fattening as much. . . ."[5] Louisa's flagging spirits were caused partially by the prospect of her first confrontation with her husband's parents, especially Abigail, whose cleverness, competence, and peppery person-

ality were famous. John Quincy's undisguised admiration for his
mother did not make it easier.

Louisa admitted that both Mr. and Mrs. Adams received her
kindly and were much pleased with the child but, she recalled,
"Had I stepp'd into Noah's ark I do not think I could have been
more utterly astonished." New England life contrasted sharply with
her experiences in France, old England, or the Prussian court.[6]

Mrs. John Quincy Adams became very ill, perhaps as a refuge. "It
was lucky for me I was so much depressed, and so ill, or I should
certainly have give mortal offense," she recorded.[7] The church, the
dressing and dinner hour, the parties, the manners, the hours of
meeting were all strange to her. John Quincy made her promise not
to talk about Berlin. She obeyed him but Epps gossiped about
Louisa's position at court, and, consequently, put her mistress in a
very unfavorable light with her New England relatives. Mrs. J. Q.
Adams was convinced that she could not "suit however well inclined." Louisa Smith, who had been like an adopted daughter to
her Aunt Abigail, was fearfully jealous of Louisa. The day that she
arrived, Miss Smith left the table crying and sobbing inconsolably.
Fortunately, President Adams took a fancy to Louisa but he seemed
to be the only one in the family who did.

In Boston, for the first time in her married life, Louisa was in
charge of the household management without the supervision of
Whitcomb, the Adams's steward. Overwhelmed by the competence
of the Boston and Quincy women, particularly Abigail, Louisa tried
to conceal her ignorance, which gained her, instead of sympathy,
criticism for what was termed her pride. Abigail's efforts to instruct
her daughter-in-law failed because Louisa was so uncomfortable that
she could not learn readily. To further the difficulty, the young
couple's means were so small that John Quincy commented frequently on his wife's expenditures and mismanagement, which kept
her constantly unhappy.

The Boston ladies took care to enlighten Mrs. John Quincy
Adams about her husband's romance with the beautiful Mary Frazier. Poor Louisa, convinced of the truth of the old French song,
"Qu'on revient toujours a ces premiers amours,"* felt assured that
she competed unsuccessfully with her predecessor in her husband's
affections. To complete her difficulties, Johnny decided that Epps

---

* "We always return to our first loves."

was an impossible expense, so that the complete care of George became Louisa's responsibility. However, the sleepless nights that John Quincy endured soon caused him to regret the loss of the baby's nurse.

The possibility of such problems had occurred to John Quincy. Before settling in Boston, he had seriously considered removing his family to New York, which he believed was the most promising spot on the continent for enterprise and industry. "What say you to joining me in the plan and going with me?" Johnny asked Tom.[8] But it was only a half-serious notion. John Quincy was probably not capable either of leaving his home territory or of disappointing his parents. Thus, as planned, in December, J. Q. Adams became a candidate for practice at the bar in Boston.

Despite John Quincy's protests, the temptation to plunge into political action was strong. His reluctance was not to public service but to having to affiliate with a party instead of being "a man of my whole country," a concept which would keep him in hot water all of his long political life.

In the spring of 1802, John Quincy was sworn in by Governor Caleb Strong as the Senator from Suffolk County to the General Court of Massachusetts. The next day he made a startling suggestion. At the federalist caucus to nominate counsellors for the Council of the Commonwealth, he suggested proportional representation of republicans, namely four. The idea was promptly rejected and, John Quincy observed, "probably forfeited whatever confidence might have been otherwise bestowed upon me as a party follower."[9]

Joshua Johnson died in April, having appointed John Quincy one of his executors, along with his son, Thomas B. Johnson, and his other son-in-law, Walter Hellen. Louisa mourned him until she became alarmingly ill. She rebelled against what she felt was the rigidity of the people around her, whom, she said, thought it a sin for her to indulge her feelings. Her father's misfortunes up to the last one, which was his removal by Jefferson from his post as Director of Stamps, and then his death, ended all hope that his affairs might be settled and his name cleared. Louisa became even more sensitive to small slights. When her son's birthday passed almost unnoticed by her Puritan in-laws, she blamed it on their annoyance that the child had not been given his grandfather's name.

According to John Quincy, the "Novitiate of my legislative labors" was not very distinguished. He said that he was not able to effect much good nor was he able to prevent much evil. There were, however, indications that he was being considered seriously for a political future. It was significant that he was honored by being asked to make two speeches, one to the Massachusetts Charitable Fire Society and one at Plymouth. But the opportunity to operate in a broader political spectrum was denied him in the November election. He opposed Dr. William Eusiis for a seat in the House of Representatives from the Boston area but lost by fifty-nine votes. Adams carried Boston and Medford but failed in Charlestown, Hingham, Malden, Chelsea, and Hull. The federalists blamed the defeat on rain, which they said kept a large number of their voters from the remotest part of town from getting to the polls. John Quincy believed otherwise, claiming that the republican party was more earnest. However, he took his failure well, saying, "I must consider it as relieving me from a heavy burden and a thankless task." Privately he wrote to Tom that "I concur with you in the opinion that the cause of federalism is irretrievable."[10]

Louisa continued delicate, her health and spirits so depressed that she thought she could please no one. Caroline came to stay after Mr. Johnson's death. She eased her sister's life by taking over the housekeeping. A much better-adjusted young woman than Louisa, Caroline became popular with Abigail and her daughter, whom, Louisa was convinced, wished that Caroline had been her brother's choice. Louisa's mother, now destitute and living with the Hellens, visited Boston in the fall. The older Adamses paid a great deal of attention to her but, Louisa said, Abigail disliked her intensely, "probably because of what Mr. Adams did for my father." When she met Mary Frazier, now engaged to John Quincy's childhood friend, Daniel Sargent, Louisa was again wracked by feelings of inferiority, and even in matters that concerned her son Louisa deemed herself ill-equipped. Now that George was eighteen months old, his father embarked on a study of education, reading works from Locke to Miss Edgeworth. He tried to share his ideas with Louisa, but she claimed she participated without benefit. Convinced that her shy, proud, silent way was contrary to that of the leading women of the day, who were showy, prominent, and with marked characteristics— just like Abigail Adams—she was very unhappy.

Louisa's discomfort at his parents' Quincy home was not shared by her husband. Though she used illness as an excuse not to go there, he felt that his native town was "almost a necessity of life."

He would arrive on Saturday and breathe fresh air until Monday. "The wharf allows me a sea bath," he wrote, and he could pass his leisure time in the library reading "Plutarch and the letters of Madame de Sévigné. The music of the birds moves me to poetry."[11]

Despite Louisa's dissatisfaction, Johnny had found a modus vivendi. Though his "remnant of leisure was small," and his "trade, the public," he filled his life with study, an occasional call for orations, "the unavoidable encroachment of dissipation," and "the summons of duty and pleasure once a week to the paternal mansion."[12] Tom acted as his unofficial literary agent, placing some of his randon pieces, such as an essay on reading in *The Portfolio*. Almost morbidly modest, John Quincy remonstrated with his brother when some praise for him appeared in the publication. He reminded Tom that he had agreed to suppress this kind of approbation.[13]

In February, John Quincy had information that he and Fisher Ames were on the list of names for United States Senator from Massachusetts to replace Jonathan Mason, who did not wish to serve again. Adams told Ames that he would withdraw his name if Ames wanted the office but was assured that Ames was on the list without his consent and would not accept. The divisive problem of Mason's successor was decided in a complicated maneuver. At a caucus at the House of Jonathan Mason, it was agreed that if Timothy Pickering failed to be elected in the first two ballots in the house, they would switch their votes to Adams. Pickering failed and John Quincy was the victor on the fourth ballot, defeating Tompson J. Skinner, the runner-up.

Although the federalists had elected him, John Quincy remained unmanageable in the Massachusetts legislature. He refused to vote with them for the removal of two jurors on the grounds that the Constitution provided for impeachment proceedings and failed to support the moneyed interests demand for the establishment of a major bank in Boston. Loss of popularity was accepted quietly by the thirty-five-year-old Senator.

However, a financial disaster that followed on the heels of his victory for the Senate seat spoiled it somewhat for John Quincy, particularly because it affected his parents. While in Europe, John Quincy had been in charge of his father's funds, which derived from the redemption of United States loans in Holland. John Adams had subscribed to them to inspire confidence in the loan. Now news reached John Quincy that Bird, Savage and Bird, the London firm with whom he had placed his father's holdings, had failed. Mortified and apologetic, Johnny sold some of his insurance-company shares and shouldered the entire debt to his father. He hated to tell John and Abigail of their misfortune and, perhaps even more, found it painful to admit his failure in judgment. Eventually the bankers paid off their indebtedness, but the last installment arrived twenty-three years later, after John Adams's death.

John Quincy's election to the Senate promised a great change for his family. George, now a precocious two-year-old, was a joy to his father and his grandfather. Louisa, however, had not yet adjusted to the United States. Even her religious opinions differed from the Adamses, although she bowed to her husband's habits out of respect to him. She was pregnant again, suffering fainting fits and a peculiar loss of feeling in her hands that required them to be tied up in laudanum poultices. Her husband was so concerned with Louisa's unhappiness and physical symptoms that he planned to take the family to Washington in the spring. They would stay with the Hellens so that Louisa's mother would be with her when the baby was born. At the last minute, the plans were changed. Very likely the Adamses wanted a native-born child.

On the fourth of July, at three in the morning, just as the first guns were fired, John Quincy and Louisa's second son was born. John Quincy was at his parents' house because his mother was seriously ill and his sister Nabby had just arrived to care for her. The baby was named John after his grandfather, which pleased Abigail although she regretted that he never resembled him.

President Jefferson ordered the Senate to meet on October 17, three weeks sooner than the time established by the former session, so that the vote could be taken on the Louisiana treaty. John Quincy and the family left Boston in plenty of time to meet the deadline but Louisa became so ill on the way that they were delayed. Her symptoms so much resembled yellow fever that the doctor was afraid to come near her. John Quincy nursed her in New York until she was able to travel. They then proceeded directly to Washington, without stopping at Philadelphia to see Tom. Louisa's first impression of the capital city was that it was a "scene of utter desolation. The roads were impassable."[14]

As the Adamses drove into the city, they passed Samuel Otis, Secretary of the Senate, carrying to Jefferson the ratification of the treaty with France ceding Louisiana to the United States. Twenty-five years later, recalling the event, Adams stated that he was sorry that he had been deprived of the privilege of voting for the treaty because he "regarded it as one of the happiest events which had occurred since the adoption of the Constitution."[15] Even before he reached his Senate seat, John Quincy Adams was in opposition to the other New England federalists, all of whom had opposed the acquisition of Louisiana.

William Plumer, a dark, sparse six-foot Senator from New Hampshire about ten years Johnny's senior, whose account of the Senate proceedings from 1803–1807 would surpass the official annals in interest, recorded New England's objections. He thought the President's request for ratification an "improper," and unconstitutional extension of his power at the expense of the legislature. He even doubted that the territory was rightfully France's to cede. Reflecting federalist opinion, he stated that the proper way to have restored free navigation of the Mississippi River would have been at the point of a bayonet. "The Senate have taken less time to deliberate on this important treaty, than they allowed themselves on the most trivial Indian contract," Senator Plumer complained.[16]

Napoleon's sale of Louisiana was a complete turnabout. He had planned earlier to establish a large and powerful French empire in the New World, bordering the Gulf of Mexico and the Caribbean Sea. His first step was the secret treaty of San Ildefonso, signed on October 1, 1800, at the summer palace of the King of Spain. In return for the retrocession of Louisiana, given in 1763, by a defeated France to her defeated ally Spain at the end of the Seven Years War, the Corsican agreed to create a kingdom of Etruria, carved from an enlarged Tuscany, for the Spanish King's daughter and her husband, the Duke of Parma. After the American wilderness, which gave the First Consul control of the commerce on the Mississippi River, was obtained, he sought the favor of the United States by acceding to the convention of Mortefontaine.

But the beautiful plot foundered on the island of Saint Domingue, France's Caribbean colony, richest in sugar of all of the West Indies. Talleyrand had long been angered at the unofficial alliance between Saint Domingue and the United States, based on American interest in the island's sugar. It was, really, a strange marriage of conflicting interests because the island's semi-independence resulted from a slave revolt led by Pierre Dominique Toussaint, born a slave, the son of a petty African chieftain from Guinea. This undersized, ugly, brilliant, talented hero, while claiming loyalty to France, as long as it convenienced him, overcame in turn the planters, his rival Benoit Joseph Rigaud, a mulatto, and the French soldiers. Americans were divided in their attitude toward Toussaint L'Ouverture, as he was called by his devoted followers. Federalists, fearing the French, saw some value in a free island. The southerners, however, fearing the example that an independent Negro country founded upon a slave revolt might have for their own slaves, opposed independence, unimpressed by Timothy Pickering's opinion that he doubted that the slaves in the United States would be infected by the independence fever.

At the end of 1801, Napoleon acted on his plan to reassert French domination in Saint Domingue. Led by Pauline Bonaparte's husband, General Victor Emanuel Leclerc, about 20,000 troops, carried by a formidable flotilla, sailed from Brest. Robert R. Livingston reported home that their plan was to proceed to Louisiana if Toussaint made no opposition, though Leclerc had no such official orders.

A series of disasters pursued the unlucky expedition, which sighted Saint Domingue at the end of January 1802. Discontented French seamen mutinied, fierce Black resistance destroyed thousands of French soldiers, aided by a virulent yellow-fever epidemic that claimed the life of General Leclerc. Napoleon soured on the project when a second expedition froze in the icebound Dutch port from which it was to set out. He turned his head away from the west to dreams of the conquest of England and, thence, all of Europe.

President Jefferson and Secretary of State Madison, in agreement that France's possession of the mouth of the Mississippi was a mortal danger, ordered negotiations with Napoleon. Robert R. Livingston in Paris was joined by James Monroe in time to participate in the biggest real-estate coup in history: the purchase of the Louisiana territory for $11,250,000—or about eight cents an acre. The mission was financed by a congressional appropriation of two million dollars, made available, in secret session, to open talks for New Orleans and the Floridas. To the envoys' surprise, Napoleon's representative, Francois de Barbé-Marbois, Minister of Finance, negotiated the offer to sell the whole of Louisiana.

Napoleon's reasons for giving up the huge area were complex. He needed money for his new offensive against Britain. Once involved in such a major war, he predicted that Great Britain would seize Louisiana. In the meantime, therefore, America could be its custodian, at a price. And after his victory over Britain and mastery over Europe, the Corsican argued, the United States could refuse him nothing, not even the return of the Louisiana Territory if that was what he wanted.

John Quincy, who had missed the drama, now involved himself in working out the details of the treaty. He had, in the absence of Vice President Aaron Burr, been sworn in by John Brown of Kentucky, president pro tempore of the Senate. Timothy Pickering, Massachusetts' junior senator though twenty-two years older than Adams, having been elected shortly after him to the sudden vacancy which arose, was already seated and had voted with the other high federalists against the Louisiana Treaty.

John Quincy, along with William Plumer, was with the majority that passed the bill for creating the stock necessary for the payment of the purchase. Pickering and the other federalists rejected that bill also, unswayed by Plumer's argument that once the Senate declared by vote that the instrument was a treaty, the faith of the nation required that the necessary appropriations be made.

Shortly after passage of the Louisiana cession treaty, Senator Adams called on Madison to enquire if the President had designated anyone to propose an amendment to the Constitution to carry through the acquisition of the territory. If not, he informed the Secretary of State, he thought it his duty to introduce such a piece of legislation. A month later, he presented his amendment which read as follows:

Congress shall have power . . . to incorporate within the union the inhabitants of all such territories, heretofore not within the limits of the United States, as have been or may be ceded by treaty . . . and to extend to the said inhabitants all the rights, privileges and immunities which are enjoyed by native citizens of the United States under the Constitution. And Congress shall also have power to make all such laws for the government of such ceded territories and of their inhabitants. . . .[17]

The proposal was inspired by Louisiana but it was equally applicable to any other alien territory that might be acquired in the future, such as Canada or the Floridas. John Quincy, already a confirmed unionist, was now displaying embryonic signs of becoming a convinced continentalist and expansionist.

By the time he submitted the amendment, Adams felt assured that no amendment that he proposed would pass in the Senate. He feared that he talked too much for a new member and must try to check himself lest he became ridiculous. But he could not refrain from declaring his views, which were decisive on just about every issue. He opposed vociferously the appointment of a committee to prepare the form of government for the Louisiana Territory. Congress had no right to establish a government without the express consent of the inhabitants of the area, he asserted. Therefore the Constitution must be amended without delay. But when his resolution was put to a test, only Pickering and James Hillhouse supported him.

Nevertheless, John Quincy's general acceptance of the Louisiana Purchase was blasted in the home newspapers, earning him "venom, because you did not vote with the Federalists throughout,"[18] Tom, now living in Quincy, wrote. The republicans, however, triumphed at the "bold and independent manner" in which Senator Adams had voted away from his party. Abigail commented to her son, in answer to him, that he must vote "as your conscience aided by your judgement should dictate."[19] But the support of the family did not mitigate public abuse. New England response to the purchase was almost entirely negative. It intensified the section's growing feeling of alienation from the center of national power because the balance of power had tipped away from them. The purchase confronted their New England homogeneity with the challenge of having to assimilate French, Spaniards, and Indians, whose background, religion, mores, and, most ominous, political attitudes differed completely from Anglo-Saxon democracy. John Quincy would soon be regarded by the federalists as a traitor to his party. The dispute that was shaping up about the twelfth amendment would again separate him from his colleagues.

Senator Adams voted against the necessary reform to the election procedure that developed from the Burr-Jefferson tie of 1800 because, although he approved of designating votes for the President and the Vice President, he was against the changes that the Senate had made in the house bill submitted to them. The Constitution provided that if no presidential candidate achieved a majority of the votes cast by the electoral college, the House of Representatives would make the choice among the five highest contenders. John Quincy wanted to keep the number at five but the Senate voted to reduce the number of eligible candidates to three, rejecting his excellent arguments on constitutional and mathematical grounds. As he promised, therefore, he voted against the twelfth amendment. Ironically, when John Quincy Adams became one of a list of presidential candidates to be voted upon by the House of Representatives in 1825, had he been one of five candidates instead of three, his chance of winning would have been greatly reduced.

It was not that Senator Adams failed to understand what qualities were necessary for success. He recorded them in his *Diary*—"firmness, perseverance, patience, coolness and forbearance." Nor did he lack the willingness to examine himself and neither did he flinch from "mortifying reflections" on his "errors, imprudences and follies" and tendencies toward "pride and self conceit and presumption."[20] The choice to battle the fierce spirit of party and to adhere to his own conscience was a free choice made with full awareness that the price might be the loss of future advancement. He would not or could not change his independent spirit. He was between two batteries, not really one of either, and was resigned to his role. "Both sides are offended at me," he wrote to Abigail. "All this I cannot help."[21] Conscience triumphed over self-analysis.

John Quincy seemed impervious to the melancholy, dreary, unfinished city of Washington which Richard Griswold of Connecticut called "a city in ruins." Louisa complained of the difficulties of transportation that were "a risk to life," the streets that were not graded, the bridges made of loose planks, the huge stumps of trees that had been cut down and then left to intercept the paths, and the roads intersected by deep ravines continually enlarged by rain. Her husband mentioned nothing of these inconveniences. He pursued an ordered schedule, rising at seven, writing in his chamber until nine, and then walking the two and a half miles from Walter Hellen's house, where he and his family were living, in time to be at the opening of the Senate. He would stay in the Senate until four or five, visiting the House if the Senate adjourned early, and then take his forty-five-minute walk home. After dinner he would play with three-year-old George in his room or spend the evening with the ladies. By eleven he was in bed.

The Hellen household was lively, constantly thronged with visitors who were attracted by the pretty Johnson sisters. John Quincy, because of his own position and his father's former position, was much courted by Washington society. However, Louisa was often accused of being proud when she went out in company because she covered her fear of making a mistake and disgracing her husband with a cold manner. Among her more agreeable evenings, she recorded, was a dinner at the White House which reminded her of European parties. The President, whom she thought ugly and awkward in manner until he spoke, provided French cuisine handsomely served, choice wine, and choice talk. Secretary Madison, a small man with a large head, she thought unassuming but a lively talker. His wife, Dolley, was described as a big woman with a fair and brilliant complexion, dressed like a Quaker. After dinner, Louisa complained, the fire was so low that the guests shivered and shook, but Jefferson, unperturbed, drew his chair to the center of the hearth in the drawing room and seemed to want everyone to go home.[22]

Discussion of the ramifications of the Louisiana Treaty spilled over into 1804. John Quincy continued his contentious behavior. His colleagues failed to accept his close examination of the details of the bills, niceties which appeared to most of them, in Fisher Ames's words, Senator Adams's "quiddities."[23] On the resolution over the taxation of Louisiana, which caused three hours of stormy debates, John Quincy contended that the Senate had no power to impose taxes on the inhabitants of Louisiana without their consent. He read from the Declaration of Independence and the Annals of the Congress of 1774–1775 to show that this was the same principle of taxation without representation about which the American Revolution had been fought. His resolutions were rejected by a vote of 22 to 4. Plumer expressed the view of some semi-supporters when he called the measures "mere abstract propositions," but Senator Adams believed that the warmth of opposition convinced Senators to vote against it "who hate me more than they love any principle."[24] It was some consolation when John Adams reassured his son that he did not "disapprove of your conduct in the business of Louisiana. I think you have been right . . . though the northern states will hate the expenses Louisiana will occasion."[25] The ex-President's support would have re-enforced Theodore Lyman's comment to Thomas Pickering, "Curse on the stripling, how he apes his sire."[26]

The Louisiana bill, said John Quincy, progressed "like a snail" until all considerations were debated by the Senate. The final struggle was over the sensitive question of slavery in the territory. Senator Adams voted against the bill, which finally passed 21 to 6, that forbade the slave trade in Louisiana. His reasoning was: "slavery in a moral sense is an evil; but as connected with commerce it has important uses. The regulations offered to prevent slavery are insufficient. I shall therefore vote against them."[27] To his mother, John Quincy explained that he adhered to his principle that "we have no right to make any *Law* for that country at present."[28]

When the Louisiana government bill came up for a vote on February 18, Adams spoke against it, at length and alone. His argument revolved around the concept that all power in a republican form of government derived from the people and the people of Louisiana had given the United States Congress no power to legislate for them. Speaking of the larger and more distant issue, John Quincy foresaw that what was being established by this bill was a colonial system of government, the first for the United States but surely not the last. He prophesied that the United States would have many colonies and, by this bill, had established a bad precedent. But notwithstanding his lone voice of protest, the bill passed handily: 20 to 5.

What seemed irrelevant in Senator Adams's impassioned pleas to the august members of the Eighth Congress achieved tremendous significance many years later. John Quincy's objection to United States action in Louisiana, "undertaking to exercise the highest powers of Government over a people without something like the consent of that people; by treaty, by popular acclamation, or at least by requiring an oath of allegiance," can be related to the modern concept of self-determination. In that sense, it was, as Adams suggested, a despotic act.[29]

His opposition to the proposed administration of the Louisiana territory did not prevent John Quincy's attendance at the feast at Stelle's Hotel given by the democratic members of Congress on January 27 in celebration of the accession of Louisiana. The President, the Vice President, and the department heads were guests. Toasts went around as was customary, but John Quincy refused to drink one proposed by Joseph H. Nicholson: "The tempestuous Sea of Liberty, may it never be calm."[30]

Republican hatred for the federal-dominated courts, fanned by President Jefferson, erupted into a sadly cruel impeachment case directed against mad John Pickering, judge of the district of New Hampshire. He was convicted, in absentia, despite a moving insanity plea sent by his son to the Senate. John Quincy argued that there was no trial because there was no appearance and that a court of law would ascertain the fact of insanity before they would allow a trial. But anxious republicans such as George Logan, who said that the accused was unfit to be a judge and therefore it was of no interest how he became so, just wanted to get rid of Pickering. The injustice of judging an insane man guilty and sentencing him, unheard, though he could not be present without hazarding his life, was of no interest to the crusaders against the federal judiciary.

On the same day that Judge Pickering was sentenced, the House of Representatives, spurred on by John Randolph of Roanoke, voted to impeach Samuel Chase, signer of the Declaration of Independence and federalist appointee. The hounding of the judiciary would be carried into the next session of Congress scheduled to act on the first Monday of the following November.

The close of John Quincy's first congressional session was, as usual, a hectic effort to push through a large accumulation of bills with very little attention paid to their contents. Senator Adams's first term was remarkable for the many bills that he, sometimes single-handedly, opposed. For example, he argued against a bill that was, supposedly, for the further protection of American seamen but was in reality intended for the protection of British seamen deserting to American ships. John Quincy pointed out that the bill violated the Law of Nations. It passed anyhow. John Quincy recorded in his *Diary* that he had better remember and practice the advice "to forget and forgive all resentments and injuries which have been excited and occasioned during the session of Congress."[31]

One of the major disappointments for John Quincy Adams was his failure to present to the Senate an amendment to the Constitution on representation that would eliminate the privilege whereby five slaves were counted as three whites for the purpose of representation, that was first developed by him in his *Serious Reflections Addressed to the Citizens of Massachusetts*, published in *The Reporter* in October 1804 under the pseudonym of Publius Valerius. In it he exposed the southern strategy of 1787 which made two unequal classes in the United States: "A privileged order of slaveholding Lords, and a race of men degraded to a lower status, merely because they were not slave-holders. Every planter south of the Potomac has one vote for himself and three votes in effect for every five slaves he keeps in bondage; while a New England farmer, who contributes tenfold as much to the support of the government, has only a single vote."[32]

In a memorandum that never was presented to the Senate, John Quincy elaborated on his thesis. He linked the immorality of slavery with the mode of representation. He said, "by making the number of slaves a component part of the right to vote," there develops "an irresistible temptation to those states which allow slavery, to increase and multiply as much as possible the number of these unhappy beings." John Quincy marshalled figures that showed that the ten non-slave states contributed three-fourths of the net revenue collected by impost, tonnage, and navigation, yet they had only seventy-eight members in the House of Representatives as compared to the South's sixty-four, fifteen of which represented the Black population. The acquisition of Louisiana would intensify the inequity; the size of the territory would probably indicate the emergence of five or six states, thereby giving to the southern states the most representation in the union. When it was realized that the free states would furnish three-fourths of the revenue for the purchase, "it must appear the most cruel of hardships, thus in a manner to lay upon them, the whole burden of acquisition which is to annihilate all their weight and influence, and to leave their interests wholly at the mercy of the rest.[33]

The close of the session coincided with the close of the winter social season which had been full of the routine balls, suppers and fêtes, crowned with the marriage of Betsy Paterson of Baltimore to Jerome Bonaparte. Now that the Washington chores were completed, Senator Adams headed for Quincy, but without Louisa and the children. Though she complained about the long separation, it was her choice. John Quincy wrote in answer to her accusation that he was cold and unkind that he understood her attachment to her family and her wish to be with them, but "I have naturally the same sentiments and affection for mine." He asked her not to let the children forget their father. "If George wants his drum he must be a very good boy," he said.[34]

In Quincy by mid-April, Johnny found his father in good health, but his mother somewhat infirm. His brother's widow, Mrs. Charles Adams, and her two daughters were there for a short time until Mrs. Adams returned to New York with her younger daughter, leaving Susan with her grandparents. Tom was now settled in Quincy and feeling reasonably happy. But John Quincy wrote to Louisa that he felt "like a fish out of water without you and my children, but I will not complain."[35] Money was really the cause of the Senator's problem. His finances were materially less than when he had married so that he could not carry the expense of moving his family twice a year. Louisa decided that she would prefer to summer with her own family in Washington rather than live alone at Quincy for five dreary months.

It was far from an ideal arrangement. The young family missed each other. His father sent George the drum he had asked for, along with drumsticks, a sling to hang it from his shoulder, and a box containing two lilliputian books. He also worried about Washington for a summer and autumnal residence and warned Louisa to be particularly careful of the evening air.

Abigail, pleased to have her oldest son at home, wrote to Louisa that he had "picked up his flesh some since his return." She had been alarmed to see how thin he was ". . . he cannot engage in any service but with his whole mind and attention and the labours and anxiety of the mind are a wearing of the flesh," she philosophized.[36]

The slow summer days filled with reading, gardening, and visiting would have been perfect for John Quincy had Louisa and the children been with him. He tried his hand at horticulture, the beginning of a life-long interest. "I pay so much attention to the poor plants from hour to hour," he wrote to Louisa, "that the only danger is of my killing them all with kindness."[37]

In Washington, Louisa was finding life without her husband very difficult. She had a return of her spasms for the first time since she reached Washington, but no fainting spells. George, now grown tall for his age, was a handful. After he destroyed all of the Hellens' chickens and drove the ducks to death, Louisa had to hire a girl just to run after him, but he obeyed no one but his mother. Baby John, now weaned, had grown handsome but also exceedingly irritable in the torrid Washington heat. Louisa confessed to her husband: "Your absence begins to be insupportable. . . ."[38]

News of the Burr-Hamilton duel and the subsequent death of Hamilton electrified America. Conversation was limited almost entirely to that incredible subject. John Quincy could not justify Burr's conduct and, after reading the correspondence between the two opponents, concluded that his actions seemed to corroborate the opinion of his character that his enemies held. But he blamed Hamilton also for not having "sufficient control over his own passions, or a sufficient elevation over the prejudices of the world" to avoid the fatal meeting.

Louisa and John Quincy differed over attendance at the funeral obsequies for General Hamilton. When Harrison Gray Otis delivered a eulogy in Chapel Church, Boston, Senator Adams stayed home. "Neither the manner of his death nor his base treatment of more than one of my connections would permit me to join in any outward demonstration of regret which I could not feel at heart," he told Louisa.[39] She answered that Gouverneur Morris's oration at Hamilton's burial in New York was "very far short of what I expected." However, she thought that her husband should have been present at the Boston services because resentment should not be carried beyond the grave.[40] Senator Adams could not let her criticism go unanswered. "The man who has injured me I can sincerely and heartily forgive. But if he has injured me without provocation, and without atonement, I can never view him as deserving marks of *honor, esteem*, or *affection* living or dead. . . . Upon this principle I refused to wear crape last winter for S(amuel) Adams and old Pendleton . . . nor will I for Hamilton. . . . I had no respect for the man."[41] In the same letter he told Louisa that Mary Frazier Sargent was dead. He admitted his early attachment for her but told his wife that on his return from Europe he felt none of it. The long separation from his wife and children, he added, would not be repeated. Next year he would bring them all to Quincy.

The publication of the pirated London edition of the *Silesian Letters* embarrassed John Quincy because included was a letter about some English people whom he and Louisa had met in Dresden, which made some allusions to their domestic history. The Senator hoped that the indiscreet paragraphs would not be noticed by the persons concerned. More seriously, the publication reminded its author of the trifling nature of the work and his hope that someday he would present something more valuable to the world.

Tom Adams, resigned to making a career of sorts for himself in his home state, ran as a federalist candidate for the legislature. When John Quincy left Massachusetts in mid-October, he thought his brother's chances slim but was much more concerned about Abigail's failing health.

Back in Washington, Senator Adams recognized that the President's popularity was contagious and widespread in all the states, including Massachusetts. "I consider the revolution there as completed," he wrote to Tom, and that in the spring both the executive branch and the legislature would pass into Jefferson's party's hands.

Along with the rest of the United States, John Adams was curious as to whether the Vice President would take his seat as usual at the start of the session. Senator Adams told him that, though indicted in New York for the challenge and in New Jersey for murder, Aaron Burr did indeed appear in the Senate and assume his position as president of that body.

John Quincy had, during the summer, confided his misgivings and self-doubts to his fond father. "Patience and perseverance," John Adams advised his son. "I have great confidence in your Success in the Service of your Country however dark your prospects may be at present. . . . You and I have clasped each other in our arms and braced our feet against the Bed-boards and Bedsprings to prevent us from having our Brains dashed against the Planks and timbers of the Ship. . . . Twenty political storms of as much danger to the Ship as this have I weathered through while the Petit Maître who now tyrannizes at our expense dared not trust his damask Person on the Sea." In answer to John Quincy's warning that their letters to each other were being read, Adams said that he would write as he pleased. "If the Peepers violate publick faith and get stung by a Wasp in the folds of the paper, let them have the Smart for their reward."[42]

The Senate was unable to achieve a quorum until the horse-racing season was over on November 16. It had been suggested that those present should do some business for the sake of the record but Senator Adams objected audibly, saying that he had "an abhorrence of tricks to save appearances." Even he realized that he had an uncontrollable "stiffness of Temper," admitting to his father that it sometimes kept him from a display of affection that he felt.

News of Tom's defeat in the November elections was not unexpected. John Quincy advised him to "keep a placid and a cheerful heart in ill-fortune," which, he pontificated, "was more worthy of merit than commanding all the votes in the world"—advice, he admitted, that he could use himself. Johnny agreed with Tom that the next election would complete the democratic revolution in Massachusetts. But their rule would be only temporary. "Change is the only unchangeable characteristic of our Government," he said.[43]

Abigail, now almost entirely recovered, was very concerned with Johnny's health. She wrote to Louisa that he had not taken enough exercise throughout the summer, spending all his time with his pen and his books. "I wish you would not let him go to Congress without a cracker in his pocket, the space between breakfast and dinner is so long that his stomach gets held with flatulence and then his food does not digest. This and a great anxiety of mind wears his constitution. The first can be cured with a dry biscuit and a glass of wine. The latter is . . . habitual. We must unite on his personal appearance."[44]

Abigail was correct about John Quincy's health. He was not seriously ill, although he had frequent colds, but felt only "indifferent" most of the time. Frustration with his role in the Senate drove him to stiffen his manner and to study harder. However, he blamed his lack of method in his study for failing to net him the results that he wanted. Despite his discouragement, he realized that "the habit had so long been fixed in me as to have become a passion, and when once severed from my books I find little or nothing in life to fill the vacancy of time."[45]

The decline of New England's power distressed the Senator. He wrote to his father that the choice of Salem's Parson Bentley for chaplain to the House of Representatives "will show you what is held out to the New England members as proof of their weight in the councils of the union and what they are willing to accept as such."[46] When all the President's nominations were confirmed without question, John Quincy commented that presenting them was a "mere formality, and a very disgusting formality."[47]

The Chase trial was but another symbol of Republican ascendancy and Jeffersonian power. In the preliminaries before the Senate, Adams detected in the actions of Vice President Burr, who had behaved in so detached a manner in the last session, some decided partiality to the prosecution. He noted that Jefferson was courting Burr for the first time since their election and realized that the Vice President wanted the Senate to send their Address to the Governor of New Jersey on his behalf to stay the prosecution against him for murder in that state.

Judge Chase, signer of the Declaration and, until now, one of the leading lights of the Supreme Court, was formally accused on January 2, 1805. His plea for adequate time to prepare his defense was rudely refused and the trial set for February 4. The accusation was in eight articles, including his conduct in several sedition trials, his withholding of legal rights from one John Fries, and the episode that set Jefferson on his trail, his harangue to a Baltimore jury in which he castigated the government for the abolition of the offices of sixteen circuit judges and the change in the state's constitution which established universal suffrage, which, he stormed, would change the republic into a mobocracy.

The day of the trial, Senator Adams entered the Senate chamber, now transformed to resemble a courtroom. Inspired by the setting of the trial of Warren Hastings in Westminister Hall, London, ten years earlier, Burr had set a small army of workmen building and upholstering. Achieving the effect of a theater, seats covered with green cloth rose in tiers facing the stage, in the center of which the President of the Senate had his chair. On either side of him, tiers of seats covered with scarlet cloth were arranged for the Senators. John Quincy, without any recorded comment, took his seat amidst this splendor. He watched the proceedings with interest and concern throughout the month's trial. The Senate met as a Court of Impeachment at 10 A.M. each morning until two or three in the afternoon. After a break for lunch, which Burr provided for them, the Senate reconvened as a legislative body until five or six.

The long trial for the survival of the federal judiciary was enlivened by the main actors: tall, burly, white-haired Judge Chase; small, elegant, severe Aaron Burr; erratic, theatrical prosecutor John Randolph; and defense attorney Luther Martin of Maryland, nearsighted, shabby, alcoholic, and piercingly brilliant.

When the vote was taken on March 1, neither side was sure about the outcome. In a tense waiting atmosphere, each Senator was polled eight times. By the fifth article, it was obvious that the trend was for Chase's acquittal. The federalists were saved, and so was the judiciary.

Until the sentence was pronounced, John Quincy refrained from commenting on the trial. "I felt the obligation of absolute silence upon pen and tongue," he wrote to his father. He had voted "not guilty" on all eight counts and after the trial confided his reaction fully. He believed that the case was part of a planned attack on the judicial branch of the government which the Administration had started with the Pickering impeachment. Having failed with Chase, Senator Adams prophesied, Jefferson would not attempt that method again. He had other ploys, such as a constitutional amendment that would make judges removable upon a joint address of the two branches of the legislature by simple majorities.

The day after the trial, Aaron Burr, no longer Vice President, took leave of the Senate. John Quincy recorded that the charming little man, thought by so many to be slippery and dangerous, delivered his farewell speech with great dignity and firmness, although with a lack of emotion. The Senate listened earnestly and attentively, many of the members profoundly moved, two of them to tears. Immediately after his address, Burr walked from the chamber. Though Adams never liked the man, he was greatly affected by his manner and appearance and in complete agreement with "his prophetic and solemn words" that "the dying agonies of the Constitution will be witnessed on the floor of the Senate," a pointed allusion to the Chase trial. The significance of the trial, said Senator Adams, was that party prosecution was disappointed. The Senate fulfilled its most important purpose, which was to check the "impetuous violence" of the House of Representatives and to demonstrate that a sense of justice was strong enough to overpower the furies of faction.[48]

After attending the marriage of Louisa's sister Harriet to George Boyd, the four Adamses and Eliza Johnson started for Quincy. A curious little incident occurred on their trip to Philadelphia. When they arrived on the packet, Aaron Burr was there. Louisa, who thought that she hated him for his duel with Hamilton, had never met him before. But in spite of herself, she was soon captivated by his manners and his charm. She reported that he was the favorite of everyone on the boat, down to the lowest sailor. By the time the trip was over, he knew the history of everyone on the vessel and was politely attentive to Louisa, and devoted to her sister. At table, he helped with the children and when, after a rough passage, they arrived at midnight, Colonel Burr, with baby John in his arms, a bundle in his hand, and Eliza leaning on his arm, walked with the Adamses to Frenchtown. He did it all with such good breeding and grace that it did not seem that he was doing anything out of the way. They laughed and talked all the way to Philadelphia so that by the time they reached there they were all quite intimate. During the time they were both in Philadelphia, they called on each other. Even Senator Adams commented, "I defy man, woman or child so to withstand the power of his fascination as to pass from him . . . without feelings of good will . . . I felt a degree of compassion for the man."[49]

The quiet solitude of their Quincy house, about two and a half miles from the Adams place, was interrupted by an unexpected offer. In August, a committee from Harvard College informed John Quincy that he had been elected Nicholas Boylston Professor of Oratory and Rhetoric. The recipient received the news with many misgivings and soon let the college know that he would take the job only on his own terms. Since he was in Washington only half the year, the required series of forty weekly lectures would have to be condensed into two lectures per week for half the year. Public declamations would have to be scheduled accordingly. Another imperative adjustment was that the authorities must waive the religious test required of a professor. "I must question their authority to require my subscription to a creed not recognized by the Constitution or laws of the State. . . . I beg to be understood that objection is to the test itself, and not to the doctrines which it prescribes," he informed Samuel Dexter. The college capitulated completely after Adams refused an alternative proposal that a substitute chosen by the administration perform the duties that the absent professor could not manage. "The duties of the office if I hold it must be discharged by myself," he said.[50]

John Quincy and his wife returned to Washington in November without the children. This was Louisa's first separation from the boys, which made her very unhappy, but money was low and the children were a burden. On the way, in Philadelphia, Dr. Rush intimated to John Quincy that Jefferson and Madison were considering a mission abroad for him. The Senator said that he would not refuse it if offered but doubted that it would be offered. Later, in December, Richard Rush wrote to ask that he be appointed secretary of the legation under him. Even when Monroe mentioned that he had heard the rumor in London, Senator Adams was skeptical.

Congress opened in December but got off to a slow start. John Quincy Adams thought that he reflected the Senate's sluggishness and had not been vigorous enough in his pursuit of his duties. In general, he believed that his political prospects were declining. He was mistaken. The independent direction that he had taken in the Louisiana question freed him from party pressure and obligation. Now his direction would be responsive to events rather than to the rise and fall of faction.

CHAPTER 9

A Man of Principle

". . . each Senator is a representative not of a single State, but of the whole Union. His vote is not the vote of his State, but his own individuality. . . ."

JOHN QUINCY ADAMS

"MY OPINIONS ON EVERY SUBJECT of moment which occur, are eventually the opinions overruled," Senator Adams complained to Abigail, "and for any purpose of public benefit to be answered, a tenth part of the time and anxiety which I give to the public affairs would be tended in all probability with the same issue. . . ." The Senator's record was beginning to look like a roster of lost causes. But, Tom pointed out to his brother, during the present session he served on more committees than before and so was receiving some recognition, particularly in his field of foreign affairs.

Most of his time away from the Senate, Adams was in his room laboriously drafting the bills that he proposed. The crowd of business was so great that he lamented "the want of *genius* because I want a mighty agent for the service of my country."[1] Time was so much a factor that personal correspondence had to be squeezed in between debates on the Senate floor which, the Senator said, probably muddled his letters into incoherence.

John Quincy and Louisa continued to live with the Hellens though Abigail had suggested that since the children were in Massachusetts, they should take lodgings nearer to the Capitol. Louisa found it hard to reconcile herself to the separation from baby John and George, who was going to school in Quincy. But her mother-in-law reminded her, somewhat harshly, good sense should make it plain that the worst thing for children was to be dragged twice a year by water or crowded stages for such distances. "I have experienced separations of all kinds from children equally dear to me, but I considered it the duty of the parent to consider the child," she wrote.[2]

There were compensations living with the Hellens. Louisa had the companionship of her sisters and she and John Quincy had the comfort of being in a warm, congenial atmosphere. Most of the members of Congress lived in rooming houses near the Capitol, apart from their wives and children, who remained in their home states.

William Plumer of New Hampshire described some of the hardships of boarding-house living. He stayed at Captain Coyle's, along with sixteen other Representatives and Senators. It was noisy and most inconvenient since he had to share a room. The most irksome aspect of the arrangement was that those of the same political party lodged in the same house. At Coyle's, Pickering, Tracy, and Davenport—all high federalists—made it uncomfortable for Plumer to invite anyone whose politics were different. If he did, "these violent inmates" treated the strangers "with rudeness & insult." Plumer could do nothing about his contention that "an interchange of sentiments tends to correct One's own errors."[3] This kind of restraint would have been unsupportable to Adams.

The lighter side of Senator Adams emerged in a piece of doggerel that he sent to Tom. It described the plight of poor Betsy, a domestic in the Hellen household.

THE MISFORTUNE
January 12, 1806

Poor Betsy was a maiden pure
Declin'd in years but so demure
    That *Man* was her aversion.
And night by night her door she barr'd
With trebl'd bolts, her fame to guard
    From slander's foul aspersion.

When lo! all in the dead of night
Came Mary, breathless with affright
    Wringing her hands and crying—

"Oh Mistress! Mistress! Rouse! Awake!
"To Betsy come, for Heaven's Sweet Sake
"Poor Betsy! She's a dying!"

The Lady—tender and humane
Starts from her bed, and flies amain
The wonder to unravel.
Flies to where Betsy lays and moans
And straightway perceives what caus'd her groans.
Poor Betsy!—was in TRAVEL!!

Tom was told to burn the poem after he read it, which, obviously, he failed to do. He was also reassured that the domestic crisis was properly resolved with a wedding and a christening.[4] Although "the power of abstraction" needed for the study of poetry, history, and philosophy was evasive after ten hours per day of "senatorial deliberation," the writing of light verse was apparently a successful form of relaxation.

Foreign affairs, John Quincy's forte, engaged much of his attention. Everyone in Washington, he observed, was "full of sound and fury" against England and Spain. The President, in his annual message, had asked for protective measures against the two powers. But Senator Adams observed, since there were two enemies at once, Congress would be very cautious about engaging in the contest.[5]

However, American consternation mounted when, as a result of the decision on the Essex case (1805), England's Rule of 1756, which provided that trade closed in peace may not be opened in war, was revived after its ten-year period of grace, during which millions of tons of American shipping enjoyed a flourishing re-export trade. Deriving from the Spanish and French West Indies, the goods were sold in Europe at a handsome profit. Now that beautiful source of income, which would not be equalled in dollar value until 1916 and probably not in real value until the late 1940s, was subject to British attack and, ultimately, the prize courts.[6]

John Quincy Adams and Secretary of State James Madison agreed that England was totally at fault. Madison wrote an opus called *An Examination of the British Doctrine, which Subjects to Capture a Neutral Trade, not open in Time of Peace* (Philadelphia, 1806), And Adams worked with a Senate committee on a series of resolutions of protest, which he drafted. They declared that the Rule of 1756 was "an unprovoked aggression" on the property of United States citizens and a "wanton violation" of neutral rights. Great

Britain must restore and indemnify immediately all American property that had been seized. And the United States was to suspend all funds and stock held by British subjects until satisfaction on the subject of captures and condemnations was given by the British government. These resolutions were all adopted, although another, proposed by General Smith and Mr. Anderson, was rejected. For the first time, Senator Adams was a successful man of both parties.

Because of the Senate's interest, Thomas Jefferson sent William Pinckney to join Ambassador James Monroe in London to try to smooth over relations between the two countries. The two Americans failed to accomplish the mission, in contrast to the success of the much maligned John Jay. A treaty was signed but it was so unsatisfactory, merely replacing the hated law of 1756 with a blockade, that Jefferson did not bother to submit the document to Congress, pretending that he withheld it because it did not contain a provision for the abolition of impressment. Again John Quincy agreed with the President. The treaty, he believed, would have involved the country in war within a year.[7]

Now that Louisiana was in American hands, Florida became very appealing, if only to fill in the southern extremity of the map. Although it was probably an inopportune time to pursue the subject because Spain, who was feeling unfriendly to the United States, showed no interest in selling, Jefferson pressed a secret bill through Congress requesting an appropriation of $2,000,000 for foreign intercourse, a euphemism for Florida. John Quincy wanted Florida also, but favored an amendment to the bill that specified the object of the appropriation. He decided, finally, to vote against the bill because, he said, it was unnecessary. West Florida, he insisted, was part of the Louisiana Purchase and so had already been bought and paid for. And two million dollars was an exorbitant price just for East Florida. In a speech on the subject, Adams was disgusted with his delivery, calling it incoherent, without order, and without self-collection, "obviously a very tedious one to all my hearers."[8] The bill passed due to the support of the President's friends, who, though reluctant, voted for it. John Quincy observed that Jefferson's whole system of administration was founded on getting legislative measures through by means of his personal or official influence.[9]

In February 1806, Marquis de Casa Yrujo, the Spanish Minister, published his correspondence with Madison in the United States

Gazette, a federal rag, printed in Philadelphia. John Quincy, who had several times been outraged by the abuse of privileges and immunities practiced by foreign ministers, decided to draft a bill that would prevent such excesses. He did not expect it to succeed but considered it his duty to open up the subject for debate.

The Senate accepted the bill and made its author the chairman of a committee to study it. At a party given by Madison for about seventy people, Senator Adams had the opportunity to talk to his host. They agreed on Madison's system of establishing permanent commercial distinctions between Great Britain and other nations, a retaliating navigation act, and aggravated duties on imports. On the subject of the foreign ministers' bill, Madison indicated that he approved of it, saying that if there had been such a piece of legislation in effect he would have been able to send Yrujo out of the country.

On March 3, the bill was debated at length. John Quincy's speech in its defense was one of his most successful, "clothed in elegant language & delivered in an impressive manner."[10] But it was doomed to failure. Even while in committee, the point had been made that the President already had the power to oust foreign officials so that the bill was unnecessary. Some Senate members objected to it because it seemed to them a direct censure of the President, which its author never meant.

Senator Adams considered the bill valuable because it went beyond the President's constitutional power, which extended the right to check nothing more than insolence. He cited the Genêt case as a good example of a situation that would have been ameliorated immediately had his bill been in effect. The bill's failure was a disappointment but Adams was more reconciled to its defeat when he heard that his father disapproved of it.[11] Adams was puzzled at the Administration's abandonment of the measure until Plumer supplied the explanation. Both the British and the French Ambassadors had intimated to the Secretary of State that their governments did not want the bill to pass.

The number of bills for which John Quincy was the scribe belied some of his pessimism over his lack of influence. He drew up articles on impressment and complained that his colleagues were hypercritical rather than friendly about changes in the wording. Then, turnabout, he stated that he had no particular attachment to his own form of expression and criticism might force him to be more accurate and precise, thereby improving his writing style for the future. The impressment bill failed, Plumer thought, because the quartet of Adams, Bayard, Hillhouse, and Pickering provoked debate, thereby stirring up antagonistic warmth and passion. Among Adams's other endeavors were bills for the encouragement of United States shipping and navigation and a bill on the Georgia land petitions.

As the session neared the end, the Senate became frantic due to unfinished business. John Quincy, along with half of the Senate, opposed the President's appointment of John Armstrong as Minister to France. Though a scholar and a writer, Armstrong's conduct had been seriously challenged for his use of the Louisiana fund when, with James Bowdoin, Minister to Spain, he had been a commissioner for settling unlawful captures made by Spain and the boundaries on both sides of the Mississippi River. The Senate tie was decided by Vice President Clinton's vote in favor of the Administration appointment. John Quincy called it "one of the most disgraceful acts of Mr. Jefferson's administration."[12]

All the New England men, except for Plumer, supported the Georgia land bill. In 1795, a corrupt Georgia legislature had sold about thirty-five-million acres at less than two cents per acre to a number of Yazoo companies. The contract was repudiated but, by that time, individuals, mostly New Englanders, had bought land from the speculators. The purpose of the bill, which passed the Senate 19–11, was to relieve the investors.

Extensive debates on the ratification of a treaty with Tripoli which Senator Adams supported revealed clearly to him the extent of politicking that the Administration indulged in during the debates on every bill. It became apparent from the way "the presidential votes" went that the President supported postponement of the bill. These voters, said Adams, were "men who get in whispers his secret wishes, and vote accordingly." In this case, however, John Quincy was somewhat confused. Madison had spent a half hour with him one evening pressing for ratification of the bill but, exchanging confidences with Plumer, the New Hampshire Senator reported that Jefferson had told him that he wanted it postponed to the next session. "How to reconcile?" Plumer asked. John Quincy answered that it was irreconcilable. There was no such thing as placing confidence in these men.[13]

Just before the close of the session, Adams presented a memorial for his brother-in-law Colonel William Smith and Samuel G. Ogden, both of whom had been involved in Miranda's attempt to revolutionize the province of Caracas in South America. Smith had subsequently been removed from his office as naval officer of the city of New York by order of Jefferson. Earlier in the winter, the Colonel told John Quincy, Miranda had revealed his project to him and asked him to come along. When the Colonel answered that he could not leave his post without the permission of Madison or the President, Miranda offered to try to arrange it while in Washington seeking their support. But the Administration did not want the United States government to interfere in the project so Smith was refused permission to go with Miranda. However, he advised the revolutionary leader, hired for him the *Leader*, a ship owned by Ogden, and helped him to buy arms, supplies, and enlisted men. The Colonel was surprised by his removal because Gelston, the Collector of the Port of New York, who knew about Miranda's activities and had given the ship clearance, was not discharged from office. Smith charged that he was being made the sacrificial lamb so that the executive could keep up the appearance that the United States disapproved of Miranda's expedition.

Somewhat later, Smith and Ogden and others were indicted by the United States Court for their part in the plot. When the trial was scheduled to be held in July, Smith made an affidavit that Madison was a material witness. John Quincy expected that the memorial would cause a disturbance among the President's men, which it did. As he expected, it was defeated after a warm debate.

At the end of April, Senator Adams started back to Massachusetts. Louisa, who was pregnant, stayed in Washington. John Quincy stopped in New York on May 1, the city's traditional moving day, to find the place in a complete bustle because of that and a warmly contested election for members of Congress and the state legislature. He saw the Smiths, whose plight was tragic. Nabby's son William, who had shipped out with Miranda, had not been heard from since March. The Colonel tried to keep up his spirits with a cheerfulness that "to my eyes have not so much rational foundation as a fairy tale," Senator Adams wrote to Louisa. The Smiths had given up their house and were living in a small cottage within the prison limits. The situation was bad, John Quincy believed, because the approval of the President and the Secretary of State to the original project would have no relevance to the legality of the endeavor.

Since he would be starting his course at Harvard shortly, John Quincy planned to find a house in Cambridge for himself and the children. He particularly wanted George with him because the child was losing his French, but the only quarters to be found were unfurnished chambers for himself, so the children stayed with their grandparents. Louisa was pleased to hear that her boys were in perfect health and anxious to see their mother. John Quincy, though disappointed his sons would not be with him, wrote proudly that John was the delight of the family. His grandfather thought that "he has more *ideas* than any other child of his age he ever knew."[14]

In mid-June, the Adams family journeyed to Boston and then to Cambridge to attend John Quincy's installation as the Boylston Professor of Rhetoric and Oratory. After waiting out a violent thunderstorm, which delayed the ceremonies for two hours, the new professor delivered his speech. It was an elegant, classical address that presented gracefully a history of the practice of the art of oratory in America. By judicious selection and the use of fortuitous phrases, Professor Adams was able to hold his audience's attention. Eloquence, he explained in his speech, "has awoke from her slumbers and shaken the poppies from her brow . . . has conquered the barbarism of Language by softening the harshness of the English into the harmony of the Latin tongue, and can control the passions of mankind by irresistible persuasion."[15] The small company in attendance at the meeting house was charmed.

A highlight of John Quincy's summer was viewing the total eclipse of the sun, the first known to be visible in Boston. Wearing special glasses for the occasion, he and other amateur astronomers, members of the Philosophical Society, gathered in Mr. Bussey's garden. It was, as always, an awesome sight. For four and a half minutes, Adams reported, the sun's face was completely covered. It was too dark to read small print and a lantern was needed to observe the thermometer which dropped eleven degrees from the beginning of the eclipse until total obscurity. Fowls roosted and the herd wound home. "The moon," John Quincy told Louisa, "appeared like a patch of court plaster upon the face of Heaven, and all around the edge of her disk was a luminous border."

Senator Adams's lodgings at the home of Dr. Benjamin Waterhouse were comfortable, particularly because of the company of the doctor, who was a man of learning with an even-tempered wife. But the teaching position was irksome. John Quincy, who felt awkward and ill-prepared, worked ceaselessly so as not to disgrace himself or the institution. Since Harvard had very high expectations from him, "Hence the present is a moment of anxiety as well as of labor, and I need all the tranquillity I can obtain to keep a due possession of myself," he wrote.[16]

Bad news came from Louisa that she had miscarried, felt very ill, and was pining for her children. John Quincy answered her rather stiffly that his thoughts turned "to the inexpressible blessings left in our remaining children." But she was not that easily placated. In August, she set out for Massachusetts and, after a very hard and long trip, reached Quincy. She was chagrined to find that her children did not know her and after she and J.Q.A. moved into their Quincy house, baby John wanted to go back to his grandmother. John Quincy's total involvement in the requirements of his professorship added to her feelings of resentment. She accused him of neglecting the children and believed that her society was proving unwelcome. Having relinquished all claim to his time in the winter, she complained, "I am the less willing to give it up in the Summer."[17]

Colonel Smith had been acquitted in July but the family in Quincy worried about young William. They did not believe the newspaper accounts that the Spanish had taken him prisoner with Miranda, but agreed with John Quincy's lament. "I wish William was at home . . . that neither he nor his father had any concern with this knight-errant expedition." The lad finally turned up in Aruba, perfectly safe and free, but his grandfather continued to be concerned that his future was ruined.[18]

Gardening became the family pastime. John Quincy, now quite a professional, taught his wife and sons to bud and graft. There were parties to attend also but, Louisa complained, they were full dress and though the cake and fruit were plentiful, there were few gentlemen and an overabundance of ladies and mosquitoes. By nine o'clock everyone went home. Weekends John Quincy spent with his father and during the week he was immersed in work and seldom home. "The cares of his family become very oppressive to him," Louisa said, but, worst of all for her, she was doomed to stay in the North when Congress reconvened.

In November, Senator Adams went to Boston and found lodgings for the family without consulting his wife. They were to board with Mr. Gulliver, but they could furnish their apartment and keep a man and maidservant. Actually, Louisa had made the decision to stay, her only alternative being to leave the children again. She was not entirely alone because her sister Caroline was with her. Once again the full responsibility for the growing youngsters rested on their mother. George had to be enrolled in a new school and, his father ordered, convinced to overcome his reluctance to learn French. John Quincy suggested a simple formula: no French—no horse. He wrote to George in French that he would buy him "le grand cheval" when he learned the language.

In New York, Adams visited the Smiths. Though Nabby was happier now about the Colonel and her son William, she needed all her courage to meet their difficulties. Smith was, as usual, perennially confident and the Senator was relieved to hear him deny any knowledge of Burr's progress.

Politics was stagnating in Washington at the beginning of the new session due to the Burr conspiracy, which no one fully understood but was the only subject that "seemed to agitate our political newes."[19] The West was inflamed over the strange reports and mysterious doings of the ex-Vice President. Rumor and reports had it that Burr had launched an expedition to separate the West, capture Mexico, take over New Orleans, or, as Burr contended, settle his Bastrop land purchase. Jefferson had been persuaded by General James Wilkinson, himself a suspected participant, and others to issue a general alarm.

At noon on Friday, January 23, 1807, the doors of the Senate chamber were solemnly shut. Mr. Giles moved that a committee be appointed to write a bill that would suspend the Habeas Corpus Act for a limited time. The need for the suspension of civil liberties, the legislative body was informed, was the danger of Burr's rebellion. Two of the principal actors, Erich Bollman and Samuel Swartwout were in Washington under arrest, and it was to prevent their escape and to help secure others who would be arrested in distant parts of the country that the bill was deemed necessary. Mr. Bayard objected. He said that the evidence available to prove a rebellion was inconclusive, and if such a rebellion ever existed it was now terminated. The writ of habeas corpus, he argued, was "the great palladium of our liberties." Its suspension "leaves our persons subject to the whim & caprice of Judges." John Quincy Adams, who with William B. Giles and Samuel Smith had prepared the bill, agreed with Bayard that habeas corpus was the great palladium of our rights "in common and ordinary cases—yet on extraordinary occasions, I believe its temporary suspension is equally as essential to the preservation of our government & the privileges of the people."[20]

Senator Adams, Plumer said, was *"passionately zealous"* for the passage of the bill. The Senate vote was unanimous in favor of it except for Bayard. But in the House the reaction was very different. When presented with the bill accompanied by an injunction of secrecy, the House declined both parts almost unanimously.

The Bollman-Swartwout case "excited such universal curiosity that we are scarcely able here to form a quorum to do business and the House of Representatives actually adjourned this morning for want of a quorum," John Quincy wrote to his father the last of January.[21] "King Burr" was the only topic of interest to the lawmakers. John Quincy thought that the Washington trial was an error and that the accused men should have been sent back to New Orleans where they had been arrested.

In his spare time, Adams worked on his lectures for his course and continued with Greek, reading through the *Odyssey* in the original. While unagitated by other matters, he said, he was able to read and understand Homer but when public business took hold of him he read without understanding.

It was a bitterly cold winter in Washington. The cold and wind were so intense that John Quincy had difficulty getting back and forth to the Capitol. In the evening the chill in his chamber made work impossible. On February 6, both Houses had to adjourn early because the windows were blown in. But Burr fever continued as intense as the cold. Because of it, business on Capitol Hill was conducted with indifference and carelessness and, John Quincy remarked, bill after bill passed without any review of the subject. Just before Congress adjourned, Jefferson received word that Burr had surrendered himself, his men, and his boats. "The termination of this Congress will leave our public affairs threatened on all sides with war, external and internal. We do nothing," Adams wrote gloomily.[22] He was happy, however, that he had succeeded in procuring the annual appropriation for the library.

Back in Boston, the Senator found his household in chaos. The family had moved, nothing was in order, and everyone was ill. Even the weather was bad. It was weeks before there was enough quiet to work. The only respite was an occasional weekend in Cambridge.

In July, Caroline Johnson, who had been Louisa's companion for the past year, was married to Andrew Buchanan. The Adams family turned out in full: the President, Abigail, Tom, who was now a judge, with his wife, the former Ann Harrod, and Nabby and her daughter. Louisa, once more, found her in-laws' habits strange. She remarked that now presents were offered and received and that the supper party was pretty but cramped.

George, just past six, was his grandfather's delight. During the summer, he fell out of the swing, breaking his collarbone and dislocating his shoulder. After the doctor set it, President Adams gave the boy a quarter for being brave. The child ran with his newfound wealth to the Common, where he met one of his schoolfellows. He sent the lad to buy gingerbread for all the boys, saying, "When I am President, I will make you Secretary of State." Great expectations had already been instilled in the child.

In August, John Quincy recorded in his *Diary*, "By the blessing of God, I have this day a third son." He was with Louisa when the child was born. At first the infant appeared dead, but he revived—in about half an hour according to his mother's account, in five minutes according to his father. The baby was named Charles Francis after his deceased uncle.

Earlier in the summer an event occurred which John Quincy believed started "the really important period of my life." It was the British attack upon the American frigate *Chesapeake*, which took place in the spring of 1807. News that the armed British ship, the *Leopard*, had fired on the American merchantman reached Boston on June 30. Senator Adams, outraged at British audacity, wanted a town meeting to protest the deed convened immediately. The federalists were opposed. Consequently, the republicans issued a call for the citizens of Boston and neighboring towns to meet at the State House to prepare resolutions of protest against the vicious attack. The meeting was not numerous but the resolutions, drafted by a committee of which Adams was a member, were unanimously adopted. Friends lost no time in telling John Quincy that he would have his head taken off by the federalists for apostasy. He said that he couldn't help it. On his fortieth birthday, which occurred the day after the meeting, he wrote, "My sense of duty shall never yield to the pleasure of party."[23] An independent was born.

On the 16th of July, aware that they had made a tactical mistake, the federalists joined a town meeting at Faneuil Hall to hear a letter read from the citizens of Norfolk describing the Virginian reaction. John Quincy Adams was named chairman of the committee to draft resolutions of a similar nature. Prominent federalists such as Harrison Gray Otis and Thomas H. Perkins were also appointed. The resolutions adopted, which were milder than the earlier set, said "that we must sincerely approve the proclamation, and the firm and dispassionate course of policy pursued by the President of the United States," that the unprovoked attack was "a wanton outrage . . . a direct violation of our national honor . . . that we remember with pride and pleasure, the patriotic and spirited conduct of the citizens of Norfolk, Portsmouth, and their Vicinities, before the orders of Government were known."

John Quincy, whose signature was on both sets of resolutions, insisted that it "was no conversion." But from that day he was given to understand that he had no communion with his party. At the beginning of the new session, October 1807, Massachusetts's senior senator "was discarded from the federal ranks" because "he had pledged himself openly to sustain the administration" in its strong position "against the wanton outrage of Great Britain."[24]

Because of the emergency, Congress assembled six weeks early. Louisa discovered that, once again without her consent, arrangements had been made for her and the children. The two older boys would stay behind and in two different places. The three remaining members of the family proceeded south, stopping off in Baltimore to visit the Buchanans. Caroline, her sister thought, was taxed beyond her strength taking care of her husband's four children by an earlier marriage.

Senator Adams returned to a discouraging situation. He recognized himself as part of a small and constantly decreasing minority, with the added disadvantage of suffering more opposition from his party friends than from his opponents. Even when they agreed with him, some legislators feared that to support an Adams measure was to lose popularity. "I am made a leader without followers," he said. Josiah Quincy, who maintained that he did not join in nor sanction any of the hostility against the fallen federalist, explained Adams's deviation from his friends with some perspicacity. He said it was "perfectly reconcilable with the peculiar texture of his mind, without resorting to any suspicion of his political integrity."[25] The tense situation that he found himself in worried Adams somewhat, but since he was incapable of considering any accommodation he could only caution himself, "Undertake little, be content with regular attendance and restrain rather than indulge debate."[26] Good advice, but contrary to the nature of the man.

At this time Adams believed that the United States could not avoid war with Great Britain. He feared that its results would be dangerous if not ruinous, but saw no way of avoiding it. The other members of the Senate, however, did not share his views. Though filled with "embarrassment, anxiety and confusion of mind," according to John Quincy, they were willing to yield to Great Britain all that she wanted.[27] It is possible that war at that time, when the nation was outraged by the Chesapeake Affair and therefore united by it, would have been more acceptable than it became five years later after the failure of the many attempts to solve the problems on the high seas with ineffective stopgap alternatives which had divided the country.

The Burr conspiracy cast its shadow over the Senate again when a decision had to be made whether to seat John Smith of Ohio, who had been indicted for treason in August as an alleged associate of Aaron Burr. Smith, who entered the Senate on November 27, prepared to take his seat, although the Senate's general reluctance to accept him was quite clear. To his great regret, John Quincy was made chairman of the committee to enquire whether Smith should not be expelled because of his connection with the conspiracy.

The committee of enquiry worked diligently, interviewing witnesses—including John Smith—and studying papers, statements, and affidavits. Even on Saturdays and on Christmas Day its unrelenting chairman held meetings. And in the evenings he pored over the material, sifting and analyzing. The last of December the long report was agreed upon by the committee in almost the exact form that Chairman Adams had written it.

The finished report was couched in such strong language that it gave "mortal offense" in New Hampshire, caused "serious regret" on the part of Rufus King and, according to Lowell, it performed "the polluting office of private revenge" for presidential vengeance. Thoroughly convinced by the carefully collated evidence that John Smith had participated in a plot to sever the Union, Senator Adams let his rhetoric master his reason. He wrote that the technical difficulty of proving an overt act of war spared John Smith, as it had his leader Aaron Burr, from conviction. The document indirectly indicted Burr, whose design, Adams wrote, had it not been stopped, would shortly "have terminated not only in war, but in a war of the most horrible description—in a war at once foreign and domestic."[28]

In a more reasonable manner, the report developed the principle that in the admission of a member to a legislative body the interest of the public was at stake, "and the interest of the individual disappears." Adams made the point that since the Constitution did not provide for recall of a legislator by his constituents, "when the darling of the people's choice has become their deadliest foe, can it enter the imagination of a reasonable man that the sanctuary of their legislation must remain polluted with his presence. . . . Must the assembled rulers of the land listen with calmness and indifference, session after session, to the voice of notorious infamy, until the sluggard step of municipal justice can overtake his enormities?" Therefore, the power of expulsion was given to Congress "to preserve the legislature from the first approaches of infection . . . its process must be summary, because it would be rendered nugatory by delay. . . ."[29] As to precedent, Adams cited the case of Blount, who, in July 1797, was expelled from the Senate for refusing to answer whether he was the author of an incriminating letter. The Senate committee had decided his guilt upon the basis of a handwriting analysis, evidence that would not be acceptable in a court of law. Implied in Adams's reasoning was the idea that the good of the legislature or the country as a whole superseded not only the individual's rights but also the right of the state or district to choose whomever it wishes as its representative. This was consistent with John Quincy Adams's fundamental concern with the Union. In this respect he would have agreed that the whole was greater than any of its parts.

The committee, therefore, "compelled by a sense of duty," submitted the resolution that, due to his participation in the Aaron Burr conspiracy, John Smith had been guilty of conduct incompatible with that of a Senator of the United States and "that he, therefore, and hereby is expelled from the Senate of the United States."[30] As expected, response from the Senators, particularly the federalists, made the bill pass "through a fiery ordeal." John Smith wrote to the Senate to complain about the committee and to ask to be heard with counsel. Senator Adams continued to examine further evidence on Smith, knowing full well that his conclusions were obnoxious to a large part of the nation. Finally the case was postponed until April to provide an interim during which tension could subside.

International problems obscured the home-grown ones. On December 18, 1807, Jefferson sent a message to Congress recommending an unlimited embargo. Immediate action was necessary, he said, because Britain had reaffirmed its right of impressment and Napoleon had ordered strict measures against American ships disobeying trade restrictions. "It was obvious that between the two, every American vessel that should be permitted to sail would go to almost certain capture and condemnation," John Quincy advised Massachusetts Governor James Sullivan. The President and Madison had great hopes for the effectiveness of an embargo as a diplomatic weapon. They reasoned that it would avoid war and, more subtly, mortally injure Great Britain by depriving her of necessary food and naval supplies customarily supplied by the United States.

The Senate committee formed to act on the President's message included a protesting John Quincy Adams. He allowed himself to be persuaded to serve on the committee only when he became convinced that there must be an embargo. However, he agreed to it with the reservation that it would be a stopgap measure of short duration. In four or five hours of debate, after submission of the measure by the committee, an obedient Senate passed the President's Embargo Act, 22 to 6. Timothy Pickering, who was loud in his denunciation, was scarcely listened to. The House passed the embargo also but only after a considerable contest.

In a letter of explanation to Governor Sullivan, Senator Adams clarified his position on the embargo. He explained that it would end impressment because British sailors in the United States would now be unemployed and so would return voluntarily to their own nation's ships, thus removing the only pretext for a quarrel between the two countries. It was "an experiment" to gauge the people's willingness to stand on their rights before the Administration entered into hard negotiations with Britain's representative, George H. Rose. In conclusion, Adams assured the Governor that the embargo would preserve peace and that it was only a temporary precautionary measure. "General embargoes of six or twelve months, of which some gentlemen talk so lightly, never entered my brain as practicable things in a great commercial country. I question whether an example of the kind can be found in history," he said.[31]

Acting on that belief, on January 11 Senator Adams offered a motion that a committee be appointed to enquire when the embargo might safely be removed. It was promptly defeated by a vote of 10–17. The embargo, a shattering blow to all commercial interests, was ill-received, particularly in New England. "A suffering community will thank Mr. Adams for proposing an inquiry," *The Repertory* wrote, but speculated that since the legislature did not know why they imposed the embargo they were not likely to remove it until it pleased the President.[32]

At this time, Senator Adams had no illusions about his position with the federalist party. Though he had never had any communication with the President except on official business, he was now considered one of his ardent supporters. "My political prospects are declining," he recorded in his *Diary*. As his term was nearing its end, he was certain that he would be "returned to a private citizen. I hope to have my mind sufficiently prepared." To his father, he admitted that his vanity might be affected but he stuck by his formula for public service—never to shrink from his country's service, never to solicit any of its favors. "I shall resume the practice of the law," he said bravely, "although this is a business for which I know myself to be indifferently qualified.[33] John Adams agreed that his son's political fate was decided. At the next Congress, he predicted, Dr. Eustis would be chosen Senator and John Quincy Adams would be numbered among the dead. "You ought to know and expect this, and by no means regret it," he cautioned.[34]

Invited to attend a meeting to discuss the next presidential election, held by the republican members of Congress, John Quincy attended, voted, but said nothing. The balloting favored James Madison for President and feeble, almost senile George Clinton for Vice President once again. John Quincy received one vote for Vice President. Federal consternation was instantaneous. "His apostasy is no longer a matter of doubt with anybody," the solid federalists raged. "I wish to God the noble house of Braintree had been put in a hole and a deep one too twenty years ago," was another sentiment.[35] Josiah Quincy, who believed that John Quincy's principles were sincere although "too pure," tried to win the renegade back by assuring him that he would receive no thanks for his conduct. John Quincy answered that to resist dissolution of the Union, or subserviency to Great Britain, he was ready "to sacrifice everything I have in life and even life itself." Neither newspaper abuse nor poison-pen letters moved him. He grew used to exhortations such as that of "A Federalist" who wrote, "Oh Adams, remember who thou art. Return to Massachusetts. Return to thy Country! Consider the consequences! Awake! Arouse in time!"[36]

But real trouble was in the making and Timothy Pickering was

its willing agent. After it became obvious that George Rose's negotiations with the Administration would fail, Pickering wrote a letter
to Governor Sullivan denouncing the embargo and, by implication,
all who supported it, and asking that the commercial states combine
to resist it. Pickering's letter was an inevitable sequel to the 1804
effort and the first appeal of a United States Senator to the Governor
of a state whose legislature had chosen him. Senator Adams considered his associate's action an unconstitutional interference with the
division of powers between the federal and state governments. A
United States Senator, according to John Quincy's political philosophy, was a representative "not of a single state, but of the whole
Union." His vote was his own individually and his constituents had
not even the right to recall him or to control his constitutional
action by instructing him.[37]

In his letter, Senator Pickering did not mention John Quincy
Adams's name but the timing of it gave away its purpose. It was sent
just before the close of the Massachusetts legislature's session in
ample time to influence the elections to the state legislature—the
one that would then vote for a Senator at the expiration of Adams's
term in March 1809. Pickering's strategy was carefully planned. It
was hoped that Governor Sullivan would communicate the junior
senator's letter to the state legislature but he did not. To take care
of this contingency, a copy of the letter had been sent to George
Cabot, who was prepared to have it published. On March 7, five
days after the letter had reached the Governor, another ploy was
attempted. Harrison Gray Otis made a motion in the state senate
that any letters received by the Governor from a Senator must be
communicated to the state senate. The motion was defeated and so,
as planned, the Pickering letter was on the press and off to a phe-
nomenal sale of some 30,000 copies in pamphlet form and over
40,000 in the newspapers before the end of March. It had the distinction of being the first public airing of differences of opinion
between two Senators from the same state.

After reading the Pickering letter, which he accepted as referring
to himself, John Quincy spent every free moment for two weeks
working on a reply, which he directed to Otis. The purpose of his
answer, he said, was not to influence elections but to "promote
Union at home and to urge to vigor against foreign hostile powers.
If Federalism consists in looking to the Boston navy as the only
Palladium of our Liberties, I must be a political heretic. If federal-

ism will please to consist of a determination to defend our Country, I still subscribe to its doctrines." That his reply would increase his difficulties and make new enemies, John Quincy was cognizant. He also adopted his father's and his brother's warning that his answer would not have much circulation because support of the embargo "will not be as catching as invective against it." Abigail was touched by her son's comment that "In a fortnight I hope to have the pleasure of seeing you, and at least at Quincy I shall be sure of meeting no altered faces."[38]

On April 9, the Adams reply to Pickering appeared in print. Though it circulated in large numbers, it could not overcome the success of the earlier pamphlet, which had enjoyed the whole field in the interim and which held the more popular position. The Adams letter was almost apologetic in its effort to be tactful about Pickering. Much of it was a philosophic restatement of John Quincy's political principles and a presentation of relevant official documents. It refuted the arguments against the embargo and was particularly eloquent against Pickering's apologia for impressment. Adams denied the statement that the number of American citizens impressed by the British was small, arose *only* from the impossibility of distinguishing between Englishmen and Americans, and that such impressed Americans were given back on duly authenticated proof. He said that he was mystified that there was such general indifference to the agony of the impressed sailor who was victimized to feed the needs of Britain's wars. "I cannot stay to account for the wonder, why, poor and ignorant as most of them are, the voice of their complaints is so seldom *heard* in the great navigating states," he wrote.[39]

John Quincy's publication of his rebellious position reaped immediate federalist vengeance. On June 2, almost a year before Adams's term expired, the Massachusetts legislature elected James Lloyd, Jr., a classmate of John Quincy's at Harvard, an eminent merchant who had served in both houses of the state legislature, to represent the state in the United States Senate starting March 1809. Lloyd won by thirty-four votes in the house, but only by 4 in the senate. Governor Sullivan observed to President Jefferson that the principal object of the federal party in Massachusetts seemed to be the political and personal destruction of John Quincy Adams. He then suggested that in Mr. Adams's interest and that of the Administration, the President should rescue him from their triumph by finding him a foreign appointment. On this subject Jefferson remained silent.[40]

John Quincy Adams sent a letter of resignation to both houses of his native legislature, stating that, "Certain resolutions recently passed by you have expressed your disapprobation of measures to which I gave my assent. . . ." Since these resolutions enjoined on the Senator "a sort of opposition to the National Administration" with which he did not concur, he had to withdraw at once.[41]

The Essex Junto pact had pursued John Quincy into cover. He was then deserted by almost all of his former political friends and many of his personal friends as well. There were a few exceptions, such as William Emerson, John Gardner, and Josiah Quincy. In the legislature all disclaimed him. Christopher Gore wrote to Rufus King that when John Quincy Adams walked down State Street at the hour of exchange, he seemed totally unknown. George Henry Rose commented with satisfaction, writing from England to Pickering, "In Professor Adams's downfall, at which I cannot but be amused, I see but the forerunner of catastrophes of greater mark. . . ." Ralph Waldo Emerson recalled that when he entered Harvard he heard stories of the numbers of coaches in which John Quincy Adams's friends came from Boston to hear him give his first lectures. After his political disgrace, his students continued to attend his classes but the coaches from Boston did not come.[42]

The republicans, however, saw great value in their distinguished convert. They offered him the congressional seat from his district, which he refused, partly because it was Josiah Quincy's office and partly because he had no stomach for further politicking. Outwardly he seemed calm, writing his Harvard lectures and working in his garden, but in the bosom of his family he expressed his true emotions. Louisa said "the dreadful restless anxiety of my husband almost made me crazy. It was too distressing to see him at such times for he could not control his feelings."[43]

The new session of Congress started with former Senator Adams in Boston. He thought that non-intervention would be better policy than a continuance of the embargo but, "at all events," he wrote to William Branch Giles in Washington, "Anything But Submission."[44] He favored non-intercourse because it would remove "some of their appeal to the people from the New Tories," John Quincy's term for partisans of a French war who favored submission to Great Britain. They were not the whole of the federalist party but its policy makers, the political descendants of the Tories of the Revolutionary War.[45]

The year 1809 looked very unpromising. Removed from public life and with his "private concerns . . . under no small embarrassment," John Quincy had only the comfort of his own conscience's approval. The embargo, though the law, was flouted by the Massachusetts courts, whose juries refused to convict a person under the law. John Quincy's gesture was being proved meaningless, at least in his own New England.

At the end of January, Adams was in Washington again, to represent Mr. Peck before the Supreme Court in the case of Fletcher v. Peck. He had hoped to remain unknown on his trip south but all the way, although no one said anything directly, there was much curiosity and speculation about why he was travelling to the capital. The former Senator had grown very absent-minded and often seemed distracted by his own thoughts. Louisa wrote that she was not surprised that he had forgotten his watch in Baltimore, just that he had kept it so long. She reminded him that due to the pressure of business he had become more and more prone to such accidents in the past year and should, therefore, just laugh at them.

The rumor had circulated around Boston that Madison would appoint John Quincy Adams Secretary of War. Both John Adams and Tom had heard it and asked Louisa if her husband would accept the post. She answered that she did not know but rather thought that he would not.[46] John Quincy denied knowledge of all rumors.

Fletcher v. Peck was heard in the Supreme Court starting on March 2, the Court meeting from 11 A.M. to 4 P.M. Although he was scrupulously prepared, Attorney Adams complained that he did not do well when speaking in public. He said that he lacked clarity in arrangement and method and that his argument was "dull and tedious almost beyond endurance." He was surprised that the Court heard him through. The following day, Adams's colleague, Robert G. Harper, argued the case, as did Luther Martin, Fletcher's attorney.

On Inauguration Day, March 4, the Court sat until twelve and then adjourned so that the judges could participate in the ceremonies. John Quincy went to the House, which was crowded, to hear the President-elect make a very short speech in a voice so low that he could not be heard. Then the Chief Justice administered the oath before the assemblage of all the other justices, who were present in their robes. Afterward, the reception was held at Madison's house because he had not yet moved into the presidential home. At 2 P.M., the festivities over, the Court reconvened to hear Martin complete his argument. After dinner, John Quincy, his mother-in-law, and Mrs. Hellen went to a ball at Long's, formerly Stelle's, in honor of the new Chief Executive. They found that the crowd was excessive, the room suffocating, and the entertainment bad.

At the ball, John Marshall mentioned to Mr. Cranch that the Court was reluctant to decide Fletcher v. Peck because it seemed contrived in order to get the Court's judgment. But on the 11th, the Chief Justice read a written opinion reversing the Circuit Court because of a defect in the pleadings. Verbally, Marshall added that, with only five judges attending, no opinion would have been given even had the pleadings been correct. The case was reargued the following term, achieving fame because it was the first case in which the Supreme Court held a state statute unconstitutional. However, this time Adams was not available to argue the case.

A few days after Madison's inauguration, at the President's request ex-Senator Adams called on him. He told him that he proposed to nominate him Minister Plenipotentiary to Russia. The past summer William Short had been proposed for the post but the Senate had rejected him. Now the Russian Emperor again asked for an exchange of Ministers. The purpose of the mission was to cultivate the Emperor's friendship and to be ready to negotiate a maritime treaty as soon as peace came. The new Minister would be expected to leave as soon as possible and to remain an indefinite time, perhaps three to four years. John Quincy consented to all the conditions.

However, the Senate rejected the proposal of sending a Minister to Russia, while making it clear that it was the mission that was rejected and not the man. John Quincy was not very disappointed. It was just as well for him and certainly for the family to stay at home, he argued, although he appreciated the President's recognition of him. "I continue to grow fat," John Quincy told Louisa and his eyes bothered him, probably from too much night work. He was glad to return to Boston.

On June 26, Madison resubmitted the Adams nomination to the Senate. This time it was approved, 19–7, although both Massa-

chusetts Senators voted against their countryman. The former Senator's friends considered the appointment "somewhat like an honorable exile." Colonel Pickering remarked meanly that the best thing
to have done with Adams was to send him out of the country. Nevertheless, John Quincy agreed to go, though he had compelling reasons to refuse: the age of his parents, the infancy of his children, and
his college commitment. He also knew that his personal popularity
would be promoted more if he refused the appointment of a republican President, as John Adams would have preferred. But in spite
of all these excellent reasons, he decided that "my duty as a citizen
to accept the call of country" outweighed all other arguments.
However, he did inform Secretary of State Robert Smith that he
could not leave before August 15 because of private affairs and
his obligation to Harvard.

With Tom and his mother, John Quincy went to Cambridge to
deliver his farewell lecture as Professor of Oratory. In it he revealed
dramatically how much he had been hurt by the treatment of his old
friends. He spoke not so much to the students there as to all who
had injured him.

At no hour of your life will the love of letters ever oppress you as a
burden, or fail you as a resource. . . . In the mortification of disappointment, her soothing voice shall whisper serenity and peace. In social converse with the mighty dead of ancient days, you will never smart under
the galling sense of dependence upon the mighty living of the present
age. And in your struggles with the world, should a crisis ever occur
when even friendship may deem it prudent to desert you, when even
your country may seem ready to abandon herself and you, when priest
and Levite shall come and look on you and pass by on the other side,
seek refuge, my *un*failing friends, and be assured you shall find it, in the
friendship of Laelius and Scipio, in the patriotism of Cicero and Demosthenes, and Burke. . . .

The paragraph, Emerson said years later, "long resounded in
Cambridge." John Quincy thought that his young listeners were
entitled to some mark of appreciation from him because "they had
withstood a most ingenious and laborious attempt to ruin me in
their estimation."[47]

Before he left the country, Adams gave his lectures to Tom to be
published in two volumes, fully expecting them to be harshly handled by critics on both sides of the Atlantic. A little bitterly he said,

"To live in the memory of mankind by college lectures is not the aim of a very soaring ambition," but, at the time, he was convinced that he had no reason to expect any higher glory from posterity.[48]

News that his son would leave for such distant parts shocked his aging father, who had grown dependent on John Quincy's visits. When Tom broke the news to Louisa, she was stunned, feeling that everyone scorned her suffering as an affectation. As usual, she was not consulted about the preparations for the trip or the arrangements for the two older boys who were to stay behind. Just before sailing, she was taken to Quincy to say farewell to her sons but was not left alone with the President lest she could arouse him to pity and he would allow her to take George and John with her. She lamented, "In this agony of agonies can ambition repay such sacrifices?" Her answer was, "Never."

In their own less dramatic way, John Quincy and his parents were saddened by the departure. John Quincy wrote that his mother's farewell letter assuring him that his children would be dearer to her for the absence of their parents was so touching that it would have melted the heart of stone.

Once more a segment of the Adams clan set sail from Boston, this time for farther shores than anyone but John Quincy had travelled before. The group consisted of John Quincy, Louisa, her sister Catherine, the baby, Charles Francis, William Steuben Smith, Nabby's eldest son who was to be the secretary of the legation, and two servants, Martha Godfrey and a Black man called Nelson. Also aboard were two volunteer secretaries who were going at their own expense, Francis C. Gray and Alexander H. Everett. The ship, the *Horace*, which left from Charlestown, was fitted out to go directly to St. Petersburg.

Whatever enmity and hatred John Quincy Adams left behind because of his position on the embargo, he did not doubt that he had done the right thing. He believed his act justifiable on the ground that it was the only alternative to war. New England federalism also was left behind to carry its principles to their inevitable self-destructive conclusion. John Quincy had heard the first whispers of their discontent in 1804 and the clamor had increased and was increasing. But most important, he was leaving to engage in work that was much more congenial to his talents and his interests than the dirty battles of the political arena.

CHAPTER 10

J. Q. A. and Alexander I,
Czar of Russia

"I fear the Emperor of Russia is half an American. . . ."
LORD LIVERPOOL TO LORD CASTLEREAGH

O N BOARD CAPTAIN BECKFORD'S *Horace,* Adams spent his time
reading Plutarch's *Life of Lycurgus,* recording the temperatures
registered on his thermometer and being entertained by a "scull of
porpoises." In a six-hour calm, off the Grand Banks of Newfound-
land, he spent the night catching cod and netted sixty fish. As well
organized at sea as he was on land, the Minister to Russia rose early
as usual, read his Bible before breakfast, and then read and wrote
most of the rest of his waking hours. He appreciated the time he had
for study and meditation and found the paucity of incident not tedious but the "prosperity" of the voyage.

There was time to digest and reflect upon the instructions received from the President. They were not specially written for him
but were copies of the despatches sent to John Armstrong when he
went to France in 1806, and to William Short for his proposed
mission to Russia in September 1808. Madison wanted the American Minister to be fully aware that he was going to St. Petersburg at
the invitation of the Emperor, who had thus demonstrated friendship, "not to say partiality," towards America. Therefore the Minister's purpose must be to cultivate good will and to enlighten the

Emperor as to the pacific and just principles upon which American foreign policy was based. Since the position of a neutral in the midst of warring Europe was unpredictable, to obtain the interest of powerful and influential Russia must be the prime object of the mission.

Though in the twenty years that had elapsed since Francis Dana's unsuccessful mission to Russia, there had been no replacement for him, Jefferson had appointed Levett Harris, a Pennsylvanian, as consul to St. Petersburg. Harris, who had been surprisingly successful, had merited the attention of the Emperor, and so Madison advised Adams to confide in him and to recognize his usefulness.

John Quincy, who had accompanied Dana in 1781, appreciated fully the twenty-seven months of frustration that the American had endured waiting for the summons from Empress Catherine that never came. He wrote to Secretary of State Robert Smith that he was surprised that there was no provision in his instructions for the presents, "which [have] heretofore been considered at the Russian Court as *indispensable* on the admission of a foreign minister." Dana attributed his return home from St. Petersburg to the refusal of the Congress of the confederation to conform with the custom. The Secretary of State reluctantly agreed that if gifts were "expected," the President sent his authorization to make them.[1]

Obviously the diplomatic reasons for the mission's failure were much more complex than the gift question, as Adams and Dana undoubtedly appreciated. Dana's offer to Russia of American trade was not an unmixed blessing. The Empress feared, for example, that American naval stores could compete in the European market for Russian ones, but, more important, Russia's plans to make an advantageous partition of the Ottoman Empire depended for success upon a quiescent Great Britain, not one stirred up by a new Russo-American agreement. Hence, though Dana attributed his failure to trivia and the indifference of the French Minister, whose support for the American cause had been expected, his real problem had been that he was at St. Petersburg at the wrong time. A doubtful American trade could not compensate Russia for an enraged Britain that might jeopardize Russian hopes.[2]

J.Q.A., now approaching Napoleonic Europe, had predicted the Corsican's meteoric rise, but was premature with his statement that Bonaparte "has stretched the bowstring till it cracks."[3] By 1809, Napoleon, Emperor for five years, had become the master of most of Europe. When Russia had been defeated at Friedland in East Prussia in June of 1807, Napoleon had not pushed over her Baltic border because he preferred to be at peace with Alexander while he developed his continental system, finished off Great Britain, and prepared his eastward push through the Turkish Empire and the Near East to India. Consequently, he had designed with care the theatrical meeting with the Russian Czar that took place on a tented raft moored midstream in the Niemen River. At this picturesque spot, the Treaty of Tilsit was signed. It was said that Napoleon was much taken with the youthful, handsome, and intelligent Russian Emperor and so turned on his considerable charm while ignoring Frederick William of Prussia, who was also in Tilsit. The collaboration between the two Emperors was to be temporary, as they both realized, but sufficiently long, they both hoped, to allow Russia to realize her ambitions in the East and for France to defeat Great Britain.

As if symbolic of the troubled waters of European diplomacy into which Adams was sailing, rough weather hit the *Horace* when she entered the North Sea. Forced to land at Christansand, the American Minister had the opportunity to see at first hand the plight of American commerce in Northern Europe. He found the Captains of nearly thirty American ships which had been captured as prizes and were waiting adjudication in the Danish courts. Since there was no American agent there, the Captains had forwarded a memorial to J.Q.A. to St. Petersburg, asking him to interfere in their behalf. He was very sympathetic but, having no authority to interpose with the Danish government, was not too hopeful of results from his complaints.

The *Horace* set out again in a heavy squall of rain and wind, because time was essential if St. Petersburg was to be reached before ice closed the ports. When two British armed ships stopped them at the entrance to the Sound, John Quincy went aboard the Admiral's ship to explain that the *Horace*'s purpose was only to conduct him to his post and that the law of nations required that he be allowed to pass. The Admiral agreed and was courteous and respectful but, said the American, he never offered him a seat during the negotiations— "This he either neglected or purposely omitted."[4]

They were stopped again by the Danes near Cronberg Castle and then allowed to continue, but headwinds kept the ship from making any progress. Adams took the opportunity to travel to Copenhagen to seek relief for the American Captains from the King of Denmark or Count Bernstorff, but both were absent. He then put the matter in the hands of Hans Rudolph Saabye, the United States consul in Copenhagen. He reminded Saabye that during 1798–1799, when certain Danish property was captured by American privateers, restitution had been made. But Saabye was not too effective an advocate because he was a Danish subject and a member of a commercial house which had some interest in privateers.[5]

It was not until October 5 that the ship could sail again. From Elsinore to Copenhagen, a distance of twenty-five miles, it sailed so close to the shore that John Quincy and Louisa stayed on deck to see the beautiful variety of houses in romantic settings, particularly pleasing because the "palaces had no magnificence and the villages no wretchedness."[6] When the ship passed the small island which was formerly the residence of Tycho Brahe, the Danish astronomer, Adams peered anxiously to try to see the ruins of his observatory but could not.

Captain Beckford, doubtful that they could reach St. Petersburg before winter, suggested that they stay at Kiel or proceed overland from Cronstadt, a 1,500-mile trip. For a period of time the decision became a struggle of wills between the Captain and the American Minister. During it, the bad weather and the calms favored the Captain's plan but Adams considered reaching St. Petersburg a matter of conscience. He said that he was "in the pursuit of a public trust. I cannot abandon, upon any motive less than that of absolute necessity, the endeavour to reach the place of my destination by the shortest course possible."[7]

His persistence was rewarded, finally, by favorable winds and even a vessel from New York, the *Ocean*, with which to exchange news. On the 22nd, Adams sighted the Tolbacken lighthouse, six miles below Cronstadt, and the next day, with a strong gale blowing, a government boat carried the Adams party to St. Petersburg. It was the eightieth day from their embarkation at Charlestown.

John Quincy took five "indifferent" rooms at the Hotel de Londres, said to be the best in the city. Louisa described her room as a stone hole entered by a stone passage so full of rats that they would drag the bread that she kept for Charles from her bedtable. Her nerves were shattered for fear that during the night they would attack the baby.

As instructed, Adams lost no time in calling upon Levett Harris and, through him, announcing his arrival to Nicholas, Count

Romantzoff, High Chancellor of the Russian Empire. On October 25, J.Q.A. was introduced to the Count, who already knew of the mission through the Russian Ambassador in Paris, who had learned of it through General Armstrong. In a short but friendly conversation, carried on in French, Adams presented his credential letter and asked for an audience with the Emperor, who was ill at the time but was, the Count said, agreeable to the American mission. Adams mentioned the Danish problem. Count Romantzoff was sympathetic, but commented that his government had similar complaints.

The success of his mission, J.Q.A. worried, was endangered by the Russian-French alliance, which seemed at its peak and which the Count obviously favored. However, the American did not know that the Czar was fed up with French authoritarianism and was looking for an issue to show his displeasure.

On November 5, John Quincy Adams was presented to Emperor Alexander I of Russia. He had been fully instructed in the formalities, which he said "were much more embarrassing to an American than the business of real importance. It is not safe or prudent to despise them, nor practicable for a person of rational understanding to value them."[8] Alexander I was exceedingly cordial. At first they talked formally about politics until John Quincy said, diplomatically, that the buildings in New York and Philadelphia were handsome and convenient, suitable to citizens of a republic, but could not vie with St. Petersburg, "a city of Princes."[9] An audience with Empress Elizabeth, Princess of Baden, followed. She, childless, the wife of Alexander from the time she was fifteen and said to have an unhappy marriage, was dressed in lace with a necklace of rubies and a chain of rubies around her head.

Louisa was presented to the Empress Mother about a week later, on the same day as John Quincy, but, she complained, he and Levett Harris went off alone to the palace, leaving her to face alone the fears and fright of "presentation at the most magnificent court in Europe." She was dressed in a hoop with a silver-tissue skirt, over which she wore a crimson velvet robe that had a long train lined in white. Her shoes were white satin and over her costume she wore a fur cloak. A diamond arrow was her only ornament. Countess Letta, a handsome, fat dowager covered with diamonds, was her sponsor.

It was not long before the Adamses realized that their meager allotment from the government and modest resources would present a problem in the glittering Russian capital. Adams's allowance of nine thousand dollars a year, with an outfit of a year's salary plus a quarter's salary for his return home was ludicrous next to the splendor of the other members of the Corps Diplomatique. The extravagance of the court caused Louisa to worry that she could never afford even the number of dresses necessary to attend the required functions.

After his first dinner at the French Ambassador's estate, John Quincy realized his predicament. There were forty seated at the table for a two-hour dinner served at about four in the afternoon. After they ate, the party returned to the hall where a French actress declaimed scenes from famous plays and a full orchestra played in between her presentations. The guests then adjourned to a small theater where another actor performed sleight-of-hand. Dancing for two or three hours followed until supper was served. At 2 A.M. John Quincy and Louisa returned home.

This kind of evening was the routine in St. Petersburg. Either guests came to see the Adamses or they went to parties that did not break up until the small hours. "It is a life of such irregularity and dissipation as I cannot and will not continue to lead," J.Q.A. lamented.

Even the children participated in the exotic social scene. Louisa took Charles to a fancy dress ball at the house of the Duke of Vicenza. When he arrived dressed as an Indian chief, there was a round of applause. About forty children were present, ranging in age from two to twelve years. A gala dinner was followed by a lottery of toys, but Adams, who was disgusted by the spectacle, hurried the child away before the toys were distributed.

Louisa tried to avoid some of the expense by pleading ill health on the night of the Emperor's birthday ball. She had only one dress which she considered elegant enough for the occasion but had already worn it several times. Since the Empress Mother was notorious for her critical comments on clothes worn too frequently, Louisa preferred to avoid the situation. Unfortunately, however, the Empress Mother was informed that Mrs. Adams had visited the Spanish consul's wife for tea the night of the ball and was heard to comment that if such a thing occurred again, the American Minister's wife would be omitted from future invitations.

Louisa asked her husband to send her home in the spring so that he could keep up appearances better. But, John Quincy explained, supporting a wife in America, even in the small house at Quincy, would cost more than for all of them to be together in St. Petersburg.

Adams had wardrobe difficulties also. The clothes that he had brought with him were all wrong. He was annoyed with the living style at St. Petersburg, which was based on the principle that everyone lived beyond his means and very often failed to pay his debts. In order to avoid such a catastrophe, Adams realized that he would have to draw upon his small property at home. He did not deny that some of the festivities were enjoyable but he hoped "to come out of it still in possession of our purses and our reason."[10]

As a first order of business, Adams reopened talks with Count Romantzoff on relief for American seamen in Denmark. Again the Count was evasive, answering in general terms that only peace would bring a remedy because the French regarded all American ships as British and believed that they carried English colonial goods. J.Q.A. accepted the Count's refusal without surprise. He was amazed then to learn from the Count a few days later that the Emperor had ordered him to inform the Danish government that he wished them to restore American property as soon as possible. Unknowingly, Adams had given the Emperor a cause with which to demonstrate his difference with Napoleon.

Feeling rather pleased with himself, the American Minister then went to the French Ambassador's ice-hills where he enjoyed the sport of sliding down the slopes. It was so cold on that December 29 that the party broke up early to spare the servants, although Nelson's toes were already frozen. It is enlightening to picture portly, dignified, middle-aged John Quincy Adams descending the ice-hill gleefully, with no other conveyance beneath him but his coattails.

Adams's first winter in the Russian capital passed without serious international developments. Court functions, such as presentations to the Emperor's brothers, Nicholas and Michael, masquerade balls, and ice-hill parties, kept John Quincy busy in a manner quite opposite to either his wishes or his preferences. Unable to spend much time at home with his Russian grammar and his correspondence, he deemed his time in St. Petersburg almost entirely wasted.

However, he did make certain interesting observations. The atmosphere of Europe had changed since his last visit, when there had been "a sort of republican or democratic spirit" prevalent. There was not a republic left in Europe. "The very name of the people is everywhere buried in oblivion, king-making and king-breaking. . . .

Jacobin grubs bursting into butterfly princes, dukes and counts, conscriptions . . . famine grinding the people into soldiers. . . . This is the present history of the times."[11] But, despite republican regrets, Adams was attracted to the Russian autocrat, whom he described as young, handsome, and elegant in person and affable and condescending in manner. Alexander was firm and consistent, although often accused of some indolence. Perhaps what appealed most to the American Minister was the Emperor's spirit of benevolence and humanity, for which he had an international reputation.

Alexander succeeded his tyrannical, unbalanced father, Czar Paul I, in 1801 when he was twenty-three years old. He was educated by Frederic C. de La Harpe, the Swiss republican who has been given the credit for Alexander's liberal ideas. Influential also were the young Czar's feelings about his father's assassination, an episode that caused him to be likened to Shakespeare's Hamlet. At the beginning of his reign, Alexander made some minor reforms, such as granting amnesty to political prisoners and exiles, abolishing torture, establishing the senate as the supreme high court, and repealing the ban of foreign books. However, though he promised sweeping measures, such as a constitution for Russia, other matters successfully delayed the project.

Adams was very likely influenced in his admiration of the Emperor by his decided pro-American policy, coupled with a resistance to British influence. Of his regard for America, John Quincy wrote, the Emperor displayed a mind "capable of appreciating distant objects and remote consequences."[12] In contrast, Napoleon continued to be offensive and harmful to America, probably because his character was not admired in the United States and he had no regard for a republic. Therefore Adams saw clearly that it was prudent for him to take advantage of Alexander's good will—"a century may not give us another."[13]

Napoleon's marriage to the Archduchess Marie Louise, eldest daughter of Emperor Francis of Austria, had Europe's "utter amazement," John Quincy reported. Count Klemens Von Metternich, the Austrian Minister, arranged it for the protection of Austria, and Napoleon accepted because he wanted an heir who would be legitimately royal. Though the marriage would seem to be fatal to British influence in Austria, the English government at this time refused a French peace offer. Alexander was very annoyed by the marriage alliance. Although he had been indifferent to Napoleon's idea of marrying his sister, the Russian Emperor disliked the suddenness with which the hopeless negotiations for the Russian princess's hand had been broken off and the haste with which the Austrian liaison had been arranged. The Russo-French Alliance was speedily moving on a collision course and the two chief operators were fully aware of it.

Alexander's displeasure with France was America's gain. The Danish government heeded Alexander's wishes and gave all despatch to settling the American claims.

During the winter, Count Romantzoff asked Adams if he had been informed that Aaron Burr was in Paris and had requested permission to come to Russia. The Count had replied to the former American Vice President that Russia did not encourage individuals who fled from the laws of their own country. If Burr wanted admission to Russia, he would have to apply through the Minister from the United States. Count Romantzoff told Adams that he had seen English newspaper accounts that revealed Burr's proposal for a separation of the American states. When turned down by Britain, it was said, he crossed the Channel and made a similiar proposal to France. All governments, the Count observed, were watching Burr's movements with suspicion.[14]

Early spring was heralded by the celebration of Easter, the most sacred holiday in the Russian calendar. The Adams family attended midnight services at the cathedral and the whole cycle of court visits required at this time. The custom of giving gifts particularly in the shape of eggs intrigued John Quincy. He recorded that the peasants presented real eggs, hardboiled and dyed red; persons of higher standing gave eggs of sugar, glass, gilt, wood, porcelain, and marble, often fashioned into cups and boxes. Servants presented eggs to masters and received a gift in return. Friends presented them to each other and then embraced. It was a strange custom for a New Englander whose culture rarely called for the exchange of gifts.

On May 12, 1810, the ice broke and at three o'clock that afternoon, the governor of St. Petersburg, as was the custom, passed in the first boat to announce the event to the Emperor and to present him with a glass of water in return for which he received 100 ducats. The summer season officially begun, the nobility and the wealthy left for their summer homes. Those who stayed in town had their double windows removed and enjoyed the long evenings. It stayed light until ten or eleven o'clock.

The opening of the Baltic renewed the diplomatic struggle between France and the United States. Caulaincourt, the French Ambassador, seemed to have all the advantages over his American counterpart. He was handsome, dignified, charming, and personally acceptable due to his ambassadorial rank. John Quincy, short, stout, stiff in manner, possessor of a very modest establishment, had the additional disadvantage of only being able to deal with the Emperor through his ministers because of his inferior rank. Consequently, Adams learned almost too late what the Frenchman was urging and fulminating. Yet, to his great surprise, John Quincy discovered that he was considered a person of great consequence at the Russian court. Alexander wanted products to flow in and out of Russia because the war with Turkey required a huge army and, with her depreciated currency, she needed foreign trade. Napoleon had no interest in Russia's predicament. He cared only about the success of his continental system, whose operation could cripple Russia and destroy her military aspirations.

The French Ambassador gave a splendid ball on May 23 to celebrate Napoleon's marriage. The Adamses were obliged to go since the imperial family would be present. The Emperor was exceedingly gracious, saying to Adams, who was bald, that he failed to recognize him on the street because he looked so different without his wig. Somehow, John Quincy construed the comment to mean that hereafter he was excused from wearing a wig, which he hated, at his future court appearances.

The Adams ladies were spectacularly noticed that night. The Emperor asked Levett Harris where Louisa was sitting and then tapped her on the shoulder to tell her that she must dance the next polonaise with him. Not knowing what to do next, she was relieved when a lady of the court told her that as soon as Alexander took his place for the dance, she must walk up alone and stand beside him. She did so, awkwardly, she thought, and danced a mercifully short polonaise. But the Emperor kept her with him, conversing about what she did not know, the acoustics in the room were so bad. Five minutes later, he bowed and retired. After some prompting from some official, she took her seat. When the music struck up again, Alexander approached Louisa to ask for a dance with her sister. Catherine, unaware of the protocol, chatted and laughed with the Emperor as if he were an American. His Imperial Majesty was so enchanted that he delayed Caulaincourt's supper twenty-five minutes to prolong the polonaise. Kitty's triumph was particularly great because she had never been presented at court.

John Quincy Adams's antagonists at home did not cease trying to keep his memory unpopular. The federalist papers copied, without comment, English newspaper accounts that Adams "is the meddling advocate for the exclusion of American vessels from the Russian ports." Abigail commented that the British party wanted the Russian mission to be as unpopular as possible. To which John Quincy answered that he was amused at the extracts that she sent him.

During the summer, Caulaincourt asked the Czar directly to close his ports to the Americans. He was refused but Alexander did agree to remain at war with England and to keep his ports closed to her ships. Though American trade continued to be a direct source of friction between the two Emperors, Napoleon was able to force Denmark, Prussia, and Mecklenburg to close their ports to United States shipping. Bonaparte harassed the United States further with orders that certificates granted by French consuls in the United States carried by American vessels in the Baltic were to be considered forgeries. The Czar was advised by Napoleon that no American trade existed.

Despite Napoleonic pressure and official ordinances accepting his dicta, John Quincy Adams informed the State Department that the need for commerce by the continental powers was stronger than the power of France, whose measure of force was met with a measure of fraud to counterbalance it. All the merchants in every European port were with the British. When Adams heard about the repeal of Napoleon's Berlin and Milan decrees, he wrote to Robert Smith that it was the termination of Napoleon's beloved continental system.

Separation from their two older sons was a constant source of unhappiness to John Quincy and Louisa which they tried to assuage with letters and gifts. In May, Adams sent three packs of French playing cards and histories of Rome and France to George and a picture book to John. Tom Adams, who was in charge of his nephews' education, received lengthy letters of advice from the anxious parents. Apart from languages and classical studies, George must learn drawing to improve his taste, and fencing to quicken his eye and strengthen his wrist. J.Q.A. also urged that George be taught to shoot and, most important, "be encouraged in nothing delicate or effeminate. . . . If he goes into Boston to see a play, let him walk, skate in winter and by all means learn to swim this summer. I know there is danger in all these things but it is a world of danger in which we live, and I want my boys to be familiarized as soon as possible with its face." In turn, Tom tried to relieve the anxieties of the absent parents by sending frequent progress reports. John's rapid improvement in reading, his father wrote, was "A banquet to my soul." However, he commented sagely: "The best of all education I know is but a lottery, and without a corresponding disposition in the child, all that you can do for him is but labor lost."[15]

During the summer, the Emperor told the American Minister that he wanted Nelson, his Black servant, to enter the Russian service as a member of the Imperial family's corps of fourteen Blacks, an élite guard who took an oath to remain permanently and to wear Turkish dress. Nelson was intrigued by the benefits, such as a carriage and four always at his service and the remains of the desserts from the imperial table. The Adamses agreed to let him go but in a few years Nelson pined away in his novel surroundings and died.

The mild weather and the quiet, with the fashionable away in their summer palaces, allowed the American Minister to work on his study of weights and measures most of the time. Letters from America arrived frequently now and were promptly answered. Abigail, whom John Quincy called the "most constant and most frequent correspondent that I have beyond the seas," was the recipient of his most open letters. To her he could speak freely about the things that pleased him, such as the review in *Anthology* of his *Lectures on Rhetoric*, which praised his work while it made war on his politics. He enclosed, with some modesty, a very flattering account of his service at the Russian court which Count Romantzoff had sent to the Russian Minister in Washington to be communicated to President James Madison. He wanted her to see it also, because it was most complimentary to John Adams and it was a good answer to the allegation in the Boston *Centinel*, which said "how insignificant a figure our townsman was making at St. Petersburg."[16] In reality, not only was the American Minister treated with attention by the Emperor but also American ships were welcomed in Russian ports while being excluded by all the neighbors.

With some misgiving, J.Q.A. recorded the first snow on October 2. This first sign of winter was also the signal for the beginning of the social season. The Adamses, including young Charles, went to the German theater, which J.Q.A. and Charles, who understood the language, enjoyed, but Louisa, with no German, found boring. The Adams family, including Kitty, were being treated with unusual honor by Alexander, receiving invitations to events that were usually restricted to Ambassadors. Now that the Emperor was back in the city, he and J.Q.A. met walking on the mall in front of the Admiralty and spoke formally but with friendliness about the weather and their health. Alexander said that physically his health was fine but his difficulty was "le moral."[17]

Abigail, having read frequent complaints about the devastating expense of her son's mission to St. Petersburg, wrote to the President about it. He answered that he had not been informed by the State Department that Adams wished to return home, but that he instructed the Secretary of State to inform Adams that if his personal sacrifices were too great and he felt it necessary to retire, he would not "in retiring from them impair the sentiments which led to his appointment."[18]

James Madison wrote to Adams that he hoped that he had reconciled himself to continuing in his station and that the urgency expressed in his mother's letter was hers and not his. There would be difficulties if he were to leave, such as explaining the move to the Emperor. However, he sent documents necessary for his departure but hoped that he would continue his "valuable services."

Before the last ship was landlocked until the following June, John Quincy wrote to Robert Smith advocating the appointment of an American consul for the port of Gothenburg. He took the opportunity to suggest further that the consular system needed evaluating so that some of the common abuses, such as selling American papers to ships of other nations, could be avoided. These temptations, Adams analyzed, were the result of not paying a salary to the consul. Some of the consuls did not stay in residence when their own businesses called them away so that sometimes they were away from their posts for years, or forever. Among his suggestions, Adams included establishment of standing instructions from the President, a residence requirement, and an agreement to keep in touch with Washington.

The good will of the Czar's government toward the United States reached out in all directions. The problem of Russian interests in the northwestern area in North America looked like a source of friction when, early in 1810, Russia demanded that Americans cease their traffic with the Indians, particularly in such items as rifles and firearms. The Russian-American Company also started some agitation over the boundary, claiming that it was the mouth of the Columbia River. John Quincy expected difficulties but in the fall Count Romantzoff voluntarily informed Adams that he was ready to fix a boundary. And then added quizzically that Russian attachment to the United States was "obstinate."

Once more, a good part of the reason for the pro-American policy was the hardening of Alexander's anti-French bias. On the first of December he told Caulaincourt that he refused to shut his ports against colonial produce. The merchants of St. Petersburg had been appealing to him for a prohibition against French luxury items in order to stop the gold drain that was depreciating the currency. The Czar acquiesced and, in mid-December, issued a ukase very favorable to American shipping. Napoleon, furious, recalled Caulaincourt, which, Adams told the Secretary of State, was an indication of the point of crisis to which the two countries were coming.

The rift between France and Russia was not "of general notoriety." J. Q. Adams sent details in cipher to the State Department in which he mentioned the arrest of a Russian general, an aide of the Emperor who was suspected of having furnished the French Ambassador with Russian military secrets. The Czar was angry also at Napoleon's annexation of Westphalian cities, which stripped the Duke of Oldenburg, father-in-law of his sister, Grand Duchess Catherine. But in spite of these signs, Adams did not think that war between the Emperors was imminent. He considered 1811 as the year of preparation for both sides.

In the midst of the gathering war clouds, the Corps Diplomatique continued to entertain and be entertained. There were changes, however, in the composition of the groups. As John Quincy said, the diplomatic corps "of all the moveable sand banks in the world of mutability, is perhaps the most given to change."[19] The shining light, Caulaincourt, after three years in St. Petersburg was replaced by Count Lauristan. The former Ambassador was in Paris in disgrace, charged with pushing French demands inadequately and becoming too pro-Russian.

At this time, Adams was thinking seriously of returning home the following year to direct his children's education. Not satisfied with the schoolmaster's report of George's progress, he wanted Tom and the President to examine the child once a month in Latin and Greek. They must not only test his memory but also his mind, because a child must be taught to think. Domestic matters were also pressing. Though the Adamses had found an apartment, it was costing entirely too much. In order to cut down, John Quincy arranged for a restaurant to furnish dinners instead of continuing to employ a steward, a cook, two scullions, a porter, and a man to make fires. This arrangement lessened the bills from the baker, milkman, butcher, greengrocer, poulterer, and fishmonger, and cut down the bills for coffee, tea, sugar, wax, and candles, upon all of which items the cook and steward made a profit. Adams complained that "among the losses occasioned by it the most valuable is the loss of time swallowed up in the business of such drudgery."[20]

Mrs. John Quincy Adams was even more unhappy than her husband. Although the Emperor had shown extraordinary attention to her and to Kitty, she missed the children constantly. A polite exchange on the public walks with Alexander I did not mitigate her constant worry about George and John and her anxiety about her pregnancy. She was fearful of bearing a child in this strange land, particularly when the constant rumors of war with France increased.

Gossip that the American Minister was planning to leave Russia spread through the Russian court. On New Year's Day the Emperor mentioned it to Adams, who denied the rumor. But ten days later he did tell Count Romantzoff that he had permission to go home for personal reasons, but, in any case, would not leave before summer. The Count urged him to stay, and when the Czar met the American at the winter palace he also urged him to stay.

The winter was made exceptionally long because there had been no news from home later than July 1810. When the mails came through in June, Adams found a number of surprises. James Monroe was now his new chief, replacing Robert Smith, and there was an appointment for him to the United States Supreme Court. Even though he knew that accepting the appointment would please his parents, John Quincy could not accept. He wrote to the President that although he had been trained as a lawyer, its studies had never been congenial to him. Therefore, he felt unqualified for the post just as he had in 1801 when he was offered the vacancy on the Massachusetts Supreme Court. In any case, he would be unable to leave for the United States during the present year and, if the President wished to terminate his mission, he would remain in Russia as a private citizen.

John Adams was told the real reason for his son's objections to judicial office. He was dissatisfied with the administration of justice in both the state and federal courts. Substantive justice was sacrificed to form, John Quincy charged, and, besides, he had "heretical opinions" on the merits of common law "so idolized" by English lawyers, and the "parrots" who repeated their words in America. Remembering his experience with the John Smith report, he worried that his views would not be well received. "I have not weight and influence enough in my country to bring it over to my opinions, and I have too much independence of spirit to renounce them myself," he said.[21]

During the summer the free flow of letters from home delighted the Adamses. John's first letter arrived, meriting an immediate response from his father, who told him that he must learn not only so that his parents and friends would love him but also because it would be better when he grew up. Charles, he told the youngster, was now out of petticoats, was learning to read at home, and spoke German better than English and English better than French. But there was tragic news from America also. Nancy Hellen was dead in childbirth, along with a stillborn infant. The shock almost caused Louisa to miscarry but she recovered gradually.

Adams correctly surmised that Monroe's appointment was due to his attitude toward England, which was much more reasonable than Smith's had been. The new Secretary of State believed that of the two irritants Napoleon was the greater. However, though Adams wanted to escape war, he saw clearly that a Britain blown up by her successes in Spain and Portugal and elated over the unexpected recovery of her King's health would only redouble her insolence to America. When questioned directly by Count Romantzoff about Anglo-American relations, John Quincy parried with the statement that it depended on England. Earlier, his Imperial Majesty, on two accidental encounters with the American Minister, had asked to be informed of the precise state of relations between the two countries.

Russia's war against Turkey was not going very well at this time, if St. Petersburg's rumor, which claimed that she would restore everything that she had captured in return for peace, could be believed. The governor of Odessa, who came to the capital to discuss a peace treaty, wanted to have included in it permission from the Porte for American ships to navigate the Black Sea. Not having any authorization for such talks, Adams wrote to Monroe for instructions.

The Massachusetts elections were of great interest to the Americans in St. Petersburg because the federalist politicians talked so openly of their readiness for a dissolution of the Union and their threats to resist the laws. Consequently, the British calculated that if they made war with the United States they would have the cooperation of the Massachusetts federalists. John Quincy, very disturbed, wrote to Abigail. If the federalist party was not put down as completely in Massachusetts as in the rest of the country, the Union would be gone and "we shall have an endless multitude of insignificant clans and tribes at eternal war with one another for a rock or a fishpond, the sport . . . of European masters and oppressors," he observed.[22]

The summer visitors from America came in a continuous stream. They enlivened the social scene and kept the Adamses informed. Some of them were naturalized Americans, most of them natives of the northern and eastern states as far south as Virginia. About ninety American ships reached Cronstadt by the end of July and twenty or thirty more sailed into Archangel and Riga. Americans enjoyed a monopoly of Baltic trade, which suited Alexander because he got sugar and coffee at half cost and sold his hemp and naval stores at double.[23]

When the house that Adams had rented was bought by the Emperor, he was told that he would have to vacate it by mid-August. House-hunting was discouraging because of high rents but the family settled on a summer home owned by Count Tatischeff, beautifully situated on Apothecaries Island, about three miles from the Summer Garden Gate, within the bounds of the city but on the banks of the Neva. They moved on John Quincy's birthday, with Louisa's usual complaint that it was slow work because her husband "reads a page in every book that passes through his hands."[24] Though the house had a splendid view, Louisa fretted that the windows of the palace looked out on their house and grounds.

On July 26, the fourteenth anniversary of his marriage, John Quincy recorded in his *Diary* that he had enjoyed more felicity than befell most from that institution. Its greatest problem had been Louisa's poor health. "Our union has not been without its trials or dissensions or differences in taste and opinions on domestic economy or the education of children." Both of them, he admitted, were quick-tempered, he, admittedly, sometimes harsh. But Louisa had always been "a faithful and affectionate wife, and a careful, tender, indulgent and watchful mother to our children all of whom she nursed herself."[25] Louisa, who suffered so cruelly from a sense of her own unworthiness, would have been relieved to read the passages.

Although Adams had the idea that Monroe wanted to replace him with Robert Smith, he continued to bombard the State Department with information and advice from St. Petersburg. He assured his chief that the Czar was attached to the United States because of his natural generosity and the magnanimity of his character. It might be a good idea, he suggested, for the President, in his message to Congress, to refer to Russia's regard for American rights and make some complimentary personal reference to the Emperor. "We need not dread French influence on our trade with Russia," he said.[26] As a postscript, Adams added that the French Ambassador candidly admitted his hope that the United States and Great Britain would go to war, a catastrophe that would benefit his country.

On August 12, Louisa Adams gave birth to a daughter. The baby was christened a few weeks later by Reverend London King Pitt, the English chaplain, with Levett Harris as her godfather and Madame Bezerra, the wife of the Portuguese Minister, and Mrs. Annette Krehmer her godmothers. She was named Louisa Catherine at her father's insistence but contrary to her mother's wishes. There had been some thought of asking the Emperor to stand sponsor but John Quincy decided that America would not tolerate it. After the brief ceremony, the witnesses, the members of the diplomatic corps, and other guests stayed for dinner and an evening of cards. John Quincy played whist with some of his guests and reflected on the superiority of the Congregational Church's proper and rational baptismal rite over that of the Church of England just practiced on his daughter.

Reading four or five chapters from the Bible was a ritual that Adams performed every morning immediately upon rising from bed, the most suitable manner to start the day, he advised his son, George Washington Adams. This advice was given in a series of letters that he wrote to George to show him the best way to derive the most advantage from Bible reading. If he did not understand everything in the letters, his father wrote, he should ask his grandparents, but in any event put them in a file for a few years and then read them again. John Quincy worked very hard on the composition of the letters, which were published in 1848, but feared that the limitations of his own ignorance on the subjects made his ideas emerge undigested and confused and that he had, indeed, taken on more than he could execute.

The charming summer house from which, in the warm weather when the windows were open the Emperor's band could be heard, had to be abandoned in mid-September. Not the least of its delights to Adams was its proximity to the country seat of Count Stroganoff, a collector of antiquities, among whose treasures was the supposed tomb of Achilles or Homer that had been brought from Greece.

Without consulting Louisa, Adams found a house which she deemed too small and disliked because it was situated in a vulgar and unpopular part of the city. Its only virtue was its cheapness. "Debt or meanness is the penalty imposed by the salary of an American Minister," she grumbled.[27]

The winter of 1811–1812 set in exceptionally early. From the last of October, the river was so completely frozen over that it was passable on foot. It had been a profitable year for American trade, with 139 vessels registered under the American flag arrived at Cronstadt. But the European situation looked ominous. The American Minister wrote to Monroe that negotiations between the two Emperors were at a standstill and it could not be hoped that war would be postponed another summer. The Russians could, however, expect a decisive victory over Turkey very soon.

The Emperor and Adams continued to meet on their walks and sometimes Louisa and Charles were along. Alexander exchanged the formal comments about the weather usual between an autocrat and a mere commoner but sometimes added slightly more personal comments about young Charles's education, and, on one occasion, asked Louisa the details about her confinement. At his birthday celebration, at which the Empress appeared with the most astounding profusion of diamonds and other precious stones, Alexander noticed that Adams was wigless. Adams said that he had his Majesty's permission. Alexander replied graciously that it was not as showy but more convenient to go without it. He then wanted to know why the American Minister did not dance. John Quincy replied that he had given it up because he was too old.

"Does your Majesty dance?" Adams asked.

"No, I say, like you, I am too old," the Emperor answered.[28]

The threat of an American war "in which we could gain nothing and could not fail to lose" worried Adams, who hoped that Congress would preserve the United States from such a disaster. He believed that if his country could find the patience, both France and England would feel a compelling need for American commerce. "Their necessities will do more for the restoration of our rights than we could do by any exertion of our own forces," he observed. But his hopes were as vain as Count Romantzoff's that Napoleon's word could be depended on.[29]

St. Petersburg had a spell of cold and foggy weather in February that caused a phenomenon often talked about. A thick fog was formed due to the smoke from fires of the city settling over it and totally obscuring the sun, which continued for three or four hours. But the bitter cold did not stop the walks on the Neva. One day the Emperor and Adams discussed the value of flannel as a protection against the cold. The emperor disliked the fabric because it was irritating. The American said that he was used to wearing it in the winter and if he should leave it off he would die. Alexander explained that many Russian physicians thought it was a bad thing to wear. The two sometimes talked more seriously. The Czar informed Adams that he would not start a war with France but that he expected to be attacked. In answer to Adams's hope that war could be avoided, Alexander replied that he did not think that it could be but hoped that it would not come to St. Petersburg.[30]

In April, two days before Alexander left the capital to review his troops marshalled on the frontiers, Count Romantzoff asked to see Adams to ask him again the precise state of Anglo-American relations. Since he had not heard from home yet, Adams could only give his own opinion. The United States, he said, would protect its right of neutrality by war if it came to it but he did not anticipate war at the moment. Then the Count left the city to join the Emperor for negotiations, which he thought would result in a settlement of differences between his country and France. Count Lauriston spoke just as positively to the American Minister, who believed neither of them about amity between the two empires. Since Prussia and Austria had both allied themselves to France, Adams told Monroe, Russia would be facing a tremendous combination of power and could hardly emerge without loss.

By April's end, John Quincy was convinced by his reading of articles and despatches in European newspapers that war between the United States and England was imminent. He altered his thinking to accommodate the situation and insisted that since England's government had refused the United States its neutrality, for his country to forego the right of navigating the ocean "would degrade us from the rank and rights of an independent nation."[31] Personally, he was heartsick that his plans to have his older sons brought to St. Petersburg in the summer would have to be abandoned.

Though Napoleon had bullied Prussia and Austria into an uneasy alliance, the two countries were never ideologically proper partners for the Corsican. They were still united with Russia on the issue of the partition of Poland, whose resurrection as a country was their mutual bugbear. Nevertheless, now Alexander had to prepare for the conflict. He lured Sweden into an offensive and defensive alliance in April and, in May, presided over the Treaty of Bucharest, which ended the Russo-Turkish war. But the United States was displeased with the Czar's July Treaty of Alliance with Great Britain.

Shortly before the event, the French had invaded Russian territory and Alexander had announced to his people that he would never make peace as long as an enemy remained in arms upon his territory.[32] In response, the French Ambassador in St. Petersburg applied for a passport and, after three applications, received it. No news came through for the first few weeks of the war so that nothing was known of the movements of the armies except for handbills which reported that the Russians had been retreating in order to unite their forces. Adams received as a legacy from the departing Ambassadors whose countries were at war with Russia the archives of the French Embassy and of the Dutch and Wurtemberg legations. The French papers were stored in a large wooden chest, the Dutch in an equally large trunk, and the Wurtemberg records in a small box covered with oilcloth about the size of a writing desk. Shortly after these encumbrances were safely stored, a note with a trunk containing the Bavarian archives arrived for Adams.

Though Congress had declared war on Great Britain on June 18, it was not until August 6 that John Quincy saw an account of it in the New York *Commercial Advertiser*. He had hoped until then that the revocation of the British Orders in Council would reverse the tide towards war because now that Russia and England were allied, he felt that he was in a touchy diplomatic situation. However, Monroe made it quite clear that the United States wanted to confine hostilities to England and that the Czar's arrangements with her should not affect the friendly Russo-American relations.

The Emperor was equally disappointed by the Anglo-American

war. He had planned to solve the problems of commerce with his British alliance and now saw the benefit dissipated. Consequently, in September, Count Romantzoff presented John Quincy with the Czar's offer to mediate between the two countries. Taken aback, Adams said that he could not answer for his government but that the war was England's blame, although it was injurious to all. But he agreed to communicate the offer to the State Department if Lord Cathcart, the British Minister, would give security to his papers so that they could reach America. The novel proposal would have to wait formal responses from both sides.

Early in September, Adams received a summons to call on famous Madame de Staël, who was staying at the Hotel de l'Europe and wished to discuss a matter concerning America with its Minister. He arrived at 4 P.M. as requested, to find her holding a salon and speaking animatedly to Cathcart. When she saw John Quincy, she stopped her conversation to welcome him and "for about half an hour [I] had the opportunity to admire the brilliancy of her genius as it sparkled incessantly in her conversation."[33] Her problem concerned lands that she owned in New York State on Lake Ontario and stocks in United States funds. She asked how she could collect the interest while there was a war between the United States and England. Madame de Staël, who said that she admired John Adams's *Defence of the American Constitution,* was also a great partisan of Great Britain and so listened carefully but with no comment to Adams's explanations of such British abuses as Orders in Council and press gangs. She saw the American Minister again the next day and once more discussed politics with him for a few hours. "I found her better conversant with rhetoric than with logic," Adams commented to his father. Having incurred the enmity of Napoleon because she would not praise him adequately in her writings, Madame de Staël was on her way to Stockholm for a kind of voluntary exile.

The Adams baby, shortly after being weaned in late summer, sickened while trying to cut five or six teeth at once. A violent dysentery with a high fever developed into severe convulsions. The acute illness persisted for four weeks, during which little Louisa endured terrible suffering. On September 15, she died. Louisa, who had just heard of her mother's death, was prostrated with grief. She adored the child and had wanted a daughter for a long time. John Quincy, too, was tormented with sadness and guilt. He brooded over the passages in the Bible that implied, though indirectly, that the

death of infant children was sometimes inflicted as chastisement for
the transgressions of their parents. "If her long and racking agonies
here were an atonement for my offences, (for her own they could
not be), I may be permitted to hope that her happiness in immorality will be proportioned to the rigour of her destiny upon Earth,"
he wrote to his mother.[34] The Emperor and Count Romantzoff sent
their condolences.

There was no official news about Moscow in the Russian papers as
late as September 24, but Levett Harris told Adams that the Russian
army had retired behind Moscow and surrendered the city to the
French. Rumors about Moscow spread, but the people were afraid
to talk openly because several citizens had been made to sweep the
streets as punishment for repeating the Moscow story. On September 29, Moscow's occupation by Napoleon's army was announced
with the explanation that it was a circumstance of trifling importance to the outcome of the war. Adams agreed, because he saw that
the triumph of the French army was a mirage and that in reality
their position was desperate. They had entered an all but deserted
city, which was consumed by fires that had been started at several
points, particularly in the grain magazines. The whole district
around the city had been denuded of food and horses. Napoleon, it
was rumored, wanted to negotiate with the Russian Emperor, who
was not interested. The invader was now in a time of danger and
was involved in the kind of warfare to which he was unaccustomed,
Adams observed.

The war interfered with J.Q.A.'s plans to be free from the Russian mission in the spring. Although he wrote to Monroe that if the
President wanted to commit the mediation negotiations to another
person he would acquiesce, John Quincy implied that he wanted the
position for himself. A more pressing problem was the possibility
that the Russian court would move from the capital to the interior
of the country. In such a case, the foreign ministers would be expected to accompany them, which the American was prepared to do
unless the safety of his family was at stake.

Public relations in an autocratic society fascinated the American
Minister with the enormity of their deception. Since the war began,
official bulletins reported an uninterrupted series of Russian victories, which were officially celebrated with Te Deums, illuminations, the firing of cannon, and bell ringing, even when the French
armies advanced to Moscow. This blatant deception gave rise to

rumors of defeat and disaster that were even more unfounded than the reports of victories.

Realistically, Russia expected to be the victor. She claimed a superior army and the advantage of being on home territory. Napoleon, in enemy terrain, was hemmed in by Russian armies over whose bodies he would have to advance or retreat, and, two thousand miles from home, half of his forces were lost already. He was further handicapped by foreign allies whose armies awaited his first defeat in order to turn away from him. Emperor Alexander was convinced that his best tactic was delay.

Adams's narrative talents were employed fortuitously in relating the dramatic events of Napoleon's disastrous Moscow expedition. John Quincy wrote: "After six weeks in Moscow, he [Napoleon] found himself with a starving and almost naked army, eight hundred miles from his frontiers and exposed to a Russian winter with an army before him superior to his own and a country behind already ravaged by him and seeking only vengeance upon him and his followers." On November 30, Adams added that the Corsican was more than a month into his defeat and, if he still lived, had scarcely the ruins of an army. Thousands of his men died of famine, thousands from the extremity of the season, and, in the past ten days, according to reports, more than 30,000 surrendered after only token resistance. The French cavalry was in even worse straits than the infantry, most of the artillery was lost, and the ammunition blown up. Napoleon would probably be captured shortly, and if he escaped "would be hardly safer at the Tuileries than in Russia." His allies would not only desert him, but there would be revolution in the satellite countries, Adams predicted. "His race is now run, and his own term of punishment has commenced."[35]

At the cathedral of Kazan, the American Minister attended the Te Deum for the defeat of the enemy and watched with faint disgust while the Emperor and the imperial family prostrated themselves before the miraculous image of the Virgin. He approved, however, when upon leaving the church Alexander was greeted by the tumultuous shouts of the populace.

In early December, at a dinner at Count Romantzoff's, there was universal rejoicing. Within the last ten days, the Russian armies had taken forty to fifty thousand prisoners with their equipment. There had been nothing like it since the days of Xerxes, John Quincy commented. One of the most interesting aspects of the victory was the behavior of the Russian peasants, whom Napoleon expected would either welcome him as a liberator or, in the crisis, demand their freedom from the Emperor. Instead, the church and the priesthood had convinced them that Napoleon was, indeed, the anti-Christ.

The Russians were disappointed that the French Emperor had succeeded in evading personal capture. They had to be content with the final estimate of the extent of his failure—about nine-tenths of his invading army, according to Adams, "were prisoners or food for worms." At least 100,000 former Napoleonic soldiers were in the Czar's power. "From Moscow to Prussia, 800 miles of road have been strewed with his artillery, baggage, wagons, ammunition chests, dead and dying men, whom he has been forced to abandon to their fate . . . the two Russian generals who have conquered Napoleon and all his Marshals are *General Famine* and *General Frost*."[36] The opportunity to be such a near-witness to an epic made Adams ponder even more fondly on the advantages of peace. Bonaparte, he said, exemplified for him the saying: "On what foundation stands the warrior's pride!"[37]

His conviction that Alexander wanted peace increased Adams's belief in the Czar of Russia's "personal virtues." He told Monroe that he believed that the Emperor was sincere in his quest for universal peace and in his assertion that he did not seek the enlargement of his dominions. Proof of his sincerity was his rejection of a birthday celebration as inappropriate in the midst of the country's sufferings.

Attempting to explain the American declaration of war against Britain to Russia's satisfaction, Adams told Count Romantzoff about the evils of the press gang and the attraction of the American merchant marine to British sailors. American vessels offered better food, better pay, and more humane conditions than their English counterparts. Therefore, the British lost English sailors and then more than made up the difference by stealing men from American ships. As for the progress of the mediation offer, the Count revealed that the English had neither accepted nor rejected it but intimated that the United States would reject it. Part of the British delay was based on their expectation that the coming presidential election would bring peace. If New York's De Witt Clinton, the federalist candidate, defeated Madison, their assumption was that peace would be made on their terms and, John Quincy commented, "the *maritime rights* of men stealing will be sanctioned forever."[38]

One of Adams's missions during the winter was to present the proposal of Robert Fulton, the inventor of the steamship, who wanted the Emperor to grant him the exclusive right to construct and use such ships on all the Russian rivers for a period of twenty years under the condition that in three years time he would have the first of these ships in use. The advantage that Fulton offered, the American Minister told Count Romantzoff, was that navigation in steamships eliminated dependence on winds and currents.

By the end of November, Adams wrote to Fulton that Alexander granted his request on the condition that it was worded so as to make clear that the first boat must be ready in three years. He also explained that he could not accept any remuneration for his part in arranging the deal because it was his duty and pleasure to promote the just interests of American citizens.

In his annual New Year's greetings to his beloved parents, John Quincy commented on the severe Russian cold—seventeen straight days with below-zero weather. He was physically and spiritually sick of the climate and, he observed, it "is certainly contrary to the course of nature for men of the south to invade the Regions of the North—Napoleon should have thought of that."[39] It had not been a happy year because of the death of little Louisa Catherine. In an interesting note in his *Diary* that suggested a connection with the loss of his daughter, Adams wrote that religious sentiments had become "daily more constantly habitual to his mind. They are perhaps too often seen in this journal. . . ."[40]

The winter of 1813 continued to be the most rigorous the Adamses had yet endured. But it was lightened by the engagement of Louisa's sister Catherine Johnson to Nabby's son, William Steuben Smith. They planned to be married in a few weeks and then to return to America the following summer.

The American war preyed on Adams's mind. He believed that impressment was the chief cause for it, that a war need not have been started over such an issue, and that peace might be made without resolving "the sailor's cause." He was disturbed also by the news from Britain of the election of America's enemy, George Canning from Liverpool, a city whose trade with the United States had flourished for nearly twenty years. Canning fulfilled Adams's fears when his first speech included the question as to why in six months of war the United States's seaports had not been destroyed.[41]

Though Russia had sustained a brilliant victory in the winter campaign, she had lost the most lives and the most property. Napoleon's friends thought that his "transcendental genius" would still prevail, but John Quincy disagreed, calling him fortune's "cast-off favorite."[42] Alexander was now at Wilna but had not carried his Chancellor with him, which gave rise to the rumor that Romantzoff's influence was running out.

All the news about the progress of the American war came to St. Petersburg through the British, who spread the idea that, in America, the war was regarded as "Mr. Madison's war" and that his opponents wanted to stop it. Consequently, the British were very cooperative about giving permission to Americans coming from the rest of Europe to land in England and to embark from there. The English newspapers also enjoyed spreading the story that the American Minister to France, Joel Barlow, left Paris for Wilna to go along with two other foreign ministers of governments allied with France. Adams denied that this was Barlow's motivation. Actually, Madison sent Barlow to France to intercede with Napoleon for a more reasonable attitude toward American commerce. He had been met with evasion in Paris but Bassano, Napoleon's Minister of Foreign Affairs, had informed him that the French Emperor would meet him for discussions in Poland. So Barlow, with his nephew as his secretary, had set out on the long, dangerous journey to Wilna. After Napoleon's defeat at the Beresina, Barlow, who stayed at Wilna from mid-November to December 5, in the hopes of having his promised meeting, gave up and started back to Paris. He was taken ill with a fever and lung inflammation on the road and, in a little village near Cracow, unable to get adequate medical attention, died. At the outbreak of the war, Prince Kurakin, then the Russian Ambassador to France, had entrusted the Russian archives to Barlow's care. Now Adams was asked to find out what happened to them. John Quincy felt that this was his responsibility as the only accredited Minister of the United States in Europe and so sent a representative to Vienna to try to find out about Barlow's death and the missing archives.

In March, Alexander's mediation offer was presented by Daschkoff, the Russian Minister in Washington to Secretary of State Monroe. Madison was in a difficult position because if he did not meet the peace offer, every home faction that opposed the war would be stirred up, but were he to show enthusiasm for it it might weaken the American military position. He decided, finally, not to wait until he heard from England but to send over commissioners at once. Secretary of the Treasury Albert Gallatin, whose enemies at home were making his job intolerable, requested that he be sent to Russia as one of the commissioners. He believed that his only future lay in diplomacy and this might be a good place to begin. Madison was willing to risk the censure resultant from acceding to his request because he thought that Albert Gallatin would make an excellent negotiator. His other choices were J. Q. Adams and James A. Bayard.

News that Madison had been re-elected reached St. Petersburg in late March along with the easing of the weather. That Elbridge Gerry was the new Vice President came as a complete surprise to the American Minister. The Russians were in the midst of Lent, theaters were closed, no balls or assemblies were allowed, and only concerts were permitted among the pleasurable amusements. During the first and last weeks of Lent, fasting was so vigorous that the people lived on bread and dried mushrooms. John Quincy informed Abigail that the Russian peasant believed murder to be a crime for which atonement was possible but there would be none for eating animal food at Lent. The orthodox religion again repelled the Puritan Adams when he saw the two Empresses prostrate themselves before an old picture called a miraculous image of the Virgin Mary in gratitude for the victory of the Russian troops at Berlin.

Charles and Louisa had both had a miserable winter, suffering continually from the bitter cold. Adams fretted about his absent sons, now at Hingham Academy about five miles from Quincy. Tom was requested to urge George to write more regularly and to be made aware that he must prepare seriously for college by devoting himself to his Latin and Greek. He must have a more regular and complete education than his own, John Quincy reminded Tom. His sons, he hoped, would be more accomplished scholars than their father.

John Adams had heard of John Quincy's appointment to the peace commission through a letter from Monroe which stated that the Minister to Russia "has obtained the entire approbation of the President." Monroe also mentioned that in case of peace with Great Britain, the mission to London would be offered to John Quincy. However, it was very painful for the aging ex-President to advise his son that he must not refuse a share in the peace negotiations. "My first wish *is* that you return to me," he said, "but I cannot be so selfish."[43]

When the orders arrived from the State Department, Adams was informed that Gallatin would be at the head of the peace negotiations because of his top-ranking position as a member of the President's Cabinet, but Adams would be the head of the commission for a treaty of commerce with Russia as the accredited American Minister there. Adams received $13,500—$4,500 applicable to his salary as Minister to Russia, the remainder for an outfit for the extraordinary mission.[44]

English newspapers, John Quincy's source of news, carried the story that Daschkoff offered the Russian mediation to Madison and was accepted in early June. The British paper predicted that the British would refuse, a judgment with which Romantzoff agreed. Adams was skeptical also that Gallatin and Bayard were the chosen commissioners. He could not see Gallatin spared from his duties as Secretary of the Treasury, and Bayard and Gallatin had always been so opposed to each other politically that he was doubtful that they would be joined in a commission. Count Romantzoff answered wisely that in the American form of government such a pair would be reasonable.

John Quincy saw that he was wrong when he read in the *National Intelligencer* that the two men had left for Russia on the first of May. At the same time he learned that the British had refused the mediation, saying that their differences with the United States involved "certain principles of the internal government of England . . . of a nature which they did not think suitable to be settled by a mediation."[45] Since the mediation was cancelled, Adams speculated that Madison had given orders to one of the commissioners to succeed him and the other to go to some post—France, Count Romantzoff suggested.

The burial of Field Marshal Kutuzov Smolensky was a magnificent spectacle. Adams took Louisa and Charles to the Kazan Church to see the preparations for the ceremony and on June 5 the American delegation, consisting of Adams and William Smith, stood for four hours through the funeral ceremony, during which the prince was buried in the wall of the church. Admiral Kutuzov, the prince's nephew, was so moved that he had a violent, almost fatal asthma attack after performing the last duty to the corpse.

Most of July, John Quincy waited anxiously for Gallatin and Bayard to arrive at St. Petersburg. News came that they had reached Elsinore and, with it, the first official information that John Quincy was one of the peace negotiators under the Emperor's mediation plan. Levett Harris was appointed Secretary of the Legation. On the 21st, the two commissioners arrived, having been delayed by the east wind prevailing in the North Sea and the Baltic, carrying a cargo of letters and despatches from the United States.

Officially informed that he was not being replaced, Adams told Romantzoff that he was staying and that William Crawford was going to be the Minister to France. He detected some coldness in the Count's manner, which he attributed to the diminution of the Russian's prestige with the Czar. Alexander was absent from the capital with the army fighting Napoleon and, significantly, had taken with him Count Nesselrode. Romantzoff's unpopularity was supposed to have been caused by his strong views on neutral rights and his unfriendliness to England. The mediation, a favorite idea of Romantzoff's, having been given the cold shoulder by the British government, the presence of the American commissioners was an embarrassment to Romantzoff. The envoys, aware of the Count's ebbing fortunes, hated to remain in the capital to aggravate their friend's position. But Romantzoff was staunch in his pro-mediation position and, when the Americans arrived, he wrote to the Emperor suggesting a renewal of the mediation offer to England and, further, did his best to make the Americans comfortable.

John Quincy, in his role as chief negotiator for a treaty of commerce with Russia, drafted a proposal in French and sent it to Romantzoff. Bayard, immediately difficult, wanted the document written in English before he would deal with it but, after some discussion, they agreed to a mutually acceptable note. The inherent difficulty of the commission method became obvious at once when it took a week for the three men to do a job that one of them would have accomplished in two hours. "In the multitude of counsellors there is safety, but there is not despatch," Adams commented.

The envoys were pleasantly surprised that the Emperor replied to the Chancellor's request by directing him to advise Count Lieven to renew the Emperor's mediation proposal. When Romantzoff read the draft of his message to the commissioners, Gallatin objected to some of the wording, which was immediately changed. The quibble was over the word "suspend" in regard to impressment rather than "abandon," the heart of the negotiation according to the Secretary of the Treasury.

Except for John Quincy, the American commissioners were not given a definitive answer and the Senate confirmations of the appointments had not arrived. War news from America was particularly negative while reports of Massachusetts opposition to it were unsettling.

A possible link with Alexander was General Moreau, a friend of the elder Adams and of Albert Gallatin, who was in St. Petersburg on his way to join the Russian Emperor at Prague. He had decided to leave the service of France because he was an anti-Bonapartist and promised to put in a good word for the American commission. However, he was mortally wounded in the battle at the gates of Dresden and it was Adams's sad duty to attend church services for him in October.

The English delay meant that by the time her answer came, if it came, ice would have closed down the Russian ports and closed the American commission in with it. An unexpected upset changed plans further. Gallatin was turned down by the Senate, who approved the appointments of Adams and Bayard. Now the Secretary of the Treasury felt free to devise his own schemes to further the possibility of arranging peace. His idea of going himself to Alexander's headquarters was discouraged vigorously and successfully by Adams, but he was determined to stop off in England on his way home to see what he could do. Bayard decided to go with him.

Great Britain turned the mediation down definitively by November but offered a direct negotiation instead. The greatest loser from the change was Count Romantzoff, who was maligned by Lord Walpole, newly arrived Ambassador from England to Russia.

In January, Bayard and Gallatin made up their minds to start home, an option that was not open to Adams. As John Adams said, "One thing is clear in my mind and that is you ought to be home. . . . The wandering life that you have lived as I have done before you is not compatible with human nature. . . . You were the greatest comfort to my life, and of that I am deprived."[46]

Bayard and Gallatin planned to reopen peace talks by direct negotiations while en route home from England. When they left St. Petersburg, Adams observed that Bayard was no more palatable to him than he had been as a fellow Senator in Washington. Although an eloquent speaker in assemblies, Adams saw little else that was good in him. He resented Bayard's repeated efforts to turn Gallatin against him. Now that he knew Gallatin personally, John Quincy believed that his desire to accomplish peace was sincere and ardent and that he was quick, penetrating, and of sound judgment.

The total collapse of the mediation effort seemed to presage the end of Count Romantzoff's career. He told Adams that he was determined to leave office. "My feelings are entirely American," he said, "and were it not for my age and infirmities I would go now to that country." The sixty-year-old Chancellor informed John Quincy in February that official communications were now to be addressed to his replacement, Senator Wedemeyer. Of Romantzoff the American wrote, in farewell, "I esteem and respect his character."[47]

During the winter, Adams suffered from a severe case of jaundice that made him listless and lethargic. He picked up, however, when he heard that he, Bayard, Henry Clay, and Jonathan Russell had been appointed to treat directly with the British government at Gottenburg upon the direct invitation of Lord Castlereagh. "This opens upon me a new prospect of futurity, and a new change in the scenery of life," he said.[48]

While Adams readied himself to leave the Russian capital, news reached there that Paris had been taken by the allies. The marvellous tidings were celebrated by brilliant illuminations and transparencies which honored the Emperor by repeating the letter A in thousands of forms. Crowds of carriages blocked the streets and everywhere people walked about in a holiday mood. Reports followed that the Emperor of France had abdicated and that Europe was at peace. "I commenced my journey to contribute if possible to the restoration of peace to my own country," Adams wrote hopefully.[49]

Louisa and Charles stayed behind with the Smiths. Charles was now in school, and since Gothenburg was not so far distant from St. Petersburg it seemed best for John Quincy to go alone. "Now I am a wayfaring man separated from all my family," John Quincy said, echoing his father's words.[50]

CHAPTER 11

The Little Congress of Ghent

"It is from Vienna and not from America that the balance of peace or war will preponderate."

JOHN QUINCY ADAMS

WHEN JOHN QUINCY Adams arrived at Reval, "the merry bells were ringing all their most laughing peals," to celebrate the fall of Paris and Bonaparte.[1] A statue of Alexander I was carried into the marketplace and crowned with a wreath of laurel leaves. The Emperor of Russia was the undoubted hero of all the rejoicing multitude who filled the streets with revelry or attended the churches to hear the solemn Te Deums sung.

Adams shared the enthusiasm of the crowd for the Russian Czar. He judged him a moderate, fair, and humane man who, it was to be hoped, would secure a solid peace and avert the possibility of another disaster likely to be sparked by the restoration of the ineffectual Bourbons and the humiliation of France. The stability of Europe would have important bearing on the peace talks about to begin between the United States and Great Britain.

Though it was mid-May, the intense cold and adverse winds delayed Adams's voyage to Stockholm. He spent the time catching up on entries to his *Diary* and reading the *Memoirs of Sully*, Henry of Navarre's Minister of Finance. On board the *Ulysses*, the cold was still so intense that the American had to walk briskly up and down the decks to warm his fingers enough to be able to hold a pen, but the ship was able to sail. On May 25, he landed in the Swedish capital.

Jonathan Russell, the new American Minister to Sweden, was already comfortably settled there. He had news that Albert Gallatin was now a member of the mission and was in England, with Bayard, urging that the seat of the negotiations be moved either there or to Holland. Clay, who was in Gothenburg, had already agreed to a change. Adams did not want to make the move, for many reasons "too tedious to mention." In the meantime, he moved into Russell's lodgings.

John Quincy was occupied for the next few days with a file of American papers that caught him up with events in the United States, and a delivery of more than thirty letters that put him in touch with his family and friends. Abigail informed her son that the federalist party had opposed the appointments of Clay and Russell but favored his. However, she warned, he should not forget that, in the past, the federalists had sacrificed both his father and him to their own interests.

The proposed change of venue irked Adams. His first impulse was to return immediately to St. Petersburg but further reflection convinced him that he must overcome his pique and proceed to Gothenburg as ordered. In the back of his mind, he worried that wherever the conference was held, the negotiations might not succeed.

Before he changed his mind again, Adams ordered his carriage to be readied, horses to be supplied at each stage, and a post map of Sweden to study. As he travelled through Sweden, he noted that the country had changed for the worse since his last visit. Then it had been poor but happy, now it appeared more prosperous but also more miserable. Before he left Stockholm, Adams found out that the three British commissioners were: Lord Gambier, Dr. William Adams, and Henry Goulburn. En route, despatches revealed that the meeting place had been changed from Gothenburg to Ghent, Flanders. The *John Adams*, Captain Samuel Angus in command, stood ready to carry the American delegates there.

Jonathan Russell and his young son joined Adams on June 11 and they all immediately boarded the *John Adams*. John Quincy, who admitted to his wife that he had grown fat since he left St. Petersburg and had benefitted from the change of air and scenery, also stated that he was depressed about the mission. "I am resolved to keep my dolefuls as much as possible to myself," he added.[2]

The ship landed the Americans at the Helder, from whence they proceeded by land to Amsterdam. Clay had not yet arrived but Adams and Russell stayed at the Arms of Amsterdam, a hotel that John Quincy had frequented since 1780. As soon as Russell had enrolled his son in a school, the Adams carriage continued its journey.

Although there was not time to stop at The Hague, John Quincy was overcome with nostalgia when the carriage passed some of the familiar scenes. "It was not in my command of language to express what I felt in passing through the yard of the house in the wood, and thence through the town along the road between the Canal to Delft. It was a confusion of recollections so various, so tender, so melancholy, so delicious, so painful, a mixture so heterogeneous, and yet altogether so sweet, that, if I had been alone, I am sure that I should have melted into tears."[3]

On Saint John's Day, the two Americans arrived at Ghent. Adams took lodgings at the Hotel des Pays-Bas on the Place D'Armes and settled down to wait for the rest of the American commissioners and their British counterparts. Though Belgium's fate was not yet established, all the nations coveted her. John Quincy predicted that English gold would turn the scales and that she would become nothing more than a British province. "The British government has substantially brought us upon British ground without our being aware of it," he observed to Louisa.[4] At the moment Ghent was bristling with activity in expectation of a visit from the Emperor of Russia and the King of Prussia, whose troops had a garrison in the city. Despite the preparations for the royal guests, the Mayor was exceedingly gracious to the Americans, offering to provide them with a meeting place.

His "being first here" pleased Adams, who hated "being waited for," but he could not reconcile himself to not having had a voice in the decision to move to Ghent. He was certain that he could have persuaded the others to stay at Gothenburg instead of giving the British the advantage of negotiating in a spot that was comfortably far from pro-American Russia.

By the end of June, except for Gallatin who had travelled to Paris from London, all the American commissioners had gathered at Ghent. Once Clay delivered the mission's papers to Adams, it was agreed that regular meetings would take place at their chairman's apartment.

The general mood of the Americans was one of watchful pessimism. John Quincy, an expert in foreign affairs as well as in pessimism, commented to his father that conciliating the British and American pretensions "will be found more unnatural than your and mine wandering life."[5] Therefore, it was likely that the time spent in Ghent would be of short duration. The others disagreed with him, predicting that they would all spend the winter there.

While they waited for the British plenipotentiaries, the Americans, except for Adams, tried to have as pleasant a time as possible. He complained about his comrades' frivolity. "They sit after dinner and drink bad wine and smoke cigars, which neither suits my habits nor my health, and absorbs time which I cannot spare."[6] John Quincy tried absenting himself from the festive board but when Clay indicated his displeasure, he reappeared at the evening meals. And when his colleagues and Captain Angus toasted him on July 11, his forty-seventh birthday, he was very touched.

In June, while in Paris, Albert Gallatin, accompanied by Levett Harris, had an audience with Alexander I, who remained exceedingly friendly to the United States. The Russian Emperor said that he had made two attempts to conciliate England but she would not tolerate a third. Britain had not forgotten "your former relations to her," he explained. From St. Petersburg, Louisa corroborated the impression. It was publicly rumored that the Emperor had declared that he intended to turn his attention immediately to the affairs of America and "was determined to procure them a good Peace."[7] This did not surprise John Quincy, whose admiration for Alexander was undiminished because only Russia took no dishonorable revenge against France.

Gallatin finally joined the rest of the waiting Americans on July 6. They had now become friendly enough to set up bachelor quarters in one house rather than continue at the hotel. Though it was a difficult task to reconcile the tastes and the requirements of five prominent and somewhat egocentric gentlemen, with the help of the Mayor of Ghent, a month's trial lease at the Hotel d'Alcantara on the Rue des Champs was agreed upon. Adams described their landlord as a jack of all trades, a Frenchman who kept a shop stocked with perfumes, millinery, prints, drawings, and handsome second-hand furniture. A former cook, he was prepared to provide his guests with the best food and wine. However, Adams was skeptical about the wine so they agreed to begin taking his wine, but with the understanding that if it was not satisfactory they would take their business elsewhere. Russell, to insure honest competition, ordered a supply of wines from Paris.

During the honeymoon period, the commissioners got on very well despite the strain of daily meetings, which Adams called to keep his colleagues alert. He kept them busy by assigning them various preliminary tasks. It was a period of adjustment that afterwards helped the five to achieve if not always complete agreement at least the ability to hide their differences from their opponents, thus avoiding the outward hostility that had marred the negotiations during the first peace commission in 1783.

The American Commission represented all the sections of the United States except for the republican south. Ex-Senator James Bayard, nicknamed "the Chevalier" after the French knight "without fear and without reproach," was a moderate federalist somewhat out of favor for having accepted the post from the arch-republican President James Madison. Bayard's justification was his desire for a just peace. During the negotiations he was ill much of the time from the effects of a severe case of dysentery that he had contracted in Russia.

A former war hawk, Jonathan Russell of Rhode Island, felt a natural affinity for a fellow hawk, Henry Clay, with whom he had travelled from Sweden. Russell was hostile to both Gallatin and Adams, although the latter thought that Russell and he were friends because they had carried on an animated correspondence when Russell was in Paris and London and J.Q.A. in Russia. During the negotiations, Russell's tendency to side with Clay earned him the title of Clay's "overzealous adjutant." However, his expertise on commercial matters made him a suitable representative of American mercantile interests.

Henry Clay, thirty-seven years old, was younger, more charming, more aggressive, and more given to the pursuit of pleasure than the others. Tall, lanky, blond and blue-eyed, he liked women, gossip, drinking, gambling, and success. His carousing disgusted Adams and caused a certain amount of tension in the bachelors' paradise.

The oldest commissioner, the closest to the Administration, and, so far the most distinguished member of the team was its logical head, Albert Gallatin—he was not the leader only because of the Senate's interference. A native of Switzerland, dark, large-nosed, and aristocratic looking, Gallatin was witty and urbane. He had been Jefferson's Secretary of the Treasury as well as Madison's and was used to dealing in committee. His value as a negotiator would emerge clearly during the proceedings.

John Quincy, head of the Commission, had in middle-age become only more precise, more conscientious, and, unfortunately, more stubborn. His appearance had not improved. Neither his mother nor his wife had succeeded in correcting the carelessness of his dress. He was short, bald, and stout, with a small mouth like Abigail's, which gave him a slightly peevish look. His eyes, whose tendency to water had started in his youth, were now permanently afflicted. He had a cold, bristly, introspective personality coupled with an independent integrity that dazzled an opponent. He related poorly to people but his intellect and scholarship gained him respect. Like his father, he had a deeply ingrained mistrust of Great Britain. In order to deal with his opponents he would have to curb his antipathy and turn it into a positive kind of caution.

The Americans awaited the British commissioners with a distinct feeling that they had been abandoned. Even in the House of Commons, questions were asked about the peace negotiations with America. Lord Castlereagh himself asked if the persons sent to Gothenburg by the American government had been forgotten. The delay was, of course, deliberate on the part of the foreign office. It was hoped that the British Generals would deliver some **stunning** victories during the summer campaign and so assure for Canada the territory that she wanted. Britain was annoyed, also, at Russia's championship of her former colonies and of France's partiality to the United States.

Nevertheless, the British administration was less hostile to America than the unsophisticated British public. The press, partly government-inspired, had primed the people to expect a peace that would deliver such territorial gains as Northern New York, the American bank of the St. Lawrence River, the East bank of the Niagara, and the return to Spain of the Louisiana Territory. They assumed that the fisheries would be barred to the Americans and that the military posts in the Northwest would be returned to them. But Castlereagh, who was now evaluating the expense of the American war and worrying about the strength of Britain's position at the Congress of Vienna due to convene in October, was interested in settling with the United States.

Finally, on August 8, the American and British plenipotentiaries met at the Hotel de Pays Bas. The three British negotiators were in no way equal to their distinguished American counterparts. They were solid, workmanlike representatives who were willing to be puppets of their foreign office. Vice Admiral James Lord Gambier, the head of the Commission, was a newcomer to the field of diplomacy. He had been a post captain in 1794 and subsequently a junior lord of the Admiralty until the burning of Copenhagen, for which he had been awarded his title. However, his forty-five years of service in the Navy gave him expertise in maritime problems. His affable, well-bred manner pleased Bayard and his position as Vice President of the British Bible Society reconciled him to J. Q. Adams.

Dr. William Adams, an Admiralty lawyer, was another one of the trained nonentities. The story was told that when Lord Liverpool was questioned about Dr. Adams, he could not remember his name. Adams, whose knowledge of Admiralty law was reputed to be formidable, prided himself on his wit and blunt humor. His adversaries, however, often found his comments cutting and nasty.

Young Henry Goulburn, who arrived in Ghent with his wife and small son just recovered from "infantile fever," carried the heaviest work load of any of the British commissioners. The Americans wrote him off as quarrelsome and obstructive but his later career, which was in domestic rather than foreign affairs, proved to be distinguished. Castlereagh did not choose the young man in order to insult the United States, as some thought. The truth was that Liverpool's pallid Ministry, subject to the machinations of such renowned statesmen as Canning and Lord Wellesley, had no one better to offer.[8]

John Quincy opened the negotiations with a firm assertion of his prerogative as head of the American Commission. With no reason given, he refused to meet at the British headquarters in the Hotel du Lion d'Or and demanded that the three Britishers come to the d'Alcantara. As chairman, Adams asserted his right to sit at the head of the table, present the formal statements to the British, and prepare the first draft of all the papers. At the first meeting, Adams and Gambier started the session with appropriate reassurances about their desire for peace and expectations of success. Though the Americans were, in reality, on the defensive, the British were at the disadvantage of having little power to operate on their own. They were also at the psychological disadvantage, shared by their manipulators, of underestimating their opponents.

Serious differences became apparent immediately. Goulburn proposed the terms as follows: recognition of the British right of impressment and the permanent pacification of an area that would become an Indian buffer state between the United States and Canada, as the sine qua non for the conclusion of a treaty. His orders also assumed a revision of the border between the two countries and of the right of Americans to fish and to land and dry their fish on the Grand Banks, a dearly held New England right that John Adams had secured in the Treaty of 1783, as a concession not to be renewed without an equivalent. John Quincy replied quietly that his group would have to consult on these matters. Hereafter, he conceded, meetings would be held alternately at the British and American headquarters.

Monroe had sent explicit orders that impressment of American seamen must cease. In June of 1813, he had written that "If your efforts to accomplish this should fail, all further negotiations will cease, and you will return home without delay."[9] Therefore Adams was convinced, after this first encounter, that the talks would not continue long since Britain would not terminate the war without establishing her maritime rights. He wrote to Louisa that he would keep her informed of the news at Ghent but that she must receive information "in the most exclusive confidence. . . . Say not a word of it to any human being, until the result shall be publicly known."[10]

At the second meeting John Quincy informed the British that his delegation was not instructed on Indian pacification, the boundaries nor a reopening of the fisheries question, which effectively stopped any further exchange until the British could consult their government. It was agreed to wait until a messenger could be despatched to London and return with the required instructions. In the meantime both sides would draw up a report of the proceedings and then collate their versions.

"We live in perfect harmony," Adams informed Louisa. Even the landlord was giving satisfaction. Their dinners were convivial occasions that included their secretaries, who lived at the hotel on the Place d'Armes. The very ghosts had been discouraged. The house the Americans were living in was said to be haunted, which had made hiring servants difficult. Now everyone agreed that "the perturbed spirits" had forsaken the house.

The preparation of the draft to be sent to Monroe rewakened all of Adams's insecurities. Bayard dealt the first blow. Instead of amending the head of the Commission's proposals, he drew up a rival draft. It was even more humiliating when Gallatin took both drafts to correct and reconcile and, instead, dropped J.Q.A.'s version completely and presented a third draft of his own, which was immediately accepted by all.

During the suspension of talks, the commissioners from both sides were constantly entertained at fêtes and balls. Lord Gambier told Adams that he remembered meeting his father when, as a boy, he stayed with his uncle in Boston in 1770. The two Adamses compared notes about their family genealogies to discover that they were not even remote cousins. Dr. Adams's family originally came from Wales and settled in Essex. There are "neither Essex kindred nor Welsh blood in our pedigree," John Quincy wrote to his father, somewhat relieved that he did not have to claim kinship to the unpopular doctor. He remarked also, with some irony, that the British Adams's arms were a red cross, whereas the American Adamses had none other than the stars and stripes.[11]

The day before the Commission reconvened, Lord Castlereagh passed through Ghent on his way to Brussels. He visited the British team but did not meet with the Americans. Castlereagh commented to Lord Liverpool that he was surprised that the Americans neither called upon him nor requested to see him, "and I thought my originating an interview would be considered objectionable and awkward by our Commissioners."[12] Probably the Americans looked at the matter quite differently if, indeed, they were aware at the time that Castlereagh was in Ghent or would have welcomed a meeting. They, too, were busy with instructions from their superiors, which arrived at this time in code, keeping Hughes, Adams, and Gallatin at work deciphering until one in the morning.

The August 19 meeting took place at the Chartreux, a former monastery at which the British contingent was staying. It proved to be very frustrating to the American five. William Goulburn presented the new set of Castlereagh-inspired instructions which in no way offered any modification of their former position. On the contrary, other demands were added, such as a military road from Halifax to Quebec which would lop off a corner of Maine, the continuance of the British right to navigate on the Mississippi, and the acceptance of the Indian boundary set up at the Treaty of Greenville in 1795 as the permanent Canadian-American border. These demands thinly disguised British fear of America's inevitable continental expansion. In answer to Gallatin's question as to what would happen to the hundred thousand American citizens already settled in the proposed buffer state, Dr. Adams answered callously that they would have to shift for themselves.

The meeting broke up with the understanding that a written answer would be presented to the British team before the next meeting. With a feeling of defeat, the American commissioners returned to Bachelor Hall. Only Clay, an experienced gambler, had the perspicacity to detect that the outrageous demands were a massive bluff by Lord Castlereagh.

Adams presented the draft of a response on the 21st to an unreceptive audience. Gallatin criticized it for its harshness, Clay for its figurative language, which, he said, was improper for a state paper. Russell smugly agreed with the two critics and then proceeded to amend the structure of every sentence while the Chevalier tried to put the document into his own language. All agreed that John Quincy's version was too long and too full of argument about the Indians. The next day they deleted half of it. On the following day, after wearisome hours of "sifting, erasing, patching and amending," they adopted an answer with barely one-fifth of John Quincy's original version still intact.[13] The product was a typical, dignified, tightly argued Gallatin concoction which rejected the Indian proposal and the other territorial demands.

Now all the Americans believed that their position guaranteed the termination of the conference. Bayard, Clay, and Gallatin planned to return to the United States. Adams decided to go back to St. Petersburg by way of Vienna in order to carry the official documents of the negotiation to Emperor Alexander. In the meantime, the commissioners entertained many of their compatriots who were passing through Ghent to other places in Europe. The city was a thoroughfare for Americans in Europe who, it seemed, came, looked at their peace commissioners, and then left. One gentleman, however, reported to Adams that he had recently seen his sons. John "is the very picture of You" and George was "a *fine, tall, stout* boy," he said.[14]

Both sides felt that breaking off negotiations was an advantage for the other. Goulburn advised Bathurst that the United States had no real intention of making peace but was seeking, rather, a means of reconciling its people to the continuation of the war. The British demand for an Indian boundary provided that excuse and thus

American desire for negotiating was over.[15] The Americans, with reason, diagnosed the British actions as a delaying ploy, though they had not read Liverpool's letter to Castlereagh which said, "If our commander does his duty, I am persuaded we shall have acquired by our arms every point on the Canadian frontier which we ought to insist on keeping."[16] John Quincy agreed with the reasoning of his colleagues and saw a further, more subtle motivation for the prolonging of the war. The basic rift between the two nations, he said, was England's jealousy of the rapid increase in population and settlements that characterized the United States. Great Britain had "an impotent longing to thwart their progress and stint their growth." With this sentiment prevailing in the British councils, "It is not in the hour of their success that we can expect to obtain a peace upon terms of equal justice or of reciprocity."[17]

At state occasions during which the two sets of negotiators found themselves dinner partners, off-the-record comments were sometimes exchanged. Clay told Goulburn that the Americans considered the British proposals equivalent to a demand for the cession of Boston or New York. And on that same evening, Bayard took Goulburn aside to try to reason with him. The British terms were ruining all prospects of peace and were sacrificing the federalist party as well. It was in England's interest, the Chevalier insisted, to support the federalists by making peace. The present demands as presented could not now and would never be accepted.[18]

John Quincy wrote to Monroe that the Indian question was basic to America's future. To stop the settlement of the wilderness was "incompatible with the moral as well as the physical nature of things." He believed that the Indians should be properly compensated for their land and moved to emptier regions but that neither Indians nor any other people who were wandering hunters could be said to have real possession of the land. "To condemn vast regions of territory to perpetual barrenness and solitude that a few hundred savages might find wild beast to hunt upon it, was a species of game law that a nation descended from Britons could never endure," he said. To doom naturally fertile land "to be forever desert by compact" would be "an outrage upon Providence, which gave the earth to man for cultivation, and made the tillage of the ground the condition of his nature and the law of existence."[19] That the great American continent in a period of less than two centuries would be threatened by overpopulation and industrial pollution was understandably beyond the imagination of the American commissioner.

The various informal confrontations between the British and American peacemakers were emotionally trying. Though all tried to maintain an appropriate equanimity, tempers sometimes flared. John Quincy told Louisa that at one private dinner the Chevalier and Dr. Adams got involved in some unfortunate asperities during which the British lawyer exposed a plentitude of his famed overpretentious wit. And Goulburn, more in the confidence of the British government than any of his peers, was often violent and bitter against the United States.

On September 5, the British answer arrived. It was a sixteen-page memo filled with such proposals as changing the Maine boundary and making the Great Lakes a British sea. To add to its insulting nature, there were gratuitous statements alleging that the "declared object" of the United States was to conquer and absorb Canada. Clay, perhaps somewhat pricked by conscience, angrily suggested that the note should be answered in one page. However, Adams and Gallatin insisted on a more cautious analysis. And on the next day Gallatin delivered an interpretation that the others could accept. Though Bayard was willing to concede a little, neither Adams nor Clay wanted any stipulation about the Indians in the treaty. As to the allegation about Canada, since American ships were subject to seizure by the superior British Navy, this should be sufficient pledge for Canada's security. Returning to Indian matters, Adams wanted the point included that British employment of the Indians in their war effort was contrary to the laws of war. The other commissioners were willing to accept the substance of John Quincy's statements but, as usual, made a multitude of amendments.

The final draft deplored the British introduction into the treaty of a sine qua non that had not even been mentioned before the third meeting. Once again the American Commission declared to the British plenipotentiaries that they had no authority to deal with them on the interests of Indians living within the boundary of the United States. They also criticized the British "for the employment of savages whose known rule of warfare is the indiscriminate torture and butchery of women, children and prisoners. . . ."[20] The Maine boundary, it concluded, was not at issue.

Despite the contents of their proposals, the British did not want the peace talks abandoned. Goulburn, who had been responsible for introducing the Indian sine qua non into the discussion, now informed Earl Bathurst that the subject seemed to be more offensive to the Americans than the military occupation of the lakes. The chief objection, he explained to the London office, was the invasion of the American right to extend their population over the whole of the unsettled country. It was probably impossible to conclude a good peace, he added gloomily.

The third British note arrived on September 20 without the sine qua non but continued the same overbearing, insulting, and inflexible attitudes. Gallatin, who scanned the note with Adams before the others, handled his dejection better. "Mr. Gallatin, having more pliability of character and more playfulness of disposition, responds to my heat with a joke," Adams wrote. On the day of the autumnal equinox, Gallatin was delegated to answer the British note, which challenged American claims of innocence in regard to imperialistic designs on Canada. The British note, for example, cited the proclamations of Generals Smyth and Hull as ample evidence of American plans to take over Canada.

Once again exercising his prerogative, Adams wrote a reply, including pointed remarks similar to those expressed to Monroe on the moral and religious duty of the United States to cultivate Indian territory. It was adopted by his colleagues, but only after resolving objections to almost every word. John Quincy was now convinced of two things; one, that if any member objected to anything he had written all agreed, and secondly if he objected to anything Gallatin wrote, unless it was voluntarily abandoned by the Secretary of the Treasury, it stayed because all the other members of the Commission supported him. Obviously, only Adams's prose ran "the gauntlet of objections." His style displeased his colleagues, particularly when he made reference to God, Providence, or heaven. Clay immediately labeled such phrases as cant and Russell laughed. Poor John Quincy questioned, privately, whether there was some basic fault in his composition.

The note to Britain denied American designs on Canada and disdained any responsibility for the war cries of Generals on active duty. As for the Indians, the commissioners declared that the United States had always dealt fairly with Indian land but retained the right to cultivate the territory within its domain.

Gallatin had definitively emerged as the natural leader of the American contingent. Even Adams admitted that "Mr. Gallatin's influence increases over all of us." The opposition accepted this truth also. Goulburn analyzed the Secretary's ascendancy as an understanding of the English position that he was able to perceive because he was less like an American than any of his colleagues.[21]

At the end of September, George Boyd, John Quincy's brother-in-law, arrived in Ghent with despatches from the State Department that were somewhat discouraging. Since money had become a problem, Gallatin was asked to negotiate a loan, preferably through Holland. However, the Ghent social scene distracted the commissioners. The round of balls and card parties, some of which even Adams attended, passed the time. Clay, whose propensity for pleasure annoyed Adams, went off to Brussels with Hughes "upon a party of pleasure," John Quincy recorded with disapproval.

On October 1, Gallatin accosted Adams with the devastating news that on August 25 British troops had invaded Washington and burned the public buildings. The London *Courier* reported: "The Capital of America, the City of Washington, has been taken and *Destroyed* after the American army had been defeated by less than $\frac{1}{4}$ of their number." Adams immediately personalized the disaster, worrying about his parents and children and visualizing Boston as the next victim of the British sword. If this event did not arouse the American people, he wrote to Louisa, they might as well "take the oath of allegiance to the maniac [George III]."[22]

Gallatin, whose home on Capitol Hill had been burned by the British, took a much more relaxed attitude toward the episode. He was relieved that his valuable possessions were saved, and remarked that the destruction of Washington would remain a monument to British barbarity. When Madame de Staël wrote from Paris that she was fearful for her American property, he advised her that to sell at a loss would be foolish. The United States always made good on its obligations, as had been proved by her payment of the Revolutionary War debts. American political morality, he added proudly, was sounder than that of any of the European powers.[23]

When Lord Bathurst read the news of General Robert Ross's sack of Washington, he wanted to order the enforcement of the Indian convention, which would have ruined negotiations. But Liverpool advised delay. "Let them feast in the meantime on Washington," he said.[24] The British reasons for continuing the peace talks had not really changed. The military victory served best as a face-saving device with the British people in case some of the settlement terms disappointed them.

Adams's judgment was hampered by his chronic pessimism. He

was so certain that the British would now demand unconditional submission that he drafted a letter to Count Nesselrode to be presented to the Emperor, relating the discouraging history of the negotiations. His production was accepted without comment by his colleagues, who regarded it as part of his mission to Russia.

A fourth British note, fifteen pages long and as offensive as the others, arrived on October 8. Though it abandoned almost all of the previous demands, it included meaningless insults, such as innuendos about the legality of the Louisiana Purchase. The stumbling block, this time, was an ultimatum demanding the restoration to the Indians of all the possessions, rights, and privileges that they had enjoyed before the war.

Again the Americans set to work to develop an answer. And again, Adams and Gallatin produced versions which differed in tone. Indignant that hitherto the American commissioners had been too defensive and cautious in their answers, John Quincy wanted to respond in the style of a retort. Gallatin wrote in his usual style. The others, although anxious for peace, were satisfied with neither draft. Henry Clay announced that he would provide a draft. It was, like its author, very direct, proposing agreement to Indian pacification based on a quickly settled peace. Adams hated it and would have preferred to break off negotiations rather than accept it, but he did not have the support of the others. They were willing to go along with Clay as long as no important yield would be made in the future. At the pace that the peace talks were going, it looked as if the commissioners would winter in Ghent. Adams believed that the deliberations at Vienna would also serve to delay them.

Bathurst answered in a few days with a greater frankness than had been evident previously. He proposed that, apart from the Northwest proposals already presented, settlement should be made on the principle of uti posseditis (state of possession). To be exact, the British would have Fort Michillimackinaw, Fort Niagara, and all the country east of the Penobscot, which reduced the earlier demand for half of Maine and the entire south bank of the St. Lawrence to a demand for Moose Island, a right-of-way across the northern angle of Maine, and the two forts.

The reason for the reduction of demands was not a sudden burst of good will. While the British Cabinet had been meeting on the subject, news had arrived that the British invasion of New York had collapsed and General Prevost with his large forces had retreated to

Canada. The London *Times* called the situation "a lamentable event in the civilized world. . . . The present American government must be displaced or, it will sooner or later, place its poisoned dagger in the heart of the parent state."[25] Although the *Courier* insisted that until the "late disaster" was wiped away, peace with America was neither desirable nor practical, the *Morning Chronicle* openly admitted that the game of war was ended.[26] In pro-American Paris, crowds gathered in the Palais Royal Gardens to cheer each recital of the Plattsburgh defeat.

The fifth British note, though it had the "same dilatory and insidious character" as the others, was shorter. But it offered no accommodation of the differences. Its answer, swiftly drafted by Gallatin, suffered few alterations. Adams was now certain that his country must prepare for another year of war, "while they [the British commissioners] are sporting with us here, they are continually sending reinforcements and new expeditions to America."[27] When the British team received their answer, refusing their base of uti posseditis, they were amazed and sent a special messenger to London to ask confirmation for breaking off the negotiations.

Somewhat relieved that the ordeal, whatever the outcome, was almost over, the American five relaxed and tried to enjoy the lively social life that the friendly citizens of Ghent offered them. Hatred and bitterness towards the British was so widespread because of the quartering of soldiers and the dumping of English manufactured goods that the Americans were fêted for being Britain's enemies.

Adams, Gallatin, and Bayard were made honorary members of the Society of Fine Arts and Letters and the other two were given a similar honor by the Society of Agriculture and Botany. At his installation, Adams answered the toast proferred to him, "Success to the pacific labors of the American negotiators," with, "Prosperity to the City of Ghent and to the Society of Fine Arts and Letters within its walls. May its artists always worthily support the glory of the country of Rubens." It was met with a burst of applause.[28]

In the midst of a windy monologue that Adams was subjecting his colleagues to during one of their daily meetings, the sixth dilatory and evasive note from the British arrived. The subject was one on which he and Clay differed sharply because it concerned the welfare of their respective sections. The westerner ardently opposed allowing the British free navigation on the Mississippi River and Adams, New England's loyal son in spite of everything that had happened, was adamant about the right to dry fish on Canadian shores. John Quincy recorded with pride that during their exchanges, he kept constant guard on his temper while Clay lost his continually and then lapsed into peevish silences. At one point the Kentucky war hawk thundered that the Mississippi right was too much to give up "for the right of drying fish upon a desert."[29] Adams's answer was a dignified silence.

The final disposal of the matter was ingenious. Clay suddenly proposed Adams's argument that the fisheries' right was irretrievably linked with the recognition of American independence and hence required no further negotiation. Displaying tact for once, John Quincy went along with his own position and Gallatin, protesting, was carried along by the others to a unanimous acceptance.

Until the 10th, the writing and the revision process continued with the five never managing to all get together at once. When they finally convened, they immediately erased about three-fourths of what Adams had prepared, including his "most important paragraph," which was a proposal to conclude the peace on the basis of the state before the war, applied to all the subjects in dispute between the two nations. Gallatin agreed to the statement but Clay said it was an offer to be made only as a last resort. Adams thought that the British would refuse the offer but it would serve a purpose. If there was a rupture, the blame would be theirs and not America's. Clay, grumbling, agreed to it but reserved the right to refuse to sign the final treaty. Hughes, the Commission's secretary, who feared that the agitated commissioners would change their collective minds, snatched the note and rushed it over to the British headquarters immediately after dinner. Again the members of Bachelor Hall settled down to the usual two-week interval of waiting.

In London, on November 3, the British Cabinet met on the American question for the first time. The English position in Europe was weak. Not only was there a crisis at the Congress of Vienna over Poland, but it was seething with plots against King Louis. The Cabinet offered the Duke of Wellington a choice either to go to America or to Vienna. Liverpool tried to cajole him to take over the American command by offering him full power to make peace or to renew the war with full vigor. Wellington refused America on the reasonable grounds that if there were a major explosion in Paris or Vienna, he would be there to deal with it, but it would take several months for him to make preparations to depart for America, and furthermore, since he could not get there before spring, he might be too late to save the situation. He advised Castlereagh that it would be best to conclude the war in America as soon as possible.

While waiting, John Quincy decided that he was pleased that the treaty draft contained his proposal. He was prepared to take full responsibility and bear the entire blame "if ill ensues." If, however, the British accepted the proposal, peace could be concluded in twenty-four hours. His mind at rest, he went to the theater weekly, which was as much of the local talent as he could endure. The Americans gave the British a dinner which, although not gay, went off in suitable style. Adams laughed at the naïveté of his namesake, who bragged that he had not attended a play in England in ten years and raved about the antics of an Indian juggler who balanced straws upon his nose.

The American commissioners received news from America that their despatches had been published along with their instructions, and that they were having the very desirable effect of uniting all factions in support of the war. When the British plenipotentiaries heard of the public action they were astonished. Goulburn could hardly restrain his temper and Liverpool called it "scandalous." Gallatin, somewhat alarmed, feared that negotiations would be broken off. Adams, however, was gratified that the President approved of their rejection of the British proposals and authorized the commissioners to conclude the peace on the basis of the status before the war, "precisely the offer which we have made in our last note and of which I have found it so difficult to obtain the insertion," he recorded.[30]

A new rejection of all the American demands arrived on November 27. But, curiously, the note also abandoned everything inadmissible to the Americans in their own demands. Adams, usually the most negative of the five, had to admit that the objects upon which the enemy insisted were too trifling to war over and that "we have everything but peace in our hands." Clay agreed that the British wanted an end to war. Though their statements on impressment, the blockade, and the Indian question were rejected, the Americans were neither surprised nor chagrined. Only the Mississippi-fisheries problem remained, along with the disposition of the Passamaquoddy Islands. Adams saw through the disposition of the Passamaquoddy Islands. Correctly, he attributed the British intention to conclude peace to their failure to achieve the ascendancy at the

Congress of Vienna, their disappointments in America, and the refusal of their own people "to squander their blood and treasure for a
war of conquest."[31]

Inevitably, Clay and Adams clashed over the final question. Clay
paced around the room, his arms waving in anger, running his fingers through his hair, shouting his objections. Adams, calm but
adamant, said that he would be ashamed to go home without either
the Moose Islands or the fisheries rights. Clay, hitting below the
belt, murmured about traitorous New England. Both Gallatin and
John Quincy pleaded and cajoled and Bayard dithered until the rest
of the Commission voted Gallatin's resolution into effect. Clay's
anger was not as durable as Russell's perfidy, however, for eight
years later the Rhode Islander would try to use the episode to ruin
John Quincy Adams's political career. The next day, Clay tried
again, this time attempting to isolate Adams who, consequently,
agreed to draft a proposal for the Mississippi that would limit British access to it. The last of November, over Adams's violent protest,
it was agreed to drop the subject of the sale of captured American
Negro slaves by British Captains who, under the guise of rescuing
them from slavery, sold them to planters in the West Indies. And,
also over Adams's protest, the British were invited to set a date for
the next meeting. They arranged it for the next day.

On December 1, at noon, nearly two and one half months after
their last meeting, the two sets of peacemakers faced each other at
Chartreux. For three hours, John Quincy complained, he and his
colleagues were submitted to the Englishmen's "airs of arrogance
and intimated threats," although, he noted, Lord Gambier never
resorted to bullying. There were fireworks over the Mississippi and
fisheries rights. At one point, John Quincy enraged his opponents
by suggesting that if the British had unlimited access to the Mississippi, the Americans might assume the same privilege for the St.
Lawrence. In the end, both parties were confused. Adams wrote,
"An adversary who, after demanding empires as an indispensable
preliminary falls to playing pushpins for Straws, deserves anything
but confidence."[32] But reports of the possibility of peace were circulated all over England. The *Times*, formerly contemptuous of
America, published a letter from Canada that said if England
wanted to defeat America she must send troops not by the tens of
thousands but by the hundreds of thousands.

By Friday, December 10, the Americans had their answer. It

was a blow to Adams. Lord Bathurst offered to negotiate both the fisheries and the Mississippi in the future for a fair equivalent. The New Englander could not accept the implication that these rights had been forfeited by war and in this he found himself to be alone. Though the catching and curing of fish was of profound interest in Massachusetts, it was not particularly so anywhere else. The quibbling between the two sets of adversaries was entirely indecisive and, in two hours, the British left, after arranging to meet again on Monday.

Throughout the weekend the Rue des Champs rang with the Clay-Adams quarrel. Never once would John Quincy relinquish his position. Would they be willing to give up Moose Island if it were located in Delaware or Kentucky, he asked Bayard and Clay. Gallatin, finally, resumed the leadership and proposed that the ante bellum status quo be insisted upon and be interpreted to include the Treaty of 1783, thus encompassing the points in conflict. "Splendid," said Adams. But Clay swore that he would not sign the treaty on that basis and Russell concurred. Gallatin, by his silence, indicated that he withdrew the offer but when everyone quieted down he said he would try again for the Passamaquoddy Islands and the fisheries.

Eight irritable commissioners reconvened on December 12 for another inconclusive session and, on the way home, Adams predicted a rupture. Clay, of course, disagreed. Bayard was uncertain but declared the Passamaquoddy Islands lost. Gallatin said he would sleep on it. While his colleagues attended the Municipal Ball at which "Hail, Columbia" was played to honor the Americans, Adams stayed at home to draft the note for the British commissioners.

Most of the Adams draft concerned the islands in conflict. He said that to except the Passamaquoddy Islands from the principle of mutual restoration of captured territory must force the American commission to conciliate beyond its authority or to terminate by their refusal. Unable to leave the touchy Mississippi-fisheries problem alone, he suggested that the only claim that Britain had to the navigation of the Mississippi was the one granted by the former peace treaty. "If she founds it on that article, she must admit the claim of the United States to the fisheries within British jurisdiction secured by the same treaty," he asserted logically.[33] Therefore, he concluded, the undersigned offered to agree to a new article on the subject or to be silent in regard to both.

The struggle resumed at the Hotel d'Alcatara. In ever-changing pairs and threes, the commissioners agreed and disagreed with each other but never kept to one position long. Gallatin, who felt most responsible to the Administration, was not ready to make the fisheries an ultimatum. Adams also worried that there was a great danger in polarizing the sections of the United States. And the financial predicament of the country was also disturbing. Alexander Baring had written to Gallatin from London that America's outstanding debt to his bank alone was more than $200,000. "Our finances are in ruin," Adams declared.

During a noon recess, John Quincy took one of his long tramps along the canals to try to clear his brain with fresh air and physical activity. Bayard, with the same idea in mind, joined him. They tossed the problem of the Passamaquoddy Islands back and forth but were no more successful at reaching a conclusion than the full complement had been during the formal session. At dinner with the American commissioners that evening, Lord Gambier remarked that he wished the Americans could come to a conclusion without another reference to England. John Quincy Adams's instinctive reaction to that was a more intense distrust of England for being so inflexible over trifles.

The depth of bitterness and anger that he felt towards all the adversaries, except for Lord Gambier, made it a constant and increasingly difficult struggle to suppress his emotions. They were being constantly aroused by the Britishers "overbearing insolence and narrow understanding." He was both proud and amazed that he was able to keep on drinking and eating terms with them.

By Wednesday the 14th, further discussion about the fisheries made it quite clear that, as so often in the past, J. Q. Adams stood alone. He reported in his *Diary*: "I further said that if they were all determined at last to yield the fishery point, I thought they were wrong not to give it up now, and sign the treaty without another reference to England as well as without my signature. I could not sign it, because I could not consent to give up that point."[34]

At this stage, Russell turned nasty and accused Adams of being unable to give up the fisheries because his father had obtained the privilege in the 1783 peace treaty. Adams did not deny this but insisted that it was not his only motivation. He said once again that he owed a duty to Massachusetts and was being asked to make a double sacrifice—the fisheries and Moose Island. Russell refused to accept the explanation, merely commenting that he did not think it proper to continue the war for them. Later on, he told Clay that Adams adopted the most extravagant opinions in the heat of the moment and then defended them with such obstinacy that he was soon reduced "to the miserable alternative of being constantly absurd or ridiculously inconsistent."[35]

Adams won this time. His exhausted colleagues agreed to try once more for the fisheries right but, if it failed, they would sign the treaty. The note went off, agreeing to the omission of the Passamaquoddy Islands from the territorial restoration but insisting that the claims in the area be settled promptly after the termination of the war. As to the Mississippi-fisheries problem, that was to be omitted from the treaty. Clay was disgusted and called it a "damned bad treaty." Adams didn't deny this but speculated on whether Clay realized how often his temper got the best of him. "We have the same dogmatical overbearing manner, the same harshness of look and expression, the same forgetfulness of the courtesies of society," he said about his cigar-smoking, hard-drinking, gambler colleague. But, Adams added, Clay, being ten years younger, could be more easily excused for his faults.[36]

At the termination of the treaty talks, Adams recorded his impressions of his fellow commissioners. The Chevalier, he conceded, had the most perfect control of his temper of the five. His was the most deliberate coolness, which denoted real self-control. Though Gallatin was not up to Bayard's standards, he seldom yielded to temper and could recover quickly. His uniqueness was his blend of stubbornness and flexibility, his greatest fault ingenuity bordering on ingenuousness. Russell, the youngest, took the least active part in the proceedings. Less social and more solitary than the others, he took offense when none was offered and deferred most to Clay, least to Gallatin and Adams.

Having taken the position that he would not sign the treaty unless the British met his demands, Adams lapsed into "a state of peculiar anxiety." He did not expect that the finished product would give the British any more satisfaction than the Americans. The essential difficulty, he pointed out, was that after the peace was made the sources of dissension would still be so numerous that the peace would be as hard to hold as it had been to obtain.

However, on Thursday, while taking one of his interminable walks, Adams looked up to see Bayard waving at him vigorously.

When he caught up with the Chevalier, who was breathing with very great difficulty because of his damaged lungs, he was told that the British answer had come and that it was close to an acceptance.

That evening the five Americans gathered in Adams's room to make the final arrangements. A messenger had been sent to Bordeaux to warn the *Transit* that a copy of the treaty would soon be ready for its trip across the Atlantic. At this zero hour, the realization that the treaty failed to satisfy the war hawks' hopes hit Clay. He rebelled against the document and tried to get Adams to side with him, a move that gave John Quincy the great satisfaction of being able to deny him. Gallatin responded with one of his infrequent violent flareups of temper. Everyone subsided at once and, in the lull, Hughes was sent to arrange the final interview with the British commissioners.

The British Cabinet, having decided to get rid of the American war, wanted the negotiations closed. However, Liverpool, still suspicious of Madison, told Castlereagh that he feared some trick about getting the treaty ratified. If this should happen, he suggested, the eastern states must immediately be given the proposal of a separate peace, "and we have good reason to believe that they would not be indisposed to listen to such a proposal."[37]

New England's disaffection, the British figured, was their hidden weapon. During "Mr. Madison's War," many New England merchantmen continued to trade between British ports and the Spanish peninsula under the protection of licenses issued by their enemy. Contraband trade was so extensive that at the end of 1813, Congress passed a more sweeping Embargo Act than Jefferson's hated one. Federalist Cyrus King thundered, "If a simple king of England, by his corrupt servants chastised New England with whips, the administration here chastised her with scorpions. . . . The states of New England can never be satellites."[38]

The embargo was repealed by the spring of 1814, but the British summer campaign intensified New England's grievances against Washington. No longer handicapped by the Napoleonic War, the British Navy blockaded New England ports and raided her coastline. In July, Moose Island and Eastport, Maine, were captured. In September, General Sherbrooke took Eastern Maine. With the rape of Washington fresh in their minds, the people of Massachusetts were convinced that Boston was next. New England's paranoia rose to the surface again. She was to be abandoned by the national Administration, she charged, because of republican hostility. Although the War Department offered to keep the Massachusetts militia within the state if it was placed under the command of the regular army, Governor Caleb Strong refused indignantly as did his fellow Governors in Connecticut, Vermont, and Rhode Island when the time came. The federalists were resentful that despite the huge war taxes that Massachusetts paid, and the large numbers of troops that she contributed, for a technicality and in direct opposition to states' rights, she was abandoned to defend herself. Some of the federalists were so outraged that they counseled ignoring local defense but soon realized the folly of their position and joined the all-out effort to work on the city's fortifications.[39] However, the irritants that made New England feel alienated from the rest of America were intensified by the crisis. Convinced that commerce was her lifeline, Madison's anti-British policy was interpreted as anti-New England. Given this frame of thought, what followed was logical. On October 6, 1814, Massachusetts called for a New England convention to be held at Hartford to review their grievances and, possibly, to convene delegates from all parts of the United States to revise the Constitution. Two months later, the Convention, heavily represented from Massachusetts, Rhode Island, and Connecticut and rather sparsely from Vermont and New Hampshire, met in secret session. At the same time that the peace commissioners at Ghent were completing their labors and John Quincy Adams was fighting bravely for the fisheries' rights for his native state, a parcel of influential New Englanders were planning to solve their problems in their own style.

At the December 3 noon meeting, the British commissioners demanded that the treaty be ratified without exception, knowing that the American system allowed for Senate changes. The final decisions concerned the restitution of captured territory except for the islands in Passamaquoddy Bay, the restoration of vessels captured at sea after the peace, and the release of prisoners. Any money dispersal, such as the advance made by each government for prisoners, was to be made in specie, the British insisted. John Quincy noted that his adversaries always had an eye for profit. The three-hour conference terminated in an agreement to meet again at three the following afternoon at British headquarters to sign the six copies of the treaty.

Adams labored over the preparation of the copies to meet the deadline. And when the two parties got together, there were few differences to rectify. Lord Gambier and John Quincy Adams formally exchanged their documents. The British leader said, appropriately, that he hoped that the peace would be permanent. Adams, speaking for the Americans, commented prophetically that he hoped that this would be the last treaty of peace between Great Britain and the United States. At 6:30 on Christmas Eve, 1814, mission accomplished, the American commissioners left the old monastery to return to their own quarters.

Anthony Baker, entrusted with the treaty, jumped into his carriage to start for Ostend, where a ship waited to carry the completed peace treaty to England. It was agreed that official notice of the signing of the agreement should not be given until Baker had time to deliver the information to the British government.

On Christmas Day, Christopher Hughes sailed from Bordeaux on the *Transit* with his copies of the Treaty of Ghent. None of the eight commissioners was completely satisfied with the new treaty. For the Americans, its greatest value lay in what it omitted rather than what it settled. Impressment, absent from the document, became an academic issue at the close of the Napoleonic Wars, for the British no longer needed an excess of manpower for their warships. Neutral rights, the fisheries and the Mississippi, cleverly unmentioned, by implication remained as before the war. Territorial disputes were postponed until tempers calmed and joint commissions could operate in a temperate atmosphere. Even the guarantees made for the benefit of the Indians, the red herring with which the British started the talks, had a confused termination. The Indians were to have their prewar rights restored, the treaty stated, but there was no guarantee for the future included. Essentially, the treaty achieved the cessation of hostilities on land and sea. American dreams of Canadian conquest and British dreams of repossessing Maine and controlling American expansion were abandoned.

After some reflection, the initial sense of disappointment that engulfed the American contingent was replaced with a positive feeling of accomplishment. They had, as Russell said, done their practical best. Gallatin wrote to the Secretary of State in the same vein, saying that the treaty was as favorable as existing circumstances allowed. Adams informed Abigail that the United States lost no essential right and gained "to our country the power at our own option to extinguish the war."[40]

In retrospect, the peace was a very fortunate one for the United States. It united the country and it demonstrated to an astounded

Europe that the absurd new transatlantic republic could hold triumphant Britain at least at a stalemate. Most important, perhaps, it established the pattern for the settlement of future disputes between the United States and her northern neighbor. The concept of joint commissions replaced the martial solution. In time, as a consequence of the Treaty of Ghent, Canada and the United States would have the longest unguarded frontier that the world has ever seen.

Inevitably, it was circumstances beyond their control that contributed a great deal to the degree of success achieved by the American commissioners. The little congress of Ghent was negotiated while preparations were being made for the big Congress of Vienna. Alexander of Russia, for reasons of his own, stretched his powerful arm benignly over the fortunes of the American republic, contributing to England's dilemma. She had more at stake, therefore, than the comfort of a handful of Indians and some American wilderness. The sacred balance of power had to be maintained in a realigning Europe that threatened to upset it. And the exhaustion of the British people who had endured too much war and had to pay for it heavily in blood and taxes was another peace factor.

At Ghent, also, the alteration of circumstances changed the original canvas. Having just defeated Napoleon, the conquest of the United States looked like an easy military achievement. It was a great surprise to the foreign office when the intrepid Duke of Wellington turned down the offer of carte blanche in the American war. The burning of Washington aroused British hopes to a fever pitch only to have them sharply deflated by news of the inexplicable rout at Plattsburgh.

A major British disadvantage was one that they never accepted. Among the American negotiators was a top Cabinet officer who had served with distinction in two presidential administrations, a future President, and a future Secretary of State. The pale puppets that the British offered were outclassed even if they had not been powerless pawns.

Though the Treaty of Ghent was not a spectacular achievement, it was a respectable addition to John Quincy Adams's list of accomplishments. To be honest, Adams was not at his best in a group effort. During the negotiations he was often pessimistic, quarrelsome, irritable, and touchy. But he managed to save the fisheries for his ungrateful home state and to preserve the Adams tradition of service to Massachusetts.

CHAPTER 12

The Second Adams
at the Court of St. James

"My son! No man except your Father was ever placed in more delicate or dangerous Situations than you are!"

JOHN ADAMS

THE DISMANTLING OF the peace mission caused more ill-feeling among the American commissioners than all but the most tense moments during the peace talks. Once Anthony St. John Baker carried a copy of the treaty to London, Mr. Carroll, Clay's secretary, carried its twin to England and thence home to Madison, and a third copy in the care of Christopher Hughes journeyed to the United States via France, there was nothing official for the commissioners to do but wait for ratification. In the interim, they decided to dispose of the residue of their five months' collaboration—the books, maps, papers, and other effects.

Gallatin suggested that everything be sent to London for the use of the mission that was going there to negotiate a treaty of commerce. Clay immediately disagreed, insisting that the State Department was the proper repository for the historical records. Adams, however, declared that "the custody of the papers would, at the termination of the mission devolve upon me, subject to the orders of our Government and I should take charge of them accordingly."[1] Still carrying a grudge from their terminal quarrels regarding the treaty, Clay "kindled into flame." He said that he was physically and morally revolted at such a pretension and scoffed at precedent. Echoing him, Russell called for a vote, which Adams refused, to Clay's further indignation. The Kentuckian then, quite tactlessly, reminded John Quincy that his position of being first in the mission was only accidental. Adams acknowledged the truth of the statement but nonetheless refused to relinquish his right. Gallatin mediated, suggesting that the subject be abandoned for the time being.

The truce lasted a few days until Clay resumed his campaign for the job of carrying the papers to Washington. Adams told him that he would deliver the documents to any person named to him in writing by a majority of the Commission and authorized to give him a receipt for the papers. Clay muttered that he would obtain such a paper and, the next day, arrived at Adams's room with a letter signed by Bayard, Russell, and himself demanding the papers. Adams said that he was not aware that a vote had been taken and once again claimed precedent and usage. In a letter to the three suppliants, he observed that their note was not the act of the majority of the mission because it was signed without consultation with the body as a whole. His objection, basically, was that some of the original papers were such that it would have to be decided to whom they should go. Clay was "cavilling upon a bagatelle merely because it would be convenient for him to have the papers," Adams recorded and finally he told Clay that he would keep the papers and act according to his judgment.

The city of Ghent was delighted at the successful completion of the peace talks. The Mayor, dressed in full regalia and flanked by four adjutants, paid a ceremonial visit to the American team. On December 8, the representatives of the United States entertained the British commissioners and nineteen other dignitaries at a gala dinner. Adams found out from Lord Gambier that his brother and Baker had been delayed by an accident on the way to Ostend but had embarked for Britain by three in the afternoon on Christmas Day and therefore had already delivered the treaty to London.

Bachelor Hall was broken up the last of the month. The Commissioners left the Rue des Champs for the Hotel des Pays Bas. A curious indication of American popularity was evidenced at their landlord's sale of the American delegation's personal possessions. For a week or ten days, an auction of their supposed effects, many of them purchased for the occasion, brought exorbitant prices from the memento-hunting citizens of Ghent. An old worthless inkstand was sold for thirty francs and, worst of all, dozens of bottles of bad wine were bought by eager purchasers, though the five Americans had not left a bottle behind.

In January, Lord Gambier and Dr. Adams returned to London, leaving only Goulburn to do the honors at the official peace dinner given by the principal gentlemen of the city. Everyone was required to appear in full uniform for the gala, which irked Adams. The large hall was decorated with British and American flags intertwined together and olive trees planted in tubs. Goulburn and Adams were seated between the Intendant and the Mayor and, as the dignitaries entered, "Hail, Columbia" was played and then "God Save the King." The two tunes were played alternately and incessantly all evening until both Americans and British agreed that it was tiresome. John Quincy gave the next to the last toast: "Ghent, the city of peace; may the gates of the temple of Janus, here closed, not be opened again for a century." The numerous company danced with vivacity until about ten o'clock.

Though he denied it, Adams relished the sentiment that was circulating throughout the city comparing the congress of Vienna unfavorably with the congress of Ghent. "Le Congrès danse, mais il ne marche pas,"* it said, and then recommended that it take a lesson from Ghent where, one morning, when nobody expected it, it was found that a treaty had been made and all was settled.[2]

After a last unsuccessful attempt to wrest the Commission's papers from Adams before leaving Ghent, Clay cooled off. He decided that he did not want Washington to know about the "scramble" over a few books and documents. Bayard and Clay left together in the diligence for Lille. A week later, Gallatin took off for Geneva to visit friends and relatives in his native city before proceeding to Paris. Though James Gallatin indicated that his father would be pleased with the Russian mission, Adams thought that he could be placed in a more useful post. Once again, John Quincy asserted that the former Secretary of the Treasury had "contributed the largest and most important share to the conclusion of the peace," adding that there had been more agreement between him and Gallatin than between any of the other members of the mission.[3]

At six o'clock on the morning of January 26, Adams left Ghent with sincere regret. He recorded that he had lived in the city for

---

* "The Congress dances, but it does not work."

seven months and two days and that it was "the most memorable period of my life." Nowhere else had he experienced such affectionate treatment from the people of a foreign land. In six hours he reached Brussels after travelling on snow-covered roads on the coldest day of winter. Sledges would have been the ideal way to travel. In Brussels, Adams gave in to intense fatigue and accompanying depression. "I suffer from inertia," he complained and predicted that it would take ten to fifteen days before the attractions of Paris would be strong enough to put him in motion. He did move himself enough to visit a famous private collection of paintings where he was very impressed with Guido's *Holy Family*, because the head of the Virgin seemed to him the most perfect ideal ever painted.[4]

Renewed in spirit after about a week, Adams started for Paris. The only sign of war that he found along the way was the bridge over the Oise, which had been blown up but was being repaired. On February 4, he arrived at the Hotel du Nord, Rue de Richelieu, which had been recommended by Gallatin. Although all that was available was a second-floor apartment with two small rooms directly on the street, he took them.

Paris was delightfully familiar. With Crawford as his sponsor, Adams was presented to King Louis, who asked the inevitable royal question—was he related to the celebrated Mr. Adams? Immediately, the social round of parties and dinners started. "The tendency to dissipation at Paris seems to be irresistible. There is a moral incapacity for industry and application . . . against which I am as ill guarded as I was at the age of twenty," he admitted.

Though it was more than thirty years since he had been in the French capital, Adams thought everything looked very much the same. He made nostalgic visits to all the houses in which his father had lived. The greatest changes, he observed, were in the area around the Tuileries. But the theater was, as always, his greatest source of recreation. An excellent performance of Moliere's *Les Fourberies de Scapin* amused him but at the same time repulsed him because of its contempt for old age, irreverence for the paternal character, and the complacency with which fraud and swindling was presented. A French friend pointed out that in real life mankind was like Scapin, a truth that Adams recognized but regretted. What passed for rigidity in his personality was possibly an intense, almost romantic desire to see the world as he wished it to be.

Madame de Staël's invitation to dine with her, given in St. Petersburg, could now be accepted. Bonaparte's fall had restored her to favor in her native land and her outspoken criticism of British vandalism in Washington made her a distinguished friend of the United States.

Now that the Louvre was turned into a museum open to the public, John Quincy said that while he waited for his call to Britain he would visit it daily. The great collections at the former palace were greatly enhanced by Napoleon's questionably acquired treasures.

Adams analyzed the British delay as an effort to feel out their power in those areas of the treaty that had not been resolved, such as the fisheries. Based on hints from the British negotiators, he warned Monroe that when the New Englanders went to the fishing grounds as usual, they would be stopped by force. The United States must then protect the right by force or negotiate. "It is probable that the real object of the British government in disputing the right at present, as well as in the adherence to the claim of the islands in Passamaquoddy Bay, is to make them an *equivalent* for obtaining the cession of the territory necessary for the communication between their *provinces of New Brunswick and of Canada.*"[5]

In early March, all of the American commissioners except Russell were in Paris. They were all concerned about Bayard, who was confined with a severe cough, fever, and an ulcerated throat, from which he never recovered although he was able to return home before he died. However, the Chevalier was the first to learn and reveal to the group the news that Napoleon had escaped from Elba and landed in France near Cannes, reportedly with 12,000 men and four pieces of cannon. The King, he revealed, immediately declared the former Emperor a rebel and a traitor.

By March 11, *le Moniteur* admitted to Bonaparte's progress within eight leagues of Lyons. That evening many people left Paris in a state of panic. After attending a pantomime at the Porte of St. Martin, Adams found numerous patrols of soldiers, national guardsmen, and sentinels stationed at the street corners. Clusters of people surrounded pillars and lampposts to read the placards announcing the latest news. When Adams joined them, a soldier came up to him and whispered in a low voice, "Dispersez-vous, Messieurs, dispersez-vous."

In Britain, news of Napoleon's escape was an additional blow to national pride. Already disturbed by the Treaty of Ghent, which the people had received with little enthusiasm, the return coincided with news from the United States that General Andrew Jackson had vanquished England's forces at New Orleans.

Paris was in a turmoil. The Palais Royale was placarded with appeals to arms against Bonaparte and heartening reports that the former Emperor had no more than 12–13,000 men at Lyons. Several army officers assured Adams that the King's government would hold because there was strong support for it, including that of the armed forces who, though they had served Napoleon in the past, would now remain faithful to the legitimate King. Sentiment in Paris appeared to be pro-Bourbon. Even though the theaters were half empty, shouts of "Vive le Roi" were as hearty as ever. Nonetheless, rumor persisted that Bonaparte would be in Paris in less than a week and would enter like a conqueror without spending an ounce of gunpowder on his march. Adams did not believe the prediction possible.

But he was less certain of his judgment when he heard that early in the morning of March 20, the King left the Tuileries for the north because Napoleon was expected within the next twenty-four hours. However, the city still seemed unanimously in favor of its present regime and that night at the opera, the cries for the King were as boisterous as ever and the walls of the Palais Royale were covered with anti-Bonaparte placards.

By the following day, the fickle Parisians had done a turnabout. Great crowds of people lined the boulevards, shouting "Vive l'Empereur." Cries of "Vive le Roi" were stilled. The grand entry was scheduled to take place through the Porte St. Antoine after four in the afternoon. John Quincy walked on the boulevards until 5:30, mingling with the crowds, hoping for a glimpse of him. Two or three troops of horses of his company entered but there was no sign of the Emperor. Though the crowd shouted enthusiastically for the horsemen as they passed, many of the people whom Adams overheard talking remarked on the inconstancy of the people. Almost miraculously responsive to business, the print shops had replaced portraits of the Bourbon family with prints of Napoleon, Marie Louise, and the King of Rome. A trooper advised Adams at six o'clock that it would be about an hour before Napoleon entered, so Adams went home to dinner and then returned to find the crowds dispersing because the latest report was that he would not enter Paris that way.

At the Théâtre Français that evening Adams noted that the actors were listless and uneasy. However, many in the audience wore a cockade. After the performance, on the way home, Adams noticed that the columns of the Palais Royale were now covered with two Napoleonic proclamations, one to the people and one to the army. A bonfire in the garden was consuming the Bourbon placards. While he was at the theater, Napoleon had entered the city at the head of the same troops that had been sent to oppose him.

The next day, Adams walked to the Place du Carrousel where he saw troops passing in review before the Emperor. The soldiers seemed enthusiastic, but the people scarcely managed to cheer. An hour later he returned to his hotel without getting a good look at Napoleon, who stayed in the palace.

Returning from his nightly visit to the theater on March 23, John Quincy was relieved to hear his wife's carriage arrive in the courtyard. He had been expecting her for about a week. She had left St. Petersburg forty days earlier. Louisa Adams, two decades later, wrote a spirited account of her hazardous journey across most of Europe with her small son. She left the Russian capital on February 12 in extremely cold weather with a newly employed French nurse and two servants. The Russian government arranged the trip and, at first, except for the weather, everything went well.

At Riga, the party rested for four or five days while the carriage was fixed. Taking stock, Louisa found that all her provisions were frozen, even the Madeira wine, and that Charles's silver cup was missing. The Governor graciously entertained Mrs. Adams, who spent most of her time at the mansion. Proceeding to Courland, the snow was so deep that the carriage had to be dug out frequently, and when the Adams party reached Mittau, friends warned Louisa that the roads were unsafe and that one of her servants was a well-known desperado from that town. She answered bravely that she knew of his past history but had promised to return him to his country. Privately uneasy, but determined to continue to Paris, she was thoroughly frightened when her driver admitted that he was lost. Baptiste, the reprobate, agreed to take one of the horses and get help, and succeeded in persuading a Russian officer to guide them to an inn after rewarding him with a handsome present. Louisa hid her bags of gold and silver from her servants, just carrying small amounts with her each day. She also kept her letters from the Russian government close to her at all times.

The party crossed over a corner of Poland, fording a frozen river that was tested for safety with poles. At the border of Russian territory, the guards were impudent and had to be shown the official letter before they allowed Louisa to continue. For a way, the road was so close to the sea that Charles wanted to know if they were going into the "great water."

From Koenigsberg, where they rested for a day and Louisa bought some amber and delivered her letter of credit, they went on to Berlin. Baptiste started to become disagreeable and threatening until Louisa told him that he could leave her employ if he wished, and that she had lived in Prussia for years and was acquainted with the King. He refused to leave, promising to be on his good behavior, but his attitude continued threatening, which frightened the other servants.

Louisa stayed in Berlin for a week while her carriage was overhauled. She recalled that it had been fourteen years since she had arrived there as a bride. The city was now very French, she observed, and she enjoyed visits with some of her old friends. In contrast to her happy memories of the Prussian capital, Louisa reflected that she had never felt at home in St. Petersburg. Except for the kindness of the imperial family, "I quitted its gaudy loneliness without a sigh except that which was wafted to the tomb of my lovely Babe."

Outside of Berlin, the roads passed through barren pine woods filled with bands of soldiers straggling home. At dusk Louisa would put on her son's military cap with its tall feather and lay his toy sword across the windows of the carriage, because her friends told her that anything military escaped attack. The servants laughed at her subterfuge so she put the insignia away before coming to the night's hostel.

Louisa was startled when she heard that Napoleon had returned from Elba, because of a curious incident that occurred just before she left St. Petersburg. A Russian countess, a friend of a friend of hers with whom she was dining, read her cards and predicted that about halfway through her journey a great man would set Europe into a fresh commotion. Louisa, she prophesied, would learn this en route and would have to change her plans. There would be difficulties but a safe conclusion to the journey.

Outside of Frankfurt, the carriage passed through a battlefield where ten thousand men had fallen. Louisa almost fainted from the stench and horror. When the servants arrived in Frankfurt they announced that they would not continue any further because they feared that war would recommence. Louisa's banker urged her to remain in the city until the situation was more clearly resolved, but she would agree only to a change of route. The only servant who could be persuaded to go with her to Paris was a clever, fourteen-year-old boy who had served in the Russian campaign and regaled his new mistress with anecdotes about Napoleon.

The travellers reached Carlsruhe without incident but Louisa was disappointed that Princess Amalia had fled to Munich and that the rumor that Napoleon had been shot was untrue. When the Adams party reached the Rhine, their real troubles began. The military stopped the carriage at Strasbourg and questioned the travellers closely. By this time, Louisa was exhausted and ill and in very poor shape to endure the angry questions from rough soldiers who stopped the carriage at every barrier and the endless nights in lonely, dilapidated inns. Good accommodations at Château-Thierry and a bottle of the best champagne that Louisa had ever tasted was a welcome respite until the evening was spoiled by a bullying gendarme, who frightened Charles by telling him to be a good boy and say nothing.

The next day the Adams carriage drove into the midst of the imperial army. Louisa was unaware of the problem until she heard curses flying at her from a number of women who were following the soldiers. "Tear them out of the carriage, they are Russians! Take them out and kill them!" they screeched. The soldiers grabbed the horses' heads but Louisa had enough presence of mind to show her credentials. An officer called out that the carriage belonged to an American lady going to meet her husband in Paris. "Vive les Américains!" the soldiers shouted. To which Louisa was forced to answer, "Vive Napoléon!" Taking no chances, a number of soldiers were directed to walk by the horses and to fire at the driver if he made a suspicious move. General Michele, who had taken charge, rode beside the carriage, warning Louisa that her position was precarious because the army was thoroughly undisciplined. He advised her to appear confident and to answer the vivas with enthusiasm. He gallantly offered to find lodgings for the American party and complimented Louisa on her French. Small Charles sat by his mother's side "like a marble statue," completely terrorized by the noise and confusion. All along the way, soldiers pointed bayonets at the carriage and called out awful oaths and threats.

The innkeeper was cajoled into housing the Adams party only if Louisa would agree to stay in a darkened room and conceal both her servants and her coach. Faint and ill, shut up in her chamber with the shutters tightly closed, Louisa neither could nor would sleep. All night long soldiers crowded into the inn, screaming and drinking. At one point the lady innkeeper crept into Louisa's room with some hot coffee and apologized for having to leave her alone. During the night, soldiers burst into the Adams room and grabbed Charles, forcing him to burn his Prussian cap.

Louisa left the next morning as soon as it was light and reached Châtillon sur Marne at nightfall unmolested. The innkeeper there warned her not to proceed to Paris because a major battle was shaping up at the gates. By this time Louisa was almost out of money, worried that her husband did not know her new route, and completely out of patience. She decided to risk proceeding to the outskirts of Paris where she might be able to contact John Quincy. The trip was easy, because her coach was almost the only one on the road, and, being an impressive equipage with six horses, the rumor spread that the lady was one of Napoleon's sisters coming to join him. On the 20th of March, Louisa arrived at Meaux, where the hostess told her terrible tales of the Cossacks and showed her the graves of six local girls who had been their victims. Louisa understood then the hatred displayed on the road when the Frenchwomen thought that she was Russian.

Except for a broken wheel that required fixing and forced Louisa to traverse the bandit-ridden forest of Bondy twice, the last lap of the trip to Paris was uneventful. The cost of the St. Petersburg to Paris journey, including the purchase of the carriage, meticulously computed by Louisa, came to $1,606.38 after all the currencies were translated into American dollars.[6]

Having been proved wrong about Napoleon's resilience, Adams tried a number of times to get a look at him. He succeeded in getting a clear view of him several times at the theater, where he marveled that the populace now shouted wildly its enthusiasm for him. John Quincy attributed the Emperor's successful restoration to the core of faithful former soldiers who rallied round him in the towns along the route to Paris.

During one of several interviews with M. de Caulaincourt, Duke de Vicence, a fellow diplomat from St. Petersburg once again in high office, Adams discussed Franco-American relations. Crawford, the American Minister to France, was not able to talk to the Duke because he did not have credentials for the new government. The Duke complimented John Quincy on the "bonne paix" that he had negotiated, to which Adams replied that it might be so considered particularly since the Americans had to contend with Great Britain alone without a friend in Europe. To the Duke's comment that the Emperor of Russia had manifested some interest in the welfare of the United States, the American answered that after the failure of his mediation effort, Alexander left the United States to fight her own battle.

The first reports about the reception of the Treaty of Ghent at home reached the American commissioners about the end of March. They knew already that the defeat of the British pleased the continental powers. Once the treaty was accomplished, from Paris to Stockholm, from Copenhagen to Amsterdam, congratulations poured in to the headquarters of the American team at Ghent. But even more satisfying was the reaction of their own countrymen, particularly the President. Madison termed the peace "highly honorable to the nation." Proof of its success was the speed and unanimity with which it was ratified. As soon as the messengers arrived in New York with the document, the rejoicing started. The Battery shook with the noise of cannon exploding and a torchlight parade snaked through the tortuous streets of lower Manhattan. The Quaker city of Philadelphia broke its accustomed Sunday quiet with the ringing of peace bells. Even Boston, formerly resistant and resentful, rejoiced unrestrainedly. Business was closed and the people milled in the streets, openly celebrating. In Virginia, where the blockade had caused a good deal of suffering, there was joyful relief. All through America the good news spread that peace had broken out.

Though spring in Paris was lovely as usual, Adams was getting impatient that his instructions to Great Britain were taking so long. "I have never been charged with a public trust from which there was so little prospect of any satisfactory result, or which presented itself with so little anticipation of anything agreeable to myself or my family," he complained to his father, whose notes on the fisheries question he was studying. The problem, John Quincy explained, was that, unlike the peace treaty, where anxieties were shared with others, this mission would have to be faced alone. Part of his consternation was that both Gallatin and Clay, already in England, had talked with Lord Castlereagh and sent back discouraging reports about Britain's reluctance to negotiate fruitfully.

In early May, the three Adamses visited Lafayette at La Grange. The General's castle was an old granite structure with four turrets, dating back to the time of Louis le Gros, set in a park planted with willows, poplars, firs, and locusts, much in the English style. The moat and drawbridge had been turned into a winding stream. Lafayette was proud of his flocks of merinos, cattle, and horses, which he proudly showed off to the Americans.

Shortly afterward, Adams's credentials arrived from America and his passports from England. The departure was postponed only long enough to say farewell to Lafayette, whose parting advice to the American Minister was to make clear to Castlereagh that England would be working against her own self-interest by starting war again.

Reflecting on his Parisian visit, John Quincy decided that it was, in many respects, the most agreeable interlude of his life. He was able to enjoy the French capital at a time that he had leisure and respite from worry about his country's welfare. He had been exposed to the gloomy court of Louis XVIII, to the splendid circle of the Duke of Orleans, and, finally, to a few glimpses of Napoleon. Sightseeing had been uninterrupted by business. Museums, courts of law, mechanical models, a Gobelin tapestry, deserted churches and catacombs had filled his days and stimulated his mind. He had the avid curiosity and the boundless energy that was to characterize generations of American travellers in Europe. Thomas Jefferson, given John Quincy's letters to read by his proud mother, commented aptly: "What lessons of wisdom Mr. Adams must have read in that short space of time! More than fall to the lot of others in the course of a large life."[7]

Laden with letters and packages to be carried to England, the Adamses left Paris on May 16. John Quincy and Louisa travelled in one carriage, Charles and his nurse in another. When they reached England, the countryside was in early verdure and the orchards in full bloom. The road from Dover to London seemed familiar to Adams even after eighteen years, but there were signs of hard times along the way, evidenced by the many homeless beggars and paupers who wandered about. When they arrived in London, the Adams party went straight to 67 Harley Street, Cavendish Square, which had been rented for them.

At the first meeting between Lord Castlereagh and Adams, which took place at the end of May, all of the essential British-American problems were reviewed. Adams informed the British Minister that the President of the United States proposed as a solution to the sensitive problem of impressment that all foreign seamen not already naturalized be excluded from the naval and merchant service of the United States. Castlereagh responded that he appreciated the American action but that he could not recognize naturalization and abandon the right to allegiance of all British subjects. In regard to the joint commissions provided for in the Treaty of Ghent, Lord Castlereagh obligingly asked what would be the most convenient season for them to work. Summer, Adams replied. The subject of the restoration of slaves was postponed until Clay and Gallatin and the British commissioners could meet with them. Adams's initial appraisal of Lord Castlereagh was that, though handsome, his manner was cold, if not absolutely repulsive.

The social round began at once for the new American Minister. At the endless dinner parties, the conversation was centered on discussion of Napoleon's chances for success. All agreed that it was most unpromising but it was commonly believed that after his defeat the Corsican would seek refuge in America.

George and John Adams joined their parents in London. John Quincy admitted that they looked almost like strangers after the long separation, but he embraced them with delight, "fresh from the headquarters of good principles." They carried with them news of the whole family. George was now fourteen, tall for his age but somewhat nervous and inclined to frequent illnesses. John, his grandfather's favorite, was small but full of energy.[8]

The preparation of the new commercial treaty was not a congenial task for Adams. Once again he was part of a team, one of whose members was Henry Clay and another Albert Gallatin, who had dominated the Ghent negotiations. Furthermore, the other two Americans had laid the groundwork for the negotiations, having been in London for the past two months. To complete the feeling that the situation was a duplicate of Ghent, Goulburn and Dr. Adams were on the British team. The third Englishman was Frederick Robinson, the Vice President of the Board of Trade, a pleasant and distinguished man.

The American commissioners had a tough assignment. They must persuade Britain to give up her discriminating duties against the United States and to allow her to trade with the British East Indies The British, always quick to seize an advantage, immediately thought in terms of an equivalent, such as the fur trade with Indians in the American Northwest, which the Americans immediately turned down. Finally, on June 7, the British commissioners accepted Gallatin's draft and promised to meet in two days with their answer. Clay and Gallatin were impatient to go home but agreed to stay a little longer. When the British failed to meet the deadline, Clay, disgusted, wanted to leave, because he did not think the negotiations would ever be completed.

It was almost ten days before the counter treaty was delivered, and then it was so different from the American version that Adams thought it was useless for his colleagues to wait around any longer. The limited terms offered included a most favored nation status only in Europe and limited trade rights in four Indian cities for a two-year period. And for this small concession an equivalent was demanded. Three disgusted Americans, Clay stating loudly that he had been deceived, prepared an answer.

Two days later at the Board of Trade, the talks were resumed. Adams took little part in them because there was constant reference to meetings that took place before he came. However, despite Clay's pessimism and British obstinacy, Adams concluded that Britain would admit the United States to her India trade because it was advantageous to her. But no agreement was reached in the next few days and, on June 21, news of Wellington's victory at Waterloo suspended the talks.

John Quincy took his family out in their carriage to see the celebration for the great victory over Napoleon. They were disappointed at the lack of splendor and the lack of imagination displayed. The illuminations were small, just spelling out "Wellington and Bleucher," "Victory," "GPR," and "GR." There were a few bad transparencies. By midnight all the revellers were gone and the Adamses retired with them.

The familiar pattern of Clay's demands that the negotiations be broken off, Gallatin's pleas for patience, and Adams's aloofness terminated on July 3. Abruptly, terms were agreed upon. The four-year treaty had only two significant articles, Adams informed his father—the abolition of discriminating duties and the admission of American commercial vessels to four British settlements in the East Indies. Britain lost the Indian fur trade and the United States failed to penetrate the West Indian trade, an error on the part of the British, J.Q.A. said, because it would cause distress to the British West Indies.

Adams and Gallatin had an irritating dispute over the placing of the signatories' names at the end of the treaty. John Quincy had received "a rap on the knuckles from home" because in the Treaty of Ghent the Americans had signed under the British and the King of Great Britain was named before the United States in all the copies. When Adams told this to Clay, he said it was of no consequence and left the room. Gallatin, however, was annoyed when he heard that Adams had copied the new treaty with the United States and Great Britain alternating for first place. "Oh, that is entirely wrong; it will throw the whole business in confusion," Gallatin said and wanted it changed. Adams refused. "I will not sign the treaty without the alternative observed throughout," he declared, and added, "The treaty itself I very much dislike, and it is only out of deference to you and Mr. Clay that I consent to sign it at all. . . . We obtain nothing by it but what we should obtain by the regulation of this Government without it."[9] The dispute proved to be superfluous because the British accepted the arrangement of names with no comment.

When it was time for the treaty makers to part, Henry Goulburn said to Adams, "Well, this is the second good job we have done together." "Yes," answered John Quincy, "and I only hope we may do a third, going on from better to better."[10] Despite his lukewarm attitude toward the two treaties, Adams noted on his forty-eighth birthday that the past year had been the most important one of his life in relation to public affairs.[11]

Though he loved and respected his parents tremendously, John Quincy sometimes found their meddling in his affairs very annoying. He hated nepotism and was more than a little put out when he discovered that his father had arranged that his grandson, John Adams Smith, be given the post of secretary to the English legation. The new American Minister had already requested that the post be given to Alexander Hill Everett, which made the situation doubly embarrassing. Further, John Quincy was still angry with his older nephew, William Steuben Smith, who had been with him in St. Petersburg. The young man had excellent qualities, his uncle admitted to Abigail, but "he has been unfortunately deficient in that without which no good qualities can avail—prudence."[12] The protest came too late, however, because young John was already on his way to London and turned out to be a model secretary and a very great asset to the legation, which his uncle was very glad to admit.

The frustrations of group authorship had disturbed the former Harvard Professor of Rhetoric. After the continual rejection of his drafts by his colleagues at Ghent, Adams questioned his ability to turn out a stylish well-reasoned piece of work. However, he consoled himself with the thought that whether he could convince an antagonist or gain support for his cause, "whatever error there may be in the performance of it, let there be none of neglect and no deficiency of earnest zeal."[13]

Of the many treaty articles that Adams now had the responsibility of seeing implemented, the most difficult for the New Englander were those concerning the restoration of American slaves who had been captured or "rescued" by the British during the war. In a letter to Lord Castlereagh written in August, Adams said: "I trust it will remain evident that in evacuating all places within the jurisdiction of the United States and in departing from their waters, the British commanders were bound not to carry away any slaves or other private property of the citizens of the United States which had been taken upon their shores."[14]

The matter was discussed at great length between J.Q.A. and Lord Liverpool, the Prime Minister. The British, Lord Liverpool said, understood the regulation concerning slaves to apply only to slaves taken in forts and on the battlefield and not to those who had taken refuge under the protection of the British army and Navy. Adams answered stiffly that the United States had no intention of disguising its intentions. The object was the restoration of all property, including slaves, which were property. The only mitigating circumstance for Adams's discomfort at having to pursue the painful subject was his knowledge that British hands were not entirely clean in this matter. Some of the slaves, John Quincy informed Lord Liverpool, had been enticed from their masters by British officers with promises of freedom and then callously resold into slavery in the West Indies. Adams said that he could provide a list of such transactions. It was then the Prime Minister's turn to be uncomfortable.

Liverpool was very cooperative about the other parts of the treaty. He said that orders had been given to surrender Fort Michilimackinac. There was, however, some difficulty about the Island of St. Helena. Since Bonaparte was to be imprisoned there, Liverpool explained, by general agreement of the allies all ships but those of the East India Company were to be excluded from the port.

Though the island was of no importance to American shipping, Adams considered the principal significant and so neither agreed nor disagreed.

Impressment, the most highly charged wartime question, was only of academic interest. The wars over, British seamen were starving in London ports and asking the Admiralty to exclude foreigners from sailing on their vessels. A large part of Adams's time was spent in listening to the applications of seamen who needed relief. In a memorandum to Lord Castlereagh, the American Minister stated, with some dry humor, "Should every person presenting himself to the American consulate as an American seaman be received as such, and conveyed to the United States at their expense, a charge heretofore made, though utterly without foundation, against the American government, of inviting British seamen into the service of the United States might recur with an appearance of plausibility."[15]

The fisheries problem was never long out of J.Q.A.'s mind. In every letter, John Adams prodded his son not to give in "one tittle or iota,"[16] advice which was hardly necessary. However, John Quincy advised his father, their native state must pass a law declaring its rights to the fisheries so that it would be clear that humiliating British acts, such as intimidating fishermen by warning them sixty miles off the shores, would not be tolerated. Massachusetts must protest these outrages and not use them in factional strife as a fault with which to taunt the federal government. If this continued, Adams warned, the British would end up by ordering Americans from the fishing grounds.

Officially, John Quincy and the British were contesting the matter on the grounds that the American claim that the fisheries was an age-old right versus the British demand for an equivalent. J.Q.A. maintained that the Treaty of 1783, which basically acknowledged American independence, could not be annulled nor could any of its parts. The fisheries were essential to the livelihood of a multitude of Americans devoid of any other, Adams argued. The British Minister answered that it was the drying and the curing on the shores that had the bad consequences, because the American fishermen, being closer, could get to stations before the British and would get the best fishing, drying, and curing places, which led to quarrels and blows, a situation that existed even before the war. Adams then suggested that American liberty be limited to unsettled and uninhabited places. Lord Bathurst, the Secretary for War and Colonies, who had been conducting the interview with Adams, was conciliatory and agreeable, just as Lord Liverpool had been. Adams, however, assured Monroe that, no matter how eloquent, the arguments of a British Minister could have no weight with him because "Our determination to maintain the right will continue it."[17]

In November, John Quincy had so severe an inflammation of the eyes that Louisa had to write his letters. The expense of living in England coupled with his growing agreement with his father's assertion that he could do no good for his country there increased his desire to return home in the spring. To save money, the family was living in the suburb of Ealing, in a charming residence aptly named "Little Boston." The entire property was bordered with laurels and surrounded by a garden. George and John were at school studying the classics and mathematics. "I am happy to assure you that the Yankee boys have done no dishonor to the reputation of their country," John Quincy wrote to his father. However, Louisa reported that Charles had forgotten his Russian and German and seemed unable to concentrate on his studies so that he was not thought of too highly.[18]

As the post-war Minister to England, J.Q.A. was, as his father continually insisted, in an unenviable position. The basic antagonism between the former mother country and her rapidly expanding and potentially powerful offshoot was unabated and further complicated by unfinished business, such as boundaries, trade, the fisheries, and unsettled claims, whether they be those of indigent seamen or slave properties. That the two countries would eventually become steadfast allies was unclear in 1816.

Adams worried that peace was proving to be a burden for Great Britain's finances and that she might seek a reason for making war, in which case the United States would be her logical enemy. It was obvious that England must look with disfavor on the rise of any other commercial nation. Americans, for their part, found it hard to forget England's recent interest in New England dissidents. The expansion of the American Navy, one of Adams's favorite schemes, was being carefully watched and then openly debated in the British Parliament. Rivalry over the world's carrying trade was soon to be intensified in the Western Hemisphere with the continuous dispute over the West Indian trade and the newly emerging Latin American countries.

Lord Castlereagh, who recognized the diversity of Anglo-American differences, asked Adams which one he would like to treat with first. Adams selected the problem of seamen, because of anxiety over it in the United States and because it had been the principal cause of the late war and the most likely source of future danger. Castlereagh liked President Madison's proposal to limit navigation in American ships to American seamen. It was a solution to impressment that "would rather make any arrangement between the two nations unnecessary," he suggested.[19] He was also receptive to J.Q.A.'s threefold plan to solve the dilemma of American seamen recently discharged from the British service into which they had been impressed and who were now unemployed and starving. The provisions were: to help to send them back to the United States; to allow those who were entitled to pensions to receive them in America; to inform Adams of the names of destitute American seamen so they could be taken care of.

Next in importance, Adams said, was the problem of disarmament on the Great Lakes. Once again the American proposed his government's plan that there should be no new armament on either side. Castlereagh countered with the suggestion that the Lakes, including the shores, should belong to one party, thus creating a wide separation between the territories and the elimination of the need for armaments. Otherwise, the British Minister insisted, the United States would have an advantage because she could rearm quicker. Though Castlereagh offered to submit the American proposal to the Cabinet, Adams wrote to Monroe that it did not look hopeful.

The next hot issue was Florida. Castlereagh began by denying the rumor that Spain had ceded the area to her, a denial that Adams accepted. They had quite enough territory, the Englishman asserted. Both Ministers then claimed that they were neutral to Spain. To the question of what was Britain's attitude toward South American independence, Castlereagh did not say.

Adams told Castlereagh that at Lord Liverpool's request he had amassed evidence on the subject of slaves taken from America and then resold by British officers in the West Indies. The British Minister took the lists of slaves and the names of the vessels and agreed to study them and to check them against British records. The fisheries were touched on briefly. Castlereagh, acknowledging Adams's long, impassioned note on the subject, asserted that he did not wish to prevent American fishing and agreed to enter into negotiations as provided in the treaty.

The office of the American legation was now located at 13 Craven Street, the Strand, a narrow street which ran from 10, the Strand, to the Thames Embankment. The quarters also served as Adams's London residence when he could not make the trip to Ealing. Official obligations, such as the Lord Mayor's dinner in honor of the Austrian archdukes, had to be honored, particularly since John Quincy was a favorite of the whig Mayor, who liked Americans. At this dinner the Duke of Kent gave a toast to the perpetuity of friendship between Great Britain and the United States, to which John Quincy answered in kind and was well applauded. Though he was an experienced guest at the endless diplomatic dinners, he was never satisfied with his own performance. He often chided himself that he had spoken too much or too little and considered himself weak at extemporaneous speaking. He confessed that he got through it only by thinking about what he would say all through dinner, "a process not remarkably favorable to the enjoyment of the conviviality of the table." He never grew accustomed to "tablecloth oratory."[20]

Due to the lack of a proper letter, Adams's presentation to Queen Charlotte was delayed for months. When he was presented, she was unusually cordial to him, despite her reputation of coldness to Americans. Her husband, George III, was in seclusion because of his madness. John Quincy heard later from the Archbishop of York that the King had been confined in two or three chambers in Windsor Castle for nearly five years. Though he was blind, he recognized people by their voices. His favorite amusement was playing the piano and devoting himself to the details of his dress.

Middle-age was getting the better of John Quincy Adams. His eyes were at least as good as they had been before his severe attack in the fall, but he complained of what was probably arthritis in his right hand. He noticed the difficulty first in his second winter at St. Petersburg, but it had become progressively worse since then. It was painful for him to hold a pen, and, though he could manage if he wrote slowly, he feared that if his correspondence increased he would have to employ an amanuensis. Increased girth was another problem. He left Russia a skeleton but had been "redeeming flesh" so rapidly since that he worried he would become unwieldy and lazy. Portraits of him at this time would make his father's title of "His Rotundity" most appropriate. Abigail recommended that he go to Bath for his rheumatic disorders, which ran in the family. Tom had been ill with rheumatic fever in January.

During the spring, lacking direct orders from Monroe, J.Q.A. was forced to refer to Washington the conclusion of his solutions for American-British differences. Charles Bagot, who was to go there as the new British Minister, was made aware of the discussions. Nevertheless, Adams was relieved to hear Lord Castlereagh declare his determination to avoid collision over the fisheries and willingness to eliminate unnecessary naval forces on the Great Lakes. The matter of discrimination against American ships in Irish ports, part of Britain's policy to limit Irish emigration, was settled favorably. Lord Castlereagh agreed to remove the discrimination but refused to give up the right.[21]

No matter how hard he resisted, a healthy part of Adams's time had to be devoted to state functions. The marriage of Princess Charlotte to the Prince of Saxe-Coburg consumed several days of festivities. Louisa attended the wedding in a white-net dress without a hoop, richly embroidered in silver, with a blue train embroidered to match and trimmed in net. Adams was elegant in a blue-cloth coat embroidered in gold, and a white waistcoat. In the course of paying formal calls, John Quincy and Lord Walpole found themselves in the same room. Adams, who had not seen Walpole since St. Petersburg, introduced himself again. Lord Walpole, without altering a muscle of his face, commented to him, "You've grown fatter," and then left the room.[22]

A much more congenial hobby for John Quincy than the social scene was hunting down books that his father wanted in the many marvelous old bookshops of London. Old John Adams, though half blind and very feeble, looked forward to the parcels of books sent home from abroad. He had requested as many copies of the British edition of the *Silesian Letters* as J.Q.A. could locate. "If I was not poor," the old gentleman wrote in a shaky hand, "I should plague you to death in hunting Books for me all over Europe. Oh! what a Building I should erect of Quincy North Common Granite, capable of holding the Library of Alexandria! . . . This is a rage; a mania; a delirium or at least an Enthusiasm which I desire you to correct in me and in yourself and in your son George."[23] He didn't mean a word of the latter statement, really, for bibliomania was one of the most endearing Adams traits. The aging ex-President wrote frequently to his son and to his grandsons. His letters, full of affection and astute comments, unlike many of the letters of his contemporaries, kept gratuitous advice and lectures to a minimum. His comments were interesting, and his pen, though often sharp, had something to say. When reporting the death of his son-in-law, Colonel Smith, he wrote: "He undesignedly did more Injury to me and my Administration than any other Man." He referred to the fact that the ubiquitous Colonel was taken in by Miranda.[24]

His small leisure, John Quincy complained to his parents, deprived him of time to spend with his sons. Though they were good-tempered boys, their father regretted that they were constantly attempting to escape from their studies, which, of course, he realized, made them much like other children. George, he felt, however, had reached the age at which it was useless to impose learning as a task if he had no interest in it for his own gratification. "If I could inspire the souls of my three boys with the sublime Platonic idea of aiming at ideal excellence. If I could persuade them to soar for the standard of emulation to the lofty *possible* instead of crawling upon the ground with the dirt-clogged *real*— But I have not the time."[25]

But despite his protestations, John Quincy had great expectations for his oldest son, which were shared by the young man's grandfather. John Adams wrote to the boy: "I agree with your amiable young friend Claudius Braceford in his opinion that nature designed you for the Senate rather than for the Field. . . . I know that gratitude, not ambition dictated your Christian name. But have care that you do not make it an Object of your idolatry."[26]

Money continued to be a nagging problem which, as J.Q.A. said many times, was inevitable in the American foreign service. He tried to squeeze some small concession from the State Department by informing them of comparative salaries and apprising them of the difficulties under which an American Minister operated. Adams could not return the hospitality that was accorded him by the British government and the diplomatic corps or even show the proper civility to visiting Americans. He concluded that unless the American government changed its attitude, permanent missions would have to be given to men of large fortunes who were willing to spend liberally.

The development of Massachusetts politics was discussed animatedly in an exchange of letters between the two Adamses. J.Q.A. had sacrificed loyalty to his own state for the best interests of the Union as long ago as the embargo controversy. The subsequent history of the federalist party had only convinced him of the correctness of his action. He observed the further decline of the party in its failures in Vermont, New Hampshire, New York, Connecticut, Maryland, and Massachusetts. "I contemplate their complete overthrow in another year," he commented in the summer of 1816. Though the dismemberment of his state through the separation of Maine would obviously occur within the next few years, his ability to tolerate the idea so well only re-enforced his self-knowledge that, if anything, his national feelings had grown. He commented that the doctrine of states' rights was all right for large states but good for nothing for weaker states and bad for the nation.

John Quincy Adams harbored intense feelings of nationalism and patriotism but always reserved the right to be independent and to count his conscience as his final arbiter. When he read the famous toast attributed by the newspapers to Stephen Decatur—"Our Country! In her intercourse with foreign nations, may she always be in the right; but our country, right or wrong"—he said that he could never join in the sentiment. "I cannot ask of heaven success, even for my country, in a cause where she should be in the wrong," he wrote. His toast, he said, would go: "May our country be always successful, but whether successful or otherwise, always right." Patriotism that was incompatible with the principles of eternal justice was unsound.[27]

Before the close of the summer season, the Adamses attended a healthy round of functions. At a dinner given by the Lord Mayor, J.Q.A. was more than a little put out by the Duke of Wellington. The great man allowed himself to be introduced to Adams once again and neither recognized nor remembered him. Wellington sat through the dinner with a grave, stern face, occasionally allowing a pleasing smile to pass over his face, but, being completely without small talk, yawned through the dinner. However, when it came time for the toasts, "bore the daubing of flattery spread over him . . . with moderate composure," Adams noted.[28] Adams was pleased to record the final event of the busy social season, the Queen's evening party in honor of the Prince Regent's birthday. Too large a portion of the past six months had been consumed by pointless festivities.

At their summer meeting, Adams and Lord Castlereagh reviewed their differences but found little common ground upon which to resolve them. The British refused to allow American trade with the British West Indies and Lord Castlereagh denied any knowledge of the boarding of American merchant vessels on Lake Erie, although accounts of it were in all the English newspapers. Lord Castlereagh seemed rather distant and vague, a state of mind that Adams attributed to the pressure of business.

At a dinner party given by the Marquis d'Osmond, the French Ambassador, Adams had the opportunity to meet George Canning for the first time. Notably anti-American, Canning actually behaved very cordially. Both he and Lord Liverpool asked many knowledgeable questions about the forthcoming American elections. Adams told them that Monroe would most likely be the next President. Liverpool asked if he might be opposed because he was a Virginian, to which John Quincy answered that it was a ground for objection but would not matter. Canning struck the American Minister as the most able of all the Cabinet Ministers whom he had met.

Though Lord Castlereagh persistently refused to discuss the British West Indies trade and all questions of neutral right in time of war, Adams still included the subjects in his lengthy and thorough note to him. Since they were important matters, Adams wrote to Monroe, an attempt must be made to persuade the British to discuss them reasonably. He suspected that it was not Lord Castlereagh who was making the difficulties but the Colonial Department. Consequently he was forced to the logical conclusion that nothing could be accomplished unless there was a change of Ministry, which was most unlikely because the rise of the price of corn had removed a great deal of the country's agricultural distress. England was enjoying also a revival of manufacturing and an increase in commercial revenue. She was definitely emerging from her post-war slump. Negotiations broke off in September because Lord Castlereagh had to go to Ireland, ostensibly to visit his father but really, it was said, to go on an electioneering campaign. "Oh, that I could make a visit to my father," J.Q.A. said wistfully.[29]

Warnings that staying in England much longer would be poor business on many scores came frequently from John Adams. He predicted that further absence might make it necessary for his son to renounce a public career forever. For the sake of the children also, John Quincy must bring his family back to America. J.Q.A. agreed, hoping that George would be able to get into Harvard early because of his proficiency in Latin and Greek. "I trust he will become a scholar," he said.[30] By the end of November there was reason to hope for an early return. Newspapers throughout the United States, John Adams wrote, were announcing "somewhat impudently" that J.Q.A. was recalled and would be appointed Secretary of State in the new President's Cabinet. "I hope it is true . . . I hope you will accept."[31]

By Christmas even John Quincy had to take the rumors about the Cabinet offer seriously. Although he had received no official advice, letters of congratulations and inevitable job solicitations were arriving daily. He did not know how to answer them. His own decision must wait until he was forced to make the commitment. Characteristically, he had overwhelming self-doubt as to his ability to fulfill the position and insisted to himself that since his native state did not esteem his services, he had regarded the English mission as the conclusion of his official career. Adams was being only partially honest, because he had heard suggestions that he would succeed Monroe from the time that he had arrived in England as the American Minister.

In America, the Adams appointment was accepted as a certainty and was a favorite topic of conversation. President Monroe's motivation for choosing the New Englander was attributed to his desire to lessen jealousy against the Virginia dynasty and to placate Adams's section of the country. Some commentators regarded the appointment as an intention to declare J.Q.A. for the next Presidency, for the position of Secretary of State had become the bridge to the White House. Others, rather malevolently, saw the appointment as a perfect opportunity for Adams to hang himself, which, they predicted, he would do promptly. Clay and the western clique were noisily opposed to the appointment, while Crawford was said to be sulky and threatening to retire. According to Crawford, Jonathan Russell made a deliberate effort to stop Adams's appointment and to urge Clay's instead.[32]

President Monroe wrote to Thomas Jefferson explaining his action. It would be bad for the country to draw a Secretary of State from Virginia, the South, or the West, he asserted. An appointment from those areas would set the whole country north of the Delaware against the approaching Administration. With this in mind, he had decided on John Quincy Adams, who, "by his age, long experience in our foreign affairs and adoption into the republican party, seems to have superior pretensions to any there." In much the same vein, Monroe wrote to Andrew Jackson, specifying that "By this arrangement [Adams's appointment] there can be no cause to suspect unfair combination for improper purposes." The Union would be served.

On March 5, with only one dissenting vote, as Harrison Gray Otis "had the satisfaction to inform" John Adams, Monroe's appointment of John Quincy Adams was accepted by the Senate. On the following day, a Mr. Cook of Kentucky was employed as a special messenger to deliver the President's letter informing the American Minister to England of his appointment. "Respect for your talents and patriotic services has induced me to commit to your care, with the sanction of the Senate, the Department of State. I have done this in confidence that it will be agreeable to you to accept it, which I can assure you will be very gratifying to me," the President wrote. No man, surely not one dedicated to public service, could resist that appeal.

While waiting for Castlereagh's summons, Adams studied the state of the British nation. He noted that while the peace of Ghent calmed discontent in America and seemed to cool party spirit, in England it spread disaffection and treason so widely that the government had to defend itself much in the manner of France before the Revolution. At the opening of Parliament, which the Adamses tried to watch from their carriage but were unable to because of the jam, there was violence. When the Prince Regent appeared in his elaborately gilded, tasteless, and clumsy state coach, drawn by eight cream-colored horses gorgeous in golden harnesses and sky-blue-silk ribbons, the crowd hissed and groaned. A window was broken by bullets or stones thrown by persons in the crowd, many of them wretched and menacing-looking. The Regent was uninjured, but ill-feeling was unassuaged.

Requests for parliamentary reform of the House of Commons, such as annual meetings and the franchise for all taxpayers, met no success. As a gesture to the starving, the Regent and his Ministers sacrificed part of their salaries but this did not increase their popularity. John Quincy predicted that the Administration would resort to repressive measures and silence the opposition with imprisonment and executions. On March 4, a bill to suspend habeas corpus passed both Houses with large majorities, along with three other bills that limited seditious meetings. Adams told the Earl of Harroby that habeas corpus was the distinguishing feature of liberty, but that he had voted to have it suspended in the case of Burr. The Earl then wanted to know what had happened to Burr, to which Adams replied that he was living in New York in obscurity.

Finally, in March, Lord Castlereagh sent for Adams. He apologized for his inability to see him sooner but said that the press of business had prevented him. However, he was ready to make certain propositions. They turned out to be scanty. The West Indies was still forbidden to American shipping, but he offered privileges in Bermuda. In the half hour allotted to Adams more time was spent in apologizing for the little time he had than in discussing matters of importance. Adams wrote to Monroe that, though Castlereagh denied it, the small concessions offered were probably in answer to Congress's act prohibiting clearance for ports to which vessels of the United States were not admitted.

Adams received Monroe's letter of appointment on April 16. Only too well he knew what "hard knots" he would have to untie, but nevertheless the next day he sent off his acceptance with the promise that he would try to leave for the United States during the following month. He was sorry to have to move out of "Little Boston," "one of the most delightful spots" in which he had ever resided. Passage was engaged on the *Washington*, which was to depart for New York the first week in June. Books and the Copley portraits of John Adams and Abigail Adams Smith were gathered for the journey. George, who had been on a tour of Paris, Brussels, and Ghent with friends of the family, returned.

While in London, Adams spent a good deal of time with seventy-year-old Jeremy Bentham, an exponent of the utilitarian school of philosophy that advocated "the greatest good for the greatest number." On their walks in Hyde Park and Kensington, they exchanged their views. Bentham expounded on reform in Britain, which, he admitted, would lead to the abolition of the Crown and the peerage and, since they would not go without a struggle, would probably mean civil war. Adams was more perturbed about Bentham's comments on religion. He feared that the philosopher was an atheist who spoke with reserve to spare the American's feelings. Before Adams left England, Betham sent him a very large package containing twenty-five copies of almost all his works, which he wanted distributed, one to the Governor of every state and the rest to suitable people.

Once again the problem of official gifts spoiled Adams's leavetaking. It was customary for Great Britain to bestow a gift of £500 on departing Ministers. John Quincy thought this procedure, apart from its unconstitutionality, degrading. It was like "beggars receiving alms from opulent princes." The practice of giving money "has not even the palliation of sentimentality to plead in its favor." When the master of ceremonies was informed of the American Minister's refusal of his gift, he was displeased because he usually received a ten per cent cut. The final audience with the Prince Regent was no more successful than his offering of gifts. Adams remarked acidly that he was "a Falstaff without the wit, and a Prince Henry without the compensations."[33]

Previous to Adams's departure, Castlereagh requested an interview to give the new American Secretary of State an overview of Britain's foreign policy. After asserting his country's desire for peace, Castlereagh asked about Spanish-American relations. Adams answered frankly that the two nations had serious misunderstandings over territorial boundaries and over commercial differences and that Spain was intractable. Castlereagh asked tentatively how the President would respond to an offer of mediation by Great Britain. Adams's answer was a non-committal explanation that he was not empowered to accept such a suggestion but it would surely be taken as a peaceful offer. Privately he recalled Britain's intransigence against the United States at Ghent, though, in all fairness, her position could be attributed to war. Castlereagh then touched on the desire of the United States to obtain the Floridas. West Florida was included in the Louisiana Purchase, Adams answered, because it had been part of the original French colony.

William Wilberforce, a member of the party in Parliament derisively called "the Saints," because of their agitation against the slave trade, made it his business to see Adams before he left the country. He projected a plan that would authorize the cruisers of all nations opposed to the slave trade to search and capture slave-trading vessels of those nations whose laws forbade the trade. Adams regarded this as a device to give Britain the right, in practice, to continue her wartime habit of searching and seizing other nations' ships, particularly since Britain was the only nation that had a fleet of cruisers that patrolled the waters in which the slave trade was carried on.

Another M.P. then offered the idea that every cruiser should carry an officer from each participating power, but both Wilberforce and Adams predicted that such a scheme would just lead to quarrelling. The issue was dropped abruptly when Adams brought up the cases of British officers who had taken slaves from the United States and then resold them. Wilberforce said that he was amazed at the information and disappointed at the failure of his conference.

A few days before Adams's departure, Castlereagh and he had a final, short meeting. If Florida was ceded to the United States what objection would she then have to the Mississippi River as her boundary, Castlereagh asked. Adams replied by pointing to the whole expanse of territory marked Louisiana on the British Minister's map and said that would be the objection. Smiling, Castlereagh commented that Spain was not the easiest of parties to deal with but he could say the same of the United States. Even at the last moment, he was evasive about British policy toward South America. Adams interpreted his hesitation to mean that Britain would side against the revolutionaries but would urge Spain to allow free trade, at least for the British. "In all her mediations, or offers of mediation, her justice and policy will be merely to serve herself," Adams wrote.

Robert Stewart, Lord Castlereagh, and John Quincy Adams never met again. Though they were both gifted men who developed mutual respect for each other, there was never any real sympathy between them. Adams's pride and sensitivity made him suspicious of the handsome, successful Englishman.

Adams departed from Europe with the conviction that the War of 1812 had left a determined antagonism against the United States. This feeling was shared with Great Britain by Spain, France, the Netherlands, Naples, Denmark, and the Barbary states, for all of them begrudged the United States her potential power. Even Russia, he asserted, had developed some coldness toward her former favorite. The Old World hoped that the burgeoning American nation would not remain united and would, instead, break up into several warring nations. Hence the new Secretary of State would base his political philosophy on the principles of union and national expansion. The keynote of his foreign policy was to be peace—"An efficient revenue and a growing navy, these are the pillars of my peace," he said.[34]

"London, farewell!" Adams wrote on June 10, with a sense of finality. In five days, the Adams family was on board the *Washington* en route to the United States. The days of wandering over the map of Europe were over. His country never again allowed John Quincy Adams to leave its shores.

CHAPTER 13

Mr. Secretary Adams

"Of the public history of Mr. Monroe's administration all that will be worth telling to posterity hitherto has been transacted through the Department of State."

". . . gifted and trained as a statesman, he was accomplished as a scholar, fervent as a patriot, and virtuous as a man."

(of John Quincy Adams)
RICHARD RUSH

A FAIR, LIGHT BREEZE floated the *Washington* to the wharf in New York on August 6, 1817, after a quiet, fifty-day voyage, during which John Quincy Adams read and wrote in his *Diary*. His return to America after eight varied and eventful years was a triumph. James Monroe had awarded him the highest office in his Administration, one that had, in the past two Administrations, led to the office of the Presidency. However, Adams was perplexed with mixed feelings. He was pleased at the prospect of seeing his aged parents but his mind was disturbed by "an anxious forecast of the cares and perils of the new scene upon which I am about to enter."[1]

With some impatience, Adams got through a ceremonial dinner at Tammany Hall that 100 guests, including powerful Governor Clinton, attended in his honor. Only delays in unloading their baggage kept the Adamses from leaving for Quincy at once. John Quincy engaged passage on the steamboat for New Haven on August 15 and then sat too long at his writing desk and missed the departure. The family had to be contented with the slower packet to Newport and Providence.

A few days later, at about ten in the morning, a carriage and four carrying John Quincy, Louisa, and the boys arrived at Peacefield. Abigail ran to the door and, in a moment, had young John around her neck with George right behind, crying, "Oh, Grandmother, Oh, Grandmother!" Charles, shy because he did not know her so well, hung back. The rest of the Quincy family gathered within half an hour. Uncle Peter Adams came first and shortly afterward Tom and his wife and five children.[2]

Delighted to find his parents in perfect health, John Quincy submitted to "the continual dissipation" of his visit home. He knew that it gave his father great pleasure to attend a public dinner given by the citizens of Boston to his distinguished son. The 200 guests included such notables as Governor Brooks, Judge Story, General Dearborn, and President Kirkland of Harvard.

To Louisa's despair, it was decided to leave the children at Quincy to continue their education under the guidance of their grandfather and their Uncle Tom. George, now John Adams's constant companion, was found to be deficient in mathematics, so, to prepare him for entrance into Harvard, he spent most of the year at Cambridge being tutored by Samuel Gilman. The two younger boys, whose travels had put their classical studies in arrears, were enrolled in the Boston Latin School. They lived with Dr. Welsh during the week and returned to Quincy for Saturday and Sunday to be spoiled by John and Abigail. Charles did very well, his brother reported, but was homesick.

After taking six stages and six steamboats, John Quincy and Louisa reached Washington on September 20, where they stayed with Louisa's sister until their house would be ready. In October, they moved into the house, rented from Daniel Brent for $650 a year. It was located about a mile from the Capitol and a mile and a half from the State Department on the northeast corner of 4½ Street and F Street NE.

On the evening that he arrived at the capital, Adams called on the President, who was about to leave Washington because his mansion had just been freshly painted and plastered and was temporarily uninhabitable. Two days later, Adams was sworn in as Secretary of State. He appointed Daniel Brent his chief clerk, established office hours from 9–3, and started to deal with the flock of office seekers who were deluging him by mail and in person. More difficult to handle were requests in behalf of others from old friends, as, for example, William Plumer, who sought a clerkship for a protégé. In less than a month, the strain of work affected Adams's eyes so severely that he had to retire by ten o'clock in the evening. He complained that the business of the office was so burdensome that he did not see how he would get through the winter.

At the end of October, Adams attended his first Cabinet meeting. He had given some thought to what would be an effective Cabinet. It must be composed of individuals, "equal in trust, justly confident of their abilities, disdainful of influence, yet eager to exercise it, impatient of control." Only Jefferson, of all the former Presidents, had had a Cabinet that harmonized. Adams's attitude toward the post of Secretary of State that was "my place is *subordinate*. That my duty will be to support and not to . . . oppose the President's Administration. . . . If I can't, my duty is to withdraw from public service."[3] Monroe's conception of a Cabinet was similar to Adams's. He perceived it as an advisory body whose members were congenial and whose function was to promote national harmony. He hoped to have in it representatives from all the sections of the country, an ideal he did not achieve because he could not find anyone from the West.

Monroe's Cabinet was the most distinguished assembly of talent since the distinguished first Cabinet of George Washington. Most of its members were nationally, even internationally, known, an asset in the first Administration and a near-disaster in the second, when the Cabinet became the arena in which the struggle for the succession to the Presidency was played out.

William Crawford, the Secretary of the Treasury, had been Monroe's chief rival for the Presidency. Although the Georgian had made no effort to get the nomination, with the support of John Randolph and Georgia's boss, Nathaniel Macon, he received fifty-four votes to Monroe's sixty-five in the congressional caucus. Madison had nearly been thwarted in his desire to see the office go to James Monroe, the last of the Revolutionary War heroes eligible for the Presidency.

A handsome giant of a man, Crawford had triumphed over vicious opposition within his own state. A duel with John Clark, the leader of the opposition, had cost him a permanently shattered wrist. In many ways, Crawford, a representative of the planter class, was the ideal politician. Coupled with an easy, genial manner, he had a clear, incisive mind and a soaring ambition to get to the top.

The War Department was headed by John C. Calhoun, former war hawk from South Carolina, whom A. J. Dallas called "the young Hercules who carried the war on his shoulders because of his active advocacy of a strong and effective army and navy." Tall, blue-eyed, a Yale graduate, Calhoun, of Scotch-Irish descent, was a wealthy planter, who, at this time, was a nationalist. In the Cabinet he would be closest in ideology to Adams and in almost constant conflict with Crawford.

Attorney General William Wirt, famous for his eloquence at the bar, was often absent from the Cabinet in order to take care of his extensive legal practice. Like Adams, he was a literary man whose volumes of essays had enjoyed some distinction. At the same time that he was appointed to Monroe's Cabinet, his biography of Patrick Henry was published. Wirt hardly knew which event pleased him more.

A contemporary who wrote anonymously but has been identified as George Waterton of the Library of Congress sketched an incisive portrait of John Quincy Adams at this time. The Secretary of State was "short, thick and fat . . . neither agreeable nor very repulsive." He was, the description continued, vigorous and healthy, regular in his habits, and moral and temperate in his life.

Sedate, circumspect and cautious; reserved, but not distant; grave but not repulsive. He receives but seldom communicates, and discerns with great quickness motives, however latent, and intentions however concealed. . . . Mr. Adams has more capacity than genius; he can comprehend better than he can invent; and execute nearly as rapidly as he can design. . . . He has all the penetration, shrewdness and perseverance necessary to constitute an able diplomatist, and eloquently to enforce what would conduce to the welfare interests of his country. . . . In short there is no public character in the United States, that has more intellectual power, the moral inclination to be more useful, or that will labor with greater assiduity to discharge the important duties he owes to himself and to his country.[4]

Monroe conducted a Cabinet meeting by presenting several written questions to the Secretaries. At the first gathering, the questions all concerned the State Department. The President requested opinions on South American independence, relations with Spain, and the piratical assemblages at Amelia Island and Galveston. Though the other gentlemen were "backward in their opinion," Adams answered all the questions explicitly. He advised that the marauding parties at Amelia Island and Galveston be broken up immediately, that the United States attitude toward Spain should await Mr. Erving's next despatch from Madrid, and that the President should recognize the independence of Buenos Aires. Though Monroe postponed consideration of the last suggestion until further study, Adams had effectively launched his career as America's greatest Secretary of State. Later that night, alone with his *Diary,* John Quincy was no longer as positive as he had been in his public statements. He complained that he was not yet fully organized and not yet ready to work out an effective method. In a short time, however, he instituted all sorts of innovations in his department, and sent out instructions to his Ministers abroad that were models of perfection.

In November, in a despatch to Richard Rush, his Minister to England, Adams brilliantly summed up the requirements of the United States for fruitful negotiations—reassessment of American entrance into the British West Indies trade, the fisheries privilege, and impressment. Adams had little hope that Rush could achieve any further favor from the British but he suggested that some consideration might be wrung from informal conversations with individual members of the British Cabinet. In regard to impressment, for example, Rush must point out that in the next war the United States might be the belligerent and Great Britain the neutral, at which time the United States would not allow "their rights of war to be less extensive than those of Great Britain." None of the European powers, least of all Britain, should suppose "that we shall indulge their commerce with privileges of neutrality which, while we ourselves were neutral, were denied to us."[5]

In his standing instructions to American diplomats Adams reflected his own experiences. Any treaty must vary the order of naming the parties and the signatures affixed to it must be alternated also. Under no circumstances might American Ministers accept presents from European sovereigns. It was the duty of American Ministers to observe and report the attitudes and conditions of the country to which they had been sent, and "an active and discreet" correspondence with other American Ministers abroad, along with a "friendly intimacy" with the Corps Diplomatique would serve to garner valuable information for the home office. These instructions, neatly written in Adams's precise, clear hand, were sent, without benefit of

secretarial help, to his overseas staff so that they might try to duplicate their chief's sterling record of service.

All matters of protocol with foreign dignitaries was a responsibility of the State Department. It was therefore John Quincy's responsibility to convey Monroe's requests to the diplomatic corps. The
fifth President made it clear to Washington society as soon as he
took office that neither the freedom of the Jeffersonian Administration nor the relaxed charm of the Madison era, presided over by the
matchless Dolley, would be continued by the harsher, more formal
Monroe. His model was George Washington's dignity and ceremony. Adams must, consequently, tell the foreign ministers not to
visit the President casually. It was particularly painful to convey this
order to the Chevalier Correa de Serra of Portugal, an intimate of
the past three Presidents and a man of great culture and learning.
Happily, the Chevalier made it easy for Adams, insisting that he
thought the new rule quite proper. He asked, then, if he might visit
John Quincy as an individual. "I'd be quite happy," Adams answered, with great relief.[6]

A romantic plot that involved the Bonapartist exiles in America
diverted the State Department at this time. "Le plan est à peu près
celui du Colonel Burr,"* De Neuville wrote. In some respects it was
reminiscent of Burr's activities in the West which had taken place
ten years earlier. The French Minister made the accusation that an
American-based association called the Napoleonic Confederation
planned to invade Mexico and to declare Joseph Bonaparte, now a
resident of the United States, King of Spain and the Indies. Adams
promised both the French and Spanish Ministers that he would give
them complete cooperation in foiling any illegal acts but refused to
arrest Bonaparte, explaining that the American government could
not order arbitrary seizures. Further reflection on the "plot" by
both Monroe and Adams made them doubt De Neuville's motives.
The so-called conspiracy seemed to be nothing more than a plan for
French refugees to settle on the Tombigbee River. One of its directors, General Charles L'Allemond, who was being heralded by De
Neuville as another Burr, promised Adams that there would be no
military adventure from the settlement. Though some of the members of the French party may have dreamed of rescuing the great
Napoleon from his St. Helena prison, a mild show of force by Span-

* "The project is about the same as Colonel Burr's."

ish troops at the site of the settlement was quite sufficient to discourage them from any thought of founding an independent state.[7]

When Congress met in early December, Adams was amazed at its freedom from factionalism. On almost all subjects, he commented, "there would scarcely be diversity of opinion enough to take the yeas and nays." Division was shaping up, however, over the Spanish-South American struggle. Because these matters were of great interest for commercial and political reasons certain Americans were intent upon manufacturing controversy over the issue in order to involve Congress. There was in that body already an outspoken advocate of South American freedom—Henry Clay, the Speaker of the House of Representatives. "Mr. Clay had already mounted his South American great horse," John Quincy recorded in December.[8] When Clay failed to get appointed Secretary of State, he refused both the Ministry to England and the position of Secretary of War, deciding instead to use his position of power in the House to force the recognition of Buenos Aires and, perhaps, Chile and thereby discredit the Administration which opposed it.

At the end of 1817, Adams admitted to pride in his new position, but was overwhelmed with work and responsibilities. Social obligations made "late hours, idle habits and waste of time." Even the weather was against him, for a spell of five days of intense cold made it impossible to write at all. His children, whose education had to be supervised over a long distance, were causing problems. John's grumbling and "very badly written" letters irked his father. "You boast of your studying hard, and pray for whose benefit do you study?" Adams asked. "Is it for mine, or for your uncle's? Or are you so much of a baby that you must be taxed to spell your letters by sugarplums? Or are you such an independent gentleman that you can brook no control and must have everything you ask for? If so, I desire you not to write anything to me."[9]

George was being just as trying, having procrastinated in his studies. His father ordered him to try for entrance into the freshman class at Harvard at the end of the winter vacation and to spend the interval preparing himself seriously. Adams accused the lad of wasting his time with Mr. Gilman reading the *Greek Testament* and other books he knew perfectly well instead of working on his deficiencies. "George, my dear George," he concluded, "let another praise you not your own lips."[10] But when George was admitted to

Harvard in March, his father relented and wrote to him, asking to be told all about his college studies.

Florida, a thorn in the State Department's side for the past fifteen years, became an active issue at the beginning of 1818. The area was increasingly important to the United States because its rivers were a convenient outlet for the enlarging communities of Mississippi, Alabama, and Georgia. The difficulty was Spain's unwillingness and inability to keep the Indians, who threatened the borders, under control.

As early as 1802, Charles Pinckney had been instructed to propose to Spain that she sell the two Floridas to the United States. The offer was rejected at the same time that Napoleon agreed to the Louisiana Purchase, which only compounded the problem because neither the eastern nor the western boundaries of Louisiana had ever been clearly determined. Now in 1818, the United States claimed the territories between the Mississippi River and the Perdido as part of the Louisiana Purchase, which Spain disputed. The treaty language was so ambiguous that even minute examination of the treaty could not offer any solution, and to complicate the picture further, in 1810, the American government had occupied Western Florida. Assurances had been given to the Spanish Governor that an equitable solution would be found, but the status quo of 1810 remained.

Monroe informed Adams that he had information that Don Luis de Onis, the Spanish Minister, was instructed to dispose of Florida on the best terms that he could get. However, after spending an hour with the Spaniard, urging him to make a proposal of what his country wanted to exchange for Florida, Adams was only able to achieve Onis's request for an American proposal.

The possible negotiation was interrupted by the news that the Amelia Islands, situated in St. Mary's River between Georgia and East Florida, had surrendered to the United States. Somewhat earlier, Gregor MacGregor, a piratical Scotsman with a long record of smuggling and murder, seized Amelia Island, a famous base for international pirates, under the questionable authority of the revolutionary armies of South America. He boldly set up a mock government there and issued commissions to United States citizens. Not satisfied with those excesses, he added an illicit traffic in runaway slaves. These unfortunate victims were encouraged to escape to the island and then were callously resold into slavery.

While MacGregor was absent from Amelia Island in October, a rival pirate, Louis Aury, arrived with 150 followers and declared Amelia Island part of the republic of Mexico. Monroe, upon hearing the news, sent out an expedition to capture the island under the No-Transfer Act of January 15, 1811, which allowed him to occupy any territory east of the Perdido and south of Georgia that had been occupied by any foreign government.[11]

At a January Cabinet meeting, the question of withdrawing the troops from Amelia Island made clear the lines along which Monroe's Cabinet divided. Calhoun and Adams wanted to keep possession in order to use it for subsequent bargaining with Spain, but the President and the others favored withdrawal. Adams commented that it seemed that Crawford's "point d'honeur is to differ from me, and to find no weight in any reason assigned by me." But about Calhoun the Secretary of State had nought but praise. He "thinks for himself . . . with sound judgement, quick discrimination, and keen observation," supported by "powerful eloquence."[12] After another meeting, unexpectedly, Monroe changed his mind. He would keep the island for the present, to which all agreed. Monroe's message to Congress explained his position but was, to Adams's taste, too apologetic. Monroe said, "The Establishment of Amelia Island has been suppressed, and without the effusion of blood. . . . In expelling these adventurers from these parts it was not intended to make any conquest from Spain."[13]

The Amelia incident was no sooner settled than Charles Bagot delivered an offer from his government to mediate the differences between Spain and the United States. The Administration opposed the idea completely but Adams was not that certain, even though he too suspected the purity of the British offer and remembered that Britain had been more the friend of Spain than of the United States. However, his refusal to Lord Castlereagh was carefully wrought. The Secretary of State pointed out that American public opinion was so strongly anti-Spanish at this time that if Great Britain played the role of mediator some of the irritation would be turned against her.

The diplomatic aspect of the Spanish troubles was only one phase of the problem. Congress continued to make the recognition of the independence of the Spanish colonies "an apple of discord among ourselves." And many serious statesmen, among them J.Q.A., questioned the nature of these revolutions. They bore little resemblance to the American Revolution, Adams observed. "Ours was a war of freedom for political independence. This is a war of slaves against their masters." It disturbed him that during their wars, the South American patriot leaders had not shown the slightest regard for individual rights or personal liberty. The press, for example, was no more free in Buenos Aires than in Madrid.[14]

The Adamses adjusted to Washington social life as easily as they could. During the spring season, they gave several parties and dinners. Louisa, however, was critical of the lack of sophistication and the gross impoliteness that she often saw displayed. She was particularly shocked by a small incident that occurred at one of Hyde de Neuville's dinners. A Chinese sang a Chinese song which produced such a roar of laughter that the poor man left the room crying. Louisa Adams, herself, was causing some consternation because she refused to return the calls of the ladies of the Congress, a matter that was shaping up into a tempest in a teapot.

On May 4, Adams was summoned to the President's house. Calhoun and Crowninshield, the Secretary of the Navy, were already there and Crawford arrived shortly afterward. The hastily assembled Cabinet was asked to consider despatches that had just come from Andrew Jackson containing the account of his progress in the war against the Seminole Indians. The General wrote that he had taken the Spanish fort of St. Marks in Florida, where they had taken refuge and then hung some of the prisoners, "as it appears without due regard to humanity," Adams interpolated. The General also reported that he was about to execute a Scotsman by the name of Arbuthnot who had been found among them. Thus was Andrew Jackson's rape of Florida first recorded in J.Q.A.'s *Diary*. At first, most probably, Adams was most concerned with the effect this bombshell would have on his negotiations with Onis which had been in progress for the past several months. Their discussions had been concentrating on the western boundary of the Louisiana Purchase. Adams, following Monroe's guidelines, offered the Colorado River as the southwestern boundary, to which Onis answered that, of course, the Secretary meant the Colorado of Natchitoches and not the Western Colorado. He meant by the Colorado of Texas, the Colorado of Texas, Adams answered testily. Onis's reply was to send a messenger to Madrid. The Don intended to keep the United States boundary as far east as he safely could, but Adams, who never lacked stamina to maintain his position, refused to withdraw from his line.

The two therefore remained separated by an expanse of territory that included much of what is present-day Louisiana and Texas. Adams hoped that Jackson's peccadillo might be a welcome distraction that would have positive repercussions.

The Jackson episode had its origin in the Treaty of 1795 with Spain, in which she agreed to restrain the Indians in her territory. This promise, always very indifferently fulfilled, became a travesty during the War of 1812, when Florida was used as a base by the British. At the war's end, Colonel Nicholls, a British adventurer, established a fort on the Appalachicola, fifteen miles from its mouth, from which he encouraged Indians and runaway slaves to harass the borders of the United States. Such was the setting for the series of events that developed into the current emergency.

In November 1817, General Edmund Gaines's troops, unable to bring back some Seminole chiefs and warriors for a conference, burned their village, Fowltown, and killed some of the inhabitants. The Seminoles retaliated a few weeks later by ambushing an American hospital ship and killing thirty-four soldier patients, seven women, and Lieutenant Scott, the officer in charge, who, it was alleged, was tortured to death. Calhoun sent General Gaines orders to attack the Seminoles and, if necessary, pursue them across the Georgia border. However, if they sought refuge within a Spanish fortress, he was to give up the attack and await further orders from the War Department.[15]

When Gaines was ordered to Amelia Island on December 26, Andrew Jackson was appointed to replace him. Before the orders reached Jackson, he had seen Gaines's communication from the War Department. The Tennessee General took it upon himself to write to Monroe and to advise him to take stronger action. In this January 6 letter, he said: "The whole of East Florida [should be] seized and . . . this can be done without implicating the Government. . . . Let it be signified to me through any channel (say Mr. J. Rhea) that the possession of the Floridas would be desirable . . . and in sixty days it will be accomplished."[16]

Jackson's letter arrived while Monroe was ill in bed. The unfortunate circumstance caused a much debated controversy over whether the President acted on the General's challenge or not. Monroe said that he did not read the letter but turned it over to Calhoun, who read it without comment. Then the letter was put away and forgotten.

Jackson's account was quite different. He said that Monroe read the letter and then, through John Rhea, sent permission to seize East Florida and Pensacola. Rhea's letter, received before Jackson reached Fort Scott, was saved until April 12, 1819, and then, following Monroe's wish as reported by Rhea, Jackson burned it.

At a later date this real or imagined letter caused a dying Monroe much anguish. Which of the two usually truthful men lied in this case cannot be definitely established. But it is interesting to note that John Quincy Adams's account of the reception of the news of Jackson's seizure of Florida indicated that Monroe and the rest of the Cabinet were truly startled by the event. It does not seem possible that Monroe as well as Calhoun and Crawford behaved as if the Jackson sortie was a complete surprise to them.

Jackson left Tennessee with about 1,000 men whom he had ordered out while the Governor was away, and met General Gaines on February 14, to find that the supply line had broken down. Starvation travelled with Jackson's army as it moved to Fort Early, Fort Scott, and then across the Georgia border. The General established Fort Gadsden on the site of the former Negro bastion on the Appalachicola, from where he planned his campaign against St. Mark's. On April 7, Jackson seized St. Mark's, sent the Spanish officials to Pensacola, and took over. Inside the fort, he found the septuagenarian Scottish trader, Alexander Arbuthnot, whom he immediately arrested and held for trial. Jackson's army pursued the Indians further into a remote village on the Suwanee River, which he found deserted because obviously it had been warned. That night army pickets caught Robert Ambrister, a former British Marines lieutenant, who had on him some damning evidence that also implicated Arbuthnot.

Jackson was completely convinced that he was correct in his suspicion that the Seminoles were being stirred up by foreign agents. With every intention of making the two captives examples for all meddling Europeans, he summoned a court martial at St. Mark's and, on April 26, tried the two British subjects. They were both found guilty and immediately executed. Jackson, thoroughly satisfied with his disposal of the agitators, seemed to have no misgivings about the fact that he, an American officer, had just executed two subjects of King George III on Spanish soil.

Jackson's adventure was not over yet. He received information, never authenticated, that Pensacola was the center of Indian activi-

ties, and was further annoyed by Spanish Governor Massot's order
that he must withdraw from Spanish soil. Instead, he occupied St.
Michael's, a fort overlooking Pensacola, and forced the Governor to
flee to the fortress of Barancas, which defended the harbor. The
Governor, who declared that he would never give in, capitulated
four days later after Jackson attacked with some artillery. The
American General then appointed Colonel King the new Governor
of Pensacola and declared American revenue laws in force. By May
30, Jackson was on his way back to Nashville, a conquering hero.
About three weeks later, Don Luis de Onis was horrified to read an
account of Jackson's exploit in the *National Intelligencer.* He hastened to demand an explanation from the Secretary of State.

The other aggrieved government made its protest known at a
small musicale given by Hyde de Neuville. Charles Bagot protested
to Adams about the execution of Arbuthnot and Ambrister, and
General Jackson's statement that their presence in Florida was the
"greatest perfidy" on the part of Great Britain. Adams turned off the
attack by answering that he was sorry that any white men, particularly Englishmen, were found with the Seminoles. About two weeks
later, since the copies of the court martial proceedings had not arrived in Washington, all that Adams could tell Bagot for the diplomatic bag to England was "this measure was not authorized by the
Government and was unexpected," but that Jackson's dispatches
would surely disclose his motives.

At this critical moment, Monroe departed from Washington for
his Virginia estate, leaving his Secretary of State to cope with the
Spanish crisis. On July 7, Adams was roused from his bed by a
servant from the Spanish Ministry who delivered a note announcing
Onis's return to Washington and his desire for an interview as soon
as possible. At 11 A.M., de Neuville arrived at J.Q.A.'s house as an
advance agent, asking if he could tell Don Luis that Jackson had
received no instructions to take Pensacola. Adams answered that
after having read Jackson's despatches, he believed that the President would approve them and find them justified. The Frenchman
cooled down after he heard that and appeared convinced. Adams
told him firmly that "however we deprecate war as an evil, we are
not to be frightened with it as a bugbear."[17]

Somewhat later, when Don Luis arrived accompanied by De
Neuville, both of them "looked tragical." Adams stayed calm but
told them that the United States could not allow its women and

children to be butchered by savages whom the King of Spain's officials were unable to control. De Neuville accepted Adams's dramatics but Onis was harder to impress. With some malice, he told John Quincy that his new instructions from Spain would have made a treaty possible were it not for this unfortunate episode.

On July 11, his fifty-second birthday, Adams asked of heaven "above all" for the fortitude to keep his integrity and accept the dispensation of Providence.[18] It was a virtue that he would need to sustain the mostly fruitless, lengthy talks that went on between him and Onis. But although, despite his threat, Onis had no intention of breaking off talks, he remained intractable about the western boundary. His offer rested stubbornly on the Calcasieu and Mermentau Rivers, two small waterways that were safely within the state of Louisiana, the historical boundary between Spanish and American lands established in 1806–1807. Adams said quietly that this was impossible.

Resolution of the Jackson affair progressed no more smoothly. Of all the members of the government, Calhoun was the most hostile to the General. He believed that Jackson wanted war in order to command an expedition against Mexico, and he was personally affronted at Jackson's blatant disregard of the War Department directives. On July 25, Monroe, back from Virginia, met with the Cabinet from noon until five to deliberate on the crisis. All the members except Adams agreed that Jackson acted "not only without, but against, his instructions," thus committing unjustifiable war against Spain. Adams disputed this analysis, arguing that there was only an apparent, not a real, violation of his instructions and that his action was justified because of the misconduct of the Spanish commanding officers. He contended that the General's actions were not directed against Spain but were necessary to terminate the Indian war. Having accepted Jackson's own justifications, Adams added, "Our frontiers could not be protected while the Indians could have safe refuge in Florida."[19]

A week of Cabinet meetings was consumed in deciding what disposition should be made of Jackson's acquisitions. Crawford wanted Pensacola restored at once, lest the United States be involved in war and the American people withdraw their support from the Administration. Adams disagreed completely, recommending instead that all the public documents be presented to Congress. Otherwise, he argued, if Jackson were put down, he would resign his commission, continue his attack against the Administration, and carry a large portion of the public with him. Finally, it was decided that Adams should prepare an answer to Onis which would then be submitted for review to the others. Though tormented by a terrible attack of palsy in his right hand, Adams worked long hours on his reply, which the Cabinet went over piece by piece, striking out every part that justified Jackson's proceedings. Instead they decided that Monroe should write a friendly letter to Jackson and include the letter to Onis, which dissatisfied the Secretary of State. He tried once more to persuade his colleagues to accept Jackson's actions, using the argument that since Jackson took Pensacola because the Spanish Governor threatened to drive him out, therefore he was motivated by self-defense against the Spanish officers, not hostility to Spain. Jackson's friends, Adams warned again, would say that after using his services the Administration had sacrificed him to his country's enemies, just as England had treated Sir Walter Raleigh. Wirt began to be swayed by Adams's arguments, but Monroe and Calhoun were inflexible.[20]

Anxiety over the Spanish muddle, coupled with the heat of the Washington summer, gave John Quincy insomnia. He revolved the dilemma round and round in his head during his fevered, sleepless nights. If Jackson's conduct was accepted, the Monroe Cabinet exposed itself to the accusation that it had started a war with Spain without a declaration of war by Congress, which was unconstitutional. If, however, Jackson was disavowed, his supporters would be offended and Monroe would "encounter the shock of his popularity and have the appearance of truckling to Spain."[21]

On July 23, Adams sent the official answer to Don Luis de Onis. It defended Jackson. Gently and tactfully, Onis was reminded of Spain's treaty obligations to maintain peace and harmony among the border Indians. Her failure to do this, Adams explained, made it necessary for the American General to cross the border in pursuit of the hostile Indians, which he did, under orders. All of Jackson's actions were endorsed as necessary "upon the immutable principle of self-defence." The President, he added, was persuaded that the Spanish officers at St. Mark's and Pensacola acted "contrary to the express orders of their sovereign" and should be punished. In the meantime, the United States President would order the restoration of Pensacola to any person authorized to receive it, but St. Mark's, being in the heart of the Indian country and remote from Spanish settlements, could be surrendered only to a force strong enough to control the Indians.[22]

Monroe was so totally absorbed in the Florida problem that he would talk of nothing else. When Adams mentioned the proposed negotiations with England, South American independence, or any other pressing matters, he would be answered with something about Jackson or Pensacola. Clay's use of the issue to discredit the Administration bothered Monroe terribly. Adams, who was not surprised, regarded it as part of the Speaker's presidential strategy, for he was convinced that if there was no Virginian available to replace Monroe, Congress would seek a former one, such as Clay or Crawford.

The Jackson issue persisted through the summer. The British Minister badgered Adams whenever possible over the execution of two of his country's nationals. Although editors of New York and Georgia newspapers had managed to publish full accounts of the court martials, the official proceedings had not reached the capital. At the end of August, however, Don Luis was placated by the news that St. Mark's and Pensacola were to be delivered over to their former commanders and that he would have proposals to form a base of a treaty soon.

Just as Don Onis was momentarily quieted, controversy over South America flared. Manuel H. de Aguirre, an unofficial but very vocal representative from Buenos Aires was pushing for immediate recognition of his country. Adams was equivocal. He was convinced that the South American cause was just but did not consider that sufficient reason for the United States to recognize countries whose state of independence was not clear enough. There was considerable pressure from many United States citizens, who openly favored the revolutionaries for economic reasons as well as ideological ones. The case of the disguised warships, built in New York for the use of South American rebels, became an embarrassment. The Spanish consul in New York City saw through the ruse and was able to get Aguirre, who was deeply involved in the scheme, arrested and imprisoned. Aguirre was outraged that the Washington Administration would not listen to his appeal for diplomatic immunity, though Adams explained that he represented a country that the United States did not recognize. Eventually, Aguirre appealed his case in the New York Courts successfully and the ships sailed for South America.[23]

John Quincy and Louisa were able to leave for home at the end of summer. Old John Adams, who had been urging his son to come home for months, was most successful with his argument that "children must not be forgotten in the midst of public duties." Difficult as it was to leave Washington with so many matters pending, J.Q.A. convinced himself that he ought to visit his parents to pass "a few days with them while the candles burn." It was a fortunate decision.

Not long after the Adamses returned to Washington, a letter came from Harriet Welsh, now Abigail's companion and John Adams's amanuensis, carrying the sad news that Abigail Adams was gravely ill. Louisa offered to go to Quincy to nurse her mother-in-law but was afraid to leave her husband who was in "an extreme stress of mind." His anxiety was so great that he was unable to share his hopes and fears even with his father. He just lived from mail to mail in a miserable silence. "In the agitation of my own heart I knew not how to order my speech," he said when the news reached Washington that Abigail was dead, after a three-week struggle with typhoid fever.

The bond between J.Q.A. and his mother was deep, subtle, and complex. As a lad, because of his father's constant absences on Revolutionary War business, Abigail depended on her eldest son. As he grew older, she saw that her hopes and her ambitions must center upon him, the most stable and the most gifted of her children. During John Quincy's youth, Abigail advised, directed, and admonished freely but after the Mary Frazier romance was broken some of that ease of communication died with it. The letters between mother and son were still loving and interested but John Quincy kept his heart to himself and was most reluctant to let his mother in on his romance with Louisa. What John Quincy never lost was a need for his mother's approval and a tremendous desire for her comfort when his career was going badly. At the end, Abigail displayed some timidity. One of her last letters to Washington, a note written to Louisa, said: "My love to my Son. I have not the Heart to ask him to wrote tho it would give me so much pleasure. . . ."24

After her death, John Quincy poured out his feelings about his mother to his father and to his sons. He dwelled on her warm and lively relish for literature and for social activities, her sense of patriotism, her profound but not intrusive sensibility, her stoical acceptance of her illness, and her devotion to doing good, sometimes secretly. The hardest thing for him to accept was the knowledge that most of his life had been lived far from her and that he had seen her only at distant intervals. Yet the consciousness of her existence was "the comfort of my life," and without it, Adams said, "the world feels to me like a solitude."

Although Tom wrote that their father had displayed great fortitude at the funeral, John Quincy worried that he would not be able to endure separation from his wife of more than fifty years. He decided that, instead of visiting his parents for Christmas, George, who had been such a comfort to his grandfather, should stay with him at Quincy. Louisa wrote to her oldest son that she consented to this arrangement "with a pang that made me sick" but "your grandfather deserves my gratitude" because of his kindness "despite the unfortunate matters after my marriage."[25]

Even the day that news of his mother's death reached him, "I was compelled reluctantly to devote . . . to the duties of my office, to prepare the draft of a despatch with instructions to A. Gallatin and R. Rush," Adams wrote.[26] It was time to renew the convention of 1818 and to rehash once more the perennial problems: the fisheries, the boundaries, and impressment. So much emotion about these questions had been expended in the past that until mutual suspicion and pride could be replaced by reason and logic, neither the American Secretary of State nor the British Cabinet and their emissaries would succeed in settling the differences. Monroe decided to order Gallatin to leave his Paris post to work with Richard Rush in London. The two Americans found that their British opposite numbers were their old friends, Henry Goulburn and Frederick Robinson, now president of the Board of Trade.

Shortly after Gallatin reached London, Lord Castlereagh invited the four commissioners to his elegant country seat at North Cray, where they were lavishly entertained and impressed with his private menagerie of lions, ostriches, and kangaroos. Lord Castlereagh, who was preparing to go to the conference at Aix-la-Chapelle, was relieved to see that Adams's agenda matched his own—commercial relations, the northwestern boundary, the fisheries, and the slaves carried off by the British at the end of the War of 1812.

Back in London, the negotiations proceeded agreeably, meetings were held, and written proposals were exchanged, but there was basic disagreement over all the issues except slave compensation. Gallatin, particularly, noticed the difference in climate from the time of the Ghent negotiations and the commercial negotiations that followed. Now the British were forced to treat the American demands with more dignity, and Lord Castlereagh, who was far ahead of the British public in understanding, realized that their colonial navigation system was outdated. Congress had passed retaliatory laws that limited British rights in American ports because of their discrimination against American shipping. The most recent of these acts, passed shortly before Gallatin went to England, declared that the ports of the United States were closed to every British ship coming from ports closed to ships of the United States. Monroe wanted Britain to open up her West Indian trade to the United States, but was not willing to go as far as Rufus King, who thought that negotiations should be dropped unless that point could be achieved.

Monroe's Cabinet locked horns on a number of the issues that were being considered for the convention. Castlereagh's solution to impressment, which advocated that both countries restrict the hiring of naturalized sailors or totally exclude each other's seamen from their respective services either on public or merchant vessels, did not go down well. Calhoun adamantly opposed it, although, after hours of discussion, Crawford and the President started to change their minds and Wirt was inclined to go along with Monroe. Adams rejected the idea completely, viewing it as a compromise that was "contrary to the free, generous and humane character of our institutions."[27]

The Cabinet objected also to Castlereagh's offer that the United States join in a treaty with Great Britain abolishing the slave trade, as did Spain, Portugal and the Netherlands. Adams tried to liken such an agreement to the joint committees that were designed to settle border disputes, but the other Cabinet members recoiled. Attorney General Wirt asserted that the arrangement, which would place United States Courts under the law of nations, was unconstitutional. Adams took exception to his interpretation because the power to make treaties was without limitation under the Constitution; therefore, since they then became the law of the land, there would be no question of unconstitutionality.[28] But in the final instructions to the American commissioners, Adams was forced to write that the President accepted Lord Castlereagh's project as indicative of understanding between the two nations, but his invitation to join with Britain must be rejected. Although the United States wanted to stop the slave trade, there were articles in the British treaties that were unacceptable under the American Constitution.

He cited particularly the establishment of a court that consisted partly of foreign judges. Also, the disposal of Negroes found on board slave-trading vessels would pose a problem for the United States because it could "neither guaranty their liberty in the States where they could only be received as slaves, nor control them in states where they would be recognized as free."[29]

Behind the circuitous reasoning lay the American fear of the impressment gang, which eliminated any desire to participate in the British treaty. In order to apprehend the piratical slavers, officers of foreign warships would have to board and search United States ships, which "would meet with universal repugnance in the public opinion of the country," Adams noted. The peculiar institution, in short, made United States participation in an international effort to eliminate the slave trade an impossibility. Once again, Adams was placed in a position where he had to justify slavery but, in this case, he also was hostile to the right of search.

When the President's instructions arrived in London, the commissioners observed that Congress was pressing economy. They were asked to propose to Great Britain some way of accomplishing the new treaty in a less expensive manner than the Treaty of Ghent had provided. Otherwise there was nothing startling in the instructions, certainly not the Secretary of State's explicit recommendations concerning the fisheries.

The convention arranged in London was, on the whole, favorable for the Americans. The boundary line between the United States and Canada that ran from the Lake of the Woods to the Rocky Mountains, the joint use of the Columbia River, and the slave indemnities agreed upon were quite satisfactory. It was an accomplishment of Rush and Gallatin that they were able to persuade Great Britain to give up their irritating demand for navigation of the Mississippi. But although Robinson offered what seemed like a reasonable compromise in regard to the West Indies trade, Gallatin's demand for complete reciprocity could not be met. The Englishman explained that the pressure of vested interests, such as Nova Scotia and New Brunswick fish and lumber, Irish salted provisions and flour, English shipping and the needs of the West Indies planters made one hundred per cent concession possible. However, Gallatin got the impression that Robinson intimated that, with patience, all the barriers would come down.

The disposition of the fisheries question was not wholly satisfactory, Gallatin admitted to Adams. During negotiations, quarrels arose over the American demand that the fisheries be secured as a permanent right. "The right of taking and drying fish in harbors within the jurisdiction of Great Britain particularly on coasts now inhabited was extremely obnoxious to her, and was considered as what the French civilians call a servitude," Gallatin wrote.[30] Richard Rush soothed Adams successfully by pointing out that the language secured the future and was the only way to reach agreement. The British, it had to be conceded, were generous in the sweep of fishing grounds they allowed.

The ten-year convention was signed by the four commissioners on October 20 and approved by the British foreign office, though not without some misgivings about the vagaries of the American ratification system. Their fears were unnecessary, however, because the Senate passed the treaty unanimously a few months later. It was popularly acclaimed in the United States but the British public was dismayed by the fishery articles and by the acceptance of the United States claim to the Pacific Northwest. Adams was reasonably satisfied with the treaty and much relieved that it was settled. Apart from some unpleasant newspaper notice, England accepted the Arbuthnot-Ambrister executions with much less protest than Adams would have predicted. Apparently Lord Castlereagh wanted to attend to the important conference at Aix-la-Chapelle without the ghosts of his unfortunate countrymen haunting him. Once again taking the bold approach, Adams sent Rush all the data about Jackson's victims, with orders to tell Lord Castlereagh that the United States hoped that the British government would completely close all their concerns with the Indians and Negroes of Florida.

A small matter of confidence disturbed John Quincy's equilibrium at this time. A rumor spread through Washington that the American Secretary of State was going to be the representative of the English Prince Regent at the christening of Charles Bagot's infant daughter. Upon learning the news, Monroe, very agitated, asked Adams about it. He answered, stiffly, that the Prussian Minister, whose monarch was a relation of the Prince Regent, was going to do the honors, though he was not surprised that the false rumor had been spread. "There had been a spirit at work ever since I came to Washington very anxious to find or make an occasion of censure upon me," he complained to Monroe, who agreed and advised him that his only recourse was to follow his own course.[31] When he returned home, Adams found out from Louisa that it was all over town that she was to hold the Bagot baby during the christening. Adams was perturbed by the incident because he felt that the President's questions indicated a lack of confidence in his prudence.

Added years and increased successes failed to change John Quincy's lack of confidence. He deplored his social behavior, observing helplessly that he either talked too much or too little, although people liked him better when he talked freely instead of remaining silent and reserved. A loose tongue, Adams said, often meant that he became dogmatic and peremptory in tone and manner, "especially offensive in persons to whose age or position others consider some deference due."[32] A serious social crisis had been gathering momentum over the convention of paying and receiving calls. Before Christmas, an anonymous card addressed to the heads of departments appeared in the Washington *City Gazette*, reproaching them for not returning visits. Adams admitted to Monroe that he had been remiss and that, most likely, the rebuke was meant for him. This was only step one in a nonsensical political charade to be played out during the Monroe Administration over this issue. It was obvious that Adams was the target, and he, who should have known better, allowed himself to be trapped into it.

The intricacy of the Spanish intrigue suited Adams's talents much better than parlor intrigue. In November, John Quincy Adams wrote a letter to George W. Erving in Madrid, in defense of the Administration's stand on Jackson, that was a brilliant model of diplomacy and patriotic apology, a masterpiece that Jefferson called "one of the ablest compositions . . . ever seen both as to logic and style. . . ." In these instructions, Adams placed Jackson's sorties into Florida and seizures of Spanish forts in the light of a holy war against red, black, and white miscreants who used Florida for their illicit purposes completely uncontrolled by irresponsibile or inadequate Spanish officers.

We have proof, he wrote, that "negro-Indian Banditti were as hostile to Spain as to the United States." Where then was Spain's indignation against British agents such as Arbuthnot and Ambrister, Erving was told to ask Pizarro. "If a whisper of expostulation was ever wafted from Madrid to London, it was not loud enough to be heard across the Atlantic nor energetic enough to transpire beyond the walls of the palaces from which it issued, and to which it was borne."[33] The Spanish King must be told about the atrocities committed in the "creeping and insidious" war against the United States and Spain. Point out that Jackson, with proof of the guilt of Arbuthnot and Ambrister, by the lawful ordinary usages of war could have hung them both without the formality of a trial, yet he gave them both the privilege of a court martial, Adams ordered.

The Secretary of State was on strong ground when he spoke of Spain's weakness, and he used his advantage forcibly. The tone of the note was bold and vigorous, the case ably argued. For once Adams was able to give his pen freedom to vent his indignation without restraint. His skill and enjoyment of the task shone on every page. Though evidence pointed to the certainty that King Ferdinand and his advisers had decided before the note reached Spain that they had better come to terms, the Jackson episode helped rather than hindered the Florida negotiations. General Jackson, with the now complete endorsement of his country, had demonstrated that it was within the physical power of the United States to take Florida by force if she so wished.

Adams advised Rush to present the American position on South America with equal confidence and firmness. The United States remained neutral because, despite their differences, she desired Spain's friendship. Nevertheless, the United States realized that Spain would never be able to restore her authority in Buenos Aires or in Venezuela; therefore the right of recognition could not be withheld for long. Another important factor that Rush might convey to Lord Castlereagh was that piracy, now flourishing under the flags of the emerging South American nations, could be controlled only if recognition was granted. "They cannot be expected to feel bound by duties of sovereign states when they are denied their rights." If Britain felt the same way on this subject, the President would be very satisfied, Adams noted.[34] Great Britain was indeed in a conciliatory mood. At the same time that Adams sent these instructions to Rush, Castlereagh advised Bagot on the "unfortunate sufferers," Arbuthnot and Ambrister. Whatever their intentions, he said, their activities were such as to have deprived them of any claim on their government for interference on their behalf.[35]

The year 1819 started as usual with the annual visit to the President's house, which was more crowded than ever before. The Adamses reached the mansion safely despite serious difficulty with one of their horses, which had suddenly become vicious. The day was particularly notable because J.Q.A. started Volume VI of his

Diary. On the flyleaf he wrote a paraphrase of some lines from Pythagoras:

> Let not thine eyelids close at parting day
> Till, with thyself communing thou shalt say,
> What deed of good or evil have I done
> Since the last radiance of the morning sun?[36]

The seesaw negotiation with Onis continued. Adams favored asking Congress to authorize Monroe to hold Pensacola, St. Mark's, and possibly all of Florida if Spain was unable to control her Indians. Onis demanded Jackson's punishment for his unlawful behavior in Florida without orders and a proper indemnity for the damages suffered. But, in reality, Onis had received new orders to conclude the treaty and intended to do so.

On January 3, Hyde de Neuville, still the faithful, unofficial go-between, whispered to Adams that the new Spanish Prime Minister, Marquis de Casa Yrujo, was more inclined to peace than Pizarro, the foreign minister who had broken off discussions with Erving in order to dramatize his disapproval of Jackson's invasion. According to the Frenchman, Spain was willing to extend the United States boundary to the South Sea (the Pacific Ocean). However, she was most unhappy about the possibility of premature recognition of the rebellious South American colonies and was concerned about the western boundary, particularly Texas.

About two weeks later, Onis presented his new instructions to Adams and, as heralded, said that he was authorized to agree to a line from the Missouri to the mouth of the Columbia River on the South Sea. Since he offered no change in the other boundaries, Adams refused the offer and started work on a new proposal, which was to take a line due north from the Pawnee bend of the Red River to the Arkansas and to follow the course of that to its source in latitude 41°, and thence by that parallel to the South Sea. Spain was forbidden by this treaty to form a settlement north of the Snowy Mountains. Monroe asked Adams to see de Neuville before he submitted the new proposal to Onis in order to tell him that, because of his government's interest in a mutual settlement, the United States would agree to a modification of the western line in order to accede to Spain's complaint that the former line ran within four or five leagues of Santa Fe. De Neuville, upon reviewing the proposals, pleaded for more concessions, particularly that the Snowy Mountain restriction be limited for a ten-year period. Adams refused because, he explained, Americans were disgusted with boundary commissions, having had more than their fill with the two British-American ones that had proved to be both slow and expensive.

The following day, Adams was mortified to discover that he had read the map carelessly and proposed the wrong line to De Neuville. The error, fortunately, was remediable because the Frenchman had not discussed the precise line with Onis. Chance, by which "I always understand a superintending Providence, has redeemed the fault of my own carelessness," he wrote piously in his *Diary*. De Neuville did mention that the "laboring point" would be the line to the South Sea, which Onis would offer somewhat differently, the southern branch of the Columbia River, so that the line would terminate at its mouth. Adams thought it peculiar that, having admitted the United States to the South Sea, Spain would now fuss over "four or five degrees of wilderness which never will or can be of any value to her."[37]

The Cabinet unanimously approved of Adams's new offer to Spain, but Clay, who complained that the price offered to Onis was too high, prepared to make further trouble. Adams, who had met Jackson for the first time about ten days earlier, discussed Florida with him. The General thought that most of the nation would be satisfied with the western boundary as long as Florida was included, but, he warned, the new territory would bring the United States once again into collision with the Indians, who were being moved west of the Mississippi.

After some further exchange between Onis and Adams, the Spanish Minister submitted a seventeen-article treaty which the Secretary of State read to Monroe and then took home to revise. When the Cabinet reviewed the treaty, they were ready to give in on several points, but Adams stood firm and proposed to add to the treaty the stipulation that all grants prior to January 24, 1818, should be valid only as they would be to the King of Spain. In a subsequent meeting, Adams was authorized to accept the longitude of 100° from the Red River to the Arkansas and the latitude 43° to the South Sea if he could not obtain a better deal. The long-drawn-out negotiations were driving John Quincy to the end of his patience. All other business in the State Department was in arrears.

De Neuville, who seemed completely in rapport with Onis, predicted again that there would be difficulties over the new counter project. A minor difficulty hinged on Adams's contention, from which he refused to move, that West Florida to the Perdido belonged to the Louisiana Purchase. A major difficulty was Onis's insistence that the middle of the rivers serve as the boundaries and that free navigation be allowed for both nations. It was a point of honor which Don Luis could not abandon without humiliation, De Neuville explained. Adams, who was no stranger to humiliation, did not understand. He countered with the argument that it would take a century to settle what was the middle of the Sabine, Red, and Arkansas Rivers and it was of no importance to Spain, who would never have settlements on these rivers. The United States, however, would have settlements there in a few years and the inevitable disputes over islands in the rivers would cause constant friction with Spain. The French Minister, accepting the sense of Adams's reasoning, promised to try to persuade Onis. Adams was equally unsympathetic with Onis's anxiety over the difficulty of justifying to his government the sale of Florida for only $5,000,000. Florida had always been a burden to Spain so that, actually, the price obtained was something to brag about rather than fret about, Adams told the Spanish Minister.

Onis, who had been confined to his bed with chilblains for ten days, arrived at the State Department on February 18 with a draft of the treaty in Spanish. But, since he had assumed the middle of the rivers for the boundaries instead of the western bank of the Sabine and the southern bank of the Arkansas, Adams told him that the United States would not accept it. To the Secretary's astonishment, Onis answered that, while visiting the President the night before, he had consented to the middle of the river boundaries. Adams was silent on that matter but remained inflexible about changing the price offered for Florida from $5,000,000 to $6,000,000 as Onis demanded.

At the Cabinet meeting the next day, Adams tactfully avoided any reference to Monroe's commitment. Instead he quietly urged that the banks of the rivers be designated as the boundaries, patiently explaining the danger of accepting Onis's proposal. The President took the position that the point should not endanger the conclusion of the treaty, until Secretary of the Navy Thompson found out from Adams that Onis had all but given in and said, "Then insist upon it by all means."[38] Thompson's comment turned the tide. Monroe agreed.

The time was approaching when the President would have to inform Congress that the treaty was not yet settled and steps would have to be taken to occupy Florida. Onis, still reluctant, called at Adams's house to make another attempt for more money and his middle of the rivers boundaries. Adams was insistent that the United States had yielded so much that the Spanish court should be grateful to Onis for the treaty he had arranged. Don Luis answered that the Secretary of State was more difficult to deal with than the President and then agreed to accept the treaty.

On Washington's birthday, February 22, at 11 A.M., Adams and Onis exchanged treaties. Later, on his way home, John Quincy found out from Mr. Fromentin, a Senator from Louisiana, that the Senate had already received the treaty, read it, and seemed universally satisfied with it. "It was, perhaps, the most important day of my life," Adams wrote. But there lingered with him a superstitious caution that made him add: "May it speed as it has begun!" The treaty's greatest achievement, its author noted rightly, was "the acknowledgement of a definite boundary line to the South Sea." Like a second Balboa, John Quincy claimed his country's right to stretch across the North American continent from sea to sea. His *Diary* was entrusted with the full record of the event, whose inception was on October 31, 1818, the day that Adams first proposed the path to the South Sea in a conference with Onis. J.Q.A. wrote: the proposal "is known to be mine perhaps only to the members of the present Administration, and may perhaps never be known to the public— and if ever known, be seen and easily forgotten." And then, at one in the morning, fearful of too much happiness, he added, "Yet let me not forget that in the midst of this hope there are seeds of fear, the ratification of Spain is yet uncertain."[39]

On the 24th, the treaty was passed unanimously by the Senate. On that same day, a committee of five members of Congress made a report censuring Jackson's Florida campaign, one of the most immediate and prominent causes that sparked the treaty.

The Adams-Onis treaty was a major victory for Monroe, his Administration, and, most of all, his Secretary of State. Monroe admitted that he expected no more than Florida. Onis, who was still annoyed, published an article in which he said that Florida was traded for Texas, which was untrue and a typical example of sour grapes and hindsight. The real bonus for the United States was the pathway to the Pacific Ocean which Adams had maneuvered. As the historian, Samuel F. Bemis, said, the treaty was "the greatest diplomatic victory won by any single individual in the history of the United States."[40]

On March 4, General Andrew Jackson dined with Louisa and John Quincy, having refused an earlier invitation because he vowed not to be seen socially until the charges against him were dismissed. Clay-Crawford politicking, which had hoped to discredit Jackson, Monroe, and Adams, had failed, although Adams was certain that he had really been the chief target. "They involved me and me alone in the whole responsibility of all his [Jackson's] acts."

Both Charles Bagot and Peter Poletica, the Russian Minister, believed that Adams's motive in defending Jackson was the furtherance of his political ambition to be President. They were mistaken. Adams was a committed nationalist who wanted the hero of New Orleans cleared so that the United States would be cleared with him. Also, there was some malicious pleasure to be derived from twisting the lion's tail. The Adamses, father and son, disliked British pompousness and condescension and it was a pardonable pleasure for John Quincy to contemplate the predicament of his opposite number in London, who would have to accept the executions of Arbuthnot and Ambrister with only a feeble roar. There had been a small risk involved, Adams recognized, but he had been willing to take it. Consequently, the United States emerged from the diplomatic tangle stronger, richer in land, and with increased prestige. Adams must be given the greatest share of the credit. He stood up to the President, his colleagues in the Cabinet, and the American Congress.

As J.Q.A. sensed, it all had gone too well. The blow fell on March 8 and it was the President who broke the news to the Secretary of State. Through a careless reading of the dates on the King of Spain's grants of lands in the Floridas, John Quincy failed to notice that some land grants that he had thought annulled by the treaty actually predated the January 24 cut-off date. As soon as he could escape from his dinner with Jackson, Adams called on Hyde de Neuville to ask him "if it had not been constantly understood by him and by Mr. Onis that the grants of land in Florida, said to have been made last winter by the King of Spain to the Duke of Aragon, Count Pinon Ristore and Mr. Vargas were null and void?" The Frenchman answered, "Unquestionably," agreeing to go to Onis at once.

It was a care-clouded countenance that John Quincy presented to his guests at Louisa's evening party, from which Onis was absent because of the death of the Spanish Queen. He was relieved a little when De Neuville arrived, explaining that he was late because he had stopped off to see the Spanish Minister who agreed to testify to the understanding upon which the treaty had been signed. But the error spoiled the Secretary of State's pleasure in his accomplishment. "Never will this treaty recur to my memory but associated with the remembrance of my own heedlessness," he lamented. And what rankled the most was that Monroe received the first inkling that something was amiss about the Florida grants from Henry Clay.

Upon further thought about the tangle, several disquieting facts disturbed Adams. Onis admitted that the land grants in question had not been made through the Minister of Foreign Affairs but by some private intrigue. Even more disturbing than that was Adams's assessment of Onis. Though he had taken a perfectly honorable position on the grants, John Quincy doubted him. "He is a man of mental reservations, hackneyed in the ways of Spanish diplomacy . . . scarce a doubt in my mind that he did intend to cover the grants . . . cold, calculating, wily, always commanding his temper, proud because he is a Spaniard, but supple and cunning," an analysis not likely to give his opponent much comfort.[41]

However, when Onis left for Spain to take his daughter to the husband whom she had married by proxy, Adams regretted his departure. His potential for trickery notwithstanding, the Spaniard represented the most important transaction in which J.Q.A. had been engaged alone. Adams asked him to carry back to Spain Monroe's request that the King change his decree ordering the death penalty for foreigners who joined the South American revolutionaries.

John Quincy imagined himself back in Europe each time that there was a formal meeting between the President and a foreign dignitary. Monroe, dressed in a half-military uniform all in black, held an audience like a sovereign. The foreign ministers, who were expected to attend in full court dress, were received by the President standing in the center of the drawing room with the Secretary of State on his right. Monroe would accept the despatch or letter from the Minister and then hand it over to Adams, just as in England the Prince Regent would hand a paper to Lord Castlereagh. Like a monarch, Monroe would answer the Minister's address with a brief comment, such as, "The United States takes a great interest in everything that concerns the happiness of their sovereign," after which there would be no further conversation.[42]

John Quincy's favorite among the Corps Diplomatique was the Portuguese Minister, Chevalier Correa de Serra, now sixty-eight years old, a witty man of extensive literary and scientific knowledge. Adams understood him very well but Monroe disliked him, because, Adams judged, the President was without relish for literature or philosophy.

Charles Bagot returned to England in April. Although he came after the war, he had been immensely popular. Tall, handsome, young, and aristocratic, he was always discreet if, perhaps, not strikingly intelligent. Adams commented wryly that "a man of good breeding, inoffensive manners and courteous deportment is nearer to the true diplomatic standard that one with the genius of Shakespeare, the learning of Bentley, the philosophical penetration of Berkeley, or the wit of Swift!"[43] But he was sorry to see him leave.

When Adams took over the State Department he found it in great disorder. Accounts and expenses were not kept, nor were papers properly filed. Daniel Brent, the Chief Clerk, was ordered to start an account book and to list all receipts and appropriations in it, thus instituting the first accounting system the Department had ever known. Adams also continued to perfect his set of instructions for Ministers sent on foreign missions. The task, Adams wrote, required knowledge of the political and economic relations between the two countries and a "mind fertile in expedients to suggest useful hints to the Minister."[44] The Secretary of State had to be an expert on all things because he had no staff but the Chief Clerk, whose job was mostly clerical.

By May, old John Adams was propagandizing for his son's annual visit to Quincy. He wrote to Louisa, whose alliance with his interests was certain, "If the President can wander round the Universe and leave all the business of the Public to two or three of his Ministers—I am sure your husband can come to Quincy and to Boston for a couple of months."[45] Louisa was particularly receptive that year because she was worried about George's lungs, which had been affected by a severe cold. "I am half crazy wanting to go to you and afraid to leave your father," she told her oldest son.[46] However, State Department business kept Adams from leaving Washington even though the summer of 1819 was particularly hot, with myriads of flies, bugs, and vermin adding to the discomfort.

As John Quincy feared, Spain's Council of State did not want to ratify the transcontinental treaty. They were dissatisfied with the amount of territory that had been given away and the absence of a clause that guaranteed that the United States would not recognize the independence of Spain's South American colonies. John Forsyth, the American Minister to Spain, wrote that the Marquis de Casa Yrujo, who favored the treaty, had been dismissed from office and subsequently banished. Monroe's Cabinet met in August to consider the problem. All agreed that since Onis had been given full power to negotiate the treaty, Spain was bound to honor it. Adams was instructed to advise Forsyth to remain in Madrid and to tell the Spanish government that if ratification did not arrive before Congress met, Florida would be occupied. Since nothing further could be done, the Adamses left for Quincy and stayed there until October.

On his return to Washington, Hyde de Neuville greeted Adams with encouraging news about the Spanish treaty. The King of Spain's confidential committee, appointed to examine the treaty, returned a report that was favorable to the United States. Monroe, however, was hesitant about taking the full responsibility for the situation and, at the same time, reluctant to ask Congress to order the taking of Florida. A report had come from Gallatin saying that France opposed violent measures, which added to the President's indecision. By way of compromise, Adams suggested that all solutions wait on news from Spain. Monroe said that he would think about it, but it was obvious to Adams that when he heard suggested strong measures the President recoiled, whereas now that he suggested limited action there was a much more favorable response. Oddly enough, it was now Crawford who was urging the President to take action.

Upon examining his own state of mind, John Quincy realized that he had genuine second thoughts about a hard stand. He feared that Spain might make the choice of going to war with the United States. A few days later, Adams found the formula that pleased the President—a recommendation to Congress that they pass an act authorizing the occupation of Florida contingent upon the arrival of the King of Spain's Minister. In his third annual Message to Congress, Monroe presented such a proposal, adding that Great Britain and France both stated that they favored the treaty while Russia had intimated approval also.

Having scaled the heights of diplomacy in his great transcontinental treaty, Adams now plunged into foolish controversy over Washington protocol. It seemed evident that his enemies promoted the importance of the matter in order to spoil his achievement. Monroe told Adams that some Senators complained that he refused to pay them first visits, to which Adams, who thought that the matter was finished, answered that he would abide by the rules of the majority of the heads of departments. He spoke carefully but was smarting under the President's comment that his action had occasioned "uneasiness, heartburnings, and severe criticism."[47]

After the department heads discussed the matter for two hours without coming to an agreement, it was decided to leave it to individual preference. Adams tried to convince the others that their visits and those of their wives should be made on the basis of friendship and not rank. Crawford and Calhoun said smilingly that they agreed, but that their wives chose to visit all the members of Congress. At that point, John Quincy realized that he and Louisa were in disgrace with all the members of Congress whose wives were in Washington.

The matter did not stop there. Three days later, on December 23, the President called at the State Department to tell Adams that Ninian Edwards, a Senator from Illinois, personally friendly to him, commented that he was fearful that the Senators would use the issue for political purposes. Adams knew that Edwards told the truth because both Senator Gaillard of South Carolina and Representative Brown of Louisiana declined invitations to dine with the Adams family because they had not previously received visits.

John Quincy attempted to retrieve the situation by writing a pair of letters of explanation, the first to James Monroe, the second to Vice President Daniel D. Tompkins. The letters were not among John Quincy Adams's happiest efforts. Rather painfully and in a stilted manner, they explained that it had been his impression that the policy on visiting followed when he was a Senator had not changed. Fulsomely, he declared his reverence for the Senate, a body over which his father had presided and in which he had served. Both he and Mrs. Adams, he said, wanted to give no offense and were "entirely disposed to conform to any pattern which they advised." Though the letters sounded repellently obsequious, John Quincy did not conceal his true sentiments successfully. In both letters, the line that rang the most true said, "I have invariably considered the government of the United States as a government for the transaction of business, and not ceremonial. . . ."[48]

This shabby tempest in a teapot had some significance for John Quincy Adams's future. It demonstrated that if he aspired to the Presidency he would either have to develop some knack for political expediency or overwhelm the public with superior and popular achievements.

CHAPTER 14

The Heir Apparent

"Distress'd, O God, in body and in mind,
Still to thy pleasure be my soul resign'd
In just proportion let my strength compare
With all the trials I am doom'd to bear."

JOHN QUINCY ADAMS

THE SECRETARY OF STATE thought that his lot was a hard one but he was pleased to have all three of his sons with him during their winter holidays. Charles Francis was already living in Washington, a student at Dr. George E. Ironside's Washington Literary Institute, affiliated with St. Patrick's Catholic Church. But George and John had come down from Harvard. His parents agreed that George, almost nineteen now, had "improved generally" and was a valued companion to his father, although still subject to periods of depression and nervous irritability. Young John, however, suffered from overexuberance and a lack of seriousness that made him want to do nothing during his vacation except complain that he was bored.

John Quincy, who abhorred idleness, insisted that the young men spend a good part of their time attending congressional debates as an important extension of their education. He also planned a dinner for their benefit that would introduce them to the twenty-two most striking members of Congress. On the guest list were such celebrities as John C. Calhoun, Thomas Hart Benton, Foote, General Bloomfield, Roberts, Storrs, Taylor, and Warfield. There is no record of the reactions of George, John, and Charles, but Louisa attested to the success of the party. The gentlemen went away *"gay, to say the least,"* she commented.[1]

On the morning of February 4, John and George started back to Cambridge. That evening, to his father's surprise and annoyance, John reappeared, announcing that he had lost his trunk and all his clothes. Apparently fearing John Quincy's displeasure, the boy stood there ill and feverish while his father fumed and his mother fussed. In a day or two, recovered and provided with new clothes, he was sent off again and Louisa was once more "left to mourn."[2]

The demands of Washington society were met stylishly by Mrs. John Quincy Adams, although she wrote in her *Diary* that she was constantly apprehensive. She blamed her husband because he never pushed her forward or encouraged her. However, she entertained regularly at Tuesday socials that were attended by 50–100 guests and sometimes included music and dancing. At frequent intervals, the Adamses gave great balls. Opening the Washington house to its full capacity, Louisa, despite her frequently delicate health, would sparkle graciously. It was the Secretary of State who suffered the greatest anxiety on these occasions. He always worried that no one would come to his party or, if he had guests, they would not enjoy themselves and the ball would be a dismal failure. On January 16, after fretting terribly during the first hours of his gala because only five guests came, he was inordinately pleased that before the evening was over, he was host to 300 ladies and gentlemen who obviously enjoyed themselves immensely. When his company left, to the surprise of the musicians and the servants, their sedate employer danced a sprightly reel with his wife and children.[3]

A few weeks later, John Quincy and Louisa attended a ball given by Mr. Gales. This time Adams danced publicly "to the astonishment of all the world." George read his mother's account of the event with roars of laughter, which rather annoyed her, although she had to confess that, at the time, Senator Walker had been so affected that she thought he would fall on the floor. The circumstance caused such a buzz of talk that for a week, Louisa told John, it "almost pushed the Missouri Question out of Congress."[4]

The Missouri controversy came as an unexpected difficulty, particularly to the southern bloc in Congress. James Talmadge of New York set it off by proposing an amendment to what was thought to be a routine House bill requesting admission to the union for prop-

erly qualified Missouri. The amendment proposed that the further
introduction of slavery into the area be prohibited and that all the
children of slaves born within the state after its admission into the
Union be set free after reaching the age of twenty-five.

The Talmadge proposal, superficially a direct challenge to slavery, stirred up other divisive issues between the sections of the
United States. Hatred between the North and South had intensified
as a result of the War of 1812. The South resented New England
anti-war activity and the North, just as bitterly, resented the domination of national parties by the southern bloc, which had caused
the domination of the Presidency by the Virginia dynasty and the
virtual extinction of the federalist party.

Economic differences between North and South caused further
difficulties. The nation was in the midst of a crippling depression,
for which the two sections had opposite solutions. The manufacturing North wanted higher tariffs while the cotton-growing South,
which depended on foreign commerce, deplored the idea.

Because of these differences, the balance between the slave and
the free states had to be kept with mathematical exactness. Since
1788 when slaveholding Kentucky and free Vermont were admitted
at the same time, the states came into the union two-by-two, like the
animals in Noah's ark. Now, the separation of Maine from Massachusetts gave the North another potential two Senators, making the
extension of the Mason and Dixon Line west a necessity for the slave
bloc. They needed westward expansion also because of its rich virgin land, to which they could migrate, leaving behind their barren
ground. Missouri was rightfully theirs, they argued, because she had
been an area in which slavery was permitted, even when France and
Spain held the Louisiana Territory.

At the start of the great Missouri debate, John Quincy Adams
noted that the slave owners were better represented than their opponents. Apart from Rufus King, no member of Congress could
equal the brilliance of William Pinckney or James Barbour. Adams
realized full well that the slave men had a more immediate stake in
the outcome. Much of northern apathy was due to their inability
to perceive the evils of slavery, while the southerner was convinced
that for economic survival he must have it.

Everything in Washington stood still while the Missouri debates
took place. The President's Cabinet meetings had to be postponed
because Calhoun and Thompson were absent, listening to Pinckney's

eloquence. Louisa Adams and her sons were present also, but they were disappointed because they felt that Pinckney's much-admired speech was totally convincing only to those who already supported his cause. Pinckney argued that Congress had no power to forbid slavery to an emerging state because it was a limitation to the sovereignty of a future state and all states must be equal. It was an ingenious argument indeed but did not fool the anti-slave faction.

The publication of Rufus King's earlier speeches on the Missouri problem made Adams wonder if the Senator from New York was aware that by contributing to the furor over the matter he was contributing to the possibility of the dissolution of the Union. "No man," John Quincy said, "ought to take an active part in that discussion without being first prepared for that and reconciled to it, because it must end in that."[5] However, when King debated the question in February, Adams went to hear him. He said nothing new, the Secretary of State observed, but in a grave, dignified manner, "he laid down the position of the natural liberty of man, and its incompatibility with slavery in any shape." He was effective and powerful, Adams added, for the great slaveholders in the House, "gnawed their lips and clenched their fists as they heard him." Later, at Calhoun's house, the only topic of conversation was King's speeches. With some satisfaction, Adams noted that "the slave holders cannot hear of him without being seized with cramps."[6]

It was quite true that fluency and facility continued to be notably limited to the slave faction. Adams said if only one man would arise "capable of communicating those eternal truths that belong to this question, to lay bare in all its nakedness that outrage upon the goodness of God, human slavery . . . such a man would perform the duties of an angel upon earth."[7] Nonetheless, J.Q.A. gave no opinion on the matter himself, wanting to avoid being drawn into the controversy as long as it could be managed.[8] He discussed his views with his friends and his colleagues but refrained from writing or stating them publicly. And in his *Diary*, he admitted his pessimistic forebodings, which, he felt, the public was not yet ready to hear. "I take it for granted that the present question is a mere preamble, a title-page to a great tragic volume," he wrote, unable to believe with the ever-hopeful Monroe that the question would be "winked away" by compromise.[9]

The present struggle, according to Adams's analysis, was between human rights and the United States Constitution, both of which he

was sure would suffer as a result of the confrontation. Though there
was a clear moral and political duty to prevent the extension of
slavery from the Mississippi River to the Pacific Ocean, yet there
was no constitutional power to prohibit slavery in any state and,
some argued, in any territory. The regulation, exclusion, or abolition of slavery was among powers reserved to the states, though
Congress could prohibit slavery in interstate commerce, Adams
thought. He believed that Congress could proscribe that slavery
may never be established in a state as they did in Ohio, Indiana, and
Illinois, but where slavery existed and slaves were held in great
numbers, as in Missouri and Arkansas, Congress had not been given
the power to eliminate it, nor would it be practical. However, if a
provision could be obtained excluding the introduction of slaves
into future territories, it would be a great and important achievement. While suggesting the position taken in the future by the free
soil party, Adams was preparing his mind for the acceptance of the
Missouri Compromise.[10]

Calhoun did not agree with the Secretary of State that slavery
would dissolve the Union. If it did, he argued, the South would
have to form an offensive and defensive alliance with Great Britain.
To which John Quincy answered, wickedly, that would be like returning to a colonial state. But the rest of the country would enjoy
universal emancipation. "Slavery is the great and foul stain upon
the North American Union," he concluded.[11]

Few were politically naïve enough to give credence to the notion
that the motives of northern politicians were wholly humanitarian.
The partisans of slavery accused King of using the issue as a tool
with which to make himself the head of half of the people in the
Union. If this was so, the New York Senator was overestimating
popular sentiment against slavery. "The people do not feel it in
their purses," Adams said correctly. Though northern and southern
members of Congress were torn asunder over Missouri, Abro K.
Paris, five times Governor of Maine, wrote from Portland that the
subject was scarcely mentioned there. To the "down-easters," the
matter was of little interest aside from the difficulty that it produced
in regard to their entrance into the Union.[12] Statements from the
press in Philadelphia, Baltimore, Cincinnati, and Pittsburgh confirmed that the American public regarded the Missouri commotion
as a Washington political quarrel. The average citizen suffering
from the effects of the panic of 1819 and the major depression that

followed it would have preferred some relief in the form of higher tariffs, a national bankruptcy law, and extension of time for the payment of his debts to the government for public land to debates over slavery. Only in the South did the question "come home to the feelings and interest of every man in the community."[13]

Thanks to brilliant maneuvering on the part of Henry Clay, the Missouri Compromise was successfully guided through Congress. Maine was admitted as a state and the people of Missouri were authorized to form a state government. Missouri and Arkansas would be slave states but in the remainder of the Louisiana Territory, north of the latitude of 36° 30', slavery was prohibited. By a vote of 90–87, the House concluded days and nights of stormy debate. Adams, who had predicted such a compromise, was not surprised. The fault was in the United States Constitution, he said again, and therefore its remedy must be in a new organization of the Union. The essential error was in human nature, which demonstrated once again that self-interest triumphed over freedom, aided, he was sorry to note, by accomplices from the free states.

Monroe now made it impossible for Adams to remain silent on the issue. The President, who had allowed Clay to manage the job of effecting the compromise rather than leading the enterprise himself as a modern President would have, asked his Cabinet to submit in writing answers to two questions: 1. whether Congress had a Constitutional right to prohibit slavery in a territory, and 2. whether the section of the bill which set up the slavery interdict at 36° 30' was applicable to the territorial state only or extended to it after it became a state. Adams, along with his southern colleagues, answered yes to both questions. He favored the Missouri Compromise only because he was convinced that it was the best that could be achieved under the Constitution and because he was unwilling to hazard a split in the Union. His conscience, however, forced him to say that "if the Union must be dissolved, slavery is precisely the question upon which it ought to break."[14]

Despite the fact that John Quincy's role in the Missouri controversy was, at best, peripheral, the problem was important in the development of his political thought. From that time on, his antislavery views were clear and his understanding of the challenge that "the peculiar institution" offered uncomfortably keen. He foreshadowed the Wilmot Proviso, which proposed at the time of the Mexican War that all territory ceded by Mexico should be free, when just before the compromise was passed he told Ninian Edwards that had he been a member of Congress he would have offered a resolution that his Spanish treaty should not be ratified without a stipulation prohibiting slavery in the territory to be acquired. He also expressed surprise that no northern or eastern member made such a proposal.[15] The Missouri question had, however, affected sentiment about the still-unratified Adams-Onis treaty.

Before the compromise, there had been universal support for the transcontinental treaty but now the northern members indicated that they would not vote for taking Florida if Spain refused to sign. The Missouri question sickened them for slave states. They didn't want Florida for a gift. The South and West were also unhappy about the treaty because it did not include Texas, which they now wanted badly, to add to the roster of potential slave states. As early as February, Poletica predicted that the Secretary of State, without the Florida treaty, had his chances of becoming President almost entirely destroyed and even ran the risk of being replaced after Monroe's re-election.[16]

From the perspective of his office at the State Department, Adams viewed Monroe's first presidential term as a period of the greatest national tranquillity that the nation had ever enjoyed. However, he foresaw that the second term would "be among the most stormy and violent."[17] Party lines had broken down and in their place was personal ambition.

Equally dismal was the state of American foreign relations. Britain showed no signs of relenting on her restrictions on West Indian trade, France was pressing absurd claims and refusing to settle reasonable ones demanded by the United States, and the Spanish delay was robbing the Administration of any credit for the Florida treaty. Claims for indemnity from the Netherlands, Naples, Sweden, and Denmark for depredations against American commerce were hopeless. Portugal was angrily demanding claims against the United States while South America was disheartened because America refused to send military aid. John Quincy's general gloom, however, was centered on the failure of Spain to ratify his treaty. It was "gone forever," he assured Monroe.[18] A good deal of John Quincy's anger was directed against Clay who, he said, tried to trap him into some statement about the matter in order to discredit him in the House. Crawford, too, Adams carped, wanted the next Presidency and intended to get it. Adams censured him for making an annual report on finances without showing it to the President, a custom that started with Alexander Hamilton and which John Quincy judged to be unconstitutional. Monroe agreed that the practice was wrong and asked his Secretary of State to look into the law on the matter.

Monroe, however, blamed some of the Spanish difficulty on the former Senator from Georgia, whose activities as Minister to Spain were proving to be an embarrassment to the Administration. Forsyth, who disliked the Spanish and had neither the inclination nor the tact to conceal it, was the subject of a complaint concerning his ill manners from the Spanish foreign office. The President's response was to favor his recall with positive disapprobation, which Adams opposed. Crawford immediately joined the President with a demand that Forsyth be censured, a position that Adams interpreted as a criticism directed at him. Crawford's stand was particularly strange because he had been Forsyth's sponsor against John Quincy, who recognized from the outset that the Georgian lacked the "experience, prudence, sincerity . . . and delicacy of sentiment" necessary to carry out his mission.[19]

As Adams suspected, somehow he was blamed for the appointment, which Louisa said that she could hardly bear because her husband had been so opposed to Forsyth. Poletica reflected the general opinion when he wrote to his home office that Forsyth was now almost generally disapproved of and the fault was attributed to Mr. Adams.[20]

The status of the Spanish treaty was now a political issue, for there was no great interest in the country for it. Clay hoped that it would be defeated so that Congress and the executive would wrangle over the Florida issue. The matter was complicated abroad by disturbances in Spain which threatened revolution. Should this occur, the country would most likely lose interest in South American revolutions and hence Spain's chief reason for settling her differences with the United States would disappear. Forsyth wrote that Spain probably wanted the United States to take Florida so that she could insist on confirmation of the grants. For all these reasons, Adams advised the President not to postpone urging Congress to take measures for reprisals against Spain and not to wait for the arrival of the Spanish King's new envoy, General Vives. Monroe, before he accepted the counsel, decided to consult his Cabinet.

At the Cabinet meeting, John Quincy was surprised that Calhoun sided with him. He said that popular feeling would be against yielding to the interference of other countries and that America should take advantage of Spain's position. Crawford immediately advised the President to take advantage of Spain's position. For once, Adams switched his position, saying a bit pompously that "true magnanimity was . . . the highest wisdom of a nation."[21]

But the Secretary of State changed his mind again when he heard from Gallatin that Don Francisco Vives, the King of Spain's envoy who had just arrived in New York, did not have the ratification with him but was empowered to agree to the United States's taking possession of Florida if he was satisfied with her stand on South American recognition and piracies. This irked Adams. When Monroe suggested peaceably that Florida should not be a cause of war, John Quincy snapped back that Florida could be occupied without risk and it could be that no other course could be taken with honor.[22]

The longer the ratification process dragged on, the more Adams was exposed to its political repercussions. The western interests, as Daniel Trimble, a Congressman from Kentucky, told J.Q.A., wanted the treaty set aside and, instead, the recognition of the South American revolutionists and the Rio Grande as the western boundary. "I understand the map of the country rather too well to suppose it would ever be possible for me to do anything that could make me popular in the Western country," he answered. And, he added, the majority of the House "would not accept the province of Texas as a gift unless slavery should be excluded from it." Since the Missouri debate, Adams told Trimble, the extension of the Union for any length of time was precarious and, most likely, Louisiana and slavery would ultimately "break us up."[23] In defense of his treaty, Adams offered the observation that negotiation implied concession on both sides. The treaty gained for the United States the Mississippi and all its waters, Florida, an acknowledged line to the South Sea, 17° latitude on its shores, and five million dollars of indemnity for American citizens. All that was given up to Spain was her claim from the Sabine to the Rio Grande.

At first, General Vives, newly arrived in Washington, appeared to be more of an obstruction than a solution to the diplomatic impasse. The Cabinet decided to ask Vives point blank if he had the power to grant ratification if satisfied with his findings. Vives responded that he did not and that he could only give a pledge for future performance. Calhoun protested that this could mean a new negotiation, which would be intolerable and therefore the matter should be brought to a close. When Vives received this information, he changed his tune and admitted that he had authorization to give the pledge of the King's ratification upon the arrival of his emissary from Washington at Madrid.

Crawford grumbled that notes would be sent back and forth endlessly and that he preferred the affair to be brought to a close. Consequently, Adams wrote a strong note to Vives saying that the President was surprised that he was not the bearer of a ratification when, by the usage of nations, nothing can release a sovereign from the obligation of a promise, and that six months was the conventional time for ratification. However, Monroe, always more conciliatory than the others, agreed to give any necessary explanations if, upon receipt of them, Florida would be delivered but that otherwise explanations were undignified and a waste of time.

At this stage, De Neuville offered to renew his services but was refused. Instead, the tedious, awkward exchange of notes continued. The note from Vives would be received, handed over to J.H. Purviance, the only translator for the State Department, and then carried by Adams to the President. After conversation with him, the Secretary of State prepared the draft of an answer according to his own ideas, which he again delivered to Monroe, who then assembled the Cabinet. The draft would be discussed by everyone and alterations, additions, and omissions proposed, after which the final note was sent.

Adams was thoroughly disgusted with the exercise in futility which Vives was causing. The members of Congress were full of curiosity about the exchanges which were supposed to be secret but, due to the number of people involved in the negotiations, were subject to many leaks. The negotiations "might as well be carried on in a public square by the sound of the trumpet as here," Adams grumbled. Even the newspapers were filled with utterly erroneous falsehoods, such as the absurd assertion in the Washington *Gazette* that Vives attended a party where several heads of departments ignored him.

On April 29, Adams arranged a serious conference with Vives. He was pleased to find the Spaniard, who asserted that he was a soldier first and a diplomat second, very reasonable. The General admitted that the account given the King about many recent events had been highly colored. Adams, in his turn, explained that the United States was a neutral in the dispute between Spain and South America and therefore it would be a breach of neutrality to stipulate recognition of South America in a treaty. As a result of the conference, Vives agreed to write a despatch home saying that he was satisfied with all explanations, which he fully believed would release the ratification. Monroe, upon hearing an account of the meeting, had visions of final success which Adams did not share. A successful revolution in Spain had limited the authority of King Ferdinand VII to give away Florida unless the Cortes (the Spanish parliament) considered the transaction as already completed.[24]

Once the obstacles to the Spanish treaty seemed insuperable, it was time to assign blame. Inevitably, the public and the newspapers dwelled on the confusion over the King of Spain's grants and cast the entire blame on Adams. "I cannot escape consciousness of that inadvertence," he admitted, and, realistically, Crawford and the President should have shared the blame because they too knew of the grants. For several other reasons also Monroe should have been held accountable for Spain's refusal to sign the treaty—his proposal to Great Britain for joint recognition of Buenos Aires, his failure to issue a proclamation against Long's expedition into Texas, and the strong leaning toward South American independence evident in his congressional messages.

Adams thought that the note which he sent to Vives was not strong enough. He told De Neuville that General Vives, once in Washington, denied his power to give the United States possession of Florida but in Paris he had told Albert Gallatin and Baron Pasquier that he had such power. De Neuville seized the opportunity to suggest that Vives, who passed through London on the way to America, might have visited with Lord Castlereagh—a mere conjecture, Adams thought, a typical ploy to stir up anti-British feeling.

May came, and still there was no resolution of the matter. Louisa watched her husband grow thin and anxious, "his mind kept up on the rack night and day." Wherever he went he was "lost in Spanish reveries."[25] On May 6, at the Cabinet meeting, there were differences about whether Congress should be asked to authorize the President to occupy Florida. Calhoun opposed it because Congress was about to adjourn and it was bad diplomacy to start relations with the new Spanish government on a note of hostility.

Both the President and the Secretary of State continued to pass sleepless nights over the handling of Vives and the message to be sent to Congress. Monroe came up with the idea that Adams see

Poletica to inform him of the latest developments. However, Adams pointed out that after their experience with De Neuville's meddling it would be best to avoid Poletica's inevitable assumption that Russian influence with Spain was being sought. Finally, Monroe decided to send a message to Congress along with the Adams-Vives correspondence, with the recommendation that action on the treaty be postponed until the next session in deference to the revolution in Spain. Adams had to explain to Vives that under the American system of Government Congress must know everything and nothing could be communicated to them without the public knowing about it as well. It seemed conclusive that Adams's Spanish policy was a failure.

On May 10, Clay made a resolution that an appropriation be provided for one or more Ministers to be appointed by the President to the new governments of South America, which, to Clay's surprise and everyone else's, passed the House. Adams took this as another blow directed against him as the chief exponent of the Administration's South American policy. Had the treaty been ratified, it would have been a "splendid success for him and the administration," he speculated, but instead Clay was using it for his own ends.

Just at this time, the Speaker announced his retirement from public life because of the embarrassed state of his private affairs. According to rumor, his financial problems were due to losses at the gaming table. However, Adams commented, he doubted that retirement blocked his prospects. Politicians in the United States always found the means to keep themselves above water as public men. And Clay, he said, "in politics, as in private life" was essentially a gamester. With a vigorous intellect, an ardent spirit, and a handsome elocution, his mind was very defective in elementary knowledge, and he had an "undigested system of ethics." John Quincy was convinced that Clay made "the most indefatigable efforts" to present him as exclusively responsible for everything unpopular in Monroe's Administration and to deprive him of his portion of anything popular.[26]

During the spring of 1820, the country was agitated by the death of the naval hero Commodore Stephen Decatur as a result of a duel with Commodore James Barron. The acrimonious exchange of letters between the two naval officers which resulted in the challenge and the encounter occurred because of Decatur's opposition to Bar-

ron's re-enstatement in the Navy. When Adams heard that Decatur
was mortally wounded, he immediately went to his house to offer
every assistance, but there was only faint hope for his life. The
Commodore died at eight in the evening. John Quincy wanted to
have a law passed against duelling, but as Louisa put it, "the people
of our country still seem to possess a little of their aboriginal barbarism, and I feel that he will have few supporters," which was
indeed the case.[27] About 10,000 attended Decatur's funeral, including Adams, who walked with Crawford in the procession. Though
he disapproved of the manner of his death, Adams said that Decatur
was "a spirit as kindly, as generous and as dauntless as breathed in
this nation, or on this earth."[28]

Before Hyde de Neuville returned to France at the end of May,
he persuaded Adams to present him to Monroe at a private audience. It was an honor that the Frenchman wanted so badly that the
Secretary of State prevailed upon the President to give it. Though
de Neuville said that he would return to America the following
spring, Adams was convinced that he would never see him again.
Perhaps it would be better if he did not return, Adams reflected, "to
part in peace once in a life with a diplomatic man is as much as can
be reasonably anticipated."[29] De Neuville, like so many other
prominent Frenchmen, had lived in exile in the United States for
several years. He returned during the restoration and then fled to
England during Napoleon's hundred days. An ultra-royalist, his zeal
was troublesome to the King and his party, so they sent him to the
United States "into honorable banishment."[30] His wife, with whom
Louisa was quite friendly, was amiable, charitable, and discreet.
And De Neuville had been universally beloved and esteemed. John
Quincy said that he had never had so good an opinion of any other
statesman's moral qualities except for Count Romantzoff.

At this time, John Quincy accepted the office of president of the
Academy of Arts and Sciences at Boston. With sincere modesty, he
wrote that he was "mortified at being raised to the head of a learned
society with qualifications so inadequate to the Station," but he was
terribly pleased. It would be an "object of pursuit" when he retired
from public life, which he was certain would occur at the end of
Monroe's Administration if not before. He told his *Diary* that he
feared retirement only because of "dread of dejection of spirits and
atrophy of mind."[31]

So many department matters were pending during the summer

that Adams wrote to his father that he doubted if he would be able
to make his annual visit. "I am handcuffed by Spain, fettered with
the census, and chained to the floor with a load . . . of Weights and
Measures," he said.[32] Since the census was one of the State Department's duties in those simplistic times, it was John Quincy's chore to
prepare the third census. On looking for instructions from the past,
he discovered "to my great astonishment . . . that there was not a
line to be found upon the subject. . . ." Some information buried in
old copies of the *National Intelligencer* proved to be so useless that
Adams had to spend his time devising methods to fulfill the requirements of the law which asked for much more information than in
the past. The new census was directed to include accounts of manufacturing concerns, manufactures, numbers of persons engaged in
agriculture and commerce, and, in addition, statistics on the ages of
slaves and persons of color and all persons over the age of forty-five.
Instructions had to be written for the marshals who were taking the
census and forms devised to garner the needed information. Finally,
ten forms were constructed for the field workers and a complete
records system so that the 1830 census takers would not have to start
all over again.

While working on the administrative details, a task he deplored
but did very well, Adams also devised a method of keeping a register
of current public officers of the United States. He also drafted a
form of instructions for the Ministers going abroad from his department. Each new Minister would be equipped with a manual on the
keeping of accounts, the correct way to write despatches, methods of
correspondence with their colleagues, deportment towards sovereigns, relations with consuls, passports, the alternative in signing
treaties, and declining gifts. In addition, each Minister would carry
with him a set of the laws of the United States, Niles's Register, and
Waits's *State Papers* and *Commercial Digest.*

As the summer progressed, the weight of work increased until 3
A.M. became John Quincy's regular rising hour and there still was
not enough time for his tasks. Some good news arrived from Tom
Adams. George had been awarded the Boylston prizes for declamation. John Quincy was rather surprised because he knew "the party
prejudices against his name and connections."[33]

Despite all the hard work, none of the diplomatic issues was
resolved. Though it was probable that Congress would go into session again without the Spanish treaty ratification, the President was

reluctant to take forcible measures. He was equally disinclined toward recognition of the South American republics although Adams urged that the recognition of Colombia should be simultaneous with the taking of Florida. Failure to recognize South American countries was intensifying the number of cases of piracy and slave-trading in which American vessels were involved, particularly those out of Baltimore. Such ships used South American commissions though the Captains were from Baltimore and there was not a South American among the crew. It was amazing, John Quincy noted, how these ships managed to go to sea right under the noses of all the United States revenue officers. Portugal, among other nations, complained about the piracy committed by vessels fitted out in American ports. Adams assured Abbe Correa that he and Monroe wanted very much to put down these practices.

In October, the new house which John Quincy bought, located on F Street NW, was ready for the family to move into. Louisa expected it to be uncomfortable because it was so small. They added a coach house and stable and did some interior remodelling so that the rooms could be opened up for parties, but Mrs. Adams always considered it as a temporary residence because her husband hinted continually that he would not be in Washington much longer.

Stratford Canning, the newly arrived Minister from England, was as enthusiastic as Lord Castlereagh about persuading the United States to cooperate with his country in a mutual search plan to eliminate the slave trade. It was once again John Quincy's task to rehearse the familiar arguments against the plan. Patiently, he reminded Canning that the United States had engaged in one war with Britain over the searching of her vessels and did not want another. Canning chose not to see the analogy. Instead he urged the same slave-trade plan at several meetings despite the constitutional argument that Adams offered. To distract him, John Quincy proposed other areas of concert for the two nations, such as uniformity on weights and measures. He promised to send Canning a copy of his book, which was now in its final draft.

In November, James Monroe was re-elected President almost unanimously. The only electoral vote that he lacked was cast for John Quincy Adams. There had been rumors reported by Louisa almost a year earlier that her husband would be proposed for Vice President if Daniel Tompkins was elected Governor of New York. Louisa considered this plan one way of kicking John Quincy upstairs because "his talents are feared and his disinclination to every kind of intrigue dreaded and looked upon as censure to others."[34] John Quincy heard similar rumors about Clay's promotion to Tompkins's position, which, it was said, failed because the caucus called in April was attended by no more than forty members, some of them among the President's most intimate friends.

Opposition to the Administration focused on Tompkins, who was often absent from the Senate and was frequently too drunk to attend to business. What opposition there was to Monroe was subordinated to the general desire to show political unanimity, for early in his first Administration it had been decided that he would have a second term.

However, there was one man who did not go along with the general apathy. In mid-November, William Plumer, now a New Hampshire elector, wrote to his son in Washington that a portion of New England wanted to give J.Q.A. their votes for the Vice Presidency, not to defeat Tompkins but to prepare the public for Adams's candidacy for the Presidency in 1824. Young Plumer was instructed to visit Adams without delay and to ask him, in confidence, whether he objected to this idea. The proposed visit was made but there were two versions of what happened. According to Plumer, Jr., he handed his father's letter to the Secretary of State, who read it, expressed obligation to Plumer for his thought since this was his first indication of New England's support, but said that he earnestly and sincerely desired no person to give him a single vote for the Vice Presidency.

Adams recorded in his *Diary* that the younger Plumer asked for his approval of his father's plan, which he refused, saying that he wanted the incumbent elected unanimously. And he particularly did not want the vote to take place in Massachusetts because it would be awkward for his father, who was one of the electors.

Young Plumer's letter to his father revealing John Quincy's attitude did not reach its destination until after Plumer left for Concord to cast his vote. In the interval, the New Hampshire elector had made up his mind that he would vote for J.Q.A. for President and Richard Rush for Vice President simply because he preferred them to Monroe, whose failure to balance income and budget expenditures added three million dollars to the public debt, and to Tompkins, whom he found worthless. At no time did Plumer try to influence his colleagues to go along with him. Few newspapers picked up the news of Plumer's vote except for the Portsmouth *Oracle*, which reported both the vote and the reasons for it accurately. Plumer, Jr., believed that the vote reflected the feelings of a large, disgruntled majority who had no means of expressing their position.[35]

When John Quincy learned that he had been the recipient of the one vote that deprived the President of the unanimous vote of the electoral college, he was surprised and mortified. "I was sorry because it implied Plumer's disapprobation of the Administration, when I think that it has been on the whole wise, honest and patriotic," he wrote. However, he foresaw great trials for the next four years because of internal divisions.[36] The tone of J.Q.A.'s *Diary* entry and its nature hinted at his real concern that Plumer's well-meant gesture might harm his popularity with Monroe or in some way lessen rather than increase his chances in 1824.

As a result of Plumer's single-vote gesture, a legend grew that the purpose of his vote was to deprive anyone other than George Washington from enjoying the honor of unanimity. But there is no evidence for this fable, which did not come into existence until thirty years after Plumer's death, sixty years after the vote was cast.[37]

On Christmas Day, Adams decided to relax with his family and to develop the literary tastes of his children. After breakfast, he read them Alexander Pope's *Messiah*, a favorite of his from the time that he was younger than Charles and an appropriate poem for the season. He was disappointed that no one except George showed the slightest interest. Charles, his father observed, had a fondness for books and a meditative mind but refused to learn anything from others. "Literature has been the charm of my life," John Quincy wrote, "and could I have carved out my own fortunes, to literature would my whole life have been devoted. I have been a lawyer for bread, and a statesman at the call of my country. It would have been a great comfort to me if all or either of my children inherited this propensity."[38]

John had recently been a source of great anxiety to his parents because of his involvement in a student rebellion at Harvard. At the height of the crisis, Louisa advised the boy that should he be expelled, his parents would try to find him a situation in the Navy. "My children seem to have some intemperate blood in them and are certainly not very easy to govern," Louisa despaired. Finally, John was able to report that everything was straightened out and he was permitted to come to Washington, although under a cloud. His mother admitted candidly that when she took a good look at her two older sons, she found them very little changed. George was as eccentric as ever and John as wild.[39]

The pressure of having everyone at home for the holidays proved to be more than Louisa could bear. She suffered from terrible headaches, which she tried to conceal from the family so as not to spoil their vacation but she found that noise was particularly impossible. Mary Hellen's violin lesson, then Charles's dancing master for three hours, and finally George's and Charles's practicing on the flute and the violin were too much. When poor Louisa complained, she was accused of being ill-tempered, which wounded her feelings. Her husband then told her that she was whimsical and fanciful.[40] Part of the difficulty was that the Adams household was quite large at this time, with the addition of Mary, Johnson, and Thomas Hellen, the orphaned children of Louisa's sister.

In January, a domestic crisis threw the entire family into a frenzy. George got into a controversy with a young man named Martin over Fanny Johnson, a coquettish house guest of the Adamses. Martin had, apparently, followed Miss Johnson to Washington. She confided to her admirer that George Adams told her that Mr. Otis said that Martin told him that he was engaged to Fanny. Martin, apparently frightened by the idea that he was being seriously involved with the girl, denied that he had said any such thing and demanded an apology or satisfaction from George. In his effort to explain what he had really said to Mr. Otis, George became so agitated at having appeared to have misrepresented that he was very upset. Louisa, observing her son's confusion, wormed the story out of him and then related the whole episode to his father.

John Quincy called his son into his office to talk to him and while he was with him the cook came to tell Louisa that Mary Hellen was in a fainting fit and had been delirious for several hours. There was no sleep for the family that night, which was passed in soothing the hysterical young ladies and making plans for George, whose character was at stake. Finally, his father suggested that George draw up a statement of his words and show it to Fanny. If his version differed from hers, she should write down what she thought that she had heard.

The next day, Mary was better and Louisa presented George's paper to Fanny. The girl stated that she never said what Mr. Martin accused her of but, after much talk, refused to sign the paper, demanding that Mr. Martin be sent for, to meet with her and George. When John Quincy, very annoyed by this time, refused to allow Mr. Martin to come into the house, the quarrelling escalated until the house was bedlam, with John and Johnson Hellen urging George to fight and everyone else thoroughly irritable and somewhat scared by the possibilities.

The matter was suddenly and amicably settled after J.Q.A. and Otis met. George apologized to Otis for any misrepresentation of facts of which he had been guilty and Otis, upon hearing the full story about Martin, decided that the young man had behaved very badly and refused to have anything to do with him. Fanny Johnson, the cause of the rumpus, departed about ten days later, to the relief of the older Adamses but the young men were left in the depths of "the belle passion."

John and Charles returned to Cambridge on February 8, although Charles was very reluctant to go. His mother said that despite his discouragement he showed a great deal of fortitude. Because of George's foolish entanglement, his father decided that he should study law in Washington with William Wirt. Louisa worried that he would be too near Mary Hellen, for she had many objections to their marriage.[41]

Canning and Adams continued to spar with each other whenever they met. The British Minister had the knack of engaging John Quincy in long conversation and then driving him into an outbreak of temper. Adams, aware of this phenomenon, complained that he spoke to the British Minister with more freedom than caution while Canning managed to remain very reserved.

A sharp disagreement flared over an account in the *National Intelligencer* of Virginia Representative John Floyd's bill for the reoccupation of the Columbia River. Canning demanded to know what the government's intentions were. Adams explained that the members of the United States legislature were independent of the executive and that he could not present himself to be questioned by a foreign minister. They argued but met several times on the matter.

In order to explain the American position, Adams made an analogy—if Richard Rush heard a member of Parliament speak of the expediency of sending troops to the Shetland Islands or the establishment of a new colony in New South Wales and then demanded an explanation from Lord Castlereagh and talked about treaty violations, he would be doing the same thing as Canning proposed. A lively exchange followed.

CANNING: Have you any claim to the Shetland Islands or New South Wales?

ADAMS: Have you any claim to the mouth of the Columbia River?

CANNING: Why, do you not *know* that we have a claim?

ADAMS: I do not *know* what you claim nor what you do not claim. You claim India. You claim Africa. You claim—

CANNING: Perhaps a piece of the moon.

ADAMS: No, I have not heard that you claim exclusively any part of the moon, but there is not a spot on *this* habitable globe that I could affirm you do not claim; and there is none which you may not claim with as much color of right as you can have to the Columbia River or its mouth.[42]

The two diplomats continued to bicker about the extent of British claims to the Northwest until Canning referred to the rights of Russia and Spain. Adams answered sharply, "Russia and Spain are the guardians of their own rights. Have you, Mr. Canning, any right to speak in their name?" Canning declared that the two countries were close allies of his. "Yes, sir . . . we know that very well, but they have not authorized you to speak for them," Adams asserted. Canning was incensed. "And do you wish me *to report to my government* what you have now said to me?" he asked. Adams replied, reasonably, "Sir, you may report to your government what you please . . . provided you repeat nothing but the truth, as I have no doubt you will."[43] They parted at that point but John Quincy was certain that the matter of the Northwest would come up again very soon. Two days later when Adams and Canning met in the House of Representatives, where the debates on the Missouri question were going on, Adams observed that Canning was still so full of resentment that but a bare salutation passed between them.

In a despatch to Richard Rush, the Secretary of State mentioned Canning's zeal over the mutual search of suspected slave-trading vessels. He told him that Monroe offered Britain a concert of operations between the armed vessels of the two countries patrolling the coast of Africa. Remind the British that last year four vessels engaged in the traffic were captured by United States cruisers and condemned, he ordered.

On February 10th, General Vives called on Adams and, quite unexpectedly, told him that after an eighty-eight-day passage from Spain, Mr. de Barros had arrived with the ratified treaty. It had been known for two months that the messenger was on his way, but John Quincy, who had suffered so many unexpected misadventures with the document, feared that if the messenger had met with an accident and his arrival was prevented until the congressional session was over, there might be serious consequences. Adams hastened to tell the President, who was greatly satisfied. With little fanfare, the treaty was ratified by the Senate, sustaining only four negative votes. Two of the dissenters owed loyalty to Clay, one cast his veto because of hatred for General Jackson, and Trimble of Ohio dissented because, said Adams, of "some maggot in the brain, the cause of which I do not perfectly know."[44]

The day that the ratifications for the Florida treaty were signed, Adams wrote, "I consider the signature of the treaty as the most important event of this Union." But he could not forgive the two years of "perfidious fraud, sordid intrigues, of royal treachery, of malignant rivalry, and of envy marked with patriotism, playing to and fro across the Atlantic."[45] He blamed Onis for his mock sickness and his use of De Neuville to carry out his double dealing. He blamed Clay, who snickered at the simplicity with which Adams had been bamboozled, and Crawford, who exulted in the slur on his sagacity.[46] Underneath it all, he could not forgive himself for his carelessness.

On the very same day, John Quincy sent to both houses of Congress his monumental report on weights and measures, the most important literary labor of his life. A modern historian called it the "classic document of the Age of Mercantilism . . . philosophy, ethics, political economy, and policy integrated in a government report."[47] For more than three years Adams had labored on it lovingly. Unlike so many contemporary reports, which are the works of committees of experts, this was a one-man job in which every word, every reference, and every conclusion was Adams's own work. He had spared no effort to study the works of others in the field but his was, without doubt, the most complete, the most scholarly, and the most relevant.

Adams admired the French system of weights and measures, which originated with "her revolution," for its attempt "to improve the condition of human kind" and its uniformity. A system of common instruments, he argued, would "furnish the links of sympathy between the inhabitants of most regions; the metre will surround the globe in use . . . one language of weights and meaaures will be spoken from the equator to the poles." Weights and measures, he said, had a unifying effect on all mankind because they were indispensable instruments for every individual every day. Hopefully, France, Great Britain, and the United States would unite in a mutual effort to promote a single universal system that would then be finally established by a general convention to which all the principal nations would assent. Such an achievement should be possible, he said, because, unlike other plans of moral and political improvement, "not excepting the abolition of the slave trade itself," there should be no great "counteracting *interest* to overcome," only prejudices, usages, and natural jealousies. Adams commented on the strange truth that all nations use the same weapons "for the wholesale trade of human slaughter" yet they refuse to weigh by the same pound, to measure by the same rule, or to drink from the same cup.

With literary skill and a remarkably novel approach, Adams developed a pseudo-scientific topic into a social document. Though France was the first to realize that uniform weights and measures involved "the interests, the comforts and the morals of all nations and of all after ages," the final prevalence of the metric system beyond France would have to wait for other nations to realize its benefits.[48]

Calhoun, whose intellectual capacities Adams respected, read the book and reported on it favorably, but ventured to suggest that its length might be a problem for most readers. John Adams corroborated that sentiment when he expressed his admiration for his son's great task but confessed that at his age he was too overwhelmed by its mass of historical, metaphysical and political data to read it all.

Nevertheless, with the greatest pride, Adams sent copies to some distinguished colleagues in the field. One went to Jean Baptiste Joseph Delambre, distinguished French astronomer and author of a book on the metric system. Another volume also travelled to France for Talleyrand, who first proposed a uniform system of weights and measures for civilized nations. And yet another copy was sent to Britain to the Earl of Carysfort, whose father had been the chairman of a House of Commons committee on weights and measures in 1758.

In March, James Monroe's second Inauguration was a modest

spectacle. He requested that the heads of the departments assemble at his house and then accompany him to the Capitol. The ladies of the Cabinet were to go on ahead where seats had been engaged for them. At a quarter to twelve, Adams arrived at the President's house to find him dressed in an old-fashioned suit of black broadcloth with shoe and knee buckles. The President, riding in a plain carriage with four horses and one Black footman, headed the procession, followed by the Secretaries, each in a carriage and pair. There was no escort and no crowds along the way. However, when they arrived at the Capitol they found a great mass of onlookers milling about, which made it difficult for the dignitaries to enter the building. No soldier or constable was present to ease the entrance of the President and his cortege. Instead, after a few minutes of severe pressure, the mob gave way so that Monroe and his Cabinet could push their way into the rotunda and proceed to the hall of the House of Representatives where the ceremony was to take place.

The President sat on a platform in front of the Speaker's chair with the Chief Justice on his right and the department heads sidelong at his right. The House was crowded with guests who talked loudly and freely even during the President's taking of the oath and his address, so that it was hard to hear. Monroe spoke in a low, grave voice. When he finished, several people came up to shake hands with him. At his departure, a cheer rose from the gallery and the Marine band played.

John Quincy returned home with his family and then immediately went back to the President's house to congratulate him. In the evening, the Inaugural Ball was given at Brown's Hotel, another function that John Quincy and Louisa had to attend. The President retired soon after supper and, at last, the Secretary of State and his wife could go home, finishing an exhausting day about midnight.

A few days later, Clay, who had resigned his position of Speaker and been replaced by John W. Taylor of New York, commented to Adams that Monroe's election gave the impression of unanimity but that he had not the slightest influence with Congress and his career was considered closed. Adams ignored the implications of the sentiment, preferring to take it as Clay's way of magnifying his own importance. Instead, he commented that he regretted their differences over South American recognition but felt that maintenance of strict neutrality was fundamental to liberty and union. Once again,

Adams warned that the South American countries showed no prospect of establishing free or liberal institutions of government.

Much of the spring was concerned with controversy over equalization of duties with France negotiated with Hyde de Neuville, who was back again at his old post. France's claims against the United States for the capture of two ships, the *Jeune Eugénie*, a suspected slaver, and the *Apollon*, accused of smuggling goods from the River St. Mary in Florida to the United States between the time of the signing and ratification of the transcontinental treaty, were a source of much acrimony. Monroe considered the problem critical because he felt that the French attitude was typical of that of many European sovereigns, who thought of the United States as the "natural ally" of their rebellious subjects. If practical, then, he argued, war was not an impossibility and therefore, without making any concession, Monroe cautioned Adams to be as conciliatory as possible.

An important, far-reaching interruption to his regular duties occurred when, during the late spring, the citizens of Washington asked John Quincy Adams to deliver the annual Fourth of July oration. The furor that resulted from the occasion came as a surprise to all parties involved. Adams prepared an address with care that was unusual for this routine annual occasion. Then, in an academic robe, which served as a professional disguise, Adams addressed a packed hall from the rostrum of the House of Representatives. Louisa said that he looked better than she had ever seen him. The theme of the speech was a response to an annoying article which had appeared in the *Edinburgh Review* of May 1820, suggesting that the United States join with British liberals to support reform and freedom in Spain, France, and Italy, and to the question often posed by British publications, "What has America done for Mankind?" The speech was also a response to Henry Clay's farewell address to his friends made in Lexington, Kentucky, also in May in which he proposed that a "counterpoise to the holy alliance should be formed in the two Americas, in favor of national independence and liberty, to operate by the force of example and moral influence . . ."[49] Though Clay asserted that he meant measures short of war, his opponents, including J.Q.A., interpreted his proposal as a direct call to action. And in his Fourth of July speech, the Secretary of State enlarged on the dangers of engaging in a crusade for democracy.

The diplomatic corps was present in the hall to listen to the oration, but fortunately Canning was visiting at Harper's Ferry.

Since traditionally these speeches included a denunciation of England, it was the better part of wisdom for the Englishman to absent himself. It was particularly politic on this occasion.

The address began with a graceful and erudite history of the progress of the British people from a nation founded on conquest, living under despotism until it partially emerged from that condition. At that state, a portion of their people became "willing exiles" in the wilderness of the western world because they "were the exiles of liberty and of conscience." Adams described how, in 150 years, successive colonies were founded until the number grew to thirteen. However, from their infancy, these offshoots were treated with neglect, harshness, and injustice, the "sufficient cause in the laws of moral and physical nature" which made the independence of the colonies a necessary act. After this historical recital, Adams picked up the original manuscript of the Declaration of Independence and, with a flourish, read it to the audience.

Having provided a sensation, he said gratuitously that he did not want to revive past anger but rather have his auditors dwell on "the interest" which "spreads as it grows old" in the "first solemn declaration by a nation of the only *legitimate* foundation of civil government. . . . It swept away all the rubbish of accumulated centuries of servitude." What followed was the routine praise of the patriots and a fiery blast against the destruction of war, during which "some of the fairest of your fields were ravaged . . . towns and villages were consumed with fire . . . the harvest of your summers were blasted; while the purity of virgin innocence, and the chastity of matronly virtue were violated." The progress of the nation from its first floundering under the Articles of Confederation to the peaceful development of its permanent Constitution was duly noted. Thus far the pattern was still conventional, if more intensely articulate than the usual Fourth of July speech, except for one significant consideration: the orator was the United States Secretary of State. It mattered little that Monroe and his fellow Secretaries were unaware of the contents of the speech nor was it significant, because had they seen it most likely, as Adams asserted, they would not have been concerned.[50]

With or without consensus, J.Q.A. took this opportunity to enunciate some very important and prophetic positions on the South American crisis, using the Independence Day pastime of insulting the British as his cover. There was ironically, however, no evidence that the importance of what the Secretary of State said was understood at the time. On the contrary, most of the noisy controversy that developed after the speech concentrated on the propriety of Adams's having made the speech while in such high office. What was unnoticed was that John Quincy, quite deliberately, was answering both Edinburgh and Lexington.

In its May article, the *Edinburgh Review* suggested that the Holy Alliance be challenged by the concerted efforts of the United States and England. Clay in his Lexington speech had suggested a sort of Pan-Americanism. Neither idea pleased Adams. Referring back to his Publicola letters, in which he had predicted the essence of Washington's farewell address, its non-intervention policy, Adams declared that he did not want to go abroad "in search of monsters to destroy." The United States was "the well wisher of the freedom and independence of all." She was the champion and vindicator only of her own. "She well knows that by once enlisting under other banners than her own, were they even the banners of foreign independence, she would involve herself beyond the banners of extrication." And, further, in reference to South America, "she has abstained from interference in the concerns of others, even when the conflict has been for principles to which she clings, as the last vital drop that visits the heart." In conclusion, John Quincy orated grandly, "[United States] glory is not *dominion* but *liberty.* Her march is the march of the mind. She has a spear and a shield: But the motto under her shield is—*Freedom, Independence, Peace.*"[51]

Response to the speech was a mixture of praise and denunciation. Most of the negative press was centered on Adams's heavy sarcasm against the British, such as: "Ye chivalrous knights of chartered liberties and the rotten boroughs! Ye improvers upon the sculpture of the Elgin marbles! Ye spawners of fustian romance and lascivious lyrics."[52] Some of those who were angered were Anglophiles from the Northeast. Critics in the press of other parts of the country, such as the Philadelphia *Aurora* and the Richmond *Enquirer*, questioned the sincerity of J.Q.A.'s Anglophobia, suggesting that it masked his and his father's partiality for England in an attempt to acquire more votes in the next presidential election.[53]

In a number of letters to friends about his address, Adams enlarged on his theme while professing amazement that the speech received such wide notice. He said that he accepted the invitation to speak because he wanted to say these things. England's deep-seated enmity to the United States was a phenomenon that he had often noted while he was overseas, and its basis, Adams believed, was her desire for revenge for the two defeats she had suffered at American hands and envy of American growth and prosperity. His aim, John Quincy told Robert Walsh, was not so much to disparage British literature and science as to point out the importance of native achievement, particularly the invention of the steamboat. As to criticism for his reference to George III's insanity, Adams defended it by reminding his critic that the Declaration of Independence was, after all, directed against the King.

For Adams the most serious purpose of his address was to demonstrate from the moral and physical nature of man *"that colonial establishments cannot fulfill the great objects of government in the just purpose of civil society,"* which not only identified the nature of the struggle of the United States for freedom from England but also interpreted the current struggle of Spain's South American colonies. It foresaw the fall of the British Empire in India and said something about the future of the United States as a colonial power, a notion abhorrent to Adams. He labelled great colonial establishments "mighty engines of *wrong* and it will be the duty of the human family to abolish them as the slave trade."[54] With some bitterness, Adams blasted his New England critics, whose animosity he traced back thirty-five years to his Commencement oration. Trust in him, he noted, had come not from his own Eastern politicians but from the Virginia Presidents.

Nonetheless, many of Adams's enemies found reason to damn the speech mercilessly, or to be triumphant about the ill way in which it was received. Henry Clay wrote to Caesar Rodney with some disgust that "of its author, I will only repeat, what I have often said that it furnishes further proof of his total want of judgment. . . . He ought never to have undertaken the task, and if he did, he ought never to have published the composition."[55] Henry R. Warfield said, "I wish Quincy wou'd make one or two more fourth of July speeches— one or two more such specimens wou'd effectually Silence his pretensions. . . ." A friend, possibly Eligius Fromentin, wrote to Clay: "Poor Adams will have to make his exit without time or opportunity to thank his friends (if he has any) for past favours. . . . What with his 4th of July garlands—flowers of etiquette. . . ."[56]

Since the Fourth of July interruption did not add anything to the solution of the difficulties with France, who was proving adamant, Adams asked Monroe, who readily assented, for two months' leave to return to Quincy. Louisa, at Peacefield since early in the summer, had reported that her father-in-law was more feeble and changed than she had ever seen him, but in tolerable spirits.

Before he left Washington, Adams informed Canning that the United States's plan for combatting the slave trade by keeping their cruisers on the African coast to cooperate with the ships of other nations was just as effective as Britain's mutual search treaties. It would be best, he said, hoping to close the matter, if each nation, agreeing as it did on mutual purpose, applied its own means effectively. In consequence, on August 20, American naval vessels cruising on the coast of Africa were ordered to carry out the laws against the slave trade. But Canning was only partially appeased and stubbornly still hopeful that his way would prevail. He wrote to his home office that he had reason to believe that all members of the American Cabinet were not equally opposed to a limited right of search and some accommodation might still be arranged.

The visit to Quincy was made but abruptly terminated. Daniel Brent, chief clerk for the State Department, had been sending on to his chief all the important despatches that came through his hands. Adams was particularly uneasy about the French negotiations and the news from Florida. Jackson, who had been appointed Governor of Florida, was now involved in a quarrel with the former Spanish Governor Callava over some discrepancies in the inventory discovered when the General took over Pensacola. The differences escalated into a scandal when Jackson suspected the honesty of Eligius Fromentin, one of the new federal judges. The precipitating episode concerned a poor woman, one of the heirs of someone named Vidal, whose case Forbes and Company had been handling for sixteen years with no results. The woman went to Jackson with the allegation that Callava held papers that supported her claim against the other contestants but would not give them to her. Jackson sent for the papers from the ex-Governor. When he was informed that Callava refused to surrender them, he ordered him arrested and the papers taken. The next morning Judge Fromentin, who was involved with Callava and the Pensacola agent of the trading concern, Forbes and Company, displayed his friendship for the ex-Governor by issuing a writ of habeas corpus to him. Jackson considered this an act of contempt on the part of the judge and overrode him by summoning Callava to an interview. All three, intensely angered, sent appeals to Monroe.

The President called a Cabinet meeting on October 23 to discuss the dispute. For several days the Secretaries wrangled with Adams, standing alone in firm support of Jackson. Monroe, Wirt, and Calhoun favored Jackson's action on the documents but denied his right to override Judge Fromentin. The public, as usual, was entirely sympathetic to Jackson and inflamed when newspaper reports indicated that the Administration might censure him. The difficulty was settled when Jackson, ill and in a foul humor, went home to Nashville and subsequently sent in a letter of resignation. The Florida interlude was only a source of annoyance to the General, who had expected patronage for his friends to be available. Monroe accepted the resignation on December 31, inserting in his letter assurances that he entertained the same sentiments as always for Jackson's integrity and ability. Several months later, although the term had not quite expired, Fromentin returned to New Orleans and died there before the year was out.

Adams, left with the job of settling the charge against Jackson made by the Spanish Minister in behalf of Don Jose Callava, pointed out that the Spanish Governor should have left Pensacola months earlier and that Jackson's request for public records indispensable for settling the Vidal case was made in behalf of orphans who needed them. Further, Callava's attempt to carry away papers was a violation of the treaty. Jackson was pleased with Adams's letter, which he said was "just like himself, a bold, manly and dignified refutation of falsehood, and justification of justice and moral rule."[57] Monroe, who was much less tolerant of Jackson's peccadillos than the Secretary of State, told Adams that if there was to be a break with Spain, he preferred it to be over South America rather than over an obscure woman at Pensacola.

On November 5, Hyde de Neuville arrived at Adams's house in a very belligerent mood to renew the subject of the *Apollon*. In no time they quarrelled over whether de Neuville had included the phrase "as a private individual," when he announced his prediction that if satisfaction was not given to the French government for the French ships in three months France would retaliate by detaining American ships in her waters. Adams said that he was happy that this was only De Neuville's private opinion and he would report it to the President. First the Frenchman responded with "All right," and then, rising from his seat, shouted in a peremptory tone, accompanied by vehement gestures, that if Adams intended to report to the President he should tell him that in his opinion France ought to declare war. With that, he rushed from the room, through the inner and outer door, and into the street. Antoine, John Quincy's valet, saw him go and shouted after him that he had forgotten his overcoat. De Neuville turned back, put on his coat, and left without saying a word. Adams was amused by the exchange but so disturbed by the state of Franco-American relations that anxiety awakened him at three in the morning and he could not get back to sleep. Monroe was surprised and annoyed when Adams told him about the Frenchman's bizarre behavior. In answer, J.Q.A. said that the *Apollon* matter would have to be included in the Message to Congress or the Administration might appear to be concealing the truth. The situation was already awkward because although the seizure of the ships was legal, Crawford and Gallatin did not support the action. Monroe agreed to mention the French dispute in his message in a moderate manner, which disappointed John Quincy, who believed that French hostility to the United States was reaching crisis proportions.

Adams believed that a liberal principle of commercial relations with foreign nations was one of the basic ingredients of national independence. The United States had made her first treaty with France who, at the time, had been extraordinarily accommodating, much more so than she had ever been with another country. In the present negotiations with France, Adams said disapprovingly, despite America's acceptance of discriminating duties which were unsatisfactory, France was still not satisfied and wanted more inequality in her favor. "I am glad she has not accepted our offer," he concluded.[58] Somewhat more persuaded now of its wisdom, Monroe included in his annual message both a review of the United States commercial system and an account of France's intransigence over the *Apollon* matter, "a cause of very great regret," he said.[59]

Though still puzzled and doubtful about the democratic potential of the new Spanish American states, Adams could no longer question the fact that their cause was gaining rapidly. By 1822, San Martin, who had freed Chile, was in Lima and the rest of Peru was about to fall to him and to Bolivar, who was coming up from the north. With Mexico in the hands of the revolutionaries, it was obviously only a matter of the timetable before all of Latin America would free itself from Spain.

However, at this time there was disturbing evidence of European activity in the newly emerging nations. Buenos Aires had been involved in a plot with France to establish a monarch there, until it was exposed and then thwarted. Britain was openly giving naval aid to the rebels in Chile as she had in Venezuela. Both Peru and Mexico were, it was said, ripe for the establishment of a monarchy.

Both in spite of these situations and because of them, on March 8, 1822, Monroe sent a special message to Congress saying that Colombia, Chile, Peru, Mexico, and Los Plata (Argentina) had achieved "such decisive success" in their contest with Spain that they deserved to be recognized. If the war continued, however, Monroe promised, perfect neutrality would be maintained. No unfriendliness to Spain was meant, only strict accordance with the law of nations and justice to all parties. Congress, if it concurred, should make the necessary appropriations.[60] This placid, uninspired message, which was probably meant to keep Spain quiet, did achieve a congressional appropriation of $100,000 for the setting up of missions in the new countries.

A protest from Don Joaquín de Anduaga, Spain's Minister to the United States, was prompt in arriving. John Quincy answered it by asserting that the United States "yielded to an obligation of duty in recognizing the independence of these provinces." It was "the mere acknowledgement of existing facts," in no way preventing Spain from trying to recover her colonies. With some asperity J.Q.A. suggested "the time is at hand when Spain's European friends and Spain herself" should realize that nothing will serve "the welfare and happiness" of Spain as well as universal concurrence in recognition.[61]

Stratford Canning, who had been the victim of American one-upmanship, quoted a conversation with Adams in which the American Secretary of State had described Spain as a man under the pressure of a nightmare, longing to raise his arm but unable to stir a muscle.

"So, Mr. Adams, you are going to make honest men of them," Canning asked. "Yes, sir!" answered the American Secretary of State. "We proposed to your government to join us some time ago, but they would not, and now we shall see whether you will be content to follow *us*."[62]

Recognition once granted, Monroe was in a quandary whether to send a Minister to Colombia immediately or to merely receive Torres as Chargé d'Affaires. He considered asking Clay to accept a South American post, but felt that he had been so hostile to the

. Abigail Adams. Engraving
fter a painting by Gilbert
tuart. *Courtesy of The New-
'ork Historical Society, New
'ork City.*

2. John Adams. Lithograph
by N. Currier. *Courtesy of
The New-York Historical Society, New York City.*

4. J. Q. A. at 16. Engrav
by Sidney L. Smith afte
drawing by Schmidt made
The Hague in 1783. *Cour*
of *The New-York Histor
Society, New York City.*

5. George Washington in
1791. Painted from life on
Marble at Philadelphia by
Archibald Robertson. *Courtesy of The New-York Historical Society, New York
City.*

6. J. Q. A. in 1795. Painting by John Singleton Copley. *Courtesy, Museum of Fine Arts, Boston. Gift of Mrs. Charles Francis Adams.*

7. Louisa Catherine Johnson Adams. Painting ascribed to Edward Savage ca. 1801. *Courtesy of Adams National Historic Site, National Park Service, United States Department of the Interior.*

Thomas Jefferson. Engraving by H. W. Smith after a painting by Gilbert Stuart. *Courtesy of The New-York Historical Society, New York City.*

9. James Madison. Painting by A. B. Durand after Gilbert Stuart. *Courtesy of The New-York Historical Society, New York City.*

10. Albert Gallatin. Etching. *Courtesy of The New-York Historical Society, New York City.*

11. James Monroe. Painting by Asher B. Durand. *Courtesy of The New-York Historical Society, New York City.*

12. Louisa Catherine Adams in 1816. Engraving by G. F. Storm after a painting by C. R. Leslie. *Courtesy of The New-York Historical Society, New York City.*

13. J. Q. A. in 1818. Plaster bust attributed to George Cardelli. *Courtesy of The New-York Historical Society, New York City.*

14. J. Q. A. as Secretary of State, 1819. Engraving by Francis Kearney ca. 1824 from Charles Bird King portrait of 1819. *Courtesy of The New York Historical Society, New York City.*

A FOOT-RACE

16. William H. Crawford. Engraving by A. B. Durand after a painting by J. W. Jarvis. *Courtesy of The New-York Historical Society, New York City*.

17. J. Q. A. in 1825. Bronze medal by Moritz Furst. *Courtesy of The New-York Historical Society, New York City*.

A Foot-Race (*left*). A caricature of the election of 1824 engraved [by] David Claypool Johnson. In the foreground, at the right, the three [chief] candidates can be distinguished. J. Q. A. is slightly ahead with [Cra]wford and General Jackson nose and nose. John Adams stands [beh]ind his son waving his hat and saying, "Hurra for our son *Jack*." [Cla]y, in black boots, at the right, looks defeated but quizzical. Adams [is u]nkindly treated with such bad puns as "Like enough he'll never [get] the better of his Quinsy." Jackson seems to be the people's fa[vori]te. The Capitol dominates the background as the symbol of the [seat] of power which will finally decide the contest. The President's [chai]r is perched coyly in the center of the scene. *Courtesy of The [New]-York Historical Society, New York City*.

18. J. Q. A. in 1826. Engraving by Thomas Gimbrede. J. Q. A.'s seal appears under the portrait. Its motif of the eagle and lyre has been used by the artist on the draperies and the chair. *Courtesy of The New-York Historical Society, New York City.*

JOHN Q. ADAMS.

President of the United States

19. Andrew Jackson, Daniel Webster, and Henry Clay. Engraving by John Sartain. *Courtesy of The New-York Historical Society, New York City.*

20. Martin Van Buren. Engraving by N. Dearborn. *Courtesy of The New-York Historical Society, New York City.*

21. Rufus King. Painting. *Courtesy of The New-York Historical Society, New York City.*

22. "Peacefield," the "Old House" in Quincy, Mass. *Courtesy of Adams National Historic Site, National Park Service, United States Department of the Interior.*

23. J. Q. A.'s bedroom in the "Old House." The pictures over the mantle are scenes of Silesia brought back by J. Q. A.; the tiles around the fireplace were a present to Abigail from John Quincy and Louisa purchased in Prussia. *Courtesy of Adams National Historic Site, National Park Service, United States Department of the Interior.*

24. J. Q. A. in 1831 or before. Marble bust by Horatio Greenough. *Courtesy of The New-York Historical Society, New York City.*

25. J. Q. A. in 1834. Painting by Asher B. Durand. *Courtesy of The New-York Historical Society, New York City.*

26. Charles Francis Adams in 1829. Painting by Charles Bird King. *Courtesy of Adams National Historic Site, National Park Service, United States Department of the Interior.*

27. Abigail Brooks Adams in 1829. Painting by Charles Bird King. *Courtesy of Adams National Historic Site, National Park Service, United States Department of the Interior.*

28. James K. Polk. Painting by Joseph Dickinson after an original by Healy. *Courtesy of The New-York Historical Society, New York City.*

29. J. Q. A. Lithograph by B. F. Butler made in 1848 from an 1843 daguerrotype by Philip Haas. *Courtesy of The New-York Historical Society, New York City.*

30. The United States Senate Chamber in 1846. Painting by Thomas Doney. J. Q. A. is the fourth figure to the left of the Speaker. *Courtesy of The New-York Historical Society, New York City.*

31. J. Q. A. in 1848. Stipple engraving by Richard Soper from a sketch made by Arthur J. Stansbury of J. Q. A. a few hours before his death. *Courtesy of The New-York Historical Society, New York City.*

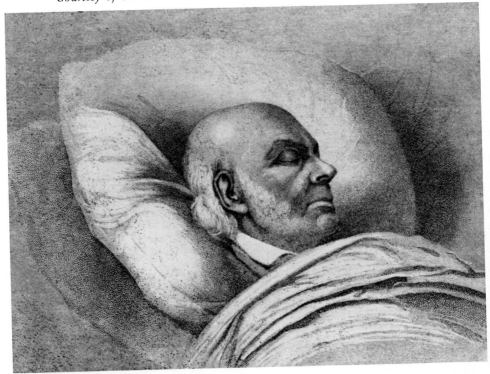

Administration that he did not deserve the recognition. Adams, who probably wished his antagonist thousands of miles away, doubted that Clay would take anything but Mexico or Colombia and anyhow was fearful of his tendency to entangle the United States inextricably in Latin American politics. Adams recognized that Clay was a talented man but was repelled by his ambition which, he commented, made him not very scrupulous and "too much addicted to intrigue."[63]

A few months later Adams seemed to change his mind about offering the Colombia mission to Clay. Though doubtful that the Kentuckian would accept it, he thought that it would be a popular move in the West and flattering to Bolivar, with whom Clay had corresponded for a long time. Adams recorded smugly that in pursuing a generous policy towards him, "as an enemy and rival, I do some violence to my inclination, and shall be none the better treated by him; but I look to personal considerations only to discard them, and regard only the public interests."[64]

Adams always believed that Clay was the deus ex machina in a controversy that developed into a vigorous paper war between John Quincy and Jonathan Russell. The complicated, time-consuming dispute started with Congressman John Floyd's resolution of January 1822, asking President Monroe to deliver to the House of Representatives all correspondence relating to the Treaty of Ghent and, in addition, the protocol of the negotiations. His rationale for the request was a sister resolution, just introduced, which concerned the occupation of the Columbia River and the reorganization of the Indian Service. Since the problem of European influence over the Indians had been exhaustively discussed at the Ghent peace talks, he agreed there was an apparent need for complete transcripts of the proceedings. In their anxiety to complete the negotiations, the American commissioners had relayed brief condensations of their final discussions and so the complete record was not filed at the State Department until a later date.

Among the letters and documents sent to Congress in answer to Floyd's call was a letter that Jonathan Russell had written to Secretary of State Monroe on December 25, 1814, in which he said that he would explain in a future letter why he disagreed with a majority of his colleagues who had been willing to trade the right of British subjects to navigate the Mississippi River in return for the fisheries privilege for American citizens.

In April, once more acting on a resolution introduced by Floyd, the House sent to Monroe for Russell's second letter, dated February 11, 1815. The letter was not in the files, so Daniel Brent, aware of this, on his own initiative, went to Russell's lodgings and asked if he had a copy. Russell said that his daughter had just lately sent him a draft. Mark it a duplicate, Brent advised, and Russell, agreeing, did. The letter was seven folio sheets of denunciation of the Ghent mission for proposing the article recognizing the fisheries right and the British right to navigate the Mississippi, a proposal with which he had concurred at the meetings. The letter had been written in Paris at a time when all the other commissioners had been present and yet he had said nothing to Adams about his intention of writing such a letter.

Adams thought that Russell's motive at that time was to play upon the sectional prejudices of a Virginian Secretary of State who served under a Virginian President and to give the New England Adams "a secret stab in their esteem for future effect." Now, Adams analyzed, the time had come to use it "to deny my chances of popular favor in the western country" and Floyd's willing collaboration in the scheme had been enlisted.[65]

In the meantime, Monroe conducted his own private search for the letter in demand, and found it among his papers dated February 1815 and marked "private." When his experienced eye compared the two letters, Adams was not surprised to find many differences. The modern version had been altered in order to glorify Clay and Russell at the expense of the other members of the Commission. Most damaging was a prophetic passage, absent from the original, that assumed knowledge of Jackson's victory at New Orleans, a piece of news that had not yet reached Paris at that time. Other slips were the inclusion of passages that assumed knowledge of the convention of 1818 by which the United States would achieve the fisheries without the Mississippi equivalent.

Monroe was dismayed when Adams pointed out the discrepancies in the two letters, and added to his verbal report a list of 172 variations, which he punctuated with some pungently sarcastic remarks on Russell's prophecies. However, in spite of the evidence, the President did not want to send the two letters to the House because, he argued, it would ruin both men. Adams disagreed, believing rather that if the documents were withheld it would appear that the Secretary of State was afraid. When Monroe continued to be upset but indecisive, John Quincy realized that the President and he had a conflict of interests. It was best for Monroe to take the path of impartiality but he must commit the letters and his findings to Congress.

The two principals in the dispute met in an office of the State Department at the end of April. Adams had no compunction about confronting Russell with the observation that his letter was an extraordinary paper and his conduct relating to it equally extraordinary. Russell during the exchange that followed said, "I have acted from no motive of hostility against you," which was too much for John Quincy. "Mr. Russell, I wish not to enquire into your motives. Henceforth, as a public man, if, upon any occasion whatever, I can serve either you or your constituents, it will afford me as much pleasure as if nothing had ever occurred between us; but of private and individual intercourse, the less there is between us from this time forward the more agreeable it will be to me," Adams answered. "I wish you well," Russell replied and left the office.[66]

Monroe, still hoping to avoid the issue, suggested that the House be informed that the letter had not been found in the State Department files. "It is impossible that the fact will not become notorious," Adams persisted. "It cannot but appear that it is known to you from my report."

"*Your* report?" Monroe replied. "To *my* report. It is no report at all until I have accepted it."

"I ask no favor, nothing but a hearing," Adams persisted stiffly, somewhat disturbed that he and his superior had come so close to a quarrel.

Finally, on May 4, Monroe acceded to Adams's wishes and made known to the House of Representatives that Russell's letter, "purporting to be the duplicate of a letter" written in February 1815, communicated a difference of opinion between him and his colleagues. The Secretary of State, he added, one of the two other living commissioners, wanted to answer it, "a claim which, on the principle of equal justice, could not be resisted." Therefore Monroe would hold up the delivery of the letter unless the House, knowing the circumstances, called for it.[67] Floyd took Monroe's hint and remained silent, but Adams was not content to leave it be. He prevailed upon Timothy Fuller to call for the Russell letter and any communication from any other member of the Ghent mission relating to it. On May 7, after dining with the President, John Quincy rode with him to the Capitol where he was to sign fifty or sixty bills into law, carrying the two editions of Russell's letters and his own remarks on them. At the House, the documents were received and ordered to be printed, but not immediately read. Acceding to Monroe's request, John Quincy had softened some of his harsh expressions, somewhat mollified also by George Hay's assurance that his paper was so unanswerable the less severe he was the more powerful the effect.

Russell was not ready to give up the battle he had started. On his way home, he stopped in Philadelphia to deliver to Robert Walsh, publisher of the *National Gazette,* another copy of his famous February letter, which Walsh published on May 10 along with an editorial vouching for the exactness of the copy. It was not an exact copy but one that differed in several ways from both the original and the duplicate. Adams immediately dubbed it the "triplicate."

When Walsh received Adams's letter exposing Russell's fraud, he published the Secretary of State's remarks, and then wrote to his friend that the publication of all the papers "was desirable for your interests. . . . You have forever stifled mysterious hints and vulgar clamour on the subject of the negotiation at Ghent."[68]

The Russell controversy dominated a good part of J.Q.A.'s thinking for the next six months. He knew, intellectually, that persecution (and so he regarded it) "makes a man an egotist in spite of himself and egotism always ended by making itself tedious,"[69] but he found it impossible to stop justifying, explaining, and renewing the controversy over and over again for his friends and correspondents. Charles Jared Ingersoll was given the credit for "the first intimation of the subfluvial torpedo which was from the turbid bottom of the Mississippi to blow me up. But I had no suspicion that Mr. Jonathan Russell had volunteered to be chief engineer for the explosion."[70] Though Adams lamented that the matter took up too much of his time, he could not stop brooding over the "miserable plot against me, devised by Clay at Ghent, and in which he has made a tool of Russell."[71]

Jonathan Russell, now at home in Meriden, Massachusetts, tried to extricate himself from the mess he had created by appealing to Clay for confirmation on some of the points. "I showed you at the time the letter which I wrote at Paris & you coincided with me in the grounds there taken for our opposition—I shall state this fact & hope should occasion require you will confirm it," he wrote in early June. Somewhat plaintively, he added, "It consoles me not a little that Adams by avowing in his rage, that the free navigation of the

Mississippi is of no more importance than the right to us of navigating the Bridgewater Canal or the Danube has settled his fate in your quarters and will gain him nothing here—A line from you under existing circumstances would be particularly satisfactory."[72] When Clay, who was away at some watering place, received the letter more than a month after it was sent, his answer was prompt and painfully candid. Upon reading the President's communications and Adams's remarks, he said, "the variance between your two letters has given in the public judgement, a great advantage to Mr. Adams, at least for the moment." He suggested, even more brutally, that if his former colleague had no satisfactory explanation, "it will do you a lasting prejudice." Clay then bowed out of any involvement with the unfortunate Russell by asserting quite clearly that it would be painful to him to be drawn into the controversy and that he resented the incorrect accusation that he prompted the call for Russell's letter.[73]

Most observers believed that Russell had injured himself more than Adams. Amos Kendall wrote dejectedly to his friend Clay that many who were formerly opposed to Adams now favored him. Stratford Canning informed London that the public was excited in no small degree by the dispute but the regret must be Russell's. With great persistence, the belief continued that Clay was involved in the business. Crawford, who would have liked to see Clay discredited along with Russell, wrote to Albert Gallatin that the object of the plan was to help Clay by demonstrating that western interests could not be safely trusted to anyone living in the Atlantic states.

The paper war continued to rage, with John Quincy wielding his pen without respite. His articles appeared in the *National Intelligencer* and the Richmond *Inquirer*, and then were copied all over the country. "I will treat Jonathan Russell as mercifully as possible consistently with the duty of exposing him in his true colour. . . . If he wishes for peace he must hold out the white flag," Adams told a friend.[74] The controversy, he wrote to his wife, who was in Philadelphia to take care of her ailing brother, was a struggle "between life and death—or for more; that is for the character of an honest man."

Throughout a broiling Washington summer, Adams labored over his vindication. Even on July 26, his twenty-fifth wedding anniversary, he stayed at his desk a hundred miles from Louisa, who was still in Philadelphia. Though he had exhausted the newspapers—for, he judged, writing there any more would look like "mangling a

fallen enemy"—his wrath was still not assuaged. He decided to write
a book that would give a chronological, comprehensive account of
the case. His wife, he wrote to Louisa confidentially, must not try to
dissuade or discourage him. "At every step I take, I want a friendly
adviser, and have had none but you."[75] She must burn the letter
after she received it or be careful that it did not fall into anyone's
hands. Actually, John Quincy was annoyed that Louisa was not with
him at this critical time. He expressed some of his irritation in
answer to her report that friends in Philadelphia were saying that
his "delicacy" about not seeking the Presidency was unsuited to the
times. "It suits my temper to be thus delicate. Do they call it aristocratic hauteur and learned arrogance? . . . It is not their cringing
servility nor insatiate importunity," he answered. His anger made
him press heavily on his pen. His characteristically careful script
was askew, the paper badly blotted. "They and you think I am
panting to be President, when I am much more inclined to envy
Castlereagh the relief he has found from a situation too like
mine."[76] The distraught Adams did not mean the last remark. Castlereagh's suicide, which he had accomplished by cutting his throat
with a small penknife, shocked John Quincy profoundly. Earlier he
had commented to Louisa, "What must have been the agonies of
that mind, which in the midst of a career of unparalleled success
was driven to suicide from despair!"[77]

After the publication of J.Q.A.'s volume, *The Duplicate Letters,
the Fisheries and the Mississippi, Documents Relating to Transactions at the Negotiation of Ghent,* a brief exchange between Adams
and Clay took place in the *National Intelligencer.* Clay, after expressing regret over the unhappy controversy, wrote that he questioned some of the statements in the book and promised that at
some future time "more propitious than the present to calm and
dispassionate consideration" he would give the public his narrative
of the transactions. Adams answered that he concurred with Clay in
regret that the controversy arose, but remarked pointedly that he
found consolation in the reflection that "from the seedtime of 1814
to the harvest of 1822, whatever he had written had been in the
face of day, and under the responsibility of my name."[78]

It was now conclusively evident that the Russell plot had misfired
and Russell was the one shot down. He was not re-elected to Congress and even Timothy Pickering, arch enemy to the Adamses, said
that Russell was a man *"fairly done over."* Pickering was even will-

ing to forgive John Quincy for his Fourth of July speech.[79] However, for the general public, as John Sloane rightly observed to Henry Clay, the rights and wrongs and the intricacies of the debate soon became obscured. The Adams-Russell controversy turned into a personal contest that entertained them as they watched to see which party would be the most cutting and sarcastic.[80]

The dog days of the summer were not confined to "drudging like a slave in self-defense against brother Jonathan."[81] There were further nuisances, such as persistent office seekers and nasty comments about John Quincy's attire. Louisa was upset by an attack in a Philadelphia paper that accused the Secretary of State of wearing neither a waistcoat nor a cravat and sometimes going to church barefoot. Adams admitted that occasionally in the extreme heat, instead of a cravat he wore a black-silk riband around his neck, but that when the fever heat subsided he resumed his cravat.

For recreation, while keeping bachelor quarters with George, Adams indulged in his passion for the theater, a source of amusement that had not failed him in forty years. In a charming "confession," John Quincy wrote to Louisa that the first woman he had loved was an actress with whom he never spoke and probably never saw off the stage. She belonged to a company of child players who performed at the Bois de Bologne, near Passy, where he lived with Dr. Franklin and his father. She was, he told his wife of twenty-five years, "the most lovely and delightful actress" that he ever saw but he had not seen her since he was fourteen and she appeared to be about the same age. "Of all the ungratified longings that I ever suffered, that of being acquainted with her, merely to tell her how much I adored her, was the most intense." He said that he was tortured by the desire for nearly two years and dreamed of her for at least seven. He learned from her the lesson of "never forming an acquaintance with an actress," an injunction he would lay upon all of his sons. As for his theatrical tastes, he liked tragedy but admitted that he preferred Joseph Jefferson, an English-born actor who played comedy roles, to them all. "The broader the farce, the more I enjoy it," he said.[82]

The Czar decided the British-American dispute over the slaves captured by the British in the War of 1812 in favor of the Americans. Adams was pleased to receive Middleton's note informing him that the convention was concluded. But a new problem arose immediately to take the place of the others—Cuba.

Mr. Barnabe Sanchez proposed, in strictest confidence, that the Cubans should declare themselves independent of Spain, without United States cooperation, and then ask admission to the Union. Adams believed that this was an ardent desire of both Calhoun and Jefferson, and perhaps it had some merit. It would avert the double danger that the island presented due to its perilous closeness to the new United States acquisition, Florida, the possibility of its falling into the hands of Great Britain or being revolutionized by Negroes. The matter had serious international implications because he feared that the new masters of Spain might trade Cuba and possibly Puerto Rico as well for an alliance to protect them from the aggression of the Holy Alliance.

Adams was determined that no advice should be given to Cuba but rather that she must be told that the President did not have the power to promise admission into the United States and, even if he had, friendship with Spain would not allow such a move. And, since relations with Great Britain seemed to be improving at last, the Secretary of State did not want to risk an action that might result in war—a war, Adams told the Cabinet, that must be won by Britain because of her superior Navy. After the victory, he reminded them, she would take over Cuba.

In no time, rumors about an American takeover of Cuba spread through the United States and, inevitably, to London. George Canning, Castlereagh's successor, seriously concerned, wrote to his cousin Stratford ordering him to find out the truth. His answer, that the United States had no intention of taking over the island, put Canning's mind at rest, although he was not completely convinced. It then became the turn of the United States to be anxious. A British squadron was ordered to Cuban waters ostensibly to protect her shipping from pirates. Though Canning explained the mission and the ships were recalled after Spain promised to settle the claims, the United States remained uneasy.

The Adams family was reunited for the 1822 holiday season. Young John, whose poor standing in his class made his father exile him the past winter, had improved his academic record somewhat and arrived at his parents' home as lively and animated as ever. Charles had put in a very difficult year at Harvard. Almost two years younger than his fellow students, he was near the bottom of his class, and wanted to leave college. John Quincy, not in the least resigned to accepting disappointment about his youngest son, advised him that he should at least finish the freshman year. "If I must give up all expectations of success or distinction for you in this life, preserve me from the harrowing thought of your perdition in the next," he wrote.[83] Charles arrived in Washington much grown and changed, Louisa said, looking much more like her now than his father. "It was the most social Christmas I have passed for many years . . . that is, freer from family bickerings and nonsense," Louisa recorded happily.

1822 had been a good year for J.Q.A. despite the constant pressure of State Department business and the Russell attack. The device that had been designed to destroy his presidential hopes now looked as if it would enhance them by giving him a sort of popularity that he seldom achieved. "Secretary hunting" notwithstanding, promises of support and encouragement came in from several unexpected quarters. In the meantime, there was still a sizable span of time to be filled as Secretary of State.

Old John Adams wrote tongue in cheek to Louisa that two years hence, when his son would be disgraced and turned out of office at Washington, he would return to Massachusetts and immediately be teased into being Governor. There would be no peace, he predicted, until he returned to private life and then he would be "as much flattered as I am."[84] John Quincy may well have been amused by his father's letter, but he knew, as did his wife, that, disgraced or not, he would stay in public life as long as he was wanted.

CHAPTER 15

President Monroe's Message

*"These United States of America which we have seen arise and grow . . .
have astonished Europe by a new act of revolt, more unprovoked, fully
as audacious, and no less dangerous than the former."*

PRINCE METTERNICH

*"I have now less than two years, at the utmost extent, to continue in my
present office. The great object of my desire is to leave the business of
the office in a situation as advantageous as possible for the country."*

JOHN QUINCY ADAMS

SOUTH AMERICA WAS very much on the President's mind. The
time had arrived, he wrote to James Madison, when "it became
our duty" to recognize the countries to the south and to maintain
friendly relations with them, which was a euphemism for developing satisfactory trade relations with them. John Quincy Adams, who
echoed these views, referring to them as duties "of the highest
order," was consulted as to the best candidates to go on the missions.
Monroe wanted the nominations to be sent to the Senate as soon as
possible.[1]

Adams immediately suggested Andrew Jackson for the Mexican
post, which surprised the President and annoyed him a little. "What
about the General's quick and violent temper?" Monroe asked.
Adams defended his protégé, saying that despite his uneven temper
Jackson's actions had always been calm and deliberate. Arbuthnot
and Ambrister seemed to have been forgotten. However, on further
consideration the Secretary of State decided that Jackson would
probably turn down the job, since he had just been unanimously
elected as a candidate for the Presidency by the members of the
Tennessee legislature. And to send him abroad might look like an
attempt to get him out of the way. Monroe agreed.

The chore of designing the instructions to be sent with the new Ministers to South America, Caesar Rodney to Buenos Aires and Richard C. Anderson to Colombia, devolved on Adams. He took their authorship with the utmost seriousness because, he realized, they would set the tone of the political and commercial relations between the two hemispheres, and since they would be a prominent part of Monroe's Administration, they must reflect his ideas and opinions. The resulting instructions were so excellent that they met with the President's complete approval. "It marked an epoch" in our relations with the independent governments of South America, Monroe said.

All of John Quincy's reservations about the nature of the South American revolutions showed through his comments. He feared that "the subordination of the military to the civil rights of the people" had not been achieved. He worried about the fate of a system of civil liberty which did not rest on religious freedom: "the control of a bishop of Rome and a conclave of cardinals on the banks of the Tiber over the *freedom of action* of American nations on the shores of the Orinoco, or the Magdalena, is as imcompatible with their independence as the arbitrary mandate of a Spanish monarch and a Council of the Indies at Madrid."[2] It was the duty of the United States to exert its moral influence over "our southern neighbors" and to provide a good example for them, he insisted. Slightly racist overtones crept into his instructions when he referred to the peoples of Colombia as a heterogeneous mass of Creoles, Indians, and Negro slaves, who had suffered centuries of Spanish tyranny.

Adams feared that South American ties with Europe would be greater than those with her North American neighbor. Rodney was cautioned to assert his influence to prevent Buenos Aires from inviting a European prince to rule over her, for she, more than any of the other new nations, had been the scene of intrigue because her government was so tainted by corruption.[3] However, the greatest threat to the United States's influence in South America was England, the commercial colossus whose ships were everywhere. Adams instructed both Rodney and Anderson to insist on complete commercial reciprocity from their respective nations, based on the most favored nation policy.

Though anxious for the new markets that South America offered and for the fostering of good relations with the countries, John Quincy was not yet prepared to accept Clay's statement made at Lexington in 1821 that all the New World nations should participate in an American system. No doubt Adams had Clay in mind when he said to Anderson "Floating, undigested purposes of this great American confederation have been for some time fermenting in the imagination of many speculative statesmen."[4] The Secretary of State was restrained also in his response to the proposed Colombian Confederacy. Its emphasis on total separation from Europe appealed to him but to concur entirely, "a more particular and definite view of the end proposed" would be necessary. Basic American isolationism underlay his hesitation. Nevertheless, despite all his restrictions and reservations, Adams rejoiced in the emancipation of the South American continent, which, he wrote, "opens to the whole race of man prospects of futurity in which this union will be called in the discharge of its duties to itself and to unnumbered ages of prosperity to take a conspicuous and leading part. It invokes all that is precious in hope, and all that is desirable in existence to the countless millions of our fellow creatures which in the progressive revolutions of time this hemisphere is destined to rear and maintain."[5]

The winter of 1823 was less charged with political crisis than the previous years. Louisa gave frequent parties that were attended by great crowds. Because of the expense, music was sometimes omitted but the animated, pleasant conversation that Louisa's two young nieces provided more than made up for it. John and Charles visited in February. Their mother reported proudly that John was much improved and that Charles gave "strong indication" of being "everything our hopes have taught us to anticipate."[6] Optimistically, she wrote that they might still do honor to the name they bore.

Trouble developed in the spring. John, almost ready to graduate, was in disgrace at Harvard for his participation in the student rebellion. Esprit de corps made his involvement mandatory, he explained to his mother. Louisa implored him to try to influence his classmates and to obtain pardon for himself. "You owe it to yourself, but still more to your father," she cried. He neither would nor could do anything about it, and was expelled along with his companions.[7] "We must submit," Louisa said, but her husband was both disturbed and annoyed. He tried to straighten the matter out but it was not until 1873 that Harvard decided to grant John Adams and the other culprits, posthumous degrees.

A minor skirmish that proved that the Adams's enemies would never stop persecuting them on the same familiar grounds occurred at this time. Congressman Alexander Smyth charged the Secretary of State with falsifying the *Journal of the Federal Convention*, which had been published under his direction in 1819. After careful comparison with the original revealed errors in punctuation which were entirely due to the carelessness of the printer, Smyth was forced to drop his accusation. However, before the "conspiracy of the colons and capital letters" was resolved, the two men had engaged in a spirited exchange in the *National Intelligencer*. Adams reported a four-hour "inquisitorial screw," during which Smyth attacked John Adams, Thomas Paine, John Quincy's vote in the Senate on the embargo, and pronounced a dissertation against hereditary honors.[8]

In March, French troops crossed into Spain, starting a chain of events that resulted in the formation of a major policy statement by the United States of America. The purpose of the invasion, carried out by the Duke of Angoulême at the head of a hundred thousand French troops, was to act on the frantic request of King Ferdinand, who pleaded that under the secret treaty signed at the Congress of Verona by Austria, Prussia, Russia, and France, he should be restored to his throne. Canning, who had tried to prevent Paris from acting, declared England's neutrality, thereby separating herself from her former allies. In a state paper, Canning warned France that if she occupied Spain it would mean war with Britain. Fearing that the profitable trade that Britain had been developing with Spain's former colonies would be jeopardized and, more interested in that trade than she had been because tariffs against British goods were being raised all over the continent, the British Minister issued the warning. He said that although England had not formally recognized the former Spanish provinces in America, she neither intended to appropriate "the smallest portion of them nor to tolerate any such attempt by France."[9]

Upon hearing of the French invasion, Adams advised Hugh Nelson, the new American Minister to Madrid, what his position must be in the war between France and Spain "now commencing." Since the result of the conflict must be that Spain's dominion in North and South America would be "irrevocably gone," the danger lay in the possibility that Cuba and Puerto Rico, still Spanish dependents, might be transferred to another power. "The islands from their local position, are natural appendages to the North American continent; and one of them, Cuba, almost in sight of our shores." Therefore, for geographical, commercial, moral, and political reasons, "it is scarcely possible to resist the conviction that the annexation of Cuba to our federal republic will be indispensable to the continuance and integrity of the Union itself."[10] The real danger was that Cuba would be transferred to Britain, a possible disaster that had already been discussed. Nelson's most important assignment, therefore, was to give "earnest and unremitting" attention to any negotiation move between Spain and England. The Spanish government must know that the United States would frown on a transfer of Cuba to any other power. Such a transfer, contrary to the will of the inhabitants, would give them the right to declare their independence and the United States the justification to support them in achieving it.

England's declaration against the latest activity of the Holy Alliance pleased Monroe, Adams, and the American public. Stratford Canning informed his cousin George that such was American sentiment, boasting that even Adams "has caught something of the soft infection." He ventured to suggest that this would be a good moment to bring the two countries closer together, since France, America's traditional ally, was "quite out of fashion."[11]

At this critical time, Stratford Canning was preparing to leave the United States. Poor health was his excuse, but it was not a secret that the Englishman resented his forced sojourn in the American wilderness and disliked his mission to keep "the schoolboy Yankees quiet." John Quincy said of Canning: "He is a proud, high-tempered Englishman, of good but not extraordinary parts; stubborn and punctilious, with a disposition to be overbearing which I have often been compelled to check." Adams judged that what the Englishman most lacked was suppleness. In fairness, however, the Secretary of State conceded that Canning was not false, was courteous, privately moral, and, most important, sincere. In his *Memoirs*, Canning described Adams fairly although without love. He was "much above par in general ability, but having the air of a scholar rather than a statesman, a very uneven temper, a disposition at times well-meaning, a manner somewhat too often domineering, and an ambition causing unsteadiness in his political career."[12]

Though the two men wrote about their respect for each other, their meetings brought out the worst in one another. Adams admitted that of all the foreign ministers with whom he had to do business, Canning most severely tried his temper. Canning could not wait to go home, although he was leaving behind only a chargé,

Henry Addington, who was most certainly in a weaker position to negotiate than his superior.

Before he left, Canning made one last attempt to convince Adams that the United States should participate in Britain's anti-slave-trade treaty. He had no success nor was he any luckier in his attempt to extract a direct proposition on the northern boundary from the American Secretary.

One of their last exchanges, which occurred during a discussion about the recognition of the South American countries, was typical of their ability to irritate each other.

CANNING: So, Mr. Adams, you are going to make honest people of them?
ADAMS: Yes, sir, we proposed to your government to join us some time ago, but they would not, and now we shall see whether you will be content to *follow* us.[13]

Physical confrontation with Canning made Adams more waspish than usual, but he did very little better when he had to write to the Englishman. After repeating the standard American arguments against allowing ships of other nations to seize the ships of the United States for any reason, Adams drew a rather unfortunate comparison. The forcible seizure and abduction of American sailors, he said, was "more atrocious than the slave-trade itself." The slave was only deprived of his rights and not necessarily forced to the violation of his duties, "forced to fight against his friends and to shed his blood in a cause which his soul abhorred."[14] Undoubtedly, although having to deal with a junior diplomat might pose some problems, Adams was not sorry to see the last of Stratford Canning. The feeling was mutual.

It was no longer possible for the United States to avoid a clarification of her position on the continent she now regarded as her own. On June 28, at one o'clock, the President and his Cabinet convened to discuss the instructions to be sent to Henry Middleton, United States Minister to Russia. Emperor Alexander I's Ukase of 1821, asserting that Russia had the right to the Northwest Territory to 51° north latitude and forbidding the approach of foreign vessels within 100 miles of the coast, must be answered.

John Quincy Adams took the position that no other country's territorial right should be admitted on the North American continent. After the Secretary of State read the pertinent Russo-American correspondence to the Cabinet, everyone agreed that Middleton should offer the Russians an article similar to the one with Great Britain, which kept the whole coast open for a definite number of years. If that proposal failed, as it probably would, Russia should be offered a 55° boundary on the condition that the western coast be free for trade with the natives as previously.

For several days, Adams steeped himself in the literature on the subject. He read Cook's *Third Voyage,* Coxe's *Russian Discoveries,* Humboldt, Mackenzie, and Lewis and Clark. As he wrote a draft of the instructions, he commented ruefully, "I find proof enough to put down the Russian argument; but how shall we answer the Russian cannon?"[15]

When he heard that Christopher Hughes was carrying Middleton's instructions to St. Petersburg, Baron Tuyl called at Adams's office to ask if he might inform his government that orders about the negotiation of the northwest coast question were on their way. After Adams agreed, the Russian Minister then wanted to know as much about the arrangements as the Secretary of State would see fit to reveal. With a great deal of tact, Adams told him that the United States would contest the right of Russia "to any territorial establishment on this continent . . . we should assume distinctly the principle that the American continents are no longer subjects for *any* new European colonial establishments." Tuyl took the news rather well. They spoke for an hour, after which the Russian observed that there would be difficulties but they would not be insurmountable.[16]

In his letter to Middleton, Adams ordered him to tell the Russian government that the United States admitted no part of their claims. The rights of the United States were founded firmly on the treaty with Spain of 1819 (Adams-Onis), the American discovery of the Columbia River from the sea and then by land (the Lewis and Clark Expedition), and lastly by the settlement at its mouth in 1811. "This territory is to the United States of an importance which no possession in North America can be to any European nation, not only as it is but the continuity of their possession from the Atlantic Ocean to the Pacific Ocean, but as it offers their inhabitants the means of establishing hereafter water communications from the one to the other."[17]

The substance of the American "no further colonization" principle was clearly stated once more that same day in a letter Adams wrote to Richard Rush in London. In it he stated the right to settlement in semi-mystical terms. It was not simply because of conquest and settlement and exploration, but it was "by the finger of nature" that the United States should form any and all future establishments on the northwest coast of America. "A necessary consequence of this state of things will be, that the American continents, henceforth, will no longer be subjects of colonization." Therefore, Rush must propose a 51° latitude boundary between the United States and Great Britain, but, since the line runs on a 49° latitude to the Stony Mountains (the Rockies), "should it be earnestly insisted upon by Great Britain, we will consent to carry it in continuance on the same parallel to the sea."[18]

Adams included a favorite project in his instructions to Rush—the regulation of neutral rights in time of war which might, hopefully, be slipped into the new convention with England. Calhoun, who came in while Adams was reading his draft of the Rush letter to Monroe, expressed doubts about its acceptance at this time. Adams agreed with him but still wanted to present it to all the maritime powers, Russia, France, and Great Britain, so that eventually it would "bear a harvest of happiness to mankind and of glory to the Union." Calhoun, though skeptical, saw no objection to its inclusion and so Monroe asked Adams to circularize the rest of the Cabinet on it.[19]

At fifty-seven, Adams felt that all the subjects with which he was dealing were important and that time pressed because he had only two more years to complete his work in the State Department. On his birthday, he recorded: "I task my faculties to their full endurance. . . . The head and heart need aid and guidance."[20] But neutral rights in wartime, he confessed, was his greatest enthusiasm. He would die for it with joy and go before "the throne of omnipotence with a consciousness of not having lived in vain for the world of mankind." However, when Monroe asked him to strike out a reference to the Holy Alliance in arguing for those rights in the paper directed to the Russian Emperor, Adams acquiesced though he regarded it as the mainspring of his argument to Alexander.

Before leaving for Quincy, Adams got into a major disagreement with Calhoun over aid to Greece, then in the process of trying to free herself from Turkey. Adams opposed going to the rescue of Greece because he did not think lightly of war with Turkey. He also vetoed a suggestion to send a secret agent to Greece to determine the truth about what was going on there, because, he said, "Our agents never will be secret."[21]

John Quincy worried about George, who had broken his arm in late spring and had been very ill ever since. The shock had thrown him into very low spirits and even his father's indulgent attitude toward him had not quieted his fears that the arm, which continued to be awkward, would become a permanent affliction. At Quincy, J.Q.A. found further cause for concern. In the two years since he had seen his father, John Adams's eyesight had grown dim and his limbs stiff and feeble. He was so bowed with age that he could scarcely walk across the room without assistance. Disturbed by his ninety-year-old father's condition, John Quincy persuaded Gilbert Stuart to paint a portrait of the old man. Stuart made numerous difficulties but finally agreed to paint "a picture of affection, and of curiosity for future times."[22]

During midsummer, significant developments that did not become known in the United States for several months occurred in England between Richard Rush and George Canning. The British Minister courted the American in a whirlwind romance that he hoped would gain him cooperation from across the sea. France's establishment of power in Spain was a threat to Britain's flourishing trade in South America. She feared that France or the Holy Alliance might try to take over Spain's former colonies there.

As soon as Rush received John Quincy Adams's instructions, he asked for a meeting with Canning. At the conclusion of their August 16 conference, Rush commented offhandedly about Canning's note to Sir Charles Stuart, the British Minister in Paris, in which he stated that he was satisfied that France had no designs on Spain's late American possessions. Canning unexpectedly, and to Rush's amazement, answered with a question about what his government would "say to going hand in hand with this, in the same sentiment."[23] He added that he hoped that Rush's new powers would allow him to make such a commitment. Rush, confused, told him that he could not but was diplomatically encouraging.

A few days later Canning put his proposal in writing. If the United States and England could understand each other on the Spanish American colonies, would it not be beneficial that the principles be clearly settled? "For ourselves we have no disguise."

1. We conceive the recovery of the Colonies by Spain to be hopeless.
2. We conceive the question of the Recognition of them, as independent states to be one of time and circumstances.

3. We are, however, by no means disposed to throw any impediment in the way of an arrangement between them and the mother country by amicable negotiations.
4. We aim not at the possession of any portion of them ourselves.
5. We could not see any portion of them transferred to any other Power with indifference.[24]

The offer was blatant. In a series of notes sent from Liverpool, where he was visiting, Canning wooed the bewildered Rush, who had not the power to act but was certainly willing to be wooed. He approved of the principles that Canning had set forth but intimated that he would like to see the Englishman's good faith demonstrated by the recognition of at least one of the South American countries. If that were done, he hinted, even without instructions it might be possible for him to act. Though he had the traditional American fear of entangling alliances and involvement in the web of European affairs, Rush believed that Canning had already acted against the threat of French colonization in South America.

Canning's motives during this period were characteristically pragmatic. He wanted France to be confronted by a combination of American and British seapower in order to deter her from any further adventures. In order to achieve American support, Canning set up a minor flirtation with Christopher Hughes, who had stopped off in Liverpool on the way to his Scandinavian diplomatic post. The British Minister visited Hughes aboard his ship, invited him to sit in his box at the theater, and spent several hours talking to him about Latin American matters.

The climax of Canning's attentions was a toast proposed at the Mayor's banquet on August 25: "The force of blood again prevails, and the daughter and the mother stand against the world." This, the Englishman commented, was his answer to J.Q.A.'s Fourth of July speech of the preceding year.

About six months later, Canning wrote to Charles Bagot, then serving in St. Petersburg, that, in August, Rush was willing to "say, swear, sign anything" with perfect certainty of not being disavowed to stop the continental powers or Spain if England recognized the Latin American states. However, since she was unwilling to do so, "Our flirtation therefore went off; but it left a tenderness behind it."[25] What actually happened was that the whirlwind courtship was over before the American State Department could act. After

Canning returned to London, two conferences with Rush convinced him that he was wasting his time. Instead, he decided to iron the matter out with France, which he finally achieved, wringing from them satisfactory assurances that there would be no intervention in South America from that quarter.[26]

John Quincy Adams was still in Massachusetts when Rush's correspondence reached Washington on October 9. Monroe took the documents with him to Oakhill for further study and then forwarded them to Thomas Jefferson with the request that after he read them he send them to James Madison. Monroe wrote: "Has not the epoch arriv'd when G. Britain must take her stand, either on the side of the monarchs of Europe, or of the U. States?" His own impression, the President revealed, was "that we ought to meet the proposal of the British govt.," and make it known that "we would view an interference on the part of the European powers and especially an attack on the Colonies by them, as an attack on ourselves."[27]

Jefferson answered the letter a week after he received it, calling the question raised in it "the most momentous which has ever been offered to my contemplation since that of Independence." He advocated that the United States should never entangle herself in the "broils of Europe" but that North and South America should have their own system. However, England, in this instance, by her "mighty weight" could "emancipate a continent at one stroke." Therefore, he also believed in a concert with Canning which, because of England's great fleets, would prevent rather than provoke war.

As requested, Jefferson forwarded Monroe's letters and enclosures to Madison. From the third Virginia hilltop, the former President advised that efforts must be made to defeat "the meditated crusade" by the Holy Alliance against Spain's revolutionized colonies. He held similar views to Thomas Jefferson's own cooperation with England.

Though Monroe's initial impulse was to accept Canning's proposal, he was not prepared to make a final judgment until he had consulted with his Administration. On November 7, he convened his Cabinet to go over the confidential Canning-Rush file. Adams, consistently suspicious of British diplomacy, doubted that Canning's object was to stop the Holy Alliance. He said that Britain feared that the United States would try to acquire some of the former Spanish-American possessions and wanted to eliminate the possibility by making an alliance. Calhoun was for joining Great Britain even if the United States had to pledge not to take Cuba and Texas. Adams answered quickly that this country had no intention of seizing either area but since either one might ask for union with us but never with Great Britain, "we give her [Great Britain] a substantial and inconvenient pledge against ourselves, and really obtain nothing in return."[28] Samuel Southard, the new Secretary of the Navy, whose predecessor now sat on the Supreme Court, agreed.

Monroe, opposed to any course that would place the United States in a position subordinate to England, suggested sending a special Minister to protest any interference by the Holy Alliance in this hemisphere. Adams questioned the wisdom of attending a Congress of the Holy Alliance even if invited. He preferred taking the opportunity to answer the communication that Baron Tuyl, the Russian Minister, had delivered recently, which declared that the Emperor would refuse to receive any Minister from the South American governments. Through such a statement, Adams argued, the United States could declare her principles to Russia, France, and the others rather than "come in as a cock-boat in the wake of the British man-of-war."[29] There was general agreement.

After the meeting broke up, John Quincy remained behind. He observed to Monroe that the group of instructions and responses to Baron Tuyl, Rush, Middleton, and the Minister to be sent to replace Albert Gallatin, who had returned from Paris, "must all be parts of a combined policy and adapted to each other; in which he fully concurred."[30] Calhoun, who met Adams outside, wanted to know what Great Britain's objections were to South American recognition. Aversion to fly in the face of the Holy Alliance and her treaties with Spain, Adams explained.

Monroe, however, was alarmed "far beyond anything I could have conceived possible," Adams recorded, with the fear that the Holy Alliance was about to restore her former American colonies to Spain. Calhoun who seemed to be the nervous Nellie of the episode, encouraged his anxieties. At a Cabinet meeting on the 15th, Monroe revealed that Cadiz had been surrendered to the French, a piece of news that had Calhoun "moonstruck." He was convinced that the Holy Alliance with a force of 10,000 men would easily take Mexico and then move on to the rest of South America. Adams did not deny that it might be possible for them to make a temporary impression for three, four, or five years but no more believed that such a restoration would be permanent than that "the Chimborazo will sink beneath the ocean." The United States had no right to dispose of the South American nations "either alone or in conjunction with other nations," he asserted.[31]

Rush's communications arrived at this time. They revealed that Canning had changed his purpose, that he was less alarmed than earlier, and that he must have been offered some inducement after France's triumph in Spain. Adams, however, interpreted England's alarm as merely an affectation in order to obtain from the American government a premature commitment against the transfer of Cuba to France or her own acquisition of the island. Having failed, he returned to the "old standard of British belligerent policy."[32] Adams knew nothing of the Polignac Memorandum, the pledge of the French government that it would not appropriate any Spanish-American possessions nor participate in any display of force against these colonies. Even Rush did not learn about the agreement until shortly before Monroe addressed the American Congress on the subject. Yet Adams, across the Atlantic, with only Rush's documents in his hands, was able to analyze British thinking with astonishing accuracy.

From one to five in the afternoon of November 21st, the Cabinet discussed what notice, if any, should be taken of the Greek struggle for independence and of Spain's invasion by France. Adams had with him his draft of an answer to Rush regarding Canning's proposals. The Secretary of State also mentioned that he wanted to prepare a confidential paper for Baron Tuyl which would moderately but firmly express dissent with Alexander's anti-republican principles and to explain America's position. At the same time, he would declare his country's intention to abstain from interference in European politics with the expectation that the European nations would neither spread their principles to the American continents nor use force against any part of it.

Monroe approved of Adams's idea and then, "in a tone of deep solemnity and high alarm," read the first version of his message, later known as the Monroe Doctrine. The basis for his sketch on foreign affairs, with occasional variations, was a paper that Adams had given him several days before. The draft spoke pointedly against France's invasion of Spain and broadly acknowledged Greek independence, recommending to Congress that an appropriation be made for sending a Minister to them.

Calhoun approved completely of the President's address but

Adams expressed the wish that the President reconsider the whole subject lest it come "like a clap of thunder" to the nations and be regarded as a "summons to arms—to arms against all Europe, and for objects of policy exclusively European—Greece and Spain."[33] For more than thirty years the United States had looked on Europe "safe in our distance beyond an intervening ocean, while Europe had been in convulsions and almost every nation had been, in turn, overthrown, revolutionized and counter-revolutionized." Now this message "would have the air of open defiance to all Europe" and might cause Spain, France, and Russia to break off diplomatic relations. Perhaps the quiet of the last seven years could not continue, but "if we must come to an issue with Europe, let us keep it off as long as possible."[34]

Calhoun disputed with Adams the statement that there was tranquillity in the nation. On the contrary, he maintained that the thinking part of the United States expected that the Holy Alliance would attack South America and that, therefore, the President should sound the alarm.

The next day, Adams saw Monroe privately to urge him again to leave out of his message any passages that the Holy Alliance could construe as aggression against them. This Administration, John Quincy urged, should be "looked back to as the golden age of this republic." To accomplish this, "we should retreat to the wall before taking to arms" and be sure that the Holy Alliance be put in the wrong. Instead of aggressiveness, Adams's strategy was "earnest remonstrance" against European interference in the Western Hemisphere. The United States must make "an American cause" and adhere to it. Monroe agreed to consider this concept for his new draft and then hold another Cabinet meeting. And after the next meeting, with much gratification, Adams saw that the new draft was in the spirit that he had urged.[35]

On November 25, Southard, Calhoun, and Wirt met with Adams and Monroe. Crawford was missing because he was still convalescing from a stroke. Adams's paper came under a heavy barrage of criticism, particularly by the President, who had reservations about its extreme republicanism, which might put off the British. Adams could not see it. He felt that nothing that the United States would do now would result in war. The restoration of South America to Spain would be to no nation's interest, he asserted, and the only bait that the Holy Alliance could hold out for England was

Cuba, which neither they nor Spain were in a position to give. "My reliance upon the cooperation of Great Britain rested not upon her principles, but her interest," Adams said, "and my whole paper was drawn up to come in conclusion precisely with Canning's declaration and to express concurrence with it."[36] The Secretary of State had the support of both Southard and Wirt.

On the same day, Adams presented the draft of his state paper to Russia. He tried to achieve a tone that was at once conciliatory, firm, and comprehensive. It began with a strong statement of American republicanism and then dwelled upon the long years of friendly relations that had existed between the two countries despite war and revolution. He noted gracefully the friendship and good will that had always been extended by Emperor Alexander. In answer to the Emperor's notification that his own and his allies' political principles determined them not to receive any agent from the new governments in South America, Adams asserted that the United States, "faithful to *their* political principles," recognized these countries. As to the Emperor's hopes that the United States preserve neutrality between Spain and South America, the answer was that his country would preserve it as long as Europe and the imperial government of Russia kept it.

The last part of the Adams paper concerned the new American foreign policy. It was the President's understanding, he wrote, that the allied monarch's declarations guaranteeing tranquillity in all the states of the civilized world were limited in application to the affairs of Europe, "not intended to embrace the United States of America nor any portion of the American Hemisphere." The United States "could not see with indifference" European force, other than Spanish, exerted to restore Spain's former colonies or establish monarchies there or transfer any of her possessions in the American hemisphere to any other European power.[37]

With more than usual brilliance, Adams established with England and Russia that the area in which the United States would take a stand would be exclusively American. European concerns were separate and none of the United States's business. To Wirt's question whether it was any advantage to the United States to commit herself to a course of opposition against the Holy Alliance, Adams had a ready answer. The stand must be made.

The next day at the Cabinet meeting, Wirt again expressed his doubts that the American people as a whole were ready to support a war for the independence of South America. It was undignified and dishonorable to menace but not strike, he asserted, and this might well have been the trap that Canning had prepared for the Administration to fall into. Hence Monroe ought not to pledge the nation to war without knowing "the sense of the country."

Calhoun was worried about other matters. He felt that the great object to be achieved was to separate Great Britain from the Holy Alliance. Since she could not resist them alone, he argued, if the United States stayed out of the picture Great Britain would be forced to go along with them, and South America would be reconquered. For the United States the next step would be that "violent parties would arise in this country, one for and one against them, and we should have to fight upon our own shores for our own institutions."[38] He favored the President's message but "an ostentatious display of republican *contrasted* with monarchical principles, always showing superiority of the former," should be omitted in the message to the Emperor because it might be offensive.

Adams did not accept the assumption that the Holy Allies intended to attack the United States and set up a monarchy. He rather suspected that their plan would be to invade South America, particularly Mexico, and first set up the standard of Spain, but their ultimate goal would be to recolonize and partition the area among themselves. For example, Russia might take California, Peru, and Chile; France could absorb Buenos Aires; Britain would take Cuba for her share in the scramble. Where would the United States be with France in Mexico and Great Britain in Cuba, the Secretary of State asked.

Monroe suggested another line of reasoning which Adams accepted as a possibility. If the Holy Alliance should attack South America, Great Britain would resist them alone and, because of her unmatched seapower, defeat them alone. Hence South America would be under British protection and would become her colonies. Adams said, "My opinion was, therefore, that we must act promptly and decisively."[39]

The Russian Minister must be answered directly, Adams told the Cabinet. Since the Holy Alliance had chosen "to edify and instruct us" with an account of their principles, they must be answered in kind. However, John Quincy, who had witnessed the Emperor's many kind acts of friendship toward the United States when he had been the Minister at the Russian court and who had a personal attachment to Alexander, did not believe that "there was one word in my draft that would give him offense."[40] Southard, Wirt, and the others, who continued to scrutinize and object to many of the details in the paper, were unconvinced. Adams, whose former experiences with this sort of thing made him very sensitive, insisted stubbornly that from the first line to the last, his memorandum's object was to answer, compactly and significantly, both Great Britain and Russia. Southard finally agreed.

Monroe kept the paper overnight for further deliberation. He approved of the despatch prepared for Rush but wanted it modified so as not to refuse outright any cooperation with Great Britain, even if she failed to recognize South American independence.

The next day, Daniel Brent carried Monroe's note to the Secretary of State with the draft of his observations to Baron Tuyl, and instruction for him to see the Russian Minister immediately. After making an appointment with Tuyl for three in the afternoon, John Quincy made one last appeal to the President. "I cheerfully gave up all the passages marked for omission except one," he recorded. He wanted to keep the second paragraph, the heart of the paper, which stated that the fundamental principles of the United States were liberty, independence, and peace. Without them, "the rest was a fabric without foundation," Adams argued. The remarks could not offend Alexander unless he planned to invade South America, in which case the paper would serve as a protest against it. John Quincy pleaded with Monroe that the effect of the paragraph would be, first, to persuade the Emperor of Russia, then, if that failed, to be the United States manifesto to the world. As an apology for his insistence, Adams declared that he considered the paper "the most important that he had ever written."

Monroe answered that he thought the exposition of principles in the rest of the paper sufficiently clear without the disputed paragraph, which might give offense because it seemed to censure the principles of the Holy Alliance. Furthermore, because of the gravity of the situation, it was particularly important that the measures be adopted with the complete unanimity of all the members of the Cabinet. However, with good grace, he agreed to re-examine Adams's original draft and come up with his final decision.

Baron Tuyl arrived at the State Department before the President returned the draft to Adams, but while they were talking about the advantages and disadvantages of making the Russian-American exchanges public, Daniel Brent called the Secretary of State out of the room to give him the President's note. The original draft was accompanied by a letter expressing Monroe's unresolved fear that the paragraph of principles contained a direct criticism of the Holy Alliance. However, he consented to the reinsertion of the lines in question because of the importance that Adams attached to them. John Quincy returned to the room and read his paper to Baron Tuyl, omitting the contested paragraph. Tuyl listened, thanked the American Secretary, and promised to send a copy to his court. He could not foretell anything about its reception. He was perfectly certain, however, of the Emperor's friendly attitude toward the United States. "In a republic, republican principles must prevail . . . but . . . difference of principle did not necessarily involve hostile collision," he observed. As to the publication of the notes and papers, Baron Tuyl now wished none of them published, particularly when he found out that, once alerted, Congress could call for all the correspondence. After Adams assured him that his confidence would not be abused, the Baron departed.

Gallatin arrived on his heels, reporting that the President had just read to him Adams's observations on the Russian communiqués. He, too, thought that the questioned paragraph would be offensive to the Emperor. Liberty meant nothing to Alexander, Gallatin asserted, and, as to independence, the Russian monarch meddled with everything. Ever since the Bourbon restoration in France, the newly returned Minister told Adams, the Russian Ambassadors interfered in the smallest details. Though the Emperor earlier in his life had inclined toward liberal opinions, now he was much changed.

Despite Gallatin's objective opinion, Adams was convinced that his paper was marred by the omission of the paragraph so essential to its theme. Late in the same afternoon, he went to see Monroe again to tell him about his interview with Tuyl and his decision to read the paper without the offending section. To others, it was "a hornet of a paragraph," as Wirt had characterized it, but to Adams it was the "cream of my paper."

Perhaps the most interesting and important aspect of the battle of the paragraph was the rather uncharacteristic reasonableness displayed by the often irascible Secretary of State throughout the whole episode. Though he fought hard, he gave up finally. Adams said it was in recognition of Monroe's superior authority and his responsibility for everything that occurred during his Administration. Adams's detractors suggested, however, that it was a political move to ensure the President's support in 1824.

In the despatch sent off to Richard Rush a few days later, Monroe again used his blue pencil freely, amending John Quincy's and then his own drafts. Adams's interest, however, was in reasserting his lack of confidence in England's position, which he described as "negotiating at once, with the European alliance and *with us,* concerning America, without being bound by any permanent community of principle."[41]

Monroe's seventh annual Message to Congress, delivered on December 3, 1823, was unusually lengthy and comprehensive. From the outset, it stated that a view of public affairs would be presented in greater detail than usual because of the "vast extent of the interests on which I have to treat," and their importance to every part of the Union. Early in the address, Monroe said that a precise knowledge of the relations between the United States and foreign powers was particularly necessary. After mentioning the work of the commissioners on boundaries working under the Ghent treaty and the French claims, the President touched upon Russia and the northwest coast. While discussing the problem, he asserted the principle: "That the American continents, by the free and independent condition which they have assumed and maintain, are henceforth not to be considered as subject for future colonization by any European powers." Thus he publicly acknowledged John Quincy Adams's noncolonization principle.

A series of diverse concerns were then covered: the African slave trade, the appointment of Ministers to the South American countries, public finance, the state of the army and the Navy, the post office, manufacturers, and the Chesapeake and Ohio Canal. Adams was relieved that his conservative position on America's role in Greek independence was upheld in the modest statement "that she [Greece] may obtain that rank [independence] is the object of our most ardent wishes." There was no request for a congressional grant for ships or anything else to go to her aid. The reason for the United States's reluctance to engage in the Graeco-Turkish struggle soon became clear.

The heart of Monroe's foreign policy statement emerged near the end of his message. Although the citizens of the United States favored the liberty and happiness of their fellowmen across the Atlantic, in "the wars of the European powers in matters relating to themselves we have never taken any part, nor does it comport with our policy to do so." The United States was, by necessity, more immediately connected with matters in her own hemisphere. "We owe it, therefore, to candor and to the amicable relations existing between the United States and those powers to declare that we should consider any attempt on their part to extend their system to this hemisphere as dangerous to our peace and safety. With the existing colonies or dependencies of any European power we have not interfered and shall not interfere," Monroe said. The attempt of any European power, he reasserted, to meddle with the governments who have declared and maintained their independence would be regarded as unfriendly to the United States.[42]

On the same day that the presidential message was delivered, Adams called on Henry Clay, now in Washington and newly elected to his old post of Speaker of the House of Representatives, in order to discuss funeral arrangements for the Prussian Minister, who had died the day before. Clay offered the comment that the foreign policy part of Monroe's speech was the best. As an early advocate of South American independence, he approved of it without limitation. Even if it led to a war against all of Europe, it would be worth it, he said. Adams acknowledged that such a war might be inevitable. He also noted in his *Diary* that Clay's attitude toward him seemed markedly different, much more agreeable.

The President's message was published immediately in the United States, and as quickly as possible in the newspapers of Europe and South America. The home press concentrated on the President's bold warning to the Holy Alliance. The pro-Administration *National Intelligencer* was enthusiastic as expected, but even in the hinterland there was a minimum of opposition. However, Robert Walsh in the *National Gazette* was one of the few editors who wrote about the non-colonization principle. It "forms quite an epoch in our relations with Europe, and cannot fail to have produced a new sensation in all her leading courts," he commented.[43]

Many Congressmen did not share the press's sanguine attitude toward the threats against Europe implied in the message. John Randolph of Roanoke, a spitfire himself, declared that Monroe's statements were quixotic and the South American states that were free should defend themselves. He was joined in his sentiments by a fellow Virginian, who denounced the doctrine as indirectly leading to war, a prerogative that belonged not to the President but to Congress. Though the public admired the doctrine's nationalism, Congress worried about the nation's military strength.

George Canning was very disapproving. He told Richard Rush that if Britain was to be repelled from the shores of America, it didn't matter whether it was effected by Russia's Ukase, barring her from the sea, or the American President prohibiting her from the land.

The President's message was "the exclusive topick of European conversation, and has attracted all eyes to our Hemisphere," Christopher Hughes wrote from Stockholm. He felt that it was an important factor in the councils of the continental governors and might be a prominent cause for keeping the peace of the world.[44]

French liberals applauded the American President's announcement. Lafayette called it "the best little bit of paper that God has ever permitted any man to give the world." However, on the Paris Bourse, which did not list Spanish-American issues, Spanish issues slumped and the purchase of them went way down. This was due, most likely, not to fear of Monroe but to the fear that now Great Britain would recognize South America, or to the possibility of an Anglo-American accord.

The courts of Europe, unprepared for Monroe's message, were unpleasantly shocked. Though they called it blustery, peremptory, and arrogant, no nation chose to make a formal protest. However, there is no evidence that it was fear of the United States, as Monroe hoped. Most of the European leaders, while amazed at the United States's insolence, doubted that she had the military power to back it up. A number of the members of the diplomatic corps attributed the contents of the message to the politics of the coming election. The French chargé said that all the members of the Cabinet, including the Secretary of State, were seeking popularity and one sure way to get it was by showing the courage to challenge the monarchies of Europe.

The Spanish chargé attributed the message to the decay of Monroe's party and the possibility that, therefore, he would not be able to transmit his office to the Secretary of State. Hence, he reported, J.Q.A.'s election was improbable at the moment but a strong foreign policy might yet achieve it.

Though the Old World might mock at the puny naval strength of the United States—forty-four vessels as opposed to France's 183 and

Russia's 300—the American nation's moral commitment to her southern neighbors could not be shrugged off. Particularly, the continental powers worried about Anglo-American accord. Though they predicted, hopefully, that there would be sound commercial jealousy between the two Anglo-Saxon nations, it was apparent that Britain had shunned the Holy Alliance.

Latin America failed to respond to Monroe's pronouncements with the expected enthusiasm. Partly, the nations were in ignorance of the danger to themselves posed by the Holy Alliance. They did not expect European interference and, had it come, their natural impulse would have been to turn to Great Britain. Past experience had made her Navy familiar with the South American cause and she had been outspoken in her opposition to France's invasion of Spain. In 1823, Great Britain's trade with the new Latin American nations exceeded that of the United States by about twenty-three million dollars and she was known to be generous in extending financial aid.

Some of the Latin American countries were hostile toward the United States. They resented the Adams-Onis treaty, United States neutrality during their wars of independence, and the use of her Navy to defend United States commerce. Mexico distrusted the United States because of her proximity. In a letter written from Buenos Aires the year after the Monroe Doctrine was presented, John Murray Forbes informed Monroe that the highest classes were overwhelmingly pro-English. "Your *Splendid Message* . . . produced an electrical effect on the Republican Party, whose numbers I am sorry to say are few, but was received with an unwelcome apathy by the men in power. . . . I caused it to be faithfully and elegantly translated and printed and I disseminated it through the Provinces and beyond the mountains."[45] However, Colombia and Brazil officially endorsed the message and Chile referred to the United States as her best and most powerful friend.

It has been suggested that Adams was not as averse to British cooperation in Latin America or as determined to reject Canning's overtures as has been traditionally accepted. He might have accepted it as long as the United States was not barred from Cuba in the future. Evidence for this position was based on the conversations between the English chargé, Henry Addington, and John Quincy Adams as reported back to Canning. According to the British diplomat, Adams appeared receptive, conciliatory, and even pleased with the report of the Canning overtures. The real issue, said Addington, was British recognition of the Latin American countries. The Secretary of State would have regarded the recognition of one of them as a pledge of good faith.

Adams may have expressed cordiality to Addington as a diplomatic maneuver, although it was more characteristic of him to err on the side of frankness, not deception. There is no indication, however, in his *Diary* or papers that he really preferred a cooperative venture with Britain. On the contrary, there were many colorful expressions of distaste for involvement with a country that Adams basically distrusted. Such an accord was much more characteristic of Monroe, particularly in view of the advice of the two Virginian ex-Presidents. After the message was delivered, Monroe wrote to Jefferson saying that he still awaited news from Rush on Canning's proposal, and it was not until February 2, 1824, that Rush's letter containing the British Minister's explanations for abandoning the project arrived in the United States.[46]

Inevitably, the question of who was the true author of the Monroe Doctrine became a game that historians chose to play and that biographers were obliged to engage in. John Quincy Adams was the early starter but was soon overtaken by the sponsors of the other favorites, Monroe and Thomas Jefferson. In establishing Adams's claim for the lion's share of the credit, there were certain indisputable factors. Adams was clearly dominant at the Cabinet meeting that finally ironed out the wrinkles in Monroe's thinking on the South American question. The part of the message that stated that North and South America were no longer scenes of future European colonization, the non-colonization principle, Adams claimed as his own. "That this principle thus inserted was disagreeable to all the principal European sovereigns I well knew, and that those of Great Britain, France and Russia had explicitly expressed their dissent from it, notwithstanding which, I adhered to it,"[47] he wrote. Adams's many years of diplomatic experience abroad convinced him that there was a natural schism between Europe and America. Europe could not be trusted, nor could the continents be linked in a sincere alliance. It was not hard for him to resist George Canning's siren song of cooperation. Not only did distrust for the former mother country motivate him but also a sense of pride that made him recoil from being the echo of British policy, particularly in view of their position on Cuba and failure to recognize South American independence. His fine intuitive sense convinced John Quincy that the Holy Allies were not seriously contemplating the restoration of the American colonies to Spain.

The final praise or blame for any national policy can never be clearly assigned. The supporters of one candidate or another for the laurel wreath often have their own motivations for choosing the winner. Adams claimed the no-colonization policy for his own. It fit in with his notions that had been expressed as a very young man in the Publicola papers and then reflected in George Washington's farewell address. But the general principles in the document known as the Monroe Doctrine, as in all major expressions of national thought, were "blowing in the wind." The American people accepted the idea of manifest destiny with mystical certainty, and so they had to accept its implied corollary—United States domination of the American hemisphere.

CHAPTER 16

A Pyrrhic Victory

"Such is the misfortune of our government that the question who shall be our next President sets aside, in innumerable places, the enquiry of what is just, what is honorable, what is for the public good."

WILLIAM PLUMER, JR.

THE ELECTION OF 1824 was unique, baffling, and unpredictable. The continuation of the Virginia dynasty seemed unlikely because there was no legitimate heir. Politically, parties had succumbed to the malaise of the era of good feelings, carrying with them the once-powerful congressional caucus. Instead of party candidates, there was a multitude of individuals, all of whom claimed to be republicans, contending for the executive office. The federalists, badly defeated in the 1816 election, did not choose to compete again in a national contest. Their strength was dominant only in Delaware; even in New England they were small in number and out of office.

Able candidates with sizable followings emerged throughout the 1824 contest. Several occupied seats in the President's Cabinet, which caused Monroe to decide to take no part in favor or against anyone. John Eaton, who backed an outsider, General Andrew Jackson, described the situation. President Monroe, he said, "like an old father . . . stands surrounded by three full grown sons, each seeking the inheritance on his departure. John Q. from the favors bestowed by the old man in his life time has been deemed a favorite always; J. C. [Calhoun] however . . . sets up also pretensions to the inheritance. William [Crawford] and the old gentleman . . . constantly disagreeing . . . hence not quite as friendly as father and son should be; be this as it may, it seems pretty well settled that the Virginia estate, if not already done will be apportioned to the Latter."[1]

Henry Clay, another major candidate, exerted his influence in the legislature, a situation that was uncommonly strong because, from the start, the number of candidates indicated the likelihood that the election would eventually be decided in Clay's bastion, the House of Representatives. However, he was somewhat unrealistic, equating his acceptability in the House with enthusiasm for his presidential candidacy. New Hampshire's representative, William Plumer, Jr., commented that, as Speaker, he respected Clay's talents and integrity, but "I fear that his fast ambition would prevent him from being a safe and useful president of the nation."[2]

There were others who entered the lists briefly or fluttered on the outside of the circle: De Witt Clinton from New York, a state that was already pinpointed as a critical one in the election, or possibly Rufus King, perennial federalist favorite. The earliest formal candidate was William Lowndes of South Carolina, whose state legislature proposed him in December 1820.

Lowndes's nomination gave Timothy Fuller the excuse to approach the prickly Secretary of State on the subject of his candidacy. "I can do nothing either to canvass for myself or to counteract the canvassing of others," was J.Q.A.'s disappointing answer. In private, however, John Quincy had no scruples about recording his feelings about his rivals. Crawford, a particular irritant, he likened to a worm, "preying upon the vitals of the Administration within its own body," the mover of the anti-Jackson group, responsible for the difficulty with Spain and the constant assailant of the War Department.[3]

No less active in discrediting the President and, consequently, his Secretary of State was Henry Clay, particularly on the South American issue. And Crawford, with smug complacency, immediately reported all of Clay's activities in vivid detail to J.Q.A.

Nevertheless, Adams would do nothing to promote his future election, which irritated his supporters into harsh recriminations. They complained that he refused to excite attention or gain friendship, that he was "retiring, unobtrusive, cool, and reflecting," that he remained silent when he should speak up. In answer, Adams said, "I only want what is freely bestowed."[4]

John C. Calhoun's entrance into the race in January of 1822

upset J.Q.A.'s friends. They had accepted Crawford's strength in the South and Clay's in the West but had not counted on Calhoun's receiving bids from members of the important contested states of Pennsylvania and New York. Heretofore, Calhoun had favored going north for the next President, choosing Adams, "a man of talents, of integrity & correct political opinion."[5] But recently it appeared that Adams had become rather unpopular in New England and would be deserted in New York and Pennsylvania. Crawford, on the other hand, was gaining and might win, so Calhoun had decided to enter the race. William Plumer, Jr. was unimpressed with the elaborate explanation. He attributed Calhoun's candidacy to a simple case of presidential fever. Adams responded to the news with some heat. He called it "an elaborate system" to degrade and vilify him, but he had done nothing and would do nothing for his own defense. His public acts must explain his views and his character. In this paranoid outburst, he said that he would rather return to private life than make any bargain or be obligated to a single individual, though that individual could make him President of the United States. He was referring to New York's Van Buren, who had made overtures to him in behalf of his Bucktails but had received no promises in return. Adams thought that faction less likely to be his friends than the Clintonians, whose views were closer to those of the North.

At this stage, Adams relented a little, agreeing that since some steps had been taken by the other candidates, perhaps he would no longer object to begin with the endorsement of the republican members of the Massachusetts legislature, stipulating that the federalists should not be present at the caucus lest they do more harm than good. Adams was a reluctant activist, but far from naïve. In January 1822, taking stock of the political activity that was raging around for all the candidates, he concluded that it might be preferable to wait until the time of election was closer. Otherwise, it might be playing into the hands of the opposition, who wanted a congressional caucus for an election three years in the future. The Secretary of State's intuition was accurate, for election fever subsided almost spontaneously in early 1822, succumbing to premature haste.

It was widely accepted that, as Jeremiah Mason told Rufus King, Monroe intended *"bona-fide*—to make his Secretary of State his eventual successor and that he will in due time, give evidence of such intention."[6] The opponents took this seriously and spared no effort to discredit J.Q.A. "As for the *Professor*," a Clay adherent wrote derisively, "he has too much *water in his Eyes* to see common things—and I doubt much whether he gets his native state. The old school Federalists regard him as an apostate and the Republicans can't forget his family." Another adherent observed that John Quincy was "too Cold—& has not the popularity—he is hated—his Father's memory is enough." Thomas Hart Benton concluded, "John Q. seems to be going off."[7] Clay, who was the recipient of this anti-Adams literature, expected to take the West easily. Then in July 1822, he and the rest of the candidates were startled by the action of the Tennessee legislature, which proposed the hero of New Orleans for the Presidency.

From his eyrie on the mountaintop, Thomas Jefferson observed the contest with assumed objectivity. He saw the presidential race as narrowed down to the two strongest contenders, Crawford and Adams. His preference was for Crawford, "a republican of the old school" who was not singed with any old federalist doctrine or new republican principles.

Although there were no pollsters at the time, the presidential election was the daily theme for newspapers and their readers, particularly in Washington. The consensus seemed to be that New England was for Adams, without enthusiasm. He also had many friends in Virginia and Maryland, his partisans insisted, although the party structures there opposed him. Clay's friends worked for Ohio, critical for them, they thought, even knowing that Clinton or Adams had the preference there. Calhoun was the decided favorite in Pennsylvania.

In November 1822, John W. Taylor told Adams that Clay was coming to the next Congress to regain the Speaker's chair and promote himself into the Presidency. Taylor approached Adams because he had been told that there was some understanding between Clay and him or their friends that the two factions would move in concert. John Quincy denied the rumor and disclaimed an understanding with anyone.[8] However, he thought that Clay planned to get what support he could so as to make a bargain in the House. With nine western states lined up, he could either force Crawford's friends to join him and become President or, if Crawford was the strongest in the House, consent to his being President at the price of making him Secretary of State first, and then heir apparent. Despite

J.Q.A.'s attitude, the rumor was strong that friends of Adams and Clay would unite to make them President and Vice President respectively.[9]

The interaction of Adams's reluctance to help himself and his friends' resultant frustration was best expressed in a graceful paper that John Quincy wrote in answer to a letter from Joseph Hopkinson of Philadelphia to Louisa Adams. During the summer of 1822 Louisa had been a guest at the Hopkinson summer house in Bordentown, New Jersey. A frequent topic of conversation had been John Quincy's indifference and neglect in advancing his own cause. At the end of the year, Hopkinson wrote a confidential letter to Louisa on that theme, concluding with some very strong statements. Mr. Adams's attitude was calculated "to chill and depress the kind feelings and fair exertions of his friends. . . . I may indeed say that he is not merely neutral on this subject but rather shows a disposition to discourage any efforts in his behalf." The truth was that his adherents were somewhat afraid of the caustic Secretary of State, for Hopkinson added sheepishly, in a postscript to his letter, "You will understand I would not dare to say or write half of the above to Mr. A., but you may do what you please with it."[10]

Louisa gave the letter to her husband, who read it and then drew up a reply which he called The Macbeth Policy. It was based on a quotation from Shakespeare's *Macbeth*:

"If chance will have me King; why, chance may crown me.
　　　Without my stir."[11]

In applying the lines to the present situation, Adams said, "Ought we not to realize that kings, crown and chance are out of the question" and that "the choice of ten millions of people by their delegated agents must award it?" However, he admitted, in this system the prize was given by "politicians and newspapers" and the man who waits for it, "by chance or *just right* will go barehanded all his life."

The point, therefore, was whether the citizen who desired the choice to fall upon himself should assist those who want to help him in its pursuit. John Quincy's answer was that, despite the law of friendship, "he who asks or accepts the offer of aid to promote his own views necessarily binds himself to promote the views of him from whom he receives it." This principle, applied to the election of the President of the United States, therefore, gave Adams no alternative but to accept "no aid on the score of friendship or personal kindness."[12]

Adams applied his principle immediately to Robert Walsh, whose support John Quincy's friends wanted him to seek. Walsh was free to pursue any line he wanted in his editorial capacity, Adams asserted. If he had no choice among the candidates, let him pursue a guarded neutrality. In his own correspondence with Walsh, Adams observed that "though not unfriendly in the main," he had "never struck me as manifesting any partiality of any kind in my favor."[13]

In the winter of 1823, Adams was quite pessimistic about his chances. All parties disowned him, he said, so "where is the buoyant principle to bring me up?" His only hope would be a strong public interest in his favor based on his talents and services. However, he admonished himself, he "must not repine at their choice. . . . Merit and just right in this country will be heard . . . if they are not heard without my stir I shall acquiesce in the conclusion that it is because they do not exist."[14]

The state of New York was the greatest unknown factor in the approaching election. Though it was agreed her politicians would not give her votes to a losing candidate, they carefully avoided expressing preference. One-third or one-quarter of the Albany legislators seemed to be for Adams, but they would give him their support only as long as they expected his victory.[15]

Good news was a scarce item for the Adams supporters at this time. Even in New Hampshire, which Plumer guaranteed for Adams, the legislature did not want to commit itself before the next session. John Quincy's mail, however, was filled with strange requests and stranger invitations. An Ohioan wrote that it had been alleged that there was not a single candidate who was not a slave holder, including Adams. When a New Englander explained that there were colored people among the Secretary's servants but that they were free, all did not accept the explanation. Adams, he advised, must make a clear statement. Dr. John R. Delaney from Jeffersontown, Kentucky, invited the Secretary of State to a barbecue of 1,000 of his supporters, the most influential men in his county, he claimed, but probably Clay would get the state.[16]

In August of 1823, Jefferson expressed himself in favor of Crawford, saying that, with John Quincy Adams, he had "a long acquaintance, but little intimate because little in political unison." With Crawford, on the other hand, he had "a short but more favorable acquaintance because always in unison."[17] Jefferson thought that in the end, the number of candidates would be reduced to two—"a Northern and a Southern one, as usual." He told Gallatin that it was only an illusion that parties no longer existed. There were the same parties as before but they did not go under the names of republicans and federalists. Many now debating in Congress who call themselves republicans were preaching "the rankest doctrines of the old Federalists." Pennsylvania and New York, he prophesied, would decide the issue. "Among the smaller motives, hereditary fears may alarm on one side, and the long line of local nativities on the other."[18]

In September 1823, William Crawford was stricken with what appeared to be paralysis and for a year was a physical wreck. There was much talk and speculation among the politicians, friends, and enemies regarding the prognosis of his disease, but since candidates were not expected to travel about and canvass their supporters, public information about the Georgian's health was vague and it never became a real campaign issue.

Just at this time, a pamphlet was published that its author hoped would blast the reputation of both Adamses. William Cunningham, an old and intimate friend of John Adams, had shot himself the previous May. His son, Ephraim, came into possession of a correspondence between his father and John Adams that had been written during 1804, 1808–1809, and 1810, in which the former President had written frankly and somewhat overexaggeratedly against the Jeffersonians. Cunningham's pledge to John Adams not to publish the letters during his lifetime was ignored by Ephraim. It was too lethal a weapon against one of the leading presidential contenders to be suppressed. Benjamin Leigh commented to Clay, his favorite, that "To you and me, however, it sheds no light upon the character of the father or the son. It furnishes evidence indeed which a large part of the public might not have possessed," but he did not believe that it would change the issue of the election. "We may content ourselves with the son as our next President," he said, blaming it on the irreconcilable division between the South and the West. John Quincy agreed that he was no better and no worse for the pamphlet. The heavy loser was old John Adams, who worried that the indiscreet correspondence would spoil his autumnal friendship with Jefferson. But the sage of Monticello wrote, "It would be strange indeed if, at our years, we were to go an age back to hunt up imaginary or forgotten facts to disturb the repose of affections so sweetening to the evening of our lives."[19]

In order to promote his candidacy, General Jackson's friends persuaded him to run for the Senate against his chief Tennessee rival, Colonel John Williams. His subsequent election made the hero of New Orleans an impressive candidate, although a good part of official Washington underrated him. Congressman Plumer was surprised when he heard Adams characterize Jackson as a very prominent and formidable opponent who was both strong and meritorious. John Quincy, whose admiration for the warrior who seemed so unlike him was of long standing, preferred the General to the other candidates, saying that, unlike the others, he would administer the government with integrity and disinterestedness, free from all bargains, compromises, coalitions, or corruptions. Jackson, he said, would not take all the western states, if Clay appeared to be a loser, but he would be certain of some of them. Pennsylvania would go for him and the mass of people everywhere.

Jackson's difficulty, Adams told Plumer, was that his character was not understood. No man acted with more deliberation or listened more readily. But when he made up his mind to act, he was inflexible. The rapidity with which he executed his plans was mistaken for rashness when it was really the result of profound calculation. His actions, if sometimes hasty, were always based on justice and the public good. As President, he might commit some trifling indiscretions, but it would not affect his wise administration of the government. After Jackson, Adams preferred Clay because he had "a root of principle" which made him a safer man than Crawford or Calhoun. The treachery of the Secretary of War was not that he expected to win the election, but that he hoped to develop some political strength and then put himself at the head of the opposition party in order to make trouble for whoever was to be the next President.[20]

The close-knit Adams family was very involved emotionally with the election struggle. George and Charles discussed their father's prospects on the numerous occasions that they met at Quincy. Old John Adams followed his son's progress with much trepidation. He wanted the victory very much. Johnson Hellen, now practicing law in Rockville, Maryland, was so engrossed in the political contest that his Aunt Louisa thought his health would suffer. Louisa had mixed emotions about it. She declared that in her husband's eight years of service as the Secretary of State he had served his country better than anyone else. If he lost the election, it would be a disgrace to the country, not to him. But she considered a private station as glorious as the Chief Magistrate's and, as far as she was concerned, " 'tis in comparison perfect freedom to the prison house of the State." In the meantime, she dreaded the new year, "which will probably be fraught with good and evil." The weather was abominable, hopefully not an omen for what was to happen "in the course of the impending question."[21]

Charles Francis was in Washington for his winter vacation, rather pleased that he was bringing his father a good report from Harvard. He marvelled at the Secreary of State's coolness in the face of all the election turmoil and the condition of the house, which was all topsy-turvy. The Adamses were giving a huge ball in honor of the anniversary of the Battle of New Orleans at which its hero would be honored. A few weeks earlier, Jackson had given a dinner, which included Clay, Crawford, and Adams. The ball was to reciprocate for the invitation.

The Adams house, which Louisa often complained was crowded for their social occasions, was enlarged by opening up the entire downstairs. The doors were removed between all the first-floor rooms and twelve pillars were set up to give the impression of a large ballroom. Adams was moved from the library and study upstairs to John's sitting room to make further space for the festivities.

Though tempers were short while all this change was going on, Louisa was so absorbed in the party preparations that she was at her best. She enjoyed having the family gathered around her, working under her direction at making decorative wreaths and then hanging them up.

On January 8, the day of the party, the family worked all day arranging the supper table, which had sixty places laid, although most of the guests would have to eat standing. At 4:30, almost before the candles were lit, the guests started to arrive and were met at the door by Mr. and Mrs. John Quincy Adams. As they entered the transformed house, they saw the panorama of rooms hung with laurel wreaths intermixed with roses arranged in festoons. Each wreath had a small illuminating lamp at its center, which cast a soft glow on the ceilings. John Quincy's bookcase, too heavy to move upstairs, stood at the end of the room, obscured by greenery. Its top was a forest of flower pots interspersed with illumination lamps. The chandelier was woven with greens and from its arms festoons were suspended, which were looped and then attached to the top of the pillars. The floors were chalked with designs of eagles, flags, and the motto "Welcome to the hero of New Orleans."

General Jackson arrived between eight-thirty and nine. Louisa took him around the room, introducing him to the guests, who milled around, anxious to shake hands with him. At this time there were about a thousand guests, some of whom climbed on chairs and benches to get a glimpse of the honored guest. All the members of Congress had been invited except for Alexander Smyth and John Floyd, "whose personal deportment to me," Adams said, "has been such that I could not invite them." Monroe refused his invitation because, he explained, when he had been in Virginia during the summer he had pointedly avoided meeting Crawford on a number of occasions. Now if he were to depart from this rule, it would look as if he were supporting one of the other candidates for the Presidency.

All the men except for the host were in full dress. They wore blue coats with gilt buttons, white or buff waistcoats, white neckties, high chokers, white trousers, silk stockings, and pumps. The ladies, of course, were magnificently gowned.

When supper was announced, Mrs. Adams took General Jackson's arm and lead him to the head of the table. The General gallantly drank her health and said that he was much gratified. After dinner, he retired. Later in the evening, while Louisa was sitting in the dancing room, one of the little lamps fell on her head, dripping oil down her neck and shoulders. This caused much banter among the guests, who said that she was already anointed in sacred oil. Louisa answered quickly that the only thing of which she was certain was that her dress was spoiled. At about 1:30 the last of the guests departed, all in good humor, and, Louisa judged, more contented than usual with their evening's entertainment.[22]

John Quincy Adams, an acute if sometimes acid political observer, predicted the failure in the coming election of the congressional caucus system. He had no basic objection to it, since it was not proscribed in the Constitution, but he was well aware that in reality it was caballing. "I consider it as one of the least obnoxious modes of intrigue," he commented rather wistfully, since he knew that he would not be its choice. However, he was certain that Crawford's friends would try to hold the caucus at the commencement of the next session of Congress.[23] John Quincy seemed to discount the amount of opposition to the caucus that would take place. In the fourteen months before it happened, several states, including Maryland, issued resolutions against it, and the western people were said to be entirely opposed. Calhoun was reported to have said that he preferred to trust the election to the people at large and Clay also declared against the caucus.[24]

The Crawford men, working diligently, managed to get endorsements for the caucus from the legislatures of New York and Virginia and partial declaration from Pennsylvania, which looked like a serious setback for Adams who depended on New York for his election. In order to strengthen their position, the Crawfordites decided to persuade a much-reluctant Albert Gallatin to run for Vice President. Gallatin, who was sensitive about his foreign birth and believed that his former services to his country were long forgotten, wanted to decline. The Crawfordites were insistent, knowing that Pennsylvania was important to them and assuming that Gallatin would deliver that state's vote. Now that Crawford was pronounced out of danger, Albert Gallatin was summoned to Washington. Not yet able to devise a plan "by which Mr. Jefferson can be drawn out," Crawford's supporters hoped that Gallatin's close relationship to Jefferson might bestow upon the party the Jeffersonian aura that it sought.

In its quest for the right image, the Crawford men tried to persuade Nathaniel Macon of North Carolina to attend the caucus. Gallatin's aid was enlisted to work on his old friend. With reluctance, he wrote to him. But Macon, though he preferred the Georgian to the other candidates, answered that he considered him an intriguer with whom he did not want to be closely associated. As to the Crawfordite pretensions to be the party of Jefferson, "There are not, I imagine, five members of Congress who entertain the opinions which those did who brought Jefferson into power, and they are not yet mine," Macon said. "No party," he added painfully, "can last unless founded on pure principles: and the minute a party begins to intrigue within itself is the minute when the seed of division is sown and its purity begins to decline."[25]

The caucus advocates allowed a rumor to leak out that Adams would be nominated for Vice President. John Quincy interpreted this as the first distress signal from the Crawford ranks but believed that the offer was fraudulent. He particularly disliked the idea that because of Crawford's illness the presidential duties might fall on the Vice President. Nor could he accept the North being placed below the South. The suggestion soured him on the whole idea of a caucus, which he now called slightly corrupt, contrary to the spirit of the Constitution, and in opposition to the wishes of a majority of the people in the country and a majority of the states. He made it quite clear to the Crawford henchmen that if nominated he would refuse to be a candidate for Vice President.[26] All this controversy did not discourage its supporters from scheduling a caucus despite the possibility that out of 261 members as many as 181 might not appear. The Crawfordites scornfully named the dissidents "The Holy Alliance."

During this trying winter, John Quincy, outwardly at least, remained aloof. Louisa, completely worn out by her ball, was in poor health, staying in her room a good part of the time. Before Charles left for college, John Quincy sent for him to discuss his studies, but Charles complained that his father did not understand him and underestimated him. The lad hated to leave Washington, reflecting that by next winter Monsieur[27] [as Charles called his father] "may be driving about in the wind, scarcely knowing his future home. Massachusetts may be his station, in which case I lose sight of Washington for years and perhaps for life."[28] Part of its charm was the memory of his passion for Mary Hellen, now engaged to George, but at various times the object of affection of all three of the Adams sons.

George missed all the election excitement, staying in Boston where he was studying law in Daniel Webster's office. He seemed to be happy there and greatly admired his mentor. However, Louisa was uneasy about George's relationship with Mary. Though engaged to the oldest son, she seemed to be showing marked interest in John, a situation to which George refused to react, although it was hinted at often by Charles.[29]

When the caucus finally met, it was attended by a mere sixty-six Congressmen who had been successfully threatened, coaxed, or entreated to appear. The vote was:

CRAWFORD	62
JOHN QUINCY ADAMS	2
JACKSON	1
MACON	1
Total	66

Two votes were given to Crawford by proxy, which made his complete number sixty-four. Gallatin received fifty-seven votes for Vice President. The results disappointed the Crawfordites very much.

At a meeting of the Republican Institution in Boston, on a stormy January night, Adams received some welcome if expected support. The two or three thousand people who attended the meeting were so enthusiastically pro-Adams that the Crawford men decided to remain silent. George Washington Adams was there and "did himself great credit by a few judicious remarks," P. P. F. Degrand reported. At the suggestion that Andrew Jackson run for Vice President there was a burst of applause and a consensus that he would add strength to the ticket. On Friday, January 23, 1824, the republican members of the Massachusetts legislature unanimously adopted a resolution favorable to Adams, so that now Maine, Rhode Island, and Massachusetts had endorsed him.[30]

Calhoun's cause collapsed when, at a meeting in Philadelphia on February 18, George M. Dallas, one of his leading supporters, presented a resolution recommending General Jackson for the Presidency. Immediately, conjecture raged about whether Calhoun would support Clay or Crawford and how it would affect New York. Calhoun, without too much struggle, resigned himself to expect nothing better than a second place on the ticket and was ready for the offer when it came from Jackson's friends. And, as expected, the Pennsylvania convention at Harrisburg nominated Jackson for President with but one dissenting vote and Calhoun for Vice President with eighty-seven votes. Clay received ten votes as did Albert Gallatin, and other candidates received eight votes each. A few weeks later, Adams was told that some of Calhoun's friends wanted his support for the Vice Presidency, which the Secretary of State did not take very seriously. He worried rather that the breaking of Calhoun's bubble made Jackson stronger and that Clay's support would fall to him also. Adams also believed that Jackson and Crawford thought that his prospects were desperate, and were prepared to scramble for his spoils.[31] Realistically, John Quincy's despair was as groundless as the rumor that his father had bequested his estate to the town of Quincy because he was displeased with his son.

Throughout the spring, official and unofficial Washington watched the progress of Crawford's health. He seemed to be recovering very slowly but his eyes were still so bad that he did not recognize anyone until their names were mentioned to him. The diagnosis of a paralytic stroke that was accepted at the time was wrong. He was suffering from what was probably an overdose of lobelia, a drug that had been given to him for a severe case of erysipelas and to which he was, apparently, very allergic. Though Crawford's opponents all agreed that he should withdraw from the race, his friends were determined to keep the extent of his debility out of the newspapers.

The last two years of Monroe's Administration were marred with difficulties that had political overtones. The "partyless" era of good feelings concluded in an atmosphere of party strife that reached deeply into the President's own family. The Ninian Edwards case was a good example. In early March, Edwards, a former Senator from Illinois, was appointed Minister to Mexico and confirmed by the Senate with no real opposition except from Crawford's friends, who believed him to be the author of the "A.B." letters published in 1822, which charged Crawford with some Treasury irregularities. Edwards, who wanted the Ministry, allowed Monroe to believe that he was not the author of the charges. Just as he was leaving Washington, Edwards received a congressional report questioning the evidence of the "A.B." letters. Edwards, to Monroe's embarrassment, confessed that he was the author and renewed his charges against Crawford, who was delighted at the development because it justified his accusation that Monroe opposed him. The President wanted to send a messenger to stop Edwards's departure for Mexico but Adams thought that he should stay out of it. Since Henry Clay had appointed a committee to investigate the charges against Crawford, the Secretary of State advised that it was up to them to censure one or the other. After much persuasion Monroe acceded.

At a Cabinet meeting, the President read a message to be sent to the House, stating that he had informed Edwards not to proceed on his mission but to await a call from the legislature. Adams and Monroe thought that Edwards should resign the Mexican post until the affair was cleared up, but Calhoun thought that such a move would be an admission of guilt. Monroe, who was very uncomfortable about the matter, demanded that Cabinet discussions be kept confidential.

Floyd's committee cleared Crawford entirely and, although Edwards was not formally censured, gave the impression that it believed that Edwards had concealed his authorship of the papers in

order to get the Mexican appointment. Adams thought the committee findings a "revolting injustice." However, when Monroe asked
him whether he could still send Edwards to Mexico, John Quincy
had to admit that it would be delicate and that Crawford would
demand his removal.

The Cabinet met for two days on the Edwards controversy, the
second day from 8 A.M. to 9:30 P.M. Once again Calhoun insisted
that Edwards must be removed if he did not resign, while Adams
asserted that there was nothing to justify the President's removing
him. Happily, the matter settled itself when a letter came from
Edwards resigning his Commission. After the committee report was
read in its entirety, Calhoun, Southard, and Wirt all agreed that
Edwards was a deeply injured man. But after entertaining his Cabinet at dinner, Monroe called in the Washington *Republican* and
announced the resignation of Edwards and the appointment of Joel
L. Poinsett in his place. Adams arrived home that night so exhausted that he could not write.

The Edwards affair, which made a great noise in Washington, was
judged to have improved Crawford's position. A further postscript
occurred in July when Ninian Edwards was refused admittance to
the Independence Day dinner. The President and Cabinet
promptly refused to attend, thus limiting the celebration to the
Crawfordites.[32]

Though Charles Adams and others observed that John Quincy
took the matter of the forthcoming election with "most amazing
coolness" and turned away questions with diplomatic answers, the
candidate was tortured by conflicting feelings. Uncertain whether to
hope for success or failure, philosophical indifference was the temper of mind to which he aspired, although he was aware that "to
suffer without feeling is not in human nature." Particularly distressing to him was his unique situation as a candidate. Feeling that if he
failed, it would be equivalent to a vote of censure by the entire
nation on his past services, he believed that he had more at stake
upon the result than any other individual in the Union.[33]

In the meantime, the State Department still required the attention of its chief. But even in his official capacity, Adams was not
allowed to forget that he was a candidate. When the slave-trade
convention with Britain came to the Senate to be ratified, it was
seized upon as a weapon with which to strike down the Secretary of
State. The public was told by the anti-Adams people that the treaty

merely masked the mutual right of search at sea. Forgotten was the primary purpose, the suppression of the slave trade, and ignored was Britain's reluctant agreement, at the insistence of the United States, to regard such trade as piracy under international law.[34]

John Holmes of Maine and New York's Martin Van Buren were the prime instigators of the Senate attack against the treaty. Behind them stood all the "dead set" Crawford men, who intimated that Adams had maneuvered the abandonment of a fundamental American right. Unable to muster enough votes to defeat the treaty outright, the dissidents introduced an amendment limiting the right to search to the area of African coastal waters. Adams believed that part of the Crawfordite opposition was a primal fear that a concert with Great Britain against the slave trade might become a concert with Great Britain for the abolition of slavery.[35]

Rufus King suggested to Adams that as a compromise the convention might be limited for a term of seven years, or might be made subject to annullment by either side with a notice of days or months. A limit for a term of years was less pernicious to the Secretary of State, but he lamented that any alteration would be "peculiarly ungracious from us," since the whole project was American and had been adopted by Great Britain at the insistence of the United States.[36]

Hoping to change their minds, the President sent a message to the Senate, including sections carefully prepared by Adams, outlining the history of the convention and pointing out the obligation of the United States to accept it. He explained that the United States was not giving up any sovereign right, because pirates have no rights. Monroe tried to reach the stubborn Senators by warning them that there were other important negotiations pending with Great Britain, particularly one in which nearly one-third of Maine was in contest. He argued that rejecting the convention would be injurious to mutual understanding and an embarrassment to the Administration. He said, "It must be obvious that the restriction of search for pirates to the African coast is incompatible with the objectives."[37]

Finally, Monroe asked Crawford to use his influence on his friends in the Senate in behalf of the convention that he had supported in the Cabinet. Crawford declined and, to Monroe's surprise and anger, said that he had not favored it in the Cabinet, which was a blatant lie that Monroe preferred to excuse on the basis of the Secretary's illness.

The Senate debated the treaty in late May with a fierceness that many observers saw as "an electioneering engine" directed against Adams. The treaty was passed, but with certain amendments, the fatal one being a refusal to allow the right of search for slave-trading pirates on the coast of America. It was a sensitive area for Americans who remembered that it was on the coast that the British ships waited before the War of 1812 to prey on American ships and impress the seamen.[38]

Adams, who was told the result by Rufus King, was uncharacteristically optimistic and wrong. He thought that Britain would accept the revised Treaty because the essential elements of the convention remained. But Monroe's gloomy predictions about Canning proved correct. The British Minister found the interdiction of the American coast unacceptable and closed the door for further discussion on the subject with Richard Rush. The settlement of the Maine boundary also failed at this time because Rush did not have the power to do the necessary trading. In this case, the British offered American navigation of the St. Lawrence River for a strip of Northern Maine which Britain wanted for a military road to connect with a port on the Bay of Fundy. Monroe's Administration was finishing with a whimper because of the Crawfordites' fixed idea that the President had chosen John Quincy Adams as his successor.

In June, Louisa, whose poor health continued into the spring, went with Mary Hellen and her son John to Bedford Springs, Pennsylvania. Although John Quincy felt very much alone, he wrote to her that she should stay there as long as her health improved and, if Bedford Springs became tiresome, to go wherever her inclination or health decided. After a month of isolated boredom, Adams decided to go to see his aging father. A pathetic note had come from the old gentleman introducing a Mr. Benjamin Parker Richardson. It said: "He can inform you how faint and feeble I am and how ardently I wish to see you and Mrs. Adams at Montezillo and all your family."[39] Louisa returned to Washington at the end of July rested and much more lively, but Charles got the impression from her letters that she was not anxious to come to Quincy that summer, although she saw no way to avoid it.

In June, the New Hampshire state legislature voted to support Adams overwhelmingly. About a week later, John Quincy's native state legislature voted unanimous support, the lion's share of the credit for that due to Joseph E. Sprague, postmaster at Salem, who acted as the commander-in-chief of the Adams forces.[40] But there were rumblings in the west for Jackson that seemed to indicate that he was claiming territory that Clay thought was his own. One writer called the West "the most restless part of our population."[41]

Adams seemed incapable of keeping out of either a major or a minor contretemps. No affront either real or imagined was allowed to pass by unnoticed. Charles, reading his father's piece in the pro-Adams Washington *National Journal* about the *National Intelligencer's* selective publication of the papers on the slave-trade convention, said that his comments "possessed all that bitterness and caustic severity which he is so much noted for." Although the young man believed that the printers acted in a scandalous manner, he knew that his father's outburst would be used against him. The *National Intelligencer's* failure to print all the documents caused Adams to authorize the *National Journal* to publish the official papers of the State Department. In answer to the protest of the editors of the *Intelligencer*, the Secretary of State said that he did not seek the favor of that paper. He then could not restrain himself from publishing an ill-timed article in the *Journal*, reprinted the next day in the *Intelligencer*, which had tried to pacify the incensed Secretary of State by printing all the slave-trade convention papers in an extra issue that they got out on July 15. However, Adams, once aroused, was unmanageable. Once again, in his own organ, he charged anonymously that the *Intelligencer* had deliberately garbled the documents in order to ensure their rejection. In vain, the editors pleaded that they had printed all the papers that had been available. We approved the papers, the editors argued. "It is very singular, that, to chastise the Senators who *rebelled* against the treaty, the Secretary should have bent his bow at us."

There was no agreement on whether Adams was right or wrong in attacking the *Intelligencer*. A Virginia supporter wrote to John Quincy that he had showed up the arrogance of the editors, who supposed that they had control of the "national suffrages. Your friends are delighted to see your powerful pen."[42] Clay's supporters predicted that, having alienated the affections of the newspaper, it might well turn its batteries on Adams. Perhaps it was better that their candidate did not have a press for himself since it provoked too much hostility.[43]

The *National Intelligencer* did seem to be paving the way to support Crawford. Since Jefferson's Administration, it had been almost an official paper in very confidential relationship with the Chief Executive. However, in supporting Crawford, who had been opposed to the Administration, Adams thought Editors Gales and Seaton were in a position to need his success. "If he falls, they must fall," he said.[44]

Descending, as political maneuvering frequently does, from policy to pettiness, a small balloon was sent up by John Quincy's enemies over the rather pathetic Moultrie affair. Louisa explained to Charles that Mrs. Mary G. Moultrie came to her in great misery, begging for help. After Mrs. Adams visited her and found her destitute with a dying child, she told John Quincy about the woman's plight. He endorsed a note for her for $187.50. The story, which was, reportedly, discussed at a tavern table, alleged that Mrs. Moultrie had a bad character "and it is made to look that your father *did not give the note for nothing*," Louisa wrote. She was very annoyed, although uncertain about who was the author of the slur. It came out later that Adams's assailant had been John B. Colvin, a former member of the State Department whom the Secretary had dismissed for negligence and for lampooning him in the Washington *City Gazette*.[45]

Adams resented these attacks not only because they were disagreeable, but because they wasted his carefully scheduled time. During this period, he rose at five or six and when the tide permitted swam in the Potomac for an hour or two, recording proudly that on August 5 he and John, accompanied by Antoine, who followed them in a boat, swam across the river, a distance of more than a mile. The Secretary took an hour and a half to complete the swim, only ten minutes less than John. Breakfast was at nine, writing and receiving visitors followed until one or two, then work at the State Department office until six, and then home to dinner. In the evening, Adams took a walk for about half an hour before he returned at ten or eleven. It was a full schedule, but it kept the candidate from brooding over the nearly dozen newspapers published throughout the country that poured out a continual stream of slander upon his character and his public and private reputation. Letters from well-wishers and enquiries about his opinions flooded the State Department office. Adams answered a few and felt guilty about it because it was a great expenditure of time on subjects that were personal and, of necessity, caused neglect to public business.[46]

The bitterness and violence of the presidential electioneering increased as the time grew closer, particularly since its uncertainties were as great as ever. John Quincy, who was not surprised, having experienced it many times before, confessed, "it is wholly impossible to be insensible while it is in operation." Hence he decided to take a month's holiday and return to his native state and to his father and two sons. He was too late, however, to participate in George's triumph, the delivery of the Fourth of July oration at Quincy. Charles, possibly with some jealousy, recorded that his brother's historical account of the Revolution was "a little too plain for the learned and a little too obscure for the ignorant."

Young Adams was praised far and wide by many people "from interested motives" and, Charles noted, George absorbed the compliments like a philosopher. But it was a proud day for John Adams, who overcame his exhaustion with amazing resilience. In defense of Charles, whose comments seem suspect, it must be admitted that to a modern eye, the address seems painfully dull.

Charles, who was seventeen years old, kept an uncensored record of his life at his grandfather's house in which Thomas Boylston Adams also lived with his wife and children. Young Adams was often disgusted by his uncle's excessive drinking and consequent outrageous behavior. Much of the unhappiness in the Thomas Boylston household Charles blamed on Ann Harrod Adams, an extravagant woman, though her husband could not afford it. She was, her nephew said, cunning, deceitful, hypocritical, ungrateful, and unprincipled in her revenge, directed presumably against the Adams family. Her one virtue was her kindness to her children and attachment to her blood relations.

When Thomas Adams was drinking, he behaved like a "brute in his manners and a bully in his family," said Charles. It affected the younger members of the family and made his wife suffer, but "her temper in my opinion has been his ruin." Sometimes his nephew had to stay up all night with Uncle Tom while he talked endlessly "under the influence of this fire which he perpetually takes."[47]

One day, in desperation, Charles talked to his grandfather about the situation. The old man said resignedly that something was necessary to check their pride and they had suffered bitterly: had all the sons been distinguished, they should have been crushed but now the world, while it respected them, could pity them at the same time and that pity would destroy the envy which would arise.[48] Thus the patriarch elevated a sordid domestic problem into a classical drama.

Charles, also rather patronizingly, watched the decline of George's relationship with Mary Hellen. Even at long distance it was obvious that Mary was less interested in her absent fiancé than in his brother John, who was in Washington. George stubbornly refused to accept the truth, which made his mother worry at his gullibility and tendency to see only the best in everyone.

When John Quincy and Louisa arrived at the family home on September 6, Charles rushed to meet them. His mother was a little pale but otherwise much better than she had been the previous winter and his father looked well but "very yellow or brown." Though very glad to see them, the ex-President, probably overcome with pleasure, was deaf and weak in the voice.

Family tensions surfaced almost immediately. Louisa, said her adoring son Charles, was lovely and pleasing, but his father was "impenetrating," which sent George into a sort of tantrum. His father's face, Charles explained, seldom gave a sure guide to his feelings, which made him enemies because he perpetually wore "the Iron Mask." One of his chief victims was George, who was unable to respond to his father with anything but fear. He was always afraid of decided men, even Johnson Hellen and John. Louisa confided to Charles that although Mary had been behaving in a manner unworthy of George, she was still half in favor of the marriage. John Quincy opposed it. Charles was sorry for John who, he felt, was another victim of Mary's considerable charms.

In contrast to his son's personality analysis, Adams received a letter from Dr. Tobias Watkins saying that the people of Baltimore were delighted with him. "They had been taught to look upon you as something like a Northwester in the month of January, freezing everything it touched and were most agreeably disappointed at seeing a countenance at least as gentle as that of other people."[49]

Frequent talk about future plans during the Quincy-Boston visit convinced Charles that his father had little hope of winning the election. The Adamses decided to live at the family home in a simple style. Apparently John Quincy thought that his Washington flour mill would bring him enough revenue to allow him to indulge his literary interests. The idea of returning to the practice of the law had no appeal. Charles, however, was disappointed. He had been "habituating my mind to floating visions of comfort and grandeur."

The climate and the manners of the South pleased him but he could return only if his father won the election.[50]

Almost every day John Quincy went into Boston to be entertained. But he refused to allow a public dinner to be given for him at Faneuil Hall. He was grateful to his supporters but thought that it would only add to the division of sentiment.

Unlike his son Charles, John Quincy enjoyed each visit to Quincy. It was a nostalgic homecoming from what seemed to be perpetual exile. One day he rode to the foot of Penn's Hill where he and his father had been born and noted that the house had been painted white recently. He then walked in the burying yard and looked at the granite tombstones that John Adams had erected over the graves of their ancestors, four generations, "of whom very little more is known than is recorded upon these stones," he mused. He wondered what would be engraved on the stones of the three living generations one hundred years hence. Josiah Quincy had just told him that they were the executors of John Adams's will.[51] Adams marvelled that although the old gentleman could not walk without aid, heard with difficulty, and had short span of interest, his memory remained strong and his judgments sound. He liked to have newspapers read to him and to dictate answers to the letters that he received.

The Adamses returned to Washington at the end of September. John Quincy left his father with foreboding, but told him that he would see him again next year. The visit home had been an escape from care, more complete perhaps than he wished, for he had surrendered his time to company and wrote almost nothing. "I am returning with no flattering anticipations to Washington to finish my term," he wrote, "and to meet the fate to which I am destined."[52]

On the way back, the travellers stopped at Philadelphia to visit General Lafayette, in the United States for the first time since the Revolution, accompanied by his son George Washington and his secretary Auguste Levasseur. Though Lafayette came at the invitation of both houses of Congress, his visit was unofficial because he had just lost his seat in the Chamber of Deputies to a royalist. The trip was a triumphal journey for the Frenchman. Everywhere he went, crowds met him with cheerfulness, kind feelings, and joy. Adams travelled with the Lafayette entourage on a tour of Delaware and Baltimore, where he and the General rowed to Fort McHenry.

Returned to Washington in mid-October, John Quincy and Louisa settled down to await the inevitable. De Grand wrote from Massachusetts that the federalists were very divided but everything was safe in the home state. John Adams, however, was disturbed by the confusion. "I am wearied of hearing the name of Adams treated with so little respect and ceremony," he complained. Louisa soothed the home contingent with the report that in spite of vulgar abuse and base electioneering for President, "we go on very quietly and dare meet any investigations."[53]

New England was coming through for Adams as predicted and expected, Timothy Pickering's slanders notwithstanding. John Adams rejoiced that his son received every vote in Braintree, Quincy, and Weymouth.[54] However, it was also obvious as the votes slowly filtered into Washington that the election would go into the House. Jackson, the late starter, was now regarded as a sure winner. Adams, because of New England's support, was also considered a safe victor. Therefore, since Calhoun had dropped out of the race, the third contender would have to be Clay or Crawford.

It was a chaotic election, not only because of the excess of candidates but also because of the unstructured way in which a variety of techniques were used to ensure the various candidate's elections. The congressional caucus was inconclusive, as were the several contested conventions, variety of resolutions, and abortive meetings. There were intercandidate negotiations, formal and informal, and several candidates used committees of correspondence. Newspapers took unlikely stands, while a constant supply of pamphlets and broadsides peppered the countryside. The object of the effort was to corral votes so that the voter was appealed to more than in the past. It was a complete reversal for the electors to be nominated first and then to try to influence the voters.[55] One definite fact emerged. New York was the great question mark and whichever way she went might well decide the election.

Adams had good reasons to expect popular support in the Empire State. He was the only northern candidate, which should have some appeal in a state that had been eagerly settled by New Englanders, and he was the only non-slave owner. However, the party in power, the regency, supported Crawford, and the electors were normally chosen by the legislature which was regency dominated. The consensus of opinion by the politicos was that Adams was a strong candidate, perhaps the strongest, but he probably did not have the majority to win. Furthermore, the partisans were so violent and vindictive that they never would unite.[56]

In January of the election year, a bill was introduced into the New York legislature to change the election law so that the people would choose the presidential electors. The regency, of course, opposed it and, though unsuccessful in defeating it in the Assembly, was able to do so in the Senate. Immediately, those who were not Crawford supporters, hearing that the legislature would give Crawford the state's entire vote, talked about uniting to prevent the congressional caucus proposed for April to nominate the Georgian.[57] The situation had an interesting effect on De Witt Clinton, self-appointed dark horse, who thought Crawford *hors de combat* and Calhoun and Clay without force. As for Adams, he could succeed only "by the imbecility of his opponents, not by his own strength. In this crisis might not some other person bear away the palm?"[58]

William Plumer, Jr., observing that by March Calhoun was out of the race, thought that New York had only one wise course and that was to secure the nomination for Adams, thus putting herself, as the kingmaker, at the head of the Union, to which she had long aspired.[59] It would not prove to be that simple.

Throughout the tortuous proceedings, Adams was in tactful but constant correspondence with his New York supporters. Most prominent among them were James Tallmadge, Joseph Blunt, and Micah Sterling. They tried to implicate him in their plans or, at least, get advice from him, but seldom succeeded. "I have nothing to ask but that the preponderating motive for every electoral vote may be fitness for the place rather than friendship for the man," the Secretary of State wrote pompously to Blunt. Then added that he had no power to transfer votes.

The New York struggle was further complicated because it was a gubernatorial year. The incumbent, Joseph C. Yates, was discarded because he was identified in the public eye with the failure of the electoral bill. Van Buren and the regency decided to run Samuel Young, a popular man and a likely favorite for the newly founded people's party. Consequently, the Adams friends decided to promote a state convention to take place on September 21 in order to nominate their own people's party candidate, probably Tallmadge.

At this point, Van Buren committed an enormous blunder by which he outfoxed himself. The regency decided to remove De Witt

Clinton from his position as commissioner of the Erie Canal in order to confront Tallmadge with a dilemma. If he voted for removal, he would alienate his political friends. If he voted against it, he would alienate powerful Tammany Hall and lose New York City.

As expected, the regency-dominated Senate voted Clinton's ouster. Thurlow Weed, the young editor of the Rochester *Clarion* who was present at the Senate meeting, rushed to the Assembly chamber to try to persuade Tallmadge not to fall into the prepared trap, even though he was known to detest Clinton. Speak up and denounce the plot, Weed urged without success. The Assembly voted to remove Clinton and Tallmadge went along with them.

When the news came out that Clinton, the hero of the Erie Canal, was removed from office, the people were shocked and resentful. Inevitably, a Clinton for Governor movement surged and swelled. Governor Yates, moved to action, which proved to be too little and too late, called a special session of the legislature. Since they had not amended the constitution, the people were afraid that they did not have the right to choose the presidential electors. Nothing much happened except that it became obvious that Clinton was growing stronger.

Joseph Blunt gathered from the special session that the best policy for the Adams men would be to agree to a proposition offered by the Clayites to divide the electoral vote of the state "according to our strength, which would give them 14 & 22 for our candidate." He asked Adams's opinion, as the fourteen votes might bring Clay into the House of Representatives. "When there would he be more formidable than Mr. Crawford? If he should be forced out of the field into whose scale would his friends throw their strength?"[60] These were the critical questions.

There was strong mutual distrust between Adams and Clinton. In his *Diary*, John Quincy noted that Clinton had already ruined himself financially in the bid for the Presidency and so feared corruption by which the New York legislature would sell the suffrage. "It will not be sold to me," he added virtuously.[61] Clinton told his confidante, Henry Post, that Adams was an apostate in politics and a pedagogue in private life; everything but amiable and honest. Furthermore, his father was a scamp.[62]

In the early fall there was still "triangular warfare" with the outcome difficult to know, Joseph Blunt wrote to Adams. Not only did Clay's friends hold the balance between Adams and Crawford, but also there was a new difficulty. The undoubted election of Clinton introduced the fear that he was a partisan of General Jackson, although it would be the lame duck legislature that selected the electors.[63]

As predicted, Clinton was elected Governor in November, but there was still no one group in control. Crawford had the Senate but the House was an unknown quantity. Micah Sterling, a federalist from Watertown, told Adams that although the friends of Clay were "trying to play a deep game" the state would go either for Adams or Crawford. Friends of both talked of dividing with Clay but the result would probably be that the Clayites would divide between the two.[64]

Both Adams and Crawford men preferred Clay out of the picture because he was such a powerful favorite in the House. However, intriguing in all sorts of patterns continued. Blunt said on November 8, "We have at this place Crawford agents under the disguises of Clayites & Jacksonians . . . our case grows stronger at every hour's delay." On November 8, Blunt reported, Clay's friends made a distinct proposition to divide the vote with the Adams men, which was not accepted. However, he thought that the Crawfordites would adopt the Adams ticket in the Assembly so that the two houses could go into joint ballot, since the Senate was decidedly for Crawford. This tactic was accomplished with the following results:[65]

	CRAWFORD	JQA	CLAY	JACKSON
Senate	17	7	7	0
Assembly	43	50	32	1

If the deadlock continued, New York would cast no votes. Some shrewd manipulating was needed and neither the Crawfordites nor the Adamsites lacked skill. Adams could win only if there was a merger with Clayites because only two electoral tickets could be voted according to the New York constitution.

At a secret meeting, Adams and Clay leaders agreed to support thirty Adams men and the six Clay men on the Crawford ticket. The Adamsites promised that if Clay carried Louisiana, they would give him the needed seven votes to get into the House of Representatives contest. Thurlow Weed, in order to insure the success of the plot, personally printed the ballots on the Sunday night before the Tuesday on which the election would take place.

At the tense joint meeting of the New York legislature, Lt. Gov. Root drew the first Union ballot from the box and cried out, "A printed split ticket!" Senator Keyes of Jefferson County shouted back that it was treason. For a moment a stampede of Senators out of the hall seemed imminent. The situation was eased by James Tallmadge's presence of mind. He called the meeting to order so sharply that everyone sat quietly while the count continued. The Union ticket elected thirty-two electors. A second ballot was required to choose the four Crawford electors. Though later the Adams managers were accused of betraying Clay, the agreement had been kept. Since Jackson had carried Louisiana, the Adamsites had been free to give him all their votes.[66]

Now there was no doubt that Jackson and Adams would enter the House contest. By December, Clay had yielded to the reality that as soon as the New York results were in he was defeated. He blamed it on the "fabrication of tales" that his candidacy was withdrawn and the discouragement of his friends. However, he told Peter B. Porter, "I only wish that I could have been spared such a painful duty as that will be of deciding between the persons who are presented to the choice of the H. of R."[67]

Daniel Webster exemplified the position of many northern political leaders. He said that Adams must be supported yet "we" should not quarrel with General Jackson because if he succeeded, by not quarreling the North would come in for her share in the new Administration. Plumer, to whom he addressed these remarks, quizzed him on whether he expected a Department. Webster denied that he wanted to be a Secretary or that his object was the mission to London with an unctuous, "It would be idle in me to shoot my arrow so high."[68] Plumer concluded that he plainly wanted London.

Adams was annoyed when it became apparent that Calhoun would be the next Vice President. His scheme to promote Jackson's candidacy had failed and the North did not even offer a vice presidential aspirant. This might, however, increase his own chance of success, since the North offered only one candidate while the slaveholding South and West offered several. The Adams party, he said, was homogeneous, solid, divided by no conflicting interests. Take away from Jackson the votes which the friends of other candidates gave him and he must fall far below his New England rival. Crawford, he asserted, had been destroyed by the caucus. However, he wanted his friends to make no advances to the other candidates but rather stand still and see what they do. On the whole, it seemed that Adams was neither confident of success nor despondent about defeat.[69]

George, still in Boston, expressed the sentiments of the entire Adams family when he wrote that he was "tired of this eternal excitement and eternal suspense," and that whatever happened his father would be remembered "as an ornament to the nation and an honour to the age in which he lived."[70] Louisa started her season of alternate Tuesday parties, knowing that they would be thronged with visitors who wanted to see how she behaved during the ordeal.[71]

The first intimation that Clay was interested in supporting Adams was recorded in the Secretary of State's *Diary* on December 15. Usually a rich source of information on Adams's reactions and activities, little was entered on this vital subject. On the above date, John Quincy noted only that his friend, Edward Wyer, told him that he had it on good authority that Clay would support him if he could at the same time be useful to himself. On the same day, Adams entered the information that he had a conversation at dinner with Mr. Clay.

Once Louisiana's choice of electors reached Washington, it was definite that Crawford and not Clay was the third candidate to go to the House of Representatives. The final count was:

	ELECTORAL	POPULAR
Jackson	99	153,544
Adams	84	108,740
Crawford	41	46,618
Clay	37	47,136

Consequently, Robert P. Letcher, member of the House from Kentucky, called on Adams and asked him point blank how he felt about Clay. Adams answered that he harbored no hostility against him, rather any that existed between them emanated from Clay as was demonstrated in the Jonathan Russell attack. However, having repelled the attack, Adams said that he no longer felt animosity toward anyone involved in it. Adams noted that the drift of the conversation with Letcher fitted in with Wyer's report. Clay would support him if it served himself and if Clay's friends "could know" that he would have a prominent share in the Administration that might induce them to vote for Adams despite any instructions. Letcher never professed any authority from Clay for what he said and made no definite proposal, although he asked that the interview be kept confidential.[72]

John Quincy was now the victim of a constant stream of visitors, many of whom professed that their calls were very confidential. James Barbour, Senator from Virginia, came to discuss his state's position in the coming contest. He said that Adams's unpopularity there was due to his refusal to attend the July 5 dinner, which was, therefore, insulting to Crawford. Adams explained that he did not act against Crawford but in response to the insult meted out to Edwards. This trivial concern points out one of the interesting factors in this campaign, which was the absence of any real issues, although the candidates differed on some of the questions. For example, the tariff was a controversial matter, as was internal improvements. Adams, in answer to Barbour, said that the "ultimate principle of my system with reference to the great interest of the country [is] *conciliation* and not *collision*." The tariff was satisfactory and if there should be a change, it ought to be to reduce it rather than increase it since revenues were abundant. Protection to the manufacturers was fair but if it was hard on agriculture and commerce, he would be inclined to alleviate it.[73] It must be noted that Massachusetts was, at that time, divided between manufacturing interests and commerce.

Clay dined with Adams on December 23. The conversation was not reported. Just the day before, the Kentuckian had answered Benjamin Leigh's comment that he expected to find him "at the board of general officers" with the statement that "he would not cross Pennsylvania Avenue to be in any office under any Administration which lies before us."[74] But a week later he was supposed to have written George McClure in answer to his letter asking whether he would prefer Jackson or Adams, "I have no hesitation in saying that I have long since decided in favor of Mr. Adams in case the contest should be between him and General Jackson. . . . I therefore say to you unequivocally, that I cannot, consistently with my own principles, support a military man." This would seem to set a date on Clay's decision, but the original of the letter has not been found and it was merely quoted in a letter from McClure written to Robert S. Rose on September 1, 1827.[75]

At the same time, Plumer observed that Adams appeared in better spirits than he had ever seen him, and more confident of success. In a conversation that Adams did not report in his *Diary*, Plumer quoted him as saying that he had received more or less distinct overtures from friends of Clay and Crawford. Clay's friends intimated that they might vote for him first and secure his election on the first ballot, which would give him all of New England, Ohio, Indiana, Illinois, Kentucky, Missouri, and Louisiana. Plumer then observed that thus Clay's friends would have made the President and set up their leader to be his heir apparent.[76] Webster, just returned from visiting the two Virginia ex-Presidents, reported them both to be opposed to Jackson. However, Jefferson, who clearly preferred Crawford, was willing to admit that Adams was "a very safe man."[77]

On New Year's Day, as was customary, John Quincy went to the President's drawing room, which was unusually crowded. Louisa, who was ill, stayed home. Somewhat later in the day, Letcher once again called at the State Department to discuss Clay-Adams relations, suggesting that the two gentlemen have some conversation about their differences, which Adams agreed to readily. That evening, at a dinner given to Lafayette by the members of both houses of Congress, Clay and Adams sat next to each other. Observers noted with interest that there seemed to be a complete absence of hostility between the two. Clay told his partner that he would like to have a confidential conversation upon public affairs. In his *Diary* entry, for the first of the new year, Adams wrote: "There is in my prospects and anticipations a solemnity and moment never before experienced, *and to which unaided nature is inadequate.*"[78]

By the first week in January, Adams's friends, though they knew nothing certain, believed that Clay would give his votes to their candidate. One reason was that Clay's rift with Jackson over the Seminole war was much deeper than his differences with Adams at Ghent. On January 8, Clay admitted to his crony, Francis P. Blair, that he was determined to support Adams. His letter, which he admitted was written with "too much levity," claimed that he had the friends of all three contenders pursuing him. The Adamsites, he said, approached him with "tears in their eyes," a reference in rather bad taste to John Quincy's "infirmity of a watery eye." Crawford he rejected because of his health and Jackson because of his military spirit. Thus Adams became, unflatteringly, "a choice of evils." Clay thought it significant that the Ohio delegation was supporting Adams, and, so it seemed, three-quarters of the Kentuckians. "My friends," Clay concluded, "entertain the belief that their kind wishes toward me in the end be more like to be accomplished by so bestowing their votes."[79]

Clay visited with Adams at six o'clock Sunday evening, January 9, and spoke with him for three hours. They went over their past differences and experiences that they had shared together, and their views of the present and expectations of the future. The time had come to speak freely, Clay said, for both he and his friends had now had time to get over their personal disappointments and must decide among the three candidates that were left. Clay said that although he found Jackson without any but military merit, a man ignorant of the laws and institutions of the country who had never showed any capacity as a statesman, his friends preferred him because he was a western man and they were jealous and suspicious of easterners. Clay wished Adams "to satisfy him with regard to some principles of great public importance but without any personal considerations for himself." Adams's final word on the interview was a cryptic comment that the Kentuckian stated that he "had no hesitation in saying that his preference would be for me."[80] That is all that is known about the conversations that took place.

Last-minute maneuvers kept Washington constantly excited. Through the influence of ardent Jacksonites, the Kentuckians in the capital received instructions from home to vote for the General. Though they were not decided whether they would follow orders or not, they were much shaken. Adams's friends feared that the same technique would be used by the legislatures of Ohio, Illinois, and Missouri.

The election fever pitch that was reaching its height just weeks before the House vote convinced Adams that "it would be necessary for me to anticipate the event of my election . . . for which it would be proper for me to be prepared," a cautious statement indeed.[81] By this time it was common Washington gossip that "an arrangement had been made between Mr. Clay and Mr. Adams for the former to transfer his influence to the latter and that for doing so he was to be made Secretary of State." D. P. Cook reported the news to Adams, saying that Mr. Ingham of Pennsylvania wanted him to stop it. Cook's answer to him, which he believed was the way Adams would react, was that if there were evidence of such a coalition of "corrupt character," it should be exposed and, if proved, he would hold Clay and Adams unworthy of public confidence. Cook repeated to John Quincy Mr. McDuffie's prediction that if Jackson were defeated by western votes, there would be "a tremendous storm raised" and the Administration would go out in four years.[82]

Many of the visitors who beat a path to Adams's door wanted reassurances of one kind or another. Scott of Missouri said he'd vote with the rest of the western delegations, although his own state would be angry, but hoped that he would be part of the next Administration. Adams answered that he could not go into details, but, if elected by the suffrage of the west, he would look there for support, which satisfied Scott. This was in the same spirit as the reassurance he had offered to Webster and other federalists that he would exclude no one for their political opinions or personal opposition to him. His great objective was to break up old party distinctions and bring everyone together.[83]

It seemed that, as a last resort, there would be some sort of rapprochement between the Jacksonites and the Crawfordites. Adams thought this would make the General stronger but it did not disturb Plumer. He predicted that Jackson could not swing the election even if to his certain states, Pennsylvania, South Carolina, Tennessee, Indiana, Mississippi, and Alabama, Crawford's Delaware, Virginia, North Carolina, and Georgia were added, making ten in all. Delaware and Virginia would never vote for Jackson, the Congressman predicted, and North Carolina was highly improbable—and Georgia would surely support Crawford to the bitter end. Where, then, would come the three more states required to win? Plumer could only conclude that Adams had to win.

The Secretary of State's stock rose sharply on January 24 when the Ohio and Kentucky members of Congress met publicly in one of the committee rooms and then invited in Crawford's and Jackson's leading friends to inform them that they were determined to vote for John Quincy Adams. Crawford had to make the next move but he did not control his supporters. McLane of Delaware stated that they might as well think of turning the Capitol upside down as persuade him to vote for Jackson. Now it looked as if Adams might win on the first ballot.

On January 27, a note came from Clay asking to see Adams, who had company for dinner but said he would see him at his convenience. Letcher called at the Adams house later and also mentioned

Clay's wish to see the Secretary. It was arranged for the following night, after dinner. Once again the two men sat together for a couple of hours discussing the presidential election. Clay spoke of his doubts concerning some of Adams's friends and was anxious for conciliation with Webster and Louis McLane. That is all that John Quincy confided to his *Diary.*

The dramatics were not over. Early in January, George Kremer, a muddleheaded Jacksonian from Pennsylvania, heard from James Buchanan, a pro-Clay Pennsylvanian, that there was a conspiracy in progress that Jackson should know about—Adams's friends were offering the State Department to Clay in return for his votes. Buchanan suggested that Jackson should make the same offer and announce that, if elected President, he would not reappoint Adams to the Department of State. Kremer told Buchanan that his candidate did not make deals and then wrote a clear but ungrammatical account of the exchange to General Jackson. A postscript said: "Mr. Buchanan stated that him and Mr. Clay have become great friends this winter, this he said as I ought to inform on my mind the authority from whence he had derived his information." Buchanan told the story with a slightly different twist. He had called on General Jackson on December 30 and stated that there was a report that if elected President he would reappoint Adams Secretary of State, which was "injurious to his election" because other "able and ambitious men" including Clay wanted that office. Jackson answered that he thought well of Adams but had not declared his intention about appointing him Secretary of State, that these were "secrets he would keep to himself—he would conceal them from the very hairs of his head." Apparently, Buchanan, having failed to reach Jackson directly, tried again through Kremer.[84]

Later in life, Clay wrote an account of his meeting with Buchanan, using the third person. Letcher was with him when Buchanan called telling them that Jackson was certain to be elected and that he would form the most splendid Cabinet that the country had ever seen. Letcher asked where he would find men of equal talent to Jefferson's Cabinet, which had contained Madison and Gallatin. Buchanan answered, looking straight at Clay, that he would not have to go out of this room for a Secretary of State. Clay replied lightly that there was "no timber for a cabinet officer, unless it was Mr. Buchanan himself." Clay wanted to publish this but Buchanan begged him not to.

The Jacksonian party, suddenly accepting the reality that Clay was the kingmaker and that their candidate was not the chosen one, gave way to revenge. On January 28, an anonymous letter was printed in the Philadelphia *Columbian Observer* that "exposed" the Clay-Adams "bargain" in bitter and vituperative language. "I was of opinion," the writer said, "that men, professing any honorable principles, could not, or would not be transferred, like the planter does his negroes, or the farmer does his team of horses. . . . Contrary to this expectation it is now ascertained that Henry Clay has transferred his interest to John Quincy Adams. As a consideration for this abandonment of duty to his constituents, it is said and believed should this unholy condition prevail, Clay is to be appointed Secretary of State."[85]

Clay reacted angrily. He published a card in the February 1st *National Intelligencer* saying that if the letter was genuine, he pronounced its author "a base and infamous calumniator, a dastard and liar" and challenged him to a duel. On February 3, Kremer revealed his identity as the author of the letter, ignored the challenge, and insisted on the letter's accuracy. Though he did not insist on fighting it out, Clay did demand a congressional investigation. Kremer's answer was that he would prove every charge but, when called to testify, did not appear, and so the investigation collapsed. He did send a letter, which he very likely did not write, but the important work that he had done was to expose the matter to the public, which would then make up its own mind.

John Quincy's *Diary* the last weeks before the House election carried lists of the names and views of the contemporary wheelers and dealers. The Secretary of State seemed to have forgotten his paper on The Macbeth Policy because he was surely not in retirement. He was in the midst of the scenes of action, although still hampered by "matters of delicacy." He asked Monroe, for example, to make his appointments after the February 9 vote so that they could not be said to have influenced the election.[86] He also stayed away from the House during the Kremer hearings.

Much as he wanted the election, Adams was never blinded by the glamor of being President, nor did he ever fail to see that whichever alternative faced him it would be distressing, perhaps "the most formidable is that of success. The humiliation of failure will be so much more than compensated by the safety in which it will leave me."[87] Rufus King, who was certain of Adams's success, agreed that it "would open to a far severer trial than defeat." For some respite from the election agony, Adams visited the theater whenever possible. He saw *The School for Scandal* and attended a gala performance given for Lafayette in which the famous Cooper appeared at his farewell performance in *Damon and Pythias* and *Katharine and Petruchio.*

On February 7, Clay and Adams had their final meeting before the election. On the following day, Louisa's Tuesday party was more fully attended than ever before. The entire Adams family, including George, now admitted to the bar, who had arrived in Washington a few days earlier, was present, along with sixty-seven members of the House, sixteen Senators, and at least 400 other guests. No doubt but one thought filled their minds. Were they being entertained by the man who would be elected the next President on the morrow?

On the snowy, wintery Wednesday of February 9, the patroon, old Stephen Van Rensselaer, brother-in-law of Alexander Hamilton, left his boarding house unaware that his would be the decisive vote of the day. A former federalist, Van Rensselaer would have been in favor of a northerner had he not regarded Adams as a traitor to his party, despite his personal assurance, conveyed through Webster, that Adams was not hostile to federalists. Van Buren, who favored Crawford, and did not want Adams elected on the first ballot because he wanted the credit for giving him New York, told about Van Rensselaer's vote in his *Autobiography*, claiming that the tale came straight from the horse's mouth. The patroon planned to vote for Crawford, but before the box reached him he lowered his eyes to ask God's help. When he opened them he saw, lying on the floor, a ticket with John Quincy Adams's name on it. Almost involuntarily, he picked it up and put it in the box.[88] True or not, the anecdote was irresistible. It could be said, then, that God elected Adams, or perhaps to escape Van Buren's wrath the patroon imagined the experience.

Adams was elected on the first ballot. With each of the states voting as a unit, he carried thirteen states as compared to Jackson's seven and Crawford's four. Although in five of the states, he was elected by one vote, once Jackson lost Maryland, Illinois, and Louisiana, the General could not take the election. Adams received the votes of the six New England states, New York, Maryland, Louisiana, Kentucky, Missouri, Ohio, and Illinois. Crawford had Delaware, Virginia, North Carolina, and Georgia, and Jackson the rest:

New Jersey, Pennsylvania, South Carolina, Alabama, Mississippi, Tennessee, and Indiana.

The election had clarified a number of political truths. The old party system had collapsed, a state of affairs that had caused the rank and file of the electorate to show a remarkable lack of interest in the election. In only six states did more than one-third of the eligible voters go to the polls. Altogether, the states had a turnout of 26.55 percent of the electorate. The election was, basically, a contest of personalities to select three of them to be submitted to the House of Representatives. Even such reliable old methods as the congressional caucus failed to operate in 1824.

Richard McCormick, in his analysis of the election, said that in most states there was a lack of rivalry because the political leaders and voters were heavily committed to one candidate. In the instances where there was a contest, there was no time to develop the necessary campaign machinery. Actually, the voter was not yet accustomed to a meaningful participation in a presidential election because of the congressional caucus and the custom of having the electors chosen by the state legislatures.[89]

Adams was basically in a better situation than the other candidates. He was the sole northerner and non-slaveholder and therefore the logical candidate for the northern bloc. Despite his loud protestations that the office must come to him, his *Diary* and letters are a confession that once the Presidency was within grasping distance, he displayed a natural aptitude for political maneuvering that was as inspired as some of his diplomatic efforts.

Rufus King, who understood well what the election meant to both Adamses, wrote from the Senate chamber, "I send you and your venerable father my affectionate congratulations upon your choice as President of the United States." John Quincy enclosed the note in a letter to John Adams, saying that "Mr. King will inform you of the event this day upon which I can only offer *you* my congratulations and ask your blessing and prayers."[90] The old man was blissfully happy. The hope for Johnny's future that he and Abigail had planned was now achieved. "The multitude of my thoughts and the intensity of my feelings are too much for a mind like mine, in its ninetieth year," he wrote. His joy was so great that his health and his energies blossomed like a false springtime. For the moment, forebodings were put aside. The Adams family wanted to believe the sentiments expressed in verses written to be sung at the dinner in celebration of John Quincy's election.

> To him, who alike inherits
> The *Name*, and the *place*, of his Sire;—
> Who has *won* the rank he merits,
> By a vigor that cannot tire;—[91]

CHAPTER 17

"The Prison House of State"

"For him [John Quincy Adams] I consider private station as glorious as Chief Magistrate's . . . as far as I am personally concerned 'tis in comparison perfect freedom to the prison house of state."

LOUISA CATHERINE ADAMS

O N FEBRUARY 10, the committee of notification composed of Daniel Webster, Joseph Vance, and William Archer called on the Secretary of State to bring him formal notice that the House of Representatives had chosen to make him President for four years starting on March 4, 1829. Trembling, covered with perspiration, John Quincy, following the precedent started by Jefferson when he, too, was elected by the House of Representatives in 1800 after the Jefferson-Burr tie, read his prepared written acceptance and then thrust it into the hand of Webster.

The reply, which was polite but stiff and formal, ill-concealed its author's distress and disappointment. "Could my refusal to accept the trust thus delegated to me give an immediate opportunity to the people to form and to express with a nearer approach to unanimity the object of their preference, I should not hesitate to decline the acceptance of that eminent charge and to submit the decision of this momentous question again to their determination," he said. Almost compulsively, he added that one of his three competitors in the House election was "further recommended by a larger minority of the primary electoral suffrages than mine." However, since the Constitution had not provided for the contingency "of my refusal," he would "repair to the post assigned me by the call of my country."[1]

The night before, at President Monroe's last levee, an ample crowd, including all of the former rivals for the Presidency except for Crawford, who was too ill to attend, was present. The sensation seekers were eager to see what would happen when the two most serious contenders confronted each other. When General Jackson and the Secretary of State saw each other they both looked tentatively until Jackson, who had a lady on his right arm, advanced. "How do you do, Mr. Adams," he said, entirely composed and courteous. "I give you my left hand, for the right, you see, is devoted to the fair: I hope you are very well, sir." Adams replied stiffly, "Very well, sir: I hope General Jackson is well." The verdict of the spectators was that the hero had vanquished the President-elect in that encounter.[2]

Adams decided that, wherever possible, he would retain the members of Monroe's Cabinet. He therefore visited Southard to ask him to stay at his Navy post. When Southard consented, John Quincy informed him that Crawford would be asked to stay on at the Treasury and that Clay would be offered State. It only took a few days before the news of the last appointment was out. And when Jackson heard it, he turned on his former friend and benefactor with vengeful fury. He said that John Quincy Adams was not the "virtuous, able and honest man" he had believed him to be even when rumor reported that he had made a bargain with Clay. "But when these strange rumours become facts . . . and Mr. Clay was Secretary of State . . . from that moment I withdrew all intercourse with him."[3] That mild statement was the declaration of a war that would rage for four years.

Throughout the Cabinet-making period, Adams's friends and supporters were displeased and dissatisfied. They distrusted Southard because he was not very well qualified and in the past election was suspected of having been a Jackson man and a tool of Calhoun. William Wirt, the Attorney General, was admittedly a good lawyer, but was more interested in his own practice than in the government and was no political asset. Clay's appointment was a political reality that the Adamsites were ready to accept since he represented nine western states that had never before had anyone in the executive department. Adams, who reported all his selections to Monroe, told the President that Clay was offered the State Department because of his talents and services and because it was due the western section for their support in the election.[4] Clay himself was faced with the dilemma: if he accepted the State Department he would be labelled "an unprincipled intriguer." If he declined, he would be deemed a coward rather than a man of principle. Nevertheless, most of his friends advised him to accept, which he did.[5]

Crawford's refusal to continue in office left the Treasury Department open. Adams decided to offer it to Richard Rush, his Minister to England, whom he believed to be a man of knowledge, ability, and sagacity. His appointment was viable politically for it would both please Rush's home state of Pennsylvania and free the appointment to the Court of St. James for De Witt Clinton, who had indicated that he coveted it. Though New York had to be rewarded for her major role in electing Adams, most politicos agreed that Clinton in the Cabinet would spell nothing but disaster. Plumer expressed the general view when he noted that the trio of Adams, Clay, and Clinton would defeat any possibility of amity in the President's Advisory Council.[6]

Even before the tenure of office started, Adams had no illusions about the difficulties that faced him. "I am at least forewarned," he told his *Diary*, after several friends had informed him that Calhoun planned to mastermind the election of Jackson in 1828. But in the meantime letters of congratulations poured into the house on F Street and into the State Department offices. Some of them tempered the greetings with demands for appointments.

Undoubtedly the person most pleased by the election was John Adams. A friend wrote to John Quincy that the old gentleman was "with us last night in the utmost cheerfulness, with a head as clear as usual & passing a joke occasionally" while he sat enthroned in his room in his usual armchair.[7] Jefferson, who now harbored a nostalgic kind of affection for the older Adams, although he had little flattering to say to others about his son, wrote with some trace of envy: "It must excite ineffable feeling in the breast of a father to have lived to see a son . . . so eminently distinguished by the voice of his country." He also reassured the anxious father that the Administration would not be as difficult as he feared. There "will be as immediate an acquiescence in the will of the majority as if Mr. Adams had been the choice of every man."[8] William Cranch congratulated the venerable ex-President for having "lived to see it," and because "that old Virginian aristocracy which for *24* years has been sitting like an incubus upon the administration of our country" had been defeated.[9]

Fatigued by two sleepless nights, harried by Louisa's failing state of health, John Quincy Adams entered upon the day for which he had been destined by the hopes of his parents and a lifetime of devotion to the public will. He left his house at 11:30 in the morning accompanied by a military escort and a cavalcade of citizens. Samuel Southard rode with him in his carriage. President Monroe followed in his own carriage. At the Capitol, the procession was met by the committee on arrangements which conducted them to the Senate. The august body had already been in session for an hour, during which they had sworn in the Vice President and their new members. When the dignitaries entered, the entire Senate rose.

At noon, the Senate adjourned and marched in procession to the House of Representatives. The Marshall headed the line, followed by the Committee on Arrangements, the President-elect and the President, the justices of the Supreme Court, and, finally, the Vice President, heading the Senators. Upon reaching the House chamber, Adams was given the Speaker's chair while the others were conducted to their assigned places. The recess behind the Speaker's chair and the lobby was reserved exclusively for the ladies.[10]

The President-elect rose from the Speaker's chair and, after a faltering start from which he quickly recovered, delivered his Inaugural Address. "The principles by which I shall be governed," he said, would be those of the Constitution which has "to an extent far beyond the ordinary lot of humanity secured the freedom and happiness of this people." Though there had been difficulties and trials of all kinds, ten years of peace at home and abroad had "assuaged the animosities of political contention and blended into harmony the discordant elements of public opinion." What must still be done was to give up all party rancor, "embracing as countrymen and friends" and yielding to talents and virtues alone, "not to those who bore the badge of common party." Most of the address was spent on the accomplishments of the Monroe Administrations, which, in effect, was a kind of summary of Adams's own work. In pleading for party solidarity, the new President admitted obliquely that the era of good feelings was now only a clever slogan.

But the assembled audience was not ready when the speaker tossed out his own outrageous unexpected priorities. "To the topic of internal improvement . . . I recur with peculiar satisfaction," he said, though "some diversity of opinion has prevailed with regard to Congressional powers to legislate on these issues." Now nearly twenty years had elapsed since the first national road was built, and surely it had benefitted thousands and injured no one. "I cannot but hope that by the same process of friendly, patient, and persevering deliberation all constitutional objections will ultimately be removed." In conclusion, the new President could not resist referring to his own unhappy situation. "Less possessed of your confidence in advance than any of my predecessors, I am deeply conscious of the prospect that I shall stand more and oftener in need of your indulgence."[11]

After the address, Chief Justice Marshall administered the oath of office, which Adams recited with his hand on a volume of Laws. After exchanging greetings with Monroe and others, including Jackson, President John Quincy Adams left the hall.

In front of the Capitol, military companies passed in review before their new Commander-in-Chief. Then the procession formed into the same pattern that escorted Adams to his Inauguration and returned him home, where for two hours visitors brought him their good wishes. Adams went to Monroe's to join his visitors, and then returned home again for dinner. In the evening, he attended the Inaugural Ball, which, as was customary, he left after supper was served.

At Faneuil Hall in Boston the triumphant North celebrated the installation of their native son with appropriate pomp and festivity. To the tune of "Rise, Columbia," they sang an ode composed especially for the occasion:

> Columbia's Hope!—by Science taught
> Freedom in thee prolongs her reign:
> The work abroad thy Wisdom wrought
> At home thy Prudence shall maintain.
>   Sound the Clarion—sound afar
>   Hail the North's ascendant *Star*.[12]

Jackson's outward gallantry concealed his real reaction. With petty spite, he criticized the "Star of the North" for the pomp and ceremony with which he was escorted to his Inauguration. In contrast, the General pointed to the modest manner in which Jefferson rode alone and humbly to the Capitol and then tethered his horse himself. The story, which Jackson knew was apocryphal, pleased him. He had already decided that he was the guardian of principles that extolled "the sovereignty of the people," unadorned with any forms of ceremonies.[13]

The Senate lost no time in informing the new President that they awaited his nominations. He was ready to send them. Crawford, who had tendered his resignation to Monroe just a few days before, was the only former member whose name was absent from the list. "I cannot honestly remain in the Administration, differing as I do from the President on some important principles," he explained to a friend.[14] Richard Rush would be the new Secretary of the Treasury.

Though Henry Clay strongly advised his chief to clear out his political enemies, Adams was as deaf to his pleas as he was to the many Senators who approached him with their favorite nominees. John Quincy Adams rejected out of hand the concept of rotation in office, which, he said, "would make the government a perpetual and intermitting scramble for office."[15] He had his own simple formula. "I decided to renominate all against whom there was no complaint." Hence even Postmaster General John McLean, whose partisanship for Jackson was hardly concealed, retained his job. Despite evidence of blatant disloyalty, Adams stuck to this principle throughout his Administration, horrifying his loyal adherents. He removed only twelve incumbents throughout his term of office and only for gross negligence.[16]

Since there were so few changes in Adams's appointments, there could be little comment about them. However, New Jersey, New York, and Pennsylvania didn't like the Barbour appointment. He was "more acquiesced to than approved," due to their feeling against Virginia. Rush was not opposed, although Mr. Sergeant would have been preferred by that section. "All gratified with Clay and his address producing best effect here in the north," a Philadelphia correspondent wrote to Adams, referring to Clay's explanation to his constituents on why he preferred the northerner to the southern General. Jackson was not as competent, he explained, and did not have the "prudence, temper and discretion necessary for the position of president." Also, Clay feared "the many dangers to public liberty" which proceed from "military idolatry." Adams's experience at home and abroad was cited and, in conclusion, Clay asserted that the new President was "discreet, sagacious," and would enter upon the duties of the office "with great advantage."[17] Neither this statement nor any other quelled the cries of "corrupt bargain" that pursued Adams and Clay throughout the entire Administration. It was too perfect a weapon for the opposition to give up.

The appointment to the Court of St. James had to wait until Clinton had enough time to make up his mind. When he decided that he preferred to remain as Governor of New York, Adams offered the post to another prominent New Yorker, Rufus King. Old now and looking forward to a peaceful retirement, King tried to refuse. Adams urged him to accept, telling him that the job was very important and prestigious and not inferior to heading one of the Departments. He lured him on with the bait that many of the negotiations underway with Britain were particularly relevant to the interests of New York and Maine. It was his duty, the President urged, to his country and to the federal party to accept the position and thereby heal party differences. King, bewildered by the pressure and the logic, did not know how to refuse. Persuading his son and family to accompany him, King consented and agreed to leave for England in May.[18] Clay approved of the King appointment but would have preferred General William Henry Harrison of Ohio, now a Senator, to Adams's appointment of Joel Poinsett as the first Minister to Mexico.

Clay had been quite certain that there would be only three or four votes against him when the Senate took up his nomination. He was approved, but there were fourteen nays to the twenty-seven yeas. The Rufus King nomination encountered strenuous opposition. It was referred to by some ardent democrats as "blood money" for federalist support and conjured up the nightmare of more and more federalist office seekers taking away jobs from pure-blooded, deserving party members. The South deplored the nomination because they could not forgive King's anti-slavery position during the Missouri debates and his proposal subsequent to that to use the money obtained from the sale of public lands for the manumission of slaves. It was to be expected that Ritchie's Richmond *Enquirer* would denounce the nomination but even pro-Adamsite Thurlow Weed failed to see the justification for the King appointment. The anti-Adams wing of the federalist party, with hard-core Timothy Pickering at its helm, sneered that King was just gathering his reward for supporting the Administration. Opposition also came from the West when Thomas of Illinois accused the New Yorker of open hostility to that part of the country. It was not until December 20, six months after his arrival in England, that Rufus King's appointment was ratified.[19]

The Adamses remained in their own home until the end of April because Mrs. Monroe's illness delayed the return to Virginia. When the first family moved into their official dwelling on April 20, Louisa took an instant dislike to it. A large part of the living quarters needed refurnishing and much of the furniture that was there was very shabby. The upper floor had only two south bedchambers, which were appropriated by the President. John had possession of a north chamber and sitting room, which left only three empty rooms on the same side, one of which Johnson Hellen moved into.

It seemed difficult to understand how Mrs. Monroe, a fastidious southern lady, could have endured the house, Louisa said. It did not have the comforts "of any private mechanics family and I believe it would be difficult to find such an assortment of rags and rubbish even in an Alms House." She admitted the people to see the President's house in its real state because she knew the public mind on general splendor. "Some think I did wrong," the First Lady admitted.[20]

President Adams's quarrel was not with the house but with the press of visitors who came every day. He rose at 5 A.M. so as to read his Bible and the newspapers, and work upon the public papers before the callers came on official business, to solicit for donations or just out of curiosity. The Department Heads kept him busy from eleven to four or five in the afternoon. One day he noted that he had not been without company for ten minutes from nine to five. Apart from a three- to four-mile daily walk, the harassed man had little recreation. The President, according to custom, did not attend private parties and refused invitations. So unless he entertained, the hours from dark till eleven were spent in his room signing land grants or blank patents. There was seldom time for his own writing.

As the warm weather approached, John Quincy resumed his habit of swimming in the Potomac each morning. Usually his son John and Antoine, his valet, accompanied him. On June 15, there was a near disaster. With the intention of swimming across the river, the President arranged that Antoine would accompany him in a canoe that they had used the past summer. John said that the boat was not seaworthy and, instead of going with his father, undressed at the rock and agreed to meet them in the middle of the river when they returned. Adams decided that the boat was safe enough, gave his watch to his son, made a bundle of his coat and waistcoat to take in the boat, took off his shoes, and was paddled by Antoine, who had stripped naked. Before they got halfway across the river, the boat was half filled with water and there was no container with which to bale it out. At the moment, a fresh breeze from the northwest blew down the river as if it were from the nose of a bellows. In five minutes, it made a tempest which swamped the canoe. Antoine and the President jumped overboard and lost hold of the boat, which drifted away. Almost in the middle of the river, they made for shore. Antoine, who was naked, made it easily but Adams, hampered by his clothes, had a great deal of trouble. While he struggled and gasped for breath, he said that he had ample leisure to reflect upon his folly. The loose sleeves of his shirt filled with water and hung like two weights upon his arms. His hat blew away. When he reached shore, the President took off his shirt and pantaloons, wrung them out and gave them to Antoine, who went to look for someone to send to the house for other clothes and for the carriage. Soon after he left, John arrived, having swum across the river when he didn't see the others. While Antoine was gone, John and his father waded and swam up and down the shore or sat naked basking on the bank of the river. Then John walked home but Adams returned in the carriage, half dressed, having lost an old summer coat, white waistcoat, two napkins, two white handkerchiefs, and a shoe. Antoine lost his watch, jacket, waistcoat, pantaloons, and shoes. The boat was also lost. But fortunately no one was drowned or injured, although the President had been in the water about three hours. "This incident gave me a humiliating lesson and solemn warning not to trifle with danger," Adams recorded.[21]

Louisa wrote to George with some humor that any rumor that he might hear that his father was drowned was untrue. She summed it up with: "The affair is altogether ridiculous as it turned out but might have been fatal to your mother's future peace." Her anxiety increased when, not long afterward, a sixty-year-old clerk, known to be one of the best swimmers in the county, was drowned at Adams's usual bathing place. The President considered giving up swimming but decided against it because in the Washington summer heat, he thought it essential to his health. Louisa deplored her husband's passion for swimming and said that now it kept her in "hourly terror for some horrible calamity."[22] But even when a pain in his side, attributed to swimming, incapacitated the President, he stayed away from the spot only for a few days.

Charles arrived in Washington early in the summer in order to avoid the embarrassment of attending his graduation from Harvard. His indifference to his studies had lost him any hope of being given a part in the Commencement exercises. When his petition to be allowed to leave Cambridge early arrived in Washington, his father received it with ill-concealed irritation. However, he agreed with his son that "it will be most comfortable for you to be as far distant from Cambridge on that day as you can."[23] Almost threateningly, he added, "You must decide on a profession for yourself." President Kirkland, however, granted Charles the leave and assured him that his degree would be received. With much more tact, Louisa wrote to Charles, "If you have no part assigned to you you must come on directly . . . so as to be here when General Lafayette is to pay us a visit and I want you to assist me in doing the honours of the House."[24]

The unprecedented, overwhelming reception that the American people accorded to the Marquis de Lafayette, now in the United States as the nation's guest, knew no bounds. He was fêted, paraded, banqueted, and subjected to the enthusiasm of the crowd, the reminiscences of old soldiers, and the banalities of official receptions. He and his son, George Washington Lafayette, were made honorary members of the New-York Historical Society and in Boston welcomed by 3,000 school children assembled on the Common, wearing ribbons stamped with the Frenchman's likeness. Later the Marquis visited old John Adams, whose alertness astounded him.

The large eastern cities competed with each other in the extravagances of their receptions. Ostentation was unrestrained when, at a birthday banquet in New York, the curtains at the end of the hall opened to display a transparency of Washington and Lafayette clasping hands before the altar of Liberty. At a fête at Castle Garden attended by 6,000 people, another monster transparency displayed La Grange, Lafayette's home, its moat, and five towers, with the inscription, "Here is his Home."

Even in the midst of the tense presidential election, the press never failed to report the travels and the sayings of the popular Frenchman. American outrage peaked when it was revealed that, in France, news of Lafayette's triumphal visit was suppressed by the Bourbons, who disliked the democratic Marquis.

Lafayette had planned to leave the United States at the end of 1824 but his friends protested strongly. The southern cities had issued invitations to him and besides, his admirers urged, he should stay and observe the outcome of the presidential election. Succumbing particularly to his son's urgent pleading, he spent the winter in Washington at Gadsby's Hotel. President Monroe had urged a sizable gift to compensate the General for the fortune he had lost in the two Revolutions and some of his subsequent adventures. While he was absent in Annapolis, the obliging American Congress discreetly voted him the money. The Senate approved it unanimously, but in the House some northern members thought it a most unnecessary extravagance. Some of the individual states, such as Virginia and New York, wishing to show up the penny-pinching northerners, proposed making their own donations, but Lafayette discouraged any further largesse.

The outcome of the election impressed Lafayette, who was pleased that there was no militant outburst after the results came out and instead he was able to witness a peaceful transfer of power. The Marquis' tour through the South and West was exhausting but perhaps even more successful than the one he had enjoyed the year before. However, though some of the Indian receptions pleased him particularly, he was constantly horrified by the spectacle of slavery. In New Orleans, he insisted on receiving a delegation of Negroes who had fought under General Jackson at the Battle of New Orleans.

General Jackson received the Frenchman at the Hermitage. General "Tippecanoe" Harrison entertained him in Cincinnati. All along his progress, Lafayette visited cities and counties that had been named after him. Albert Gallatin delivered a long address recounting Lafayette's achievements at a ceremony that took place at Uniontown in Lafayette County, Pennsylvania. But one of the major ceremonies Lafayette attended was in the North—the fiftieth anniversary of the Battle of Bunker Hill. After that occasion, Lafayette went to Quincy to say farewell to John Adams, who advised him not to take part in any more revolutionary projects.

Lafayette was to be returned to France in state on the new United States frigate which President Adams proposed to name the *Brandywine*, in honor of the Frenchman's first battle and first wound. It was a proud forty-four-gun vessel but, despite John Quincy's urging, it could not be readied before September. In the meantime, Lafayette would have to stay in America.

On August 6, Adams and his son John accompanied General Lafayette and his suite to Virginia to visit ex-President Monroe.

The first night after leaving Washington, they stayed at a hotel in Fairfax where the town turned out to honor the guests. The next day, somewhat delayed by a broken axle that had to be repaired before the carriage could continue, they arrived at Monroe's house where the welcome committees again flocked to see the Marquis.

Charles was very pleased at the quiet when the Lafayette party left for Virginia. He wrote to his grandfather that Lafayette "engrossed all our attention. Dinner succeeded dinner & party to party although the weather was warm." Young Lafayette was no favorite of the President's youngest son. Not only did he usurp his room but he was "rather dull."[25]

The President had no choice but to participate cheerfully in the arrangements for the nation's guest. On the hottest day of the season, he had to ride with Lafayette to Leesburg, Virginia. In the evening the party arrived at Mr. Ludwell Lee's house where a chamber with two beds was allotted to Monroe and Adams. The President wrote, "I have no pleasure in such scenes."[26] The return home was no more comfortable. Day and night, the roads were "blazing and suffocating" and unfit for "pampered horses." Near Washington, one of Adams's four horses fell and died. After four days, a tired, irritated Chief Executive reached home to find that letters and business had multiplied while he was away. It was good news that the *Brandywine* would be ready to sail the first week in September.

Louisa, who carried the burden of White House entertaining, was, candidly, fed up with the General. She complained to George that he was "so eloquent that I was half inclined to adopt your Cambridge fashion and ask him if he would let nobody speak but himself."[27] The family had a short respite from the French entourage when Lafayette went to Montpelier. "Tired of him," Charles wrote to his grandfather. He and John wanted their apartments back. "You may think these sentiments very degenerate, my dear grandfather, in a descendant of yours," the lad said, "but I advise you, we of the third generation look with more impartial eyes on *all* the actors of the revolution, and are apt to think that we have overpaid one hero."[28]

The weather cooled off toward the end of August but not Louisa's temper. She did not "hail with joy" the return of Lafayette. "I admire the old gentleman," she insisted, "but family comfort has been reduced, we are obliged to turn out of our beds to make room," and having to keep open house was a heavy expense, plus the necessity of increasing the presidential retinue of servants from sixteen to twenty.[29]

All this domestic strain did not really minimize the Adams family's concern for the Frenchman. Everyone worried about Lafayette's return to France lest the government turn their hostility against him. John Quincy, on several occasions, echoed his father's advice to the Marquis to refrain from further participation in revolutionary projects. At the age of sixty-eight he must leave revolutions to younger men, the Marquis protested. But the President observed that "there is fire beneath the cinders."[30]

The day before Lafayette's departure, his sixty-ninth birthday, John Quincy gave a great dinner in his honor. Contrary to custom, the President proposed a toast.

"To the 22nd of February and the 6th of September, the birthday of Washington and the birthday of Lafayette."

Lafayette replied, "To the 4th of July, the birthday of liberty in two hemispheres."[31]

At noon on the day of Lafayette's departure, the people began to collect and the military to form on the square. At half-past twelve, the President, Lafayette, and the Secretaries gathered in the White House drawing room to receive dignitaries, friends, and visitors and have refreshments. Afterwards, they all proceeded to the hall where Adams addressed his guest and received his answer. Both men were greatly affected.

"In your visit to twenty-four states . . . you have heard the mingled voices of the past, the present and the future age, joining in one universal chorus of delight at your approach. . . . We shall look upon you always as belonging to us. You are ours by that more than patriotic self-devotion with which you flew to the aid of our fathers. . . . Speaking in the name of the whole people of the United States . . . I bid you a reluctant and affectionate farewell."[32]

Lafayette, overcome, answered, "God bless you, sir. God bless the American people, each of their states, and the federal government."

Affectionately, the emotional Frenchman embraced all the Adamses. The President accompanied him to the door where the people waited, encircling his carriage. The Secretaries rode with Lafayette to the boat accompanied by a military escort. Then the Secretary of the Navy, General Brown, and John Adams boarded the ship with him and stayed until it was under full sail.

Henry Clay returned to Kentucky at the end of June because of persistent ill health. From there he reported to the President that in his state there was the strongest evidence of public confidence in the Administration. Even those who opposed his support of Adams were now united in general approval.[33] The illness of his young daughter delayed his return to the capital and when he finally arrived in Washington in August he had just learned of the child's death.

There was little serious business in the early months of the Administration. The most irksome problem concerned the Creek Indians in Georgia who did not want to give up any more of their land. Part of the difficulty was the division among the Creeks. The Upper Creeks living along the forks of the Alabama, on the Tallapoosa and the Coosa in Alabama, who composed the majority of the Creek nation, wanted to yield no further territory. But the chiefs of the Lower Creeks who lived in Western Georgia along the Flint and Chattahoochee branches of the Appalachicola were willing to negotiate for removal. John Quincy asked Calhoun what was the raging fever for Indian lands that possessed the Georgians. Vice President Calhoun explained that it was the lottery that the state had for disposing of them.[34] Much of the Indian land there was now coveted for its good cotton-growing potential.

The situation became critical when four Creek Indians called on the President before breakfast on May 15 with a letter from Governor George Michael Troup of Georgia announcing the murder of their chief, General McIntosh, by a party of 400. Troup asserted that Howell, the Indian agent, had instigated the massacre. Adams was shaken when he found that the situation was not as clear as it seemed. Barbour, in whose hands the papers were left, said that Troup, who represented the interests of the cotton planters, was a madman not to be trusted and that the general opinion was that this would be the beginning of a ferocious Indian war.

Upon investigation it became apparent that it was not Howell who was responsible for the massacre but members of the Upper Creek faction who were "executing" McIntosh for selling them out. The root of the difficulty was the treaty of Indian Springs, which had slipped through the Senate in March. John Quincy had signed the treaty when it crossed his desk during the first few days of his Administration, thinking that it was the proper thing to do since it had already been ratified. Now that Troup had sent for help, fearing an invasion of Creeks into Georgia, Adams acted quickly. He suspended Howell and sent General Edmund Gaines into Creek territory to await instructions. For a while it looked as if it would be necessary to recall Congress so they might vote adequate funds.

Upon discussing the problem with General Brown, Adams got further disturbing insights into Governor Troup's game. Brown also remarked on Troup's violent nature and on the advantages Georgia might accrue from an Indian war. It also became clear that the treaty of Indian Springs had been fraudulent because, although reputedly signed by the assembled chiefs of the Creek nation, it had actually been negotiated with William McIntosh, chief of the Lower Creek tribe, and seven of his allies. It provided that the Creek nation would exchange its Georgia land for equal land west of the Mississippi, an evacuation scheduled to take place within eighteen months, but no surveys would be made before September 1826. Some monetary compensation was also included.

Once more conversant with the Indian problem, Adams reversed his position about Howell, deciding that to suspend him would have a bad effect on the Indians. He also limited General Gaines's authority to protection of the Georgian frontier unless Indian outrages continued. Governor Troup, the President decided, had been exceedingly "hasty and intemperate."[35] The Cabinet agreed that a letter should go out to Troup warning him not to survey the territory prematurely.

Troup responded to Washington's admonitions in colorful and abusive language, which was answered with tactful and delicate firmness. Troup was not to be put off with soft words. The sovereignty of his state was being challenged, the Governor believed, but he limited his protest to warlike language and, for the time being, agreed not to make the survey of Creek land. The people of Georgia, her Governor declared and probably rightly, felt that the government in Washington was neglecting their interests and delaying their rights, while the treaty had given them what they wanted. "There is a spirit and feeling existing in Georgia, which would at a moment's warning march ten thousand bayonets to drive General Gaines and his little army from the territory, if it was *imprudently* required by the Governor, [who] is the *idol* of the people," a Savannah friend wrote to Rush. The President, on the contrary, he added, has no party in Georgia.[36]

Since, for the moment, the Indian situation seemed under control, Adams decided to leave Washington for Quincy. Each year, as

summer approached, there was anxiety about the old gentleman. "I
pray your father may be allowed once more to see him and that your
Grandfather's days may be prolonged until August when I hope he
will be able to visit him," Louisa wrote to George in June. Lately
reports had been optimistic that he was enjoying a "revival" since
he had seen that his son had not served an ungrateful public.[37]

His return to Massachusetts as a conqueror probably pleased the
austere President. He seldom enjoyed public adulation but this time
there were many visits and some instances of crowds collecting when
he went abroad and on his travels. While in the north, he decided to
undertake Charles's law education, but his visit with George was
worrisome. The young man seemed unhappy, restless, without direction to his life and to his future. John Quincy, while he was in
Princeton, sent him a poem which he called the "Sum total of a
Father's blessing. Health, Content, honest Fame, Peace with God."
It had several verses and concluded with:

> But all too weak is mortal speech
>   The feelings of my Heart to utter
> And words are impotent to teach
>   The lessons on my lips that flutter.
> With will unyielding *Rule thy Soul*,
>   And *spurn* the deadly draught of *Pleasure*
> Then bid Earth's orb unheaded roll,
>   And grasp at Heaven's eternal Treasure.[38]

On the same day he wrote to Honorable John Davy in Boston
about the establishment of a chair of astronomy at Harvard and the
building of an observatory. The idea was particularly brought to
mind by the appearance of a comet "which at this very time is
enlightening our starry night *unobserved*, for want of such an institution."[39] Adams offered $1,000 for a subscription for this purpose
over a two-year period. With proper application, he maintained,
further aid would come.

The journey back to Washington was tedious and disagreeable
because Louisa was ill most of the time. She dreaded returning to
the "great unsocial house" where, she declared, she would never feel
at home. The state rooms were so large that they could not be
warmed in winter so that entertaining meant inevitably getting a
terrible cold.[40]

Upon his return to the capital, Henry Clay was found to be "in great affliction." A second daughter, married and living in New Orleans, had just died. The loss of two children within a month had so debilitating an effect on Clay's health that he talked of having to retire. However, the Secretary of State told the President he was satisfied with his treatment towards him and with the Administration. This countered somewhat bad news from Joseph Blunt, who reported that the candidates nominated for the New York legislature were all anti-Administration men. Blunt tried to suggest tactfully that the "sincere and early friends" had been unrecognized and that, perhaps, some act of confidence on the part of the President would produce "incalculable benefit." Though it was understood that Adams was determined not to administer the government for personal purposes "surely a public testimony of your confidence in men, whose principles & qualifications are unquestionable should not be withheld, because those men have supported your election," he pleaded.[41] The New York Adamsites were particularly angry at the appointment of Alfred Conkling, a known Jackson man, to be district judge of the northern district. "Now the power of men bent on Mr. Adams overthrow will be strengthened," a New Yorker wrote to Adams from Albany under the name of Algernon Sidney, which he avowed was a pseudonym.[42]

John Quincy spent the better part of the month of December preparing the annual Message to Congress, "a task of great anxiety." He tried the technique of giving the draft to the members of the Cabinet, who would meet and examine it among themselves and then discuss the result with him. He wanted the benefit of their objections but had some misgivings about starting the precedent since the responsibility for the message was wholly his.[43] Nonetheless, when his first draft was ready on November 1, he could not resist reading sections of it to his Secretaries when they came to his house.

The members of the Cabinet were quite free with their advice. When it was urged that something soothing to the state of South Carolina be put in the message, Adams answered that he could not while that state persisted in violating the Constitution and the rights of foreign nations. Though Britain had complained and the State Department had promised that the cause of the complaint would be removed, the Governor of South Carolina never answered the Secretary of State's letter. The difficulty was over a South Carolina law that said that any free Negroes entering a South Carolina port would be imprisoned while in the state and not liberated until payment was made for the cost of their detention. The South Carolina law was declared unconstitutional by Attorney General Wirt and by the federal courts, but it was not repealed by the South Carolina legislature and it continued to be enforced. The South Carolina senate asserted that the duty of preventing insurrections was "paramount to all *laws,* all *treaties,* all *constitutions*" and protested the right of the United States to meddle with her domestic regulations.[44]

When the message was read in its entirety to the assembled Cabinet, except for Wirt who was absent, only Richard Rush approved of it completely. Barbour objected to the remarks on internal improvements; Clay wanted the comments on a national university expunged. He also advised that letters of marque and reprisal should be issued against France in order to collect the long-standing claims against her. Barbour opposed the idea since it would mean war and no one in the country wanted to go to war for them, he said.

When Wirt returned from Baltimore, the President read his message to him. The lawyer thought that the part on internal improvements was excessively bold and would give credence to the opposition party in Virginia, which represented Adams as grasping for power. He also feared that the references to the voyages of discovery and scientific accomplishments of the monarchies would be criticized as showing partiality for monarchies. Wirt argued his point of view with the President for two or three hours but could not change his mind. "Mr. Rush is as enthusiastic for it as Wirt is against it," Adams commented.[45]

At the first session of the Nineteenth Congress, which met on December 5, Daniel Webster successfully engineered the election of Adamsite John W. Taylor of New York as Speaker of the House on the second ballot. Though he won by only five votes, it was a significant Adams-Clay victory. Opposition to Taylor was heavily southern because of his position on the Missouri Compromise, anti-Clintonian rancor, and his attachment to Adams. The situation in the Senate was very touchy. No one faction had a certain majority so the balance was held by the Crawfordites.

After a committee composed of members from both houses called on Adams and informed him they were ready to receive any communication that he should make to them, the President replied that his written answer would be in their hands at noon. After they left, the President sent his son John with the message and its accompanying documents. He was glad that the bustle of the day kept his mind off the reception that the speech was getting. "I await with whatever composure I can command, the issue," he wrote.[46]

Insofar as the annual message presented the State of the Union, the Adams report was acceptable, even pleasing, since the President was able to report a condition of peace and prosperity. Among the matters mentioned were the Panama congress of South American nations, to which the United States had been invited, had accepted, and to which the President would soon name Ministers; the promising condition of the nation's finances; and the flourishing condition of the Postmaster General's Department. A report on American foreign relations was, on the whole, favorable. Though French claims were not resolved, the Joint Commissions with Great Britain seemed to be coming to a successful conclusion. But when John Quincy Adams presented his program, his plans and his hopes for the Union, his ideas were met with a volume of criticism and ridicule that far surpassed William Wirt's worst predictions.

Much in advance of his time, the President proposed an extensive system of internal improvements to be paid for by superfluous revenues, a national university, the development of geographical and astronomical sciences, the establishment of a uniform system of weights and measures, and the improvement of the patent system. "The great object of the institution of civil government is the improvement of the condition of those who are parties to the social compact, and no government in whatever form constituted, can accomplish the lawful ends of its institutions but in proportion as it improves the condition of those over whom it is established." Though this read like orthodox Rousseau and Locke as interpreted by the founding fathers, it clashed with the sensibilities of the States Righters and the party men.

The nationalist tones in which the President talked upset a good part of his listening audience. They were even more disturbed at his suggestion that Europe's monarchies had accomplished more in certain areas than this land of liberty. "While foreign nations less blessed with that freedom which is power are advancing with gigantic strides in the career of public improvement, were we to slumber in ignorance or fold up our arms and proclaim to the world that we are palsied by the will of our constituents, would it not be to cast away the bounties of Providence and doom ourselves to perpetual inferiority?"

The taint of monarchy had been on the Adamses since John Adams's Presidency and their enemies were always alert to revive it. The American people did not want to hear that in the twenty-five years since American independence "the Governments of France, Great Britain and Russia have devoted the genius, the intelligence, the treasures of their respective nations to the common improvement of the species. . . . Is it not incumbent upon us to inquire whether we are not bound . . . to contribute our portion of energy and exertion to the common stock?"

John Quincy's poetic plea for the erection of an astronomical observatory, "light-houses of the skies," he called them, was sneered at so derisively that the public and the press never stopped referring to the phrase with contempt. The context in which he presented the idea was unfortunate. He said: "On the comparatively small territorial surface of Europe there are existing upward of 130 of these light-houses of the skies, while throughout the whole American hemisphere there is not one."[47]

The reaction of the opposition was partially ideological. Van Buren, not yet officially linked to any faction, said that no real republican, "no intelligent friend of the reserved rights of states" could fail to see in the President's message anything but the "most ultra-latitudinarian doctrines." Jefferson thought some of the proposals unconstitutional.[48]

Adams could not understand the consternation. "I thought the power of making roads and canals given by the Constitution," he asserted. And George Washington had recommended the establishment of a national university and a military academy. Had he lived until today, Adams said, he would have seen West Point, but in this city which bears his name "the site for an university still bare and barren."[49]

The Adams program, also in the Washington tradition, was free of factionalism, but the times were awry for such a political philosophy. Though his Administration was not yet a year old, it was already condemned. Probably there was nothing that the President could have done to save it. The opposition wanted a strong party government, not a presidential program of good works.

It was still possible for the Adamses to deceive themselves that all was well. Louisa informed George that they were having a "bustling" season, "so far all gaiety, harmony, good humour." Recent confirmations of appointments by the Senate indicated a "much more quiet and agreeable winter than was at first apprehended."[50] The President was lulled into a false optimism. Fearing that his election "with perhaps two-thirds of the whole people adverse to the actual result" might precipitate violence or rejection of the House of Representatives choice, when this did not happen he mistook outward peace and prosperity for acceptance of his Administration.

Two or three thousand people attended John Quincy's first presidential New Year's Day open house, more guests than had ever come before. Most of the members of Congress and the diplomatic corps, including the British and South American Ministers were there. Conspicuously absent were the dignitaries of Russia and France, who said that they objected to the immense crowd. They had applied to Clay for permission to come at another time, but Adams declined, declaring coolly that he was unwilling either to give up two days to the ceremony or to yield to their pretensions.[51]

During the winter term the Congress spent a good part of its time debating about the sending of United States delegates to the Panama mission. In April of the preceding year, the Mexican Minister had proposed to Clay that the United States be represented at the meeting, organized because of Simon Bolivar's wish to promote the unification of South America. Clay, a Latin America enthusiast, strongly advised his country's cooperation. At the spring Cabinet meetings Clay and Barbour both pushed for involvement and were able to convince Southard in spite of his objections.

John Quincy acted on their advice immediately and approached Richard C. Anderson about attending the Congress. Anderson agreed to go. He was an excellent choice, known to be in sympathy with the Spanish-American movement and appointed in 1823 by Monroe to be the first Minister from the United States to Colombia. Accompanied by his wife and children, the new Minister went to Bogotá, where he was received with overwhelming enthusiasm and had the distinction of negotiating the first treaty between his country and an independent South American nation.

Anderson asked the President if he would have a colleague to go to the Congress with him. Adams answered that he preferred one Minister whose object would be "to consult, deliberate, and report rather than contracting positive engagements."[52] But Clay urged that two representatives be sent, suggesting Gallatin for the other

post. This indicated the importance which Clay attached to the
Congress, for Gallatin was the most distinguished diplomat of the
era. But John Quincy, certain that Congress would balk at the expense of two delegates, still thought that one was enough.

Just before Christmas, Clay urged Adams to send the message
about the Panama conference and his nominations to the Senate.
The President succumbed to Clay's pressure and chose a second
Minister, John Sergeant of Pennsylvania, a Philadelphia lawyer who
had been a member of Congress. The President's eloquent message
explained that American objectives at the Panama congress were
not to contract alliances or engage in any undertaking or project
"importing hostility to any other nation." The South American nations, "in the infancy of their independence," had sometimes
granted special trading privileges to Spain and had established
commercial relations with European powers unfavorable to the
United States. Since the adoption of principles of commerce would
be discussed at the meeting, it would be an opportunity for the
United States to urge the Adamsite doctrine that free ships make
free goods. It would be more effective, the President urged, to establish such a doctrine at a general meeting than to be forced to negotiate it in separate treaties with each of the participating nations. It
might also be possible to get a mutual agreement that would guard
against the establishment of any future European colony in the
Western Hemisphere. Adams also hoped that "the moral influence"
of the United States might be exerted there for the "advancement of
religious liberty," much needed because several of the countries had
an established church without toleration for any other sect.[53]

Although for the most part the Panama congress was popular in
the country, it was used as the major opening salvo against the
Administration. Adams recognized it for what it was at once, but
noted also that the opposition was still struggling to unite because
they were still discordant among themselves. Nevertheless, the anti-
Administration forces saw the Panama congress as a particularly
suitable vehicle for opposition since the Senate Committee on Foreign Relations had four southern members. Van Buren, who had
already discussed the strategy with Calhoun, organized the opposition with his customary skill. He decided on delaying tactics which
would hold up the ratification of the Ministers, and so the first step
was to send to the President for confidential papers and treaties with

the South American republics. Adams complied by immediately furnishing the documents.

As Adams predicted, the foreign relations committee submitted a long, intricate report against the Panama mission, summing it up with the opinion that "it was not expedient at this time" to comply with the President's request. It was still uncertain, however, how the Senate would go. Clay and Adams believed that they had a majority to confirm. Van Buren, just as uncertain, tried another trick. He proposed that the Senate should carry on its deliberations with open doors, a proposal that passed with a very close vote. Adams, much angered at "the fruit of the ingenuity" of Van Buren, answered with a message which asserted that all the communications that he had made to the Senate had been confidential and that, in the public interest, the confidence between the executive and the Senate should continue unimpaired. "I should leave to themselves the determination of a question upon the motives for which, not being informed of them, I was not competent to decide," he wrote meaningfully.[54]

A few neutral Senators were antagonized by the President's response because they thought it tactless. Van Buren and company, encouraged, continued with their delaying tactics, introducing motions that required taking separate votes and climaxing the procrastination with three weeks of secret conferences to go over the President's communications. The Senate behavior was dominated by the southern bloc's fear that slavery's continuance was threatened by the conference. It was both embarrassing and, in terms of the future, unfortunate that the slave-owning legislators had so little restraint in their insulting comments about the Latin Americans.

The pro-Adams Senators listened patiently until, on March 14, Van Buren pushed too far. He moved that the Constitution did not authorize sending representatives to such an assembly and to do so would be contrary to traditional United States foreign policy. In answer, the pro-Administration Senators defeated the motion and then confirmed the nominations.[55]

The next hurdle for the Panama project was to extract the needed funds from the House of Representatives. On March 15, Adams sent the House a message explaining to them why participation was essential. "There is scarcely one [topic] in which *the result* of the meeting will not deeply affect the interests of the United States," he asserted. For example, the invasion of Cuba and Puerto Rico by the united forces of Mexico and Colombia was among the subjects to be matured at the congress. The House voted the $40,000 requested on April 22, but before it did, a vicious speech against the project sparked violence.[56]

The Senate opposition, though defeated temporarily, did not give up. Adams's message to the House increased rather than allayed southern anxieties. The Panama congress was scheduled to discuss suppression of the slave trade, a subject uncomfortably close to emancipation, and, worse, Haiti, a country that existed as a result of a slave revolt, would be represented by a Black man. Thomas Hart Benton, Robert Y. Hayne, and John Holmes of Maine combined with others to develop a program of debates to stop it. Van Buren spoke piously in Jeffersonian measures but it was John Randolph of Roanoke who, on March 30, unleashed the furies.

Gaunt, half mad, but devilishly eloquent, Randolph rose from his seat to start a speech that went on for six hours. It was directed against the Panama mission but its sharpest thrust was against the Adams Administration, particularly the President and the Secretary of State. Literary, political, philosophical references tumbled over each other in the quixotic rhetoric of the Virginian. Following his argument was somewhat like threading through a labyrinth in Wonderland, but the intent was clear and when he wished to make his point it stood out by virtue of its audaciousness.

About halfway through the tortured prose of his oration, Randolph became more lucid and frankly offensive. "This is the first Administration that has openly run the principle of patronage against that of patriotism, that has unblushingly avowed, aye and executed its purpose, of buying us up with our own money. . . . Let Judas have his thirty pieces of silver, whatever disposition he may choose to make of them hereafter—whether they shall go to buy a potter's field, in which to inter this miserable Constitution of ours, crucified between two gentlemen suffering for 'conscience sake' under the burthen of the two first officers of this government forced upon one of them by the terms of the Constitution, against its spirit and his own, which is grieved that the question cannot be submitted to the People." In fits and starts the accusation and the distortions continued. They might have been ignored were it not for a wild analogy based on Henry Fielding's *Tom Jones*. Randolph said, "In what parliamentary debate was it, that, upon a certain union between Lord Sandwich, one of the most corrupt and profligate of men in all relations of life, and the sanctimonious, puritanical Lord Mansfield . . . on what occasion was it, that Junius said, after Lord Chatham had said it before him, that it reminded him of the union between Blifil and Black George?" In a digression he then made an accusation that has never been proved to be anything but a mirage from his teeming brain. "I then say, sir, that there is strong reason to believe that these South American communications, which have been laid before us, were manufactured here at Washington, if not by the pens, under the eye of our own Ministers, to subserve their purposes." Mockingly, Randolph accused John Quincy Adams of a determination to "become the apostle of liberty, of universal liberty," as his father at the time of the formation of the Constitution was known to be "the apostle of monarchy." The Virginian then repeated the story of his grudge against the Adamses. When he was a schoolboy in New York at the time that John Adams was there as Vice President, "I remember the manner in which my brother was spurned by the coachman of the then Vice President for coming too near the arms blazoned on the scutcheon of the Vice-Regal carriage. Perhaps I may have some of this old animosity rankling in my heart. . . ." The speech continued with increasing vituperativeness. Considering the author of the remarks, they might still have been ignored had he not worked himself up to the final insult.

Randolph said that he would have gone along with the President's right to keep his communications secret were it not for his objectionable slur on the motives of the Senate. But after twenty-six hours he had to give in. "I was defeated, horse, foot, and dragoons—cut up—and clean broke down—by the coalition of Bilfil and Black George—by the combination unheard of 'til then, of the puritan with the blackleg." Bilfil was the hypocritical malevolent youth who got the stupid hero, Tom Jones, into constant trouble while Black George was a rascal of a gamekeeper who allowed Tom to take the blame for his poaching.[57] Perhaps Clay could have ignored the literary allusion, but the term "blackleg" he couldn't stomach. Webster defined it as a swindler, a dishonest gambler.

Though Clay disliked duelling and his wife Floride was still grief-stricken over the deaths of their two daughters, he issued a challenge to Randolph. The Virginian had refused to meet General Wilkinson's challenge in 1807, but this time he was ready and would not listen to the efforts of Thomas Hart Benton and other friends to stop it. On April 8, 1826, at 4:30 in the afternoon on the Virginia side of the Potomac, the two adversaries fired at each other. There were two exchanges but the only damage was to Randolph's white flannel gown, through which a bullet passed. Both men agreed that honor had been satisfied.[58]

John Quincy, whose pen was his sword, answered Randolph's literary allusion with another. Using Ovid's lines on Envy, he applied them to John Randolph of Roanoke.

> Pallor in ore sedet; macies in corpore toto;
> Pectora felle virent; lingua est suffusa veneno.
>
> His face is livid; gaunt his whole body;
> His breast is green with gall; his tongue drips poison.[59]

The President's enmity centered on Calhoun, who had permitted the outrageous speech to go on without a word or an expression to curb it, parliamentary or otherwise. On May 1, Force's *National Journal*, the Administration's arm, carried an article criticizing the Vice President's Jacksonianism, signed "Patrick Henry." It was answered ten days later in the *National Intelligencer* by a writer who used the pseudonym "Onslow." For five months the two authors fired paper bullets at each other. Few of the knowing doubted that the true names of the authors were John Quincy Adams and John C. Calhoun, although the former never admitted it.[60]

The anger, the dissidence, the near-bloodshed that the Panama congress evoked in the United States dwarfed the pathetic aftermath. Although the congress was scheduled to meet in June 1826, Sergeant, fearing the pestilential heat of a Central American summer, got permission to leave at a later date. Anderson, on his way from his ministerial post at Bogotá to Cartagena, became ill and died on July 24, at the small town of Turbaco. Hence neither United States Minister attended the first Pan American congress. Unfortunately, however, Britain was ably represented by Edward J. Dawkins, whose mission was to carry out Canning's orders to thwart any move that would benefit the United States. Dawkins faithfully recounted to the South American delegations all the insulting remarks of the southern bloc. The Englishman's object, of course, was to promote British trade with Latin America. The congress itself accomplished little except perhaps to set a precedent for the future. But John Quincy Adams had the last word in a letter written a year after the close of the congress. He said that in order for the United States to preserve good relations with South America, she must observe and persevere in "a system of kindness, moderation, and for-bearance."[61]

The Indian problem revived when a delegation of Creeks came to Washington, with $4,000 for their expenses, to seek the support of the "Great White Father." They did not want to cede all their lands to the state of Georgia and had been given some hope by General Gaines that the boundary could be established at the Chattahoochee River. Adams, who felt as if he had been placed in the middle of the controversy, postponed the interview until he had more information. If he answered the delegation inflexibly, they would be more distressed, he reasoned. If, on the other hand, he were sympathetic "it would imply censure upon the treaty, which we must yet maintain, and would be offensive to Georgia." Georgia Senator Cobb, in a great state of excitement, threatened that unless the Administration supported his state against the Indians, Georgia would support Jackson. But Adams felt that "we ought not to yield to Georgia because we could not do so without gross injustice."[62]

Every attempt to persuade the Creek delegations to cede all their land to Georgia failed. After the Indians left the War Office on January 17, under the impression that negotiations had broken off, Chief Opothle Yoholo attempted suicide. The next day, however, when the talks resumed, the Indians agreed to accept a more western branch of the Chattahoochee as their boundary and, on the 24, a new treaty was signed at the War Office. Adams submitted it to the Senate a week later, explaining that the former treaty signed at Indian Spring the previous year could not be acted upon because the majority of the Creek nation did not accede to it. The change was minimal. The final portion of land excepted from cession was "of a comparatively small amount and importance. . . . I have assented to its exception as far as to place it before the Senate only from a conviction that between it and a resort to the forcible compulsion of the Creeks from their habitation and lands within the State of Georgia there was no middle term."[63]

It appeared that, with regret, Adams had abandoned the Indian cause. Barbour, who had negotiated with them closely, developed sympathy for Indian suffering, enough to propose that all Indians be formed into a great territorial government west of the United States. His plan was full of benevolent humanity, the President agreed, but "I fear there is no practicable plan by which they can be organized into one civilized or half-civilized government." Rush,

Southard, and Wirt agreed with the impracticability of Barbour's plan but had no other to suggest. Barbour also asked for a $50,000 appropriation for the relief of the Florida Indians, who were starving in the land to which they had emigrated. "They are where they are by our seeking," he reminded them, "and their country was exchanged as is usually the case by treaty, doubtless, with an ignorance on their part of that to which they consented to emigrate; and erroneous information on ours, as to its fitness."[64] The Secretary of War tried to put a good face on the white man's motives but revealed that he understood the red man's plight. The Indians had become an uncomfortable burden that was impossible for an Administration of good will to handle.

During the winter, the city of Washington suffered from an epidemic of influenza that did not spare the First Family. Johnson Hellen moved into the White House, too ill to follow his profession. At times the Senate was unable to form a quorum to carry on its duties. But this only temporarily halted the gaiety of the social season. The Corps Diplomatique set the style by entertaining handsomely.

George, whose persistent cough after a bad bout of influenza had his parents so worried that they begged him to come to Washington to get well, was elected to the Massachusetts legislature. John Quincy was delighted at "this first step in your advancement." His father was, of course, full of advice, some of it clearly of the "do what I say and not what I do" variety. George was admonished to follow early hours of going to bed and getting up, to avoid procrastination, and to think of the post as one of *"danger* and duty," rather than honor or "vainglorious exultation. Be mindful of your deportment to others . . . this is the greatest and most important Secret of Public Life," advised the crusty, independent President. He seemed more in character when he added that he approved his son's determination to act and vote according to his sense of right, but then cautioned him to avoid taking the unpopular side if it is wrong. "If popular sentiment be strong and urgent you must reconsider often your own impressions whether they may not be erroneous."[65]

Rufus King sent his resignation in March. The old federalist complained that his health was very bad and, in fact, Canning was proving to be so difficult that the mission was at a standstill. The British Minister refused to negotiate the interest charges that the

United States claimed on the slave indemnifications. When King had mentioned the figure of $2,000,000, Canning immediately said that it was outrageously high and would discuss it no further, not even making a counter offer.

All efforts to solve the differences collapsed after that: the Maine boundary, navigation of the St. Lawrence, and the duties on cargoes bound for the West Indies. King felt that the British were too preoccupied with their own problems. Suffering from chronic indigestion and offended by Canning's suggestion that the Anglo-American Commission on Slave Indemnities be transferred to Washington, King decided to throw over the job. He wrote angrily that Canning's plan to transfer "matters entrusted to me at this Post, is an indignity to my feelings, and evinces a defeat of confidence in me . . . which I feel cannot but impair my influence on the future execution of this trust."[66]

The President accepted King's resignation with no apparent regret and immediately offered the post to the master diplomat, Albert Gallatin. There were important matters pending between the two nations which required Gallatin, Adams thought. He offered him a "special mission" to England in which he would have ample discretionary powers to act. Gallatin accepted on those terms, but when his instructions arrived he was not satisfied. Claiming that they left him no discretion even on important points, he wrote to Adams that they made him "a mere machine. . . . I am not afraid of incurring responsibility . . . but I cannot do it in the face of strict and positive injunctions."[67] The issue was the northwestern boundary between the United States and Canada. Adams insisted that Gallatin hold out for the 49th parallel—"This is our ultimatum and you may so announce it," he said.[68] The President's motives were political. He did not dare give the Jacksonians the possibility of accusing him of giving in to the detested British.

Early in 1826, Jefferson, already in his last illness, appealed to the Virginia legislature to grant him an unusual request. He wanted to dispose of his property by lottery in order to save Monticello. The Virginia General Assembly, overcoming some opposition, gave its permission. When the friends and even former foes of the ex-President heard that the sage of Monticello was in danger of losing the home that he had made famous, they were horrified. Subscriptions for funds were started. The President's Cabinet discussed what to do about it on the fiftieth anniversary of the Declaration of Independence that Jefferson had penned. Barbour suggested that after the usual ceremonies at the Capitol, he should invite subscriptions for Jefferson, starting with his own contribution of $100. Rush thought that a meeting to raise money should be called immediately, because flooding rains that had just stopped had done great damage to the ex-President's estate.

It was too late to help Thomas Jefferson. On July 6, Governor Barbour brought Adams the news that Jefferson had died on the afternoon of July 4. The President had to decide whether he should issue an Act such as had been done at Washington's death. But after working on a proclamation for some time, he decided instead to notice the event in his next annual message. However, the War and Navy Departments ordered all the posts to pay funeral honors and officers to wear black mourning bands on their left arms for six months. A funeral service was planned to take place at the Capitol, with William Wirt delivering the eulogy.

While he was making plans and establishing protocol for honoring the third President of the United States, John Quincy was gravely concerned about his father's health. In May he had received a letter from Dr. Waterhouse that reported that old John Adams was failing rapidly. "In the *eye* of the physician," he appeared "much nearer the bottom of the hill" than when they had visited him together the past summer. Dr. Waterhouse said he was too feeble to come downstairs, "all his functions have give ground much more than his brain." The doctor said that the old man told him that he hoped that his son and his daughter-in-law would come in the summer.[69] Tom Adams's more recent letters made the President decide that he must manage to get to Quincy by the end of July or the beginning of August at the latest. If anything occurred to make it necessary "to anticipate the period of my journey, let me know," he wrote to his brother. On the Fourth of July, Dr. Waterhouse wrote that Thomas B. Adams said that his father could not hold out through the summer. He was so weak that he could hardly expectorate, which might stop him from breathing at night.[70] But it was already too late.

Susan B. Clark, a daughter of John Adams's son Charles, was in constant attendance on her grandfather. On the third of July, she wrote to her uncle, the President, that Dr. Holbrook doubted that his father would live another two days, surely not more than two weeks. The next morning the patriarch started to sink so rapidly that an express was sent for George in Boston with the hope that he would come in time "to receive his last breath." Just before the young man arrived, the ex-President was somewhat easier than he had been for the past two days. Susan Clark told him that it was the Fourth of July, the fiftieth anniversary of independence. He replied, "It is a great day. It is a good day." At 1 P.M., he said, "Thomas Jefferson survives." The last word was indistinct. He said no more. When George arrived, his grandfather seemed to know him but could not speak. At half-past six, John Adams passed away, "as quietly as an infant sleeps."[71]

On June 8, when President Adams received the news that his father was dying, he got ready to leave for Quincy, leaving each Department in charge of its head and the Cabinet in charge of the funeral honors for Jefferson. John Quincy had somehow convinced himself that his father would survive the summer, even another year, so that the knowledge of his father's imminent danger "was unexpected." At 5 A.M. the next morning, he left with his son John in his carriage with four horses. The day was hot and when he reached Waterloo, Mr. Merilly met them with the news that John Adams was dead. It had no sudden violent effect on his feelings because he expected it, he said. He tried to console himself with the fact that his father was almost ninety-one years old and had led an illustrious life. "The time, the manner, the coincidence with the decease of Jefferson, are visible and palpable marks of Divine favor," he wrote.[72]

When the President reached New York on July 11, Philip Hone, the Mayor, and the Aldermen, called with friendly condolences and stayed with him until he embarked on the steamer. It was John Quincy's fifty-ninth birthday and that evening, alone and under these peculiar circumstances, he reflected that he must wean himself away from the world and all which it inherits.

In Washington, however, Charles and Louisa and the girls celebrated the President's birthday by drinking champagne and "being very merry." Charles wrote that he supposed this "little fête" would have looked very dreadful to "the prudish citizens who make it a business to censure others" but his grandfather had been very old and no one could seriously regret his death.[73]

After four days of travelling in 96° heat, the Adamses arrived in Boston, where they were met by George. He described his grandfather's last hours and the funeral, which had been arranged by Josiah

Quincy and had taken place on Friday the seventh, with about 2,000 people in attendance.

At the Adams mansion everything seemed the same to the President until he entered his father's bedroom, where he had sat with him on the last two visits. It was an inexpressibly painful moment. "My father and mother have departed," he thought. "The charm which has always made this house to me an abode of enchantment is dissolved; and yet my attachment to it, and to the whole region round, is stronger than I ever felt before."

Under John Adams's will, John Quincy was left the family house and about ninety-three acres around it upon payment of $10,000 with interest within three years. The decision to keep the house as a place of retirement where he could go in two or three years to pursue his literary occupations had been made already. Adams wrote to Louisa that there was some question about the furniture in the house which, it seemed by the terms of the will, would have to be sold. In the meantime, he would stay in Quincy "in all possible retirement" until his return to Washington would be indispensable. She should join him with Charly and Elizabeth, his brother Tom's daughter, as soon as she could bring the horses and carriage.[74]

By the next day, plans had changed. Adams decided that the furniture must be sold at auction, therefore the domestic establishment would have to be broken up, so Louisa had better not come until she heard from him. He expected to stay about two months unless Washington public business called him.[75]

Louisa accepted her husband's desire to keep his father's house, but cautioned him about burdening himself with too much land. "The Jefferson family afford a gloomy instance of this." She also suggested that neither he nor George undertake the task of settling the estate. It would be impossible "to do strict justice to them and to your own children and . . . to give satisfaction to relatives who for years have been jealous both of your talents your station and your fortune."[76]

Louisa decided that she would not stay to swelter in the heat of Washington. Instead she went to Lebanon Springs, New York, accompanied by Elizabeth and an unwilling Charles, and against the advice of her friends, who did not know of the complications at Quincy. Johnson Hellen stayed at the President's house so that the public would not feel it had been left to servants.[77]

Letters of condolence poured into Quincy from all over the world and from people in all walks of life. The President attended many services in Massachusetts at which eulogies for his father were delivered. He was especially moved by the close of one given by Harvard's President Kirkland in which he referred to Abigail Adams. Her son wrote that it "deeply affected me, more than I was aware it was in human speech to do."[78]

On August first, Edward Everett delivered a eulogy at which a hymn was sung that characterized the nature of many of the tributes.

> Great God! how deep thy gracious ways;
> The *Sire*, removed through length of days,
> The *son* is raised by thy command,
> And *Adams* lives to bless our land.

On the next day, Daniel Webster spoke in Faneuil Hall for two and a half hours. The President admitted that he got some melancholy gratification from all these tributes but was overcome with fatigue.

Louisa was still advised not to come to Quincy, which suited her because she did not want to get involved in the settlement and was afraid that if she were there she could not steer clear of it. "Your affectionate, truly elegant present on my birthday, will be kept and cherished by me till I join the assembly of my fathers," her husband wrote to her. It was probably a translation of Lamartine's *La Mort de Socrate*, which Louisa dedicated to John Quincy "as a tribute of respect for those superior talents and requirements which all acknowledge and venerate."[79]

When Louisa asked that John and George visit her, Adams refused because he could not spare them. His business, public and private, was more demanding than it had been in Washington. The heads of the departments sent letters and papers and the estate business dragged on. George was engaged in the problems connected with the settlement of the estate and John was occupied as the President's secretary. At the end of August, however, George was sent to his mother with $500 which she needed for her expenses, but was ordered to return to Boston immediately to attend to business.

Charles complained that his stay in Lebanon was like a sentence in purgatory but his mother refused to listen to his pleas of boredom. Finally, she decided that she had had enough of the resort and started back to Washington to await her husband. Instead, George met her in New York and brought her back to Quincy while Charles continued to the capital and his studies, claiming to enjoy the solitude, relieved only by the company of Johnson Hellen.[80]

Although a daily reader of the Bible and a persistent churchgoer who often attended two services on Sunday, John Quincy never joined the church to which his forefathers had belonged for two centuries. At the same time that he decided to make the family home his permanent residence, he also resolved to make a public profession of his faith and hope as a Christian. He thought it particularly appropriate to do this directly after the death of his father.

Certain theological questions challenged John Quincy's faith. Immortality puzzled him; miracles confounded him. "The miracles in the Bible furnish the most powerful of all the arguments against its authenticity, both historical and doctrinal; and were it possible to take its sublime morals, its unparallelled conceptions of the nature of God, and its irresistible power over the heart, with the simple narrative of the life and death of Jesus, stripped of all the supernatural agency and all the marvellous incidents connected with it, I should receive it without any of those misgivings of unwilling incredulity as to the miracles, which I find it impossible altogether to cast off."[81] Christ's divinity and the trinity both posed questions for Adams. Neither the Gospel of St. Matthew nor anything that he had seen in the many exegeses that accompanied his Bible reading satisfied him either that the "doctrine of the Divinity of Christ *is not* countenanced by the New Testament" or that "it is clearly revealed. Of the question between the Unitarians and the Trinitarians I have no precise belief, because no understanding," he confessed. But these misgivings which had kept him from joining the ancestral church were no longer compelling. His faith now seemed closely bound to the affection he felt for his parents, particularly his mother. Dr. George Ellis said that when he shared a room with Adams on the occasion of the celebration for the fiftieth anniversary of the New-York Historical Society, the dignified old ex-President, with no apparent embarrassment, before he went to bed repeated in audible tones the prayer his mother taught him as a child: "Now I lay me down to sleep. . . ."[82]

On October 1, when the pastor of the church, Mr. Whiteney, before starting the service, said that those persons who had expressed their wish to join in the communion might present themselves, the President and the others so inclined rose in their places. The pastor reminded them of the engagements implied in participating in the rite—a sincere belief in the divine mission of Christ and a fixed purpose of living according to the rules of his gospel. For the first time in his life, John Quincy partook of communion.[83]

It seemed clear to Adams that he had made all the preliminary preparations for an early retirement. Nothing in the news that was coming from Washington heralded anything but failure in 1828. New York, it seemed, was lost. Adams now hoped that his sons would pursue useful professions and would prefer to live in Quincy or nearby so that he could "anticipate the pleasure of enjoying the constant society of his children" for the remainder of his days, though, he told Charles, "I've never tried to control them."[84]

On the way back to Washington in mid-October, Adams had an almost fatal accident. At the ferry crossing from Providence to Newport, a heavy gale blew, felling one of the horses, who then engaged in such a violent struggle that he almost turned over the boat. Adams noted that for many months, perhaps years, he had not been in such imminent danger. "Upon what a slender thread human life depends, and how incessantly it needs the guardian care of superior power."[85] Louisa and John, who went by land, met Adams in New York. He went ahead of them again in order to reach Washington in time for the joint ceremony for Jefferson and John Adams. Charles, who found his father looking as well as he had ever seen him, met him with the horses in Baltimore and rushed him to the Capitol. Attorney General Wirt delivered the double eulogy. Although he had preferred to speak only of Jefferson, whom he knew, he was persuaded, in the interest of national unity, to speak of them both. After the two-and-a-half-hour discourse, John Quincy returned home escorted by Captain Randolph's troop of horses.

The Panama congress, now transferred to Mexico, lacked an American delegate due to the death of Richard Anderson. Clay wrote to ex-President Monroe asking him to go but, having received no answer, decided to visit Oak Hill and talk to him. Adams also asked the ex-President to accept the mission. It will be "but setting the seal to your own work," he said persuasively. But Monroe refused, explaining that his wife's health was so poor that he feared she would die if he left her. He also had to stay home to try to retrieve his private affairs.[86] John Sergeant, still in Washington preparing to attend the second meeting of the Inter-American congress, was given a dinner by the President which all the dignitaries of the government attended. He and Rochester, the secretary, planned to embark on the *Hornet* for Tambaya about November 15.

Winter business was delayed while everyone went to the races. The President, who should have started on his second annual message, had to spend time signing land grants, patents, Mediterranean passports, and Commissions. When he asked Clay for a list of subjects from the State Department that the message should contain, the Secretary of State took advantage of the opportunity to bring up the hostility to the Administration displayed by the port collectors at Philadelphia and Charleston. Adams answered that he preferred to wait before making removals, unwilling to change his principle of not dismissing a public officer "for merely preferring another candidate for the Presidency."[87]

On October 30, the anniversary of his father's birthday, Adams wrote a sonnet in his honor. He deliberately inscribed it in a kind of shorthand that would not be easily legible, but at the same time sent a copy enclosed in a letter to his son George. Its subject matter is interesting. After speaking of his father's death, he said:

> Who but shall learn that freedom is the prize
>   Man still is bound to rescue or maintain;
> The native's God commands the slave to rise,
>   And on the oppressor's head to break his chain,
> Roll, years of promise, rapidly roll round,
>   Till not a slave shall on this earth be found.[88]

With reluctance and anxiety because of the misunderstanding with which his first message was received, John Quincy started to compose the new one. Again and again, although with misgivings, he gave the draft to the Cabinet to read and discuss. Barbour and Clay objected to some passages, Southard remained quiet, and Rush stood with his chief. Finally all agreed that the President must decide finally what should be included and in what language.

On December 4, Congress opened and asked for the message. Having promised it in writing for the next day, the President stayed up late that night, frantically revising the two copies that he would send to them. Charles described the message accurately. "It is not so very powerful [a] one as the last session, but well adapted to the present state of affairs, as it gives no hold to the enemies of the government."[89]

In mild tone, the message reviewed the year's activities and the favorable state of the union. It was a year, the President reported, in which "we continue to be highly favored in all the elements which contribute to individual comfort and to national prosperity. . . . We have peace without and tranquillity within our borders. . . ." Foreign trade relations had improved, except for those with the colonial possessions of Great Britain in America. An unusual reference was made to the death of Alexander I of Russia, a "long-tried, steady and faithful friend" of the United States. When the news of the Emperor's death reached John Quincy in February, he recorded that "through my agency he rendered essential good offices to my country. His influence upon the history of my life has been great and auspicious."[90]

In conclusion, the President paid tribute to the fiftieth anniversary of the day "when our independence was declared" and to two of the principal actors in that scene—"the hand that penned the ever-memorable Declaration and the voice that sustained it in debate who were by one summons, at the distance of 700 miles from each other, called before the Judge of All. . . . They departed cheered by the benediction of their country, to whom they left the inheritance of their fame and the memory of their bright example."[91]

Now that the members of Congress were back in the capital, Adams's list of visitors swelled. Even his evening hours were absorbed with them. On the ninth of December, his records showed that eleven Senators and thirty-three members of the House called. But it was not yet clear in what spirit Congress had assembled, whether they would be more conciliatory than the previous year or less. The parties were dividing, although the composition of them was not yet clearly defined. It seemed that Adams and Clay represented the national republicans while the Jacksonian party was just forming. Calhoun was certainly with them, expecting to carry the South. Van Buren and the northern contingent were not yet committed. Any vague hope that the President had held that he would be able to unite the factions into a Utopian sequel to the era of good feelings was now abandoned.

CHAPTER 18

The Tragic Presidency

"My anticipations for the two succeeding years call for more than Stoic fortitude."

JOHN QUINCY ADAMS

O N DECEMBER 16, just returned from England, John King, Rufus King's oldest son and secretary of the American lega- tion in London, dined with the President, bringing with him the convention that settled the amount of the indemnity for the slaves carried away during the War of 1812. Albert Gallatin negotiated the treaty, which required Great Britain to pay the sum of $1,204,960. John Quincy was very pleased, "in better spirits during the last week than I have ever known him," Charles said.[1]

But in reality, this was small comfort. Larger, more complex, and more charged problems with the British remained unresolved, in- cluding one that related to a pet Adams principle, complete mari- time reciprocity. When Gallatin arrived in England, he found that by Orders in Council, England had forbidden all trade in American vessels between the British West Indies and the United States. The move was justified, the British claimed, because the American Con- gress had failed to act on an 1825 Act of Parliament. What was even more serious, the British refused to negotiate on the subject.

At first Gallatin was puzzled by the extreme hostility to the United States that met all his attempts to reason with the foreign office, particularly Canning. After research, thought, and some information he gathered while in France on a brief trip, Gallatin deduced that Canning was, simply, angry at the American system of government. He resented the contents of a personal letter of instructions that Adams had sent to Richard Rush and which had been published by order of the American Senate. He fumed at a report, published by a congressional committee headed by Francis Baylies, that enumerated the claims of the United States to the Oregon Territory. Gallatin tried, with gentle reason, to explain that these acts were in keeping with the American system. The disgruntled Englishman replied that American congressional committees had too much power and their freedom of language was likely to enmesh their country in war. Gallatin wrote to Adams that he was certain that the Baylies Report had been, at the least, the immediate cause for the British Order in Council.[2] He reassured the President that Canning's malice was not directed toward him. On the contrary, Canning's chargé, H. U. Addington, told Adams that Canning preferred his election to that of any of the other contenders, particularly since another's election would have lost Adams the State Department.[3]

The British interdict was not scheduled to go into effect until December 1 so countervailing measures could not be taken until then. Adams, who expected that the opposition would make the most of their opportunity to use the subject to attack him, believed that Congress should pass an act totally excluding American ships from trading with British colonies in the West Indies and in all of North America. However, provision should be made to reopen trade immediately upon Britain's capitulation. Adams decided to recommend his proposal but to go along with whatever the legislative branch decided.[4]

The rebellious Congress had no intention of bailing out the President. In February a bill was introduced into the Senate that provided for retaliation against British shipping, which, just as Adams expected, was immediately subjected to Van Buren's manipulations. He managed to get it amended in such a way as to have its meaning twisted and made an embarrassment to the Administration. It passed the Senate but was stopped in the House, which was still presided over by Adamsite John W. Taylor. A conference committee failed to resolve the differences between the two houses, so since Congress was about to adjourn the matter was left in the hands of

the Chief Executive. He had no choice but to prohibit trade between the United States and the British colonial ports as spelled out
in previous congressional acts. However Adams took the mildest
course possible, following up his mandated act with lenient Treasury orders.[5]

Partially in defense of and partially in explanation of his decision,
John Quincy wrote to Gallatin that the British action "has taken us
so much by surprise that a single short session of Congress has not
been sufficient to mature the system by which we may most effectively meet this new position assumed by the colonial monopoly of
Great Britain."[6] Though the Senate, in this instance, had taken the
British side, Adams warned Gallatin that this did not mean that
they would feel the same about issues such as the Northwest, the
navigation of the St. Lawrence River, and impressment. On the
contrary, "one inch of ground yielded . . . one step backward . . . one
hairsbreadth of compromise" on these matters would inflame Congress. In a more cheerful mood, Adams observed that since Britain
was undergoing great changes in her political and social system, she
would stay where she was. Unfortunately, however, Gallatin was
unwilling to stay at his post another year or two when "some turn in
the tide of affairs might have occurred" and he could then, with his
"conciliatory management of debatable concerns," improve Anglo-
American relations.[7]

Gallatin had no illusions about his assignment. He called it "the
most laborious foreign mission" at this time. Most of his time was
consumed by the Oregon question. The President had given him an
absolute mandate to insist on the 49th parallel as the division between the territory of Great Britain and the United States. As a
committed nationalist and expansionist himself, besides being convinced that it was the will of the people, Adams could accept no less.
Throughout the year and a half of tense negotiations, Gallatin
loyally adhered to his chief's orders. But, privately, he disagreed in
principle. Gallatin was a limitationist, certain that the Oregon Territory, separated as it was from the rest of the United States by the
Great American Desert, then considered an insuperable barrier,
would never be a permanent part of the United States. Eventuallly,
he thought, it would become an independent Pacific republic. Jefferson, who held this view, had passed it down to his political heirs
—Gallatin, Monroe, Crawford, Clay, Thomas Hart Benton, and,
probably, Madison.[8]

The struggle that was going on in London, therefore, was really between the two supernationalists, Adams and Canning. Gallatin was only the able, diplomatic puppet of his President. Though Oregon was of little interest to the British public, it was of critical importance to the commercial enterprise, the Hudson's Bay Company, which had a monopoly on its fur trade. The independent American trappers could not compete with the powerful British company.

Canning successfully convinced an apathetic British Cabinet that Oregon was important because of the future possibility of a flourishing trade with China. The British therefore countered the demand for the 49th parallel boundary with the proposal that the boundary be placed midstream in the Columbia River, an arrangement that could have deprived the United States of what is now two-thirds of the state of Washington.

Gallatin's instructions were to obtain a straight line on the 49th parallel to the sea. The one concession he was authorized to offer was free navigation on the Columbia River and its tributaries for all British subjects. Therefore, it was not long before it became obvious that settlement could not be made. Neither side was willing to yield, so the negotiations drifted into a discussion of renewal of the joint occupation agreement. Canning offered a fifteen-, twenty-, or even twenty-five-year extension, which appealed to the British since it would have allowed the Hudson's Bay Company ample time to establish a firm hold on the area. Gallatin refused, stating that he was briefed only for a ten-year extension of the original agreement.

Suddenly in June, the British plenipotentiaries accepted a simple renewal of the ten-year agreement, but wanted, in addition, certain declarations. Both parties should agree not to exercise any exclusive sovereignty or jurisdiction over the territory and the United States was not to set up a fort in the area of a territorial government. Gallatin, somewhat nonplussed, rejected the additions. He said that he was authorized to arrange a free trade agreement, a compact of joint exploitation open to commerce and settlement by both parties, without the need of further clarification. The American Minister argued that the Hudson's Bay Company was, in effect, a territorial government because it had a monopoly in the Northwest and its own security system. The United States, on the other hand, might need military posts to protect American traders and settlers from the Indians and the Indians from aggressors. Since an incorporated

monopoly was contrary to the American system, a territorial government had to be maintained for the sake of peace. It took a good
deal of flat, hard bargaining before Gallatin was able to persuade
the British that he could not accept the bans that they suggested. In
the end, a simple renewal of the old agreement was achieved. Gallatin fooled himself that Canning was willing to "let the country
gradually slide into the hands of the United States." Adams, more
hardheaded and more concerned with retaining the territory, did
not agree. He continued to distrust the British, while Gallatin, internationally minded, hoped for Anglo-American accord.[9]

Under no circumstances was Adams in a position to yield to the
British. Politically, his Administration could not have sustained the
congressional rage that would have ensued had any "American" soil
been given to the hated British. Though the final settlement of the
Oregon question was deferred for the time being, it was perhaps just
as well, for the "temper of the parties" was not propitious to a
benign solution. Somewhat disappointed, without ever having expected anything else, Adams had to console himself with the
thought that negotiations had managed to keep the peace. During
this winter of his discontent, a curious, even ludicrous relationship
evolved between Adams and his would-be assassin. In November
1826, Dr. Huntt came to the President to tell him that Dr. George
Todson, an assistant surgeon who had been cashiered by a court
martial for embezzlement of public stores, and whom, consequently,
Adams had refused to renominate to the Senate, had determined to
murder him. Huntt's informant was Colonel Randall, Todson's
lawyer, who believed that his client was serious.

Randall called on Adams himself and repeated that Todson was
completely capable of assassination, was utterly mad on the subject,
and might well make such an attempt on one of the President's
solitary, early-morning walks. Adams answered that he could not
reverse the court martial against Todson nor could he guard himself
"against the hand of an assassin." Randall, who was a phrenologist,
then added that his apprehension was intensified because of Todson's extraordinary organ of destruction, which lightened the matter
for Adams, who had no respect for the "science" of phrenology.

The next month, Todson managed to meet Adams and to demand that his nomination be sent to the Senate. When the President answered that he was willing to consider the doctor's threat
against his life as a momentary alienation of the mind, Todson nei-

ther denied nor disavowed his threats, merely saying that he gave up the idea when he was told that Adams showed compassion for him. The President, still refusing to accede to any of Todson's requests for office, wrote piously that "My life is in the hands of a higher power than the will of man."

Todson became a constant suppliant. In December, he asked for his expenses to return to New Orleans, saying that his assassination threat was absurd and that he was destitute. Adams refused him and he went away. In March, Todson, still in Washington, came to the President's house and asked for remission of his court martial, which required the payment of $47.00. To this Adams assented. But later in the month the doctor reappeared, grateful for the remission of the debt, but seeking further favors. Adams said that he could do nothing for him. In a week Todson was back, complaining that his fiancée's parents objected to his poverty and to the shadow on his character caused by his dismissal. Once more, the President said that he could do nothing and the doctor left quietly.

In June, Southard told the President that a vessel carrying some 112 Negroes, who had been illegally imported into the United States and were being transported back to the African colony, was delayed because the ship's surgeon had died at Savannah. Adams suggested Dr. Todson for the position, but Southard had heard so many negative things about the man that he did not want to give him the job. However, in time he was persuaded to relent. When Todson came to thank Adams for his intervention, the President warned him that his future would depend on the propriety of his conduct. Todson returned in December, having almost succumbed to African fever, with a report that the colony would prosper if given aid and not permitted to fall victim to the spirit of mercantile speculation among the colonists.[10] The following June, the President tried to send the apparently rehabilitated doctor with a company of displaced Indians. After that, Dr. Todson dropped from the annals of history, of interest only because of what he threatened to do and for President Adams's method of dealing with him.

Georgia's Governor Troup refused to be intimidated by either the President or the Congress. He continued with his program to oust the Creeks from Georgia land as rapidly as he could, sending his surveyors into the Indian land despite the law. When the Creeks retaliated by arresting the intruders, Troup ordered out the state militia to protect them and to see that the survey continued. Upon hearing the news from Georgia, Adams hastened to consult his Cabinet about taking steps. It was within the power of the executive to order out federal troops to arrest the surveyors but the President doubted the expediency of such a move. Clay advised sending the troops but, once again, Adams wanted Congress to act before he engaged in conflict. He would send a message to them, and in the meantime, at Barbour's suggestion, he would send a federal agent to warn the Georgians.

"This is the most momentous message I have sent to Congress," Adams wrote in his *Diary*. In the February 4 communication, the President informed the Congress that "under color of legal authority from the state of Georgia" surveys were being made of Indian lands in direct violation of the treaty of Washington made with the Creeks. So far, Adams said, he had abstained from military force to oust the surveyors because Georgia intimated that she would resist any such force and "a conflict *must* have ensued, which would itself have inflicted a wound upon the Union and have presented the aspect of one of these confederated states at war with the rest." However, if the state of Georgia persisted in the encroachment of Indian territories, "a superadded obligation even higher than that of human authority will compel the Executive of the United States to enforce the laws . . . by all the force committed for that purpose." This would be resorted to only if all other expedients failed.[11]

Adams worked long hours, often until midnight, researching the history of United States-Indian legal relations in the journals of Congress and the speeches of Washingon. He concluded that the problem had now become a conflict between the rights of the states and of the federal government, although the issue had been debatable ground more correctly under the Articles of Confederation than at the present time.[12]

Troup did not accept Adams's ultimatum gracefully. He angrily wrote to Rush that "from the first decisive act of hostility, you will be considered and treated as a public enemy." He promised, further, that he would resist any attack by the United States. Since the President had referred the subject to Congress, each house took up the challenge in its own way. The lower house, still partial to the Administration, reported that the United States should purchase title to all Indian lands in Georgia and, in the meantime, the treaty of Washington was in force. The hostile Senate committee, headed by Benton, adopted the concept that the treaty of Indian Springs vested the title to the lands in Georgia and, therefore, the state could not be attacked by the United States. For better or worse, the issue settled itself in November when the Creeks agreed to a treaty giving up all their claims. The Cherokees, who on July 26, 1827, attempted to solve their conflict with Georgia by adopting a national constitution similar to the United States Constitution, and declaring themselves an independent nation, fared no better. The Georgia legislature passed a law that all white persons in Cherokee territory were immediately subject to Georgia law and, in 1830, the Act would be extended to include the Indians.[13]

The humane Adams Indian policy which attempted to delay the removal of the Indians ended in futility. Andrew Jackson, a renowned Indian fighter, was the hero of the times and the country's sympathy rested with him and with his harsh Indian policies. Finally, all that Adams accomplished in Georgia was to alienate the state.

During the winter of 1827, Charles, barely twenty, fell in love with Abigail Brooks, a daughter of Peter C. Brooks of Medford, Massachusetts, a very wealthy businessman who had served as a federalist in the Massachusetts legislature for many years. Abby and Charles met while she was visiting her sister and brother-in-law, Mr. and Mrs. Edward Everett, who were living in Washington because Everett was a Congressman from Massachusetts. After a short acquaintance, Charles decided to declare his serious intentions. Both fathers thought that the couple was too young to marry but finally consented to an engagement. John Quincy wrote to Mr. Brooks that he had made it a rule to allow his sons freedom to make their own choices "in that most important of all connections, the partnership of life." But, although he approved most highly of his choice, Charly was under twenty-one and had not completed his education. The President agreed to recognize the youth's proposal to become engaged but did not want him to marry before he was of age. Charly, Adams told Mr. Brooks, had a sedate and considerate character, a studious disposition, and a high and delicate sense of humor, habits that were domestic and regular, and a generous and benevolent temper. Hence, an early marriage was more congenial to him than it would be to a youth of more ardent passions. Should you agree, he told Brooks, my hopes are for their "highest happiness."[14]

The course of true love never did run smooth. On March 6, Charles was shaken by a letter that Abby received from her father ordering her to delay her answer to Charles for the present. She was away from home, he said. They were both very young and her parents had no personal knowledge of the young man.[15] Everett wrote to his father-in-law for more specific instructions and then, humanely, carried off his wife and sister-in-law to Harper's Ferry for a short vacation. Charles stayed home and suffered, finding the situation "extremely painful" and trying to refrain from being angry with Mr. Brooks.

When the Everett party returned from the Shenandoah Valley, there was a second letter from Mr. Brooks mailed the day after the other, withdrawing his request for the delay and giving his full consent. Charly observed that he could have been spared the week's pain but concentrated on enjoying the remainder of Abby's visit before she had to return to Medford.

Congress adjourned quietly on March 3. The night before, John Quincy and his two sons rode to the Capitol where, assisted by Clay, Rush, Barbour, and Southard, the President read bills for four or five hours and then stayed until 2 A.M. signing about forty of them into law. It was obvious to him that his Administration had run into an immoveable wall of opposition. None of the nationalist measures that he had advocated in his hapless first annual message had been acted upon. The newspapers and the public had developed an indifference to the Washington scene and instead became absorbed in the constant anti-Administration tirades of such newspapers as the Albany *Argus,* the Richmond *Enquirer,* and Duff Green's United States *Telegraph* on the monotonous subject of the corrupt bargain charge.[16] The only bill that pleased Adams to sign or that seemed to him of any lasting benefit was the half million dollars appropriated yearly for the gradual improvement of the Navy.

The burden of office was becoming heavier and lonelier for Adams. "I can scarcely conceive of a more harassing, wearying, teasing condition of existence," he said pathetically. Retirement could not be worse than "this perpetual motion and crazing cares." His loss of privacy was one of the most painful prices paid for public life. "I can never be sure of writing a line that will not someday be published by friend or foe. . . . This condition of things gives style the cramp." Even physically, the strain was showing. He complained of a catarrhal oppression on his lungs which "produced listlessness and depression." Louisa also noted that he was more unwell than he had been in years and was losing weight fast.[17]

The beauty of nature, which he observed minutely on his daily walks, was one of the few continuing sources of pleasure for the President. He noted "the putting forth of the leaves" and asked Rush to help him with the project of procuring seeds and plants from foreign countries so that he could plant them in the garden of the Columbian Institute. The subject of the production and growth of fruit and forest trees absorbed a lot of his reading. In his *Diary*, he recorded the trees he observed, the trees he planted, and their progress. On April 24, he wrote, "This A.M. with Antoine, planted 4 rows of large Pennsylvania walnuts, 9 Quincy walnuts, 8 hazelnuts. . . ." It was a wide new field that had opened to him but, he said with regret, in the remnant of his life still left to him there would be little time to explore its possibilities.[18]

The psychological importance of this new avocation was intuitively understood by Adams. "My health and spirits droop and the attempt to sustain them by . . . botany, the natural history of the trees, and the purpose of naturalizing exotics, is almost desperate."[19] When friends and relatives went abroad, he requested clippings of plants. Thomas B. Johnson, his nephew, who sailed to the south of France for a year or two to recover his health, was asked to send home a box of acorns from the cork oak packed in sand, and a small jar of olives which propagate in the sand.[20]

As the weather grew warmer, Adams eyed his swimming hole with interest. But his health was still "drooping." He had no particular complaints, only a loss of appetite, general weakness, and a weight loss so great that he could scarcely wear his last year's clothes. The certainty that his career was finished added to his despair. All around him he saw only treachery and plotting. Van Buren, who had just returned from a tour of the South begun at the close of the last session of Congress, was now General Jackson's man, Adams observed accurately. "He is now acting over the part in the affairs of the union which Aaron Burr performed in 1799 and 1800: and there is much resemblance of character, manners, and even person between the two men." However, Van Buren had "improved as much in the art of electioneering upon Burr as the State of New York has grown in relative strength and importance in the Union. . . ."[21] Van Buren's trip had been more successful than Adams realized. The New Yorker had welded a North-South alliance, laying a foundation for the democratic party, thus reviving the two-party system.[22]

Adams had not changed his mind about electioneering. "They

work by slander to vitiate public opinion, and pay for defamation to receive their reward in votes," he said. When some friends urged him to attend a celebration of the opening of the Pennsylvania canal and to meet the German farmers and talk to them in their own language, the President refused. This mode of electioneering suited neither his taste nor his principles. "I think it equally unsuitable to my personal character and to the station in which I am placed," he said.[23] It disgusted Adams that politics and electioneering seemed to be the only subject of discussion for men in the public service. In several states at this time there were meetings, counter meetings, committees of correspondence, delegations, addresses for and against the Administration. Thousands of people, said Adams, were engaged in little else but working up the passions of the people in preparation for the election, still more than eighteen months distant.[24]

His basic principles of living became almost an obsession with John Quincy. A friend brought him a signet ring which he had commissioned him to have executed in London from his own design. The device was a cock with the motto, "Watch." It symbolized the precept of Jesus, who had used the cock as a monitor to call to duty the disciple who had denied him, to pray as well as watch. Though Adams was not satisfied with the ring, finding it crudely done, he wrote a poem, which he sent to his son George, called *Watch and Pray: Sonnet to Chanticleer.*

> Minstrel of morn whose eager ken decries
> > The ray first beaming from night's regions drear;
> > Herald of light, whose clarion sharp and clear
> Proclaims the dawning day-star of the skies.
>
> Bird of the brave, whose valiant heart supplies
> > The beak of eagles and the falcon's spear;
> > Bird of the lofty port, disdaining fear,
> Unvanquish'd spirit, which o'ercomes or dies.
>
> Bird of the faithful, thy resounding horn
> To thee was given the child of man to warn
> > Of sinking virtue and of rising day.
> Oh, while from morn to morn I hear thy strain,
> Let the shrill summons call me not in vain
> > With fervor from on high to Watch and Pray.

George, who had been ill most of the winter, met with a minor accident in the early summer. When Louisa read his letter, she burst into tears and insisted on going to Boston immediately. Neither John Quincy nor anyone else was able to dissuade her. She departed accompanied by two servants, leaving Mary Hellen to take care of the family.[25]

Adams rejoiced "with trembling" at Louisa's news that their son's health improved during the next few weeks. Louisa, much relieved, arranged that John and Johnson Hellen would meet her in New York on the way back to the "Presoliad." However, the President, with Charley as his secretary, decided to go to Quincy for the months of August and September, staying with his brother's family. When she received the news, Louisa arranged to go to Long Branch. John Quincy "swooned" at the thought of staying in such a place and could never be persuaded to either visit her in such a watering place or vacation in one.

On July 31, an hour before he was scheduled to leave for home, Adams received despatches from Governor Cass of Michigan reporting that hostilities had broken out with the Winnebago Indians. Adams almost postponed his journey, but his miserable health, complicated by sleepless nights and his doctor's diagnosis of erysipelas which the northern climate was supposed to help, persuaded him that he had better not change his plans. His mental condition was equally poor. For the last several months, he had been so depressed that he sometimes wished that his life was terminated. The curtailment of his swimming to between ten to twenty minutes a day frustrated him almost more than anything else.[26]

While in Baltimore, Adams saw John Sergeant, newly returned from Tacubaya, Mexico, where the proposed congress had never been held. Sergeant brought back a disquieting report about the American Minister, Joel Poinsett, whose recall, he said, might be demanded by the Mexican government. This news was not entirely unexpected, for Clay had mentioned in May that Poinsett seemed to be mixed up with party movements and political Masonry in the border country.

A month later Henry Clay wrote to Adams that Poinsett must be recalled immediately, and at the same time Richard Rush indicated that he would like to replace him. Adams decided to postpone his decision until he returned to Washington. The charges, which were vague, Poinsett denied. Somehow the American had become involved with Masonic societies which turned out to have political repercussions. However, as soon as he had discovered this to be true, he had withdrawn. Adams believed that to recall Poinsett now would be to yield to congressional zeal and pressure.[27]

In reality Poinsett had tried to deal with the anti-American setup in Mexico caused by British influence. In order to neutralize the power of the pro-British Scottish-rite Masons, he encouraged the organization of York-rite Masons and suggested that they function as political clubs. When the Mexican government got wind of this, they demanded Poinsett's recall, to which Adams had to accede. It was quite clear that meddling with Mexican internal affairs was acceptable only when the British and the French Ministers indulged in the sport. After their revolution against Spain, control of the Latin American countries had fallen into the hands of the landed upper classes, who related better to aristocratic France and Britain than to republican United States.[28]

The reunion of the Adams family in New York, the first time all the clan had been together since March 1825, was not a huge success if Charles's account can be taken at face value. George's manners were strange; Louisa was neither in good health nor in good spirits and the President was depressed.[29] The next day after dinner, the contingent bound for Quincy took leave of Louisa and boarded the steamboat. Twenty-six hours later, the President was in Quincy.

Adams's health improved immediately. "My native air is as cheering to me as ever," he wrote. Immediately he plunged into an energetic program of planting and botanical experiments.

Louisa was not as fortunate. John, who accompanied her on this year's trip, proved to be as unsatisfactory a companion as Charles had been the year before. He was a "tyrant," she told Mary Hellen, "who will have everything his own way." She complained that all the Adams men were peculiarly severe and harsh towards women without consideration for their constitutional weaknesses. It was her fate to live among beings "utterly superior to myself and to wage eternal war against the scorn and contempt which has long been my portion. . . ." In a paroxysm of self-pity, Mrs. Adams lamented that she could not meet the exactions of her husband and children, who took her sickness for ill-temper and her sufferings for unwillingness. She warned Mary Hellen that tenderness was an essential ingredient for a woman's happiness, but it was a trait that she would not find if she connected herself with an Adams.[30]

While in Massachusetts, John Quincy arranged for Charles, who had just become twenty-one, to enter Daniel Webster's law office and to lodge at a boarding house at 3 Cambridge Street, Boston, run by Mrs. Ann Wilson. An earlier plan, favored by both the President and his wife, was to set up Charles and George in a house with Louisa Smith to take care of them. It had to be abandoned because George was unhappy with it. Adams went to Medford to visit Charles's future parents-in-law and was satisfied with their kind reception. It was proving to be a very restful and satisfying vacation— reading, working in the seedling nursery and the garden, bathing at light tide, excursions, visits, dinners, and fishing. However, Adams asked his wife to send John back to Quincy as soon as she could spare him.[31]

John joined his father at the family mansion as requested, but he brought discouraging news from the capital. The Adamsites were very despondent and "look very blue." This did not make the President any more willing to change his style in any way. He told George Sullivan of New York that he could not receive the support of any man who expected any personal consideration in return and was aware that the New Jersey *Patriot* turned against him because Stockton did not get the job as district judge. "The loss of political, and what is far more bitter, of personal friends for the faithful and fearless discharge of my duty is a calamity in which I have been for twenty years steeped," he said, and even more pointedly added, "If the sole object of a President of the United States were to secure his own re-election perhaps the exclusive appointment of his friends to office might be in his hands an effective electioneering engine."[32]

George brought his father the news that George Canning was dead. That he was "an implacable and rancourous enemy of the United States," Adams regarded as certain. But, he told Rush, "his death buried in my bosom all the feelings of resentment which his conduct towards us had kindled," and aroused the hope that his successors would be better and wiser men. However, Gallatin soon discovered that Huskisson was just as intransigent to the United States as his predecessor because he had an "undue and illiberal jealousy" of the growth of American shipping and navigation.[33]

Adams's return to Washington was as close to a triumphal tour as the cold, austere, uncharismatic President enjoyed during his term of office. A committee requested that he spend a few days in New York but he was unable to accede because letters urging his immediate return to Washington had come from Clay. However, when John Quincy's steamboat docked at Philadelphia, a great crowd of people was assembled to greet him with three cheers and accompany him to the United States Hotel where they cheered him again. Southard met him there with the news that Clay's letter was about an impending war with the Winnebago Indians but later despatches explained that the two Indians who had been involved in the murders that were to touch off the war had surrendered to the United States authorities and the crisis was over. Adams stayed in the city of brotherly love for another day, receiving a constant stream of visitors, including Count de Survilliers, the title by which Joseph Bonaparte was known while he lived in Bordentown. A letter came from a Baltimore committee asking the President to visit that city, to which he acceded.

Before he left Philadelphia, Adams boarded the battleship *Pennsylvania*—136 guns, which would be the largest ship to float upon the ocean. Built chiefly of oak, the President noted that she looked like a city. When several thousands gathered on the wharf, the President told those nearest to him that he would shake hands with them all if they would clear a path for him, which they did. And as the ship left the pier, he heard three cheers, which greeting he returned by waving and shouting, "God bless you all!" to the orderly crowd. The unaccustomed public adulation pleased Adams. "I trust that no vain or unworthy sentiment of excitation mingles with the cheering glow of thoughts and the solemn reflections which they excite in my mind," he wrote. The Adams partisans in Philadelphia were smugly confident that the presidential visit would help them to carry the election for congressional candidate, John Sergeant.

In Baltimore the reception plans were delayed because of the funeral of Colonel Howard. Adams solved the dilemma by attending the funeral, which took most of the day. On Sunday, he went to a Roman Catholic church, which was not unusual, where he was interested to see two large pictures presented by the late and present Kings of France. After that, a crowd of 20,000 people of all classes and all political opinions came to see the President. The clamor was no less than in Philadelphia but somewhat less pleasing. Some of the visitors were drunk and boisterous, but many said that they hoped Adams would be re-elected. The political truth was, however, disquieting. The week before, there had been an election for members of the state legislature in which the friends of the Administration both in the city and the country around Baltimore had been unsuccessful. Nevertheless, the memory of the cordiality that he experienced from "multitudes of our fellow citizens" warmed the heart of the crusty President. He told his son George that their continuous and affecting kindness was entitled "to all my gratitude."[34]

Louisa, a practiced observer of Adams habits, also noted that the receptions in the two great cities of the East were a joy to her husband. "If he would only lend himself a little to the usages and manners of the people without hiding himself and too modestly rejecting their civilities, no man could be more popular because his manners are simple, unostentatious, and unassuming," she observed to Charles. She had sent the carriage and coachman for the President, who was escorted to the turnpike by a committee of about twenty gentlemen. At the start of the highway, Adams got out of the carriage, the men dismounted, and he thanked them. The contingent of notables returned to Baltimore and the Adams coachman whipped up his horses and drove back to the President's house, where they arrived by four in the afternoon. Louisa was unwell, but not confined to bed, and had invited Clay, Rush, Barbour, and Southard to dine with them that evening.

Returned to his desk, piled high with mail, Adams complained that of all the letters he had been doomed to read since he had become President, one small file would keep those worth preserving. About 150 people visited him on the first work day back in Washington, 100 of whom were mail contractors who had agreed to carry the mail for the next three or four years. Adams received them in the winter parlor, shook hands with them, served them cake and wine, and then personally conducted them on a tour of the President's house. He offered a toast—success to all "through the highways and byways."[35] Their mission reminded him of his internal-improvements program, which would increase the post roads and hence the numbers of those who carried the mail on them.

Adams partisans brought the President increasing evidence that his declining popularity was due in part to his policy of public appointments. New York City was lost, Joseph Blunt said, although he had some hope for the state. General Jackson had active political workers who were influencing public opinion for him. Their avowed policy would be that "party services shall be rewarded," which made their partisans active and zealous. "Your friends," the desperate New Yorker dared to say, "only give lukewarm aid to the cause." Blunt begged the President to give this matter consideration. But he stood no more chance of changing Adams's ideas than did Clay, who had, once more, brought up Postmaster General McLean's insidious hostility to the Administration, lately implemented by giving out patronage to those opposed to the President. In New York, for instance, almost every officer in the customs house and post office was anti-Administration. Adams's reply to the evidence was simply that McLean had greatly improved the post office and was very likely the best head the Department had ever had. He disappointed Clay further when he refused to answer his constituents' questions about Adams's public accounts and his position when a Senator on the Louisiana Purchase. It was a lack of propriety to have correspondence with an electioneering committee on these subjects, Adams said.

The Van Buren machine was operating at top efficiency as Webster and Rochester duly noted. The northerners, hoping to counter it, suggested that Clay be run for Vice President, an idea that Southard immediately told the President he was against. Barbour, who thought New York a lost cause, was Adams's preference for a vice presidential candidate, although he realized that the subject was a delicate one.

It seemed from John Quincy's attitude that he had already admitted defeat to himself. There was a movement against the Administration in all the local parties, he noted, which could result only in disaster. It was much more satisfactory to plant trees lovingly and list each one in his *Diary*. Around his enclosure of oaks he now had a border of a chestnut, a willow, a black walnut, a persimmon, a tulip tree, and a lime. And he eased the pain of his dying hopes with the reflection that his trees would outlast many Presidents.

"Your letters are becoming a necessary of life to me," Adams wrote to Charles. The President had promised to direct his son's reading, and with increasing pleasure recommended his favorite authors and commented on them. It was "luxurious entertainment" for the harassed Chief Executive to reread classical literature and, with a scholar's glee, pass on his appreciation for Cicero, Pliny, Madame de Sévigné, Pope, Voltaire, Rousseau, and Pascal. The epistolary style, he told Charles, had been used for every kind of literary composition. Liebnitz and Newton wrote mathematical treatises in letters while Locke and Sidney used it to expound political theory, "as did your grandfather." Rousseau and Richardson wrote novels and political codes, and "for delightful letters on nothing," John Quincy advised his son to read Madame de Sévigné.

Once a week Adams sent off to Boston at least four closely written pages, which distilled the wisdom he had acquired in a lifetime of reading. After Pascal, read Plato's *Protagoras, Gorgias,* and the first *Alcibiades,* he suggested. Compare the Sophists of the age of Socrates with the Jesuits at the time of Pascal. The study of morals "gives us the wisdom and virtue of former ages for the guidance of our own conduct but the application of any lessons we have learnt must always be made by the operation of our own mind." Though he was constantly interrupted, ten times in one evening, the fond father wrote way into the night. He placed Napoleon below Cromwell, who held his usurpation until his death, because Napoleon was merely "a military and political gambler; playing every stake for himself; and doubling his stakes in utter defiance of the doctrine of chances, till it was impossible that he should not lose the game."[36]

The time for preparing the annual message was approaching, but there seemed to be no time for it because of the stream of visiting Congressmen. It was a curiosity to Adams that even those who were "bitter as wormwood" in their opposition to his Administration were ready to come to dinner, introduce their friends to the President, and recommend them for office. All were accepted, friend or enemy, except for John Randolph, whose "besotted violence" excluded him.[37]

When the third message was finally written, with little enthusiasm for it, Adams submitted it to his Cabinet. It was too long and he wanted their advice on how to streamline it. The Secretaries objected at once to the complimentary paragraphs on the Postmaster General's handling of his job. Adams acceded and abridged them. Rush persuaded the President to tone down and shorten his comments on internal improvements. Some pressure from New York supporters to add to his message a recommendation for the protection of domestic manufactures was turned down. Since his southern friends were equally insistent that he say nothing, he decided it was the safest course, particularly when taking sides could appear to be improper interference in order to influence Congress.

The Twentieth Congress was anti-Administration in both houses, a situation that had never before occurred. The first act of the newly constituted House of Representatives was to elect a Speaker who represented the majority party. Former Speaker, John W. Taylor, received only four votes, while Andrew Stevenson of Virginia won with 104 votes. Adams's loss of strength was immediately obvious. As he predicted, it was to be a Congress "unexampled in factious violence and fury."

President Adams seemed to have bowed to his fate, for his annual message was simply a workmanlike review of the past year. After commenting on its peace and prosperity, he outlined the condition of foreign affairs and reviewed the various departmental reports. Only in the last paragraphs were there some discreet suggestions, wholly undeveloped, as to what Congress might take up. He mentioned the debt that the country owed to the remaining Revolutionary War veterans, the need to extend the judiciary to meet the expanding country, and the need for amelioration of the harsh bankruptcy laws.[38] Adams was already behaving like a lame-duck President. And his appointments submitted to the new Senate continued to be based on his system of nominating for reappointment all officers whose Commissions expired unless misconduct was charged against them. That this did not suit his "Falstaff friends who follow for the reward," he accepted with good grace and thereby sealed his destiny.[39]

The growing momentum of the Jackson forces did not keep over 3,000 guests from attending the Adams's New Year's Day open house. The moderate temperature helped to bring out about two-thirds of the members of Congress, all the foreign ministers, all the heads of the departments, and a sprinkling of minor officials and private citizens. Everyone was in high good humor and conducted themselves with propriety. After the crowd left, the weary President, with nothing to ponder on but the bad news that the legislature of Georgia had nominated Crawford for Vice President just as it had nominated him for President the year before, retreated to his room. There he persevered until his *Diary* for the departed year was closed and he had prayed for strength proportional to the trials of the coming year.

Now that his own career seemed to be drawing to a close, Adams turned to his sons' prospects with added interest. The letters to Charles sounded more and more like sermons, which did not appeal to the young man, as he noted in his *Diary*. Now he, too, received the sonnet about Chanticleer and early rising which his father tediously advocated as "the cure-all for moments of discouragement and despondency." It became obvious that he placed his hopes on his youngest son. George continued almost criminally negligent with his accounts and erratic in his behavior. Early rising and regular diary-keeping were rather simplistic solutions for the emotional turmoil and constant hypochondria that George suffered from. He was beyond John Quincy's easy adage that the regular keeping of his diary helped especially in moments of great agitation, because it brought relief "to tell the tale of woe."[40]

At no time in his life did John seem a likely candidate for the Adams mantle. In November he became engaged to Mary Hellen, a blow to George, who never got over his strange infatuation for her, and a source of anger to his father. The President disapproved of marrying before one was self-supporting. Louisa, who had been in the middle of Mary's flirtations with all of her sons at one time or another, was always somewhat embarrassed that the difficult, fickle girl was her niece.

Charles received an extra hundred dollars from his father around Christmas time. It was for extraordinary expenses and to stimulate him to do some of his father's copying. Charles had been pressing for more money, claiming that he required more than his two brothers because of the expense of courting Abby Brooks. It was a match that Adams approved of. His hopes but faintly hidden between the lines, his father wrote to Charles: "All my success in the world has been the blessing of Heaven upon Drudgery. . . . May yours be more brilliant and more durable."[41]

Charles, in one of the frequent letters that examined his feelings, wrote that he disliked the idea of a political existence. Somehow John Quincy twisted this into a criticism of himself. "I've never sought office but I have no dislike of it," he said testily. "In a Republican Government the Country has a *right* to the services of every Citizen. And each Citizen is bound in duty to perform the service. . . ." Or did the older man hope that his son would succeed him as he did his father?[42]

During the early winter of 1828, preparations were made for the Adams-Hellen wedding, although Louisa reported to George, "Strange to say, neither by word or look has your father intimated the idea of such an event taking place." His disapproval was being shown by silence, which even extended to refusing to speak to Mary. Both Charles and George received wedding invitations, but neither attended.

On February 25, the wedding took place in the Blue Room at

the President's house. Unlike similar future occasions, it was a modest affair. Abigail Adams, one of the four bridesmaids, recorded that the bride looked very handsome in white satin, orange blossoms, and pearls. John Quincy wrote to Charles that he should "wish them [the newlyweds] with me all possible happiness," suggesting that he was reconciled to the event, and forwarded a piece of wedding cake.[43] The newspapers noted the occasion briefly.

Her son's marriage plunged Louisa into a depression that she could not control. Mary, she said, was "as cool, easy and indifferent as ever. . . . John looks already as if he had all the cares in the world on his shoulders and my heart tells me that there is much to fear. . . ." She disapproved of the young people's decision to live in the White House and she resented the fact that they made their plans without consulting either her or the President. "The idea of having a married son in my House has always been painfully disagreeable to me," Louisa grumbled. Consequently, she announced that she would confine herself to her room, a device that she had employed in the past when annoyed with her family. Charles, who was the recipient of his mother's complaints, remarked that she "has lost all the elasticity of her character. . . . I cannot comprehend what makes her so low."[44]

The Twentieth Congress seemed dedicated to the harassment of the President. The committees sent to the executive office about five times more requests for facts and opinions than they had to his predecessors. Sometimes the House and Senate committees made the same calls, so that double labor was required. Adams just stood by, helplessly seething at their open hostility.

Richard Rush, who had been the most stalwart defender of the President in the Cabinet, spoke frequently about how his health was being destroyed by the work of the Treasury Department. He mentioned that he would be glad to accept the mission to London or any other vacancy. Adams, who saw the bid for what it was, commented wryly that it was the "preference of the harbor to the tempest." He promised to do all in his power to gratify his friend's wishes.[45]

In pamphlets, newspapers, handbills, stump speeches, and tavern talk, the Adams Administration was reviled and accused. Even in Congress inquiries were made into the President's public conduct in the distant past, such as the vote on the acquisition of Louisiana, the Mississippi and fishery question at Ghent, and, more recently, the Panama congress. The suspicion that Adams had somehow instituted the Congress persisted. Van Buren always believed it to be a strong possibility that, although organized in South America, "the inspiration which suggested it was of Washington origin.[46]

John Randolph's tireless rancor against Adams was equalled only by that of Virginia's Governor William B. Giles. "The issue of the presidential election will kill them by the gratification of their revenge," Adams quipped.

De Witt Clinton's unexpected death at this time caused repercussions in New York that were potentially ominous to the Administration. John Quincy believed Clinton to be one of the first post-Revolutionary great men of the age but said that his mind was of secondary size. Though he and Clinton had not been friends, Adams had to recognize that now Van Buren, a confirmed Jacksonite, was most likely to be the most powerful New Yorker.

Condemned to vacate their lands, the Georgia Cherokees sent a published copy of their written constitution to the President, hoping that this would save them. Governor Troup immediately declared that this was in violation of the article in the U.S. Constitution that forbade the formation of a new state within any of the separate states. Adams did not think that the article was applicable in this case because the Indians could not, by writing a constitution, change their relationship with the United States or establish an independent civilized government within the United States. The Cabinet, after discussing the issue and failing to come to an agreement, decided to study it.

Two weeks later, the Cabinet agreed that the article in the constitution only applied to those who had been parties to the compact and therefore not to the Indians. However, Clay urged Adams to refrain from saying so to the Governor as it was up to Congress to direct the President to act on the issue. Finally, Adams ordered Secretary of War Barbour to instruct the United States agent to inform the Cherokees that their constitution could not in any way alter their relationship with the United States. In the meantime, the Governor of Georgia had declared that the jurisdiction of the state extended to Cherokee lands, regardless of their constitution.

Mounting feeling over the coming election erupted into the usual accumulation of newspaper slanders, but Russell Jarvis, a rejected office seeker, formerly an Adamsite, set off a series of events that at least struck an original note. Jarvis, a thirty-seven-year-old writer for the anti-Administration Washington *Telegraph*, a graduate of

Dartmouth College and Tapping Reeves's Law School, as was fairly common for many of Adams's enemies, did not scruple to visit the White House drawing rooms. On April 2, he came and introduced a number of ladies and other members of a party from Boston to Louisa. In the East Room, the group stood within earshot of John Adams and Reverend Caleb Stetson, pastor of the Medford Church. Stetson asked young Adams, "Who is that lady?" nodding his head at the Jarvis group. John replied in a loud voice that she was Russell Jarvis's wife and then added, as if he intended to be heard, "*There* is a man who, if he had any idea of propriety, ought not to show his face in this house." The visitors took note of the statement and left. John Adams was particularly angry at Jarvis because the newspaperman had recently revived the scurrilous story that when President Adams had been Minister to Russia he had handed over the beautiful Martha Godfrey, the Adamses' nursemaid, to Czar Alexander for lascivious purposes.

On April 8, having pondered the matter and no doubt discussed its political potential with his friends, Jarvis sent a note to young Adams. The intermediary was Alexander C. McLean, who had witnessed John's remarks at the White House levee. John acknowledged to McLean that he had made the alleged statements but refused to make a written reply. Frustrated, but unwilling to drop the matter, Jarvis waited. On April 15, John Adams, acting as his father's secretary, carried some papers containing nominations to the Senate and the House of Representatives to the Capitol. While passing through the rotunda, he was assaulted and struck in the face by Jarvis. There was some difference of opinion among eyewitnesses about whether Jarvis actually pulled John's nose as he claimed, but John did turn on him with his cane and strike at him before spectators could separate the two men.

The fracas was witnessed by William Emmons of Boston, Clement Dorsey, a House member from Maryland, and Colonel Gardner of the Post Office Department. The President did not hear of the event until that evening when Everett came to report it and to suggest that the President inform Congress officially. Adams answered that he would wait awhile because he felt that it was Congress's affair rather than his since it occurred within congressional walls. But he was quite doubtful that a body as hostile as it was would act in behalf of either his son or himself.

The Cabinet disagreed with the President. They wanted Adams

to send a message to Congress outlining the assault on his son. Clay, veteran of many duels, the most experienced member on points of honor, was adamant that a message should go at once. Attorney General Wirt, with a lawyer's caution, counselled passing by the episode without notice saying that such a position would demonstrate more calmness and dignity. He was overwhelmingly overruled.

Chief clerk of the Department of State, Daniel Brent, carried the President's message. It stated that the President's private secretary, while on public business within the Capitol, "was waylaid and assaulted." The President asked the Congress "whether any further laws or regulations are necessary to insure security in the official intercourse between the President and Congress." In its deliberations on the subject, the President said, "It is neither expected nor desired that any consequence shall be attached to the private relation in which my secretary stands to me."[47]

At once, the incident became meat for the political grinder. Committees of investigation were formed by Congress, but not in good will. Daniel Webster reported to Adams that Nathaniel Macon was the only opposition Senator who admitted that the outrage was unjustifiable. At the inevitable congressional hearings, John Adams and Jarvis were both summoned and witnesses were called. Finally, by a bare majority, Jarvis's act was censured by the House of Representatives, less because of the insult to the President's son and messenger than for its display of contempt for the sanctity of the Congress's home. As a device for forcing a duel that would involve the First Family, it failed. It did, however, re-emphasize the weakness of the presidential position with Congress.

For a time, Louisa was terrified that there was a plot to wipe out her family. She trembled every time either John or George, who was visiting Washington, went out. However, as time passed and there was no further incident, she told Charles that if the unhappy event went no further, it would have had the happy effect of uniting the family.[48]

Spring and horticulture again lifted the President's flagging spirits. His seedling trees that he had planted from nuts grew in his nursery. He particularly watched the cork oak from Spain, which was his favorite. It mortified him that, despite his efforts, the United States, unlike European nations, paid no attention to the cultivation of forest trees. In his opinion, he wrote to Charles, it was one of the most important branches of political economy. Charles answered, somewhat cruelly, that his father's passion for planting was a substitute in old age for more pungent passions. Adams denied this, saying that he did not have the means earlier in his life to indulge in these interests.[49]

Just before the Twentieth Congress retired for the summer, it passed a tariff known to history as the Tariff of Abominations. Guided to a successful conclusion by the wily red fox of Kinderhook, John Randolph said that it referred to manufactures of no sort or kind except the manufacture of the President of the United States. Its victim was to be John Quincy Adams.

Historians differ in their interpretation of Van Buren's tariff policy. Unwilling to appear to be against protection, necessary to the North and the East, equally unwilling to support a high protective tariff for fear of antagonizing the cotton-growing South which was dependent on overseas sales, a farce was arranged. The tariff bill would be written with schedules that were so ridiculous that they would be laughed into rejection, each partisan having his own motive for rejection. For example, molasses, which New England needed to have imported free, would have a high tariff on it, while woolens, for which New England competed with England, had its duties lowered. The bill's Grand Guignol design was to trap the President. If he signed it, the South would damn him for a protectionist. If he vetoed it, the North would condemn him as a traitor to his own peole. A revisionist interpretation stated, however, that its authors designed it to pass so that it would help Jackson, in the election, "preserve harmony among the New York Republicans, win the doubtful state of Pennsylvania and the northwest to Jackson's candidacy, and set the troublesome issue of the tariff at rest for the electoral campaign."[50] Both interpretations agreed that the tariff harmed the President.

Adams signed the tariff bill because he believed that since the Act was constitutionally passed, it was his obligation not to veto it. But he recognized its significance for him. In defiance of South Carolina and Georgia, he confided in Charles, "they have passed a tariff bill for the protection of American manufactures and added appendages to burden New England." It was a fitting close to a congressional session unexampled in United States history. "A majority of both houses of Congress, composed of every material of factions . . . melted by a common disappointment into one mass envenomed by one spirit of bitter unrelenting persecuting malice against me. . . ."[51] But perhaps Adams preferred the bizarre bill to one that did not protect his New England manufactures.

That the days of the Adams Administration were running out was recognized by its members as well as by its leader. Now Barbour as well as Rush sought the vacant English mission. Adams, who saw his Cabinet deserting the sinking ship, did not blame them. That spring, Clay threatened to resign because of his failing health. He must go home to die or to get better, he complained, speaking of general decay and paralytic numbness that started in his left foot and gradually rose to his right hip. Southard doubted that the Secretary of State would live out the month, but Adams disagreed, diagnosing Clay's malaise as a deep humiliation which was hitting all around him. Dr. Huntt agreed that Clay's disorder was nervous and that what he needed was relaxation from his public duties. But a trip to Philadelphia, where he consulted with two outstanding diagnosticians, revived his health and his spirits. He was loyal and would sink with the ship when that was required.

"As the rage of the tempest increases and the chances grow desperate, each one will take care of himself," Adams predicted. But he was thankful for the past services of his colleagues and not anxious to involve them in his political downfall. He appointed Barbour, who got over some last-minute anxiety about expenses, to the Court of St. James, rejecting Webster, who also wanted it. On May 24, Barbour resigned as Secretary of War and was replaced by General Peter B. Porter.

Though he had closed his ears to Clay and the others earlier, it was now painfully clear to the President that his Postmaster General was criminally unfriendly to the Administration. McLean's duplicity was utterly transparent when he engineered the appointment of Thomas Sergeant, close friend of anti-Adamsites Ingham and Dallas, as postmaster of Philadelphia. Clay and Barbour both urged McLean's instant removal, but it was too late. For one thing, he was a Methodist preacher in whose career all the Methodists in the United States felt a deep interest, which would make his removal unpropitious. And despite Adams's conviction that McLean had been all along "a supple tool of the Vice President Calhoun," he could fix on no act that would justify his removal.[52]

Even in the declining years, appointments had to be made as new jobs opened. Often they were accompanied by painful aftermaths.

The death of General Brown left a vacancy in the post of Major General that General Winfield Scott and General Alexander Macomb both claimed. After Macomb was appointed by the President, he complained that Scott refused to speak to him and refused to accept Adams's decision, declaring that he could not obey the commands of his junior and inferior officer and would appeal to Congress for redress. At a Cabinet meeting, Adams asked Rush, Porter, and Southard how he should deal with the "insubordinate and disrespectful" conduct of General Scott who, in the past, had rendered gallant services to the nation. Though he had been insubordinate, it was "in the nature of our principles and institutions to temper with kindness and indulgence even the rigidity of military discipline." However, Scott's application for a furlough in order to solicit congressional action against the President's decision was an insult. What means did the Congress have to act other than by impeaching the President, Adams asked. All the Cabinet members agreed that Scott must be refused leave and ordered back to his post.[53]

No task was too small to engage the President at this time. Luigi Persico, the Italian sculptor who was working on the pediment of the Capitol, consulted often with Adams. The design was Adams's and so he was critical of all its details. Persico's execution of the eagle, the President said, was not good. The sculptor had made it a "pouncing bird." And had the President's keen eye failed to note it, the anchor in the design would have been a Dutch one instead of an American.

The President's physical faculties were slowing down. His Potomac swimming periods were reduced to fifteen or thirty minutes a day and, instead of taking his long walks, he rode horseback for eight to fourteen miles per day. At least he was able to enjoy his plants. Before breakfast, he observed them growing in their pots and boxes, visited the garden, and devoured books on botany. In the evening, after the day's work, he paid a visit to the nursery, where he noted his observations on the growth of the trees.

On the Fourth of July, instead of the usual reception at the President's house, Adams agreed to speak at the ground-breaking for the Chesapeake and Ohio canal. Though it was a project that he supported, he predicted gloomily that whatever he said would be severely criticized. To avoid as much embarrassment as possible, he prepared his speech carefully.

Between seven and eight on Independence Day morning, Adams and his son John went to the Union Hotel at Georgetown where the officials of the canal company, the Mayors of Washington, Georgetown, and Alexandria, the department heads, the foreign ministers, and the guests had already gathered. At about eight the procession formed and, preceded by a band, walked to a wharf where they embarked on the steamboat *Surprise*, followed by two other vessels. The flotilla proceeded to the entrance of the Potomac canal where they transferred to canal boats that carried them to just within the state of Maryland, the spot chosen for the ceremony. About two thousand people were assembled to hear the President of the C & O make a short speech before he handed the President the spade. At his first strike, Adams hit the stump of a tree which was just under the surface of the ground. After repeated efforts with no results, the President took off his coat, seized the spade, and successfully raised a shovelful of earth. The multitude roared its approval. When they quieted down, the President gave a fifteen-minute address.

The Marshalls returned Adams to the White House, escorting him on horseback. It had been an exhausting day, although cool and breezy for that time of year. Adams complained that performing a part in the presence of large numbers of people made him tired and awkward; only his assault on the wayward stump had saved the day. The act struck favor in the public mind much more "than all the flowers of rhetoric in my speech," and diverted their attention from "the stammering and hesitation of a deficient memory."[54]

Washington's intense summer heat, declining health, and inability to relieve his misery with a swim of any length combined to convince John Quincy that it was time to go home. He informed his brother that he would bring along his son John, a serving man, and three horses, and would stay from six weeks to two months. Louisa did not accompany her husband. Much as she would like to see Charles, at Quincy she had "neither affection nor community." She would not live in the family house and expose herself to insults, and it would look strange if she lived at one place and the President at another. She also believed that John Quincy would rather go without her. Her plan to buy a comfortable compact house at Quincy never materialized. "For ten years, I've been led on and would have had a beautiful residence to retire to," she complained to George. When depressed, she did not hesitate to communicate her despair to her sons. "Now! All will be old, comfortless and unpleasant . . . as cold and as barren as I fear my heart has become."[55]

At Baruch's Tavern in Baltimore, a stream of visitors, mostly strangers, came from four in the afternoon until almost eleven o'clock to shake hands with the President. In the evening, in the square outside Adams's room, a Mr. McMahon, a young man who was a member of the Maryland legislature, harangued crowds of Jacksonites for almost three hours on "the unpardonable sins of the Administration and the transcendant virtues of Andrew Jackson." When Adams went to bed, he could hear McMahon's voice "like the beating of a millclapper" but was spared hearing what he was saying. The weary President, who knew that a similar pro-Administration meeting had taken place a few nights before, reflected that a stranger would think that the United States had no other occupation but electioneering.[56]

At Philadelphia, a large crowd welcomed the President, but mingled in the shouting were some voices that clearly cried, "Huzza for Jackson!" The New York reception was marred by the news that his brother Charles's widow had died.

The air of home failed to revive John Quincy as he had hoped. He was happy to find everyone well at Quincy but the journey left him feeble and in a state of lassitude that he said had never struck him before. Charles was concerned enough to write to Louisa that his father looked pale and thin. To which Mrs. Adams replied defensively that her husband injured himself from swimming, certainly did not receive benefit from gardening out in the hot sun, and overdid his riding. But he did not understand her anxiety and any opposition to his desires was ill-received and misunderstood.[57]

John Quincy's annual visit was somewhat spoiled by a conflict with Charles. When the young man received a check for $1,000 on the occasion of his twenty-first birthday, he took the opportunity to discuss his wedding plans with his father. Now that he was of age, he reminded the President, he had fulfilled the mandated waiting period and wanted to know what support would be allowed him. Adams answered with a tortuous account of his own prospects and intentions and ended by telling Charles that his present allowance would be extended. "I thought that his own views were not at all well digested but that is the usual way with our family," the disappointed youth wrote. Mr. Brooks, upon being approached the next day, was equally cautious. He discussed Abby's allowance but would give no definite date for the wedding. Charles, anxious to settle the matter, approached his father again and more directly about an increase in his allowance. It was an unpropitious moment and, apparently, he was rebuked bluntly. Charles recorded "It is very certain that my feelings were cruelly hurt, and in a manner which no subsequent kindness can remedy."[58]

Father and son were no longer cordial to each other. When they spoke, their conversation was stiff and often ceased entirely. Charles felt that he had been treated without respect and that the situation was being exacerbated because Adams would not in any way repair the mischief.

In early September, a letter from Mrs. John Adams reported that her mother-in-law was seriously ill. Adams decided that if he did not hear that she was recovering by the next mail, he would start back to Washington. The next letter disclosed that Louisa had erysipelas, or an inflammation of the head pressing on the brain and also on her heart. The President departed at once, leaving word for Charles, who was at Medford visiting Abby, to follow him immediately. Reluctantly, the young man obeyed. Louisa made a slow but satisfactory recovery, which was made much more pleasant by her youngest son's presence. John and Mary had little time for her because they were supervising the building of their house on the west side of Sixteenth Street, less than two blocks off President's Square. But when Charles left Washington on November 4, he was still as uncertain about wedding plans. Adams gave him his travelling expenses and two shares in the Middlesex Canal Company, worth about $500, but would not discuss the other matter. Charles received the gifts as graciously as he could, but was not able to erase the August confrontation from his mind. "It burns like a rankling sore; it is destined to have a material influence upon my futurity, for it cut me in the most agonized spot," he said. The young man resolved that he would continue to respect his father and perform his duties, only with a less willing heart.[59]

John Quincy resumed his executive obligations, pushing aside the looming election as well as he could. Since he would neither electioneer nor direct the activities of his supporters from behind the scenes, he spent his time riding on horseback to restore his health, and "ranged over the woods in pursuit of acorns."[60] There were frequent dinners at the President's House, handsome as ever and well attended. Adams and Clay appeared close to each other at this time, facing mutual disaster together.

Charles, who commented that the affairs of his family were "the most singular in the world for Hot Water seems our element," shared with them all the wish that the election would be over. Then, hopefully, the Adamses "might cease being the eternal subjects of contention and abuse," and ". . . as to the general prospect; whatever it may be. . . . it will turn out for the best."[61]

CHAPTER 19

Old Hickory versus
John of Braintree

". . . of all the oppositions I have lived to witness, & I have seen a number, I do not recollect one so malignant & unprincipled *as that which is organized against you."*

WILLIAM PLUMER TO JOHN QUINCY ADAMS

"I ADVISE THE FAMILY to prepare for defeat . . . the general opinion seems to be that little short of a miracle can save the P[resident]," Charles wrote from Boston on November 8.[1] The news was uncomfortably accurate and, since the election took place in the several states between October 31 and November 5, it was timely. The Jackson party was successfully achieving what Martin Van Buren, its gifted manager, referred to as the coalition of the planters of the South and the plain republicans of the North.

Though Jackson had claimed to be as aloof from electioneering as his stiff-backed opponent, he had, in reality, spent the years since the 1825 decision in the House of Representatives, ensuring that he would not be defeated a second time. Secure in his belief that he had been deprived of the Presidency by the corrupt Clay-Adams bargain, he regarded himself as the people's choice. A successful planter, a slave owner, financially much better off than Adams, nevertheless he believed in his public image, which was that of a backwoodsman-soldier, sworn enemy of the elitist present Duke of Braintree.

A search for viable campaign issues would prove fruitless in an

475

examination of the election of 1828. It was still essentially an era of personal contests. However, underneath the surface, despite the absence of discussion on the subject, it was clear that both Adams and his running mate, Richard Rush, were northerners and non-slaveholders, in contrast with Jackson and Calhoun, both southern planters and slaveowners.

A curious but interesting side issue in the campaign was the emergence of the anti-Mason party, a political force that became much more important later on, but already in this campaign was of some significance, particularly in the western counties of New York.

Information about the Morgan affair, the episode that inspired the formation of the new party, was exhaustively explored in the pages of Thurlow Weed's autobiography. But the mystery has never been completely solved. William Morgan, a Virginia-born stone mason who served as a Captain in the War of 1812, settled in Le Roy, Genesee County, New York, in 1822 or 1823. In this stronghold of Masonry, Morgan became an active, devoted member of the order until he quarrelled with his Masonic friends. As a kind of revenge, Morgan, who moved to Batavia, New York, decided to reveal the secrets of the society, finding a publisher in David C. Miller. When the Masonic brethren failed to buy Morgan's silence with a bribe, they started on a program of harassment. Several times Morgan was arrested for small debts but each time his friends bailed him out.

In August 1826, the outraged band of Masons became more militant. They participated in an attack on Miller's printing press, hoping to find and destroy the Morgan manuscript. The fire which they set was put out, however, and the angry group had to content itself with blaming Miller for setting fire to his own property in order to gain public sympathy.

In September, a warrant was issued for Morgan's arrest for the theft of a shirt. The unfortunate man was carried off to Canandaigua, where he was acquitted but then rearrested for a two-dollar debt which he admitted he owed. Without cash, he offered his coat as a barter payment but was refused and put into prison.

Mrs. Morgan, hearing of her husband's arrest, went to Canandaigua, accompanied by a local Mason and carrying with her Morgan's papers. She soon learned that her husband had been taken from his prison by "a few desperate fanatics" and conveyed in a carriage that was seen travelling in the direction of the Niagara River. From there it was deduced that he was carried to Canada. William Morgan was never seen alive again.[2]

Committees formed in the western counties to protest the outrage. Governor Clinton published several proclamations, offering rewards for the recovery of Morgan or information on his place of confinement. Some of the offenders were arrested, tried, and convicted, but Morgan's whereabouts were not revealed.

In February 1827, the people of the towns of Batavia, Bethany, and Stafford met and resolved to withhold support from all Masons who had supported the abduction of Morgan. Similar meetings occurred in surrounding areas where soon the resolutions extended their ban to exclude all freemasons from any office. Thus the anti-Mason party was born.[3]

Andrew Jackson, a Mason of long standing, remained silent on the subject of the Morgan case. Adams, also, played down the issue, despite Thurlow Weed's attempts to identify the anti-Masons with the Adamsites. Apart from the fact that many prominent figures in American history such as Franklin, Washington, and Lafayette had been Masons, Adams was aware also that his Administration contained a good portion of them, and he did not want to lose their votes. John Quincy did, however, answer in the negative a number of letters from ardent anti-Masons who questioned him on rumors that stated that he was a member of the brotherhood. For example, he was entreated by Editor W. W. Philips to make a statement in writing denying Masonic membership for the readers of the Trumansburg, New York, newspaper.[4]

It was a particularly vicious campaign that the friends of both candidates waged in 1828. Its greatest victim was Old Hickory's pipe-smoking, unostentatious, elderly wife, Rachel Donelson. The Adams-Clay press, knowing of Jackson's sentimental devotion to his wife, took particular pains to revive and embellish the forty-year-old story of their marriage.

Administration papers exposed the gossip with every questionable detail blown up to bigger than life size. Rachel Donelson, beautiful, said to be irresistible to men, married Captain Lewis Robards before she was eighteen. From the beginning, the marriage was marred by Robards's constant jealousy, which finally drove him to order Rachel out of the house. The wretched girl returned to her mother's home outside of Nashville, where Andrew Jackson became a boarder.

A brief reconciliation between Captain and Mrs. Robards was disturbed by Robards's suspicion that his wife was interested in Jackson. Some words between the two men caused quick-tempered Jackson to challenge Robards to a duel, which was refused. Instead, Jackson moved out of the Donelson house, which allowed another reconciliation between the married pair. This episode, too, was short-lived and, in July 1790, Rachel Robards eloped with Andrew Jackson.

Divorces were very complicated procedures in the eighteenth century and required a legislative act. Robards was unable to obtain any document but a bill, passed in December 1790, which allowed him the right to "sue out" a writ against his wife. If the jury, then, found that his wife had deserted him and consequently lived in adultery with another man, "the marriage . . . shall be totally dissolved."[5] Apparently Robards allowed it to be assumed that he had obtained a divorce. So in August 1791, Andrew Jackson and his Rachel, both twenty-four years old, were married and set up housekeeping in Jackson's loghouse in Bayou Pierre. Two years later Jackson was stunned to discover that Robards had not sued for divorce until that very spring. At first Jackson refused to consider the suggestion that he had best remarry Rachel, but there was a conventional marriage bond issued dated January 1794 in their names which leads to the conclusion that another ceremony did take place.

With this juicy old scandal to work with, the Adams-Clay press set about hunting up any embellishments it could discover, sending out scouts to interview the people who lived in the area where the episode had taken place. It cannot, of course, be determined whether Jackson lost or won votes as a result of this, but it was certain that it tormented the aging, retiring, and not-too-robust Rachel Jackson and probably contributed to her death.

There were other anti-Jackson canards published by the Adams-Clay interests. They did not equal in cruelty the ungentlemanly attack on Mrs. Jackson but they were sensational and damning. Under the franking privileges of several Adams Congressmen, an account of Jackson's executions of several militiamen was distributed. To give the story additional credence, it was designed to look like an official document issued by the War Department. The famous "coffin handbill," widely distributed, had drawings of black coffins purporting to symbolize the militiamen whom Jackson had executed. His "bloody deeds," the public was reminded, also included the executions of Arbuthnot and Ambrister, who now, for this purpose, became heroes.

For a time the Administration papers dwelled on Jackson's alleged connection with Burr's conspiracy but they had to abandon that attack when the Jacksonians responded with the information that Henry Clay had been Burr's lawyer during an early period of Burr's western adventures.

In retaliation, John Quincy Adams was not spared by the Jackson press. With great absurdity, he was accused of misrepresenting public accounts in order to get more money for his foreign service—"double pay," said a Kentuckian. The President was also accused of adopting European manners and habits, even to the point of prescribing "gorgeous dresses for our foreign ministers."[6]

In Congress, Jackson supporters accused the President of extravagant waste of government funds—precisely of the expenditure of fifty dollars for a billiard table. Congressmen Everett of Massachusetts and Sergeant of Philadelphia refuted the ridiculous charges by pointing out to their unreceptive colleagues that Adams's foreign accounts had been settled long ago and had been sanctioned by other Administrations. No foreign minister had received less for his services, they protested.[7]

Added as a note to a campaign biography of Jackson published by Isaac Hill, a New Hampshire newspaperman, was the old story that, while in Russia, Adams had pimped for Alexander I. John Quincy angrily protested to Everett that Martha Godfrey, the girl in question, who had been Charles's nurse at the time, was a girl of unreproachable conduct. She had seen the Emperor once when he and the Empress and Princess Amelia of Baden had sent for her and Charles. Their imperial Highnesses' interest in Martha had been piqued by some letters that she had written home to her mother, opened by the Russian post office, that repeated some stories that she had heard about the Emperor's amours. Adams was convinced that the Martha story had been furnished by his attentive enemy, Jonathan Russell.[8]

With a perverted sense of fairness, Duff Green of the *Telegraph* thought it was necessary to make it up to Rachel Jackson by attacking the integrity of the First Lady. He made fun of Louisa by ridiculing her as a snob and accusing her of friendship with royalty. He implied that he could say more damning things about her but he would refrain. As was expected, the familiar anti-Adams accusations were revived with enthusiasm, such as the allegation that the Adams family was royalist and monarchist. And the "corrupt bargain" story was appropriately overworked.

Jackson, it must be admitted, forbade his friends to use the weapon of slander against his opponent's wife, even in reciprocity. "I *never war against females* and it is only the base and cowardly that do," he wrote.[9] Nowhere in the Adams papers has a similar statement been found authored by John Quincy Adams.

The sound and fury of the electioneering signified but one thing, the inevitable defeat of the Adams forces. Though Jackson preferred to believe that his victory was the triumph of the people over the privileged classes, a close analysis of the returns does not justify that myth. Jackson was essentially a sectional or regional candidate who carried the South and the West except for Clay's Kentucky. There was some Adams support in Virginia and North Carolina, but not enough to carry those states.

Unlike the election of 1824, which had so many candidates, in 1828 the voter's choice had to be made between the two leading contenders. In the middle states, critical because none of the candidates except for Richard Rush came from that area, Jackson was able to attract the former supporters of Crawford and Calhoun and even some of Henry Clay's. Van Buren's Bucktails backed Jackson wholeheartedly, making their choice completely along party lines, because the Empire State had no favorite son in the contest. New York's advocacy of the hero was a particular triumph for the political maneuvering of the Red Fox of Kinderhook.[10]

John Quincy Adams had the overwhelming support of his native New England. It was questionable, however, whether it could be attributed to popularity. William Coleman's comment in the New York *Post* that New England would give J.Q.A. "a sulky, cold, dissatisfied support" was true of many voters, particularly federalists. A revival of bitter controversy over the Hartford convention between Adams and a group of Massachusetts federalists was a most unfortunate and ill-timed exchange for an election year. Many federalists had become Jacksonians, although most of them were from the middle states.[11]

Andrew Jackson carried every state in the West, which helped him to achieve a decisive victory. His popular vote was 647,276 votes to Adams's 508,064. But in the electoral college, the General had

178 votes to John Quincy's eighty-three. The Adams-Rush team carried the New England states, Delaware, New Jersey, six of Maryland's eleven votes, and sixteen of New York's thirty-six. The anti-Masonic party, strong in the western counties, accounted for their showing in New York. Jackson and Calhoun had all the rest of the states.

At first the Adams family seemed relieved, almost elated, that the election was over, and they were no longer burdened with office. Louisa reported that everyone was in good spirits and the President had grown very fat. Plans had been made to quit the President's mansion in February, move to a Washington residence until John Quincy could settle his affairs, and then proceed to Boston in May. John would stay behind to work the flour mill for at least a year.[12] "Your father really and solemnly and without exaggeration seems to enjoy the idea of shaking off those trammels which have bowed him to the dust," Mrs. Adams observed to Charles.[13]

Adams rented Commodore Porter's house, which caused much gossip in Washington society. It was said that the First Lady's health would not allow her to live in Boston and that the President also planned to remain in Washington. The rupture between Adams and his old friends and party was reported to be so great that returning to Massachusetts would be unpleasant.

Though the family believed that the President accepted his change of status with equanimity that was almost joy, Adams grieved privately. To his *Diary* he admitted that the sun of his political life had set in the deepest gloom. Defeat did not come easily to the proud man, born to be President, whose brief tenure in office was the least proud part of his long public life.[14]

The members of Congress called on the President in a constant stream, which further unseated the tranquillity of his mind. Even his most bitter enemies paid formal visits on the fallen chief and had to be received. From the small talk that he had to engage in, Adams became apprehensive that his retirement might not be as pleasant as he had anticipated. Friends told him that he might meet a very cool reception when he returned home in the spring. Some old federalists, he learned, were determined to break off all personal intercourse with him. "I shall go into retirement with I know not how many bitter controversies upon my hands," Adams reflected. The one pleasant event at this time was the birth of John Quincy's first grandchild, Mary Louisa, born on December 2.

The Adams party was not ready to dump their leader. John

Bailey asked the President if he would accept the Senate seat from
Massachusetts. Immediately, John Quincy answered that he would
not displace any man. Upon being assured that Nathaniel Silsbee,
the incumbent, did not want to be returned, he added another objection—he had decided "to go into the deepest retirement and
withdraw from all connection with public affairs."[15] However, he
admitted to Charles Minor, he had not abandoned his lifelong principle that if the people called for his services he would not decline
"any station" which was offered. But, at present, he did not want to
give a hint to the public that he was available.[16]

With a noblesse oblige kind of bravado, Louisa's December 18
drawing room was particularly lavish. The First Lady wrote casually
and amusingly to Charles that she borrowed lights from the dining
room and the private sitting room to light up the East Room and
had brought in all the bedroom chairs to accommodate the crowd.
"I had the band, and as I anticipated, the young folks got to dancing. Your father enjoyed himself as much as anybody," she said.[17]

Washington's unofficial society reporter, Mrs. Margaret Bayard
Smith, told a different tale. In her opinion, Mrs. Adams had gone
too far "in this assumed gaiety" and in this last drawing room substituted social, gay, frank manners for their (the Adamses) usual
"repulsive and haughty reserve." The audience chamber, "never
before opened, and now not furnished, was thrown open for *dancing,* a thing unheard of before at a drawing room!" Everyone from
the Administration was there and, Mrs. Smith pointed out, ostenta-
tiously dressed in their new Paris frocks. Though the courage that
the defeated Administration displayed in treating their failure as
one of the chances of war was admirable, their behavior at the party
was affectation, she judged.[18]

John Quincy's choice of a distraction for these painful times was
strange, but typical. During the late campaign, letters had been
published in the anti-Administration papers about Adams's relationship with Jefferson at the time of the embargo controversy, the
project for a New England Confederacy agitated in Washington
during the winter of 1803–1804, and the inextinguishable subject of
the fisheries. Adams's answer to these accusations caused a group of
"citizens of Massachusetts, residing in Boston and its vicinity,"
headed by Harrison Gray Otis, to challenge his charge that federalist leaders from Massachusetts in 1808 had for several years the object of dissolving the Union and establishing a separate confedera-

tion. The group demanded evidence, on behalf of their deceased friends and their living children, that these allegations were true. On December 30, J.Q.A. answered that he had not spoken of the federal party but of *"certain leaders* of that party." Their object, he told the group, was controversy and the October 21 statement issued in his name in the *National Intelligencer* was not meant to offend or injure any one of them. The answer was made to expressly disavow a charge laid before the public, sanctioned with the name of the late Mr. Jefferson, inputing to certain citizens of Massachusetts "treasonable negotiations with the British government *during the war,* and expressly stating that the information came *from me."*[19] A long and somewhat tedious explanation of what really happened followed. Adams noted that he had waived his scruples and the proprieties of his situation as President of the United States in consideration of his long friendship with some of the "citizens of Massachusetts" but he could not, "at this time, disclose his evidence" for which they called, nor could he divulge the names that they requested. No pressure, he concluded, "shall draw me to a disclosure which I deem premature, or deter me from making it when my sense of duty shall sound the call."[20]

After composing his reply to the Massachusetts federalists, Adams wrote confidentially to William Plumer, asking him for any material facts that he might have on the 1803–1804 New England Confederacy. The President explained his answer, saying that he declined controversy for the present but would have to decide during his retirement whether he would continue the discussion. In the meantime, he wished to collect corroborative testimony.[21] Much of his information, Adams revealed to Plumer, was collected from Uriah Tracy, then the Senator of Connecticut, who disapproved of the project but had known all about it. Now, if Plumer could see his way clear to reveal them, Adams would like the names of the members of Congress with whom he had talked, particularly the individual who had given the information about the intended meeting in Boston in the autumn of 1804 and the assurances that, despite Hamilton's death, the plan was not to be abandoned.[22]

Charles was pressed into service and directed to look up all the old documents relevant to the case. George and no one else might be shown these letters, John Quincy advised, but both of his sons should "take care to keep as much as possible aloof from my quarrels." Adams believed that the revival of federalist party supremacy in Boston had touched off the attack against him. The Massachusetts thirteen, which included Harrison Gray Otis, Israel Thorndike, T. H. Perkins, William Prescott, Daniel Sargent, John Lowell, William Sullivan, Charles Jackson, Warren Dutton, Benjamin Pickman, Henry Cabot, son of George Cabot, C. C. Parsons, son of Theophilus Parsons, and Franklin Dexter, son of Samuel Dexter, now the new elite, had seized the opportunity to fall upon him, their defeated enemy.

Charles's wish that his father's retirement would allow him to enjoy peace proved that, although he was a perceptive young man, he did not yet fully know him. "Retirement will not shield me from persecution," the President predicted. "I was born for a controversial world, and cannot escape my destiny." But, like an old war horse, he relished the fight and, in a real sense, invited it. With admirable insight, Adams remarked that a medical writer had observed that one disease sometimes became a cure for another. Reopening this old sore, the dispute over the New England Confederacy "has taken from me almost all the pain from the presidential defeat," he said. Under its stimulus, "I am recovering health and flesh til I shall be ready to exclaim with the fat **Knight** in Shakespear: 'A plague of this sighing and grief! It blows up a man like a bladder!' "[23]

The Massachusetts thirteen did not choose to wait until the President retired. They responded with "An Appeal to the Citizens of the United States" on January 28, 1829. Adams, they charged, had dishonored Massachusetts and therefore it was necessary to make this appeal because the citizens of every state in the Union had a deep interest in the reputation of every other state. The long-winded, tortuous retelling of Adams's reply was punctuated with insulting inferences. The charges, the Appeal stated, were not "an anonymous slander of political partisans but . . . a solemn and deliberate impeachment of the first magistrate of the United States, and under the responsibility of his name."[24]

Over and over again, Adams was baited to name the accused parties and to publish his evidence. Almost as a warning, the conclusion of the Appeal said: "Mr. Adams . . . by his political legacy to the people of Massachusetts, undertakes to entail upon them lasting dishonor." By reaffirming his conviction of the existence of the old secession project and then connecting it with later events, he "dooms himself to the vocation of proving that the Federal party were either traitors or dupes. . . ." The persistence and the hostile tone of Otis and company proved that the coming retirement would be marred by the open antagonism of former friends.

Adams, who by force of circumstance had made Plumer a semi-confidante in the matter, told him that H. G. Otis, now Mayor of Boston, denied that he had ever attended a meeting at which division of the Union was agitated or that there was any proposal for forcibly resisting a Congressional Act. But his name appeared on the paper that comprised the final report of the Hartford convention.[25] If Otis had heeded his advice on the embargo in 1808, he would have been Governor of Massachusetts and have had no Hartford convention sins to push on others, Adams concluded.[26]

Although he always discussed the subject in assured tones and seemed to keep his temper, John Quincy was profoundly disturbed by the controversy with the federalists. He insisted that his sons follow the arguments so that they would know that their father never deserted his friends or charged any man with treason. Most important, Adams wanted it clear that he never ceased to support the Union.[27] To further this project of clearing his name, Adams tried to persuade Charles King and his brothers to reconsider their refusal to reveal their father's opinion on the Hartford convention. But, even the forty-year friendship between Rufus King and Adams did not sway the younger Kings. They preferred to keep silent.[28]

The new year, 1829, began in gloom, John Quincy recorded. Louisa had a sleepless and painful night caused by inflammatory rheumatism and the dawn was overcast. As Adams started to write, his lamp went out, self-extinguished from lack of oil. The incident unsettled him and only prayer, the first psalm which promised that the righteous man will be blessed, comforted him.[29]

The entire Administration seemed to be dogged by ill-luck. Almost every Cabinet member succumbed to severe illness. Clay, too sick to go out, was pale, thin, hollow-eyed, his voice feeble, the very picture of melancholy. Rush complained of pains in his head and shortly thereafter became alarmingly ill. For three weeks Southard was confined to his room from which he emerged so feeble that a relapse was predicted. A mysterious malady that caused vertigo followed by a loss of sense and motion threatened William Wirt with the necessity to relinquish his law practice.[30] Washington murmured that every one of the public men due to retire on March 4 would return to private life "with blasted hopes, injured

health, impaired or ruined fortunes, embittered tempers and probably a total inability to enjoy the remnant of their lives." As the
time for Jackson's Inauguration neared, Southard continued desperately ill and Rush secluded himself so no one saw him. Clay
managed to keep his mask of smiles, though many thought that he
would never take the lead again.[31]

Melancholy as were the troubles of the fallen Adams Administration, the greatest blow fell on the victorious hero. The death of Mrs.
Jackson shocked him so severely that many predicted that the future
President's days were numbered. And, in late January, it was
rumored, though incorrectly, that the General was dead.[32]

The last levee to take place at the President's house during the
Adams Administration attracted more than 1,200 guests, some of
them frankly curiosity seekers. The party was very gay and the supper beautiful. Louisa noted, with satisfaction, that her guests enjoyed themselves so much that they did not go home until two
o'clock. She was satisfied that President and Mrs. John Quincy
Adams had taken their leave with all the grace imaginable.[33]

On February 1, the furniture was already being moved to the
Commodore Porter house on Meridian Hill that Adams had rented
until the weather was fine enough for his wife to travel north. John
and Mary's baby was christened Mary Louisa on February tenth and
on the next day the votes for President and Vice President were
opened and President-elect Andrew Jackson arrived in the capital.
For the last time, Adams was occupied with the close of the session
of Congress. As one of his last acts as President, Adams went to the
Capitol on the evening of March 2, accompanied by his son John
and Thomas Boylston Adams, Jr., to sign thirty bills into law. Several members of both houses came to say goodbye. Earlier in the
day, Seneca chief Red Jacket and his interpreter had called at the
President's house to say farewell. The chief, who had been exhibit-
ing himself at theaters, now needed money to return home. Adams
referred him to the Secretary of War. The only chore left was to see
that the President's house was readied for its new tenant. Adams
told Mr. Ringgold, Jackson's agent, to take an inventory of the
house and to tell the General that he could receive there after the
Inauguration.

Jackson had been residing at Gadsby's Hotel and holding court
there. His avoidance of Adams was noted by all the newspapers. The
Jacksonian *Telegraph* attributed it to the General's belief that

Adams was personally responsible for the story about Mrs. Jackson printed in the *National Journal*. Mr. Ringgold reported that Jackson wanted to call on the President when he came to Washington but had been dissuaded by his friends.

All the Adamses but the President were installed in the new house by the end of February. But as late as the third of March, Adams was still detained by government business, and the inventory had not been completed. However, when Calhoun explained that the tremendous crowd expected after the Inauguration might break down the rooms at Gadsby's Hotel, John Quincy promised to vacate the President's house on time. Michael Anthony Giusta, who had been in Adams's employ since Amsterdam, in June 1814 had been engaged by the new President. "This separation from Domestics who have so long lived in the family is among the painful incidents of the present time," his employer wrote.[34]

On March 3rd, the Twentieth Congress closed, and so did the Adams Administration. About noon the President went to the Capitol with his nephew and his son and signed the remaining fifteen bills. About three o'clock, a Joint Commission announced to the President that the houses were ready to adjourn. Adams answered that he had no further communication to make and wished each individual member health and happiness. Then, alone, he walked back to the President's house. During the afternoon and evening when the members of the Administration called, Adams polled them on whether he should attend Jackson's Inauguration. All except Richard Rush opposed the idea.

About nine o'clock, John Quincy Adams left the President's house for the last time as its occupant, accompanied by John and T. B. Adams, and joined the ladies at Meridian Hill. After dinner, Adams accepted the resignations of Richard Rush, General Porter, Samuel Southard, and William Wirt. The Administration of the second Adams was officially closed.

Inauguration Day, 1829, was warm and springlike. Adams had informed the newspapers that he wished his friends and the citizens of the district to refrain from the customary visit. Few came. While the hero was enjoying his ultimate victory, the defeated President rode on horseback through F Street to the Rockville Turnpike and over it until he came to the turn in the road whence he returned over College Hill and back to his new house. Near the post office he was overtaken by a Mr. Dulaney who asked how he could see John

Quincy Adams. Dulaney, who came from Waterford, Virginia, wanted to see some papers relating to the town's post office. He returned home with Adams and was given the papers.

"I can yet scarcely realize my situation," John Quincy wrote. With a feeling of despair, he begged, "from indolence and despondency and indiscretion may I specially be preserved."

Brooks Adams called John Quincy Adams's presidential career "the tragedy of our grandfather's life because it injected into his mind the first doubt as to whether there were a God and whether this life had a purpose."[35] Intuitively penetrating as many of Brooks Adams's observations were, this much-quoted one does not seem to be valid. On the contrary, ex-President Adams seemed to rely more and more heavily on divine guidance as the world turned against him, though certainly it was true that Adams's presidential years were his least glorious, for he had the dubious distinction of being his country's first minority President.

Having become the Chief Executive at the time when political parties were realigning and reasserting their power after an almost partyless era, no one was less suited to the developing situation than John Quincy Adams, non-party man par excellence. When he started his Administration, Adams had hoped to launch a fully realized program that advocated internal improvements, the establishment of a national university and a national observatory, and the promotion of scientific explorations. Almost at once his projects were humiliatingly laughed away. It was not the constitutional limitations that halted his efforts but the indifference of a Congress that preferred slandering him and denouncing him to questioning what intrinsic worth his program might have had.

Adams did not lack an understanding of the workings of Congress and politics. He was not naïve nor was he a Don Quixote tilting at windmills. His shortcoming was an inability to use the presidential power that he had through a misplaced but stiff-necked ethical sense. Perhaps it might be called a sin of pride. He had no party machinery and he spurned party machinery. He refused to help himself with the meager patronage power that he possessed. On the contrary, he was squeamish about rewarding his friends and righteous about retaining his enemies in office, allowing them to do him unquestionable harm.

When he had been Secretary of State, Adams emerged as a strong, fearless, indefatigable giant. As President, he complained constantly, suffered physically and mentally, and behaved as if he were out of his element. The last of the aristocratic Presidents, in the mold of the founding fathers, he signed all bills whether he liked them or not, as long as they were properly passed and constitutional. Perhaps Adams would have been a stronger presidential leader had he not been hampered by the factional quarrels in Congress. Much influenced by his father, who believed in presidential leadership, it would seem logical, based on the evidence of his strongly-worded first congressional message.

John Quincy blamed his failure on the restlessness and ambition of the South and West, which united "to produce the next administration." He freely admitted that he had no personal party in the past, and "never shall have one."[36] Unspoken, though it hung over his entire Administration, was any reference by Adams to the corrupt-bargain charge. Though it haunted him for the four years that he held presidential office and was kept alive by the Jacksonians, John Quincy seemed unable to bear to mention it.

Leaving the public service "with scanty resources, no light embarrassments and a family unavoidable and heavily expensive," Adams protested that he was not disappointed at the defeat. His only regret was that instead of quiet retirement to pursue agriculture, letters, and the study of the past, he would be "hunted down" in privacy as he had been in public life.[37] His life would be "militant to its close," Adams said. In a sonnet written for a young lady's album, a sentimental custom in which the elderly stateman often indulged, John Quincy expressed his feelings.

> Extract from bitterness his latent sweet
> And make in wormwood's cup ambrosial honey shed.[38]

CHAPTER 20

The Unquiet Retirement

"Quiet is not his sphere. And when a legitimate scene of action does not present itself, it is much to be feared that he will embrace an illegitimate one."

CHARLES FRANCIS ADAMS

"IT WAS MY INTENTION to bury myself in complete retirement as much as a nun taking the veil," John Quincy replied when invited to a farewell dinner for Henry Clay.[1] The raucous reception for the people's President at which Old Hickory had been nearly pressed to death by the eager crowd that milled around him and the subsequent invasion of the President's house by the rabble of scrambling, fighting partisans, had nothing to do with "Mr. Adams." The ex-President was quietly fixed at Meridian Hill.

For once, Mrs. John Quincy Adams was pleased with the house she had to live in. The original design suited her needs. There were two sets of apartments, one for summer and one for winter; two handsome parlors in the center of the home opened into each other with large sliding doors. A long room on the north side, which Mrs. Porter had used as a ballroom, was actually a passage between the two wings. There were also an adequate number of bedrooms. John Quincy had a nice study which opened on to a little flower garden and John had an office. In the garret, a large room received "the offensive billiard table." The grounds were spacious, encompassing gardens, a large working farm, and some woods, all properly fenced.[2]

Now only an observer, sometimes a gossip, Adams could not refrain from commenting about the new Administration. He noted that neither the Van Burenites nor the Calhounites were contented with the composition of the Cabinet and he revelled in the scandal it was making. The appointment of John Eaton as Secretary of War was obnoxious because of his indolence and incompetence but, most of all, because of the "shock to public morals" caused by "crowding his wife into the circles of decent social life." Pretty Peggy O'Neall Eaton, the daughter of a Washington tavern keeper, the widow of a paymaster in the Navy, and now the bride of Jackson's favorite, already had an unfortunate reputation. It was said of her, as it had been about Rachel Jackson, that she had lived with her present husband while her former husband was still alive. Though Mrs. Eaton was now "a person of dashing consequence," thanks to the President's sponsorship, the Washington ladies refused to visit her.[3] This lively account entertained Charles but he thought that he detected a false bravado in the tone of his father's letter that somehow depressed him.

Louisa deceived herself that her husband had never been happier. She said that he was so busy with self-made tasks that there was no time left for regret. His spirits were unusually good, she reported happily, and "Madamoiselle Louise," his little granddaughter, contributed considerably to his enjoyment.[4] And she, too, could not refrain from relating the "tittle tattle" of the city, particularly the "discord and confusion which bids fair soon to rival the ancient Gomorrah." The "fair Eaton," she said, assumed "the sway and every cavalier or witless damsel who will not assume her colors are to meet the frown of the modern Nero." Louisa also appeared to be in excellent spirits, "better than when we were in prosperity," Adams told George.[5]

As a last act of his public life, Adams engaged Luigi Persico to make a bust of him, suffering with resignation the two-hour sittings that the sculptor required. It was to be "a beau ideal" of the ex-President, Persico said, therefore he was forbidden to smile, for that was not presidential. Poor John Quincy commented that, consequently, he was possessed with "an irresistible propensity to laugh" and, after that passed off, he wanted to doze, "which would never do in plaster of Paris." The finished product was "the most perfect resemblance of me which my children will possess," John Quincy said and the family agreed with him.[6] Unfortunately, the bust was destroyed on Christmas Eve, 1851, when the Library of Congress, where it had been placed, was gutted with fire.

Adams became invisible to official Washington. Except for Van Buren, now Secretary of State, no member of the Administration called, although they had almost all been guests of the ex-President's in the past. "They hate the man they have wronged," he said, consoling himself with reading Cicero's *Phillipics* and writing fables in imitation of La Fontaine. The results were unsatisfactory, for he judged them ill-executed, but they had some therapeutic value. But John Quincy's Puritan soul could not be long content with a life that was, admittedly, "happier than I have ever enjoyed. . . . I must quit this Eden to go home," he decided, dreading what might wait him there.[7]

For the last few years, Louisa and John Quincy had been forced to realize that their oldest son was unhappy, nervous, and often erratic and irresponsible. His physical health was affected. He complained of rheumatism and many other ailments. Although his election to the state legislature appeared to be the beginning of a promising career, his symptoms continued. He was negligent in keeping his father's accounts for the Boston business and failed continually to write the weekly letter to Washington. John Quincy begged in vain. "I close with assurances of my constant affection and wishes for a *revival* of our correspondence," he wrote.[8]

During the summer of 1827, Louisa had gone to New York to be with George, who was suffering from a severe nervous irritability which made him fear censure even when it was not merited. Dr. Welsh advised quiet and a change of scene, but most urgently recommended that he not be harassed with business or any other cares. He was of an age when he was his own master, Louisa reminded her husband, and his parents must provide kindness blended with firmness to keep him from taking some rash steps that would ruin his future. George had confided to his mother that he thought that John Quincy would not approve of his political opinions and that it would cause his father some inquietude.[9]

Though Adams listened to the advice of his wife and the physician, he was unable to empathize with George. "Inform me whether you regularly go to your office. . . . Your mother was severely ill but the best medicine for her would be a favorable account of your health and attention to business. . . . This too would be a Panacea for your father," he wrote, without understanding that he was destroying his son.[10] Even more painful to the young man were reminders of his grandfather's accomplishments. John Quincy protested to George that he did not refer to them in order to hurt his feelings but to stimulate him to *"perseverence* in the cause of virtue, by reminding you of the blood from which you came." The distraught father could not refrain from twisting the knife. "Time was when I took it for granted that your life was sober, regular and industrious, now I need weekly assurance." And then he recommended that "as a favor" George join the Boston Society for the Suppression of Intemperance to save himself and then perhaps others from that "insatiable and all devouring calamity." Alcoholism had already devoured Tom Adams, but of course that was not mentioned.[11]

When at times George's letters came promptly and he seemed improved, John Quincy could not refrain from responding with inspirational letters that suggested universal panaceas. George must learn some stanzas from Thompson's *Castle of Indolence,* which he enclosed, and repeat them every morning with his prayers. They extolled "the simplest charms of nature" and often helped him through rough moments, J.Q.A. told him.

> I care not Fortune, what you me deny:
>   You can not rob me of free nature's grace
> You can not shut the windows of the sky
>   Through which Aurora shows her brightening face.
>
> You cannot bar my constant feet to trace
>   The wood, the lawn, the living stream at eve;
> Let health my nerves and finer fibres brace
>   And I their toys to the great children leave
> Of reason, Fancy, Virtue—Nought can me bereave.[12]

Among other cures for melancholy, Adams advocated the active keeping of a diary, which was "the time piece of life and one of the best preservatives of morals." A man who committed to paper from day to day the employments of his time, the places he frequented, the persons with whom he conversed, and the actions that occupied him "will have a perpetual guard over himself."[13]

George tried to reform many times. After his father sent him $1,000 to cover his debts, he started a diary and joined a reading group led by Dr. Channing. But he still complained of weakness and dejection. Charles, who was living in Boston, was charged to "cherish brotherly feelings" but found the job difficult.

Neither George's good intentions nor his father's patience lasted very long. Receiving notice of another sizable debt that his son had incurred, Adams offered to buy his library. "As to Books—debts for books! Of what earthly use to you are, or can be books, with such a life as you have led! The very possession of books is a perpetual sarcasm upon your prostitution of your time to licentiousness," he fumed.[14] Then the frustrated father was sorry for his harshness. "All his thoughts turn fondly to you," Louisa wrote to ease the breach. "You have become an object of the most watchful and incessant care and affection to your father. . . ."[15]

But even his mother became completely disgusted with George's behavior. In the spring of 1828, she said that she would "write to him no more—for even mercy may be trifled with until it is lost." It must be "perverseness of mind" that made him reject God's gifts to him. At that time, George declined nomination to the House of Representatives because, he told his father, he felt unable to represent his townsmen. He also withdrew voluntarily from the state legislature, claiming that his father's position made it awkward for him to stay.[16]

In the meantime, all of George's obligations remained in arrears—his accounts, the lists of his books, the payment for Thomas J. Hellen with which he was charged. Though his physical symptoms sometimes improved, his emotional state continued disturbed. Charles was unable to give him as much time as before because he was busy pursuing his romance with Abby Brooks.

The crisis of George's life was precipitated by the expected return of his parents to Quincy. Charles issued the first warning that George's state of mind was deteriorating in a letter to his mother written in April 1829. He said that he was anxious to hear when his father would come north, "as I think he shouldn't defer it very long." Rather unsympathetically, Charles described his brother's melancholia and constant complaints about his inability to work. "I do not want to alarm you," Charles prefaced his mention of the "disgusting place" where George was living.[17]

Louisa had been bombarding George with letters requesting that he come to Washington and escort his parents home. "Your health would be benefited by a change & your company delightful to me," she pleaded. She then tried to interest him in family life at the old

house. He would live with them and "Your father will have a horse
& gig & you'll have the use of it," she offered naïvely. "Charles will
electioneer for you," she added as a bonus. Adams also believed that
it would be best for George to reside with them.[18]

At first the invitation to go to Washington appeared to revive
George, but almost at once, as Charles put it, "his habitual vaccilla-
tion of mind forbids him immediately packing his trunk and being
off." Almost a recluse now, he had ceased to be able to cope with the
ordinary details of life.[19]

On April 20, Adams took matters into his own hands and issued
a clear order to George. "I wish you to come immediately upon
receiving this letter, to return with us," he said.[20] A few days after
his father's letter arrived, George set out, leaving his affairs in
Charles's hands. That astute gentleman observed that his brother,
like Uncle Tom, who was now settled in a new residence so that the
family mansion would be ready for its owner, "are both quivering
under the fear of the merited reproaches which my father can
though he will not give."[21]

About one o'clock on Saturday, May 2, Nathaniel Frye, Adams's
brother-in-law, arrived at Meridian Hill and asked Adams if he had
received any letters in the mail or heard anything from George.
When Adams said that he had not, Frye mentioned that he had seen
a short paragraph in the Baltimore *American* stating that George
W. Adams had been lost from the steamboat *Benjamin Franklin*
between Providence and New York on Thursday morning before
daylight. About a half an hour later, Judge Cranch arrived with
several letters that confirmed the awful news. One was from Charles
King and one from Davis and Brooks who had taken charge of
George's trunk and personal possessions. His body had not been
recovered.

Louisa's state upon being told the news by her husband was "not
to be described." Judge Cranch returned to the city to fetch Dr.
Huntt, who stayed until evening—"but there was no medicine for
this wound." Mrs. Frye stayed the night to help with her stricken
sister. John Quincy was so agitated that his *Diary* entry was written
in handwriting that went wild. He wanted to go to New York at
once but Mrs. Frye's earnest pleas not to leave his wife and to spare
himself finally convinced him to allow John and his nephew William S. Smith to go in his stead.

A young man by the name of Keep called on Adams with some

information on George's last days. Keep, who had been on the steamship, reported that George had been unwell for several days, suffering from hallucinations. His deranged mind imagined that people were breaking into his room, an idea that he refused to give up even after a search revealed that nothing was missing and no one was there. He also had the impression that the machinery was speaking to him, saying, "Let it be!" over and over again. On Wednesday, George had talked to Peter Jones, one of his fellow passengers, a missionary who had a few Indian boys with him, and gave him a donation. That night, young Adams went to bed at the same time as the other passengers but woke up several times during the night. He awakened a Mr. Parker at one point to accuse him of circulating reports against him among the other passengers. After Mr. Parker's denial of the charge, George went with a candle to the berths of the other passengers, looked at them, and then returned to bed. At about 3 A.M., young Adams sought out Captain E. S. Bunker to ask to be put ashore. When Bunker asked him why he wanted to go ashore, George answered that the others had been talking and laughing against him. Bunker was called away at that point so George got into a conversation with John Stevens, a Common Councilman from Boston. About ten minutes later, Stevens noticed George's hat at the end of the upper deck. Somewhat puzzled, he asked if anyone had seen Adams in the last few minutes. George was nowhere to be found. "In the wandering of his mind he had fallen overboard," his father recorded.

Louisa, prostrated by shock, became dangerously ill with a high fever and a racking cough. John Quincy did not leave her. "To me he is a ministering angel always at my side, lavishing on me the most soothing tenderness," Louisa wrote to Charles.[22] Trying to appear calm, the ex-President was overwhelmed with a grief such as "I never knew before." His former occupations were flat and all prospects "for the remannt of my life" in which he had delighted "are broken up." He felt that his mind was rambling. Only prayer sustained him. One afternoon while taking a desultory walk around the square, heavy-hearted as usual, he looked up and saw a rainbow. He took it as a sign of the goodness and mercy of God.[23]

Gradually the bereaved father restored the pattern of his life. He worked on his book about the political parties of the United States which was growing into a larger work than he had contemplated, and swam in the Potomac, but for no more than ten minutes at a time. Just before returning to Quincy, Adams had a terrible attack of inflammation of the eyes similar to the one he had suffered at Ealing, England. This malaise was followed by a bilious attack that delayed his departure for more than a week. Louisa, who dreaded the northern bleakness and its Puritan inhabitants, finally determined to stay in Washington with her daughter-in-law and granddaughter. John would accompany his father home and then return in mid-July, John Quincy to follow in October.

Charles thought that his father's return was already perilously overdue. The family mansion at Quincy was going to ruin. Adams's financial affairs needed careful attention and George's debts had to be attended to before his creditors closed in. Charles, who had been charged by his brother to look after his unfinished business, found, not unexpectedly, much that was distressing. He immediately destroyed some of his brother's papers which he felt would give the family grief but he could not eliminate everything. While examining one trunk, he came across a paper that George had addressed to him, requesting that if he died in the year 1828, his debts should be paid and the balance be given to a girl whom he had seduced and was now pregnant. The girl was Eliza Dolph, who had been a chambermaid at Dr. Welsh's where George had been living.

Before Charles could straighten out the matter quietly, a nasty episode shaped up over the misalliance. Apparently George had requested Dr. David Humphreys Storer, who was attending Eliza, to persuade Miles Farmer, who in partial payment for his services as estate agent for Martin Thayer of Amherst lived rent-free in one of his houses, to take in Eliza and her illegitimate child. Farmer took her in but complained that George's continued attentions to Eliza made the other tenants suspicious, which threatened his job. George then promised Farmer compensation but his suicide prevented the payment. Farmer now wanted Charles to make good his brother's promise.

With remarkable firmness, Charles refused to be bullied into any expenditures. He provided some money for Eliza and the child but thought that the mother "must work for herself." Eliza went back into domestic service. Farmer persisted in his demand for money, threatening a public scandal, but Charles was adamant. Failing with Adams, Farmer tried to extort money from Dr. Storer, which finally evolved into a court case.

Charles was summoned to court in February 1831, shocked that "my brother's reputation must be mangled in a Court of law." With no sympathy whatever for George's victims, Eliza and her child, he only observed that once again he was "shocked" that "the Girl" had been summoned as a witness. The worst was averted at the last minute when the case was referred to three referees so that the Adamses were spared "an exhibition before a crowded Court of the whole melancholy story."[24] Finally, Farmer received damages of two hundred dollars and had the last word when he published a long pamphlet that attacked the Adams family. When computed, George's debts amounted to one thousand dollars, which his father paid. "Poor George," as he was always called subsequently, bore a melancholy fate, his brother observed, adding callously that "on the whole, I have been forced to the unpleasant conclusion that it was not untimely. He would have lived probably to give much misery to his friends and more to himself. . . ." Charles felt the greatest amount of sympathy for his father, who "almost lived in him [G.W.A.] and the loss will to him indeed be dreadful."

While in New York, on his way to Quincy, Adams found out that George's body had been recovered at East Chester, seventeen miles from New York City. Accompanied by John and George Sullivan, Adams travelled there and dined at the house of Dr. Ten Broek where his son's watch, penknife, silver pencil case, comb, seal, pocketbook, and the key to his trunk were delivered. A copy of the coroner's inquest, delivered at the same time, stated that a youth named Waterbury who was standing on City Island saw the body drifting with the tide, watched until it came to land, and then remained with it until the coroner and jury came. The verdict was death by drowning.

In the afternoon, the tomb of Mr. Drake, where George's body lay, was opened so that his father could go in and see the coffin. A burial service was performed by the minister of the Episcopal Church in the presence of a sizable crowd of local people. After it, the Adamses and Sullivan returned to the city, John Quincy carrying with him the pathetic reminders of his lost son. When the news reached Louisa, she mourned again. To her husband she wrote, "Hope which lived in spite of reason is now dead." In her utter desolation, she begged God "to soon permit me to quit a life of such deep suffering."[25]

John Quincy was in little better shape emotionally. As the *Chancellor Livingston*, the steamboat that carried him up the Hudson, passed City Island, he said, "My sensations . . . were agonizing. The power of prayer alone is left." When he reached the paternal mansion on June 18, it was uninhabited and almost stripped of furniture. Feeling sorry for his desolate state, Louisa C. Smith agreed to keep house for him and Charles stayed with him four nights a week so that he and his brother John between them could do all the necessary business. Adams saw what friends he wished to.

Charles and Abby's wedding was to take place on September 1. Mr. Brooks had bought the young couple a house in Boston. John Quincy hoped that his son would be able to support a family. Since George's death, he spent a lot of time brooding about his remaining sons' prospects. But of the agitations of the world, Adams knew nothing, hardly looking at a newspaper. "Of public affairs I take no thought, I wish to dismiss them forever," he told Louisa, who only wished that he meant it. On his sixty-second birthday, Adams echoed the sentiment, adding that he wished only to be useful to the family.[26]

Louisa planned to come to Quincy in August with Mary and the baby because the Meridian Hill house was sold. John had to remain in Washington to look after the mills upon whose success depended Adams's ability to pay his debts. The dream of his retirement, to build a stone library to house his books and papers, would have to be suspended until finances were again stable, and the prospects were disheartening for the market was falling, due to good harvests in France and Britain, which eliminated the need for American flour.[27]

Louisa did not come to Quincy after all. She got as far as New York, where Charles met her, but she and the baby became ill and so she decided to return to Washington. Quincy was not the place for her to recapture her health or peace of mind. She was, therefore, absent from the wedding of her youngest son and Abigail Brooks at Medford. After the ceremony was performed "according to congregational form," the wedding party enjoyed a joyous supper and then Charles and his bride returned to Boston and their own house. John Quincy and his nephew stayed with the bride's parents, although Mrs. Brooks was very ill and able to attend the wedding only with "great exertion."[28] Adams gave his daughter-in-law Abigail—"a name most dear to me because it was that of my mother and sister" —a present of a cameo ring with two hands joined. He gave the couple three family portraits painted by Stuart of John Adams,

John Quincy Adams, and Louisa Catherine Adams, and for their wine cellar three dozen small bottles and one and one half dozen half magnums. Duly noted in his *Diary* was the fact that Charles's wedding day was also the anniversary of the treaty of Paris of which John Adams was one of the signatories in 1783.

A severe bout of rheumatism that almost lost him the use of his writing hand tormented Adams all fall. He spent some of his time supervising the project of having bookcases built around his bedroom to house his library, still packed in trunks and boxes and stored in Boston. Charles was unable to get home often, so Lt. Thomas Boylston Adams had been his uncle's constant companion and William Greenleaf was engaged in unpacking and then cataloguing his books, miraculously undamaged, although some of them had been in the same packages since they came from England in 1817. The library was its owner's passion, although he had never had the enjoyment of it. "No such library existed in the hands of any other individual in the United States," Adams crowed.[29]

Charles was delighted to see his father "transmogrifying" the house, happily surrounded by his battery of books. The old house, scene of the annual pilgrimage to Quincy, brought his departed parents close to the ex-President. In October, a tablet dedicated to John and Abigail Adams was unveiled in the Quincy church. The inscription, written by their devoted son, recalled the dates and incidents that made their lives particularly remarkable and memorable. For John Adams, other than the dates of his birth and death, it was recorded that he pledged "his Life, Fortune and Sacred Honour" to his country's independence and on September 3, 1783, signed the treaty of Peace with Great Britain. Of his political life, nothing was written. The son preferred to dwell upon the marriage of his parents "of more than a century. They survived in Harmony of Sentiment, Principle and Affection."[30]

One of the undertakings of Adams's retirement which never reached fruition was a biography of John Adams. Started and worked upon off and on, John Quincy was unable to sustain it. He refused also to become the president of the Columbian Institute although he remained a member. He did, however, accept an appointment to the Harvard Board of Overseers. Of the world of politics, he remained apart, only occasionally commenting to his friends on the Jacksonian era. The present problems he defined as the public lands, the Indians, the bank, and the tariff. He warned that a war with Mexico was not unlikely and that one or more of these problems might divide parties whose lines were not as yet drawn. He thought the facts "much too detestable to be ridiculous" but could not refrain from remarking to Abby that Mr. Van Buren was about to scale the Presidency of the United States, "by mounting the shoulders of Mrs. Eaton."[31]

The debate in Congress over the public lands was electrifying Washington during the first session of the Twenty-first Congress. It marked the struggle between the states' righters and the nationalists and was an attempt to break down the Union of the eastern and western sections in order to restore the more familiar western and southern coalition against New England. Its climax was the Webster-Hayne debate. Adams said of it that Mr. Webster "pulverized the Hartford convention as well as Hayne. The Otis of the East and the Hotspur of the South preach the same identical doctrine." Webster's famous tribute to nationalism—"Liberty *and* Union, now and forever, one and inseparable"—was a justification and an echo of John Quincy's stand in his reply to the Massachusetts federalists.[32]

Adams was certain that Jackson would be a candidate for re-election and would succeed. The hero of New Orleans, he judged, would continue to enjoy his personal popularity because the vices of his Administration were not the sort that affected popular feeling. "If he lives, therefore, and nothing external should happen to rouse new parties, he may be re-elected not only twice but thrice."[33]

Whether he wished to or not, Adams became the confidante of officials who were peremptorily removed from their jobs when Jackson came into office. The new President's "spoils system" ousted the son of Elbridge Gerry, signer of the Declaration of Independence and Vice President of the United States, from his job as surveyor of the Port of Boston. When Gerry protested, he was told by Jackson's representative that offices were not hereditary. Adams, who was repelled by the system, commented that Gerry's distress was great for he supported his wife and four unmarried sisters. Abrupt dismissal was a common story for those who had not been ardent Jackson supporters.

South Carolina's rebellion against the federal tariff interested Adams. Joel Poinsett told him that the state's attitude would be intensified by their new governor, James Hamilton. The former Minister to Mexico was going home to try to calm the excitement which he did not share. "There is every prospect that her bullies will succeed, to the sacrifice of all the rest of the Union, as the bullies of Georgia have succeeded in the project of extirpating the Indians by the sacrifice of the public faith of the Union and of all our treaties with them," Adams said. He was so suspicious of Jackson's good faith that he did not recognize the sincerity of the President's toast, "The Union: it must be preserved," lumping it together with the rest of the "obnoxious toasts" at the Jefferson Day dinner.[34]

In the late spring, John Quincy, Louisa, Mrs. John Adams, and the small Louisa with her nurse, Mrs. Knowland, arrived at the old house, which Charles had dutifully readied for them. Now that he had his own home, Charles preferred not to join the already crowded establishment in Quincy as his parents wished. Despite his mother's annoyance, his father's grief, and his sister-in-law's pique, Charles thought it a wise decision if only because it saved his father some expense. As the keeper of the accounts, Charles was in a position to know.

John Quincy seemed to have resigned himself to a life of literary pursuits and gentlemanly retirement. However, Charles noted in his *Diary* throughout the summer his father seemed depressed and not as pleased with his freedom as he had been the year before. Louisa was despondent, suffered a very severe attack of erysipelas, and was not enjoying the Quincy interlude. Mary was pregnant and hence did nothing but sit, and the child, in the midst of all this, was a nuisance. Charles tried to excite his father's weakened purpose to resume an interest in writing John Adams's life, but without success. Only Cicero had any intellectual appeal, particularly the first Tusculan, which discussed Cicero's contempt for death. Adams said that it was a most favorable moment for him to read it, "when I have no plausible motive for wishing to live, when everything I foresee and believe of futurity makes death desirable, and when I have the clearest indication that it is close at hand." But the Roman's arguments were hollow, for, Adams acknowledged, "the love of life and the horror of dissolution is as strong in me as it ever was at any period of my existence."[35]

John came in July, crowding the house even more and inconveniencing his parents who gave up their room to him and his family. And on September 9, Mary bore a second daughter. Since her father had returned to Washington and the flour mill, Adams took his place at the new baby's christening. She was named Georgeanna Frances. Charles assumed that the second name was a compliment to him although no one said anything. The event aroused his anxieties about his own childlessness. If John had no sons, he reflected, "what becomes of the family which we love and cherish?"[36] John Quincy was a typically doting grandfather. He wrote to John that he hoped that they could all be together at Quincy the next summer so that "the little Syren Loo Loo with Sister Baby may inhale bracing breezes."[37]

The first indication that John Quincy Adams's enforced leisure was to be interrupted appeared in J. T. Buckingham's Jacksonian paper, the Boston *Courier*, on September 6. It suggested to national republicans that they elect John Quincy Adams as their next representative from Plymouth. It would be agreeable to him, Buckingham asserted, thinking it would be a good way to get rid of the ex-President as a future political challenger.[38]

Adams did not take the suggestion seriously until he was called upon by John B. Davis and then Richard Joseph Richardson, the incumbent, who had decided to return to his Hingham congregation. Richardson said that he was certain that the local newspapers, the *Old Colony Memorial* and the Hingham *Gazette*, would support the Adams candidacy, and no other. This was important because, without a majority in the district for a candidate, under Massachusetts law, that district went unrepresented. The only question his supporters had was whether service in the House of Representatives would now seem degrading to the ex-President.

Adams replied that no person could be degraded by serving as a representative to Congress, or indeed as a selectman in his town if he were elected by the people. He was deterred only by the state of his health, his age, and how the election would turn if he were not a candidate.

The Adams family reacted vehemently to the proposal. Louisa told Charles that she was against it—"There are some silly plans going on here and God only knows in what they will end, but I fear not at all to my taste." Charles was so against the idea that he told his *Diary* that the acceptance of the post diminished the man. "He wants the profound wisdom which gives knowledge its highest lustre, he is not proof against the temporary seductions of popular distinction to resist which is the most solid evidence of greatness," he said smugly. Then, with some guilt, he added, "Yet if he is not in character like Washington, he is a very extraordinary man for the times we live in."[39]

It would have hurt the father who had said of Charles, "Your conduct since you came of age has pleased and comforted me," to read that entry. And his son's opposition to his new role did cause a temporary misunderstanding. Charles finally told his father that he opposed his candidacy, which distressed him. But, though he had a miserable night and a return of his lumbago, his determination was not altered. Unimpressed by Charles's argument that his action would become a precedent and therefore was important to the whole nation, he was equally unmoved by the Jacksonian attempts to stop his nomination, made at Halifax by the republican convention, and the following day by the national republican convention. Adams accepted the nominations, happy to be a part of the real world again. In a letter to Joseph Story he revealed his enthusiasm. "There is a typhoon raging in Europe and a hurricane in South America. . . . And what have we here?" Not only would "the burning lava" that would pour down the mountains of the world "overflow upon us" but he saw the elements of revolution in the United States—the Indians, the tariff, the railroads and the canals, cotton bagging and nullification. He had been too young for the first Revolution. He did not want to miss the second.[40]

Mary returned to Washington with her two daughters but Louisa announced that she would stay in Quincy. It was a surprising decision, particularly since the old house was not ready for winter habitation. Adams said resignedly, "The separation of families is very painful to me but I cannot help it," and prepared to make the house suitable for year-round occupancy. Louisa explained that she could not go on smoothly with her family while she held the opinions that she did on the politics of the day. Her mind and nervous system were too shaken by suffering to once again be plunged into "political machinations." She did not condemn her husband's choice but his family is and always must be secondary to a "zealous Patriot."[41]

Charles, who had always dreamed of having his mother living near him, now enlisted his brother's support to persuade her to change her mind. "Write a mild letter approving indirectly our father's course," he directed, "and perhaps request her company this winter." The letter was written, "kind and affectionate" in its intentions, John Quincy observed, but it "should have been more so in its form."[42] Louisa replied that she would prefer to stay in Quincy for the climate would not be as harmful as "a house which will become the focus of intrigue." However, she gave in to the family's pressure, and, once again, would sacrifice herself to its conveniences. And, for financial reasons, she would not try the family funds any more.[43]

The election returns, decisive and determined early, appeared in the Boston *Daily Advertiser* on November 4. Adams had received 1,814 votes out of 2,565 from the inhabitants of the twenty-two towns in the district. Arad Thompson, a Jacksonite, polled 373 votes, William Baylies, a federalist, 279, and there were ninety-six scattered votes. Adams was jubilant. He had received nearly three votes out of every four throughout the district. "My election as President of the United States was not half as gratifying to my inmost soul," he told his *Diary*, though "the dearest of my friends have no sympathy with my sensations."[44] It was a small consolation prize for the suffering of the presidential years and the domestic calamity that followed. In the year 1829, Adams said, scarce a day passed that he did not recall the scene in the French opera of *Richard Coeur-de-Lion* in which the minstrel, Blondel, sang under his monarch's prison walls:

> O, Richard! O, mon Roi!
> L'Univers t'abandonne.[45] *

John Quincy planned to leave for Washington in early December, although he was not required to be there until March 4 and the first session of the Twenty-second Congress would not meet until December 5, 1831. One of the reasons for an early return was the state of the flour mill which, Charles predicted, was the gulf into which the family finances would sink.

Louisa started out before her husband with the carriage and horses. Adams, who was delayed by the obligation to attend the probate court in Dedham in reference to John Adams's will, was forced by bad weather to take the stage to Hartford in order to catch up with Louisa. They met in the Connecticut capital and decided to take passage on the steamboat from New York, where Adams visited Monroe, who was staying with his daughter and son-in-law, the Samuel L. Governeurs. Monroe, ill and worn, was concerned about the Jackson-Calhoun controversy that Crawford had stirred up and that Adams had tried all summer to escape from.

With the Meridian Hill house sold, the new Congressman and his wife went to live with John and Mary. Much of Adams's occupation during the winter was devoted to past problems that refused to be laid to rest. Crawford, who hated the fact that he had been relegated to the scrap heap of politics, revived the Cabinet dispute during the

---

* "O, Richard! O, my King!
  The world is forsaking you."

Seminole war, in which all of its members but Adams opposed Jackson's aggressive behavior, particularly John C. Calhoun. Adams prided himself that he did not fall for the artifices of the embattled trio—Crawford, Calhoun, and Jackson. He said: "Their demerits to me are proportional to the obligations to me—Jackson's the greatest, Crawford the next, Calhoun's the least of all but darkened by his . . . icy-hearted dereliction of all the decencies of social intercourse with me, solely from the terror of Jackson, since 4th of March, 1829."[46] Therefore, he felt justified in not answering any questions directly.

Commenting on Jefferson's *Memoir* of his life up to his becoming Secretary of State, just published, Adams had little flattering to say. He was particularly repulsed by Jefferson's "treacherous and inventive memory," which had caused him to attack John Adams and later to involve J.Q.A. in controversy with the Massachusetts federalists. Jefferson appeared to Adams as a very unheroic figure. He mocked his explanation for declining an appointment as a Minister to negotiate peace with Great Britain, pleading family responsibilities. Proudly, John Quincy recalled that his father had exposed himself and his two small sons to capture by British ships crossing the ocean three times during the war. And John Jay and Henry Laurens had taken similar chances. On slavery also, Jefferson had taken the coward's way. Although he saw the discrepancy between the principles of the Declaration of Independence and the real existence of slavery, he bowed to discretion and, when his colleagues urged him to strike out such heresies as a plan for general emancipation which he had originally proposed in his revision of the Virginia laws, he acquiesced.[47]

During that winter, Adams worried about Chief Justice Marshall's health, met Benjamin Lundy, the editor of an abolitionist newspaper, and observed the progress of the Calhoun-Van Buren struggle for the succession. To his sorrow, he was made aware that the present Administration planned to sell the live-oak plantation that he had purchased for preservation. Though it was flourishing, it was to be sacrificed to "the stolid ignorance and stupid malignity of John Branch [Secretary of the Navy] and his filthy subaltern Amos Kendall."[48]

John Quincy and Henry Middleton, recently recalled from the Russian mission, had an entertaining gossip about Middleton's successor, Randolph of Roanoke. That gentleman, whose eccentricity was enhanced rather than subdued by the Russian climate, behaved like a crazy man for a few weeks in St. Petersburg and then retreated to London for the winter. He was now to be re-elected to Congress "for the people of his district are as much enamored with him as the Queen of the fairies was with the ass's head of Bottom after the juice from love-in-idleness had been squeezed upon her eyelids in her sleep."[49]

At the end of April the annual pilgrimage to Quincy was begun. Louisa, Mary Louisa and her nurse, and several servants went in the carriage, followed by Adams in the stage. The ex-President was elated to read, en route, that Jackson's Cabinet had resigned over the "Eaton malaria." Jackson, who demanded a military loyalty from his followers, was unable to keep the Eaton matter where it belonged and accused his official family of plotting to get rid of his favorite and his wife. Eaton resigned first, then Van Buren. About a week later, the President requested the resignations of Samuel D. Ingham, Secretary of the Treasury, and John Branch of the Navy.

The Quincy summer of 1831 was a return to "my plantations," its gardens and its orchards. Adams was suffering from an acute attack of eye trouble, his usual running eyes so bad that he had to curtail his literary activities. Charles kept badgering his father to get on with the life of John Adams, hoping therefore to wean him away from such hot chestnuts as anti-Masonry.

He hoped in vain. In May, Adams attended the anti-Mason convention in Boston at which Timothy Fuller presided. Certain now that Masonry would not voluntarily abjure their unlawful oaths, abolish their odious penalties, and discard their ridiculous secret pageantry, Adams believed that it was his duty as a citizen to take sides.[50] The anti-Masons hoped to make political mileage out of J.Q.A.'s presence on their platform. Hopefully it would be a blow to Clay's candidacy. Although Adams denied an inclination to take any part in the '32 contest, he admitted that the Masonic party in Massachusetts had identified itself with Clay "by winding themselves around the National Republican Party like ivy."[51]

John sent very discouraging bulletins from Washington about the condition of the family flour mill. Adams wrote irritably that their prospective losses did not disturb him as much as John's complaints, but Charles was not as generous. He blamed John for his characteristic style of making noise over his successes although none of his transactions could bear a probe.[52] However, in all fairness the recent loss of $15,000 was Adams's fault. His decision to speculate in flour to sell in the cold winter months while the mill was not operating was based on his prediction of a European war. However, the European crisis abated, flour prices dropped, and it was likely that the surplus would spoil before it could be sold.

For the third time in his life, Adams was asked to deliver a Fourth of July address. He suffered from anxiety over it—partly because the last one had proved to be so explosive and partly because it was difficult to be original on the subject. He fretted that if the oration was poor it would be an "exhibition of faculties in decay." The speech had him so upset that he broke out in boils on the right side of his face and agonized about how he would look on the dais.

The oration was delivered in about an hour and twenty-five minutes, which meant that about a third of what Adams had written was omitted. It was well received, frequently interrupted by applause, and soundly cheered at the end. Charles admired his father's natural style of delivery, contrasting it favorably with Everett's admired but studied manner. However, he noted that his father, as usual, made his points by attacking. There were some gracefully turned phrases, one of which pleased the natives exceedingly. Adams spoke of "the primitive mother of those principles which have made this day a day of glory and of joy—the Plymouth Colony."[53]

The summer could have been marred by the Farmer pamphlet about "poor George," which revealed the story of his unhappy relationship with Eliza Dolph. There were some efforts made to blackmail Charles into paying for the destruction of the pamphlet but he opposed the scheme. "We must not flinch," Charles maintained, disagreeing with Judge Hall's well-meaning advice to keep the pamphlet from Louisa. On the contrary, Charles preferred that his mother know all about it rather than be shocked by some unexpected disclosure. The family endured the embarrassment, apparently with little ill-effect.

James Monroe died on the Fourth of July, in the tradition of John Adams and Thomas Jefferson and J.Q.A. was asked by the city of Boston to deliver a eulogy on August 5 at the Old South Church. Adams, who blamed the penury and financial distress of the six previous years for Monroe's death, noted that the Monroe era was the period of greatest tranquillity that the country had ever enjoyed. Ironically, however, no one regretted the end of his Administration and he had enjoyed less popular veneration than any of his predecessors.

Weeks of laborious work were directed to the composition of the eulogy. Adams toiled through the damp and sultry summer days, reviewing the events of Monroe's life and tracing its details in the notes sent to him by Samuel Gouverneur and in the dusty volumes of Revolutionary War history in his own library. Monroe's life, he observed, spanned the country's history for a full half century.

Thursday afternoon, August 25, was dark and rainy when Charles arrived at the church with his father and mother. The place was crowded to suffocation, the heat oppressive, and the mass of people that pushed and fought to get in the front door noisy. During the delivery of the eulogy, it poured. John Quincy could hardly see his notes it grew so dark in the church, even though lamps were lit on the pulpit. Consequently he held his address so close to his mouth that the audience in the back had trouble hearing him.

Adams felt that the oration was coldly received in Boston. He blamed the hostility of the federalists, Masons, and Jacksonites against its author. Ralph Waldo Emerson, who had been present at the church, said of the eulogy that "There was nothing heroic in the subject and not much in the feelings of the orator, so that it proved rather a spectacle than a speech."[54] Yet the eulogy was popular enough to be frequently reprinted.

Charles and Abby had a baby girl on August 12, whom they named Louisa Catherine after her maternal grandmother. Her father preferred Abigail, but Abby was so opposed to the idea that he abandoned it. Because Abby was in poor health, it was decided that the young couple and their child move to Quincy for two weeks so Abby could be relieved of her household cares. Charles, who was now forced to live with them, was extremely critical of his parents' mode of life. He said that his mother was constantly ill and his niece a nuisance. His attitude was probably a reflection of his fear that he would tangle with his father over financial affairs and anti-Masonic politics. Unable, in spite of his intentions, to hold his tongue, Charles told Adams that the flour business would ruin him quickly. He was surprised that his father, instead of being angry, listened and then said he would ponder over it. As for anti-Masonry, though John Quincy turned down the offer to be the party's presidential candidate, Charles worried that his father would change his mind. It was a relief when news came from Mr. Degrand that on October 2 William Wirt received the nomination. Adams also declined a nomination for the office of Governor of Massachusetts and, instead, declared that he supported Governor Lincoln's administration. "This may perhaps put me in as bad odour with the anti-Masons as I am with the Masons," he lamented.[55] But he still believed, as he told William H. Seward, that the Masonic institution in the United States "is the greatest political evil with which we are now affected."

Before he left for Washington at the end of October, Adams toyed with the idea of purchasing the Boston *Patriot* as a speculation and perhaps installing Charles as the editor. The young man was pleased, immediately visualizing his father giving up politics and devoting himself to filling up the paper with his literary labors and completing the biography of John Adams. It was with some misgivings, then, that Charles watched his father's departure from Boston. He would have been even more disturbed had he known that his aging father was entering a political battlefield in which he would spend the next two decades.

$\star$ ┃ *CHAPTER 21* ┃ $\star$

The Call

"My election to Congress was a Call—*unsolicited—unexpected—spontaneous."*

JOHN QUINCY ADAMS

O N DECEMBER 5, the first session of the Twenty-second Congress convened and the first ex-President to sit in its chamber was given seat #23. Adams's fear that his election would be contested on the grounds of his residence in the Plymouth district was needless. The accuracy of his forecast—"I go to experience slights, mortifications—insults—loss of reputation—and perhaps exposure of myself by infirmities of temper unsuited to the trials"—was yet to be proved.[1]

The first order of business was the election of a Speaker. The two leading candidates were Andrew Stevenson of Virginia and Joel B. Sutherland of Philadelphia. Stevenson won by one vote which, Adams commented, mattered little; though both were men of principle according to their interest, "there was not the worth of a wisp of straw between their value."

John Quincy's first disappointment was his appointment as chairman of the committee on manufactures. Although it was a position of great responsibility, he felt unqualified, for it was alien from any experience in his life. He had been hoping for the foreign affairs committee but the Speaker preferred someone close to the

Administration for that office. Although "I have petitioned almost upon my knees to the Speaker to be released," Adams wrote to Charles, his appeal was in vain.[2] Stevenson would not allow Adams to accept Edward Everett's offer to give him his place on the foreign affairs committee. He must stay where he was because, the Speaker explained, the continuance of the Union was tied up with the tariff problem and his influence exerted upon the eastern states might reconcile them to certain necessary modifications in the tariff. Adams had to agree.

President Jackson's State of the Union message asked for a tariff reduction, which meant that J.Q.A.'s committee would be closely watched by the Administration policy makers. Adams agreed to consult with Louis McLane, Secretary of the Treasury, on his Department's plan. The tariff finally turned out to be a compromise between the protectionist needs of the North and the free-trade needs of the South.

At a meeting with Henry Clay, newly nominated national republican party candidate for President, and others at Edward Everett's house, anti-Administration strategy was discussed. Clay proposed immediate and total repeal of all the duties on such items as tea, coffee, spices, and indigo, and a reduction of revenue of more than seven million dollars. Adams answered that this would be in defiance of both the South and the President, which would ensure the failure of the bill. Clay responded that "he would defy the South, the President and the devil for the maintenance of the American System. There was no need to pay the entire United States debt by March 4, 1833." Adams observed, "It would be a great and glorious day when the United States shall be able to say that they owe not a dollar in the world."[3] He was uncomfortable, as always, in a party council. Besides, if any party was likely to promote his interests, it was the anti-Masons, not Clay's national republicans. Adams believed that the revision of the tariff had to be "the effect of compromise," as were the independence of the United States and the Constitution, realizing that such a solution would suit no party, hence, "the result will be—with heaven."[4]

From the moment that he entered the House, the ex-President took to it with intense, almost romantic enthusiasm. "The forms and proceedings of the House;—the colossal emblem of the Union over the Speaker's chair, the historic Muse at the clock, the echoing pillars of the hall, the tripping Mercuries who bear the resolutions and the amendments between the members and the chair, the calls of ayes and nos, with the different intonations of the answeres from the different voices, the gobbling manner of the clerk in reading over the names, the tone of the Speaker in announcing the vote, and the various shades of pleasure and pain in the countenances of the members on hearing it, would form a fine subject for a descriptive poem."[5] Adams did not write that poem, but his son Charles noted acidly: "His congressional Affairs now turn his head as much as others formerly did. He runs into everything headlong."[6]

George Washington's centennial birthday celebration was a disappointment to his admirer, John Quincy Adams. John A. Washington refused to allow the first President's remains to be transferred to the city that bore his name and entombed under the Capitol. Somehow this proposal was linked in J.Q.A.'s mind with the preservation of the Union. "I now disbelieve its duration for twenty years and doubt its continuance after five," he wrote. "It is falling into the sere and yellow leaf."[7]

An attempted rapprochement between the President and his predecessor also proved to be a disappointment. Colonel Richard M. Johnson approached Adams on Jackson's behalf, proposing that social intercourse be resumed. Adams, who claimed never to have known that the cause of the rift was Jackson's anger that he had not stopped the gossip against Mrs. Jackson in his party's press, was agreeable. But upon further reflection, he decided that the matter was a political issue. If he resumed friendship with Jackson, the federal party, now pro-Clay, would disown him. It was best to be circumspect.

Thomas Boylston Adams's death in early spring, though not a surprise, was "a deep affliction." Charles was ordered to arrange that his uncle be buried in the family vault beside his sister Abigail, George Washington Adams, and his own infant child.[8] The death made financial complications because John Quincy held the mortgage on his brother's house and farm in Braintree. He told his son to take possession of the property but see that the rents were paid to his uncle's widow and to pay for the funeral and burial. With some regret, John Quincy would have to accept Charles's evaluation of the youngest son of John and Abigail Adams—"A man who paid a bitter penance for his follies and left his Children to share the same as his only legacy."[9]

Once again, in March, John Quincy tried to get excused from

further service on the committee on manufactures, justifying his request by citing his impending trip to Philadelphia as part of a committee appointed to look into the United States Bank. In the debate that ensued, such enemies of J.Q.A. as Churchill Cambrelang of New York, William Dayton of South Carolina, James Bates of Maine, and Jesse Speight of North Carolina were loud in their assertion that only he could mend the split in the parties and make it possible for an acceptable tariff to be written. Friends such as Everett and H. A. S. Dearborn extolled his virtues but moved to postpone the motion. Finally, Adams withdrew his motion but promised to renew it at another time.

Earlier, Nicholas Biddle, president of the United States Bank since 1822, applied to Congress for rechartering. Although Jackson's hostility to the bank was notorious and its charter had four more years to run, Biddle had accepted the advice of Webster and Clay that this was a good time to make application. Congress would be sure to pass the bank bill, Clay reassured Biddle, and if Jackson vetoed it, he would make it an issue in his political campaign which was about to begin.

However, Congress did not allow the plan to go smoothly. Judge Augustin S. Clayton introduced a resolution for an inquiry into the bank, supporting his request with a long list of charges against it. It was accepted, thanks to the efforts of George McDuffie of South Carolina, who was in charge of the recharter and wanted the tariff considered first.

At the United States Hotel in Philadelphia, the bank committee, carefully weighted by the Speaker with anti-bank members, kept bachelor quarters. John Quincy said that it was very sociable and good-humored. He doubted that the tariff question would be settled at this session of Congress, so it was just as well to let the nullifiers who threatened to act if the tariff was not moderated make good their threats.[10] In the meantime, the congressional committee worked from ten in the morning to late afternoon, "chained to the bank." In the evening they visited the theater, received and paid visits.[11]

The bank committee issued a majority report, saying that their investigations had convinced them to recommend that, at present, the bank should not be rechartered, because it was an unnecessary institution, whose management was both unintelligent and dishonest. Later, some of the charges were disclaimed by certain committee members on the floor of Congress, which would have made the majority report, originally passed by a 4–3 vote, a minority report. And many agreed that the vindictive vigor with which the bank and its directors were attacked made the report ridiculous. Hezekiah Niles said that it was "the strangest mixture of *water, gruel and vinegar,* the most awkward and clumsy and exaggerated *ex parte* production that we ever read. . . . Never did a man more mistake himself than Mr. Clayton, when he thought himself capable of grappling a subject like this. . . ."[12]

George McDuffie wrote the minority report which found the bank free of all charges against it. It was not, however, strong enough for Adams. He prepared his own minority report with the concurrence of John G. Watmough, a Pennsylvania national republican. John Quincy was a staunch supporter of the bank—which reflected his social class, his respect for private property, and his belief in sound money—and offended by the idea of states issuing paper money through their own banks. Nicholas Biddle, a friend who had often entertained him and his wife, was a cultivated man with literary tastes, who was very congenial to Adams. "There is except my own son, not a man living with whom I could open in such unlimited confidence all my impressions of public duty and of unpromising anticipation as I then did with you; and in the tangled path before me, I feel the want of friendly and disinterested Counsel more than has ever happened to me through the whole of my life," he wrote later.[13] John Quincy, therefore, was anxious to "vindicate the honour of injured worth." Nicholas Biddle, he asserted, was a man of sound judgment, liberal spirit, benevolent feeling, and irreproachable integrity. He pointed out that the committee with which he conducted the investigations had a "predetermined hostility," which caused it to spend its time "prying for flaws and hunting exceptions." Whatever the bank's managers said or did, they were wrong. For example: "If they enlarge their discounts and accommodations, they supply temptations to over-trading and bring the Bank to the verge of ruin. If they contract their issues, they produce unheard of distress in the trading community."[14] The insinuations and accusations were as absurd as they were erroneous and inconclusive. Finally, Adams asserted that the proceedings of the Commission were without authority and in flagrant violation of the rights of the bank and the principles of freedom.[15]

Charles, who was at this time often at odds with his father, admired the report. "My father has exalted himself prodigiously," he wrote. "There is a high souled independence in his course which suits my particular temper exactly." However, Louisa, who was already at Quincy, had another point of view. "Mr. A———'s quite knocked up here it seems and will probably not be sent again. His Report is not admired and it is all over with him."[16]

Utterly weary of the lengthening session of Congress, Adams said that he was never so much harassed in his life. If he could come out of it "with a sound intellect I will never I think be so swallowed up with business again." At midnight he dropped to sleep over his papers to be up again at five in the morning.[17] The tariff bill, which Adams now thought was very good, still had him "chained to his desk" at the end of June. At long last it passed the House and the Senate, to be signed into law by the President on July 14. In general, the bill reduced duties to the 1824 level, and, Jackson hoped, would appease the South adequately.

The bank bill suffered a different fate. It passed through Congress, almost unanimously supported by the New England and Middle Atlantic states. However, Jackson would not be intimidated into accepting the odious institution. Clay and the opposition thought that they had him on the horns of a dilemma. If he signed the bill he would be giving in to the bank that he loathed, if he did not he would most likely lose the support of Pennsylvania, the bank's home and a pivotal state for him.

"The Bank is trying to kill me, *but I will kill it!*" the hero told Van Buren, holding his hand in one of his own and passing the other through his long white locks, while he lay stretched on his sickbed, "a spectre in physical appearance."[18] The President sent back to Congress a lengthy veto message that analyzed his reasons for rejecting the bill. Despite John Marshall's decision in McCulloch v. Maryland, Jackson considered the bank unconstitutional. At the close of his veto message, the President introduced a class slant: "It is to be regretted that the rich and powerful too often bend the acts of government to their selfish purposes," the people's friend said. "Many of our rich men have not been content with equal protection and equal benefits, but have besought us to make them richer by an act of Congress."

With a curious lack of perception, the national republicans peppered the countryside with copies of Jackson's veto message, thinking it would defeat him. Quite the contrary, the electorate loved old

Hickory's attack on the bank as a monster monopoly, some of whose stockholders were sinister foreigners and the rest of whom were members of the monied aristocracy.

Just before John Quincy's sixty-fifth birthday, an anonymous letter appeared in the Boston *Daily Advertiser & Patriot* describing him as "looking younger and sprightlier than when he stood at the head of the nation." It also complimented him for his steady and cool handling of the bank and tariff negotiations, which displayed "a promptness and decision characteristic of his patriotic predecessors of the same name, industrious for steady habits. He certainly, at this time, stands on an eminence deservedly high."[19]

At this very moment, Adams was having difficulties in the House of Representatives. A motion had been offered to censure William Stanberry of Ohio for words spoken in debate that were allegedly hostile to the Speaker. When Adams was polled by the clerk, he delivered a paper which read, "I ask to be excused from voting on this resolution, believing it to be unconstitutional, inasmuch as it assumes inferences of fact from words spoken by the member, without giving the words themselves, and the fact not being warranted in my judgment by the words he did use." Though the House refused to excuse him, Adams refused to vote, not from disrespect, he insisted, but from the conscientious motives which he had recorded. Someone in the House said that Adams could have left the chamber and so avoided voting. "I do not shrink from my duty by such an expedient," the ex-President explained. "It is not my right alone, but the right of all the members, and of the people of the United States, which are concerned in this question, and I cannot evade it."

A motion to reconsider the vote refusing to excuse Adams lost 59–74. The Speaker once more read the rule, which mandated that every member must vote, and then ordered the question repeated. Adams gave no response, just remained in his seat.

The House could no longer ignore the action of its distinguished member. According to their rules, they had to either expel him or commit him to the custody of the sergeant at arms. John Quincy said that he was greatly mortified but he remained immovable. During the debate that followed, Edward Everett remonstrated with his colleagues for even entertaining the idea of censuring Adams, of whom it might be said that no one was more assiduous in his duty. And on the next morning when the vote was taken, "the House cooled down wonderfully," the culprit observed. A motion to lay the censure resolution on the table passed 89–63.[20]

John Quincy returned to his homestead shortly after the episode of his near-disgrace, which convinced Charles that the old man was not suited for his seat in the House. The hoped-for quiet was occasionally interrupted by partisans who urged Adams, despite his determination to remain neutral, to take a stand on the presidential election. Still firmly steeped in the cause of anti-Masonry and worried about its survival, Adams was not willing to implement his convictions with public statements. He was pleased, however, when Charles came out with the statement that the Masonic society was "false and unsound . . . at variance with the foundation of society and government."[21] Pennsylvania held the balance of the next election, the ex-President said. "Let her be true to herself & all will be well."[22]

New York was hit so hard by a cholera epidemic that John, who had been suffering from severe eye trouble, decided not to come to Quincy for the summer to avoid passing through the affected city. But, in spite of the day of fasting and prayer ordered by the Governor of Massachusetts, the disease spread to Boston as well as to Philadelphia, Washington, and elsewhere. "The destroying angel is hovering over us," Adams feared. "I grow superstitious . . . I cannot reconcile it to my theory of divine benevolence that his visitation is without some great reforming and redeeming purpose."[23]

The news from Washington concerning the family flour mill continued to be very discouraging. John's illness, followed by his associate Mr. Greenleaf's, convinced Adams that the business should be given up. He told his son to prepare to shut up as soon as possible since this was probably to be his last winter in Washington, and dispose of the property as advantageously as possible. But by the time he returned to Washington, it was obvious that his popularity in the state and the Plymouth district had increased rather than waned. My father "will probably remain in Congress as long as he has a mind, and I do not see but what General Jackson may have a lease equally long of the Presidency," Charles observed.[24]

During the previous winter, Adams had composed a long narrative poem in 266 stanzas, written in the Byronic ottava rima, which he called *Dermot MacMorrogh*. Most of the stanzas had been composed in groups of two or three before their author rose in the morning. And during his afternoon walks around the capital,

Adams would compose an additional few verses which he would memorize and then write down when he returned home. In the evening, the poet read his day's composition to his wife, herself a poet of sorts. The narrative, a moral, historical tale about events in Ireland about 1172, was written to teach the virtues of marital fidelity, patriotism, and piety, Adams said.

Very nervous about the reception of his epic, Adams assured his publisher that the first edition would sell because of momentary curiosity about the author and the singularity of the subject. The whole edition did sell quickly, as did several subsequent editions.[25]

"Scarcely any man in this country who has ever figured in public life has ever ventured into the field of general literature, none as successfully," Adams recorded with satisfaction. His *Dermot Mac-Morrogh*, he bragged, was an original work of "history, imagination, and poetry." One must, however, agree with Charles that the work lacked invention, imagination, and, in common with all of John Quincy's poetry, descriptive imagery. Perhaps it would have been best, as the frank young man suggested, had the epic never been published.[26]

During the nearly six months' visit to Quincy that John Quincy and Louisa had made during the summer, Charles and Abby stayed with them at the mansion. The two families lived together quietly and happily without a single disagreeable or painful happening. It was rumored that Adams would replace Edward Livingston as Secretary of State in Jackson's new Cabinet, a move that was supposed to have been inspired by Van Buren. But John Quincy denied the possibility and, of course, nothing happened. In reality, Adams was as critical of Jacksonian policy as ever. He accused the President, whose 1832 message had just been read, of surrendering the Union "to the nullifiers of the South and the land robbers of the West . . . no more than I predicted nearly two years since. . . ."[27]

Despite Adams's disbelief in Jackson's integrity on the issue of the Union, on December 10 the President delivered his nullification proclamation. The hero said: "I consider then, the power to annul a law of the United States, assumed by one state, *incompatible with the existence of the Union, contradicted expressly by the letter of the Constitution, unauthorized by its spirit, inconsistent with every principle on which it was founded, and destructive of the great object for which it was formed.*"[28]

South Carolina passed an ordinance declaring the Adams tariff null and void and Governor Hayne countered the President's statement with a fine statement of the case for nullification. He displayed some caution, however, because the South as a whole had rejected the policy and the Carolina unionist convention, which had met in Charleston from December 10 to 14, was ready to go to war rather than accept nullification.[29]

Though the authorship of the nullification proclamation has been generally attributed to Secretary of State Livingston, its resemblance to John Quincy Adams's style and turn of thought was noted by at least two diverse readers. A New York publisher, who had just received Adams's anonymous introduction to a source book on American history that included the Declaration of Independence, the Constitution, and Washington's farewell address, remarked on the similarity between the ex-President's exposition on the Union and the President's newly issued nullification proclamation. Consequently, without consultation, he added the Jackson document to the source book.[30] Charles Francis, reading the proclamation in Boston, had the same impression. "I do know who was the author," he said positively but wrongly. He also agreed with his father that a public meeting in Boston should not be held to respond to the Jackson proclamation. "Wait at least until the whole policy of the Administration shall be disclosed. It is rotten ice," the Plymouth member advised.[31]

When Adams heard that the proposed meeting did take place at Faneuil Hall, he was amused at Harrison Gray Otis's speech, which included extracts from the last report of the Hartford convention, "his own legitimate offspring." However, he could report back to Charles that the first reports about the effect of the President's message in South Carolina had arrived in Washington. They fortified the union party and made the nullifiers lose their temper.[32]

Jackson had made clear in his December message that if an "exigency" arose and the nullifiers seized imported goods from the South Carolina customs houses or took any other overt action against the national tariff law, he would promptly notify Congress. On January 16, the President sent a special message to Congress, afterwards erroneously known as the "force bill message," asking for permission to store confiscated goods in "floating customs houses" on United States ships off South Carolina harbors. He also wanted to collect duties in cash and to be granted other powers to forestall Carolinian subterfuges to avoid collecting the tariff.

Thomas Boylston Adams, stationed in Augusta, Georgia, asked his uncle how to act if he was forced to fight against South Carolina. Unionist John Quincy Adams answered unhesitatingly that if Georgia or South Carolina resisted and used physical force to do so, their act "would be unconstitutional. . . . It would also be an overt Act of Levying War against the United States. . . . If you are unwilling to perform military duty against the Act of a State, then you would have to resign your commission."[33] In a larger sense, Adams still believed that the South Carolina rebellion was part of the "Administrative Revolution." He could not accept Jacksonian credibility.[34]

The Washington winter was so severe that the Adams house became a hospital. Louisa and John were both very ill and even the Congressman had a serious bout of fever to add to his palsy, running eyes, and rheumatism. It was hard for him to hold his pen and he was so ill for several days that he was barely able to crawl to and from the Capitol. But he got there lest he miss some important decision.

The tariff bill was now out of Adams's hands. It had been assigned by Speaker Stevenson to the committee on ways and means, whose chairman was Gulian C. Verplanck, a northern democrat. The Massachusetts delegation met to try to defeat the bill in the Senate but they had no hope of stopping it in the House. As expected, Verplanck's committee brought in a bill which almost eliminated protection, reducing the rates to about one-half of the current ones over a period of two years. After John Quincy's suggestion that the Secretary of the Treasury be asked whether the government would have enough revenue from the reduced tariff to take care of its needs was ignored, he decided to be merely a spectator at the Verplanck bill debate. Besides, he reasoned, he was still exhausted from his recent illness.

"Our slaves sail the Northern ships and run the Northern spindles," he heard Georgia's August Smith Clayton say. The Georgian's argument was premised on the concept that slaves raised and harvested the cotton that was then used in northern mills and the cloth carried overseas in northern ships. Alert now to the speaker's rhetoric, John Quincy shuddered when the southerner said: "Our slaves are our machinery, and we have as good a right to profit by them as do the northern men who profit by the machinery they employ."[35]

Age, debility, inarticulateness all vanished at once. Extemporaneously and with a passion that he never unleashed before on the floor of the House, Adams spoke. His avowed purpose was to place "*protection* itself under the shield of constitutional right," thereby giving it a last chance for salvation. He also revealed the "superabundant Protection" enjoyed by the southern slaveholders at the expense of the rest of the Union. Hoping to effectively turn the tables on his assailants, the tears rolling down his cheeks from his rheumy eyes, he rasped: "I have heard it declared by the gentleman from Georgia that the species of population he alluded to constituted *the machines of the South.* Now those *Machines* have twenty-odd Representatives in this Hall, Representatives elected not by the *machines,* but by those who own them. . . . Have the manufacturers asked for representation from their *machines?* Their looms and factories have no vote in Congress, but the machines of the South have more than twenty Representatives on this floor. . . . What I say is that the South possesses a great protected *interest. . . .*" Waving his copy of the Constitution over his head, he read the clause in it that required the return of fugitive slaves to their owners. "What, what is this but protection to the owners of the *machines* of the South?"

Then, with full awareness that he was going where angels fear to tread, Adams said, "This Constitution . . . guarantees to every state protection against domestic violence. This, to be sure, is a general provision, but everybody knows that where this sort of machinery exists there is liable to be more violence than elsewhere because the *machinery* sometimes exerts self-moving power. Such a power has been exerted. Very recently." His reference was to the Nat Turner rebellion in which sixty slaves, led by the Virginia Black, had murdered fifty-five white people. Listening to him, the southern contingent glowered with fury.

Unperturbed, the elderly statesman continued his denunciation of the slaveholding interest, using Clayton's euphemism "machine" with increasing contempt. The army protected the South, he said. Only the states with "this machinery" needed a standing army. His district of Plymouth, the whole manufacturing interest, had not one dollar's use for an army. The South needed the Navy also to police the ships so that cargoes of cotton could sail safely. Adams did not omit a barb about the generous distribution of public lands that the South had supported. "My constituents have as much right to say to the people, 'We will not submit to the protection of your interests' as the people of the South have the right to address such language to them," Adams said.

William Drayton of South Carolina, livid with anger, accused Adams of suggesting that the slave properties of the South go unprotected unless the tariff protect the northern manufacturing interests. He has "thrown a firebrand into the Hall!" Drayton shouted. Three days later, Adams said to his colleagues that it was the nullification ordinance which was the firebrand.[36]

Henry Clay, who had been listening to the debate in the House, heard the speech, and, Adams noted, made use of it. He authored a compromise tariff that was "the stab under the fifth rib to the manufacturers . . . the sacrifice of the North to the South of the free labourers to the slave-holders." It provided that there would be a reduction of duties every two years for ten years until the level was twenty per cent by 1842. Adams did not oppose the tariff but neither did he approve it, merely conceding that "it may serve the purpose of a Truce between the parties."[37] And it had the further political purpose of saving Calhoun, who had resigned from the Vice Presidency and was now a Senator from South Carolina and his fellow nullifiers.

On the same day that the House of Representatives accepted the compromise tariff, Jackson's force bill was passed. Adams voted for it although he thought that Jackson would have earned personal honor and strengthened the Union immeasurably had he put down the nullifiers. Adams saw the repeal of the nullification ordinance by South Carolina and its rejection of the force bill as a tragedy because it signified an end to the American system. "I have written its epitaph—I mourn over it as over my own child—for I and not Henry Clay was its father. It was mine as the record of its birth in the Senate of the United States of Monday the 23rd of February 1807 will testify. And now I have had the melancholy consolation of writing its epitaph."[38]

When Andrew Jackson was inaugurated for his second term as President of the United States and Martin Van Buren was sworn in as Vice President on March 4, 1833, ex-President John Quincy Adams was absent. The Inaugural Speech, Adams recorded, was brief and full of smooth professions. His evaluation of the hero had not altered.

In April, Adams set out alone for Quincy, although "dear little Louisa" stood at the door with her cloak and bonnet on, insisting to the last moment that she was going with Grandpapa. She had to wait until later when she would accompany her grandmother. The trip north was somewhat faster now that part of it was by railroad. Adams was impressed with the speed of the trains, sixteen miles in fifty minutes, but inconvenienced by the "shower of burning flakes floating around us in the cars all the way."[39]

Fanny Kemble was "the lion in Boston" that season. Adams found her very well formed and not unhandsome but merely "passable." She talked about dramatic literature with the ex-President without impressing him that she was different from any other well-educated, intelligent woman. He was somewhat piqued that she avoided discussion of her own poetic productions, and instead talked endlessly about her prowess as a horsewoman. Adams asked her if she had ever seen her aunt, Mrs. Siddons, on the stage. She replied that she had not and, until a few years earlier, had had no intention of becoming an actress herself.

John's poor health frightened his parents. His eyes troubled him and he suffered from constant debility. Adams begged him to come to Quincy to recuperate. "I entreat you not to disappoint me," he wrote. While waiting for the family to join him, Adams said that he "lived like Robinson Crusoe" in the Adams mansion. He read, strolled around the garden and nursery, and plucked up the never-ending weeds.

Josiah Quincy, now president of Harvard University, visited Adams to tell him that Andrew Jackson would be visiting Boston and that the corporation of the university had decided to bestow upon him the degree of Doctor of Laws. When Quincy intimated that Adams would be invited to the ceremony, he declined the honor, citing the strained personal relations between him and the seventh President. Furthermore, he said with more honesty than tact, "as an affectionate child of our Alma Mater," he would not want to be present to "witness her disgrace in conferring her highest literary honors upon a barbarian who could not write a sentence of grammar and hardly could spell his own name." Quincy sputtered some explanations about precedent and protocol. President Monroe, upon his visit, had received the honorary degree, therefore the corporation felt that omitting the same gesture for Jackson might be construed as party spirit. Adams was unimpressed by the argument. He commented to Dr. Waterhouse that a Doctorate for which an apology was necessary was a "cheap honor . . . a sycophantic compliment."[40]

In July, Benjamin Hallett tried to persuade Adams to consent to be nominated by the anti-Masons for Governor of Massachusetts. Though Hallett insisted that such party stalwarts as Stephen C. Philips, Edward Everett, and Daniel Webster wanted him, Adams refused because he doubted that he had the strength to hold the balance of the parties. He suggested that Daniel Webster run instead, but was told that he looked to be President of the United States. Finally, in September, after much pressure was exerted on him, Adams agreed to allow the anti-Masons to run him. And on September 12, he received that party's unanimous endorsement. Charles carried his father's acceptance to the committee. Once again, John Quincy Adams was launched "upon the strong ocean of political electioneering."

Among the remedies suggested for the ex-President's rheumatism was a trip to the White Mountains. He went with Mr. and Mrs. Isaac P. Davis for a ten-day tour, during which he admired the majesty of the Great Stone Face and revelled in the beauty of the New England countryside. However, he could not escape politics entirely. In Vermont, their annual election was going on and it became apparent that the basic struggle was between Masonry and anti-Masonry.[41]

A self-imposed summer chore was teaching small Louisa to read. He worked with her in his study, where she preferred looking at his "household gods" to mastering the alphabet. The six little bronze busts were J.Q.A.'s favorite possessions. There were two philosophers, Plato and Socrates; two poets, Homer and Vergil; and two orators, Cicero and Demosthenes. On the wall were many prints brought back from his travels, the most cherished one, an engraving of Cicero at his villa. Around the room there were mementos and *objets d'art* from Europe, but mostly there were shelves and shelves of books.

Annoyed at his lack of perseverance, John Quincy analyzed the characteristics needed for a good teacher. He gave the highest rating to soothing, coaxing, and flattering with a little, a very little, shaming. In order to try to identify with his granddaughter he set himself the task of learning Hebrew, which he had tried to do for forty years without much success. "I make my own indocility the apology for hers," he said.[42]

"I have a grandson, the first, though there are three little girls who have familiarized my ears to the appellation of grandfather," Adams told Christopher Hughes. "My hopes revive," he recorded when the news came that Charles and Abby were the parents of a fine boy. He was given the name of John Quincy Adams. On his christening day, his grandfather delivered to Charles John Adams's seal which had been affixed to the peace treaties with Great Britain. A few years before his death, John Adams had given this seal to John Quincy. It was engraved with a pine tree, a deer, and a fish swimming in the sea, and in an oval over the cartoon were thirteen stars to represent the thirteen original states. The legend, a quotation from Horace, read: "Piscemur venemur ut olim," which John Quincy translated as "fish and hunt we will as heretofore."

After his death, Adams told Charles, the seal would be his, but it was his desire that it be passed on to "your son this day baptized" if he prove a descendant worthy of it so that it would continue to be a memorial to John Adams, one of the chief founders of American independence. As an afterthought, or perhaps in recognition of the fact that Charles was his third son, John Quincy added: "And should you have other sons, I wish you to leave it to either of them at your discretion."[43]

The gubernatorial election did not look promising for the Adams candidacy, particularly since the national republican convention was not expected to support his nomination. Boston and Worcester were "hotbeds of Masonry" and almost all the printers in the state were Masons, which, of course, "infected the presses." However, even though he expected it, Adams was bitter about his rejection by the national republicans. Alexander H. Everett, who attended the convention because he thought that his brother Edward might receive the nomination, reported that Chairman William Sullivan was very prejudiced against the ex-President. Not at all surprised, because Sullivan had been one of the Otis group that had attacked him in 1829, Adams decided that the whole proceedings at the convention were impelled by the single motive of excluding him. "They had treated me much as the New York legislature had treated De Witt Clinton when they turned him out from being a Canal Commissioner."[44]

Governor Levi Lincoln blamed Adams's anti-Masonry publications for the falling off of his supporters, which had forced him to decline the nomination for re-election, but the Plymouth member refused to accept the responsibility. He argued that, quite the opposite, personal opposition to him benefited Masonry. "This will be the only cement to keep the national republican party together," he said bitterly. It was a deplorable controversy which would inevitably bring his life "to close in hopeless conflict with the world," read Adams's *Diary* entry at this time. His memoir was filled with words of doom and paragraphs of self-pity, but there was no suggestion that he considered retiring from public life.

Henry Clay, who had been touring the Atlantic seaboard cities from Baltimore to Boston, visited Adams at Quincy. "This fashion of peddling for popularity by travelling round the country gathering crowds together, hawking for public dinners and spouting empty speeches is growing into high fashion," Adams noted scornfully. His own style was to hide away from the vulgar hubbub of political activity and then, when defeated, to continue to sulk in his tent.

Louisa and the family preceded the ex-President to Washington. He followed by hack and steamboat to Perth Amboy, where he boarded the railroad cars that would carry him to Bordentown. He was in Car B, No. 1, when the train stopped, the wheels were oiled, and it continued. After travelling five miles further, the front left wheel of Adams's car caught fire, burned for several minutes, and then slipped off the rail. The train stopped only after several rear cars telescoped into the injured one which, by some mechanical miracle, had slipped onto the track again. One of the passengers was killed and many others hurt, when the twisted railroad cars piled up on the siding. Adams gave his testimony about the accident and then left for Philadelphia. "I have had a surfeit of Railroad travelling which must undergo great improvement before I shall ever be willing to trust a friend of mine to it," he said, but, refusing to give in to his own fears, continued by railroad as if the accident had not occurred.[45]

The Massachusetts gubernatorial race was indecisive and no one received a majority.

John Davis (*National Republican*)	25,149
Marcus Morton (*Democrat*)	15,493
John Quincy Adams (*anti-Mason*)	18,274
Samuel C. Allen (*Workingman*)	3,495

Now the election had to go into the House of Representatives for them to choose two candidates to go into the Senate, where the Governor would be chosen. Edward Everett tried to convince Adams that if he and Morton were chosen, the Senate would select Morton. Therefore he wanted Adams to decline in favor of his fellow Congressman, Davis. Adams did not let him know of his intentions, because he had lost confidence in the two Everetts—"both reeds shaken with the wind."

At the same time, Adams became disillusioned with Richard Rush, who had taken a stand against the United States Bank. His defection from the anti-Mason party was attributed by Adams to his passion to go to England again. Unfortunately, however, Rush's action would ruin anti-Masonry in Pennsylvania and go far to demolish it in the Union. Hence, Rush was removed from Adams's shrinking roster of friends. "It closes all confidential correspondence between him and me forever," he wrote. "And friendship! What friendship have I ever found but it has been disgraced by misconduct or betrayed by sordid interests?"[46]

As he had promised at the time that he accepted the nomination during the summer, he withdrew from the gubernatorial contest since he had not been elected by popular acclamation. Charles taxed his father for an explanation of what seemed like a reversal of his decision in 1829. Adams explained that though the cases were parallel, they were not alike in all particulars. In the earlier period, he claimed, he had the strongest popular vote although "by political legerdemain another had the votes of New Jersey, Ohio, and four votes from New York." New Jersey's vote, which would have turned the election, was lost because of "the dirty intrigue" of an accomplice of Aaron Burr. "I had beyond all question the highest aggregate popular vote," he insisted.[47] In this case, Adams reminded his son, since Davis had at least 7,000 more votes, he could only be elected by a bargain of the anti-Masons with another party to exclude the man who had the largest popular vote. Adams would not do it. Perhaps he had had enough of bargains.

Adams feared that the result of his withdrawal would be alienation from the anti-Masonic party. "My public life will terminate by the elimination from me of all mankind . . . it is the experience of all ages that the people grow weary of old men. . . . There is an ill-fortune that pursues, in old age, especially, men whom fortune has much favored in youth."[48] He was not open to persuasion. Had the national republicans endorsed his nomination, he would have felt that his Administration could have united the shattered fragment of the party that had supported his Presidency. But now, with the support of less than one-fourth of the electorate, he refused to force himself upon the people.[49]

Adams threw his support to Davis, contrary to his former statements. He gave as his reasons the change in his feeling toward Governor Lincoln, the overthrow of the national republican party in many elections, and Rush's desertion of anti-Masonry for Jackson-Van Buren Masonry, dragging the Boston anti-Masons with him. If he had not influenced them all, he had certainly carried with them their organ, the *Daily Advocate*.[50] Hence Charles was delegated to present a letter to the Speaker of the House of Representatives in Boston, withdrawing John Quincy Adams's name for Governor.

In his own style, Adams had effectively deserted the anti-Mason party and retired to his natural condition as a man without a party. It is doubtful, however, that he could have been convinced that his action would be so interpreted. His son hinted at it with no result.

Seated in his same seat, Adams again witnessed the election of Andrew Stevenson as Speaker of the House, when the Congress reconvened. The Administration forces were in full sail and New England had lost all of her influence, Adams observed. "Maine and New Hampshire are among the most obsequious Spaniels of the Collar—Connecticut has gone and Rhode Island is going over to the Kennel—Vermont alone stands erect by the triumph of anti-Masonry."[51]

The congressional session was remarkably uneventful for the Plymouth member. His anti-Masonic crusade over, it now appeared that both the anti-Masons and Masonry were in a decline. Adams's chief objection to the Masons had been to their secret oaths, rituals, and penalties. Several states, including Massachusetts, Rhode Island, and Vermont, had passed legislation forbidding the administering of extrajudicial oaths, thus satisfying his objections. He also noted with satisfaction that membership in the order had declined in some of the northern states and disappeared in others. Eventually, it became obvious that the anti-Mason party would be absorbed in the emerging whig party.

Very little was accomplished in Congress. The House, Adams predicted, by a majority of a little less than forty would sustain the President in his experiment to sweep the United States Bank and its president off the face of the earth. Adams refused to get involved in the debate. James Polk of Tennessee tried to needle him into participation by glorifying Jackson and abusing his predecessors, but succeeded only in getting a sharp response: "Whenever any admirers of the President shall think fit to pay his court to him in this house, either by a flaming panegyric upon him, or a raucous invective on me, he shall never elicit one word of reply from me." When the ex-President quoted Hamlet's lines:

> No! let the candid tongue lick absurd pomp,
> And crook the pregnant hinges of the knee,
> Where Thrift may follow fawning. . . .

Polk shrank back into his shell and said nothing. Adams sat there deaf to the nullifiers who introduced the subject into all their speeches. Some of them were eloquent, he admitted, like Pinckney, who "raved till half past three o'clock."[52]

In April, the United States Bank was battered by a series of four resolutions that were passed in the House. Adams came home from the session "exhausted, dispirited and mortified," particularly annoyed by the resolution that provided for the appointment of a select committee for a bank investigation with power to visit the bank and any of its branches. Nothing had ever been more arbitrary and tyrannical since the domiciliary visits of Revolutionary France, he fussed. "It proves how feeble even in this country are all the principles of freedom in collision with a current of popular prejudice or passion."[53]

There was an occasional happy moment. Warren R. Davis of South Carolina, while speaking on a bill for the reduction of appropriations for Ministries to Great Britain and Russia, turned to Adams and said: "Well do I remember the enthusiastic zeal with which we reproached the Administration of that gentleman, and the ardor and vehemence with which we labored to bring in another. For the share that I had in these transactions, and it was not a small one, *I hope God will forgive me, for I shall never forgive myself.*"[54] And on May 23, John Adams took his father to Georgetown to the landing place of the Chesapeake and Ohio canal. The president and directors of the company had invited two canalboats of congressional families to make an excursion to Harper's Ferry. It was a pleasant outing, during which Adams saw the junction of the Potomac and the Shenandoah rivers. However, he did not think the landscape was as sublime as Jefferson had described it. He thought it resembled the course of the Elbe River between Dresden and Bohemia but on a smaller scale. The canal was, indeed, a great work, John Quincy conceded, but he questioned its utility, predicting that railroads would take the place of canals and the horse could not compete with the locomotive.

Shortly before the end of the congressional session, news came from France that Lafayette was dead. To honor his memory, the halls of Congress and the chairs of its presiding officers were dressed in mourning. Calhoun offered a resolution, which was passed, that John Quincy Adams be asked to deliver the Lafayette eulogy before both Houses at the next session.

Meanwhile, Adams arranged his summer plans, corresponding with Charles from the empty room of the committee on manufactures. Tongue in cheek, he wrote that the office of chairman had been a sinecure this session and the use of the room one of its privileges. Though John's health had been very poor for more than a year, he would not listen to his father's pleas that he and his family should spend the summer in Quincy. "Nothing would do you as much good," Adams urged. "I wish you would think so and gratify your affectionate father." Part of his urging was due to his belief that this was his last term in Washington. He hoped that John would not settle permanently in Washington, believing it would mean irretrievable ruin for him. "Stay in Washington this winter," he advised, "but afterwards come to Quincy and manage the estate. . . . This in my belief is the only expedient now left to save your children and yourself, and to give quiet to my last hours."[55]

Exhausted from the long hours in the House—one day the session lasted for fifteen hours without intermission and refreshments— Adams looked forward to his vacation. However, once at home, he was immediately drawn into the crisis at Harvard over student disturbances which had resulted in the senior class's return home without knowing whether they would have a Commencement or not. The problem arose because President Quincy had turned over several students who had destroyed college property to the county court to be tried in September, and had expelled others. Consequently some of the seniors refused their parts for the Commencement.

Adams explained to his friend Quincy that he would have to justify his policy of abandoning students to the civil authorities like common criminals before the Board of Overseers. It was a new way of handling breaches of college discipline and Quincy had bitter enemies on the Board, particularly James T. Austen and Alexander Everett.

A committee was formed to investigate the scandal, although most of the Board was agreed that it was a violation of college tradition to go to the law and that the students were too young to be fully responsible. Adams was in a most difficult position. He wanted to support Josiah Quincy, who had been his friend for fifty years but was once again in a minority position and unable to be really effective.

It was ironical that President Quincy found himself in this position, for he had started many of the student reforms at the college. He improved their food and services in commons, had them addressed as "Mr.," personally took over parietal details, and so was confused and hurt when the students turned against him. Adams privately blamed Quincy's permissive attitude, particularly the familiarity he allowed with him and his family, for the breach of behavior. Fortunately, the committee reports and Adams's memoranda on the episode proved unnecessary because, in the end, the students capitulated and the Commencement was held.[56]

As late as the end of September, John Quincy, Louisa, and small Louisa waited for John and Mary Adams to join them. Louisa was quite ill when Mary's letter arrived, saying that her husband was detained by severe sickness. A few weeks later, news reached Quincy that John was dying. Adams immediately left for Washington, but although he arrived in three days his son was already in a coma, and died that night. Louisa, who had been unable to travel earlier, followed a month later with Charles. John Quincy found his loss "irreparable," commenting that it had "almost broken his heart." The sorrowing parents blamed themselves for not getting their son away from the unhealthy Washington climate and for pressuring him about the flour mill. Some of Louisa's anguish was expressed in a poem, written many months after the young man's death, called "John's Grave."

> Softly tread! for herein lies
> The young, the beautiful, the wise
> Sorrow untimely nipp'd the flower
> He sunk beneath her blasting power
> But left a loved and hallowed name. . . .

Still grieving but without any thought but to fulfill his obligations, Adams resumed his seat among the 188 representatives who constituted the new chamber and, on the last day of the year, delivered the oration on Lafayette, whose composition had occupied him all summer. In his thorough manner, Adams reviewed Lafayette's complex career through the American Revolution, the French Revolution, the Napoleonic interlude, and the various restorations, using original material that he had obtained from George Washington Lafayette.

The House of Representatives had been prepared to receive the Senators and their distinguished guests, all of whom crowded into the chamber. On the wall behind the Speaker's chair, portraits of George Washington and the young Lafayette were hung. In front of the rostrum, the President, the Vice President, and the members of the Cabinet were seated. At about 12:30, John Quincy Adams took the Speaker's chair and in a strong, clear voice delivered the address on the life and character of the United States's dearest foreign friend. It lasted almost three hours.

Those who expected a political speech stressing the tradition of friendship between Lafayette's country and George Washington's were disappointed. Adams merely capsulated the dead hero's life and contributions, no more and no less. He linked the two countries only when describing Lafayette as the bearer of the American principles of liberty to his native land. It was an able speech, though somewhat dull. After it was finished, the guests left at once, and business was resumed in the House. Demonstrating their approval of Adams's address, the House ordered 50,000 copies to be printed; the Senate, more modestly, ordered 10,000.

The timing of the address was touchy because good relations between France and the United States were in jeopardy. France's promise, by the Treaty of 1831, to pay the United States five million dollars for long overdue claims for shipping depredations during the Napoleonic Wars had not been fulfilled. Jackson, in his State of the Union message in December 1834, asked Congress for a law that would authorize reprisals upon French property if the claims were not paid promptly. Many thought that there would be some reference to this state of affairs in the Adams address.

The whig party was absolutely opposed to Jackson's belligerent stand. Clay, who had urged strong measures against France in this very same matter when he had been Secretary of State, now joined Webster in the position that the American people would not support the President in a French war. Adams, who needed the whigs in the Massachusetts legislature to advance his candidacy for Nathaniel Silsbee's seat in the Senate, ignored his opportunity. No doubt with full understanding of what he was doing but with the righteousness from which he could never free himself, Adams failed to make any favorable reference, even a faintly polite one, to France. Webster, whose enmity to Adams always simmered below the surface, took advantage of the omission to advise the home-team whigs to bypass the Plymouth representative and support John Davis, now the Governor, for the Senate seat and Edward Everett to fill the vacant governorship.[57] Though he would do nothing to help himself, Adams would have liked to sit in the Upper House again.

Unwilling to let the House committee on foreign affairs bury the French question, Adams proposed a resolution that the President be requested to send to the House copies of the most recent correspondence from Edward Livingston, the United States Minister in Paris. Secretary of State Forsyth provided the papers, but then there was silence from the House again. The most important concern now must be our relations with France, Adams told a friend, but that which occupied Congress much more was "the making of the next President."[58] Democrats were playing the game too. They thought that the people would blame the whig Senate for not supporting Jackson.

On February 7, Adams again brought up the French matter, proposing a resolution that required the House foreign affairs committee to make a report at once, saying whether they supported the President in "maintaining the rights, interests, and honor of the country." Perhaps, however, he suggested, the committee, like the Senate's, might prefer "to dodge the question." Speaker John Bell of Tennessee, a whig, called Adams to order sharply. "It is not permitted to speak disrespectfully of any act of the other branch of the legislature," he admonished. Adams withdrew the "horrid" phrase respectfully.[59]

Though the testy old ex-President was beginning to acquire some popularity in the House, his stand on the French matter revived fears in the hearts of the New England shipping interests that had been dormant since the War of 1812. Webster sounded the alarm again and the Massachusetts legislature responded. As a result, the whig slate was adopted: John Davis for Senator, Edward Everett for Governor, and Daniel Webster for the President of the United States. Adams told Charles not to "brood too much over my Sorrows."[60]

As soon as information that Jackson did not have the solid support of the legislature in the matter that concerned them reached

France, the French Minister was recalled from Washington and his American counterpart was asked to leave Paris, which Livingston stolidly refused to do until he had orders from home. And less than a week before the Twenty-third Congress adjourned, the House committee on foreign affairs delivered its report on the French controversy. Chairman Cambreleng reported that it was their advice to postpone the question until the next Congress, due to meet in December. In the meantime, the Committee submitted three policy resolutions: 1. the House insisted on the execution of the treaty with France with no further negotiations; 2. no reprisals on French commerce for the present; 3. preparations should be made for any possible emergency with France.

Adams proposed three alternative resolutions: 1. indemnity rights of American citizens from the French government must not be "sacrificed, abandoned or impaired"; 2. the President should take the initiative to resume negotiations between France and the United States "if compatible with the honor and interest of the United States"; 3. no legislative measures hostile to France is necessary at this time.[61] The debate on the two sets of resolutions seesawed back and forth for several days. The Massachusetts delegation let its Plymouth member know that his ideas were contrary to those of his state. Adams regretted that but said that he must follow the dictates of his heart. At the end, the debate reduced itself to two alternatives —Virginian William Segar Archer's resolution to take no action or Adams's resolution that the treaty be executed "at all hazards." Cambreleng offered a compromise. He suggested that the resolution read: "that in the opinion of the House the Treaty of the 4th of July 1831 should be maintained and its execution insisted on." Adams agreed. The house voted 212 ayes and no nays, the chair announced to the accompaniment of applause from the galleries. At midnight the House adjourned.

Adams persisted in calling the resolution his own. He believed that he had achieved it despite Cambreleng and the whole Administration party, the Georgian and South Carolinian nullifiers, Archer and Virginia hair-splitters, and the Clay and Webster whigs. "I breasted them all," he boasted to Charles.[62] The battle revitalized him, he said with some relish, and noted that if re-elected to the House a career of action was now opened "more conspicuous and more perilous than any that I have gone through."[63]

Jackson had now been granted the power to take action if he must before the next congressional session but he still lacked the necessary money to implement it. The House, therefore, added three million dollars to the Senate fortifications bill to cover any contingency. Adams voted for it but the whiggish senate objected that the President had been awarded dictatorial powers. A conference committee finally agreed on three hundred thousand dollars with the addition of five hundred thousand dollars for warship repairs. Debate continued until past midnight on March 3, the time appointed for Congress's adjournment. Since a quorum could not be met, at 3:30 A.M. on March 4, the Speaker declared the House adjourned and the fortification bill died from neglect. Adams returned home completely worn out at the time when he usually got up.

The ill-fated French question met another obstacle just when everything seemed straightened out. France voted to appropriate the money for the indemnities but demanded that the President explain the insulting anti-French statements made in his message to Congress. Jackson, as expected, refused to make an apology to France saying that his communication to Congress was no concern of a foreign nation. He retaliated by ordering Livingston to leave Paris if payments did not begin at once. It looked as if Adams's prediction of war with France was about to be fulfilled when the international scene was altered. Louis Phillipe was asked by the Queen of Spain to intervene in her behalf and there was a possibility of war with Russia. Great Britain, now in need of France to help take care of the European squabbles, tried to smooth over the silly rift over protocol. The Vice President, the Secretary of State, and Livingston, back from France, helped matters by writing a sentence into the President's next annual message that was slightly more conciliatory than the previous one. France preferred to accept it as an apology so that in the fall of 1836 payments from France could begin.

During his summer visit to Quincy, Adams heard disquieting reports from Washington. Riots had occurred when a slave belonging to Mrs. Thornton attempted to murder her and her aged mother. As a result, mobs of white people in the capital roamed through the Negro areas destroying their homes, schools, and a church. Similar riots duplicated these outrages in Baltimore and throughout the South. In Mississippi several persons were hanged for circulating abolition pamphlets and, in South Carolina, abolition literature was removed from the mails without any action being taken by Postmaster Amos Kendall. In free Boston, Adams wrote disgustedly, there were calls for a town meeting to put down abolitionists in Webster's *Morning Post* and the Jackson and Van Buren papers.[64]

The anti-slavery movement had been expanding since the emancipation of slaves in the British West Indies and the increased activities of the Colonization Society in the United States. The American and British Anti-Slavery Associations linked together to support newspapers and pamphlets, and to send them free to the South "into the midst of slaves." Adams perceived slavery and democracy as incompatible. He foresaw that the planters of the South would "separate from the Union, in terror of the emancipation of their slaves." Then the slaves would emancipate themselves by a servile war. However, he did not speculate on what his role would or should be, probably assuming that the time would be far distant enough to occur after his lifetime.

The death of John Marshall early in the summer severed another link with the early republic. A midnight appointee of John Adams, for thirty-five years Marshall had guided the Court and had exerted influence "far more extensive than that of the President of the United States." Marshall, "by the ascendancy of his genius," Adams wrote, settled many constitutional questions "favorably to the continuance of the Union." He kept Jefferson, who hated and derided him, "much under the curb." Adams feared that a successor would be appointed of a very different character.[65]

In Washington again, preparing for the new session of Congress, Adams concentrated on a scheme for expediting the passage of the general appropriations bill. He denied the rumor that he was to be made the chairman of the committee on foreign relations, calling it, a foolish tale. "There is no personal communication direct or indirect between me and the President. There will be none of my seeking." To a Boston friend, he wrote, "I stand in the House of Representatives, as I did in the last Congress—alone."[66]

CHAPTER 22

"*Old Man Eloquent*"

"*. . . that dishonest victory
At Chaeronea, fatal to liberty,
Kill'd with report that old man eloquent.*"

JOHN MILTON

IT WAS SO UNUSUAL for John Quincy Adams to be away from his seat in the House of Representatives that his absence in April 1836 was noted in the *National Intelligencer*. An abscess on his leg swelled his foot to such a size that he could not move from his couch. But after a week of confinement, the restless Plymouth representative "could crawl in a carriage to the Capitol." He was still very weak and his voice was almost gone from a catarrhal cough that was chronic but much worse in wintertime. Some mornings he arose with a congestion that took all morning to clear up. Louisa suffered extreme anxiety over her husband's health. She still reproached herself for John's death. "Did I not see my son wither before my eyes? I'll never forgive my passiveness," she mourned. Now she feared that fate pursued her once again.[1]

Most of the subjects that had concerned Adams in the previous session had righted themselves. The French problem was settled and Webster and his friends had capitulated in favor of appropriations. John Quincy's brilliant defense of the appropriations bill from Webster's charge that the fund was voted upon without the President's recommendation earned him a sobriquet that he enjoyed for the rest of his life.

Surrounded by an attentive audience of Congressmen who had left their desks to crowd around the ex-President's chair, Adams defended the appropriations bill. Since the money was to be expended only in the event that it was necessary for defense of the country prior to the then next session of Congress, an interval of nine months, "no other provision could have been made to defend your soil from a sudden invasion or to protect your commerce floating upon every sea." This then, he said, was the appropriation "so tainted with man-worship, so corrupt, so unconstitutional" that the *National Intelligencer* would rather see a foreign enemy at the walls of the Capitol than agree to it.

"Sir, for a man uttering such sentiments, there would be but one step more, a natural and easy one to take, and that would be, with the enemy at the wall of the Capitol, to join him in battering them down."

A burst of applause filled the chamber with a resonance that drowned out Speaker Polk's vigorous banging of his gavel. While the furor was raging, a member, his name unknown, dubbed the forensic hero "Old Man Eloquent." In Milton's poem, "To the Lady Margaret Ley," he called Isocrates Old Man Eloquent, referring to the story that when the orator heard the result of the battle of Chaeronea, which was disastrous to Grecian liberty, he died of grief.

The settlement of the dispute with France totally changed the political picture. The opposition was destroyed. Clay suffered a personal defeat when the whig party nominated William Henry Harrison for their presidential candidate. Adams also suspected that the Plymouth whigs, resentful of his anti-Masonry, were plotting to run an opposition candidate against him. It would close his career, he predicted. "I have no good reason for wishing that it may be otherwise."[2]

The major controversy that was to tear Congress apart for decades and expose the unmentionable subject of slavery was beginning to take shape. For the past twelve years, American settlers had been moving into the fertile lands of Texas, undeterred by differences in religion, culture, and government with Mexico. Some came bringing with them their slaves. They gave lip service to the Mexican government, but resented its attempts to abolish slavery and to restrict further American immigration. When Mexico's dictator, Santa Anna, forced the Mexican congress to abolish its constitution, the Texans declared their independence. The American President, although the allegation cannot be definitely proved, promoted the action, giving it his enthusiastic endorsement as did the southern slaveholders.

Adams believed that from the beginning of the Jackson Administration there had been a project to get Texas for the United States, re-establish slavery there, and carve out of the area five to nine slave states which would then come into the Union. Once the Texans declared themselves free, they sent commissioners to the United States to ask for recognition of their independence and to negotiate their annexation. "The whole of this stupendous undertaking has not yet been disclosed," Adams confided to Russell Freeman.[3]

Benjamin Lundy, Quaker abolitionist, who had once conceived the scheme of settling 250 families in Texas and establishing a free-labor agricultural station there to raise sugar, cotton, and rice in order to demonstrate that it could be done without Black slavery, influenced Adams's thinking about Texas. After the Texas secession from Mexico, Lundy, who now had to abandon his scheme, published a pamphlet called *The Origin and True Causes of the Texas Revolution Commenced in the year of 1835*, which advocated a moral and a political campaign to keep Texas from entering the Union. "People of the North! *Will you permit it?* Will you sanction the abominable outrage; involve yourselves in the deep criminality, and perhaps the horrors of war, *for the establishment of slavery in a land of freedom?*" he wrote. The Lundy pamphlet became the Bible of the anti-slavery supporters.

Adams was the advocate of the Lundy position and the spokesman for anti-Texas sentiment in the House. When he had, during his Presidency, twice tried to purchase Texas from Mexico, he apparently had not considered its potential as slave territory. Hence, his detractors have attributed his change in position to the change in attitude that his constituents demonstrated. But this is not valid for, at this time, Massachusetts was not heavily abolitionist. If there had been a change of heart, it was John Quincy's own.

At the end of May, by way of commenting on an appeal for help from settlers on the Alabama-Georgia border who were being massacred and whose homes were being destroyed by Indians, Adams maneuvered his discussion into a consideration of the Texas revolution. He called it a Mexican civil war, a war for the re-establishment of slavery after its abolition. Every effort was now being made, he argued, to drive the United States into a war on the side of slavery. In his anger, John Quincy shook his finger at the southern bloc arrayed before him, calling them "slave-holding exterminators of Indians." The South, he charged, was luring the United States into a possible war with England. Would England, he questioned, after emancipating slavery in their own West Indies, tolerate a naval power's conquest of Texas for the purpose of reintroducing slavery? "Are you ready for all these wars? A Mexican war? A war with Great Britain? A general Indian war? A servile war?" and then, inevitably, a civil war. "From the instant that your slaveholding states become the theater of war, civil, servile or foreign, from that instant the war powers of Congress extend to interference with the institution of slavery in every way," he warned.[4] Haynes, Waddy Thompson, Henry Wise, and Lawless protested until eight o'clock that the ex-President had wandered far from his topic. But they were visibly shaken by the tirade. The motion to help the embattled settlers was approved. Adams favored it also because, he said, it was impossible for him to keep his vote from sufferers.[5]

The Adams speech, printed in the *National Intelligencer*, was so much in demand that it was published as a pamphlet. The South and West seethed with anger over it, the North and East applauded it. Though he criticized its shortcomings, particularly its poor organization, the author observed that the cause that it touched upon would be still "left on the threshold" at the end of his life. "I can only open the door."[6]

The issue of slavery refused to be quietened. Arkansas Territory asked to be admitted as a state but in its constitution was a section that prohibited its legislature from emancipating slaves without the consent of the owners, to which Adams objected. After an all-night session, at five in the morning, he offered an amendment to the admission bill that read: "Nothing in this act shall be construed as assent by the Congress to the article in the Constitution of the state in relation to slavery and emancipation of slaves." A three-hour debate ensued, in which Wise, Cushing, Briggs, Hoar, and Hardy of New York took part. George Dromgoole of Virginia, "drunk with whiskey," and Jesse Bynum of North Carolina, "drunk with slavery," were abusive and insulting to Adams, which he ignored. Having endured the marathon meeting with only his slice of bread for sustenance, John Quincy never admitted exhaustion or despair even when, at 11 A.M. his amendment failed by a vote of 90–32. Arkansas and Michigan were admitted as a pair, one slave and one free. Congressman Stephen Phillips of the Massachusetts delegation brought John Quincy home in his carriage, "much fatigued."[7]

"I enter the seventieth year of my pilgrimage," Adams recorded on July 11 while in Philadelphia. Though not an abolitionist, he spent his birthday with Benjamin Lundy, who wanted Adams's help but was not encouraged. The two then went to a tea at James Mott's where there was a large gathering of "Friends" who talked mostly about abolition and the evils of slavery. Adams enjoyed himself but lamented "the undue proportion of talking assumed by me, and the indiscretion and vanity in which I indulged myself." He met Lucretia Mott, a feminist who would later be involved in woman suffrage, whom he described as lively, sensible, and an intrepid abolitionist.[8]

The ex-President's chief work during his summer visit to Quincy was a eulogy on James Madison, who had died on June 8, which had been requested by the Common Council of Boston. Adams, feeling that he had no choice, accepted "with an aching heart," well aware that the work would entail hours of anguish, particularly since he did not have some indispensable materials. In the course of doing his research, Adams went through Jefferson's correspondence thoroughly. It showed "his craft and duplicity in very glowing colors," John Quincy wrote in his *Diary*. His success was "a slur upon the moral government of the world and his rivalry with Hamilton was unprincipled on both sides." Jefferson's treatment of John Adams, which his son considered "double dealing, treacherous, and false beyond all toleration," particularly incensed him. And Washington was no better treated than Adams—"as far as he dared," John Quincy pointed out. However, Jefferson's attachment to Madison, his friend who would be useful to him, was "exemplary." Madison was able to moderate some of Jefferson's excessees and was, John Quincy concluded, "in truth a greater and far more estimable man."[9]

As he continued to read more of the Jefferson letters, Adams noted that the Virginian's duplicity sunk deeper and deeper into his mind. Though his hatred of Hamilton was "unbounded" and of John Marshall "most intense," Jefferson never completely shook off a warmth and intimacy with John Adams that was formed when they both worked together in the cause of independence and were abroad as joint peace commissioners after the treaty of Paris in 1783.

Jefferson's problem, Adams said, was that he always sacrificed to his ambition and, in his last years, to his envy and poverty. In his study of the Virginia and Kentucky resolutions, both of which denounced the alien and sedition laws, penned during John Adams's Administration, Adams saw the difference between the two authors. Jefferson was the ideological father of South Carolina nullification, which pointed directly to dissolution of the Union, whereas Madison, Adams maintained, shrunk from such a conclusion.[10]

All of the bitterness against Jefferson so carefully recorded in John Quincy's private diary was absent in the Madison eulogy, delivered in Boston on Tuesday, September 27. Charles and the ex-President went with Mayor Armstrong to the State House where they joined Governor Edward Everett. The procession formed there and marched up State Street, preceded by several military companies, to the Odeon, formerly the Federal State Theatre.

A crowded house listened for two and a half hours to the small, grey figure, whose voice could hardly be heard even when, with difficulty, he raised it. It was a dark day, hard for aged eyes to see the pages, especially when a heavy shower darkened the room almost entirely. Since the house was lighted only by a skylight, the speaker had to rely on his memory for much of the time. All through the speech Adams suffered a feeling that he would have to stop and publicly admit his physical inability to go on. But, despite the handicaps, the audience paid uninterrupted attention, applauding occasionally, and, at the end, bursting into a rousing ovation. The crowd, which could not have heard more than snatches of the labored delivery were really applauding their distinguished, gallant countryman, who had been the subject of the eulogy's Foreign Minister, and was standing before them, a living link with the country's earliest history.

Adams was somewhat concerned that his comments on the Alien and Sedition Acts would get him into a controversy with the Virginians, who considered themselves the heirs of Jeffersonianism. It did not stop him, for he could not lose an opportunity to defend his father's fame, vindicate New England character, and expose "the fraudulent pretenses of slaveholding democracy."[11]

On the 500-mile trip from Quincy to Washington, which was comfortable and well tolerated by Louisa, Adams found the country blazing over the election. In New York, it was assumed that Pennsylvania, Virginia, and Connecticut had gone for Harrison and to question it "would have been a passport for a Coat of Tar and Feathers," he told Charles. Delaware and Maryland had certainly gone for Tippecanoe but Van Buren might have carried Pennsylvania.[12]

On November 22, at the *National Intelligencer* office, Adams saw some returns from his own election district. At Abington all three parties voted for him but at Rochester, where the Whigs had a majority, J. Thomas won. In Weymouth the small minority of Whigs did not vote at all. Adams's victory came from the anti-Masons and the portions of the two other parties that did not venture a nomination against him but, perhaps, would have supported another candidate had there been one. This was "a perilous passage through a narrow strait, and will certainly not be repeated," he predicted, particularly hurt that the turnout for him had been so small. Only 3,785 votes had been cast when the average number of votes in the contested districts had been about 7,000.[13]

Though the results of the presidential election would not be formally announced before Congress met in December, there was no doubt that Van Buren was the victor. Adams attributed his success in Virginia and North Carolina to the "impalatable alternatives," White and Harrison, who have had "honour enough just having been designated as candidates for the Presidency." Van Buren would now have to spend his Administration playing the parties against each other, for which task he had "the hand of a master." But the future was not certain. Clay might still rally the West and South but Calhoun and Webster had two perpetual bars to their elevation. Calhoun was saddled with the stigma of nullification; Webster was afflicted with his connection with federalism.[14]

President Jackson's last message to Congress irritated Adams because of its "glorification" of prosperity and its "spice of piety." The President's view of foreign affairs was "hasty" and his notice of a commercial treaty with Siam "boastful." Adams disliked the message most because three-fourths of it was a final stab at the Bank of the United States and a commentary on the injustice of banks to the laboring poor. Two weeks later, however, Adams was surprised to hear the President's message concerning the new republic of Texas. In a reversal from the spirit of the last congressional session, which seemed to reflect the presidential position, Jackson discouraged any precipitous recognition of Texas and prescribed caution about its annexation to the United States.

On January 7, an issue erupted that Adams had long expected

would be the monster that would devour him. From the time that he first sat in the House, the Plymouth representatives had been presenting petitions on Mondays (petition day) in accordance with the first amendment to the Constitution. Many of them prayed for abolition of the slave trade in the District of Columbia, others for the abolition of the peculiar institution. Most of them were not from his own district, which did not stop John Quincy, who considered himself the servant of all the people. Sometimes the petitions came from groups of women who were anti-slavery. "I had not yet brought myself to doubt whether females were citizens," Abigail Adams's son told his colleagues, who stormed at him both because of the subject of the petitions as well as their authors.

The proper role of Congress on the controversial subject of slavery baffled Adams. He loathed the institution but he was reluctant, indeed unable, to take any position that might hasten the severance of the union. He speculated, however, that, in the case of a servile war, Congress would have complete control over the subject "even to emancipation of the slaves in the State where such insurrection should break out. . . ."[15] In Congress, Adams balked at the southern bloc's ability to get the Pinckney resolution, known as the "gag rule," passed. It read: "All petitions, memorials, resolutions, propositions or papers, relating in any way . . . to the subject of slavery or the abolition of slavery, shall, without being printed or referred, be laid on the table, and that no further action whatever shall be had thereon."[16] This was the first of a series of gag rules, each more stringent than the last. John Quincy pointed out that there was no guarantee that the House would not extend its ban on matters other than slavery which it did not wish the opposition to introduce.

On Monday, January 9, Adams rose to present his batch of petitions, starting with one from 150 women of Dorchester, Massachusetts, for the abolition of slavery. The suppliants were from Adams's own district, which, as he often observed, was very divided on the subject. His move that the petition be read was quickly countered by Georgia's Thomas Glascock. But before the Plymouth representative sat down, he extolled the motives of the petitioners and accused the House of defying the Constitution. The petition was received but it was voted to lay it on the table without being read.

Undeterred, Adams tried another ploy. He challenged successfully the right to use the gag rule from the last session, claiming that it had expired. Having temporarily subdued Speaker Polk, the elderly statesman produced a petition from 228 women of South

Weymouth and told the assembly that as part of his speech, he would read the petition.

Glascock objected loudly but not loudly enough to drown out Adams's vigorous, firm voice reading—"Impressed with the sinfulness of slavery, and keenly aggrieved by its existence in a part of the country over which Congress—"

"Has the gentleman from Massachusetts a right under the rule to read the petition?" Pinckney interrupted.

"The gentleman has a right to make a statement of the contents of the petition," Polk ruled.

"I am doing so, sir," Adams insisted.

"Not in the opinion of the Chair," Polk answered.

"I was at the point of the petition," Adams continued, "keenly aggrieved by its existence in a part of our Country over which Congress possesses exclusive jurisdiction in all cases whatever—"

All over the House there were shouts of "Order! Order!"

"Do most earnestly petition your honorable body," Adams continued.

The House was in an uproar, but Adams persisted. "Immediately to abolish slavery in the District of Columbia . . ."

"Take your seat," the Speaker ordered.

Adams obeyed, but not until he read clearly and rapidly, "and to declare every human being free who sets foot upon its soil."

Further debate failed to subdue the ex-President. He proceeded to present another petition from forty residents of Dover, which was tabled after a debate that continued on the following day. And on January 18, the House voted 139-69 to renew the gag resolution.[17]

Adams told Rowland Johnson of Philadelphia that the regulation that petitions on slavery would not be heard "will in all probability survive me," but he could not be stopped from trying to ameliorate the evil sooner. He resumed the battle on February 6, 1837, with a test case.

With some doubt as to the authenticity of a paper that was written legibly but signed by marks and scrawls, Adams stated that he would send the document "purporting to come from slaves" to the chair. Consternation overcame the House, particularly in the slaveholders section. Waddy Thompson of South Carolina moved that Adams had been guilty of gross disrespect for the House and should be severely censured by the Speaker. Dixon H. Lewes of Alabama accused the Plymouth representative of outraging the rights and feelings of a large portion of the people of the Union. To allow slaves such a privilege, he cautioned, would invite "the slave population to insurrection."[18]

Adams answered coolly, "I said I had a paper purporting to be a petition from slaves. I did not say what the prayer on the petition was. . . . This is the *fact*." If they read the petition, they would discover that it was a petition of slaves that slavery should not be abolished, addressed by a Buddy Tayloe to John Quincy Adams, Virginia, February 1, 1837. As a device to embarrass its recipient, the spurious petition failed. Adams knew that it was a forgery by a slaveholding master to dare him to present a petition allegedly from slaves. But its author failed to understand the New England conscience. Adams declared that he did not consider a forgery committed for the purpose of deterring a member of Congress from the discharge of his duty as a hoax.

Possibly some of the members who had been agitating for Adams's censure grew a little ashamed when they reflected on the "hoax." They voted to accept a set of resolutions that endorsed slavery rather than censured John Quincy Adams. The first one stated, simply, that slaves did not possess the right of petition as do "the people of the United States by the Constitution." Having established that slaves were not people, another resolution, designed just for Adams, stated that "the Hon. John Q. Adams, having solemnly disclaimed all design of doing anything disrespectful to this House in the inquiry he made of the Speaker as to the petition purporting to be from the slaves, and having avowed his intention not to offer to present the petition if the House was of opinion it ought not to be presented—therefore, all further proceedings in regard to his conduct do now cease."

But the Hon. John Quincy Adams was not willing to be bailed out on the southern bloc's terms. He asked for an opportunity "for a full hearing in my own defense." It was granted because all of his colleagues realized that they might need the same right someday. The speech that followed convinced many of his hearers that he had earned the title bestowed upon him by *The New York Times*—"The Massachusetts Madman."

Sparing no one, accepting none of the taboos imposed by the House, Adams darted from slaveholding to the sacred name of woman, and then back to the right of petition. He told the astounded audience that he did not want the resolution about him carried because it sounded like a pardon. "I have not done one single thing that I would not do over again in like circumstances." The resolution against Adams failed to pass by a vote of 21 to 105, but the resolution that slaves did not have the right to petition won by a substantial vote, 163–18. It was a personal victory for the ex-President, though he took no pleasure in it. The controversy proved to him that henceforth the question of slavery would mingle with every conflict in the union.[19]

Old Man Eloquent had been so sorely tried by the House trial that he had not written to his son in months. He only wanted to return home as soon as possible and have Charles and his family spend the summer with him. But he was in financial straits and before he could return to Quincy he had to raise two or three thousand dollars. One of his largest creditors, Antoine Giusta, the Adams's former valet, needed to be repaid the $1,000 that was owed him.

Meanwhile, the abolitionists and anti-slavery people watched Adams's activities with great interest. If he would not join them, he was certainly their most prestigious champion in the House. In a letter to Lewis Tappan, one of the founders of the American Anti-Slavery Society, Adams tried to clarify his position. "Upon the means of ridding our country of this greatest of moral ills inflicted upon us, my opinion differs from yours but this is a difference of deliberate judgement and not of principle." Most puzzling to his abolitionist friends was Adams's position on the abolition of slavery in the District of Columbia. He could support it only if the District wanted it. Sarah Grimké, who admired the ex-President's recognition of women by presenting their petitions, thought his refusal to support the abolition of slavery in the nation's capital "a surrender of moral principle to political expediency."[20] His fear was that any measures leading to the abolition of slavery would result in "a conflict for Life and Death between Freedom and Slavery through which I have not yet been able to see how this Union could ultimately be preserved from passing."[21] He had thought that slavery in the United States would perish gradually after the abolition of the slave trade and the emancipation of their slaves by Great Britain and South America, but the debates in the Virginia legislature destroyed his hopes. The assertion by southern political leaders and intellectuals that the Negro was an inferior race, born to slavery, provoked his indignation. It was brought to a boiling point when he reflected on southern demands that northern states deliver up free citizens to their revenge and accede to the strangling of free thought in the mails.

Adams recalled that in 1826, when he was President, King Christophe of Haiti told the United States agent there that he would not discuss American claims unless Haiti was recognized by the United States. "A bare hint to Congress of the possibility would have been received by the *Gentlemen of the South*" in the same spirit as his January tenth petition. "It would have suggested that negroes and mulattoes were not only human beings but capable of constituting a sovereign state and if I had escaped impeachment there would have been a Resolution carried . . . that featherless bipeds with wool for hair and their descendants till bleached into Anglo Saxons are not entitled to the rights of man," Adams wrote, confidentially, to an anti-slavery friend.[22]

An invitation to the anti-slavery convention in Boston reminded the Plymouth representative of the confusion of his position. Realistically he knew that he must be circumspect because all the political parties were waiting for him to commit an overt act which their presses could act upon. The South was in a perpetual agony of guilt and terror. The North favored the whites and feared the Blacks in the South. The politicians courted southern votes while the abolitionists "kindle the opposition against themselves into a flame" and the populace was against them. "I must pursue a road between the exposure of the last Congress and shrinking from danger," Adams advised himself.[23]

On May 6, for the first time since he left it as President of the United States, John Quincy went to the President's house. Martin Van Buren received him alone and they conversed about the terrible Washington summers, bathing and swimming in the Potomac, and the general state of European politics. Both avoided mention of the public affairs of the United States.

Adams had small respect for the "American Talleyrand." He saw some resemblance in character to Madison—his calmness, gentleness of manner, discretion, and easy and conciliatory temper. But Van Buren's obsequiousness, sycophancy, profound dissimulation, and duplicity were his own. In the last two characteristics he resembled Jefferson, though he lacked the genius of the third President. The most disgusting aspect of his character, Adams judged, was his fawning servility, which was neither like Madison nor Jefferson.

The summer at Quincy provided much needed quiet after the destructive misery of the gag rule fight. Adams enjoyed being with Charles and Abby and their children. "Grandfathers have the privilege of being foolish. . . . I claim this privilege of being foolish about my grandchildren," he wrote to Charles Davis who had complimented Abby Adams on her charming offspring.[24]

His constituents favored their Congressman with tangible evidence of enthusiastic support for his principles on at least two occasions during that season. On June 1st, a committee of the delegation in the Massachusetts house of representatives composing Adams's 12th congressional district came to visit him. Mr. Thayer read an address approving of his conduct on their behalf, particularly in the past session, and then presented him with a cane made of timber from the *Constitution*. After a brief inner struggle, John Quincy decided that he could accept the gift since it was not "of sufficient pecuniary value to be declined."

Later in July, the district convention of delegates from the towns of the 12th congressional district convened at the Town Hall to pass resolutions approving of Adams's conduct on the right of petition and his opposition to the annexation of Texas. Adams talked to them for an hour and a half, frequently interrupted by cheering and applause. At the close of the meeting, a number of copies of J.Q.A.'s address to his constituents were distributed.

Though his electorate was willing to go along with their representative in these matters, they were divided on the issues of slavery and abolition. Adams's abolitionist friends, such as Samuel Webb and Benjamin Lundy, tried to urge him to indiscreet actions "which would ruin me and weaken not strengthen their cause." Louisa, Charles, and Mary tried to divert him from all connection with the abolitionists. "Between these adverse impulses my mind is agitated almost to distraction. . . . I walk on the edge of a precipice in every step that I take," he complained.[25]

The Twenty-fifth Congress convened in special session in September, in order to deal with the economic depression that the country was suffering, but Adams's chief occupation was assorting the petitions that poured into his house in huge numbers. The petition parade started on September 20 with Adams presenting twelve against the admission of Texas. A week later, on petition day, The Madman from Massachusetts presented petitions for the abolition of slavery in the territories, for refusing admission to any new state that had slavery, and for prohibition of the interstate slave trade. But to his request that the Secretary of the Treasury report to the next session of Congress the number of slaves exported from and imported into the ports of the United States by the coastal trade, there was a resounding "No," from the servile side of the House. On the next day, Adams presented fifty-one petitions against the gag rule and 150 other petitions, many of them left over from the previous session. After they were all presented, received, and laid on the table, the petition marathon was over until the winter session.

Since Louisa had stayed in Quincy, it had become her husband's habit to retire to the committee room of the now almost defunct committee on manufactures and to spend the dinner hour there, eating his five or six small crackers and a glass of water and writing a letter or two. He said that the respite, before the evening session began, calmed him so that he was equal to resuming his active role in debate.

The special session failed to accomplish its purpose. The country was in the midst of national bankruptcy, Adams said, because of the insolvency of multitudes and because the banks' suspension of specie payments was a fraud. He suggested two remedies. 1. The Congress of the United States should regulate the currency; 2. Wipe out all debts and begin again. Detach the government from all banking and deal in nothing but precious metal. He did not believe that either of his suggestions would be followed. The basic fault was Jackson's strangling of the National Bank which, if in existence, would be the most effective instrument for controlling the state banks and restoring paper currency.[26]

Van Buren's proposal to solve the depression was an independent treasury bill which would create a sub-treasury system. Government funds would be withdrawn from the Jackson "pet banks" and placed in vaults. This would assuredly keep the money safe but was deflationary, for it deprived the banks of a substantial amount of money with which to do business. The bill passed in the Senate but was defeated in the House, 119–107. Adams supported it in principle but voted against it, fearing that the machinery would be administered by political appointees. Nothing accomplished, the members of Congress might just as well have stayed home until the regular session convened in December.

During the special session, in a debate over a bill for adjusting the remaining government claims on the deposit banks, Adams asked its author, Churchill Cambreleng, to explain some of the wording. In a surly reply, Cambreleng said that if the gentleman from Massachusetts would read the bill, he could answer his own question. It was late, the New Yorker snarled, and he could not waste his time "discussing nouns, pronouns, verbs, and adverbs with the gentleman from Massachusetts."

"Well, sir, as language is composed of nouns and pronouns, verbs and adverbs, when they are put together to constitute the law of the land the *meaning* of them may surely be demanded of the legislator, and those parts of speech may well be used for such a purpose. But, if such explanation be impossible, it certainly ought not to be expected that this House will consent to pass a law which the author of it does not understand," Adams replied.

After that introduction, the ex-President took the floor for two hours, exposing the true character of the bill by using computations drawn from the Treasury reports. He denounced the bargains made by Cambreleng and the members of the debtor states to postpone the bill in exchange for increased indulgence for their banks as a device for the Administration to get the support of the southern and western states. The bill passed due to Administration pressure but the *National Intelligencer* recommended Adams's clear and forceful speech "to all who wish to understand the questions on which it treats."[27]

Just before the end of the special session, Adams had the Massachusetts delegation to dinner. For the past three winters he had given up entertaining because of John's death, Louisa's illness, his own health, his pecuniary problems, and the feeling against him of some of the members of his own delegation. Since for the moment there was a truce, he decided to dine with them.

During the brief interval between sessions, Adams became involved in the case of a slave named Dorcas Allen. She had been sold along with her four children, to be sent south and separated from her husband. In a fit of despair and temporary insanity, she slit the throats of two of her children and then tried to kill herself. At her trial in Alexandria she was acquitted by the jury on the grounds of temporary insanity. On October 21, the *National Intelligencer* carried an advertisement for the sale of Dorcas Allen and her surviving children.

Adams, because he considered it a "case of conscience," called at the newspaper office to enquire about the case. From the newspaper files and later from Nathaniel Frye, his Washingtonian brother-in-law and manager of his flour mill, Adams pieced together the whole story. Fifteen years earlier, Dorcas Allen had been freed after the death of her mistress. She married a waiter at Gadsby's Hotel and raised a family. Years later, Rezen Orme found out that the ex-slave had never obtained a certificate testifying to her freedom, and promptly arranged to have her seized with the children and sold South. The murders occurred at this time. When Adams asked why Mrs. Allen had been exonerated by the jury, his brother-in-law enlightened him on the intricacies of southern justice. Since she was a healthy woman in the prime of life, she was worth too much money as a valuable piece of property to be hanged or put away for life.

William Seaton, editor of the *Intelligencer*, was polite to the ex-President, regretted the plight of the poor woman, but could see no redress. Since she could not prove that she was free, she was legally still a slave. Neither the judge who had been on the case nor District Attorney Francis Scott Key, both of whom Adams visited, was particularly disturbed about the case. They pointed out that Nathan Allen, the husband and father, could buy his family back and that General Walter Smith, a retired army officer, was helping to raise funds for the Allens.

Adams continued to work on the Allen tragedy. He called on Washington's Mayor, Peter Force, talked to Dorcas Allen in her prison cell, and to Nathan Allen at his home. Most important, he forced the slaver to agree to sell back the three victims for $475, the amount of his investment.

Nathan Allen came often to the Adams house, pleading silently. He needed $145 to supplement General Smith's subscription but John Quincy, after carefully consulting his own narrow funds, could spare him no more than $50. The situation looked hopeless. When Adams approached Key for some help, the district attorney warned him that there was violent hostility in Washington, as in all southern towns, against those who interfered with the working of the slave system. In Alton, Illinois, early in November, Reverend Elijah Lovejoy, a leading abolitionist who tried to establish a newspaper there, was murdered by a mob when he refused to abandon the press to them. "Such is the condition of things in these shambles of human flesh, that I can not now expose this horrible transaction but at the hazard of my life," Adams wrote.

The Dorcas Allen story had an unexpected happy ending. Mr. and Mrs. Allen came together to call on Adams and to tell him that Nathan had already bought his wife's freedom and, when they had the ex-President's fifty dollars, their two daughters would be released from jail. Adams made out the check, advised Allen to let him see that the bill of sale was in order, and then watched the pair disappear down the street. It was a greater satisfaction than he had experienced in days, he noted.[28]

"A new coat of varnish" covered Jackson's message of 1832, Adams commented about Van Buren's address to the Congress. It gave him a fit of melancholy for the future of the United States. Northern rights were being sacrificed to southern slavery and the West's plunder of the public lands. But it was time again for the presentation of the mountains of petitions. The American Anti-Slavery Society and the newly formed Female Anti-Slavery Society had mounted a campaign that threatened to drown the legislature in petitions. Before the inevitable gag resolution was passed for the current session, Adams tried to persuade the House to refer the memorials and remonstrances against the annexation of Texas to the United States to a select committee and not the slaveowner-dominated committee on foreign affairs. He failed. And he had no success either in moving to refer all petitions for the abolition of slavery and the slave trade in the District of Columbia to the committee on the District of Columbia. All the petitions were tabled. When William Slade of Vermont, an anti-Mason who was drifting into abolitionism, got the floor by a ruse and spoke for two hours against slavery, he "shook the very hall into convulsions." The slave-holding members immediately caucused in the chamber of the committee on the District of Columbia in order to draw up a new and stronger gag resolution.

The next day John Patton of Virginia presented it. When his name was called, Adams answered with "I hold the resolution to be a violation of the Constitution, of the right of petition of my constituents, and of the people of the United States, and of my right to freedom of speech as a member of this House." A veritable war-whoop of cries of "Order!" resounded from every corner of the House. The Speaker declared Old Man Eloquent's request to have his motion entered on the *Journal* out of order, and ordered him to answer either aye or no. Adams then suggested that the whole exchange be entered in the *Journal*, including the Speaker's decision. Polk did not answer. The gag rule was duly passed and established for the session. "Wind and tide are against me on this subject," Adams noted. "Between the thirst of the slaveholders for Texas and the apathy of the opposition presidential canvassers, I shall have a heavy task to preserve the peace."[29]

The New Year's recess was a break in the tension which some felt as much as or more than Adams. "Calhoun looks like a man racked with furious passions and stung with disappointed ambition, as he is," Adams observed. He met the Senator while delivering a manuscript of his speech in the office of the *National Intelligencer*.

A clear sky, bright sun, and a calm atmosphere was an auspicious beginning for the year 1838. Adams did not attend the crowded reception at the President's house. Having opposed the Administration in Congress, John Quincy could not justify a public exhibition of personal courtesy which might be interpreted as friendliness. Instead he held his own open house, attended by about 300 people, most of whom stopped after paying their respects at the President's house. Clay came and, surprisingly, Secretary of State Forsyth and Secretary of War Poinsett— "The hyprocrisy of politics, to which I am obliged to submit, as to the fashion of the world; but which I can not and never could practise."

Lt. Thomas Boylston Adams died in early 1838. His uncle was distressed, for he was almost a son to him. "I . : . flattered myself with hopes that a long career of usefulness and honour was before him to contribute with you to sustain the credit of the name and family when I shall sleep with my fathers," Adams wrote to Charles.

And the petitions never stopped pouring into Adams's house and office. One day thirty-one arrived, consuming the entire evening in assorting, filing, and entering them on the list that Adams kept. Along with them came flattering letters that might have "puffed up" his vanity, had they not been more than balanced by furious, filthy, and threatening notes, mostly from the South. The banner day was on February 14, when Adams presented 350 petitions. They broke down as follows.

158	for rescinding the gag resolution
65	for the abolition of slavery and the slave trade in the District of Columbia
17	for the prohibition of internal slave trade
4	for the abolition of slavery in the territories
2	against the admission of any new state whose constitution tolerated slavery
54	against the annexation of Texas to the United States
50	miscellaneous

350

A man named Judson offered the most original petition. He suggested that Congress should appropriate money to build a wall like the Wall of China between the free and the slaveholding states. Unamused, the Speaker ordered it laid on the table with the rest.

More seriously, a petition asked that Congress protect northerners going to the South from danger to their lives. When the motion was laid on the table, Adams said that in another part of the capital the threat had been made that if a northern abolitionist should go to North Carolina and utter a principle of the Declaration of Independence—"Order! Order!" yelled the slave bloc, the Speaker's voice among the loudest. When they quieted down, John Quincy finished his sentence—"that if they could catch him they would hang him." The Speaker ordered the gentleman from Massachusetts to take his seat, which he did. A moment later, however, he arose and presented another petition. His reference was to Senator Preston's threat to hang northern abolitionists.[30]

Party division and sectional strife emerging from the struggle over slavery resulted in a fatal duel between two members of the House. William J. Graves, a Kentucky whig, thirty-two years old, challenged Jonathan Cilley of Maine, a young freshman Congressman. The dispute was really second-hand. After Cilley charged James Watson Webb, editor of the New York *Courier and Inquirer*, with accepting a bribe for giving favorable publicity to the Bank of the United States, the newspaperman wrote a letter to Cilley challenging him to a duel. Unaware of its contents, Graves agreed to deliver it.

The Maine Congressman refused to accept the challenge because he did not consider Webb a gentleman and, besides, he had every right to the privilege of immunity for any remarks made on the floor of Congress. Graves returned the letter to Webb and then became the victim of his southern colleagues who pointed out to him that he had been insulted. Cilley, they said, had implied that he was not a gentleman. A messenger could be no better than the man who sent him to deliver the message. Graves then asked Cilley to issue a public statement declaring that he did not intend to insult his fellow Congressman. Cilley balked and, when Graves sent him a challenge, agreed to meet him—rifles at one hundred yards.

The two young men met in a Maryland field by the Marlboro Pike. Henry Wise was Graves's second. General Jones of Wisconsin acted for Cilley. At the third exchange, Cilley, who was reputed to be a master marksman, was shot in the stomach and died in a few minutes.[31]

The duel shocked the nation into action. Mostly from the North petitions poured in to Congress asking that duelling be forbidden in the District. The House, which formed a committee to investigate the subject, expected that Adams would engage himself in the reform. He had always been outspoken about his belief that duelling was uncivilized and un-Christian but felt so much in the minority that he considered it useless to attempt anything. Furthermore, he was skeptical about the project. "What influence of fear of punishment can be exerted over men who begin by deliberately staking their lives upon a feather?" he asked. He also opposed the proposal made by some horrified Congressman to try Graves for murder, a prerogative, he said, that was reserved for the Courts. "After giving Mr. Cilley the burial of a Saint, I did not perceive the Justice, Humanity or Piety of expelling all his accomplices as felons," he wrote to Charles.[32]

After Samuel Prentiss of Vermont originated an anti-duelling bill in the Senate, Adams was willing to sponsor it in the House. Passed in February 1839, the Prentiss-Adams law prohibited the giving, delivering, or accepting of a challenge to a duel within the District of Columbia, and carried a penalty of ten years' imprisonment if any of the parties was killed, five years if no such disaster occurred, and three years for assaulting a person who refused a challenge. The southern contingent, however, endorsed Henry Wise's statement, made after the bill was passed, that now any member may brand another a coward on the floor of Congress and the matter will drop without a fight.

Adams answered angrily that he acted for the independence of the members from the northern section of the United States which abhorred duelling, consequently they were being perpetually insulted by members from other sections who were under the impression that the insult would not be resented. "I am not willing to sit any longer and see other members from my own section of the country, or those who may be my successors here, made subject to any such law as the law of the duellist."[33]

Adams was optimistic that the session would not result in war with Mexico or annexation of Texas. But he was aware that "the fatal blow will only be suspended." In the meantime, he continued to present his armfuls of petitions whenever the opportunity arose.

On May 21, he presented thirty-five, "exactly the number of days since the last presentation." Most of them were against the "abomination, the fraudulent Treaty of New Echota," which ceded all the Cherokee lands to the United States and provided for the transportation of the Cherokee Indians beyond the Mississippi. They asked for justice and mercy for the Cherokee Indians.

All of the petitions were laid on the table, along with one from Stephen Taller and thirty-eight inhabitants of Jeffersonville, Gouchland County, Virginia, that sought John Quincy Adams's expulsion as a nuisance. Adams moved that the Taller petition be referred to the committee on the judiciary but it, too, was tabled.

As the dreary session continued, the intense heat almost overcame Adams. At times it was so bad in the House that he had to leave his seat at frequent intervals to go to breathe at one of the windows. But the session lingered because the northern and southern members were deadlocked over Texas.

In June, when the Iowa Territory bill was debated, Waddy Thompson said frankly that he would vote for no new northern territory "while the northern fanatics" poured in petitions against the annexation of "the great and glorious republic of Texas." Adams objected to the peculiar glory of Texas, which consisted of having made a land of freemen into a land of slaves. There was too much of that sort of glory already, he said. Shouts of "Order!" forced the Speaker to stop the Plymouth member from continuing. He was ordered to take his seat.

How to treat the right-of-petition issue so as to achieve success oppressed and dejected the ex-President. It seemed possible that the gag rule might be circumvented when the slavery faction accepted Adams's motion to refer a resolution from the Massachusetts legislature opposing the annexation of Texas to the committee on foreign affairs. Since the committee was heavily staffed with southerners, the chairman agreed to accept that petition and all the others on Texas, and to prepare a report.

It was mid-June before the committee made its report to the House. Chairman George C. Dromgoole spoke for the majority. He said that since there was no proposal in the House at that time for the annexation of Texas, it would be best to excuse the committee from further study of the subject and place the Texas petitions back on the table lest any future discussion of Texas annexation be prejudged and prejudiced. The southern bloc hoped by the ruse to silence an Adams tirade against slavery that might gain some support for his position.

At this time, Adams had consciously accepted the fact that he could not tolerate the institution of slavery either on political or on practical grounds. His support of the Louisiana Purchase and the annexation of Florida which had increased the number of slaves in the United States was part of his remote past. Now he was a gadfly who, by his eloquence and fervor would not allow the slaveocracy to forget that the issue was alive. Adams deplored its dangerous potential for splitting the union, yet he could no longer live comfortably with it. He was not yet an abolitionist, but his speeches revealed such hatred, scorn, contempt, and bitterness against the peculiar institution that all that was missing was the name "abolitionist."

Maneuvering to be recognized and to be heard during the debate that followed the committee report required the skill of a magician. Finally, Adams managed to propose an amendment that read: "Resolved: that the power of annexing the People of any independent foreign State to this Union would be usurpation of power, unlawful and void, and which it would be the right and duty of the free People of the Union to resist and annul." The ex-President had outfoxed the committee. Whether they liked it or not, the issue was launched on whether Texas should be annexed or not.

For the next few weeks until Congress adjourned, Adams occupied part of each morning hour with a speech on Texas. He complained that his speech was "cut up by the rules of the House into driblets of a quarter of an hour a day, of which the House are already so tired that they take every possible occasion to stop my mouth."[34] But his filibuster was a noble marathon. The committee was exposed for not having read the materials submitted to them and the President was censured for withholding documents relevant to Mexico. Adams also revealed the fact that Texas was still pressing for annexation.

In the course of the debate, the question of women and government came up, touching off some interesting fireworks. Benjamin Howard of Maryland commented that some of the petitions against the annexation of Texas had been signed by women. "I consider it discreditable," he said. "I think that these females could have sufficient field for the exercise of their duties to their fathers, their husbands, or their children. . . . I feel sorry at this departure from their proper sphere. . . ."

The son of Abigail Adams once again rose to the defense of the 238 women who signed the first anti-annexation of Texas petition which he had, earlier, proudly presented. Perhaps he had seen the letter that his mother had written to John Adams in March 1776. When you make the code of laws for the new government, she said, "I desire you would remember the Ladies. . . . If perticuliar [sic] care and attention is not paid to the Ladies we are determined to foment a Rebelion, and will not hold ourselves bound by any Laws in which we have no voice, or Representation."[35]

For several successive days, Adams attacked Howard for his statement that the presentation of petitions by ladies was "discreditable." Adams asked: "Was this from a son? Was it from a father? Was it from a husband that I heard these words? . . . Are women to have no opinions or actions on subjects relating to the general welfare?" In sonorous tones, Old Man Eloquent rolled off the names of great women of the past—Miriam, Deborah, Esther, Aspasia, Cornelia, Portia, Elizabeth, Maria Theresa of Hungary, Catherine of Russia, Isabella of Castile, and, finally, "the ladies of our own Revolution." He admitted that women must bear children and devote time to domestic chores, but "the mere departure of women from the duties of the domestic circle, far from being a reproach to her, is a virtue of the highest order, when it is done from purity of motive, by appropriate means, and towards a virtuous purpose."[36]

The petition of the 238 mothers, wives, and daughters of his constituents was not only, in his opinion, proper in every sense but also aptly expressed his own convictions. It read: "Thoroughly aware of the sinfulness of slavery, and the consequent impolicy and disastrous tendency to its extension in our country, we do most respectfully remonstrate, with all our souls, against the annexation of Texas to the United States."

In his own version of his speech, delivered in fragments in the House of Representatives during the morning hours of the sixteenth of June to the seventh of July 1838, Adams summed up his heroic effort in one sentence: "I do believe slavery to be a sin before the sight of God and that is the reason and the only insurmountable reason why we should not annex Texas to this Union."

When Congress adjourned on July 9, after sitting all night, it was expected that the Texas matter would be resumed at the next session. Theoretically, also, Adams still held the floor and would be able to continue his efforts the following December. However, the furor had influenced President Van Buren to back away from annexation. Sensing that their cause was to be buried for the time being, the Texas representatives withdrew their proposal for annexation on October 12.

Adams returned to Quincy at the close of the session. In September, the ladies of Quincy lionized their champion at a picnic and ball which the ex-President and his wife attended. In his speech, Adams mentioned that at the last session of Congress "the rights and reputation of the women of my country, and particularly of the district were involved." That women would be interested in such subjects as public lands, currency, exchange, manufactures, etc., he doubted. "But, for objects of kindness, of benevolence, of compassion, women, so far from being debarred by any rule of delicacy . . . are, by the law of their nature, fitted above all others for that exercise."[37] Though Adams was far from a supporter of the feminist movement which was still in its infancy, he had won the admiration of many women for his speeches in the House. Tangible evidence in the form of hand-knitted mufflers, socks, and hand warmers poured into his Washington residence.

The abolitionists and anti-slavery advocates tried to force Adams into a more militant position by threatening to oppose his re-election if he did not accept their creed of immediate abolition of slavery. Dr. William Ellery Channing and others urged him to present the test question—immediate abolition of slavery in the District of Columbia and the territory of Florida—but he refused. Not more than thirty members of Congress would vote for abolition in the capital city, he said, and the political parties were against it. "The abolitionists resort to extreme principles which retard instead of advancing their own cause," he observed sadly.[38]

As promised, abolitionist zeal endangered John Quincy's seat in November 1838. The Democrats supported an abolitionist write-in candidate at the last moment hoping that, since Adams had no formal opposition, his supporters would not bother to come to the polls. The ruse almost worked. Adams was shocked to find that he had won the election by a mere few hundred votes. It proved, he observed, that the abolitionists had no political understanding and were willing to make the Administration which they abhorred more powerful.

CHAPTER 23

"The Venerable Nestor
of Massachusetts"

"Mr. Adams loves the negroes too much, unconstitutionally."
                                                              "VIRGINIAN"

*". . . while a remnant of physical power is left me to write and speak, the
world will retire from me before I shall retire from the world."*
                                                              JOHN QUINCY ADAMS

"MUTUAL GREETINGS—cordial on the lips," Adams noted about his reception by the new Congress. But at the first opportunity they re-established the gag rule for all abolition petitions. When this annual ritual was achieved, John Quincy rose and addressed the Speaker, proposing that "no resolution of the House could add or deduct from the powers of Congress conferred by the Constitution of the United States." Hastily, before anything could come of the ex-President's resolution, the motion to adjourn was carried.[1]

Adams was overcome with disgust. Bitterly, he castigated the Congress. "When I look upon the composition of these two bodies, the Senate and the House of Representatives of the United States—the cream of the land, the culled darlings of fifteen millions of square miles—the remarkable phenomenon that they present is the level of intellect and of morals upon which they stand; and this universal mediocrity is the basis upon which the liberties of this nation repose."[2] Having vented his frustration, he proceeded to deliver the petitions that came to him. On January 17, he presented 195 of them on slavery topics.

John Quincy was as unruffled by the threatening letters that arrived daily at his home as he was by congressional displeasure. B.J. wrote twice that he would shoot Adams in the presence of the House or in the street. A Virginian ordered him to desist from using up the valuable time of Congress with "your d——d abolition petitions. . . . If you do not . . . I will let loose the reign of my Vengeance and the consequence will be that the life of our once beloved President will be no more."

The hate letters emanating from the South redoubled in viciousness against John Quincy's presentation of petitions in favor of the recognition of Haiti. "Beware, or something will come over you as a thief in the night," an Alabaman threatened. A gentleman from Georgia said that Adams "will be shot down in the street, or your damned guts will be cut out in the dark."[3]

During the brief session, Adams tried to clarify his position on slavery by proposing his own anti-slavery program, which was designed to achieve gradual and legal abolition. On February 15, 1839, he read to the House three amendments to the Constitution.

1. From and after the 4th day of July, 1842, there shall be, throughout the United States, no hereditary slavery; but on and after that day every child born within the United States, their territories or jurisdiction, shall be born free.
2. With the exception of the Territory of Florida, there shall henceforth never be admitted into this Union any State the constitution of which shall tolerate within the same the existence of slavery.
3. From and after the 4th of July, 1845, there shall be neither slavery nor slave trade at the seat of government of the United States.[4]

Adams had no hope that his modest proposal would be received or even discussed in the House. It served to explain to all the petitioners the only method by which, in his opinion, slavery could be abolished "without violence and without injustice." Ironically, the Adams explanation, when it appeared, infuriated the hard-line abolitionists. Undaunted, Adams continued to explain his own position to his anti-slavery correspondents. State legislatures must abolish slavery within themselves by declaring children born free after a given day. To abolish it "against the will of the Slaveholders themselves . . . would be in my opinion neither practicable nor just."[5]

That the slaveholders had any rights was a premise that the radicals could not even consider. Adams's tirade against the abolitionist doctrine of immediatism was written with an acid pen. "What then is the meaning of that immediate abolition which the Anti-Slavery Society had made the test of orthodoxy to their political church? A moral and physical impossibility." This unkind blow fell heavily on the abolition leaders, who were already overwhelmed by the imminent collapse of the Anti-Slavery Society. One wit retaliated with a piece against Adams that, though it did not scan, made its point.

> He that played Sir Pander
>   While wages were to be had,
> And saved slave-trading Andrew,
>   Now rails at them like mad;
> And turning to us he modestly says
>   "Your language is too bad."[6]

Despite the abolitionist newspapers' "grand chorus" against John Quincy's position paper, he was invited to attend the national anti-slavery convention to be held in Albany at the end of July. He did not go but sent a letter explaining his point of view to Reverend Joshua Leavitt and H. B. Stanton of the committee of arrangements. Immediate abolition without compensation, he reiterated, would be equal to abolition by force and could be carried out only by soldiers. Their idea, he commented, was Utopian, whereas his was not inconsistent with an abhorrence of slavery "as cordial and unqualified as that of the most devoted abolitionist."[7] Adams did not want to go to the convention because he balked at the statement of the society "That every American citizen who retains a human being in involuntary bondage as his property is (according to Exodus XXI:16) a Man-Stealer." The biblical verse read: "And he that stealeth a Man, and selleth him, or if he be bound in his hand, he shall surely be put to death."

The brief session of the Twenty-fifth Congress, which ended in early March, contributed to John Quincy's financial problems, since Congressmen were paid on a per diem basis. Charles was commissioned to dispose of some of his father's Boston real estate in order to supply him with the money needed for expenses and the trip north. Adams also was not particularly well that winter. He had a severe catarrhal cough, "which did not lay me up, though I surely thought it would lay me down." It did not, however, keep the ex-President from his commitment in New York or his visit to Quincy, "where I shall devote the ensuing season to the memory of my Father." The obligation to fasten John Adams's fame in a memoir still persisted for his seventy-one-year-old son.[8]

The New-York Historical Society had invited Adams to make an address on April 30, the fiftieth anniversary of George Washington's Inauguration. "My reputation, my age, my decaying faculties, have all warned me to decline the task," Adams said. But "the day was a real epocha in our country" and so he felt obliged to accept. As was his nature, he made himself a "self-tormentor" over the speech, losing all peace of mind while he wrote and rewrote it. The theme was unity of Washington's two great objectives—the War of Independence and the establishment of the Constitution.

Charles arrived from Boston at 6 A.M. on April 30 to accompany his father to the Washington jubilee. The two-hour discourse, which was delivered at the Middle Dutch church on the corner of Nassau Street, traced the history of the Constitution from pre-Revolutionary times until its adoption. It was a labored offering, but well received by the assemblage in the crowded church.

One of the strangest bequests that the government of the United States ever received was a gift of more than £100,000 from the estate of James Smithson. In his will, the eccentric Englishman provided that his estate should go to his nephew but, should his nephew die without heirs, the whole property was to be bequeathed "to the United States of America found at Washington, under the name of the Smithsonian institution, an establishment for the increase & diffusion of knowledge among men."[9] Smithson's nephew died without heirs in 1835.

When President Jackson was informed of the Smithson windfall he was puzzled, because the Englishman seemed to have no connection with the United States. But it was his duty to submit the offer to Congress. Congress was equally baffled and suspicious, not even knowing whether it had the power to accept the gift. To answer the question, a committee was formed with John Quincy Adams as its chairman, an assignment that he enjoyed. The subsequent report submitted in January 1836 reflected the enthusiasm of the committee chairman. "To furnish the means of acquiring knowledge is the greatest benefit that can be conferred upon mankind. It prolongs life itself, and enlarges the sphere of existence."[10]

Adams's logic convinced the House, and finally both branches of Congress passed a bill directing the President to obtain the bequest. Quite naturally, John Quincy was curious about James Smithson.

He called on Aaron Vail, the British Chargé, but was unable to find out anything reliable from him or the other members of the embassy staff. It was intimated that the man was insane, had republican tendencies, and that he was the ante-nuptial son of the first Duke and Duchess of Northumberland, hence the older brother of the late Duke. The embassy gossip was partly true. Smithson was the illegitimate son of Sir Hugh Smithson, later the Duke of Northumberland, and Elizabeth Hungerford Keate Macie, a wealthy widow, a cousin of Sir Hugh's wife. Smithson became an amateur scientist, doing most of his work in the field of analytical chemistry. Although never a famous chemist, Smithson did identify a new mineral ore which was named smithsonite. His connection with the United States was, at most, ephemeral. It has been postulated that he regarded the political freedom that America offered a more congenial atmosphere for scientific achievement than a monarchy because President Jefferson had offered political asylum to his friend, Joseph Priestley, after Britain had exiled him for his political beliefs.

Whether Smithson was an Americanophile or simply an eccentric, Adams, upon hearing that Richard Rush had obtained the bequest, went to see President Van Buren. He talked to him for nearly two hours, trying to convince him to recommend to Congress the establishment of an astronomical laboratory, which would employ an astronomer and an assistant to observe night and day and then inform the public of their findings. Another valuable addition to the scientific life of the nation, he suggested, would be a series of annual lectures on natural, moral, and political sciences. Above all, he warned the uninterested executive, "no jobbing—no sinecures—no monkish stalls for lazy idlers. . . . I feel deep responsibility as testator to the world for this."[11]

Adams became the watchdog of the Smithsonian bequest, worrying that it would be "filtered to nothing, and wasted upon hungry and worthless jackals."[12] In February 1839, he averted the attempt to siphon off part of the fund for an educational institution. However, as time went on, it became apparent that Van Buren was totally indifferent to the disposal of the money and that there were opponents to the establishment of the Institution, such as Calhoun.

When William Green, president of the Quincy Lyceum, asked Adams to give a lecture on the Smithsonian bequest, he accepted. If he could not prevent the failure of Smithson's intention, he could, by making it a subject for a lecture, leave a record for future time of what he had done to accomplish "the great design." After working on his lecture for some time, he decided that one presentation was not enough to contain all that he had to say. In order to save the fund from "misapplication, dilapidation and waste," he must overflow "into a second lecture and arouse public sympathies for the proper use of the fund," which might mean giving similar lectures wherever Adams could be heard.

Dissatisfied with the finished products, "written under the harrow of such distress of mind" and "insupportedly tedious and dull," Adams still carried them before the public. On November 13, at seven o'clock, he walked from his house to the Town Hall, already crowded to capacity. Despite a hacking cough and a good deal of hoarseness, the ex-President's voice came across with an earnest, firm vigor. The audience, made up of two or three women to one man, listened avidly throughout the hour-and-a-half speech. After it was over, a resolution of thanks was adopted and a request for him to return the following week for his second part. Satisfied, John Quincy rode home and retired to bed with a cup of spearmint tea.

Adams did not deliver his second lecture himself. On the following Wednesday, young Georgeanna Frances Adams lay dying. On Tuesday, her grandfather sat up with the mortally ill child far into the night and when he retired did not undress. He handed his manuscript to Reverend Lunt, the family minister who had been praying outside of Georgeanna's room, with instructions to read the lecture for him if he could not go to the Lyceum.

By daylight the child seemed somewhat better and likely to live for several days longer. Adams called on Reverend Lunt, advising him to go to the meeting with the lecture and wait until seven o'clock. If Georgeanna improved, he would be there but if he did not arrive by seven, he should read it. At about three in the afternoon, the child suddenly became worse. Her agonies "were terrible," her distraught grandfather recorded. At ten to six she died. Adams retired to his bed-chamber "in a state approaching stupefaction." "On this day our lovely and beautiful Fanny died," Louisa wrote, overcome with grief.[13]

When Adams failed to appear at the appointed time, Mr. Lunt read the second Smithsonian lecture. Mr. French, the schoolmaster, had been at the Adams home at six and carried the news that the child was dead. The lecture was well received in Quincy and also, on the following day, in Boston when Lunt read it for Adams before the Mechanic Apprentice's Library Association.

The first Smithsonian lecture was an historical narrative describing the nature of the bequest, the uneasiness of Congress over its acceptance, and the progress made until the present. Adams gave his opinions on how the fund should be used—not for a university, because Smithson wanted it to promote knowledge, not learning, and had chosen the United States to carry this knowledge "to the whole human family." Adams described his plan for an observatory in detail, revealing his correspondence with George B. Airy, the Astronomer Royal of the Royal Observatory at Greenwich. In an impassioned outburst, Adams implored, "Oh! My Countrymen—can you think of seeing this fund wasted upon the rapacity of favourite partisans, squandered upon frivolous and visionary mountebanks, and embezzled in political electioneering, without mortification and disgust?"[14] In conclusion, he begged his listeners to give him their sympathy and influence in support of his plan: 1. the fund should be preserved inviolable; 2. no part of it should be used for the education of children or young people; 3. the astronomical observatory. He promised that he would, if possible, resume the subject at the next session of Congress.

John Quincy Adams's watchful and persistent vigilance during ten years of service as chairman of various Smithsonian committees helped to preserve the bequest. The strange legacy had a group of supporters under Joel Poinsett, who organized the National Institute for the Promotion of Science, but it also had articulate and vituperative detractors in the halls of Congress. Debates on the Smithsonian problem became chronic as various legislators rode their own hobbyhorses. Senator Benjamin Tappan of Ohio wanted an experimental agricultural station established while Senator Rufus Choate of Massachusetts pleaded eloquently for an ample library. In the House, Robert Dale Owen of Indiana rejected musty libraries in favor of a teacher training school for the practical arts and sciences. This last proposal upset Adams who presented a novel reason for objecting to it. It was the duty of the American people themselves to provide schools for their children and they would be disgraced by using the money of a foreigner to defray such charges. It would be better to see the money thrown into the Potomac than to use it for a normal school, Adams declared. The bill was defeated.

Finally, in the summer of 1846, Congress, more from exhaustion than conviction, passed an act establishing the Smithsonian Institution. A simple building was to be erected to house a museum of scientific materials, a chemical laboratory, a library, an art gallery, and lecture facilities. At Congressman Adams's insistence, only the income from the bequest was to be used. The principal would be held by the Treasury Department.

In voting for the watered down Smithsonian bill, which lacked provision for an astronomical observatory, Adams was motivated by the realization that he could not do better. His success was in preventing the politicians from absorbing the money for their own political purposes and in preserving the spirit of the Smithson bequest—"an establishment for the increase & diffusion of knowledge among men." The achievement complemented the author of the treatise on weights and measures, the constant stargazer, and the indefatigable, if disorganized, planter of acorns and seedlings.

However, in 1839, the subject that absorbed most of John Quincy Adams's time and all of his "good feeling" was the *Amistad* case. During the summer, newspaper reports about the long, black schooner that appeared and reappeared like a ghostly apparition in the waters of the Atlantic intrigued the public imagination. Off Barnegat Bay, an American ship came close enough to the dilapidated vessel to report the presence on it of about twenty-five half-naked Negroes who indicated that they were out of food and water. The *Emmeline* took the derelict in tow but when it was apparent that the black men had armed themselves, she cast them off.

The alarm went out up and down the coast to look out for the strange ship. On August 26, at Sag Harbor, Long Island, two sea captains, hunting birds on the dunes, suddenly came upon four Blacks wrapped in blankets. By means of sign language, Captains Henry Green and Peletiah Fordham conveyed to the strangers that they were on Long Island, which was free land. The Blacks then led the sea captains to the top of a dune, from which they saw the long, low black schooner with tattered sails and no flag.

Shortly, a small boat, carrying several more Black men landed on the beach. The two captains noted that the Blacks were sketchily dressed but were adorned with necklaces and bracelets made of gold doubloons. Green and Fordham, who were already counting their fat salvage rights, were disappointed to see a United States Coast Guard brig, the *Washington*, appear off Gardiner's Point. Lieutenant Thomas R. Gedney boarded the schooner with a landing party and took off all the Blacks as prisoners. An elderly white man who spoke only Spanish appeared from below decks and threw himself, sobbing, into Gedney's arms. In a moment, another Spaniard emerged from the same place and in passable English told an extraordinary story.

After a number of conflicting stories were pieced together and a person was found to translate Mendi, the language of the captured Blacks, the drama was unraveled. The Negroes had been originally imported from Africa by a Portuguese slaver, the *Tecora*, and taken to Havana, which was contrary to Spanish law and to the treaty between Great Britain and Spain that forbade the slave trade.

Two Cubans, Jose Ruiz and Pedro Montez, bought the *Tecora*'s human cargo, planning to take them to the Cuban coastal town of Puerto Principe on a coastal vessel, the *Amistad*. The slave owners had obtained false papers from the Cuban authorities that identified the captives as *ladinos*—that is, slaves imported before the abolition of the slave trade—which was impossible, because the forty-nine male slaves and the three little girls and a boy were too young to have been imported before the 1817 Anglo-Spanish treaty. The ship left Havana harbor on June 28, 1839.

When the *Amistad* was at sea for four days, the slaves, led by Singbe or Cinque (Joseph Cinquez), revolted and killed the Captain and the cook. A day or so before the mutiny, while on deck for their daily airing, one of the Africans asked the cook, in sign language, what was going to happen to them. The answer, a grisly jest, terrified the Black men and doomed the cook. Using unmistakable sign language, the cook pantomimed the captives' fate—their throats would be cut and they would be eaten.

After their successful revolt, Cinque and his fellow captives spared Ruiz and Montez to sail the ship to Sierra Leone for them. Montez deceived his captives by changing the course at night, though during the day the Negroes understood enough navigation to judge the direction in which they were sailing. Hence the erratic course of the vessel and the dilapidated state into which it fell.

On August 29, a judicial hearing on the *Amistad* was conducted aboard the *Washington*, anchored in New London harbor. Judge Andrew Judson, who had been the prosecuting attorney in the Crandall case, which forced Prudence Crandall to give up her school for Negro children in Canterbury, Connecticut, presided. The Spaniards claimed the slaves as their property and charged the Blacks with murder and piracy. Gedney claimed the ship, the cargo, and the captives as salvage. And Angel Calderon de la Barca, the Spanish Minister in Washington, was exerting diplomatic pressure to have the *Amistad* returned to its owners and the slaves sent back to Havana.

Judge Judson was not prepared to render a final judgment. He remanded the prisoners to the custody of the United States Marshall to await trial by the circuit court when it met at Hartford on September 17 and in the meantime the terrified Negroes, who were unable to understand what was going on at their trial, were to be taken to the New Haven county jail.

It was obvious that the imprisoned *Amistad* captives were in a precarious position. Help would obviously not be forthcoming from the federal government, for Van Buren was indifferent and the Secretary of State John Forsyth, who would be required to handle the case with the irate Spanish government, was himself a Georgia slaveholder. The abolitionists and anti-slaveryites under Lewis Tappan immediately organized a committee to raise funds for the defense, and the New York *Emancipator* appealed to "the friends of humanity" for donations.

What was needed to promote their cause, the *Amistad* relief committee realized, was to find a champion who had national appeal. John Quincy Adams, the reluctant friend of abolition, would be a particularly useful ally. Ellis Gray Loring, a Massachusetts lawyer, an anti-slavery man, and a friend of the old statesman, was prevailed upon to ask for his opinion on the case. When John Quincy received Loring's letter, he debated with himself whether to display good sense and decline to get involved, thereby saving himself, or to succumb to his conscience, which urged him to accept public responsibility. His New England conscience won out and in a letter to Loring, parts of which were printed in several newspapers, Adams answered the Massachusetts lawyer's question.

The captives of the *Amistad* "were victims of the African Slave Trade . . . cast upon our coast . . . by their own ignorance of navigation and the deception of one of their oppressors . . . whose life they had spared to enable them by his knowledge of navigation to reach their native land." Their present plight "claimed from the humanity of a civilized nation compassion:—it claimed from the brotherly love of a Christian land *sympathy*;—it claimed from a Republic professing reverence for the rights of man, justice. . . . Instead they were seized, jailed, accused of piracy and murder."[15] Adams told Loring that the *Amistad* Blacks' actions on board ship, whether piracy and murder or not, had emancipated them from the condition of slaves. "They were not slaves but Masters."[16] It was clear to all that John Quincy Adams thought that the *Amistad* Negroes should go free on habeas corpus and that he was willing to serve in their defense.

When the House of Representatives convened on December 2, it could not get started because five of the New Jersey seats were contested. For three days the chamber was abandoned to complete confusion. Through it all, an eyewitness recorded, Adams sat quietly, absorbed in writing, seemingly oblivious to the disturbance around him. On the fourth day of anarchy, Hugh Garland, the clerk, started to call the rôle call again. When he reached New Jersey, Adams, hands clasped at the front edge of the desk to help him to rise, pulled himself to his feet. "I rise to interrupt the clerk!" he shouted.

"Silence! Hear him!" echoed from all parts of the House. "Hear John Quincy Adams!" In a few minutes, there was silence. Even the rudest and most rambunctious members listened.

"It was not my intention to take any part in these extraordinary proceedings," the venerable Plymouth member said. "I had hoped this house would succeed in organizing itself. . . . But what a spectacle we here present! . . . We do not and cannot organize; and why? Because the clerk of this house—the mere clerk . . . usurps the *throne*. . . . Is he to suspend by his mere negative, the functions of government, and put an end to this congress? . . . He refused to call the roll . . . compel him to call it."

A member interrupted to say that compulsion could not reach the clerk, who said that he would resign rather than call New Jersey.

"Well, sir, let him resign, and we may possibly discover some way by which we can get along without the aid of his all-powerful talent, learning, and genius!" Adams answered.

Cheers shook the Capitol. Old Man Eloquent had found a way to allow the government to continue to function.

"Who will put the question?" many voices shouted.

"I intend to put the question myself," rang out Adams's voice, carrying above the others.

Richard Barnwell Rhett of South Carolina leaped on a desk, waving his arms and shouting. "I move that the Honorable John Quincy Adams take the chair of the Speaker of the House and officiate as presiding officer till the house be organized by the election of its constitutional officers." The ayes answered in a thunderous chorus. Between Louis Williams of North Carolina and Rhett, Adams was conducted to the Speaker's chair.

Henry Wise, Adams's sworn enemy in the House, for that one occasion became a genuine admirer. "Sir, I regard it as the proudest hour of your life," he said to John Quincy, "and if, when you shall be gathered to your fathers, I were asked to select the words which in my judgment are best calculated to give at once the character of the man, I would inscribe upon your tomb this sentence: *I will put the question myself.*"[17]

Adams's ten-day reign was a trying one. The stormy sessions lasted so long that the ex-President left his post only long enough to take a cup of coffee and two slices of buttered toast. One snowy day his coachman stood outside the door of the Capitol to walk the old man home. The roads were too slippery for the horses.

It took many attempts before a speaker was elected. The Administration candidate, John W. Jones, was way ahead at first but could not get a majority. As the members deserted Jones, Robert Hunter, a Virginia whig, was able to unite all the whigs and the malcontents and so win the chair. Adams relinquished his post, returned to his regular seat, and "walked home with a lightened heart."[18] The five New Jersey whigs, whom Adams, when acting Speaker, had failed to get admitted to the House, were excluded and five democratic "pretenders" were accepted instead.

Adams, as usual, prepared to present his mountains of petitions, but the real focus of interest for those concerned with "the peculiar institution" was the court room where the *Amistad* Blacks were being tried. The Secretary of State had assured the Spanish Minister that a United States vessel, the *Grampus*, was lying in New Haven harbor ready to carry the *Amistad* defendants back to Cuba. Since the Negroes said in the Connecticut court that they were not slaves, then, the President reasoned, they should have the opportunity of proving it in Cuba.

The trial, which took place the first week in January, was attended by a tense and anxious audience. At its close, Roger Baldwin, the New Haven attorney for the Blacks, was able to convince the court of the rights of his clients. "Cinquenzo and Grabeau shall not sigh for Africa in vain," the judge ruled. "Bloody as may be their hands, they shall yet embrace their kindred." The Africans had been illegally captured, illegally transported, and illegally enslaved under the laws of Spain and under the law of nations. Therefore, they were to be delivered to the President of the United States to be transported to Africa and there to be delivered to the agent appointed to receive them and conduct them home. The judge also denied salvage rights to Lt. Gedney since, under Connecticut law, slaves had no value nor were they saleable.[19]

The President, greatly dissatisfied with the decision, complained that Judge Judson had not taken into consideration the larger political aspects of the case. Hence, under his orders, District Attorney William S. Holabird appealed the decision to the district court. When in April the Court upheld the earlier decision, the case was appealed to the Supreme Court, scheduled to meet in January 1841.

In the meantime, John Quincy's annual battle to defeat the gag rule suffered its usual defeat. He did, however, win a resolution which asked that the House be given copies of the papers and correspondence relative to the *Amistad* case that were exchanged between the President and the Spanish Minister, to which Van Buren acceded. After the material was printed and made available to the Congressmen and the public, the printing was exhausted in a few days.

Until their trial date, the *Amistad* captives were detained in their New Haven jail. Even though the anti-slavery newspapers screamed out against their captivity, Judge Thompson refused to grant them bail or even let the children go free. Consequently, the Blacks became a source of great interest to the American public throughout the United States. Their story was sympathetically dramatized in a play called *The Black Schooner* which had a successful run in New York and elsewhere. A Boston artist painted a huge canvas, depicting Singbe killing Captain Ferrer, called *The Massacre*. It was displayed in New Haven and Hartford where the public paid admission to see it and the press praised it highly.

The captives were involuntarily subjected to an education program designed by their abolitionist friends. Josiah Willard Gibbs, a Yale professor of languages, located James Covey, a seaman who understood the Mendi language, so that the Blacks could learn English, read the Bible, and be converted to Christianity.

As the bitter cold of the New England winter subsided, the *Amistad* captives were able to exercise for longer hours on the New Haven green. Though they were now less of a spectacle than when they first arrived, volunteer committees of abolitionists continued to pay the cost of their education and, more important, of their defense. By this time most of the thirty-six Africans who survived could read and write a letter in English. But they all had one wish— to go home.

The plight of the *Amistad* captives only highlighted the horror of domestic slavery for Adams. Over the loud protests of the southerners in the House, he presented his petitions whenever he could. They were, of course, all immediately tabled, but they kept alive the issues of slavery and of the right of the citizens of the United States to petition their legislature. On March 20, the Plymouth member offered to send 511 petitions to the clerk's table. When the members from Georgia roared their protests, Adams asked quietly if they would prefer him to present each one individually, a process which would take all night. The 511 petitions were immediately received.

"What a horrible exemplification of slavery!" Adams cried after he had been visited by Joseph Cartwright, the preacher of a Negro Methodist church in Washington. Cartwright had a subscription book to raise $450 so that he could purchase the freedom of his three grandchildren, all under four years old. He told Adams that it had taken him twenty years to purchase his own freedom and that of his three sons.

The congressional session had begun to be an endurance contest. On April 8, a "nuit blanche,"* the House refused to adjourn at 3:30 A.M., so Adams, exhausted, went home and slept from four to seven, breakfasted, and then returned to the Capitol at 8:30. The sleepless nights continued while the appropriations bill was being argued. During the ordeal, Adams composed "The Wants of Man," his most successful and most widely reprinted poem. Stanza XIX was particularly appropriate at this time.

> I want a keen, observing eye,
>   An ever-listening ear,
> The truth through all disguise to spy;
>   And wisdom's voice to hear;
> A tongue, to speak at virtue's need,
>   In Heaven's sublimest strain;
> And lips, the cause of man to plead,
>   And never plead in vain.[20]

On the evening of May 16, returning to the House between six and seven, Adams found that it had adjourned. As he walked into the committee room of the committee of manufactures, he tripped

* "sleepless night"

over the newly laid matting, pitched forward, fell, and dislocated his right shoulder. It was set by Dr. Thomas and Dr. May, both of whom ordered their patient to stay at home for a while. But the next morning, despite the remonstrances of his family, John Quincy was in his seat. However, when the shoulder continued to be very troublesome, in answer to Louisa's entreaties Adams agreed to stay home. Dr. May asked him if he had ever dislocated the shoulder before. Adams answered that he did not recall the incident himself but his mother had told him that when he had been two or three he had strayed into the street and a nursemaid seized his hand, giving it an involuntary jerk that dislocated his shoulder. Since then his right hand had been weaker than his left, he had never been able to write fast, and, for the past twenty-five years, could not use his forefinger and thumb. Though his right hand had been disabled many times, "a chastisement of heaven," it was his duty to write. The shoulder did not cease to be excrutiatingly painful until almost the end of June, the damage to the right hand seemed to be permanent.

The debate on the sub-Treasury bill rambled on. Adams entertained himself through the endless speeches by composing a poetical address in ottava rima to the marble statue of Clio over the clock at the front entrance to the hall. He also wrote clever, biting sketches of his colleagues, which he entrusted to his *Diary*. Walter Colquitt of Georgia was "a ranting Methodist preacher, a middle-sized man of swarthy complexion and crispy curls, between hair and wool, raising ominous conjecture of an infusion of African blood . . . low in stature, with eyes black as jet, and Ladino platitude of face. His articulation is rapid and indistinct, his gesticulation so violent and contortive, that he looks more like a stage tumbler making somersaults than like a decent pulpit preacher. . . ."[21] On Sunday, Adams went to hear Colquitt preach and found him much better as a pulpit orator. However, the subject of his sermon was the procrastination of repentance, and Adams thought there was not a member of the House who needed the practice of it more than Colquitt.

The congressional session did not close until sometime after midnight on July 21. Adams walked home exhausted, reflecting on the Twenty-sixth Congress. "The most important and the worst measures of the administration have been carried through the House by the most contemptible men in it," he commented. Congress appeared to be a degenerating institution, once again falling into "profligate factions."[22] What was to become of slavery, the public lands, the collection and disbursement of public funds, the tariff, and foreign affairs, he asked himself.

Adams spent the next few days sifting through and filing the hundreds of unanswered letters, pamphlets, and public papers that had accumulated during the session. He packed them into four large boxes, along with books, and sent them by ship to Boston. Almost half of his mail was from strangers who sent requests for him to deliver orations and lectures, all of which he turned down.

During his summer at Quincy, many attempts were made to draw the ex-President into the political agitation over the coming presidential election. As returns came in from North Carolina, Kentucky, Indiana, and Alabama for the state governments, it looked as if the whigs were the favorites. "The imposture of Jackson and Van Buren democracy would seem to be drawing to its catastrophe," Adams wrote with pleasure. Though he considered himself to be a twelve-year silent victim of Jacksonianism, he had decided never to speak out on presidential elections because of his "peculiar situation," not even when asked by the whigs of his own district who had just endorsed him. Adams admitted to John Bell, who visited him at Quincy, that the times seemed favorable for a change, which should ensure William Henry Harrison's election. The new custom of electioneering by the principal leaders was a corruption of popular elecions, Adams maintained. He sneered at the practice of touring the country and holding forth like Methodist ministers to the assembled multitude of twenty, thirty, or fifty thousands, not one of whom could hear or listened.

In September, Charles, who now had a summer house near the family homestead, Mary, and Louisa persuaded Adams to take an excursion on the Cunard steamer, *Acadia*, on its first return trip to Halifax, Nova Scotia. The land was wildly beautiful, Adams thought, and on his way home through the British provinces he observed evidence of the British government's desire to please her colonials in Canada. Perhaps she had learned something from the American Revolution.

The *Amistad* case, Judge Thompson ruled, in the April 1840 appeal, was to be tried in the Supreme Court because it had now become an issue between Spain and the United States. He could not dictate to the Supreme Court but felt that its importance required a decision by the nation's highest Court. Roger Baldwin's plea that the case be dismissed was overruled and the Supreme Court placed it on its agenda for January 1841.

The interest of the public in the *Amistad* captives was just about exhausted. Inevitably, contributions required for the defense had almost dried up, the lawyers on the case either had withdrawn or were looking for reasons to leave. Seth Staples from New York was no longer on the team, Theodore Sedgwick, Jr. was missing more often than present, but Roger Baldwin stayed on through all the appeals, finally realizing a fee of only seven hundred dollars. The committee, feeling that it needed a lawyer with prestige and ability to work along with Baldwin, approached Rufus Choate, one of New England's leading trial lawyers, but he refused because he opposed abolition. Finally, Lewis Tappan, overcoming his anger over John Quincy Adams's lukewarm position on the slavery issue, agreed with Ellis Gray Loring that Adams was their only chance.

When Loring and Tappan called on the ex-President in Quincy on one crisp October morning, Loring did the talking. Would Adams become the assistant council to Baldwin in defense of the Africans in the *Amistad* case before the Supreme Court, he asked. The Plymouth representative tried to excuse himself because of age, inexperience—it was more than twenty years since he had argued in the Courts—and his duties in the House of Representatives. But when the two abolitionists convinced him that it was a matter of life and death to the unfortunate captives, Adams capitulated. Overjoyed, the two visitors promised that Baldwin would furnish Adams with a brief.

Charles was a silent and disapproving witness at his father's meeting with Tappan and Loring. Just nominated to the Massachusetts House of Representatives by the Boston whigs, the younger Adams feared that his father's independent espousal of the anti-slavery cause might be an embarrassment to the whigs, who might then make it unpleasant for him.

In November, John Quincy travelled to New Haven to consult with Baldwin. The two lawyers worked in Adams's room in the Tontine Hotel for two hours, going over the papers and the arguments. Baldwin then took his colleague to see their clients. Adams noted that the thirty-six men (the children were in a separate house so he did not see them) were confined in one large room about thirty feet long and twenty feet wide. They slept in eighteen crib beds arranged in two rows, two deep on both sides the length of the chamber. All but one of the men was under thirty, short, under 5'6", with Negro faces varying in color from ebony-black to dingy-brown. Cinque and Grabow had remarkable faces, Adams observed. Three of the captives read part of a chapter in the New Testament very indifferently; one boy wrote tolerably well. Huddled together as they were and having no one but their teacher, Mr. Ludlow, to talk English with, Adams judged that their learning had to be very slow.

"I am here in great tranquillity," the Plymouth representative informed Charles from Washington. He had lectured all the way down from Boston to Philadelphia—at New Haven, New York in a heavy snowstorm, and the next day in Brooklyn. The old man was indefatigable.

General Harrison's election did not guarantee that the country would gain by the change, Adams warned. Jackson surrendered himself "to the dominion of the kitchen"; what would Harrison's be? With all of the problems of the nation—the Florida war, Indians, internal improvements, the tariff, the northeast boundary, slavery, abolition, impressment—who will lead Congress? Clay perhaps, he suggested. Whatever, "I shall be as I have been—a solitary." As to Charles's career in the legislature, his father told him that he must never be discouraged or soured. "Fortify your mind against disappointments. . . . Keep up your courage and go ahead!"[23]

A heavy snowfall marked the opening of the second session of the Twenty-sixth Congress. The new speaker was Robert M. T. Hunter, "an amiable, goodhearted, weak-headed young man, prematurely hoisted into a place for which he is not fit." Adams started off as usual by unsuccessfully attempting to rescind the gag rule, and when it failed submitting his quota of petitions. Among them was a petition from two chiefs of the Seneca tribe asking that no appropriation be made to carry into effect the fraudulent treaty by which they were to be driven, "like a herd of swine from their homes to a wilderness west of the Mississippi."[24]

Both the President's and Adams's New Year's Day open houses were less well attended in 1841 because of snow, hail, and sleet. Those who went to call on Van Buren were mostly whigs, his adversaries. His own party deserted him. "Nothing more uniformly exemplifies this propensity of human nature than the exit of a President of the United States," Adams commented from bitter experience.[25] But this New Year's Day he had little time for reflection. Instead he worked for several hours on the *Amistad* case.

Attorney General Henry D. Gilpin advised Adams that Van Buren stated that the *Amistad* case would not be dismissed from the Supreme Court without an argument because the Spanish Minister insisted on the delivery of the defendants to Havana. Adams protested without success. It was an abominable executive and judicial conspiracy against the lives of these wretched men, he felt. But in due course, as predicted, the motion to dismiss the appeal was denied.

"Half prepared" and with "a heavy heart, full of undigested thought, some of the justice of my cause, and deeply desponding of my ability to sustain it," Adams went to Court. There he found a welcome reprieve. Since Justice Story had not returned to Washington, Chief Justice Roger B. Taney decided to postpone the case for several weeks until there would be a full complement of nine justices.

Just prior to the new date for the Supreme Court hearing, "a severe visitation of providence" occurred. After depositing Adams at the Capitol, his coachman Jeremy Leary started to leave the yard, but in the front of the yard the noise of an exhibition of firing with Colt's new repeating gun frightened the horses. They reared up, jamming the Adams carriage against another wagon and tossing Jeremy and the footman from the box. The coachman was almost killed by the fall. Adams came to him as soon as he heard the news, bringing with him Dr. Kearney, an army surgeon. Jeremy was in excrutiating pain with a severe contusion of the back and, most serious, an internal wound in the bowel. Adams hired a messenger wagon, laid the coachman on a mattress with a pillow and blankets, and brought him home. At about 6:30 the following day, Leary died. Justice Taney agreed to postpone the *Amistad* case until the twenty-second so that John Quincy could attend the funeral "of my poor, humble, but excellent friend Jeremy Leary."[26]

With a "thoroughly bewildered mind" Adams walked to the Capitol to attend the often-delayed opening of the case. It was Washington's Birthday, which should have augured well, but he feared that only fervent prayers could carry him through the ordeal. Attorney General Gilpin opened up with the logical argument that the *Amistad* was a properly registered Spanish ship which plied the coastal trade of Cuba. The passports of the passengers were in order, which proved conclusively that the Negroes belonged to Senors Ruiz and Martez. According to the law of nations, the Court could not go behind or enquire into the validity of these credentials. The Attorney General cited many authorities from law books, but offered no argument to show that the right of property remained unimpaired by the mutiny. He insisted that the captives be returned to their owners and that the circuit court was wrong when it declared that they were free.

Roger Baldwin responded mildly and moderately in behalf of the Blacks. The case involved "considerations deeply affecting our National Character in the eyes of the whole civilized world, as well as questions of power on the part of the Government of the United States, which are regarded with anxiety and alarm by a large part of our citizens," he said. Can our government "become a party to the proceedings for the enslavement of human beings cast upon our shores and found in the condition of freemen within the territorial limits of a free and sovereign state?"[27] On the following day, the Connecticut lawyer continued his defense, arguing that the captives had the right of self emancipation but soft-pedalling his remarks so as not to activate southern prejudice, which was well represented on the Court.

Adams watched the proceedings with such increasing agitation of mind that it was little short of agony. He sat writing and rewriting his brief but nine-tenths of what he wrote, he complained, was waste paper. The skeleton of his argument was not yet put together. After the Court closed for the day, he hurried to the Library of Congress to read James Madison's speech in the Virginia convention on the double condition of slaves in that state, as persons and property. Until the moment that the Court convened the next day, the Plymouth member was in the clerk's room working on his presentation.

The black-robed justices in the full but not crowded court room and the few ladies in the gallery awed Adams. Until he rose to speak he was deeply distressed, but as soon as he started, "my spirit did not sink within me." Old Man Eloquent held the attention of the judges for four and a half hours until at 3:30 the Court was adjourned. The essence of his argument was to display "a steady and undeviating pursuit of one fundamental principle—the ministration of *justice.*" He charged that the Administration, pressured by Ministers of a foreign nation, had brought its powers to bear "in this case, on the side of injustice."[28] Justice Story reflected the amazement of all the justices when he described Adams's argument as "extraordinary—Extraordinary, I say, for its power and its bitter sarcasm and its dealing with topics far beyond the record and points of discussion."[29]

After an uneasy and restless night, Adams arose, encouraged and cheerful, ready to face the Court again, but learned that Justice Philip Barbour had been found dead in his bed. Chief Justice Taney ordered that the Court be closed until the first of March.

When it reconvened, Adams appeared at Court to finish his argument. In his four-hour speech, he recapitulated some of his earlier arguments, not sparing the Attorney General for his refusal to go behind the fraudulent *Amistad* documents. The ex-President particularly emphasized the constitutional principle of habeas corpus. If the President had handed over the *Amistad* captives to Spain, as was demanded, "What would have been the tenure by which every human being in this Union, man, woman, or child, would have held the blessing of freedom? Would it not have been by the tenure of executive discretion, caprice, or tyranny . . . at the dictate of a foreign minister? Would it not have disabled forever the effective power of habeas corpus?"

The aged orator then addressed the seven justices with a closing non-sequitur that moved the audience to solemn stillness. He referred back to the seventh of February 1804, when he had first addressed the Court. "As I cast my eyes along these seats of honor and of public trust, now occupied by you, they seek in vain for one of those honored and honorable persons whose indulgence listened then to my voice. Marshall—Cushing—Chase—Washington—Johnson—Livingston—Todd—Where are they? . . . Gone! Gone! All gone! . . . gone to receive the rewards of blessedness on high."[30] At eleven the next morning Adams arrived at the Supreme Court to hear Attorney General Gilpin's closing argument, in which he reviewed Baldwin's arguments but ignored those of the ex-President. The Court adjourned until March 9, when the decision would be delivered.

In the interval, William Henry Harrison was inaugurated as President of the United States. Adams's verdict was that the production was "showy—shabby," although he acknowledged that the demonstrations of popular feeling were unexampled since those for Washington in 1789. The procession lacked pomp and circumstance, he criticized, referring to the Tippecanoe clubs, college students, schoolboys, and about half a dozen veterans who had fought with the hero in the War of 1812 that tagged after the military cavalcade, carrying awkward and badly painted banners and replicas of log cabins. General Harrison, dressed in a plain frock coat, indistinguishable from his retinue, rode a mean-looking white horse, Adams noted. However, he admitted, the perfect order and tranquillity that marked the day was much to be admired.[31]

Justice Story, who delivered the Court's opinion in the case of the United States v. the *Amistad*, affirmed the decision of the district court except in regard to the Negroes. He ordered that they be placed at the disposal of the United States to be sent back to Africa. They were declared free.

Not waiting to hear Judge Baldwin's dissenting opinion, Adams went to the chamber of the committee of manufactures to write to Lewis Tappan and to Roger Baldwin. "The Captives are free!—" he told Tappan. "But thanks—thanks—in the name of humanity and justice to you." More reservedly, he wrote the news to Baldwin, adding that Lieutenant Gedney's claim for salvage was affirmed.[32]

There was still unfinished business. How were the captives to be returned to Africa? It was clear to Adams that it was the duty of the government of the United States to provide transportation at their own cost and, possibly, to indemify the Africans liberally for their eighteen months of false imprisonment. Acting on his conviction, the ex-President approached Daniel Webster, now Secretary of State, asking if President Harrison could not provide passage to Africa for the Blacks since they had been deprived of the vessel found in their possession and of its cargo, their lawful prize of war, which would have provided them with the money for their return trip. At first Webster seemed startled by the original proposal but finally agreed to seek passage for them on a public ship. He would speak about it to the Secretary of the Navy. Either to fortify his request or because he did not quite trust Webster, Adams advised Baldwin to send a memorial to the President requesting a vessel and, if the President could not manage it, to send a memorial to Congress.[33] Meantime, the Africans had been discharged from prison and sent to be employed and instructed in Farmington, Connecticut.

Just a month after his Inauguration, President Harrison died of complications resulting from a chill. For the first time in American history, the Vice President would become "Acting President of the Union," as Adams phrased it. It was not a happy prospect, he noted, for Tyler was "a political sectarian of the slave-driving Virginian Jeffersonian school, principled against all improvement, with all the interests and passions and vices of slavery rooted in his moral and political constitution." He was, in short, "not above mediocrity."[34]

As an ex-President, Adams was expected to be part of the funeral cortege that followed the car, driven by six white horses, upon which Harrison's remains had been placed. The procession consisted of twenty-six pallbearers wearing white scarfs, one pallbearer for each state in the Union, then the family, then John Tyler and the heads of the departments. Ex-President Adams followed with the heads of the departments of the Van Buren Administration, the justices of the Supreme Court, Senators, foreign ministers, members of the House of Representatives, and the Governors of the states and territories. All of the dignitaries were preceded by numerous and diversified military escorts. Adams noted that although the diplomatic corps was present in full costume, the British Minister was absent. Vast crowds followed the procession from the President's house to the Capitol. The city bells tolled and guns were fired from the west terrace of the Capitol. From the Capitol, the procession, flanked by the floating multitude, proceeded to the Navy yard where the body was placed in a vault.

Harrison's wife and son were too overcome with grief to attend the funeral. The family was represented by three orphaned grandsons, ranging in age from ten to fourteen. Adams, moved to compassion by them, observed that they were "just able to feel the reverses of their condition, their prospects and their hopes."[35]

Tyler's presumption that he was now the President of the United States and not the Vice President acting as President irked Adams. It was a construction in direct violation of "both the grammar and the context" of the Constitution, he asserted. The powers and the duties of the office of the President were, upon his decease, bestowed upon the Vice President but not the office.[36] Utter distrust for Tyler's principles and lack of confidence in Daniel Webster, his Secretary of State, convinced Adams that between the two of them and the manufacturing interest, his position was perilous.

When, at the special summer session of Congress, the reinstatement of the gag rule came up routinely, Adams almost prevailed in his attempt to achieve an amendment to it. Henry Wise, who led the fight against the proposal, raved about "the hell-hound of abolition," calling Adams the leader of the abolitionists throughout the

Union. Working himself up to such a pitch that his voice failed and he lost the thread of his argument, Wise carried on without abatement. Finally he became ghastly pale, said that he felt ill, slumped in his chair, and fainted. The dramatic display was somewhat effaced in value when Wise returned after the weekend somewhat subdued but still capable of six hours of continuous invective against the aged Plymouth member. At the end of his hysterical tirade, he was bowed over his desk, only capable of whispering—"Abolition, abolition"—John Quincy Adams was the arch fiend, "the inspirer and leader of all abolition."[37] Wise's histrionics prevailed. All petitions were to be hung up for the session and debate on the rule was postponed to the winter, when they would reconvene. Congressmen from New Hampshire and Maine had supported the southern bloc to make the anti-Adams victory possible.

The purpose of the special congressional session which had been called by Harrison before his death was to deal with the need to replace the hated independent Treasury system. Instead of a matter of economics, the bank issue became a power struggle between "His Accidency" John Tyler and Senator Henry Clay, who wanted to wrest the leadership of the whig party from the usurper. Clay supported a revival of the old Bank of the United States, which was contrary to the President's states' rights position. Tyler advocated a District of Columbia bank with the power to branch out in the states if the states wished it. Clay's committee wanted to pass an amendment that "branching" could not take place without the consent of the individual state. Tyler objected, complaining: "I am placed upon trial. Those who have all along opposed me will still call out for further trials. . . . Remember always that the power claimed by Mr. Clay and others is a power to create a corporation to operate *per se* over the Union. This from the first has been the contest."[38]

When the bank law passed, despite the urging of his friends, Tyler decided to veto it. As a result, Adams, who had been invited along with the President, the Cabinet, and the Congress to visit the battleship *Delaware*, decided not to go. "The feud festering between congress and John Tyler" made it "no time for festivity or hollow-hearted pageantry," he said pompously. The President did not go either.

On August 16, when the veto message was read, there was some disorder in the galleries. That evening a group of Democratic Senators, including Benton, Buchanan, and Calhoun, visited the President's house to compliment him on his courageous act. But later that same night, a boisterous mob of whig sympathizers woke up the First Family with their noisy protests and then burned the President in effigy. Adams saw nothing heroic about Tyler's setting his will against both Houses of Congress. His view was that Tyler had first usurped the title of President and was now resorting to the veto power, "the most anti-democratic institution of the Constitution." It would probably prostrate the administration, he predicted.[39]

A second bank bill was devised, reputedly after a group of congressional whigs met with the President, but somehow there was a misunderstanding, either deliberate or unconscious, because the effort was no more acceptable to Tyler than the former one. He still objected that states' rights had not been properly protected and on September 9 sent a second veto message, polite and apologetic but adamant. All over the country, whigs denounced the accidental President while the party prepared a proper rebuke.

Adams was made aware of the plan at a meeting of the Massachusetts delegation called by Secretary of State Daniel Webster, who announced that the Secretaries of the Treasury, Navy, and War and the Attorney General had decided to send in their resignations. Webster, addressing the ex-President directly, said that he felt that he had not sufficient cause for resigning his office and wanted the opinions of his compatriots. While Webster insisted that it was a matter of perfect indifference to him whether he kept the job or not, Adams was reminded of Falstaff's recruit, Peter Bullcalf, a comic prototype of double talk. Webster explained that Tyler had always treated him well and probably wanted him to stay, particularly since he was in the midst of negotiations with England. The assembled caucus agreed that Webster would not be justified in resigning at this time but they all felt that "the hour for the requiem of the Whig party was at hand."[40]

If Henry Clay believed that the mass exodus of his Cabinet would destroy Tyler's will to continue as President, he was mistaken. With effortless ease, a new Cabinet was assembled, one that reflected Tyler's states' rights whig views and that included his other allies, the conservative democrats. Now, flanked by his own supporters, he was in a stronger position than before.

On his way to Quincy after the close of the congressional session, Adams stopped off at New York to see the Tappans. He reported that he had seen the President about transporting the *Amistad* Africans home on a public ship, as Webster advised. However, Tyler wanted to shift the responsibility to the Colonization Society, which disappointed the Tappans as they had hoped to ship all the Africans home that autumn.

During the Quincy visit, Adams delivered a controversial address to the Massachusetts Historical Society on the war between Great Britain and China (the Opium War), which was still going on. He had a large audience that filled the Masonic Hall to overflowing, despite a heavy rainfall. The war was not being fought on the opium question, Adams told his listeners, but over the Kowtow, "the arrogant and unsupportable pretension of China" that she can direct her commercial relations with other nations "not upon terms of equal reciprocity, but upon the insulting and degrading forms of the relation of lord and vassal." Britain had the righteous cause, he told the amazed audience. But the New Englanders should not have been surprised to hear him say that "the duty of each [nation] is to hold commercial intercourse with the other . . . from a joint and equal moral consideration of the interests of both." Therefore, these principles of the Chinese Empire "truckled to by the mightiest Christian nations of the civilized world, have at length been brought into conflict with the principles and the power of the British Empire. . . ."[41] The audience did not show signs of disapproval although Adams's position was contrary to popular opinion. However, the speech was published only in the *Chinese Repository*, Macao, China, in 1842. Dr. John Palfrey, the editor of the *North American Review*, delicately turned it down.

John Quincy foresaw great anxiety and little possibility for improving the condition of the country by legislation as he prepared for the opening of the winter session. There was no reason to believe that he would not be alone as heretofore when he refused to accept the House rule on petitions, but he would not remain silent. And the Administration now solicited little respect from the aged Plymouth member. "There is neither spotless integrity nor consummate ability at the helm of the ship," he observed, "and she will be more than ever the sport of winds and waves drifting between breakers and quicksands."[42]

Quincy's Sage

JANUARY 1, 1842, a beautiful winter's day, marked the thirtieth anniversary of John Quincy Adams's sojourn in Washington and the twenty-fifth consecutive year of his residence there. The President's reception was so thronged that the porter had to lock out the crowd pressing for admission lest those already inside be suffocated. Adams thought that the mob must have come to see the house and not its occupant because "there has never been a time when the personal sympathies of the *people* were so utterly indifferent as they are this day to John Tyler."[1]

At least five hundred people called on ex-President Adams that day, at least twice the number that had ever been received before. A great number of the Congressmen, including almost all of the whigs, were present, as was General Edmund Gaines. The General said gallantly that he had come to see the only President of the United States he had ever seen, the others had been President of a party. John Quincy liked the compliment but attributed it to Gaines's pique at General Scott's promotion to Major General.

Among the distinguished guests at the Adams house that day was Theodore Weld, just arrived in Washington, who came with Joshua

Leavitt, an abolitionist journalist, and Joshua R. Giddings, whig abolitionist Congressman from Ohio, with whom Weld was boarding at Mrs. Sprigg's, across the park from the Capitol. Weld had been invited by the small but enthusiastic band of congressional abolitionists to head the anti-slavery lobby and to help the legislators gather material for their arguments in Congress.

Theodore Weld, who had just left "the pomp and tinsel and fashion and display of magnificence" at the President's Palace, noted that Adams's red brick house was plain and plainly furnished and his host and hostess plainly dressed—"the old gentleman *very* plainly." When introduced to him, Adams asked graciously, "Is it Mr. Theodore D. Weld?"

"Yes."

"I know you well, sir, by your writings," Adams replied. He asked for Mrs. Weld, discussed slavery, the case of the *Creole*, abolition by the Bey of Tunis, and the possibility of abolition in Cuba. When Weld met Louisa he was glad to observe that her husband addressed her as "My *dear*" as he had heard "that they lived unhappily together."[2]

Adams, who was moving gradually toward a more open concert with the abolition wing, invited Weld to dinner about a week later. It was "a genuine abolition meeting," Weld told his wife. "The old patriarch" talked with as much energy and enthusiasm "as a Methodist at a camp meeting. Remarkable man!" In the course of conversation, the host discovered that he and Angelina Grimke Weld were "blood relations" though the South Carolina Smiths, which pleased Theodore. Since Weld's father and John Quincy Adams were second cousins, "You and I must be about Sixth Cousins," he wrote happily to his beloved Angelina.[3]

The degree of closeness with which Adams worked along with the anti-slavery clique at Abolition House, as Mrs. Sprigg's boarding house was called, is subject to conjecture. However, he did call a meeting on January 15, which was attended by Seth M. Gates of New York, Joshua Giddings, and about ten others to develop a plan of action for saving the right of petition. The group approved of the idea but nothing specific was settled. A week later the friends of the right to petition met again and listened to six resolutions that Adams prepared. Once again they were polite but not enthusiastic. The difficulty was a basic difference of philosophy between the ex-President and the abolitionist wing, a problem that he refused to recognize. The abolitionists were most interested in the abolition of slavery while he emphasized the constitutional right of petition.

Another direct confrontation between Adams and the slavocracy had been boiling up in the House since the start of the session. Now that the edge that the southern bloc was able to maintain in support of the gag rule was lessened, the Plymouth member's obstinacy posed a greater danger. Old Man Eloquent must be suppressed. At the same time, Adams, who hoped to press his advantage, planned a stratagem to circumvent the gag rule. It was undoubtedly a prepared move because he told Weld the day before that he would present some petitions that would set the slavocracy "in a blaze." Weld was there to watch the conflagration, and so was Lord Morpeth, the English abolitionist.[4] Adams rose to present the petition from Habersham County, Georgia, which asked for his removal from the office of chairman of the committee on foreign relations, a post to which he had been assigned that session, because of his abolitionist bias. It charged that he had a "perfect monomania" on the subject of color. When the southerners moved to place the petition on the table because of its subject matter, Adams protested that it was his privilege to be heard in his own defense, and the Speaker was forced by House rules to accede to the "question of privilege."

Once given the permission to speak, "Old Nestor lifted up his voice like a trumpet; till slaveholding, slavetrading, and slavebreeding, absolutely quailed under his dissecting knife."[5] Desperately the southern wing, ably represented by Henry Wise, Adams's most ardent adversary, Kenneth Rayner of North Carolina, William Cost Johnson, a whig from Maryland, and dozens of others, tried to stop the embattled old man "who breasted the storm and dealt his blows upon the head of the monster."

The enraged opposition shouted questions of order, sometimes at the top of their voices—"That is false"—"I *demand* Mr. Speaker that you *put him down!*"—"What? Are we to sit here and endure such insults!"—"I demand that you shut the mouth of that old harlequin!" Frantic with frustration, the slavery members left their seats to mill around the section of the hall where Adams stood speaking without noticing the outcries. When successfully interrupted, the ex-President said in an irritating voice, "I see where the shoe pinches, Mr. Speaker, it will pinch *more* yet. I'll deal out to the gentlemen a diet that they'll find it hard to digest. If before I get through, every slaveholder, slavetrader and slave breeder on this floor does not get materials for bitter reflection it shall be no fault of mine."[6] While he was observing that there was an alliance between the southern slavetraders and northern democrats to get rid of him as chairman of the foreign affairs committee, the House voted 91 to 76 to stop him from continuing.

On January 25, Adams gave the whigs, who were thoroughly disgusted with their errant patriarch, an opportunity to suppress him. He presented a petition from Benjamin Emerson and forty-five other citizens of Haverhill, Massachusetts, praying that Congress would immediately peaceably dissolve the Union. Their reasons were: 1. no Union was agreeable that did not offer reciprocal benefits; 2. a vast proportion of the resources of one section of the Union was drained annually to sustain the views of another section without adequate return; 3. judging by past history, the Union, as it was going, would overwhelm the whole nation in destruction.[7] Adams supporters moved that the petition be referred to a committee for report and answer.

First there was an explosion, and then all Babel broke loose upon the Plymouth representative. Suggestions were made by some snarling southerners to burn the petition in the presence of the House and to others to print it so that the country could see its outrageous character. Finally, Thomas Walker of Virginia, as a question of privilege, presented a resolution to censure John Quincy Adams. A much more elaborate set of particulars against him was then formally offered by Thomas F. Marshall of Kentucky. It was, most likely, a joint prepared effort of many members of the slave interest who now thought that they had Adams safely caught and ripe for exposure before the entire nation.

The censure proposal began: "Whereas, the Federal Constitution is a permanent form of Government and of perpetual obligation until altered . . . the Hon. John Quincy Adams . . . in presenting for the consideration of the House of Representatives of the United States, a petition praying the dissolution of the Union, has offered the deepest indignity to the House of which he is a member; an insult to the people of the United States . . . and will, if this outrage be permitted to pass unrebuked and unpunished, have disgraced his country . . . in the eyes of the whole world . . . for this insult [he] . . . might well be held to merit expulsion from the national councils; and the House deem it an act of grace and mercy, when they only inflict upon him their severest censure. . . .''

The censure motion against the ex-President excited Washington and the rest of the country. The galleries were closely packed with visitors and with Senators who left their own hall to listen to Adams's reply to his persecutors. When the old gentleman rose, all eyes "met in a focus" on him. He spoke without bitterness: calm, fearless and majestic. "The highest illustration of the moral sublime that I ever witnessed in a popular secular assembly," Theodore Weld wrote of the small, bald, gray patriarch, whose hands trembled with age. Adams commenced his defense coldly and judiciously and then turned his scorn on Thomas Marshall, the handsome, vigorous nephew of his former friend, the great Chief Justice of the Supreme Court. The young man had accused Adams of having asked the House of Representatives to commit high treason by reading a petition for the dissolution of the Union.

"I call for the reading of the first paragraph of the Declaration of Independence," Adams demanded.

The clerk read, urged on by John Quincy to proceed to the "right and duty."

"Read it! Read it!" he insisted. "And see what that says of the right of a people to reform, to change, and to dissolve their government."

The clerk dutifully read from the document— "but when a long train of abuses and usurpations, pursuing invariably the same Object evinces a design to reduce them under absolute Despotism, it is their right, it is their duty, to throw off such Government, and to provide new Guards for their future security."

"Read that again!" Adams demanded, and then continued his argument. Finally, he said, "I rest that petition on the Declaration of Independence."

Henry Wise took over the southern attack, invoking Washington's farewell address, which recommended national unity and recalling Adams's support of the passage in the treaty of Ghent which provided for the payment to their owners for slaves carried off by the British. "That one should so have outlived his fame," he mourned. "The gentleman is politically dead; dead as Burr—dead as Arnold."

Adams sat silently repressing his anger, planning his answer. Theodore Weld offered to relieve him from the drudgery of gathering the materials necessary for his defense. "I thank you. I accept your offer gratefully," the old man answered. The tirades against him that he had to endure daily were draining his energies. But when he spoke in the House his voice rang out clear and hard. Weld noted in amazement that when he called on John Quincy after a long day at the House, the Plymouth representative would come to greet him "as fresh and elastic as a boy." In answer to Weld's fear that he had tired himself out, Adams replied, "No, not at all. I am all ready for another heat." And then he would review the main points of his next day's argument, rehearsing the gestures and the elocution as if he had been addressing the House.[8]

After a brief respite due to the death of Rhode Island's Senator, Nathan Dixon, Adams's "fiery ordeal" continued. Questions were brought up that were not relevant to the issue but that required answers. John Quincy was forced to refute charges relating to matters as old as political parties during the Jefferson Administration. The past was rehashed with enthusiasm but without meaning. To Weld and the abolitionists, these angry, eloquent exchanges were not even worth listening to because they avoided the basic issue: the struggle between the slaveocracy and the forces of abolition. The slaveocracy would not succeed in crushing Adams and the right, Weld predicted. "If they should *fail* it will be the most signal overthrow that has ever befallen the slaveholding host."[9]

Beneath the surface, beyond the exchanges over matters long since settled, the essential question was clear to Adams. He had received the petition and it had been his duty to present it. The right to petition was a constitutional guarantee that the southern bloc wanted to destroy in order to force the principle of slavery on the free states. Hence, on February 3, still talking in his own defense, Adams somewhat humorously reported some of the letters from the South that threatened him with assassination. Among them was a colored lithograph portraying him with the mark of a rifle ball on his forehead, with the motto, "To stop the music of John Quincy Adams, sixth President of the United States,

> Who, in the space of one revolving moon
> Is statesman, poet, babbler and buffoon.

Adams observed that these words had been used in debate by Gilmer. The only difference was that "fiddler" had been changed by "his echo" to "babbler."

The ordeal was becoming exhausting and upsetting to Louisa who was forced to see her husband go off every day to face the abuse of the House. One day, utterly distraught, she suffered a fainting fit and was miserably ill for twenty-four hours. But nothing would stop the intrepid old man, who seemed to thrive on a diet of controversy. While there were windmills to fight, Adams was pleased to be there to tilt with them. However, he wanted his speeches reported fully and accurately. His complaint that the *Intelligencer* suppressed some parts and falsified others annoyed the editors so that they retaliated by refusing to report his speeches at all.

The quantity of words that were daily tossed about in the House debate occupied about a hundred columns in the *Congressional Globe,* and much of it went unrecorded because of the shouting and carrying on. Adams, who was an expert at the lethal jibe, enjoyed the verbal duels with a youthful zest. Mocking young Marshall's legal shortcomings, he asked him where he got his law. Assuredly not from his uncle, Adams snapped and then made a nasty reference to his victim's reputation for alcoholism.

Henry Wise took on the old man next by inaccurately quoting from *Macbeth*: "Come on, Macduff/ And damn'd be he, who first cries, hold, enough."

Adams answered with a reminder to Wise of his involvement in the Cilley-Graves duel. Pointing to him, the ex-President said, "That far more guilty man came into this House with his hands and face dripping—when the blood spots were yet visible upon him. . . . It is very possible that *I* saved this blood-stained man from the censure of the House."

Wise rose angrily to a point of order. "Is it in order for the member from Massachusetts to charge me with the crime of murder and with being stained with innocent blood? . . . the charge . . . [is] a base and black lie as the *traitor* was black and base who uttered it!" he cried.

The debate looked as if it would continue indefinitely and mount higher and higher in abusive exchanges. Adams said that it would take him at least three weeks to conclude his defense. At one point, Gilmer offered to withdraw his resolution if Adams would withdraw his petition. He was refused. To withdraw it would be to sacrifice the right of petition, the right of habeas corpus, the right of trial by jury, the confidence of the post office, the freedom of the press, the freedom of speech—"every element of liberty that was enjoyed by my fellow citizens," Adams protested.[10]

The end of the seemingly endless debate came quickly and unex-

pectedly. On February 7, Adams entered the House with an out-
line of the continuance and the conclusion of his speech, which
would have taken at least a week. As soon as he got the floor, he said
that he was prepared to continue but also willing to stop and dismiss
it from consideration forever. John Minor Botts, a Virginian whig,
moved to lay the whole subject on the table forever. It was carried
106 to 93. Immediately thereafter, the acceptance of the Haverhill
petition was voted on and the House refused to receive it, 166 to
40.

The current of public opinion seemed to be swinging toward
Adams. He became the high priest of the cause of constitutional
rights. Even the abolitionists, who had rejected him in the past and
whose numbers he had never joined officially, now regarded him as
their dauntless advocate. Despite their threats, their parliamentary
devices, and their sound and fury, the efforts of the slaveholders had
failed to destroy Adams. Weld recorded: "The old Nestor turned all
their guns against themselves, and has smitten the whole host with
dismay and discomfiture." And Francis Pickens of South Carolina
summed it up effectively: "Well, that is the most extraordinary man
on God's footstool."[11]

The southern whigs had a brief period of sweet revenge after
Adams escaped their ire. Joshua Giddings presented a resolution on
the *Creole* case, which had the South aroused because they believed
that the slave rebellion that had occurred on that ship was directly
inspired by the decision in the *Amistad* case. In November 1841,
135 slaves mutinied on the *Creole*, a coastwise ship sailing from
Hampton Roads to New Orleans. The slaves killed one of the ship's
owners and then made the white crew take them to Nassau to seek
freedom on British territory. To the complete consternation of the
southerners, the British arrested those slaves who were identified as
the murderers and set the others free. Daniel Webster was deluged
with slaveholder demands for indemnification from the British for
their lost slaves.

Giddings, an ardent abolitionist, declared that Virginia had no
jurisdiction over the coastwise trade and that the laws of the United
States did not recognize the coastwise slave trade. Botts answered
Giddings's resolution with a counter resolution which proposed that
the Ohioan's "utterly unwarrantable" action be condemned by the
House. This time the southern bloc would not be cheated of its
prey. The motion was hurriedly passed by a vote of 125 to 69 in

favor of condemnation. Adams moved to give Giddings permission to be heard in his own defense, but his proposal was refused. Solemnly Giddings shook the ex-President's hand and then, resigning his seat, left the House. That evening he left Washington to return to his constituents. Six weeks later he was back in the capital, having been returned by an overwhelming vote from his 16th congressional district of Ohio.

When the attention of the House was returned to its business instead of the persecution of part of its membership, Adams was again disgusted with Tyler's leadership. The President had vetoed the tariff bill and now wanted to use the public lands money to lessen the Treasury deficits. As chairman of a special committee to report on the executive veto, Adams stated his views on both subjects. The public lands, he declared, "are the noble and appreciable inheritance of the whole nation." To use the proceeds from their sale for the ordinary expenses of government was to destroy the trust vested in Congress. In reference to Tyler's veto, Adams called it the "five times repeated stricture of the Executive cord." The congressional power to enact laws for the public welfare "has been struck with apoplexy by the Executive hand."[12] The report deplored the President's abusive exercise of his constitutional power to stop Congress and suggested that the veto power ought to be limited by an amendment to the Constitution. The House failed to sustain that suggestion by its inability to achieve a two-thirds vote. Implicit in the Adams's report was a move to impeach Tyler. But the whigs were not powerful enough to dispose of their accidental President, and Clay, who might have led such a crusade, had resigned from the Senate in March, his opposition program a shambles as a result of the presidential vetoes.

Adams did not take seriously Clay's invitation to a barbecue meeting in Dayton, Ohio, or his suggestion that he resume leadership of the whig party. It was no longer becoming, he told his friend-adversary, for him to undertake to lead in the councils of nations. Though he was despondent over the public lands policy, he was not in despair. They should both take consolation that Tyler's Administration was drawing to a close.[13]

Adams returned to Quincy in the summer of 1842 as a conquering hero. Though he protested that he was humiliated by the praise lavished on him, he was honest enough to admit that it inflated his vanity ridiculously. The Plymouth district, no longer intact as a result of the 1840 census, gave the old patriarch a glorious reception, complete with banners, toasts, orations, and verses composed to the tune of "My Country 'tis of Thee."

> Time shall touch the page
> That tells how Quincy's sage
> Has dared to live.[14]

Most heartening was the audience's adoption of resolutions upholding their Congressman's opposition to the annexation of Texas and congratulating him on his conquest of his enemies.

Without campaigning or making any effort to seek support, the newly formed 8th congressional district elected Adams in November 1842. He had been unanimously nominated by the whigs, who also passed resolutions endorsing his conduct, although in September he had declined attendance at the whig convention, citing his health and personal matters. However, he had expressed his conviction that "the welfare of the country is staked upon the harmony and prosperous issue of their deliberations." The election returns were somewhat disappointing because the four towns that gave least support to Adams were his three native ones—Randolph, Quincy, and Weymouth—and his mother's native town, Braintree. "The people are a wayward master," he commented.[15] Actually, the whigs had not done well in Massachusetts. Charles had been elected, but, in general, the democrats had triumphed.

At the start of the new session of Congress, Adams's resolution to rescind the twenty-first House rule, which excluded abolition petitions from being received, was rejected 84–93. The gap was narrowing, though the northern democrats were still allied with southern slavers. Abolition House was now the acknowledged reception center for petitions against slavery. An appeal sent out to the nation to deluge the Congress with them was signed by the whig insurgent Congressmen and, leading all the rest, John Quincy Adams.[16]

Presidential fever was again rampant in Washington. Adams, who refused to participate in any public way, enjoyed the game of picking the winner. Martin Van Buren would win in 1844, he predicted. Henry Clay had as little prospects as Tyler or Calhoun. Buchanan was "the shadow of a shade," General Scott was a "daguerreotype likeness of a candidate—all sunshine through a camera obscura." As for Judge John McLean, he was "but a second edition of John Tyler—virtually Democratic, double-dealing and hypocritical. They will go into the Democratic convention and all melt into the Corinthian brass of Kinderhook."[17]

In June, when Charles came back from the whig convention held in Worcester, his father was worried about the nature of the party. He suspected Webster of trying to "dragoon" the Massachusetts whigs from their allegiance to Clay and to supplant him. So far, Webster had successfully managed to drive John Davis into retirement and thus, Adams believed, insure the state for Marcus Morton, the radical democrat. Actually, he proved to be wrong because the whigs gained control under George Briggs, a temperance man from the western part of the state who got the nomination for Governor. Nevertheless, Adams blamed himself for "a craven spirit" that kept him from getting involved "in this mighty movement upon the history of Man." He really believed that Massachusetts, by going democratic, would be helping to prostrate the Union before the slavery faction.[18]

The Bunker Hill Monument, now completed, was to be dedicated in June. Lafayette had laid the cornerstone in 1825 and Webster had delivered the address. This time Webster would again deliver the address and the President and his Cabinet would be there as guests—John Tyler "with all his court, in gaudy trappings of mock royalty, to receive the homage of hungry sycophants, under color of doing homage to the principles of Bunker Hill martyrdom," Adams said. And Webster hoped by it "to whistle back his Whig friends, whom he had cast off as a huntsman his pack."[19] John Quincy Adams declined his invitation to the travesty.

While Tyler, his entourage, and the "godlike Daniel" celebrated the completion of the monument and feasted at Faneuil Hall, Adams stayed home visiting his seedling trees and listening to the cannonade from the town. It reminded him of the thundering cannon and the smoke of burning Charlestown that he had viewed as a child in 1775. Combining his idealized recollection of that historic day with the present scene—the pyramid of Quincy granite, Daniel Webster spouting, and John Tyler's nose, which cast a shadow outstretching that of the monumental column—he observed that he would have to be driven either to indignation or to laughter.

On the Fourth of July, Adams attended a speechmaking that gave him great pride. Charles Adams gave the annual Boston City oration at Faneuil Hall. The applause of the crowd for his "only surviving son," coupled with his memories of his last Independence

Day in Boston, which was in 1809, evoked "an agitation of my feelings" that no language could express, the Quincy sage said.

Although he had travelled extensively in Europe, Adams had never had the time to see much of his own country, even those sections relatively close to home. On July 6, the ex-President went with his daughter-in-law, her father, Peter Brooks, and his grandson, John Quincy, on a tour of Western New York, mostly for Abby's health. The trip turned into a triumphal progress for Adams. All along the way, deputations met him to invite him to visit their towns and cities.

Adams inspected Niagara Falls with his old friend General Peter Porter, who took him to all the points from which the cascades and rapids could be seen from the best advantage. It was an unusually clear day, the sun "shining in cloudless splendor, and the snowy foam of the spray reflected the burning beams in a constantly shifting rainbow, adding exquisite beauty to the awful grandeur of the falling flood," Adams wrote.

While he was at the Falls an invitation came for Adams from Professor Ormsby M. Mitchel of Cincinnati to lay the cornerstone of an observatory to be built there by the Cincinnati Astronomical Society. A year earlier, when the professor was in Washington and had asked Adams for letters of introduction so that he could seek support for the project, Adams called him an annoying, vain braggart. Now that Mitchel had achieved his project, Adams agreed to undertake the "hazardous and expensive" trip.[20]

At Buffalo, shouting multitudes met John Quincy and his travelling companions at the steamer. Millard Fillmore made a complimentary address and then he and the Mayor drove the old gentleman around the city in an open barouche. At the American Hotel, hundreds of men and women were waiting to shake hands with the celebrity and in the evening a mammoth torchlight parade was staged.

Similar attentions met the Adams-Brooks party wherever they went. The city of Rochester welcomed them with guns firing, bells ringing, and hordes of shouting people. After a day of speeches, handshaking, and torchlight parades, the Mayor took them to the railroad and presented the ladies with a basket of magnificent cherries. Canandaigua, not to be outdone, sent Francis Granger and Jared Wilson to conduct them to their town. At the outskirts, a cavalcade in military uniform welcomed their guests with a brass band and a line of carriages which formed a procession a mile long. Adams made a speech which he thought inane, "as I always do when answering compliments," but the crowd loved it. The old man had become a symbol of the early republic to the cheering crowd, and they thought him a brave and somewhat astounding warrior in the cause of liberty.

William Henry Seward came to conduct the Adams party to Auburn, but they were stopped along the way by crowds who wanted to hear a speech and to shake the patriarch's hand. At Auburn, a torchlight procession guided the travellers to Seward's house, where the retired Governor received Adams with cordiality and affection. Many felt that Adams regarded Seward as his natural successor, who would continue the work for human rights that the old gentleman knew that he must leave unfinished.

A committee of Black citizens called on John Quincy in Utica to thank him for his efforts to protect the right of petition and to promote the abolition of slavery. Adams went to a female seminary where he heard a Mr. Spencer give an address consisting of extracts from Abigail Adams's letters about her oldest son, written between 1774 and 1778. "I actually sobbed as he read, utterly unable to suppress my emotions," he wrote. "Oh my mother: Is there anything on earth so affecting to me as thy name? so precious as thy instructions to my childhood, so dear as the memory of thy life?"[21] John Quincy was so choked with emotion that he did not know how he answered Spencer's presentation.

Crowds gathered around their ex-President every time the train stopped for fire and wood. He would descend from the train, shake hands, and speak to the people until the train started again. A cavalcade of butchers and many thousands of citizens met the party at Albany. At the state capital, speeches, receptions, and dinners were given in his honor and he was conducted to the mansion house of the patroon, the late Stephen Van Rensselaer.

Finally, on August 4, at 6:30 A.M., the Adams party drove to the train station to take the Great Western Railroad to Boston. At Springfield John Quincy met his old pupil, subsequent protégé, and now alienated friend, Alexander H. Everett. He regretted that Everett was now a political outcast, a wreck of his own ambition, and the victim of one more cunning and unprincipled than himself."[22]

The adulation of the crowd, a phenomenon that was rare in Adams's long public life, had been a fatiguing but pleasant interlude. Now, back in Quincy, Lewis Tappan came to return Adams to the familiar world of controversy. Tappan had just returned from the world anti-slavery convention held in London. Before leaving in the spring, he had talked to Adams, who told him that British abolitionists could influence their government not to recognize the republic of Texas unless slavery were abolished. "I deem it the duty of Great Britain as a Christian nation to tell the Texans that slavery must be abolished—that it shall not be planted there, after all the efforts and sacrifices that have been made to abolish it all over the world. . . . If slavery is abolished in Texas, it must speedily fall throughout America, and when it falls in America, it will expire throughout Christendom."

Once in Britain, Tappan carried the ex-President's message to those whom he met. Duff Green, who was the unofficial representative of southern interests in London, claimed that Tappan did irreparable harm by testifying at hearings on the treaty being negotiated between the United States and Great Britain. "So, the reciprocity treaty is destroyed in inception," Green asserted, thanks to Great Britain and "their allies, John Quincy Adams & Co."[23]

Hardly an ally of the mother country, Adams was, on the contrary, very suspicious of her sincerity. The policy of Great Britain was to protect slavery in the southern states and Texas while "humbugging the abolitionists in England into the belief that they intend directly the reverse," he warned. Nonetheless Adams was pleased to read in the proceedings of the anti-slavery convention that a resolution had been offered and unanimously adopted honoring him for his work. "Before my lamp is burnt out, I am desirous that my opinions concerning the great movement throughout the civilized world for the abolition of slavery should be explicitly avowed and declared," he pledged. "God grant that they may contribute to the final consummation of that event."[24]

Adams was disappointed that his Fourth of July address to the citizens of Bangor, Maine, that celebrated the anniversary of the emancipation of slaves in the British West Indies, was so little noticed. He meant it to be a strong note of defiance to all slaveholders upon earth. "Are we not suffering our own hands to be manacled, and our feet to be fettered with the chains of slavery? . . . By a fraudulent perversion of language in the Constitution of the United States, we have falsified the constitution by admitting into both the legislative and executive departments of the government an overwhelming representation of one species of property to the exclusion of all others, and that odious property is slaves? . . . O, my friends, I have not the heart to join in the festivity on the first of August—the British anniversary of disenthralled humanity. . . . I would spare the blushes of my country, weigh down my spirits with uncertainty, sinking into my grave as I am, whether she is doomed to be numbered among the first liberators or the last oppressors of the race of immortal man!"[25]

Adams planned to depart for Cincinnati on October 25, allowing thirteen days to make the trip via Buffalo, Ashtabula, and Cleveland. "If a spark of your enthusiasm for the cause of Science, and the honour of our country, burns in my bosom, it shall live until the Cornerstone of Your Observatory shall have been laid,"[26] he wrote to Mitchel. In the meantime, every ounce of energy and every waking hour was devoted to the composition of the oration. Libraries were combed for material by all the Adamses and their friends so that "the transient gust for enthusiasm for the science of Astronomy at Cincinnati" could be turned into "a permanent and persevering national pursuit."[27] The work had to be completed by October 20 so that it could be copied.

That it was a long and perilous journey for an old man to make, particularly in the late fall, Adams and his family knew very well. The decision was rash but, John Quincy said, he must go, "happen what may." Louisa knew better than to try to stop him. And on the last day at home, the ex-President worked until one in the morning on a speech to his constituents. At half-past four, the speech still unfinished, he rose and, with Charles, rode to Dedham. A crowd of men and women met him, shook his hand, and then formed in a procession to go to the meeting house. A complimentary song with verses that were sung to the tune of "Auld Lang Syne" preceded the two-and-a-half-hour speech. It was a "miserable fragment" of what it should have been, Adams lamented. After the ceremonies, he, Charles, and young John Quincy returned to Quincy for dinner. The next morning at 5:15 Adams left from the Boston station for Springfield and another lecture. Exhausted but game, he read his address on "Society and Civilization" with "difficulty and hesitation."

The Indian summer weather gave way to cold and snow. The train from Albany was frozen to the ground and arrived in Utica two hours late. "There is no uniformity in human life more monotonous than that of traveling in railroad cars," the weary traveller complained. The crowds of the summer were snowed into their homes and farms. "My passage now silent and unobserved."[28] At Buffalo, Adams heard a "practical sermon" at the Unitarian church and an evening service at the Episcopal church and then went to a party at Millard Fillmore's.

In his anxiety to get to his destination in time, John Quincy embarked on the *General Wayne* in the falling snow. The steamer was buffeted about on the angry lake until the Captain anchored at a small cove on the Canadian side. Most of the ladies and almost all of the men were violently seasick, but the old gentleman, a veteran of many transatlantic voyages, was fine, just annoyed at his rebuff by Lake Erie. He rested in the Captain's stateroom and read a volume of Matthew Davis's *Life of Aaron Burr*, which confirmed his opinion of Burr's trifling and profligate character.

The next day, improved weather allowed the Captain to sail to Erie, Pennsylvania, where a reception committee met Adams and carried him to the City Hall for a complimentary address and then returned him to the steamer, accompanied by a military escort and a torchlight parade. By this time, exposure had stirred up John Quincy's catarrhal cough and he had a sore throat and a fever.

The 232 miles from Cleveland to Columbus, Ohio, could be travelled by land, on the stage over bad and extremely dangerous roads or by boat on the Ohio canal, a four-day passage. Adams decided to take passage on the *Rob Roy*, a canal boat. While he waited, the incognito he had enjoyed during most of the trip was lost in a barber shop where he was recognized while being shaved. News got around quickly that the ex-President was in town, and in no time Adams's room at the American Hotel was invaded with admirers clamoring to shake his hand and be introduced.

Very unwell, Adams boarded the *Rob Roy* at Akron on November 2. The eighty-three-foot-long, fifteen-foot-wide canal packet had over twenty additional passengers and four horses. The interior of the boat was divided into six compartments, the first in the bow with settee beds for the ladies separated by a curtain from a parlor bed-chamber. The quarters were so close that Adams found it a "trial such as I had never experienced." To make it worse, the windows of the cabins had to be closed to keep out the driving snow, which intensified the heat in the rooms that were already made unbearable by the roaring stoves. Fortunately, his fellow travellers were amiable, but nevertheless, at eleven, Adams retired with a headache, chills, and hoarseness to spend a miserably restless night.

At daylight, John Quincy went to a hotel for breakfast and then endured the inevitable reception and address at the Town Hall. He shook hands with men, women, and children, but when a very pretty woman kissed him on the cheek, he returned the salute on the lips. After that he kissed every woman that followed, "at which some made faces but none refused."[29]

The canal boat progressed at the rate of two and a half miles an hour despite the snow, but it was an uncomfortable ride. The vessel was so unskillfully steered through the 200 locks that it thumped into every one of them and struck and grazed along the sides. Adams spent part of the time playing cards with the passengers. He had often played whist but euchre was a new game for him.

William Greene, a lawyer, one of the committee of three sent by the Astronomical Society to meet Adams at Cleveland, caught up with him at Kirkenville. A stage coach awaited to carry them to Columbus, Ohio, for a gala reception by the Mayor and flattering crowds. Just before daybreak, Davis Jenkins, a mulatto, called on Adams to carry the thanks of the Negro community of Columbus for his defense of their rights. Plans to leave Columbus at eight o'clock on November 6 had to be delayed so that two military companies of Germans could escort their visitor out of the city. While waiting for them to assemble, Ohio's Governor Shannon arrived. "I cannot realize that these demonstrations are made for me," Adams noted, "and the only comfort I have is that they are intended to manifest respect, and not hatred."[30] Almost too late, the adulation of the people was being lavished on a public servant who had given a lifetime to them and had, for most of it, reaped indifference or abuse.

When the boat reached Dayton, Adams left it to ride twenty-two miles to Lebanon in a carriage provided by the Astronomical Society, escorted by a large delegation of citizens. Thomas Corwin welcomed Adams at the Presbyterian church with a splendid address that required a response. To answer a polished speech "offhand" was "distressing beyond measure" and "humiliating to agony," the former Harvard Professor of Rhetoric and Oratory complained. He returned to bed that night worn out with fatigue.

The twenty miles from Lebanon to Cincinnati was travelled in another large cavalcade of carriages. At the outskirts of the city, Mayor Henry E. Spencer, accompanied by Professor Mitchel, met the entourage to escort John Quincy Adams formally into Cincinnati. The city's honored guest was transferred to an elegant open barouche with four horses and seated with the Mayor and the professor. It was a beautiful sunshiny day but in approaching the city, which was encircled by steep hills, while turning a corner and descending one of the steep inclines, the pole of the carriage snapped off. Adams had to leave his state carriage and travel the rest of the way in an ordinary two-horse conveyance.

Arrived at Henry House, where John Quincy was to lodge, the Mayor and his guest were conducted to a large balcony in front of the house from which Spencer delivered a welcoming address. It was received with deafening shouts of applause from the assembled multitude. "My answer was flat, stale and unprofitable, without a spark of eloquence," John Quincy complained. But the audience heard his remarks with renewed shouts of welcome. The rest of the evening, Adams's rooms were the scene of a continual procession of guests that barely left him time for dinner.

All of the arrangements for the laying of the cornerstone were completed, but Adams trembled that his speech was not perfectly prepared. Though worn out with anxiety and the congestion in his chest, the intrepid statesman sat up until one in the morning working on it, until, overcome with exhaustion, the speech still unfinished, he retired to a sleepless bed. At 4 A.M. he rose and finished the address.

By daybreak, visitors, invitations, and deputations overwhelmed Adams. Finally at ten, surrounded by a dense crowd, the procession of the members of the Astronomical Society was formed. However, as Adams entered his open carriage the rain came down in torrents so that the sides of the carriage had to be raised, obscuring him from the crowds, which continued to stand in the downpour, hoping to catch a glimpse of him. The streets became a sea of mud and the horses slid and strained up the slippery hill until they reached the summit. At the top, in the midst of a circular plain, the cornerstone had been placed and a stage had been erected from which the address would have been given, but all that could be seen was "an auditory of umbrellas, instead of faces." The discourse had to be postponed until the next morning but the cornerstone was laid and Adams did read the speech he had prepared, the manuscript so defaced by the rain that it was almost illegible.

The next morning John Quincy gave his speech, a two-hour-long

address that the audience listened to without impatience or inattention. "Man is a curious and inquisitive being," he said, "and the
exercise of his reason, the immortal part of his nature consists of
inquiries into the relations between the effects which fall within the
sphere of his observation and their causes which are unseen. The
earth beneath his feet, and the vault of heaven over his head, are the
first objects in physical nature which force themselves upon his observation and invite him to contemplation." Adams then gave a
brief history of astronomy—"from the solar centralism of *Coper-
nicus,* and the planetary laws of *Kepler,* and the gravitation of *Newton,* to the celestial mechanism of *La Place,* and its improved revisal
of our own *Bowditch.*" Using his much-abused phrase "lighthouses
of the skies," the ex-President recounted the story of European astronomical societies, particularly those of England.

In the United States, he continued, the arts and sciences which
had been pursued with most intense interest were those best adapted to "our own conditions. We have explored the seas and fath-
omed the depths of the ocean and we have fertilized the face of the
land. We—you—*you* have converted the wilderness into a garden.
. . ." But the toils "upon this terraqueous globe" made us "overlook its
indissoluble connection, even physical, with the firmament above."
Then in a graceful flourish to his hosts, he concluded, "You fellow
citizens of Cincinnati—you, members of the Astronomical Society, of
this spontaneous city of the West, will wipe that reproach upon us
away. That edifice of which, under your charge, the cornerstone is
now to be laid will rise a lasting monument of your ardent and
active zeal to connect the honor of your country with the constant
and untiring exploration of the firmament of heaven. . . ." Finally,
blending science and religion, Adams said, "and may the blessing of
Him, who from his lofty throne, rules the Universe in wisdom and
goodness, crown your labors with success."[31]

Brooks Adams commented that with all its shortcomings, due to
his grandfather's limited strength and lack of time to revise it, the
address was "the most compact, suggestive and imaginative essay
upon astronomy in the language."[32] No American statesman had
done as much as John Quincy Adams for the promotion of science.
The appreciative members of the Cincinnati Astronomical Society
rewarded the old man's pluck on the spot by passing a resolution to
name the observatory hill "Mount Adams."

The hospitable western city was reluctant to let its aged lion return home. He was fêted, subjected to a complimentary speech by Judge Este of Hamilton County, which he answered "as desparation dictated," and lauded by a deputation of Black citizens. With some reluctance, he had to refuse invitations to go further west and south for he had neither the stamina nor the time before the opening of the new congressional session. He did go one day to Covington, Kentucky, with former Governor Morehead. The crowds were as enthusiastic as in Cincinnati and a pretty young woman took his hand and whispered, "The first kiss in Kentucky!" He did not re-fuse.

When Adams finally was allowed to leave Cincinnati on the *Benjamin Franklin* for Pittsburgh, he felt that his duty had been performed. At Marietta, he disembarked to visit the Indian mounds but still arrived in Pittsburgh a day earlier than expected. The festivities in his honor began on November 17 with a large procession headed by Adams, who was exhibited in a barouche with four horses. Once again, a heavy drenching rain cut short the speech-making but the crowd came in squads to John Quincy's bed-chamber to shake his hand.

After four days, Adams left Pittsburgh, flattered but claiming that it was "inexpressibly irksome" to be "held up as a show" and forced to face thousands. "The stamina of my constitution are sinking under the hardships and exposures of travelling at this season," Adams recorded. Overcome with weariness, he called his triumph "empty honors . . . carrying with it no solid permanent opinion."[33] Though he voiced these reservations, the intrepid ex-President continued his amazing journey without omitting any of his obligations. He stopped at Jefferson College in Canonsburg and then travelled twenty-five miles by stage in a snowstorm to Brownsville. He took the railroad from Cumberland to Washington City and then rode to Harper's Ferry for dinner. Finally the B & O took him to Baltimore and then to Washington, where he was grateful to go home. "I have little life left in me," he confided to his *Diary*. All the adulation and demands of his journey were "so adverse to my nature that it has, in great measure, solved the continuity of my existence, and I am like one coming out of a fainting fit."[34] Brooks Adams believed that John Quincy had committed suicide for the sake of science, which was, probably, a romantic exaggeration. Part of what Adams suffered from was a complete letdown after the excessive admiration that he rejected so piously. He realized also that the people of the

United States did not appreciate the importance of science as a principle of political action. The slave oligarchy, he accused, systematically suppressed all public patronage for any "progress of the mind," astronomy particularly.

Louisa was frightened when she saw her returned Ulysses. His chronic cough was worse than she had ever heard it and his "debility and exhaustion beyond description." The family physician agreed that his symptoms were dangerous. Adams, as usual, paid little attention to wifely anxieties. "It would be a glorious moment for me to die, so let it come," he told a horrified Louisa. To Charles, he wrote that he came home "half dead—but am getting better." Somewhere in between was an accurate appraisal of the old gentleman's condition. Whatever, he was far from finished with the world. There was still unfinished business.

CHAPTER 25

The Final Battle

"Mr. Adams is a man of great powers, but chiefly he is a sincere man, and not a man of the moment and of a single measure."

RALPH WALDO EMERSON

"IN THE HOUSE, the life and death struggle for the right of petition was resumed," Adams recorded on December 20, 1843. Though the democratic majority was about two-thirds, Adams's motion to expunge the anti-petition rule had a vote of 91–94. Only three voters were responsible for retaining the gag rule. The slavers were "Up in a panic."[1]

On New Year's Day, the Adamses received an uninterrupted stream of visitors. Lest he forget the coming struggle in the House, among the callers were some of John Quincy's bitterest enemies, both from the North and the South. Among them was Charles Jared Ingersoll, "the cunningest and most treacherous cat of them all." At about three in the afternoon, Adams disengaged himself from the throng and walked to Mrs. Madison's house to pay his customary courtesy call. That night he reflected, "Tomorrow recommences the struggle which, for me, can terminate only with my life."[2]

Preparation of his report on the Massachusetts resolves, which Charles Francis had written and then guided through the state legislature, occupied most of Adams's time. The resolves offered an amendment to the Constitution abolishing the privilege of the slave states to count every five slaves as three free men for the purpose of representation in the House of Representatives. The new proposal was almost a duplicate of the one Adams had supported when he was a Senator.

The House committee to consider the Massachusetts resolutions only appeared to consist of six members from the free states and three from the slave states. Joseph R. Ingersoll of Pennsylvania, for example, was "the impersonation of that state's desertion from the standard of liberty and Edmund Burke," and the New Hampshire democrat in the panel was another northern deserter. "With such a committee you can imagine how I get along," Adams told his son.

The committee on rules for which Adams was to make another report was no better. "The New York Kinderhook democracy repudiated the gag only for outward show," he claimed. "They wanted a compromise and the south will bully them into a gag." And, as he predicted, both of his efforts were unsuccessful. The gag rule was "repurchased for the benefit of the Northern man with southern principles," and the Massachusetts resolves were "turned over to Virginia slave breeders."[3]

"Dies Irae," John Quincy wrote about the *Princeton* tragedy. He and the Adams ladies had been invited by Captain Robert Stockton to a party on board the warship *Princeton*, which was to make a cruise down the Potomac, during which the "Peacemaker," a new supergun would be demonstrated. Adams could not go because he did not want to miss attendance at the House, and Louisa was expecting houseguests. Isaac Hull Adams, John Quincy's nephew, represented the family.

While the ex-President was at dinner with some friends, including Richard Pakenham, the new British Minister, John Barney stormed into the room, rushed over to General Scott, and told him, with loud groans, that the President wanted to see him. The "Peacemaker" had exploded when charging its second round, killing Abel P. Upshur, who had succeeded Daniel Webster as Secretary of State, Thomas Walker Gilmer, the Secretary of the Navy, and five others.

Adams believed that John C. Calhoun's appointment as Secretary of State meant that Texas annexation would be consummated. It was already evident that British Minister Pakenham would make no resistance. Adams was so annoyed with Calhoun that when he met him at a meeting of the National Institute he could do no more than shake hands with him in silent disapproval.

The annexation of Texas had become the controversial issue upon which the election of 1844 would be based. Both Henry Clay and Martin Van Buren had come out against it, whereas it was "John Tyler's last card for a popular whirlwind to carry him through," as Adams commented.

At the first whig convention, held in Baltimore, Henry Clay received the nomination for the Presidency, Theodore Frelinghuysen for the Vice Presidency. The news, which was received in Washington by telegraph, pleased Adams, who considered the Kentuckian's prospects better this time than ever before. He also sincerely believed that his former Secretary of State's success would be in the best interest of the country.

The democratic national convention unanimously elected James K. Polk of Tennessee for their presidential candidate and, after Silas Wright of New York declined the nomination, George M. Dallas of Pennsylvania for his running mate. Adams's fears were justified. The convention passed a resolution for the immediate occupation of Texas and Oregon.

When the treaty for annexing Texas to the United States which was submitted to the Senate in late April failed to get the required vote, Adams deemed it a deliverance from a conspiracy comparable to Cataline's. "May it prove not a mere temporary deliverance like that, only preliminary to the fatal successful conspiracy of Julius Caesar." The annexation of Texas, he predicted darkly, would be the first step to the conquest of Mexico, of the West Indies, "of a maritime, colonizing, slave-tainted monarchy and of extinguished freedom." He prayed that the country be delivered from such a fate, thankful that the first session of "the most perverse and worthless Congress that ever disgraced this Confederacy has closed."[4]

One of the pleasantest happenings for Adams that spring was the presentation of a gift so tempting that the old Puritan could not find it in his heart to follow his usual custom of refusing all such offerings. A group of admirers sent him a milk-white ivory cane a yard long, made of one elephant's tooth, tipped with silver. On its top, the American eagle was inlaid with gold and a ring under its pommel was inscribed with the name John Quincy Adams and the words "Justum et Tenacem propositi virum."* The accompanying letter said that when the gag rule was finally abolished, the date was

---

* From Horace: "The just man and firm of purpose."

to be inserted under the ring's inscription. Adams considered the cane as a trust to be returned when his mission was completed.

A different kind of gift flattered him just as much. When Captain Daniel Parker wrote, saying that he had named his ship, *John Quincy Adams*, the ex-President responded with appreciation for a "disinterested regard." The Adams family would be pleased to accept the Captain's invitation to see the ship, he replied.[5]

The intensity of the capital's summer heat became more unbearable each year for the aging Adams. By the end of June, despite his seventy-six years, Adams could not keep himself from his river bath any longer. At five in the morning he went in his barouche to his old, favorite spot, managed with some difficulty to undress, got into the water, swam for about five minutes, and then came out refreshed. The next day he repeated the exercise, swimming for ten minutes and then emerging, convinced that swimming prolonged his life.

The secret wedding of Julia Gardiner and President John Tyler in New York City electrified the nation. The ceremony was a quiet one for it was only four months since the bride's father had lost his life in the *Princeton* explosion. Adams wanted only to avoid the inevitable celebrations when the newlyweds returned to Washington. With his pen dipped in acid, he recorded that Captain Tyler and his bride were the laughing stock of the city. Unable to forgive the President for his assumption of the war power "as a prerogative" and the veto power as "a caprice," he vented his hostility by terming the wedding arrangement a "revolting indecency," and accusing Tyler of "performing with a young girl from New York the old fable of January and May."[6]

While travelling to New York, on July 11, his seventy-seventh birthday, John Quincy had an accident that fortunately turned out to be trivial. He and Louisa alighted from the railroad train at about ten at night onto an unrailed floor that was raised four feet above the ground. Unaware in the dark, Adams stepped off the platform and pitched forward, drawing his wife, whose arm was linked with his, over him. While falling, John Quincy was convinced that he had been killed and his wife's shriek convinced him that she was killed also. Fortunately, all that happened was that Louisa fainted, but revived immediately, and Adams had a bruise as big as a dinner plate on his thigh. Since no bones were broken, the elderly pair took the ferryboat to New York as soon as they recovered their wits and then proceeded immediately to Quincy.

Despite Adams's valiant fight to abolish the gag rule, he displeased the abolitionists because he was opposed to the immediate abolition of slavery in the District of Columbia and the territories. Consequently, the liberty party, which held a convention at Dedham in October, nominated Appleton Howe of Weymouth to run for Adams's congressional seat. Howe, who had been a state senator from Norfolk County for several years, received thirty-six of the fifty-five votes, Adams received fourteen. "I hope I may not take it too much to heart, but that it will prepare me for retirement for the rest of my days," John Quincy said unconvincingly. Since he expected opposition from the democratic party as well, he was preparing for a real possibility.

James Polk's election, which was announced by the firing of guns on the receipt of the election returns from the western counties of New York, was accepted by Adams as the signal for his retirement from public life. Though the idea of forced retirement was bitter medicine for the proud ex-President to accept, he spent the few days before the Massachusetts election contemplating the defeat he now considered inevitable. On November 11, he went to the Quincy Town House, tore off his own name from the whig ticket and deposited the remainder in the ballot box. That evening, Price Greenleaf brought the returns from Braintree, Randolph, and Hingham. They were more favorable than the candidate expected but not sufficient to resolve his doubts. But the next day, Charles drove out to Quincy with the Boston *Atlas*, which gave the election figures. The whig ticket had been sweepingly successful. In the eighth district the returns were:

Adams	8,401
Wright	5,328
Howe	850

It was a clear victory that surpassed the majority in 1842 by about 500 votes.

On his way back to Washington, Adams stopped in New York to attend a dinner at the New-York Historical Society in honor of its president, eighty-three-year-old Albert Gallatin. It was a nostalgic meeting for the two old men. In his remarks at the dinner, Adams said of Gallatin that "among all the public men with whom I have been associated in the course of my political life, whether agreeing or differing in opinion with him, I have always found him to be an honest and honorable man."[7] It was a fair estimate, candidly given. Adams hated the speech that Luther Bradish, former Lieutenant Governor of New York, made about him. He "toasted me—or roasted me—with a speech so fulsome that it overset all my philosophy, and I stammered a reply the only palliation of which was its brevity."[8]

"We are all in the dolefuls [over the presidential election] but wailing won't help," Adams wrote to Charles from Washington. He realized that New York had been the pivotal state and that Clay lost because the liberty party candidate got enough votes in the burned-over district to split the whig vote and thus secure the state for Polk. It was painful to him to witness his defeat, he told Clay, for he had hoped that under the Kentuckian's guidance the country would have recovered from its downward trend.[9]

When Congress opened, John Quincy was prepared to respond to the customary resolution to reinstate the standing rules, including the gag. And on December 3, he read his proposal—"Resolved: That the twenty-fifth rule [gag rule] for conducting business in the House . . . is hereby rescinded." Ignoring a motion offered by Jacob Thompson of Mississippi that his proposal be tabled, Adams called for the yeas and nays on his motion. The clerk was ready to begin the call when he was interrupted by the arrival of John Tyler, Jr. with the President's Annual Message. Immediately, Thompson tried to delay the vote by demanding that the message be read at once, but Adams insisted that the vote be taken on his resolution. First the clerk polled the members on the motion to lay the Adams resolution on the table. It failed, 81 to 104. With rising hopes, Adams listened to the roll call on his resolution. It was carried—168 votes to 80. "Blessed, forever, blessed be the name of God," John Quincy cried.[10]

The abolitionist Congressmen gathered around their champion. He had won his eight-year fight to stop the slavocracy from depriving the American people of their constitutional right to petition their government on the subject of slavery and the slave trade. Adams's practical way, though less dramatic than the activist abolitionists wanted, had secured them the setting in which they could continue their work. Politics had done the rest. The resolution carried because the northern locofocos had united with the northern whigs against the southern bloc. They were taking their revenge on their peers, who had forced them to give up their favorite, Martin Van Buren, and accept Polk.[11]

The South was frustrated and infuriated by the repeal of the gag rule. South Carolina's legislature denied the right to Congress to legislate on the slave question. It was a "flagrant outrage" that would result in the dissolution of the Union, they declared.

Adams, triumphant, took his cane to be engraved with the date of the rescinding of the gag rule—December 3, 1844. He then turned it over to the patent office, where he asked that it remain.

Even in the midst of their rejoicing, the cloud of Texas annexation hung over the anti-slavery faction. Van Burenites combined to make the gag rule repeal possible, but the slavers could look for support in Congress from expansionists who followed the American continental dream. The Tyler Administration might still have the last word.

In order to simplify the vote on annexing Texas a joint resolution was introduced that only required a majority vote. Adams sat "a silent witness" to the proceedings for more than a month but finally could stand it no longer. In the hour allotted to him he "barely reached the threshhold of his speech." And, on the next day, January 5, 1845, "the hour of doom" occurred. The joint resolution was passed in the House, 120–98. Hardly more than a week before the new President's Inauguration, the joint resolution was accepted by both houses and quickly signed into law by Tyler. Just as quickly, he sent the annexation proposal to Texas to forestall the imminent treaty of peace and mediation with England and France which would have stopped the annexation. The republic of Texas, with but one dissenting vote, agreed to annexation by the United States.

The next step was inevitable. "It is a signal triumph of the slave representation in the Constitution of the United States," Adams wrote when the Senate agreed to the admission of Texas to the Union by a vote of 27–25. "The heaviest calamity that ever befell myself and my country was this day consummated," the distracted ex-President exclaimed the next day. He had taken no part other than silent voting. Afterward, he concluded, "I regard it as the appoplexy of the constitution."[12]

With "an unusual degree of pomposity," Polk was inaugurated, without the attendance of ex-President Adams, who was invited but did not go. The new President's half-hour Inaugural Address was delivered to "a large assemblage of umbrellas," for it rained hard throughout the ceremony. Polk went to both of the balls that were given that night in his honor. One cost ten dollars per ticket, the other five. Polk dined "with the true blue five dollar democracy," Adams commented maliciously.[13] The Adamses were invited to both dinners but attended neither.

That summer in Quincy, a realization of encroaching age crowded in on Adams. On the anniversary of his marriage, he said, "Forty eight years have since passed away. A small remnant only can be before us. . . . We have enjoyed much. We have suffered not a little."[14] For the past thirteen years, John Quincy recalled, he had been the only member of his past and present generation alive. And, in August, after attending the Harvard Commencement he noted that 1845 marked the sixtieth year of his membership in Phi Beta Kappa.

The state of his health made it necessary for Adams to give up his summer sea and river bathing. The shower bath also had to be abandoned because the jar was too great. Even participation in social and civic occasions was seriously curtailed. What energy was left in the small gray form had to be garnered for the congressional battles that never ceased.

However, his interest in literature and history never dimmed. Adams differed with Horace Walpole's statement that "History is and must be false." He acknowledged that it could only be imperfectly known to the actors and contemporaries, but he agreed with Voltaire who said that "posterity [was always] eager for details." The past of the United States would require from the historians the keenest perception and profoundest meditation to assign to its leaders "their proper station and weight, as elements in the complicated and wondrous tale," he advised a friend.[15]

Delivered safely at his house in F Street by Christopher Hughes on December 1, Adams prepared for participation in the first session of the Twenty-ninth Congress. The Texas crisis was over. As he advised a New Hampshire correspondent, resistance to "annexation of the Lone Star to the great Constellation" must now be abandoned."[16] The concentration of interest had shifted to Oregon.

John Quincy directed all his energies to reading the discussions on the subject by the past Secretaries of State Daniel Webster, Abel Upshur, John Calhoun, and James Buchanan, and of the British

Ministers Henry Fox and Richard Pakenham. Adams's conclusion after exhaustive study was that Polk's Inaugural speech notwithstanding, the United States had an unquestionable title to 54° 40′. President John Quincy Adams had renewed the treaty with Great Britain which, for an indefinite period of time, provided joint occupation of the Oregon Territory between 42° and 54° 40′. His arrangement also had provided that either party to the agreement could cancel it on a year's notice. This arrangement had sufficed until 1843, when American settlers, in large numbers, started to migrate to the jointly shared area. These American pioneers and their friends were now pressing for American acquisition of Oregon. "The reoccupation of Oregon!" was their battle cry. Polk was in a dilemma. In his campaign strategy he had undertaken to capture the West under the banner of Oregon and the South under the banner of Texas. But the South did not want Oregon. Having just obtained a potentially favorable balance of free and slave states with Texas, they were not pleased at the idea of unbalancing again by the acquisition of northern, non-slave soil.

Inevitably, Polk's first annual message to Congress referred to his Texas-Oregon commitment. It was also a restatement of the Monroe Doctrine. "The United States, sincerely desirous of preserving relations of good understanding with all nations, cannot in silence permit any European interference on the North American continent, and should any such interference be attempted will be ready to resist it at any and all hazards." John Quincy Adams's non-colonization policy had come to roost in Oregon. Polk asked that Congress support him in his determination to give Great Britain the agreed-upon one year's notice to terminate the joint occupation treaty.

Adams, who believed sincerely that the American title to 54° 40′ was legitimate, predicted that the final border settlement would be a continuation of the 49th parallel to the sea. "And Mr. Polk will finish by accepting it."[17] Yet the ex-President took no part in the debate. He had a nervous tremor that made writing impossible without an instrument to steady his hand, which had on its ivory label the motto, "Toil and Trust." The southerners, however, wanted Adams's support. They felt that if he had opposed war with Mexico over Texas logically he must oppose Oregon's annexation because of the possibility of war with England. Robert B. Rhett of South Carolina, the leader of the battle against the President's resolution, addressed the old diplomat directly. "The gentleman from

Massachusetts across the way had shown himself a hero by voting against the last war with England but now was rabid for war with her."

Adams, who felt that the statement was "a dead set" against him, rose and asked if Rhett meant him. When the South Carolinian acknowledged that he did, Adams answered that he had been the Minister to Russia when the War of 1812 was declared and had been in St. Petersburg for three years before. He was, however, willing to impute the charge as one based on ignorance and not viciousness.[18]

As the debate continued, Adams noted that the Polk Administration was "flinching upon the Oregon Controversy." The Administration papers were preparing the public for acceptance of a British offer of the 49th parallel to the Pacific Ocean describing it as the offer made by Adams. The abolitionists, who needed as large a bulk of Oregon as possible to balance Texas, urged Adams to speak in the debate. But his wretched health and grief over the death of his grandson, Arthur, discouraged him. However, when Thomas B. King of Georgia addressed him personally, on February 19, he could not ignore him.

"Was the title of the United States to the whole of Oregon to latitude 54° 40' clear and indisputable?" King asked.

Adams rose to answer. The question, he explained, could have two constructions, one with reference to right and wrong, another with reference to fact. As to right, the title of the United States was clear and indisputable.

"Then why did not the gentleman from Massachusetts give that definition when he was Secretary of State?" King persisted.

Adams pointed to the Bible and asked the clerk to read the twenty-sixth, twenty-seventh, and twenty-eighth verses of the first chapter of Genesis. They were "what I conceive to be the foundation of our title," he explained.

As instructed, the clerk opened the book that always lay upon the table in front of the Speaker and read:

26 And God said, Let us make man in our image, after our likeness: and let them have dominion over the fish of the sea and the fowl of the air, and over the cattle and over all the earth, and over every creeping thing that creepeth upon the earth.

27 So God created man in his own image, in the image of God created he him; male and female created he them.

28 And God blessed them, and God said unto them, Be fruitful And

multiply, and replenish the earth, and subdue it: and have dominion over the fish of the sea, and over the fowl of the air, and over every living thing that moveth upon the earth.

There, said the man who read the Bible daily all his life, was "the foundation of all territorial rights. . . . There, sir, in my judgment is the foundation not only of our title to Oregon, but the foundation of all human title to all possessions."

Adams was not finished with the Bible lesson that he had designed for his colleagues. The clerk must read the eighth verse of Book II of the Psalms.

Ask of me, and I shall give thee the heathen for thine inheritance, and the uttermost parts of the earth for thy possession.

Now, Adams cried excitedly to the clerk, turn back a verse or two and you will see to whom it was said that He would give them.

Psalm 2,6 Yet I have set my King upon my holy hill of Zion.
7 I will declare the decree: the Lord hath said unto me, Thou art my Son; this day have I begotten thee.

Then Adams displayed the vast scope of his knowledge of history. By that same biblical right, he maintained, Great Britain held Ireland. By that same power, Pope Adrian gave Ireland to Henry I of England.

Undismayed by erudition, King charged Adams with inconsistency for having agreed to a joint occupation in 1818 and 1827 and now being ready to put an end to that compact. It was in the interest of the United States, then, to leave the territory free and open, Adams replied. Now—"I want the country for our western pioneers . . . to go out and make a great nation . . . instead of it being hunting grounds for the buffaloes, braves, and savages of the desert."[19]

That afternoon the vote was taken in the House. By a majority of 163–54 the President was asked to give Great Britain the year's notice that had been provided for in the 1827 treaty. On April 27, President Polk gave the former mother country notice that the joint occupancy agreement was terminated.

Adams never believed that there was real danger of war with England over Oregon because, in his opinion, Polk would never have risked it for 54–40, and Britain was always ready to concede the 49th parallel. Though he proved correct, Robert Dale Owen, the social reformer Congressman from Indiana, stopped by John Quin-

cy's desk at the House to tell him that he planned to go to England
to preserve an amicable adjustment between the two countries.
Adams wished him success but pointed out that England had no
right in Oregon of permanent possession. He abhorred war, the ex-
President added, but "there are, and always have been . . . times and
occasions of dire necessity for war; and philosophically speaking, I
believed that war was not a corrupter, but rather a pacifier of the
moral character of man."[20]

Historians dispute whether the Oregon settlement was a true
compromise, a fair exchange, or a defeat for Great Britain. Britain
gave up the area in the Northwest encompassing the Columbia
River in 1846, but perhaps this made up for the United States's
abandonment of a portion of Maine that was rightfully hers in the
Webster-Ashburton negotiations of 1842.[21]

Even before peace with Great Britain was absolutely sure, the
continentalist aspirations of Polk and his supporters catapulted the
United States into another war. On May 11, the President sent a
message to both Houses of Congress declaring that "Mexico . . . has
shed American blood on American soil. . . . War exists."[22] Adams
called the document a "recommendation of circumlocution" but it
passed the House 174–14. The ex-President was against it, remarking that only one-half of the delegation from Massachusetts voted
for "this most unrighteous war."

Adams opposed both the war and Polk's presumption in ignoring
the constitutional right of Congress to declare war. In this interpretation, he was joined by Benton, Calhoun, and other members of
both Houses. But Adams said nothing aloud in the House chamber.
He was too tired and too discouraged. His son's career seemed more
important at the moment. "Proceed—Persevere—never despair—
don't give up the Ship," he wrote to Charles. "The Mexican War
and the free trade tariff will in time give you topics to handle not
yet disclosed."[23]

Old Man Eloquent was now in his eightieth year, weighed down
by constant fatigue and the endless session of Congress. One hot
summer morning at dawn, he rose and, drawn by an irresistible
urge, walked over to the lower Tiber bridge to his old bathing spot.
He bathed and swam for about five or ten minutes and then came
out. Before he entered the water, he overheard three young men,
none of whom he knew, say, "There is John Quincy Adams." For
the next day or two it was hot enough to bathe but when the temperature dropped to 74°, the daily swim was abandoned.

In August, the first session of the Twenty-ninth Congress finally adjourned, permitting Adams to leave for his "earthly home." It had become more of a refuge than ever now that his faculties were declining daily. But later in the summer, he felt strong enough to preside over a meeting at Faneuil Hall that concerned a slave who had escaped from New Orleans in a merchant vessel from Massachusetts commanded by a Captain Hannum. When Hannum discovered the fugitive, without a warrant, he shipped him aboard another vessel back to his master in New Orleans. An attempt to follow the ship with a writ of habeas corpus for the captive failed. The meeting was held to clarify the facts in the case and to prevent a repetition.

The hall was filled to every nook and cranny and the galleries were crowded with ladies. John Quincy Adams was assigned to the chair by acclamation and among the speakers that evening was Charles Francis Adams. At the close of the session, the hall rose to give their aged champion of freedom a vote of thanks.

Another expedition that summer was made to Long Pond in Wayland to break ground for an acqueduct to Boston. Adams enjoyed it but paid the price with excessive fatigue, a sore throat, and an attack of palsy so severe that he could hardly write.

This year the whig convention unanimously nominated Adams for re-election to the Thirtieth Congress. He was now associated with the radical branch of the whig party called the "conscience whigs." That the slave power sneered "at *conscience*, as in days of yore our pilgrim forefathers were called *puritans* in derision" was not something of which to be ashamed, he told John Palfrey. On the contrary, it should be inscribed on our banners and preserved, if need be, "with martyrdom in the cause of Liberty."[24]

When Adams was re-elected he considered it an endorsement by his constituents of his position on the Mexican War. The first report of the returns on his contest were incorrect. An error from Roxbury, when corrected, increased his majority from 237 votes, as first recorded, to 651.

Louisa, Mary, and Mary Louisa preceded John Quincy to Washington, accompanied as far as Philadelphia by Charles Francis. The ex-President moved into his son's house at 47 Mount Vernon Street, Boston, joining his daughter-in-law and her five children. This annual visit before his return to the capital had become a pleasant conclusion to his summer vacation.

On Friday, November 20, Adams rose as usual between four and five and went through his morning routine of washing and then massaging his palsied limbs with a horsehair strap and mitten. After he breakfasted with the family, Dr. George Parkman called for him to walk over to the new medical college. While they were strolling slowly, Adams suddenly felt that he was unable to walk, his knees buckled, and he started to sink to the ground. Dr. Parkman saved him from falling and then assisted him to stagger back to his son's house. The family physician, Dr. Jacob Bigelow, in consultation with Dr. Jackson, took care of the ailing ex-President, diagnosing the attack as a slight paralytic stroke. Adams reported that he had little or no pain but his speech and right side were affected. "From that hour I date my decease, and consider myself for every useful purpose to myself or to my fellow creatures, dead; and hence I call this and what I may write hereafter a posthumous memoir," Adams wrote morbidly in his *Diary*.[25]

The newspapers throughout the country printed the news of Adams's illness. Charles, who was on his way back from Philadelphia, read about it while on the Long Island Railroad. Louisa saw an account in the Washington papers and then received more details in letters from Abby. She left the capital immediately, accompanied as far as Baltimore by her nephew. From there she travelled alone by steamboat and railroad, reaching Boston on the twenty-fourth.

Adams recovered slowly and uneventfully. On New Year's Day he took his first ride in the carriage for about an hour. For the next few weeks he continued the daily ride until the twenty-second, when he walked on the street in Boston. The next two Sundays he went to the First Congregational church by carriage and the following week walked there for both the morning and the afternoon services and took communion.

The following month, Adams, Mrs. Adams, Charles, and the nurse left for Washington. They made the trip in easy stages: railway to Springfield where they stayed overnight, the next day by rail to New Haven through Hartford. At New Haven, which they reached at five in the afternoon, they boarded a steamer for New York, arriving at nine in the evening. The next day it rained so the Adams party remained indoors at the City Hotel. On the eleventh, they set out for Philadelphia by the Camden Railroad and took lodgings at the Union Hotel in Chestnut Street, avoiding any company. On the twelfth, Louisa's seventy-second birthday, they travelled by railroad to Baltimore, dined at the United States Hotel, and then continued the trip to Washington. The carriage awaited them at the station and, about eight o'clock, deposited them at their house on F Street.

The very next day, looking frail but determined, Adams entered the House of Representatives for the first time since his illness. All the members rose to greet him and business was suspended while he was conducted to his usual seat, hastily surrendered by the representative who had been assigned it at the beginning of the session. Adams took his seat and, in a voice quavering with weakness and emotion, said, "Had I a more powerful voice, I might respond to the congratulations of my friends, and the members of this house for the honor which has been done me. But, enfeebled as I am by disease, I beg you will excuse me."[26]

Certain that he would die if he gave up public life, as he told Louisa, Adams attended the House regularly. He was no longer burdened with any committee duties except for his favorite, the Library of Congress. When the roll call was taken for votes, however, the old gentleman always responded, sometimes with his independent approach as evident in the past. He was one of four members to support Massachusetts Congressman Charles Hudson's antiwar resolution, which proposed that American forces be withdrawn to the east bank of the Rio Grande and that peace terms be negotiated with Mexico without demanding any territorial cessions.

During the three remaining weeks of the session, Adams participated in debate only once. A proposal of a $50,000 appropriation to compensate the owners and other claimants of the *Amistad* for the loss of the ship and the slaves was tacked on to an appropriations bill for the payment of civil and diplomatic officials and had the endorsement of the Secretary of State James Buchanan and President Polk. In a voice that was hardly stronger than when he resumed his seat, Adams defended the separation of powers guaranteed in the Constitution and the freedom of the *Amistad* captives. Since the Spanish claims were illegal, to pay them would be a slur on the Supreme Court's decision and a robbery of the people of the United States. The vote, which was taken on March 2, split along sectional lines. The constitutional argument could not supersede the basic difference between the pro-slave and anti-slave members. The measure was defeated by a combination of northern and western votes but the Spanish government did not allow the matter to rest. It was regularly revived throughout the next decade until after the Civil War. Once slavery was abolished in the United States, Spain had to accept the fact that the *Amistad* claims died with the peculiar institution.

John Quincy seemed to be quietly preparing for the end of his life. In May, he turned over to Charles all the trusts that were still committed to his care. "It has been my earnest endeavour to discharge them all faithfully," he told his son, "but ⸳ ⸳ the 20th of November, last, I have been disabled both in body and mind, to fulfill the obligation . . . upon you therefore rests many of my responsibilities for the remnant of my days and which will continue after my decease."[27]

The bracing New England breezes of Quincy convinced Adams that he could return to Congress in December, although he still doubted that he would be able to resume an active role in debate. His hopes focused on the abolition of slavery, but feared "the consummation is not to bless my eyes nor to delight my years in my present state of existence."[28] Too feeble to accept the many invitations that came, Adams still kept up a limited correspondence. He told Brantz Mayer, who sought his advice on writing a history of the Mexican War, that an historian "must have neither Religion or Country." His own impression of the war, he said, was that "there was no aspect of right or wrong of which we can claim the benefit in the controversy."[29]

Mr. and Mrs. John Quincy Adams celebrated their fiftieth wedding anniversary on July 27 at a quiet family celebration in which the ex-President took a lively interest. Henry Adams, in his famous autobiography, sketched a charming vignette of his grandmother at this time. Louisa seemed "singularly peaceful, a vision of silver gray, presiding over her old President and her Queen Anne mahogany; an exotic, like her Sèvres china; an object of deference to everyone, and of great affection to Charles; but hardly more Bostonian than she had been fifty years before, on her wedding day, in the shadow of the Tower of London."[30]

Never too old or too feeble to make an effort in the cause of science, particularly one of his "lighthouses of the skies," Adams went with Edward Everett, now president of Harvard, to view their observatory. He wanted to present a memorandum "so it will redound to the promotion of Science."[31]

On the way back to Washington, while John Quincy and Louisa were in New York, a committee of the Anti-Slavery Society called on them. They wished to express their thanks to Adams for his work in

Congress and elsewhere in behalf of the cause. However, the committee arrived after the Adamses left, so Lewis Tappan sent a copy of the resolution to Washington. When Congress met again, the old veteran unknowingly got involved in a whig in-fight that placed him in conflict with his son. The whigs, who had a small majority in the House, expected to get the speakership, but the "conscience whigs" wanted an assurance from Robert Winthrop, the caucus candidate, on his position on the Mexican War, the extension of slavery, and his choice for committee heads. Winthrop refused to be bound by any pledge and so Palfrey, Giddings, and Tuck did not vote. Winthrop was elected, finally, on the third ballot by a majority of one.

Among Winthrop's supporters was John Quincy Adams who had, at one point, asked Palfrey to give up his opposition to him. When Charles, who stood with the "conscience whigs," realized what his father had done, he wrote to Louisa, *"Don't let my father play* into their hands. I won't ask him to help us—All I want is to have him stand aside and see fair play. . . ."[32]

Adams was appalled when he saw what political use was made of his vote for Winthrop. It had not been meant, as the Boston *Atlas* and *Daily Whi* implied, that he regarded his son's position as visionary and erroneous. On the contrary, he assured Charles, he admired his "honest and sincere views of the course of your country." The vote for Winthrop had been a sentimental one because Winthrop's father had stuck with J.Q.A. when his other friends had deserted him.

Anxious to make amends, Adams wrote effusively that "from the time when the Creator established the relation of father and son, between men on earth no more truehearted, faithful and affectionate son than you have been to me ever existed." He suggested that this letter be published and that "he may perhaps hereafter assign his reasons for voting for Winthrop."[33]

Louisa responded to Charles with some further insight into John Quincy's condition at this time. His father's health, she wrote, "renders him at times the creature of impulse." He intended no wrong "to you or to *his friends* but the allurement of flattery; and that desire which has ever possessed him, of striking out a new path for *himself,* led him to this. . . ." He believed that he was rendering his son and friends "a great conciliatory service."[34]

In order to spare the old gentleman, the abolitionist members had taken over the presentation of petitions. But on December 20, Adams insisted on presenting two that prayed for peace with Mexico. He had the satisfaction of hearing them turned over to the committee on foreign affairs instead of laid on the table as they would have been before the gag rule was rescinded.

On the New Year, Adams wrote another fulsome letter to Charles. His thoughts, he said, turned to him and to his family "for all the blessings which you have been and still are to me." Perhaps still brooding over the fiasco of the Winthrop vote, he advised Charles to have "a stout heart and a clear conscience, and never despair."[35]

At the beginning of the year 1848, many friends and observers noted that Adams seemed to have renewed vigor. He attended a reception given by the Mayor of Washington on February 17 and on the next day conducted a meeting of the Library of Congress committee and, in the House, supported a bill to aid the descendants of John Paul Jones. That Saturday evening, the Adamses entertained at an open house for many guests. Though the aged statesman appeared in good spirits, one friend reported that he told him in confidence that he did not expect to survive the entire congressional session and he kept reminding Louisa where he had put his will. As always, Adams attended church twice on Sunday and also wrote some verses for Caroline Edwards. And he talked about attending the Washington's Birthday ball with Louisa, who was a patroness.

On January 21, John Quincy rode to the Capitol seemingly in as good health as usual. A discussion developed on the floor about a resolution to thank certain military officers for their services in the Mexican War. When the Speaker called the question, Adams's loud, strong "No" could be heard above the clamorous ayes.

While the clerk read the words of praise for the warriors who had conquered in the Halls of Montezuma, an abolitionist reporter who had his eyes on the rebellious old gentleman saw him flush at the temples, move his lips in an attempt to speak, clutch at the corner of his desk with his right hand, and then slump over to the left.

"Mr. Adams is dying!" shouted Washington Hunt of New York, who sat near him. Davis Fisher of Ohio, whose seat was next to John Quincy's, responded quickly enough to catch him in his arms before he could fall to the ground.

The agitated House members crowded around their stricken patriarch. A few of them carried him to the Speaker's table, while others brought a sofa, laid him on it, and bore him to the rotunda.

Four Congressmen who were physicians advised that the patient be taken to the east portico, but it was too damp and drafty, so, at Winthrop's invitation, the sofa, with Old Man Eloquent prostrate upon it, was carried into the Speaker's chamber. There friends and physicians stayed with him.

By this time the news had spread throughout the capital that John Quincy Adams was dying. The Senate and the Supreme Court rose immediately.

Reviving a little, Adams called for his sometime enemy Henry Clay, who came at once, weeping, and clasping his hand. The spectators watched the stricken man as he tried to form words. Some thought that he murmured, "Thank the officers of the House." But a few minutes later, quite intelligibly, he said, "This is the last of the earth: I am content."[36]

Louisa, who had been summoned, was too late to see her husband conscious. Charles left for Washington as soon as he heard of his father's collapse, but was too late to see him alive.

Adams lingered in a coma during the twenty-second of February. The Washington's Birthday balls and celebrations were cancelled, and each day the House met and then adjourned without conducting any business. On the following day, at 7:20 P.M. John Quincy died. It was fitting that his end came in the midst of the political arena in which he had waged his battles for freedom and union. It was not for him to close his eyes in the quiet and seclusion of his Quincy home.

The bereaved nation bestowed on Adams all the funeral honors and pageantry that could be devised. His body lay in a silver mounted coffin on a catafalque in front of the Speaker's platform. Daniel Webster wrote the inscription engraved upon it, and all the nation's dignitaries, the President, the Supreme Court, the officers of the Army and Navy, the diplomatic corps, and the Congress attended his funeral service. Charles Francis Adams, Mary Hellen Adams, her daughter Mary Louisa, and Isaac Hull Adams represented the family. Louisa was too bereaved to attend. It was the most impressive funeral procession that the nation's capital had ever seen, "a splendid pageant," Polk called it. From the Capitol the body was borne to the congressional cemetery until it would be shipped to Quincy.

A committee of one member from each state and territory of the Union escorted John Quincy's remains to the family tomb in

Quincy. All along the route of the funeral train, flags flew at half mast, stores were closed, and the people stood with bowed heads.

The people of the United States mourned their ex-President for his more than half a century of unbroken public service and because, a child of the Revolution, his life linked their glorious past with their uncertain present. Controversial, independent, stubborn, austere, crusty, difficult as he had been to his friends, to his enemies, and even to his family, in the last few years of his life he had become unpredictably popular and beloved. In death he was an awesome figure. Those who mouthed the eulogies and arranged the obsequies were not able to evaluate their hero's accomplishment with any sense of the perspective of history. Many great men who knew him and worked with him recorded their impressions. All agreed with Van Buren that he was honest and incorruptible, the least venal of men. Forgotten was the accusation of the corrupt bargain which had victimized him for so much of his life. However, it was Isaac E. Holmes, a South Carolinian, a member of the slavocracy that he hated, who expressed it all best. "When a great man falls, the nation mourns; when a patriarch is removed, the people weep."

NOTES

CODE

APM	Adams Papers Microfilm
JA	John Adams
AA	Abigail Smith married to JA
JQA	John Quincy Adams
LCA	Louisa Catherine Johnson, wife of JQA
CA	Charles Adams, son of JA and AA
Mrs. CA	Sarah Smith, sister of WSS and wife of CA
TBA	Thomas Boylston Adams, son of JA and AA
Mrs. TBA	Ann Harrod, wife of TBA
AA$_2$	Abigail Adams Smith, wife of WSS and daughter of JA and AA
WSS	William Stephens Smith, brother of Mrs. CA and husband of AA$_2$
GWA	George Washington Adams, son of JQA and LCA
JA$_2$	John Adams, son of JQA and LCA
Mrs. JA$_2$	Mary Catherine Hellen, niece of LCA and wife of JA$_2$
CFA	Charles Francis Adams, son of JQA and LCA
ABA	Abigail Brooks Adams, wife of CFA

Chapter 1

NOTES

1. JQA to Robert Walsh, May 1, 1836, APM #152
2. The quotations and the descriptive material comes from JQA to Reverend W. B. Sprague, October 31, 1830, APM #150
3. Lyman H. Butterfield (ed.), *Diary and Autobiography of John Adams*, Volumes I–IV (New York, 1964), Vol. III: 257, 261–262
4. *Ibid*, 262
5. *Ibid*, 263
6. *Ibid*, 270
7. *Ibid*, 275
8. *Ibid*
9. *John Adams Diary*, I: 264–265
10. *Ibid*, 312–313
11. *Ibid*, 305
12. *Ibid*, III: 292
13. Lyman H. Butterfield (ed.), *Adams Family Correspondence*, Volumes I, II (Cambridge, Massachusetts, 1963), I: 91
14. *John Adams Diary*, II: 86
15. *Adams Family Correspondence*, I: 114
16. *Ibid*, 145
17. *John Adams Diary*, II: 157
18. *Adams Family Correspondence*, I: 167
19. Lawrence H. Gipson, *The Coming of the Revolution* (New York, 1954), 231

20. *Adams Family Correspondence*, I: 252
21. *Ibid*, 284
22. *Ibid*, 288–289
23. JQA to Anny Quincy Thaxter, July 31, 1838, APM #153
24. *Adams Family Correspondence*, I: 332
25. *Ibid*, 352
26. *Ibid*, 388
27. *Ibid*, II: 45
28. *Ibid*, 80
29. *Ibid*, 87, 98
30. *Ibid*, 27–28
31. *Ibid*, 56
32. *Ibid*, 166
33. *Ibid*, 177–178
34. *Ibid*, 186, 204
35. *Ibid*, 254–255
36. *Ibid*, 261
37. *Ibid*, 266
38. *Ibid*, 269
39. *Ibid*, 271
40. *Ibid*, 301
41. *Ibid*, 373
42. *John Adams Diary*, IV: 4
43. *Adams Family Correspondence*, II: 390
44. *Ibid*, 391

Chapter 2

NOTES

1. *John Adams Diary*, IV: 6–7
2. *Ibid*, 12
3. JQA to John M. Murdagh, May 30, 1832, APM #150
4. *John Adams Diary*, IV: 12
5. *Ibid*, II: 295
6. *Ibid*, IV: 42
7. *Ibid*, 66
8. Charles Francis Adams (ed.), *Letters of Mrs. Adams, The Wife of John Adams*, Volumes I, II (Boston, 1848), I: 126–127
9. Charles Francis Adams (ed.), *Memoirs of John Quincy Adams*, Volumes I–XII (Philadelphia, 1874–1877), I: 9
10. *Ibid*
11. Charles Francis Adams (ed.), *Letters of John Adams*, Volumes I, II (Boston, 1841), II: 30
12. *John Adams Diary*, II: 347
13. *Ibid*, 385
14. Adams, *Letters of JA*, II: 49
15. *John Adams Diary*, II: 362
16. *Ibid*, 385
17. *Ibid*, IV: 174
18. *Ibid*, 201

19. *Ibid*, 213
20. Adams, *Letters of AA*, I: 149
21. *Ibid*, 151–153
22. Adams, *Letters of JA*, II: 76
23. Worthington C. Ford (ed.), *The Writings of John Quincy Adams*, Volumes I–VII (New York, 1913–1917), I: 4
24. AA₂ to JQA, May 24, 1781, APM #125
25. JQA to JA, August 21, 1781, APM #125
26. *Ibid*, October 11, 1781
27. JQA to AA, October 12/23, 1781, APM #125
28. JQA to JA, January 1/12, 1782, APM #125
29. AA₂ to JQA, August 13 (?), 1782, APM #125
30. JQA, *Writings*, I: 7–10
31. *John Adams Diary*, III: 108
32. *Ibid*, 149–154
33. JQA, *Writings*, I: 14
34. Adams, *Letters of JA*, II: 106
35. Adams, *Letters of AA*, II: 43–44
36. JQA, *Memoirs*, I: 21

Chapter 3

NOTES

1. JQA, *Writings*, I:17
2. *Ibid*, 17–18
3. Robert East, *John Quincy Adams, The Critical Years: 1785–1794* (New York, 1962), 41
4. *Ibid*, 45
5. Henry Adams, *Historical Essays* (New York, 1891), 94–95
6. *Ibid*, 103
7. *Ibid*
8. *Ibid*, 118 (Rustication meant that a student was suspended)
9. JQA, *Writings*, I: 28
10. Adams, *Historical Essays*, 94–95
11. JQA, *Writings*, I: 28–29
12. East, *JQA*, 77
13. *Ibid*, 80; Lawrence Shaw Mayo, "Jeremy Belknap and J. Q. Adams, 1787," *Proceedings* of the Massachusetts Historical Society, Vol. LIX, 1925–1926, 203–210
14. *Ibid*, 86
15. Charles Francis Adams, Jr., *Life in a New England Town: 1787, 1788* (Boston, 1903), 14
16. JQA, *Writings*, I: 33–34
17. *New England Town*, 16, 23
18. *Ibid*, 36
19. *Ibid*, 45
20. *Ibid*, 46
21. JQA, *Memoirs*, VII: 307
22. *New England Town*, 74
23. *Ibid*, 69
24. *Ibid*, 84

25. *Ibid*, 94
26. *Ibid*, 127
27. *Ibid*, 152
28. Elizabeth Shaw to Abigail Adams, September 21, 1788, APM #371
29. *New England Village*, 120
30. APM #223; East, *JQA*, 123–124
31. Bridges to JQA, February 28, 1789, APM #372
32. JQA to Thomas N. T. Curtis, July 1, 1844, APM #154
33. *New England Village*, 178–179
34. JQA, *Writings*, I: 44–49

Chapter 4

NOTES

1. John Allen Krout and Dixon Ryan Fox, *The Completion of Independence* (New York, 1944), 13
2. JQA to CFA, March 26, 1828, APM #148
3. JQA, *Writings*, I: 57–58
4. Samuel Eliot Morison, *The Maritime History of Massachusetts* (Boston, 1921), 44; JQA, *Writings*, I: 55–56
5. *Ibid*, 61
6. East, *JQA*, 140; JQA to Robert Walsh, March 12, 1829, APM #149
7. Page Smith, *John Adams*, Volumes I, II (Garden City, New York, 1962), II: 815
8. East, *JQA*, 142
9. JQA, *Writings*, I: 70
10. *Ibid*, 74; 80–81
11. *Ibid*, 88
12. *Ibid*, 98
13. *Ibid*, 90; East, *JQA*, 145
14. JQA, *Writings*, I: 66
15. *Ibid*
16. Philip S. Foner (ed.), *The Complete Writings of Thomas Paine*, Volumes I, II (New York, 1945), II: 1320
17. Lester J. Coppon (ed.), *The Adams-Jefferson Letters*, Volumes I, II (Chapel Hill, North Carolina, 1959), I: 246
18. JQA, *Writings*, I: 113
19. *Ibid*, 127
20. *Ibid*, 127, 129
21. East, *JQA*, 156
22. JQA, *Writings*, I: 135–136
23. *Ibid*, 142
24. *Ibid*, 144–145
25. *Ibid*, 146–147
26. *Diary of John Adams*, II: 354
27. JQA, *Writings*, I: 150
28. *Ibid*, 152
29. *Ibid*, 160
30. *Ibid*
31. *Ibid*, 177
32. East, *JQA*, 188–192

33. JQA, *Writings*, I: 185–186
34. *Ibid*, 148
35. Samuel Flagg Bemis, *American Foreign Policy and the Blessings of Liberty* (New Haven, 1962), 262
36. Adams, *Letters of JA*, II: 162–164
37. JA to JQA, May 26, 1794, APM #377
38. JQA, *Memoirs*, I: 32
39. Adams, *Letters of JA*, II: 152

Chapter 5

NOTES

1. JQA to JA, July 18, 1794, APM #126
2. *Ibid*
3. Adrienne Koch and William Peden (eds.), *The Selected Writings of John and John Quincy Adams* (New York, 1946), 239–240
4. JQA to AA, July 20, 1794, APM #126
5. JQA to John Gardner, October 26, 1794, APM #126; JQA, *Memoirs*, I: 40
6. JQA, *Memoirs*, I: 41–45
7. JQA to JA, October 23, 1794, APM #126
8. JQA, *Memoirs*, I: 48–51
9. JQA to Dr. Thomas Welsh, October 27, 1794, APM #126
10. R. R. Palmer, *The Age of the Democratic Revolution*, Volumes I, II (Princeton, New Jersey, 1959, 1964), II: 177–178
11. JQA to AA, October 25, 1794, APM #126
12. JQA, *Writings*, I: 209–214
13. *Ibid*, 224–227
14. JQA to JA, November 9, 1794
15. JQA, *Writings*, I: 297
16. *Ibid*, 248–250
17. JQA to Sylvanus Bourne, January 8, 1795, APM #126
18. JQA, *Writings*, I: 275
19. *Ibid*, 379
20. *Ibid*, 331–333
21. JQA to AA, May 15, 1795, APM #128
22. JQA, *Writings*, I: 348–353
23. *Ibid*, 363
24. JQA, *Memoirs*, I: 99
25. *Ibid*, 99–101
26. *Ibid*, 81
27. JQA, *Writings*, I: 381–390
28. Adams, *Letters of JA*, II: 81; AA to JQA, February 10, 1795, APM #375; JA to JQA, August 20, 1795, APM #375
29. JA to Abigail Adams, August 25, 1795, APM #380
30. JQA, *Writings*, I: 419
31. *Ibid*, 417
32. Edmund Randolph to JQA, August 14, 1795, APM #380
33. John C. Miller, *The Federalist Era: 1789–1801* (New York, 1960), 169–170; Joseph Charles, *The Origins of the American Party System* (New York, 1961), 107
34. JQA, *Writings*, I :427–428

35. JQA, *Memoirs*, I: 126
36. JQA, *Writings*, I: 423

Chapter 6

NOTES

1. JQA, *Writings*, I: 424
2. *Ibid*
3. JQA, *Memoirs*, I: 133, Edmund Malone, *An Inquiry* (London, 1796) (The book is a refutation of the authenticity of most of the items that Adams saw)
4. JQA, *Writings*, I: 450
5. JQA, *Memoirs*, I: 141
6. *Ibid*, 145
7. JQA, *Writings*, I: 440
8. *Ibid*, 449
9. *Ibid*, 450
10. *Ibid*, 459
11. JQA, *Memoirs*, I: 167
12. JQA, *Writings*, I: 447
13. *Ibid*, 478
14. JA to JQA, April 5, 1796, APM #381
15. JQA to AA, February 28, 1796, APM #381
16. *Ibid*, March 30, 1796
17. The quotations are from LCA, *Record of a Life, My Story*, July 23, 1825, APM #265
18. *Ibid*
19. JQA, *Writings*, I: 494
20. *Ibid*, 449–508
21. JQA to AA, June 30, 1796, APM #381
22. JQA, *Memoirs*, I: 173
23. LCA to JQA, July 4, 1796, APM #382
24. LCA to JQA, July 24, 1796, APM #382
25. JQA to AA, July 26, 1796, APM #128
26. JQA, *Writings*, II: 2
27. JQA to LCA, August 10, 1796, APM #382
28. AA to JQA, August 10, 1796, APM #128
29. JQA to LCA, September 12, 1796, APM #382
30. *Ibid*
31. JA to JQA, October 28, 1796, APM #128
32. *Ibid*, November 11, 1796
33. AA to JQA, November 11, 1796, APM #128
34. JQA to LCA, November 12, 1796, APM #382
35. JQA to AA, November 14, 1796, APM, #128
36. LCA to JQA, November 25, 1796, APM #382; LCA, *Record of My Life*, APM #265
37. LCA to JQA, November 27, 1796, APM #382
38. JQA to LCA, December 26, 1796, APM #382
39. LCA to JQA, December 20, 1796, APM #382
40. JQA to LCA, November 21, 1796, APM #382
41. JQA, *Writings*, II: 21
42. *Ibid*, 43
43. *Ibid*, 55

44. *Ibid*, 65
45. LCA, *Record of My Life*, APM #265
46. LCA to JQA, January 6, 1797; JQA to Joshua Johnson, January 9, 1797, APM #383
47. JQA to LCA, January 10, 1797, APM #383
48. LCA to JQA, January 17, 1797, APM #383
49. LCA to JQA, January 20, 1797, APM #383
50. LCA to JQA, January 31, 1797, APM #383
51. JQA to LCA, February 7, 1797, APM #383
52. JQA to LCA, February 12, 1797, APM #383
53. JQA to LCA, February 22, 1797, APM #383
54. JQA to LCA, February 27, 1797, APM #383
55. JQA, *Writings*, II: 111–113
56. Bemis, *American Foreign Policy*, 272–277
57. JQA, *Writings*, II: 155
58. Adams, *Letters of JA*, II: 252
59. JQA, *Writings*, II: 155
60. *Ibid*, 156
61. JQA to LCA, March 21, 1797, APM #383
62. JQA to LCA, April 13, 1797, APM #383
63. JQA, *Writings*, II: 162
64. LCA to JQA, May 26, 1797, APM #383
65. JQA to LCA, May 31, 1797, APM #383
66. *Ibid*, June 6, 1797
67. JQA to Joshua Johnson, June 6, 1797, APM #384
68. JQA, *Writings*, II: 180
69. LCA, *Record of My Life*, APM #265
70. Joshua Johnson to JQA, July 19, 1797, APM #385
71. LCA, *Record of My Life*, APM #265

Chapter 7

NOTES

1. JQA, *Writings*, II: 253
2. JQA, *Memoirs*, I: 203
3. *Ibid*, 207
4. JQA, *Writings*, II: 234
5. *Ibid*, 278
6. Miller, *Federalist Era*, 211
7. JQA, *Writings*, II: 281
8. *Ibid*, 310
9. LCA, *The Adventures of a Nobody* (Washington, 1840), APM #269
10. LCA, *Record of My Life*, APM #265
11. LCA, *Nobody*, APM #269
12. JQA, *Writings*, II: 291
13. *Ibid*, 294
14. JQA, *Memoirs*, I: 219–220; Thomas Boylston Adams, *Berlin and the Prussian Court in 1798* (The New York Public Library, 1916), 20–21
15. Miller, *Federalist Era*, 243
16. JQA, *Writings*, II: 360–365; Samuel Flagg Bemis, *John Quincy Adams and the Foundations of American Foreign Policy* (New York, 1949), 100

17. JQA, *Writings*, II: 370
18. LCA, *Nobody*, APM #269
19. JQA, *Writings*, II: 394
20. *Ibid*, 393
21. *Ibid*, 435
22. LCA, *Nobody*, APM #269
23. JQA, *Writings*, II: 451, 454–455
24. *Ibid*, 168
25. John Quincy Adams, *Letters from Silesia* (London, 1804), 86–90
26. *Ibid*, 108
27. *Ibid*
28. *Ibid*, 178
29. *Ibid*, 250
30. *Ibid*
31. JQA, *Writings*, II: 480
32. *Ibid*, 484
33. *Ibid*, 487
34. Janet Whitney, *Abigail Adams* (Boston, 1947), 280
35. TBA to JQA, December 6, 1800, APM #399
36. *Ibid*
37. AA to JQA, January 27, 1801, APM #400
38. JQA, *Writings*, II: 493
39. *Ibid*, 508
40. *Ibid*, 522; Linda K. Kerber and Walter John Morris, "The Adams Family and the Port Folio" (*William and Mary Quarterly*, July, 1966), 458
41. JQA, *Writings*, II: 522
42. JQA to JA, May 16, 1801, APM #400
43. LCA, *Nobody*, APM #269

Chapter 8

NOTES

1. JA to JQA, September 12, 1801, APM #401
2. JQA, *Memoirs*, I: 247
3. JQA to TBA, September 27, 1801, APM #401
4. JQA to LCA, September 29, 1801, APM #401
5. JQA to AA, November 6, 1801, APM #401
6. LCA, *Nobody*, APM #269
7. *Ibid*
8. JQA to TBA, November 28, 1801, APM #401
9. Henry Adams, *Documents Relating to New-England Federalism 1800–1815* (New York, 1877), 57
10. JQA, *Memoirs*, I: 256; JQA to TBA, November 10, 1802, APM #401
11. JQA to TBA, July 25, 1802, APM #401
12. *Ibid*, January 2, 1803
13. *Ibid*, January 10, 1803
14. LCA, *Nobody*, APM #269
15. Adams, *New-England Federalism*, 53
16. Everett Somerville Brown (ed.), *William Plumer's Memorandum of Proceedings in the United States Senate 1803–1807* (New York, 1923), 13

17. JQA, *Writings*, III: 20–22
18. TBA to JQA, December 21, 1803, APM #402
19. AA to JQA, December 11, 1803, APM #402
20. JQA, *Memoirs*, I: 276
21. JQA to AA, December 22, 1803, APM #402
22. LCA, *Nobody*, APM #269
23. JQA, *Writings*, II: 30
24. JQA, *Memoirs*, I: 287
25. JA to JQA, February 25, 1804, APM #403
26. JQA, *Memoirs*, I: 287
27. Plumer, *Memorandum*, 14
28. JQA to AA, January 24, 1804, APM #403
29. JQA to TBA, January 27, 1804, APM #403
30. Plumer, *Memorandum*, 123
31. JQA, *Memoirs*, I: 311
32. JQA, *Writings*, III: 70
33. *Ibid*, 98
34. JQA to LCA, April 9, 1804, APM #403
35. *Ibid*, April 15, 1804
36. AA to LCA, May 21, 1804, APM #403
37. *Ibid*
38. LCA to JQA, June 26, 1804, APM #403
39. JQA to LCA, July 28, 1804, APM #403
40. LCA to JQA, August 5, 1804, APM #403
41. JQA to LCA, September 2, 1804, APM #403
42. JA to JQA, November 9, 1804, APM #403
43. JQA to TBA, November 26, 1804, APM #403
44. AA to LCA, December 3, 1804, APM #403
45. JQA, *Memoirs*, I: 327
46. JQA, *Writings*, III: 83
47. JQA, *Memoirs*, I: 320
48. *Ibid*, II: 37
49. JQA to TBA, April 1, 1803, APM #404; Anecdote from LCA, *Nobody*, APM #269
50. JQA, *Writings*, III: 129

Chapter 9

NOTES

1. JQA, *Memoirs*, I: 395
2. AA to LCA, January 19, 1806, APM #404
3. Plumer, *Memorandum*, 158 (This theme is developed brilliantly in James Sterling Young, *The Washington Community 1800–1828*, New York, 1966)
4. JQA to TBA, January 20, 1806, APM #404
5. *Ibid*, December 10, 1805
6. Marshall Smelser, *The Democratic Republic 1801–1815* (New York, 1968), 144
7. Bemis, *JQA and American Foreign Policy*, 138
8. JQA, *Memoirs*, I: 400
9. *Ibid*, 403
10. Plumer, *Memorandum*, 445
11. JQA to JA, March 28, 1806, APM #404

12. JQA, *Memoirs*, I: 421
13. Plumer, *Memorandum*, 472; JQA, *Memoirs*, I: 432
14. JQA to LCA, May 10, 1806, APM #404
15. JQA, *Writings*, III: 145
16. *Ibid*, 151
17. LCA to JQA, July 2 and 20, 1806, APM #404
18. JQA to LCA, July 20, 1806, APM #404
19. JQA to TBA, January 7, 1807, APM #405
20. Plumer, *Memorandum*, 585–587
21. JQA, *Writings*, III: 159
22. JQA to AA, February 13, 1807, APM #405
23. JQA, *Memoirs*, I: 469
24. Adams, *New-England Federalism*, 185; JQA, *Memoirs*, II: 161–162
25. JQA, *Writings*, III: 172
26. JQA, *Memoirs*, I: 402
27. *Ibid*, 476
28. JQA, *Writings*, III: 182–183
29. *Ibid*, 176–176
30. *Ibid*, 184
31. *Ibid*, 185–187
32. *Ibid*, 187
33. JQA, *Memoirs*, I: 498
34. JQA, *Writings*, III: 189
35. *Ibid*, 233
36. APM #405
37. Adams, *New-England Federalism*, 195
38. Worthington C. Ford, "The Recall of John Quincy Adams in 1808," Massachusetts Historical Society *Proceedings*, XLV, 362
39. JQA, *Writings*, III: 207–208
40. *Ibid*, 236–237
41. Adams, *New-England Federalism*, 372
42. Ralph Waldo Emerson, *Letters and Social Aims* (Boston, 1894), 120
43. LCA, *Nobody*, APM #269
44. JQA, *Writings*, III: 248
45. Adams, *New-England Federalism*, 130–131
46. LCA to JQA, February 16, 1809, APM #407
47. Emerson, *Letters*, 120–121; Ford, *Recall of JQA*, 167–168
48. JQA, *Writings*, III: 334

Chapter 10

NOTES

1. JQA, *Writings*, III: 328
2. Davis Griffiths, "American Diplomacy in Russia, 1780–1783," *William and Mary Quarterly*, July, 1970, 379–410
3. JQA, *Writings*, III: 333
4. JQA, *Memoirs*, II: 28
5. JQA, *Writings*, III: 350
6. JQA, *Memoirs*, II: 38
7. *Ibid*, 43

8. *Ibid*, 50
9. *Ibid*
10. JQA, *Writings*, III: 396
11. *Ibid*
12. *Ibid*, 399
13. *Ibid*, 404
14. *Ibid*, 406–410
15. *Ibid*, 530
16. JQA to AA, December 17, 1810
17. JQA, *Memoirs*, II: 186
18. James Madison to AA, August 15, 1810, APM #410
19. JQA to AA, APM #411
20. JQA, *Memoirs*, II: 194
21. JQA, *Writings*, IV: 146
22. JQA to AA, June 30, 1811, APM #411
23. Henry Adams, *History of the United States of America*, Volumes I–IX (New York, 1962), V: 423
24. LCA, *Nobody*, APM #269
25. JQA, *Memoirs*, II: 282–283
26. JQA, *Writings*, IV: 165
27. LCA, *Nobody*, APM #269
28. JQA, *Memoirs*, II: 332
29. JQA to AA, January 1, 1812, APM #413
30. JQA, *Memoirs*, II: 352; JQA, *Writings*, IV: 306
31. JQA, *Writings*, IV: 45
32. JQA, *Memoirs*, II: 383
33. JQA, *Writings*, IV: 45
34. JQA to AA, n.d., APM #414
35. *Ibid*, November 30, 1812
36. JQA, *Memoirs*, II: 422
37. *Ibid*, 423
38. JQA to JA, January 12, 1813, APM #415
39. JQA to AA, December 31, 1812, APM #414
40. JQA, *Memoirs*, II: 436
41. JQA, *Writings*, IV: 427; JQA to JA, January 12, 1813, APM #415
42. JQA, *Writings*, IV: 432
43. JA to JQA, April 22, 1813, APM #415
44. James Monroe to JQA, April 17, 1813, APM #415
45. JQA, *Memoirs*, II: 479
46. JA to JQA, November 28, 1813, APM #416
47. JQA, *Memoirs*, II: 579
48. *Ibid*, 584
49. *Ibid*, 602
50. *Ibid*, 608

Chapter 11

NOTES

1. JQA to LCA, May 13, 1814, APM #418
2. *Ibid*, June 11, 1814

3. JQA, *Memoirs*, II: 650
4. *Ibid*
5. JQA, *Writings*, V: 57
6. JQA, *Memoirs*, II: 656
7. LCA to JQA, June 4, 1814, APM #418
8. Wilbur Devereux Jones, "A British View of the War of 1812 and the Peace Negotiation," *Mississippi Valley Historical Review*, December, 1958, Vol. XLV, No. 3, 481–487
9. Adams, *History of United States*, IX: 11
10. JQA, *Writings*, VII: 74
11. *Ibid*, 75
12. *Ibid*, 90
13. JQA, *Writings*, V: 93–94; JQA, *Memoirs*, VI: 21
14. JQA, *Writings*, V: 12
15. *Ibid*, 111
16. *Ibid*, 103
17. *Ibid*, 119–120
18. *Ibid*, 92–93
19. *Ibid*, 115–116
20. *Ibid*, 125
21. Henry Adams, *The Life of Albert Gallatin* (New York, 1943), 281
22. JQA to LCA, August 22, 1814, APM #419
23. Adams, *Gallatin*, 533
24. Bradford Perkins, *Castlereagh and Adams: England and the United States, 1812–1823* (Berkeley, 1964), 89
25. Adams, *History of U.S.*, IX: 35
26. *Ibid*, 35–36
27. JQA, *Writings*, V: 164–165
28. JQA, *Memoirs*, III: 58–59
29. *Ibid*, 63
30. *Ibid*, 70
31. JQA, *Writings*, V: 220
32. *Ibid*, 226
33. *Ibid*, 233–234
34. JQA, *Memoirs*, III: 119
35. Fred L. Engelman, *The Peace of Christmas Eve* (New York, 1963), 279
36. JQA, *Writings*, V: 240
37. *Ibid*, 217
38. Samuel Eliot Morison, *Harrison Gray Otis, 1765–1848, The Urbane Federalist* (Boston, 1969), 346–347
39. *Ibid*
40. JQA, *Writings*, V: 248

Chapter 12

NOTES

1. JQA, *Memoirs*, III: 130
2. JQA, *Writings*, V: 263
3. *Ibid*, 267
4. *Ibid*, 273

5. *Ibid*, 284
6. LCA, *Narrative of a Journey*, APM #269
7. Cappon, *Adams-Jefferson Letters*, 503
8. JQA, *Writings*, V: 318
9. JQA, *Memoirs*, III: 243
10. *Ibid*, 248
11. *Ibid*, 250
12. JQA to AA, June 30, 1815, APM #414
13. JQA, *Memoirs*, III: 252
14. *Ibid*, 337
15. JQA, *Writings*, V: 451
16. JA to JQA, June 17, 1815, APM #414
17. JQA, *Memoirs*, III: 387
18. JQA, *Writings*, V: 448; LCA to AA, January 23, 1816, APM #429
19. JQA, *Writings*, V: 492
20. JQA, *Memoirs*, III: 379
21. *Ibid*, 330
22. *Ibid*, 352
23. JA to JQA, July 3, 1816, APM #432
24. *Ibid*, June 25, 1816
25. JQA to AA, June 6, 1816, APM #432
26. JA to GWA, June 16, 1816, APM #432
27. JQA, *Writings*, VI: 61
28. JQA, *Memoirs*, III: 413
29. JQA, *Writings*, VI: 109
30. *Ibid*, 116
31. JA to JQA, November 26, 1816, APM #434
32. JQA, *Writings*, VI: 133–134
33. JQA, *Memoirs*, III: 528–529
34. JQA, *Writings*, VI: 143; JQA to JA, May 29, 1816, APM #432

Chapter 13

NOTES

1. JQA, *Memoirs*, IV: 3
2. Whitney, *Abigail Adams*, 325
3. JQA to AA, April 12, 1817, APM #437
4. JQA, *Writings*, VI: 519–520
5. *Ibid*, 243–244
6. JQA, *Memoirs*, IV: 28
7. Bemis, *JQA and Foundations of American Foreign Policy*, 306
8. JQA, *Memoirs*, IV: 28
9. JQA to JA$_2$, November 17, 1817, APM #440
10. JQA, *Writings*, VI: 279
11. *Ibid*, 286
12. JQA, *Memoirs*, IV: 36
13. James D. Richardson, *Messages and Papers of the Presidents, 1789–1908* (Bureau of National Literature and Art, 1908), II: 23–25
14. JQA to TBA, April 24, 1818, APM #443
15. George Dangerfield, *The Era of Good Feelings* (New York, 1952), 126

16. Marquis James, *The Life of Andrew Jackson* (Indianapolis, 1938), 283
17. JQA, *Memoirs*, IV: 105
18. *Ibid*, 107
19. *Ibid*
20. *Ibid*, 113
21. *Ibid*, 115
22. JQA, *Writings*, IV: 387–391
23. Arthur P. Whitaker, *The United States and the Independence of Latin America: 1800–1830* (New York, 1964), 235
24. AA to LCA, April 15, 1818, APM #443
25. LCA to GWA, December 7, 1818, APM #445
26. JQA, *Memoirs*, IV: 155
27. *Ibid*, 148
28. *Ibid*, 151
29. JQA, *Writings*, VI: 471
30. Adams, *Gallatin*, 572
31. JQA, *Memoirs*, IV: 178
32. *Ibid*, 131–132
33. JQA, *Writings*, VI: 490
34. *Ibid*, 525
35. *Ibid*, 515
36. JQA, *Memoirs*, IV: 203
37. *Ibid*, 236
38. *Ibid*
39. *Ibid*, 275
40. Bemis, *JQA and Foundations of American Diplomacy*, 340
41. JQA, *Memoirs*, IV: 306
42. *Ibid*, 314
43. *Ibid*, 339
44. *Ibid*, 340
45. JA to LCA, May 18, 1819, APM #447
46. LCA to GWA, April 22, 1819, APM #447
47. JQA, *Memoirs*, IV: 479
48. JQA, *Writings*, VI: 569; JQA to Daniel D. Tompkins, December 29, 1819, APM #447

Chapter 14

NOTES

1. LCA, *Diary*, February 4, 1820, APM #265
2. *Ibid*, February 4, 6, 1820
3. *Ibid*, January 16, 1820; William P. Cresson, *James Monroe* (Chapel Hill, 1946), 367
4. LCA to JA₂, February 28, 1820, APM #449
5. JQA, *Memoirs*, IV: 517
6. *Ibid*, 522–524
7. *Ibid*, 525
8. LCA, *Diary*, February 15, 1820, APM #265
9. JQA, *Memoirs*, IV: 495
10. *Ibid*, 529–530
11. *Ibid*, 531

12. *Ibid*, 533; Glover Moore, *The Missouri Controversy: 1819–1821* (Lexington, 1966), 170–171
13. Moore, *Missouri Controversy*, 171–173; JQA, *Memoirs*, IV: 533
14. JQA, *Memoirs*, V: 12
15. *Ibid*, 54
16. JQA, *Writings*, VII: 15
17. JQA, *Memoirs*, IV: 497
18. *Ibid*, 502
19. *Ibid*, 522
20. LCA, *Diary*, March 11, 1820, APM #265; JQA, *Writings*, VII: 5
21. JQA, *Memoirs*, V: 30
22. *Ibid*, 60
23. *Ibid*, 68
24. *Ibid*, 83
25. LCA, *Diary*, May 4, 1820, APM #265
26. JQA, *Memoirs*, V: 59, 92
27. LCA, *Diary*, March 23, 1820, APM #265
28. JQA, *Memoirs*, V: 94
29. *Ibid*, 138
30. *Ibid*, 136
31. *Ibid*, 138
32. JQA to JA, July 19, 1820, APM #450
33. JQA to TBA, September 12, 1820, APM #450
34. LCA, *Diary*, February 17, 1820, APM #450
35. Lynn W. Turner, *William Plumer of New Hampshire: 1759–1850* (Chapel Hill, 1962), 317
36. JQA, *Memoirs*, V: 79
37. Turner, *Plumer*, 319
38. JQA, *Memoirs*, V: 219–220
39. LCA, *Diary*, November 15, December 21, 1820, APM #265
40. *Ibid*, January 9, 1821
41. *Ibid*
42. JQA, *Memoirs*, V: 232
43. *Ibid*, 253
44. *Ibid*, 286
45. *Ibid*, 289
46. *Ibid*
47. William Appleton Williams, *The Contours of American History* (Chicago, 1966), 214
48. Adrienne Koch and William Peden, *Selected Writings of John and John Quincy Adams* (New York, 1946), 309; Adams, John Quincy, *Report on Weights and Measures* (Washington, 1821)
49. Whitaker, *Independence of Latin America*, 345
50. JQA, *Writings*, VII: 114
51. Edward H. Tatum, Jr., *The United States and Europe, 1815–1823: A Study in the Background of the Monroe Doctrine* (New York, 1967), 244; JQA, July 4, 1821, Address, APM #452
52. *Ibid*
53. Whitaker, *Independence of Latin America*, 366
54. JQA, *Writings*, VII: 202
55. James F. Hopkins (ed.), *The Papers of Henry Clay*, Vol. 1–3 (Lexington, 1965), III: 107

56. *Ibid*, 150, 200
57. JQA, *Writings*, VII: 189
58. JQA, *Memoirs*, V: 417
59. Richardson, *Messages*, II: 100
60. *Ibid*, 116–118
61. JQA, *Writings*, VII: 219
62. *Ibid*, 217
63. JQA, *Memoirs*, V: 496
64. *Ibid*
65. *Ibid*, 497
66. *Ibid*, 504–507
67. Richardson, *Messages*, II: 138–139
68. Robert Walsh to JQA, May 22, 1822, APM #455
69. JQA, *Writings*, VII: 260
70. *Ibid*, 261
71. JQA, *Memoirs*, VI: 40
72. *Papers of Clay*, III: 223
73. *Ibid*, 252–253
74. JQA, *Writings*, VII: 280–281
75. JQA to LCA, September 6, 1822, APM #456
76. *Ibid*, October 7, 1822
77. JQA, *Writings*, VII: 309
78. *Papers of Clay*, III: 323
79. JQA, *Writings*, VII: 284
80. *Papers of Clay*, III: 341
81. JQA, *Writings*, VII: 284
82. JQA to LCA, August 28, 1822, APM #456
83. JQA to CFA, May 18, 1822, APM #455
84. JQA to LCA, December 25, 1822, APM #457

Chapter 15

NOTES

1. Whitaker, *Independence of Latin America*, 374–375
2. Koch and Peden, *JQA Writings*, 347
3. JQA to Caesar Rodney, May 17, 1823, APM #460
4. JQA, *Writings*, VII: 471
5. *Ibid*, 422
6. LCA, *Diary*, APM #265
7. LCA to JA₂, May 10, 1823, APM #460
8. JQA, *Memoirs*, VI: 127
9. Perkins, *Castlereagh and Adams*, 312
10. JQA to Hugh Nelson, April 28, 1823, APM #459
11. Dexter Perkins, *The Monroe Doctrine: 1823–1826* (Cambridge, 1932), 60
12. Tatum, *United States and Europe*, 236–237
13. *Ibid*, 236–237
14. JQA, *Writings*, VII: 514
15. JQA, *Memoirs*, VI: 159
16. *Ibid*, 163
17. *American State Papers*, Class 1, Foreign Relations, V, 436–437

18. JQA to Richard Rush, July 22, 1823, APM #462
19. JQA, *Memoirs*, VI: 165–166
20. *Ibid*, 146
21. *Ibid*, 173
22. *Ibid*, 176
23. Perkins, *Castlereagh and Adams*, 316
24. *Ibid*, 316–319; Bemis, *JQA and the Foundations of American Foreign Policy*, 377
25. Perkins, *Castlereagh and Adams*, 322
26. *Ibid*, 324
27. Armin Rappaport, *The Monroe Doctrine* (New York, 1966), 59
28. JQA, *Memoirs*, VI: 178
29. *Ibid*, 179
30. *Ibid*
31. *Ibid*, 186
32. *Ibid*, 188
33. *Ibid*, 192–196
34. *Ibid*
35. *Ibid*, 197–199
36. *Ibid*, 199–204
37. Memorandum on a Conversation with Baron Tuyl, November 25–27, 1823, APM #463
38. JQA, *Memoirs*, VI: 206
39. *Ibid*, 208
40. *Ibid*, 209
41. Worthington C. Ford, "The Genesis of the Monroe Doctrine," *Massachusetts Historical Society Proceedings*, Second Series, XV, 391
42. Richardson, *Messages*, II: 207–209
43. Whitaker, *Independence of Latin America*, 525
44. Christopher Hughes to JQA, February 11, 1824, APM #464
45. Whitaker, *Independence of Latin America*, 537
46. Rappaport, *Monroe Doctrine*, 233–250
47. JQA, *Memoirs*, VI: 218

Chapter 16

NOTES

1. Bassett, J. S., *The Life of Andrew Jackson*, 2 Vols. (New York, 1911), 327
2. Everett Somerville Brown (ed.), *The Missouri Compromise and Presidential Politics, 1820–1825, From the Letters of William Plumer, Jr.* (St. Louis, 1926), 51
3. JQA, *Memoirs*, V: 298, 315
4. *Ibid*, VI: 63–64
5. Brown, *Presidential Politics*, 71
6. JQA, *Writings*, 278
7. Clay, *Papers*, III: 185, 196, 202
8. JQA, *Memoirs*, VII: 14
9. Brown, *Presidential Politics*, 77, 82
10. JQA, *Memoirs*, VI: 130–131, 132
11. Shakespeare, William, *Macbeth*, Act I, Scene 3, lines 144–146
12. JQA, *Memoirs*, VI: 138
13. *Ibid*, 134

14. *Ibid*, 137

15. Clay, *Papers*, III: 412; JW Taylor to JQA, April 18, 1823, APM #459

16. Dr. John R. Delaney to JQA, July 5, 1823, APM #459

17. JQA, *Writings*, VII: 320

18. Adams, *Gallatin*, 591–592

19. Cappon, *Adams-Jefferson Letters*, II: 601

20. Brown, *Presidential Politics*, 93–94

21. LCA, *Diary*, APM #265

22. JQA, *Memoirs*, VI: 228–229; Aida DiPace Donald and David Donald (eds.), *Diary of Charles Francis Adams*, Volumes 1, 2 (New York, 1967), I: 32–38; LCA, *Diary*, January 8, 1824, APM #265

23. JQA, *Memoirs*, VI: 19

24. Brown, *Presidential Politics*, 93–94

25. Adams, *Gallatin*, 596

26. CFA, *Diary*, I: 82; JQA, *Memoirs*, VI: 246–247; Brown, *Presidential Politics*, 95–97

27. Charles often referred to his father as "Monsieur" and his mother as "Madame"

28. CFA, *Diary*, I: 89

29. LCA to GWA, February 12, 1824, APM #464

30. PPF DeGrand to JQA, February 16, 1824, APM #464

31. JQA, *Memoirs*, VI: 265

32. *Ibid*, 396–397

33. CFA, *Diary*, I: 31; JQA, *Memoirs*, VI: 324

34. JQA, *Memoirs*, VI: 310, 321

35. *Ibid*, 328

36. *Ibid*, 329

37. Richardson, *Messages*, II: 246

38. *Ibid*, 347–349

39. JA to JQA, July 24, 1824, APM #465; PPF DeGrand to JQA, June 11, 1824, APM #465

40. Wm. Claggett to JQA, June 10, 1824; PPF DeGrand to JQA, June 11, 1824, APM #465

41. Amos Lane to JQA, June 22, 1824, APM #465

42. JG Jackson to JQA, August 6, 1824, APM #465

43. Clay, *Papers*, III: 818–820

44. JQA to RS Garnett, July, 1824, APM #465

45. CFA, *Diary*, I: 274–275; LCA to CFA, July 27, 1824, APM #465

46. JQA, *Memoirs*, VI: 402–406

47. CFA, *Diary*, I: 161, 164, 167

48. *Ibid*

49. Tobias Watkins to JQA, September 6, 1824, APM #466

50. CFA, *Diary*, I: 318

51. JQA, *Memoirs*, VI: 417–418

52. *Ibid*, 418

53. PPF DeGrand to JQA, October 16, 1824; JA to JA₂, October 16, 1824; LCA to CFA, October 17, 1824, APM #466

54. GWA to LCA, November 10, 1824, APM #466

55. Roy Nichols, *The Invention of American Political Parties* (New York, 1967), 271; *Clay Papers*, III: 888

56. *Clay Papers*, III: 524

57. CFA, *Diary*, I: 67

58. DeAlva Stanwood Alexander, *A Political History of the State of New York, 1774–1832* (New York, 1906), 334

59. Brown, *Presidential Politics*, 105
60. Joseph Blunt to JQA, August 8, 1824, APM #465
61. JQA, *Memoirs*, VI: 408
62. Alexander, *New York*, 335
63. Joseph Blunt to JQA, October 4, 30, 1824, APM #466
64. Micah Sterling to JQA, November 5, 1824, APM #466
65. Joseph Blunt to JQA, November 8, 9, 10, 1824, APM #466
66. Alexander, *New York*, 340–341; B. O. Taylor to JQA, November 16, 1824, APM #466
67. Clay, *Papers*, III: 892
68. Brown, *Presidential Politics*, 119–120
69. *Ibid*, 120–121
70. GWA to LCA, December 8, 1824, APM #466
71. LCA to GWA, December 14, 1824, APM #466
72. JQA, *Memoirs*, VII: 446–447
73. *Ibid*, 450–452
74. *Clay Papers*, III: 901
75. *Ibid*, 906
76. Brown, *Presidential Politics*, 123–125
77. *Ibid*
78. JQA, *Memoirs*, VI: 458
79. Glyndon G. Van Deusen, *Henry Clay* (Boston, 1937), 186; JQA, *Memoirs*, VII: 461–462
80. JQA, *Memoirs*, VI: 465; Brown, *Presidential Politics*, 131
81. JQA, *Memoirs*, VII: 471
82. DP Cook to JQA, January 21, 1825, APM #467
83. JQA, *Memoirs*, VI: 473–475
84. Bassett, *Jackson*, 357
85. *Ibid*, 459–460
86. JQA to James Monroe, February 3, 1825, APM #467
87. JQA, *Memoirs*, VI: 489
88. Martin Van Buren, "The Autobiography of Martin Van Buren," *Annual Report of the American Historical Association for the year 1918*, Vol. II, 150–152
89. Richard McCormick, *The Second Party System: Party formation in the Jacksonian Era* (Chapel Hill, 1966), 330–333
90. JQA to JA, February 9, 1825, APM #467
91. J. Percival, *Ode*, March 4, 1825, APM #468

Chapter 17

NOTES

1. Richardson, *Messages*, II: 292–293
2. Bassett, *Jackson*, 365–366; JQA, *Memoirs*, III: 502
3. Bassett, *Jackson*, 366–367
4. JQA, *Memoirs*, VI: 507–508
5. Brown, *Presidential Politics*, 139–142
6. *Ibid*, 142–143
7. PPF DeGrand to JQA, February 15, 1825, APM #467
8. Cappon, *Adams-Jefferson Letters*, II: 609
9. William Cranch to JA, February 17, 1825, APM #467

10. *Arrangements*, March 4, 1825, APM #468
11. Richardson, *Messages*, II: 294–299
12. Thomas Wells, *Star of the North*, March 4, 1825, APM #468
13. Bassett, *Jackson*, 367
14. Leonard D. White, *The Jeffersonians* (New York, 1965), 64
15. JQA, *Memoirs*, VI: 521
16. White, *Jeffersonians*, 381
17. Josiah Quincy, *Memoirs of the Life of John Quincy Adams* (Boston, 1860), 143–144; Joseph Blunt to JQA, April 17, 1825, APM #469
18. JQA, *Memoirs*, VI: 523; Rufus King to JQA, April 4, 1825, APM #469
19. Robert Ernst, *Rufus King: American Federalist* (Institute of Early American History and Culture at Williamsburg, Virginia, 1968), 394–395; Robert V. Remini, *Martin Van Buren and the Making of the Democratic Party* (New York, 1959), 95
20. LCA to CFA, April 20, 1825, APM #470
21. JQA, *Memoirs*, VII: 27–29
22. LCA to GWA, June 13, July 23, 1825, APM #470
23. JQA to CFA, July 17, 1825, APM #148
24. CFA, *Diary*, II: 3
25. CFA to JA, August 8, 1825, APM #471
26. JQA, *Memoirs*, VII: 42–43
27. LCA to GWA, August 13, 1825, APM #471
28. CFA to JA, August 21, 1825, APM #471
29. LCA to GWA, August 22, 1825, APM #471
30. JQA, *Memoirs*, VII: 48–49
31. Brand Whitlock, *Lafayette* (New York, 1929), 282
32. *Address to Lafayette*, September 7, 1825, APM #472
33. Henry Clay to JQA, June 25, 1825, APM #470
34. Frederick Jackson Turner, *Rise of the New West, 1819–1829* (Gloucester, Massachusetts, 1961), 310; JQA, *Memoirs*, VI: 245–246
35. JQA, *Memoirs*, VII: 11
36. W. Hardin to Richard Rush, September 12, 1825, APM #472
37. LCA to GWA, June 5, 1825, APM #470; Benjamin Waterhouse to JQA, July 4, 1825, APM #471
38. Poem to GWA by JQA, October 16, 1825, APM #472
39. JQA to Honorable John Davy, October 16, 1825, APM #148
40. LCA to GWA, November 6, 1825, APM #472
41. Joseph Blunt to JQA, October 29, 1825, APM #472
42. Algernon Sidney to JQA, September 3, 1825, APM #472
43. Quincy, *JQA*, 149–150
44. *Ibid*, 152; Turner, *Rise of New West*, 308
45. JQA, *Memoirs*, VII: 64–65
46. *Ibid*, 72
47. Richardson, *Messages*, II: 316
48. Remini, *Van Buren*, 102
49. Richardson, *Messages*, II: 312
50. LCA to GWA, December 23, 1825, APM #473
51. JQA, *Memoirs*, VII: 98–100
52. *Ibid*, 15–16
53. Richardson, *Messages*, II: 318–320
54. *Ibid*, 327
55. Remini, *Van Buren*, 107
56. Richardson, *Messages*, II: 329–330

57. Register of Debates in Congress, Nineteenth Congress, 1825–1826, 389–406
58. Van Deusen, *Clay*, 220–222
59. Henry Adams, *John Randolph* (Boston, 1883), 189
60. Dangerfield, *Era of Good Feelings*, 363–364
61. Whitaker, *Independence of Latin America*, 602
62. JQA, *Memoirs*, VII: 79, 92
63. Richardson, *Messages*, II: 325
64. James Barbour to JQA, February 14, 1826, APM #474
65. JQA to GWA, May 25, 1826, APM #148
66. Rufus King to JQA, March 29, 1826, APM #475
67. Albert Gallatin to JQA, June 30, 1826, APM #476
68. Frederick Merk, *The Oregon Question* (Cambridge, Massachusetts, 1967), 66
69. Benjamin Waterhouse to JQA, May 12, 1826, APM #475
70. *Ibid*, July 4, 1826
71. JQA, *Memoirs*, VII: 133; GWA to JQA, July 9, 1826, APM #476
72. JQA, *Memoirs*, VII, 124–125
73. CFA, *Diary*, II: 67
74. JQA to LCA, July 14, 1826, APM #149
75. *Ibid*, July 15, 1826
76. LCA to JQA, July 18, 1826, APM #476
77. *Ibid*, July 20, 1826
78. JQA, *Memoirs*, VII: 134
79. JQA to LCA, July 24, 1826; CFA, *Diary*, II: 42
80. CFA, *Diary*, II: 78
81. JQA, *Memoirs*, VII: 176
82. Samuel Flagg Bemis, *John Quincy Adams and the Union* (New York, 1956), 106
83. JQA, *Memoirs*, VII: 149
84. JQA to CFA, September 15, 1826, APM #149
85. JQA, *Memoirs*, VII: 151
86. *Ibid*, 158
87. *Ibid*, 163–164
88. JQA to GWA, October 30, 1826, APM #148; JQA, *Memoirs*, VII: 164
89. CFA, *Diary*, II: 91
90. *Ibid*, 112
91. Richardson, *Messages*, II: 350–364

Chapter 18

NOTES

1. CFA, *Diary*, II: 93
2. Adams, *Gallatin*, 620; Raymond Walters, Jr., *Albert Gallatin* (New York, 1957), 334–335
3. JQA, *Memoirs*, VII: 234–235
4. *Ibid*, 213–214
5. George Dangerfield, *The Awakening of American Nationalism* (New York, 1965), 264
6. Adams, *Gallatin*, 624
7. *Ibid*
8. Merk, *Oregon*, 117
9. *Ibid*, 183

10. JQA, *Memoirs*, VII: 190–193, 215, 242, 244, 248, 288–289, 292, 378–379
11. Richardson, *Messages*, II: 370–373
12. JQA, *Memoirs*, VII: 231–232
13. Turner, *Rise of the New West*, 313
14. JQA to P. C. Brooks, February 23, 1827, APM #148
15. PC Brooks to Abigail Brooks, March 1, 1827, APM #479
16. Remini, *Van Buren*, 137
17. JQA, *Memoirs*, VII: 235, 242; LCA to JQA, March 25, 1827, APM #429
18. JQA, *Memoirs*, VII: 261–262
19. *Ibid*, 291
20. JQA to TB Johnson, July 17, 1827, APM #148
21. JQA, *Memoirs*, VII: 272
22. Remini, *Van Buren*, 146
23. Quincy, *JQA*, 158
24. JQA, *Memoirs*, VII: 281
25. CFA, *Diary*, II: 140–141
26. JQA, *Memoirs*, VII: 310–312
27. JQA to Henry Clay, August 31, 1827, APM #147
28. Whitaker, *Independence of Latin America*, 590–595
29. CFA, *Diary*, II: 148
30. LCA to CFA, August 19, 1827; LCA to Mary Hellen, August 19, 1827, APM #482
31. JQA to LCA, August 28, 1827, APM #147
32. JQA to George Sullivan, September 22, 1827, APM #147
33. JQA, *Memoirs*, VII: 328; JQA to Richard Rush, September 20, 1827, APM #147
34. JQA to GWA, October 20, 1827, APM #147
35. JQA, *Memoirs*, VII: 340
36. JQA to CFA, November 7, 19, 25, December 12, 1827, APM #148
37. JQA, *Memoirs*, VII: 366
38. Richardson, *Messages*, II: 378–392
39. JQA, *Memoirs*, VII: 366
40. JQA to GWA, January 1, 1828, APM #148
41. JQA to CFA, January 7, 1828, APM #148
42. *Ibid*, January 29, 1828
43. Anne Hollingsworth Wharton, *Social Life in the Early Republic* (Philadelphia, 1902), 225; CFA, *Diary*, II: 218
44. LCA to CFA, February 26, 1828, March 10, 1828, APM #485
45. JQA, *Memoirs*, VII: 403
46. Van Buren, *Autobiography*, 202
47. Richardson, *Messages*, II: 400
48. LCA to CFA, April 17, 1828, APM #148; JQA, *Memoirs*, VII: 508–515; Bemis, "The Scuffle in the Rotunda," *American Foreign Policy*, 279–288
49. JQA to CFA, May 11, May 28, 1828, APM #148
50. Remini, *Van Buren*, 170–172; Bemis, *JQA and the Union*, 90
51. JQA to CFA, May 28, 1828, APM #148
52. JQA to CFA, July 7, 1828, APM #148; JQA, *Memoirs*, VII: 540
53. JQA, *Diary*, June 28, 1828, APM #39
54. *Ibid*, July 4, 1828
55. LCA to CFA, July 30, 1828, APM #486; LCA to GWA, September 30, 1828, APM #487
56. JQA, *Diary*, August 5, 1828, APM #39
57. LCA to CFA, August 18, 1828, APM #487
58. CFA, *Diary*, II: 271, 279

59. *Ibid*, 303
60. JQA to GWA, October 5, 1828, APM #148
61. CFA, *Diary*, II: 301

Chapter 19

NOTES

1. CFA to LCA, November 8, 1828, APM #488
2. Thurlow Weed, *Autobiography* (Boston, 1883), 240
3. *Ibid*, 242
4. WW Phelps to JQA, March 3, 1828, APM #485
5. James, *Jackson*, II: 65
6. Daniel Trimble to JQA, September 4, 1827, APM #482
7. Quincy, *JQA*, 168
8. JQA, *Memoirs*, VII: 415–416
9. Bassett, *Jackson*, 394–395
10. McCormick, *Second American Party System*, 333–334
11. Shaw Livermore, Jr., *The Twilight of Federalism, The Disintegration of the Federalist Party, 1815–1830* (Princeton, 1962), 240–243
12. LCA to CFA, November 15, 1828, APM #488
13. *Ibid*, November 20, 1828
14. JQA, *Diary*, December 3, 1828, APM #39
15. *Ibid*, December 9, 1828
16. *Ibid*, December 11, 1828
17. LCA to CFA, December 18, 1828, APM #489
18. Margaret Bayard Smith, *The First Forty Years of Washington Society* (New York, 1965), 248
19. Adams, *New England Federalism*, 50
20. *Ibid*, 62
21. JQA to William S. Plumer, December, 1828 (?), APM #148
22. JQA to William Plumer, December 31, 1828, APM #148
23. JQA to CFA, December 31, 1828, APM #148
24. Adams, *New England Federalism*, 63
25. JQA to William Plumer, January 26, 1829, APM #148
26. JQA to CFA, January 29, 1829, APM #148
27. JQA to GWA, February 22, 1829, APM #434
28. JQA to Charles King, March 4, 1829, APM #149
29. JQA, *Diary*, January 1, 1829, APM #39
30. Smith, *First Forty Years*, 256–257
31. *Ibid*, 259; JQA, *Diary*, January 4, 1829, APM #39
32. LCA to CFA, February 1, 1829, APM #490
33. *Ibid*
34. JQA, *Diary*, February 28, 1829, APM #39
35. Henry Adams, *The Degradation of the Democratic Dogma* (New York, 1919), 10
36. JQA to Jeremiah Coudy, February 24, 1829, APM #148
37. JQA to CFA, January 13, 1829, APM #148
38. JQA to GWA, January 19, 1829, APM #148

Chapter 20

NOTES

1. JQA, *Diary*, March 6, 1829, APM #39
2. LCA to CFA, March 19, 1829, APM #148
3. JQA to CFA, March 8, 1829, APM #148; Smith, *The First Forty Years*, 288
4. LCA to CFA, April 3, 1829, APM #480
5. *Ibid*, March 12, 1829; JQA to GWA, March 13, 1829, APM #148
6. JQA to CFA, March 30, 1829, APM #148; JQA, *Diary*, March 30, 1829, APM #39; Andrew Oliver, *Portraits of John Quincy Adams and his Wife* (Cambridge, Massachusetts, 1970), 165
7. JQA, *Diary*, April 14, 30, 1829, APM #9
8. JQA to GWA, July 15, 1827, APM #481
9. LCA to JQA, July 26, 1827, APM #481
10. JQA to GWA, October 28, 1827, APM #148
11. *Ibid*, November 18, 1827
12. JQA to GWA, December 19, 1827, APM #148
13. *Ibid*, November 28, 1827
14. *Ibid*, January 21, 1828
15. LCA to GWA, March 7, 1828, APM #480
16. CFA to JQA, May 6, 1828, APM #485
17. CFA to LCA, April 14, 1829, APM #491
18. LCA to GWA, April 8, 1829; JQA to CFA, April 16, 1829, APM #491
19. CFA to LCA, April 18, 1829, APM #491
20. JQA to GWA, April 20, 1829, APM #149
21. CFA, *Diary*, II: 370
22. LCA to CFA, May 7, 1829, APM #491
23. JQA, *Diary*, May 4, 1829, APM #39
24. CFA, *Diary*, II: 403–404
25. LCA to JQA, June 16, 1829, APM #491
26. JQA to LCA, June 24, 1829; July 11, 1829, APM #149
27. JQA to JA₂, August 2, 1829, APM #149
28. JQA, *Diary*, September 3, 1829, APM #39
29. *Ibid*, October 6, 17, 1829
30. Bemis, *JQA and Union*, 125
31. JQA to ABA, January 31, 1830, APM #149
32. JQA to Joseph Blunt, March 4, 1830, APM #149
33. Quincy, *JQA*, 197
34. Allan Nevins (ed.), *The Diary of John Quincy Adams* (New York, 1928), 403–404
35. *Ibid*, 404
36. Marc Friedlaender and L. H. Butterfield (eds.), *Diary of Charles Francis Adams*, Volumes 3, 4 (Cambridge, Massachusetts, 1968), III: 317
37. JQA to JA₂, October 29, 1830, APM #150
38. CFA, *Diary*, III: 321
39. *Ibid*, 329
40. JQA to Joseph Story, October 23, 1830, APM #150
41. CFA, *Diary*, III: 348
42. JQA to JA₂, November 13, 1830, APM #150
43. CFA, *Diary*, III: 349
44. JQA, *Memoirs*, VII: 245–247

45. *Ibid*

46. Nevins, *JQA Diary*, 410

47. *Ibid*

48. *Ibid*

49. *Ibid*, 416

50. JQA to Richard Rush, May 23, 1831; JQA to Timothy Fuller, June 6, 1831, APM #150

51. JQA to Richard Rush, June 17, 1831, APM #150

52. CFA, *Diary*, IV: 79–80

53. JQA to John Marston, July 14, 1831, APM #150

54. Bliss Perry, *The Heart of Emerson's Journals* (New York, 1958), 51

55. JQA to JA₂, October 7, 1831

Chapter 21

NOTES

1. JQA to CFA, November 27, 1831, APM #150

2. *Ibid*, December 15, 1831

3. Nevins, *JQA Diary*, 429

4. JQA to Joseph Sprague, February 2, 1832, APM #150

5. Nevins, *JQA Diary*, 430

6. CFA, *Diary*, IV: 20

7. Nevins, *JQA Diary*, 431

8. JQA to CFA, March 15, 1832, APM #150

9. CFA, *Diary*, IV: 259

10. JQA to LCA, March 24, 1832, APM #150

11. *Ibid*, April 12, 1832

12. Bray Hammond, *Banks and Politics in America: From the Revolution to the Civil War* (Princeton, 1957), 394–396

13. JQA to Nicholas Biddle, November 18, 1835, APM #150

14. Register of Debates, 22nd Congress, 1st Session, 408, 410; Hammond, *Banks*, 395

15. Quincy, *JQA*, 204

16. LCA to Mrs. JA₂, May 29, 1832, APM #152; CFA, *Diary*, IV: 305

17. JQA to LCA, June 6, 1832, APM #150

18. Van Buren, *Autobiography*, 625

19. CFA, *Diary*, IV: 327

20. Quincy, *JQA*, 203–207; CFA; *Diary*, IV: 330

21. CFA, *Diary*, IV: 349

22. JQA to Ingersoll, August 22, 1832, APM #150

23. JQA to Robert Walsh, September 15, 1832, APM #150

24. JQA to JA₂, October 5, 1832, APM #151; CFA, *Diary*, IV: 370

25. JQA to Robert Walsh, October 19, 1832; JQA to Melvin Lord, November 27, 1832; JQA to Benjamin Waterhouse, November 2, 1832, APM #151

26. JQA, *Memoirs*, IX: 24; CFA, *Diary*, IV: 390–391

27. Nevins, *JQA Diary*, 433

28. Richardson, *Messages*, II: 643

29. William W. Freehling, *Prelude to Civil War, The Nullification Controversy in South Carolina, 1816–1836* (New York, 1965), 268

30. Bemis, *JQA and Union*, 204

31. CFA, *Diary*, IV: 419, 422–423

32. JQA to CFA, December 25, 1832, APM #151
33. JQA to TBA, January 17, 1833, APM #151
34. JQA to Richard Rush, March 6, 1833, APM #151
35. Register of Debates, 22nd Congress, 2nd Session, February 2, 1833
36. JQA to JA₂, March 13, 1833, APM #151; Register of Debates, 22nd Congress, 2nd Session, 1639–1651, February 7, 1833
37. JQA to Benjamin Beuler, March 21, 1833, APM #151
38. JQA to CFA, April 20, 1833, APM #151
39. JQA to LCA, April 20, 1833, APM #151
40. JQA, *Memoirs*, IX: 4–5
41. JQA to Richard Rush, October 1, 1833, APM #152
42. JQA, *Memoirs*, IX: 13
43. JQA to CFA, October 27, 1833, APM #152
44. JQA to Richard Rush, October 1, 1833, APM #152; JQA, *Memoirs*, IX: 20
45. JQA to CFA, November 10, 1833, APM #151
46. JQA, *Memoirs*, IX: 38, 40
47. JQA to CFA, December 2, 1833, APM #151
48. JQA, *Memoirs*, IX: 53
49. JQA to Benjamin F. Hallett, December 16, 1833, APM #151
50. JQA to CFA, December 21, 1833, APM #151
51. *Ibid*, December 3, 1833
52. JQA, *Memoirs*, IX: 107, 111
53. *Ibid*, 122–123
54. *Ibid*, 135
55. JQA to JA₂, July 9, July 23, 1834, APM #152
56. JQA, *Memoirs*, IX: 157–158
57. Bemis, *JQA and Union*, 311
58. JQA to Benjamin Pickman, January 20, 1835, APM #152
59. Register of Debates, XI: 1233–1359
60. JQA to CFA, February 10, 1835, APM #152; JQA, *Memoirs*, IX: 207–208
61. Register of Debates, XI: 1507–1508
62. JQA to CFA, March 5, 1835, APM #152
63. *Ibid*, April 8, 1835
64. JQA, *Memoirs*, IX: 251–252
65. *Ibid*, 461
66. JQA to Benjamin F. Hallett, December 26, 1835, APM #152

Chapter 22

NOTES

1. JQA to CFA, April 25, 1836, APM #152; LCA, *Diary*, April 20, 1836, APM #268
2. JQA to CFA, May 3, 1836, APM #152
3. JQA to Russel Freeman, 1836 (?), APM #152
4. JQA, *Memoirs*, IX: 287; Register of Debates, XII. Part IV, May 25, 1836 (for the House)
5. Quincy, *JQA*, 243–244
6. JQA, *Memoirs*, IX: 298
7. *Ibid*, 294; JQA to Friend E. L. Atlas, Jr., June 25, 1836, APM #152
8. JQA, *Memoirs*, IX: 302–303
9. *Ibid*, 304–306

10. JQA to Edward Everett, October 10, 1836, APM #152
11. JQA, *Memoirs*, IX: 310
12. JQA to CFA, November 11, 1836, APM #152
13. *Ibid*, December 12, 1836
14. *Ibid*
15. JQA to Solomon Lincoln, April 4, 1836, APM #152
16. Register of Debates, XII, Part III, 3758–3778, May 18, 19, 1836
17. *Ibid*, 1314–1339
18. Quincy, *JQA*, 252
19. JQA to CFA, March 23, 1837, APM #153
20. Bemis, *JQA and Union*, 349
21. JQA to Charles Hammond, March 31, 1837, APM #153
22. JQA to E. Wright, Jr., April 16, 1837, APM #153
23. JQA, *Memoirs*, IX: 349–350
24. JQA to Charles Davis, July 25, 1837, APM #153
25. JQA, *Memoirs*, IX, 365
26. JQA to William Foster, July 2, 1837; JQA to Charles Davis, July 25, 1837, APM #153
27. Quincy, *JQA*, 322, 325
28. JQA, *Memoirs*, IX: 418, 421
29. *Ibid*, 454, 457
30. *Ibid*, 496–499
31. *Ibid*, 497; Bemis, *JQA and Union*, 377
32. JQA to CFA, March 19, 1838, APM #153
33. Quincy, *JQA*, 322, 325
34. JQA to Abbot Lawrence, June 27, 1838, APM #153
35. *Adams Family Correspondence*, I: 370
36. Quincy, *JQA*, 276–282
37. JQA, *Memoirs*, IX: 381
38. JQA to Charles P. Kirkland, October 15, 1838, APM #153

Chapter 23

NOTES

1. JQA, *Memoirs*, X: 49
2. *Ibid*, 79
3. JQA, *Memoirs*, X: 95; Bemis, *JQA and Union*, 375
4. Congressional Globe, VII: 218; JQA to Joshua Leavitt and H. B. Stanton, July 1, 1839, APM #153
5. JQA to Samuel Webb, April 23, 1839, APM #153
6. Gilbert Hobbs Barnes, *The Antislavery Impulse, 1830–1844* (New York, 1964), 166–167 (The poet referred to Adams's support of Jackson's French policy in 1836)
7. *Ibid*
8. JQA to CFA, April 23, 1839, APM #153
9. Walter Karp, *The Smithsonian Institution* (Smithsonian Institution, 1965), 9
10. Quincy, *JQA*, 265
11. JQA, *Memoirs*, X: 244–251
12. *Ibid*
13. LCA, *Diary*, November 20, 1839, APM #268

14. Wilcomb E. Washburn (ed.), *The Great Design, Two Lectures on the Smithson Bequest by John Quincy Adams* (Washington, 1965), 65–68
15. Hartford *Daily Courant,* December 30, 1839
16. JQA to Ellis Gray Loring, November 19, 1839, APM #153
17. Quincy, *JQA,* 298–300
18. JQA, *Memoirs,* X: 165
19. Hartford *Courant,* January 15, 1840
20. John Quincy Adams, *Poems of Religion and Society* (New York, 1850), 2
21. JQA, *Memoirs,* X: 316
22. *Ibid,* 338
23. JQA to CFA, November 28, 1840, APM #154
24. JQA, *Memoirs,* X: 399, 406
25. *Ibid,* 387
26. *Ibid,* 427–428
27. Charles Warren, *The Supreme Court in United States History,* Volumes 1, 2, (Boston, 1926), II: 73–74
28. JQA, *Memoirs,* X: 431
29. Warren, *Supreme Court,* II: 76
30. Bemis, *JQA and Union,* 410
31. JQA, *Memoirs,* X: 439–440
32. JQA to Lewis Tappan; JQA to Roger Baldwin, March 9, 1841, APM #154
33. JQA to Roger Baldwin, March 17, 1841, APM #154; John W. Barber, *A History of the Amistad Captives,* 361–363
34. JQA, *Memoirs,* X: 456–457
35. JQA to CFA, April 7, 1841, APM #154
36. JQA, *Memoirs,* X: 463–644
37. *Ibid,* 479
38. Robert Seager II, *and Tyler too: A Biography of John and Julia Gardiner Tyler* (New York, 1963), 154
39. JQA to LCA, August 25, 1841, APM #154
40. JQA, *Memoirs,* XII: 16
41. *Proceedings of the Massachusetts Historical Society,* XLII, June 1909–1910, 295–325
42. Quincy, *JQA,* 343

Chapter 24

NOTES

1. JQA, *Memoirs,* XI: 48
2. Gilbert H. Barnes and Dwight L. Dumond (eds.), *Letters of Theodore Dwight Weld, Angelina Grimke Weld and Sarah Grimke, 1822–1844* (Gloucester, Massachusetts, 1963), 885–886
3. *Ibid,* 890 (Actually JQA was mistaken: the South Carolina Smiths and the Massachusetts Smiths were not related)
4. *Ibid,* 899
5. *Ibid*
6. *Ibid*
7. JQA, *Memoirs,* XXI: 711
8. *Weld-Grimke Letters,* 905–906
9. *Ibid,* 909
10. *Congressional Globe,* XI: 208

11. *Weld-Grimke Letters,* 911
12. House of Representatives Report #998, 27th Congress, 2nd Session, "Respecting the Veto on the Tariff"
13. JQA to Henry Clay, September 20, 1842, APM #154
14. JQA, *Memoirs,* XI: 251–253
15. *Ibid,* 268–269
16. Barnes, *Antislavery Impulse,* 195
17. Nevins, *JQA Diary,* 549
18. *Ibid,* 381
19. *Ibid,* 550
20. *Ibid,* 400
21. *Ibid,* 400
22. *Ibid,* 405
23. Barnes, *Antislavery Impulse,* 290
24. JQA, *Memoirs,* XI: 40
25. Quincy, *JQA,* 400–401
26. JQA to Mitchel, October 3, 1843, APM #154
27. Adams, *Degradation of the Democratic Dogma,* 66
28. JQA, *Memoirs,* XI: 413
29. *Ibid,* 419
30. *Ibid,* 423
31. John Quincy Adams, *An Oration delivered before the Cincinnati Astronomical Society* (Cincinnati, 1843), 12–63
32. Adams, *Degradation of the Democratic Dogma,* 72
33. JQA, *Memoirs,* XI: 439
34. *Ibid,* 438

Chapter 25

NOTES

1. JQA, *Memoirs,* XI: 460
2. *Ibid,* 466–467
3. JQA to CFA, January 15, February 22, 1844, APM #154
4. JQA, *Memoirs,* XII: 49
5. JQA to Daniel P. Parker, July 30, 1844, APM #154
6. JQA, *Memoirs,* XII: 66–67
7. Adams, *Gallatin,* 676
8. JQA, *Memoirs,* XII: 108–109
9. JQA to CFA, November 26, 1844; JQA to Henry Clay, January 4, 1845, APM #154
10. JQA, *Memoirs,* XII: 116
11. Charles Sellers, *James K. Polk, Continentalist, 1843–1846* (Princeton, 1966), 168
12. JQA, *Memoirs,* XII: 172–174
13. *Ibid,* 178–179
14. *Ibid,* 205
15. JQA to Brantz Mayer, October 29, 1845, APM #154
16. JQA to Augustus Harms, November 1, 1845, APM #154
17. JQA, *Memoirs,* XII: 221
18. *Ibid,* 230–232
19. Congressional Globe, 29th Congress, 1st Session, 1845–1846; JQA, *Memoirs,* XII: 242–245

20. JQA, *Memoirs*, XII: 254–255
21. Bemis, *JQA and Union*, 494; Merk, *Oregon Question*, 189–216; Sellers, *Polk*, 357–359
22. Richardson, *Messages*, IV: 437
23. JQA to CFA, June 29, 1846, APM #155
24. JQA to John G. Palfrey, November 4, 1846, APM #155
25. JQA, *Memoirs*, XII: 279
26. Quincy, *JQA*, 425
27. JQA to CFA, May 11, 1847, APM #155
28. JQA to Julius Rockwell, June 13, 1847, APM #155
29. JQA to Brantz Mayer, July 6, 1847, APM #155
30. Henry Adams, *The Education of Henry Adams* (New York, 1931), 18–19
31. JQA to Edward Everett, September 10, 1847, APM #155
32. Martin Duberman, *Charles Francis Adams, 1807–1886* (Boston, 1960), 447
33. JQA to CFA, December 7, 1847, APM #155
34. Duberman, *CF Adams*, 447
35. JQA to CFA, January 1, 1848, APM #155
36. "This is the last of earth, but I am composed" has been reported as JQA's last words but I think that JQA would have preferred the other rendering immortalized by William Seward in the great eulogy he delivered to the New York State legislature.

BIBLIOGRAPHY

Manuscripts

Adams Family Papers, Massachusetts Historical Society (Microfilm edition at
    Columbia University)
De Witt Clinton Papers, New York Public Library
Albert Gallatin Papers, New-York Historical Society
Rufus King Papers, New-York Historical Society
James Monroe Papers, New York Public Library
John W. Taylor Papers, New-York Historical Society

Newspapers

Boston *Columbian Centinel*
Hartford *Daily Courant*
New York *Evening Post*
Niles's Weekly Register (Baltimore)
Washington *National Intelligencer*
Washington *National Journal*
Philadelphia *National Gazette*
Richmond *Enquirer*

Printed Primary Sources

ADAMS, CHARLES FRANCIS (ed.), *Familiar Letters of John Adams and his Wife*
    Petersburg to Paris in February, 1815," *Scribner's*, XXXIV (October,
    1903)
ADAMS, CHARLES FRANCIS (ed.), *Familiar Letters of John Adams and his Wife*
    Abigail Adams during the Revolution, New York, 1876
—————— (ed.), *Letters of John Adams*, Vols. I & II. Boston, 1841
—————— (ed.), *Letters of Mrs. Adams with Appendix containing Letters Ad-*
    dressed by John Q. Adams to his Son on the Study of the Bible. Boston,
    1848
—————— (ed.), *Letters of Mrs. Adams, the Wife of John Adams*, Vols. I & II.
    Boston, 1841
—————— (ed.), *Memoirs of John Quincy Adams Comprising Portions of His*
    Diary from 1795–1848, Vols. I–XII. Philadelphia, 1874
ADAMS, CHARLES FRANCIS, JR., "Correspondence of John Quincy Adams, 1811–
    1814," *Proceedings* of the American Antiquarian Society U.S. XXIII
    (April, 1913)
——————, *Life in a New England Town 1787, 1788*. Boston, 1903
ADAMS, HENRY, *The Degradation of the Democratic Dogma*. New York, 1919
——————, *Documents Relating to New England Federalism*. Boston, 1906

————, The Education of Henry Adams. New York, 1931

————, Historical Essays. New York, 1891

ADAMS, HENRY, II, The Adams Mansion, The Home of John Adams and John Quincy Adams, Presidents of the United States. Quincy, Massachusetts, 1935

————, The Birthplaces of Presidents John and John Quincy Adams in Quincy, Massachusetts. Quincy, Massachusetts, 1936

————, A Catalogue of the Books of John Quincy Adams Deposited in the Boston Athenaeum with Notes on Books, Adams Seals and Book Plates. Boston, 1938

ADAMS, JOHN QUINCY, American Principles: A Review of Works of Fisher Ames. Boston, 1809

————, Argument of John Quincy Adams Before the Supreme Court of the United States in the Case of the United States vs. Cinque and other Africans. New York, 1941

————, Dermot MacMorrogh or The Conquest of Ireland: An Historical Tale of the 12th Century in Four Cantos. Boston, 1832

————, The Duplicate Letters, the Fisheries, and the Mississippi. Boston, 1822

————, Fourth of July Address, 1821. Cambridge, 1821

————, Letters on Silesia. London, 1804

————, The Lives of James Madison and James Monroe. Buffalo, New York, 1850

————, Letters on the Masonic Institution. Boston, 1847

————, Lectures on Rhetoric and Oratory, Delivered to the Classes Of Senior and Junior Sophisters in Harvard University. 1810

————, Oberon Translated from the German of Wieland (1799–1801). New York, 1940

————, An Oration delivered before the Cincinnati Astronomical Society on the Occasion of Laying the Cornerstone of an Astronomical Observatory on the 10th of November, 1843. Cincinnati, 1843

————, Parties in the United States. New York, 1941

————, Poems of Religion and Society. New York, 1848

————, Report on Weights and Measures. Washington, 1821

————, Letter of the Hon. John Quincy Adams in a Reply to a Letter of the Hon. Alexander Smyth to his (Va.) Constituents. Washington, 1823

ADAMS, MISS ABIGAIL, Journal of Miss Adams. New York, 1841–42

ADAMS, THOMAS BOYLSTON, Berlin and the Prussian Court in 1798, Journal of Thomas B. Adams, Secretary of the United States Legation at Berlin (ed. by Hugo Paltsits) New York, 1916

American State Papers, Foreign Relations, Ed. by Walter Lowrie and Matthew Clark. Vols. I–VI. Washington, D.C., 1832–59

BAKER, GEORGE F. (ed.), The Life of William Seward with Selections from His Works. New York, 1855

BALDWIN, ROGER S., Argument before the Supreme Court in the case of the United States vs. Cinque and other Africans of the Amistad. New York, 1841

BARNES, GILBERT H., and DUMOND, DWIGHT L. (eds.), Letters of Theodore

Dwight Weld, Angelina Grimké Weld and Sarah Grimké, 1822–1844. Gloucester, Massachusetts, 1963

BROWN, EVERETT SOMERVILLE (ed.), *The Missouri Compromise and Presidential Politics, 1820–1825: From the Letters of William Plumer, Jr.* St. Louis, 1926

———, *William Plumer's Memorandum of Proceedings in the United States Senate, 1803–1807.* New York, 1923

BUTTERFIELD, LYMAN H. (ed.), *Adams Family Correspondence,* Vols. I & II. Cambridge, Massachusetts, 1963

———, *Diary and Autobiography of John Adams,* Vols. I–IV. New York, 1964

CALHOUN, JOHN C., *Works,* Vols. I–VI. New York, 1853–1855

CAPPON, LESTER J. (ed.), *The Adams-Jefferson Letters,* Vols. I & II. Chapel Hill, North Carolina, 1959

Congressional Globe. Washington, D.C., 1834–77

DONALD, AIDA DI PACE and DONALD, DAVID (eds.), *Diary of Charles Francis Adams.* Vol. I, Jan. 1820–June, 1825; Vol. II, July, 1825–September, 1829. Cambridge, Massachusetts, 1964

FONER, PHILIP S. (ed.), *The Complete Writings of Thomas Paine.* Vols. I & II. New York, 1945

FORD, WORTHINGTON C., "Letters of William Vans Murray to John Quincy Adams, 1797–1803," *Annual Report* 1912 of American Historical Association

———, *The Writings of John Quincy Adams.* Vols. I–VII. New York, 1913–1917

FRIEDLAENDER, MARC, and BUTTERFIELD, L. H. (eds.), *Diary of Charles Francis Adams,* Vols. III & IV. Cambridge, Massachusetts, 1968

GALLATIN, COUNT (ed.), *A Great Peacemaker: The Diary of James Gallatin, Secretary to Albert Gallatin 1813–1827.* New York, 1914

HAMILTON, STANISLAUS M. (ed.), *Writings of James Monroe.* Vols. I–VII. New York, 1898–1903

HOPKINS, JAMES F. (ed.), *The Papers of Henry Clay.* Vols. I–III. Lexington, Kentucky, 1965

HUNT, GAILLARD (ed.), *The Writings of James Madison.* Vols. I–IX. New York, 1906

KING, CHARLES R. (ed.), *The Life and Correspondence of Rufus King.* Vols. I–VI. New York, 1894

KOCH, ADRIENNE, and PEDEN, WILLIAM (eds.),*The Selected Writings of John and John Quincy Adams.* New York, 1946

"Letters of James Lloyd, 1815–1824," Massachusetts Historical Society *Proceedings,* October, 1911–June 1912, V. 45

MOORE, JACOB BAILEY, *Vindication of Mr. Adams's Oration.* Concord, New Hampshire, 1821

MORRIS, ANNE CAREY (ed.), *The Diary and Letters of Gouverneur Morris.* Vols. I & II. New York, 1888

NEVINS, ALLAN (ed.), *The Diary of John Quincy Adams.* New York, 1928

———, *Polk: The Diary of a President, 1845–1849.* New York, 1929

The Register of Debates in the Congress of the United States. Vols. I–XIV. Washington, D.C., 1825–1837

RICHARDSON, JAMES D. (ed.), *Messages and Papers of the Presidents, 1789–1908.* Vols: I–III. Washington, 1908

RUSH, RICHARD, *Memorandum of a Residence at the Court of London from 1817–1825.* Philadelphia, 1845

SEWARD, FREDERICK H. (ed.), *Autobiography of William H. Seward.* Vols. I–III. New York, 1877–1891

VAN BUREN, MARTIN, "The Autobiography of Martin Van Buren," *Annual Report* of the American Historical Association for the year 1918 (Vol. II)

WASHBURN, WILCOMB E. (ed.), *The Great Design: Two Lectures by John Quincy Adams on the Smithson Bequest.* Washington, D.C., 1965

WEED, THURLOW, *Autobiography.* Boston, 1833

Selected Secondary Works

ADAMS, HENRY, *Life of Albert Gallatin.* New York, 1943

———, *History of the United States of America,* Vols. I–IX. New York, 1962

———, *John Randolph,* Boston, 1883

ALEXANDER, DE ALVA STANWOOD, *A Political History of the State of New York, 1774–1832.* New York, 1906

ALLEN, H. C., *Great Britain and the United States: A History of Anglo-American Relations.* New York, 1955

AMMON, HARRY, *James Monroe: The Quest for National Identity.* New York, 1971

BAILEY, THOMAS A., *America Faces Russia,* New York, 1950

BANNER, JAMES M., JR., *To the Hartford Convention.* New York, 1970

BARBER, JOHN W., *A History of the Amistad Captives.* New York, 1840

BARNES, GILBERT HOBBS, *The Anti-Slavery Impulse: 1830–1844.* New York, 1964

BARTLETT, C. J., *Castlereagh,* New York, 1966

BASSETT, J. S., *The Life of Andrew Jackson,* Vols. I & II. New York, 1911

BEMIS, SAMUEL FLAGG, *American Foreign Policy and the Blessings of Liberty and Other Essays.* New Haven, 1962

———, *John Quincy Adams and the Foundations of American Foreign Policy.* New York, 1949

———, *John Quincy Adams and the Union.* New York, 1956

BENTON, THOMAS HART, *Thirty Years' View,* Vols. I & II. New York, 1854

BOBBÉ, DOROTHIE, *Mr and Mrs John Quincy Adams.* New York, 1930

———, *De Witt Clinton.* New York, 1962

BRANT, IRVING, *James Madison,* Vols. I–VI. Indianapolis, 1941–1961

BROOKS, PHILIP C., *Diplomacy and the Borderlands, the Adams-Onís Treaty of 1819.* Berkeley, 1939

BRUCE, WILLIAM CABELL, *John Randolph of Roanoke, 1773–1833,* Vols. I & II. New York, 1922

BRUUN, GEOFFREY, *Europe and the French Imperium 1799–1814.* New York, 1938

BURT, A. L., *The United States, Great Britain and British North America.* New York, 1961

BUTTERFIELD, LYMAN HENRY, *Butterfield in Holland*—a Record of L. H. Butterfield's pursuit of the Adamses abroad in 1959. Cambridge, 1961

CHARLES, JOSEPH, *The Origin of the American Party System*. New York, 1961

CLARK, BENNETT CHAMP, *John Quincy Adams, "Old Man Eloquent."* Boston, 1932

COIT, MARGARET L. *John C. Calhoun: American Portrait*. Boston, 1950

CRESSON, WILLIAM PENN, *James Monroe*. Chapel Hill, 1946

DANGERFIELD, GEORGE, *The Awakening of American Nationalism*. New York, 1965

———, *The Era of Good Feelings*. New York, 1952

EAST, ROBERT A., *John Quincy Adams: The Critical Years 1785–1794*. New York, 1962

EMERSON, *Letters and Social Aims*. Boston, 1894

ENGELMAN, FRED L., *Peace of Christmas Eve*. New York, 1963

ERNST, ROBERT, *Rufus King: American Federalist*. Williamsburg, 1968

FALKNER, LEONARD, *The President Who Wouldn't Retire: John Quincy Adams Congressman from Massachusetts*. New York, 1967

FAY, BERNARD, *Franklin: The Apostle of Modern Times*. Boston, 1929

FORD, WORTHINGTON C., "The Genesis of the Monroe Doctrine," Massachusetts Historical Society *Proceedings*, Second Series, XV

———, "A Lost Opportunity—Internal Improvements," Indiana Historical Society *Publications*, VI (No. 1, 1916)

———, "The Recall of John Quincy Adams in 1808," Massachusetts Historical Society *Proceedings*, XLV

FREEHLING, WILLIAM W., *Prelude to Civil War: The Nullification Controversy in South Carolina, 1816–1836*. New York, 1965

GIPSON, LAWRENCE, *The Coming of the Revolution*. New York, 1954

GREEN, CONSTANCE MCLAUGHLIN, *Washington: Village and Capitol: 1800–1878*. Princeton, 1962

GRIFFITHS, DAVID M., "American Commercial Diplomacy in Russia: 1780–1783," *William and Mary Quarterly*, July, 1970

HAMMOND, BRAY, *Banks and Politics in America: From the Revolution To the Civil War*. Princeton, 1957

JAMES, MARQUIS, *The Life of Andrew Jackson*, Vols. I & II. Indianapolis, 1938

JONES, WILBUR DEVEREUX, "A British View of the War of 1812 and the Peace Negotiation," *Mississippi Valley Historical Review*, December 1958, Vol. XLV, No. 3

KARP, WALTER, *The Smithsonian Institution*. Washington, 1965

KERBER, LINDA K., and MORRIS, WALTER JOHN, "The Adams Family and the Port Folio," *William and Mary Quarterly*, July, 1966

KETCHAM, RALPH, *James Madison*. New York, 1971

KROUT, JOHN ALLEN, and FOX, DIXON RYAN, *The Completion of Independence*. New York, 1944

LAFEBER, WALTER, *John Quincy Adams and the American Continental Empire*. Chicago, 1965

LIPSKY, GEORGE A., *John Quincy Adams: His Theory and Ideas*. New York, 1950

LIVERMORE, SHAW, JR., *The Twilight of Federalism: The Disintegration of the Federalist Party, 1815–1830.* Princeton, 1962

LOGAN, JOHN A., *No Transfer: An American Security Principle,* New Haven, 1961

McCORMICK, RICHARD, *The Second Party System: Party Formation in the Jacksonian Era.* Chapel Hill, 1966

MALONE, DUMAS (ed.), *Dictionary of American Biography,* Vols. I–XXII. New York, 1935–1958

MALONE, EDMUND, *An Inquiry into the Authenticity of Certain Miscellaneous Papers and Legal Instruments attributed to Shakespere etc.* London, 1796

MANNING, CLARENCE A., *Russian Influences on Early America.* New York, 1958

MARTIN, CHRISTOPHER, *The Amistad Affair.* New York, 1970

MAYO, LAWRENCE SHAW, "Jeremy Belknap and JQ Adams, 1787," Massachusetts Historical Society *Proceedings,* October 1925–June, 1926

MERK, FREDERICK, *The Oregon Question.* Cambridge, 1967

MILLER, JOHN C., *The Federalist Era: 1789–1801.* New York, 1960

MOORE, GLOVER, *The Mississippi Controversy: 1819–1821.* Lexington, 1966

MORISON, SAMUEL ELIOT, *Harrison Gray Otis, 1765–1818: The Urbane Federalist.* Boston, 1969

——, *The Life and Letters of Harrison Gray Otis,* Vols. I & II. Boston, 1913

——, *The Maritime History of Massachusetts.* Boston, 1921

——, *Three Centuries of Harvard.* Cambridge, 1937

MORSE, JOHN T., JR., *John Quincy Adams.* Boston, 1882

NEWSOME, ALBERT RAY, *Presidential Election of 1824 in North Carolina.* Chapel Hill, 1939

NICHOLS, ROY, *The Invention of the American Political Parties.* New York, 1967

OLIVER, ANDREW, *Portraits of John Quincy Adams and his Wife.* Cambridge, 1970

PALMER, R. R., *The Age of the Democratic Revolution,* Vols. I & II. Princeton, 1959, 1964

PARMET, HERBERT S., and HECHT, MARIE B., *Aaron Burr: Portrait of an Ambitious Man.* New York, 1967

PERKINS, BRADFORD, *Castlereagh and Adams: England and the United States, 1812–1823.* Berkeley, 1964

PERKINS, DEXTER, *The Monroe Doctrine 1823–1826.* Cambridge, 1932

POWELL, J. H., *Richard Rush: Republican Diplomat 1780–1859.* Philadelphia, 1942

PRENTISS, H. P., *Timothy Pickering as the Leader of New England Federalism, 1800–1815.* Salem, Massachusetts, 1934

QUINCY, JOSIAH, *Memoirs of the Life of John Quincy Adams.* Boston, 1860

RAPPAPORT, ARMIN (ed.), *The Monroe Doctrine.* New York, 1966

REMINI, ROBERT V., *The Election of Andrew Jackson.* Philadelphia, 1963

——, *Martin Van Buren and the Making of the Democratic Party.* New York, 1959

ROSEBOOM, EUGENE, *A History of Presidential Elections.* New York, 1964

SCHLESINGER, ARTHUR, *The Age of Jackson.* Boston, 1945

SEAGER, ROBERT II, *And Tyler Too: A Biography of John and Julia Tyler.* New York, 1963

SELLERS, CHARLES, *James K. Polk Continentalist, 1843–1846.* Princeton, 1966

SEWARD, WILLIAM H., *The Life and Public Services of John Quincy Adams.* New York, 1855

SMELSER, MARSHALL, *The Democratic Republic, 1801–1815.* New York, 1968

SMITH, MARGARET BAYARD, *The First Forty Years of Washington Society.* New York, 1965

SMITH, PAGE, *John Adams,* Vols. I & II. Garden City, New York, 1962

SPRAGUE, WALDO CHAMBERLAIN, *The President John Adams and President John Quincy Adams Birthplaces.* Quincy Historical Society, 1959

TATUM, EDWARD H., JR., *The United States and Europe 1815–1823: A Study in the Background of the Monroe Doctrine.* New York, 1967

TURNER, FREDERICK JACKSON, *The Rise of the New West, 1819–1829.* Gloucester, Massachusetts, 1961

TURNER, LYNN W., *William Plumer of New Hampshire, 1759–1850.* Chapel Hill, North Carolina, 1962

VAN DEUSEN, GLYNDON, *Henry Clay.* Boston, 1937

——, *The Jacksonian Era, 1828–1848.* New York, 1959.

——, *Thurlow Weed: Wizard of the Lobby.* Boston, 1947

WALTERS, RAYMOND, JR., *Albert Gallatin.* New York, 1957

WARREN, CHARLES, *The Supreme Court in United States History,* Vols. I & II. Boston, 1926

WESTON, FLORENCE, *Presidential Election of 1828.* Washington, 1938

WHARTON, ANNE HOLLINGSWORTH, *Social Life in the Early Republic.* Philadelphia, 1902

WHITAKER, ARTHUR PRESTON, *The United States and the Independence of Latin America: 1800–1830.* New York, 1964

WHITE, LEONARD D., *The Jeffersonians.* New York, 1965

WHITLOCK, BRAND, *Lafayette,* Vols. I & II. New York, 1929

WHITNEY, JANET, *Abigail Adams.* Boston, 1947

WILLIAMS, WILLIAM APPLETON, *The Contours of American History.* Chicago, 1966

——, *American-Russian Relations, 1781–1947.* New York, 1952

WILTSE, CHARLES M., *John C. Calhoun, Nationalist, 1782–1828.* Indianapolis, 1944

YOUNG, JAMES STERLING, *The Washington Community, 1800–1828.* New York, 1966

Index

Index